At the top of this oil-on-panel painting Elizabeth I is seen in her royal closet in the Chapel Royal, St James's Palace, giving thanks for an answer to her prayer of state for the defeat of the Spanish Armada, depicted below, in 1588. See p. x for a full description. (Reproduced by kind permission of the Parish Church of St Faith, Gaywood)

The Chapel Royal
ancient & modern

David Baldwin

Duckworth

First published in 1990 by
Gerald Duckworth & Co. Ltd.
The Old Piano Factory
43 Gloucester Crescent, London NW1

ISBN 0 7156 2349 4

British Library Cataloguing in Publication Data

Baldwin, David
  The Chapel Royal : ancient and modern.
  1. London. (London Borough) Westminster. Places. Chapels
  Royal. St James's Palace. Chapel Royal, history
  I. Title
  942.132

  ISBN 0–7156–2349–4

Photoset in North Wales by
Derek Doyle & Associates, Mold, Clwyd.
Printed and bound in Great Britain by
Ebenezer Baylis & Son Ltd, Worcester

Contents

This book
is dedicated by
gracious permission
to
Her Majesty The Queen.

In memory of the late Colin Scull,
former Serjeant of the Vestry of
Her Majesty's Chapel Royal.

Preface

This book would not have been written had it not been for the specific request and encouragement of the Sub-dean of the Chapel Royal, Canon Anthony Caesar.

My grateful thanks for their assistance go to my wife Andrea, and my children Katherine and Andrew, for displaying a degree of patience I had no right to expect but which made the completion of this work possible.

To my brother Robert, Head of Navigational Sciences at the National Maritime Museum, Greenwich, goes my gratitude for sharing his unique knowledge of maritime history.

To my parents, Sir Peter and Lady Baldwin, go my thanks for providing me with the word-processing facilities, and for their unflagging and loyal encouragement, not least in the initial editing of the text.

The helpful assistance in numerous forms, on occasion from overseas, of Mrs Jessie Smith, Tony and Cora Anne Johnson, Christo and Isobel Kollias, Mrs Marguerite Baldwin, and Sir Richard and Lady Hayward was a great incentive to complete this work.

I must, too, record the unseen encouragement afforded me in my boyhood by my late uncle, Professor Kenneth Baldwin, consultant to the Food & Agriculture Organization of the United Nations, for his willingness to let me browse through his own fascinating library, which has at last borne fruit in this book. My hope is that it will one day be added to the ranks of the books contained therein.

I owe a great debt of gratitude to numerous academic establishments and repositories. Among those to whom I am particularly indebted I wish to record my special gratitude to my colleagues, friends and staff of the following establishments: H.M. Chapel Royal, the Lord Chamberlain's Office, the Public Record Office, the Royal Collection and in particular the Registrar, Marcus Bishop, the Royal Library, the Guildhall Library, the National Maritime Museum, the Carisbrooke Castle Museum, the Bishop Cosin Library, Durham University Library, St Paul's Cathedral, Lambeth Palace Library, the Bodleian Library, the College of Heralds, the British Library and in particular Michael Boggan, the British Museum, and Durham University Department of Archaeology and in particular Dr Colin Haselgrove. I am very grateful for encouragement from all quarters of T.R.H. The Prince and Princess of Wales's Office and from that of the Marshal of the Diplomatic Corps, and for specialist naval contributions from Edward Cadwallader, Keeper of the Closet. I am also grateful to everyone at Gerald Duckworth & Co. Ltd. for seeing the book

ix

through to publication.

My thanks go to Elizabeth Wiggins, Librarian at the National Maritime Museum, Greenwich, for compiling the index, and to her colleagues David Spence, Jim Stevenson and Barry Cash for their photographic services.

I am indebted to my generous sponsors Mrs Jessie Smith, Mrs Marguerite Baldwin, H.M. Chapel Royal, and Rothmans of Piccadilly, for making this publication possible.

In order to avoid a mountainous sea of capitals consequent upon the mention of so many office holders, lower case has been used for titles extensively in this book. This style differs at times from the conventions embodied in the Public Record Office Guide, but is in no way intended to be a reflection on the dignity or otherwise of the office or title.

D.J.P.B.

Note on the frontispiece

This oil on panel depicts Elizabeth I at St James's Palace and Tilbury in 1588. Bequeathed to the Parish Church of St Faith, Gaywood, by Thomas Hares (1572-1634) who was Rector of the Parish for 36 years, the panel shows events surrounding Elizabeth's visit to Tilbury to address the volunteers. Tilbury Fort can be seen to the left of the panel, while beneath the queen mounted on horseback surrounded by her forces is a paraphrase of her speech to the troops. At the top Elizabeth is shown at prayer before her visit to Tilbury. This is probably the only known depiction of the royal closet at the Chapel Royal at St James's Palace in the sixteenth century. The queen is kneeling with a large prayer book open in front of her resting on a gold cushion with red trimming and gold tassels – an item mentioned in the Old Cheque Book account of her visit to the Chapel at St James's on Easter day 1593, while on the left is a throne of black velvet with gold fleurs-de-lys and her monogram. Above her is a black and gold canopy, behind which is the curved shape of the turret wall with two windows, the right-hand one containing ecclesiastical stained glass through which her prayer 'Blessed be the great God of my salvation' is wafting. This window is evidently meant to convey the Chapel Royal beyond and is surrounded by black, gold and red tapestry. By the time Elizabeth went to address the assembled troops at Tilbury from St James's, the Spanish Armada had passed up the North Sea. She was concerned to thank God for this but knew that a threat still existed from the Duke of Parma's forces across the English Channel.

1

The Origins of the Chapel Royal

Ostorius led his enthusiastic soldiers forward. They crossed the river without difficulty, and reached the rampart. But then, in an exchange of missiles, they came off worse in wounds and casualties. However, under a roof of locked shields, the Romans demolished the crude and clumsy stone embankment, and in the subsequent fight at close quarters the natives were driven to the hilltops ... It was a great victory. Caratacus' wife and daughter were captured: his brother surrendered. He himself sought sanctuary with Cartimandua, queen of the Brigantes. But the defeated have no refuge. He was arrested, and handed over to the conquerors.

So wrote the Roman senator, consul, and governor of Western Anatolia, Publius Cornelius Tacitus, who was born in AD 56. In this account[1] Tacitus was describing the victory of the Roman army under Aulus Plautius and Publius Ostorius Scapula over the British under the leadership of Caratacus, king of the Silurians, in the year AD 51. The British war was in its ninth year, and as Tacitus observed, 'Caratacus, whose many undefeated battles – and even many victories – had made him pre-eminent among British chieftains'[2] was taken to Rome along with his entire family. He adds 'the reputation of Caratacus had spread beyond the islands and through the neighbouring provinces to Italy itself'[3] and that the people of Rome were 'curious to see the man who had defied our power for so many years'. It was fifteen years beforehand, in 36, that Caratacus had inherited the crown of the Silurians from his father, king Cunobelinus. Upon his accession Caratacus had three sons, Cyllin (Cyllinus), Lleyn (Linus) and Cynon. He also had two daughters, Eurgain and Gladys (who later adopted the name Claudia).[4] Upon their capture in 51 they, too, were taken to Rome. They were all paraded before

[1] Tacitus, *Annals* 12.33-40, *Histories* 3.45. In 1990 Colin Haselgrove and a team from Durham University discovered the site of queen Cartimandua's palace, where Caratacus was betrayed, on a hill in the Pennines above Stanwick in Teesdale. See John Crossland, 'British traitor's palace unearthed', *Daily Telegraph*, 15 April 1990, and *Current Archaeology*, April 1990.

[2] Tacitus, *Annals* 12.33.

[3] Ibid. 12.36.

[4] See Sir John Rhys & D. Brynmor Jones, *The Welsh People*, 2nd rev. ed. (Fisher Unwin, London, 1900), p. 38.

The Tofts settlement, Stanwick, North Yorkshire. View of the 1989 excavations, showing the foundations of timber buildings belonging to the first century AD settlement of queen Cartimandua of the Brigantes. (Photograph reproduced with the kind permission of Dr Colin Haselgrove)

Claudius Caesar, but on reaching the dais Caratacus spoke, saying: 'Had my lineage and rank been accompanied by only moderate success, I should have come to this city as a friend rather than a prisoner, and you would not have disdained to ally yourself peacefully with one so nobly born, the ruler of so many nations.'[5] Claudius promptly pardoned the family but with the proviso that they be confined to Rome for seven years – though during this time they enjoyed semi-regal status at the Palatium Britannicum.

During this time of confinement Pudens, a Roman senator and relation of Aulus Plautius, became engaged to Gladys, who had been adopted by Claudius Caesar and thereby assumed the family name of Claudia. Pudens and Claudia were duly married in AD 53 at the Palatium Britannicum – the first Christian church in Rome. Christian because Caratacus' sister, his daughters Eurgain and Gladys, and Linus his son, were all converted to Christianity in Britain before their captivity in Rome. The poet Martial, writing in c. AD 68 in Rome, asked 'Since Claudia wife of Rufus comes from the blue-set Britons, how is it that she has so won the hearts of the Latin people?' He refers to Rufus as her 'holy

[5] Tacitus, *Annals* 13.32.

2

The Tofts settlement, Stanwick, North Yorkshire. View of the 1984 excavations, showing an arc of stone walling dating to the late first century AD. Queen Cartimandua's palace is known to have been circular and it was there that Caratacus and his family were handed over to the Roman army, as described by Tacitus, in AD 51. (Photograph reproduced with the kind permission of Dr Colin Haselgrove)

husband', and in an earlier epigram specifically mentions that 'The foreign Claudia marries my Rufus Pudens'. Martial describes her as 'Foreign Claudia native of the Britons' (13B, XI, 53). Rufus Pudens, Roman senator, is referred to in the New Testament when Paul sends greeting from Corinth to 'Rufus chosen in the Lord, and his mother, and mine' in Rome (Romans 16:13). Caratacus himself was converted in Rome between 51 and 58. There was even contemporary suspicion that Aulus Plautius' wife, Pomponia Graecina, had adopted Christianity. St Paul arrived in Rome in 56 and found the Caratacus family of Christians, and the next we hear of them all is from Paul himself.

In his Second Letter to Timothy from Rome Paul wrote, 'Greetings from Eubulus, Pudens, Linus, and Claudia, and from all the brotherhood here'.[6] This strongly implies that the Caratacus family also knew Timothy, while Paul himself tells us in the same letter that 'I have no one with me but Luke',[7] and gives instructions to Timothy to come before winter and bring with him 'the cloak I left with Carpus at Troas, and the books, above all my notebooks'.[8] If Timothy did indeed bring these items,

---

[6] Second Letter of Paul to Timothy 4:21.
[7] Ibid. 4:11.
[8] Ibid. 4:13.

3

Stanwick, North Yorkshire. Aerial photograph showing the Iron Age earthworks (foreground) and the Tofts settlement area (top left-hand corner, to the left of the church). (Photograph reproduced by kind permission of the Archaeology Department, Durham University)

their contents would have been shared with the Caratacus family at the Palatium Britannicum.

Tacitus records that in 57, a year after Paul's arrival in Rome, 'the distinguished lady Pomponia Graecina, wife of Aulus Plautius – whose official ovation for British victories I have mentioned – was charged with foreign superstition and referred to her husband for trial'.[9] She was in fact acquitted and lived to a very great age, but it can be assumed that by 'foreign superstition' was meant Christianity and that it was probably her young newly married relations, Pudens and Claudia, who had converted her.

A year later, in 58, Caratacus returned to Britain leaving Pudens, Claudia and Linus in Rome. Pudens died a Christian martyr in AD 96 and Claudia in AD 97. Their four children Timotheus, Novatus, Praxades and Prudentiana were, according to the Vatican librarian cardinal Baronius' *Annales Ecclesiastice* (1601 edition, vol. 2, sec. 8-148) instructed in Christianity by Peter and Paul. Linus would have been about twenty-two when his father returned to Britain and must have met Peter on several occasions before being consecrated by Paul as bishop to lead the church upon Peter's death. Both Peter and Paul were martyred in about 65 and Linus duly became bishop of Rome in succession to Peter. That the Linus

[9] Tacitus, *Annals* 13.32.

4

of the Second Letter of Paul to Timothy and the Linus who became bishop of Rome in succession to Peter were one and the same person was attested by such credible authorities as Irenaeus and Eusebius.

Caratacus returned to Britain as a Christian convert and thereby reintroduced Christianity to court circles. His son Cyllin had a son Coel, who in turn had a son Lucius – the future king Lucius of Britain. The Venerable Bede, writing in AD 731, had this to say of Lucius:

> In the year of our Lord's incarnation 156, Marcus Antonius Verus, fourteenth from Augustus, became emperor jointly with his brother Aurelius Commodus. During their reign, and while the holy Eleutherus [bishop of Rome, 167-182] ruled the Roman church, Lucius, a British king, sent him a letter, asking to be made a Christian by his direction. This pious request was quickly granted, and the Britons received the faith and held it peacefully in all its purity and fulness until the time of the emperor Diocletian.[10]

Bede's statement is of course very suspect in its generality, for it is accepted by most scholars of the early church that Christianity was introduced to Britain by several routes. The strong traditions surrounding the foundation of Glastonbury by Joseph of Arimathea, and the secret adoption of Christianity by certain Roman soldiers who were subsequently posted to Britain are evidence for this. But of great significance in Bede's statement about king Lucius is the fact that Lucius must have known of Christianity to be in position to ask the bishop of Rome, Eleutherus, to make him a Christian. Could it be assumed that this knowledge was the result of his great-grandfather's conversion and adherence to Christianity in Rome and his return as a Christian to Britain? This would seem a reasonable assumption. The adoption of the Christian faith seems to have been a common occurrence within the royal family of Caratacus and Lucius. Certainly Christianity was strongly

---

[10] Bede, book 1, ch. 4. The sources used by Bede were numerous and most interesting. His principal authority was abbot Albinus who succeeded Hadrian as abbot of the monastery of St Peter and St Paul in Canterbury in 709. He it was who advised Bede, through the good offices of the future archbishop of Canterbury, Nothelm, of noteworthy facts in the history of the province of Kent and the surrounding region. Nothelm himself visited Rome during the pontificate of Gregory II (715-731) and obtained permission to research the papal archives for Bede. As Gregory had been librarian of these archives prior to his elevation much cooperation was forthcoming. The letters of Gregory I and other popes were found, copied, and taken to Bede. Abbot Albinus also furnished information about the bishops under whom the provinces of the East and West Saxons, the East Angles and the Northumbrians were converted, together with information about their kings – so important to the story of the Chapel Royal, as we shall see. Bishop Daniel of the West Saxons advised upon the history of his province as well as upon the adjoining province of the South Saxons and the Isle of Wight. The monks of Lastingham advised upon the spread of Christianity among the Mercians and the East Saxons, while the abbot Esi advised upon the East Angles. Bishop Cynibert advised upon the province of Lindsey, and the monks of Lindisfarne upon the Northumbrians.

established in areas outside the influence of the Roman army, suggesting its arrival in these parts through other sources. Tertullian of Carthage, writing about 192, stated that 'In Britain obedience to Christ is acknowledged in districts inaccessible to Roman arms'. In these 'Celtic' areas the earliest church practices and traditions were to live on and provide the basis for many arguments with, and surprises for, St Augustine and his colleagues upon their arrival in Kent to 'convert' Britain to Christianity in 597. It also resulted in British kings practising variously Celtic and Roman traditions, depending upon the source of their conversion.

What, we must ask, were the early church practices that the royal family of Caratacus and Lucius must have adopted? For the answer to this it is instructive to turn to the letters of Pliny the younger to the emperor Trajan, written in about 98. From him we learn that Christians:

> met regularly before dawn on a fixed day to chant verses alternately among themselves in honour of Christ as if to a god, and also to bind themselves to abstain from theft, robbery, and adultery, to commit no breach of trust and not to deny a deposit when called upon to restore it. After this ceremony it had been their custom to disperse and reassemble later to take food of an ordinary, harmless kind, but they had in fact given up this practice since my edict issued on your instructions, which banned all political societies.[11]

It may well be that the 'fixed day' was the sabbath, while the practice of chanting 'verses alternately' was a sort of antiphonal psalm chanting, and the 'food of an ordinary, harmless kind' was the occasion for celebrating the holy eucharist with bread and wine.

Just forty years before Pliny wrote this Caratacus was released and returned from Rome to Britain. The gap narrows to twenty years when one reads that Pliny interviewed people who had been Christians 'twenty years ago' – and that 'this made me decide it was all the more necessary to extract the truth by torture from two slave women, whom they call deaconesses. I found nothing but a degenerate sort of cult carried to extravagant lengths.' This observation is significant in that it shows that there appeared to be no other religious practices associated with Christianity than the ones already clearly described for the emperor Trajan.

It would not seem far-fetched in the least to suggest that the simple Christian practices that Pliny noted in the Roman provinces of Bithynia and Pontus (modern Turkey) in 78 were the same or similar to those practised twenty years previously in Rome by Caratacus and brought to Britain by him in 58.

Apart from those already outlined in Pliny's letters, what other practices constituted the 'purity and fulness' to which Bede referred? We

---

[11] Pliny the younger, *Letters to Trajan* 96.

have very little direct evidence, but we can venture more detail by adopting an indirect approach, turning again to Bede and the Vatican archive accounts of St Augustine's mission to England – to 'a barbarous, fierce, and pagan nation, of whose very language they were ignorant' – or so Augustine's missionaries thought!

St Augustine landed at Thanet in 597 only to discover that the king of Kent, Ethelbert, 'had already heard of the Christian religion, having a Christian wife of the Frankish royal house named Bertha, whom he had received from her parents on condition that she should have freedom to hold and practise her faith unhindered with bishop Lindhard, whom they had sent as her helper in the faith'.[12]

This tells us more about the Frankish Chapel Royal than the English – in so far as the Frankish 'royal house', of whom Bertha was a member, was fairly well steeped in Christianity. Her parents were Christians and evidently a bishop, Lindhard, was attached to the court, with a duty to obey the wishes of the king. He was thus ordered to accompany the royal Bertha on her journey to marry the Kentish king Ethelbert.

But, to return to the Kentish royal court, we learn yet more from St Augustine's questions written before 600 in Kent to pope Gregory at Rome. Among the nine questions he asks advice about are two of great significance for our story:

> *Question 2:* 'Since we hold the same faith, why do customs vary in different churches? Why, for instance, does the method of saying mass differ in the holy Roman church and in the church of Gaul?'
> *Question 7:* 'What are to be our relations with the bishops of Gaul and Britain?'[13]

St Augustine was puzzled at finding a Christian episcopal church hierarchy already established in Britain. It was similar in its customs but its teachings differed in many respects from those of Rome.

St Augustine's arrival in Kent with his mission to Christianise Britain in fact provided the occasion for an amazing episcopal muddle. Expecting to find a pagan nation to convert, St Augustine to his surprise found an existing church with bishops and, indeed, an archbishop (of Chester) with his own pallium! Pope Gregory at Rome set the scene for a 'showdown' with the existing British church by ordering St Augustine to defer to the church in Gaul and its archbishop because the latter's pallium was as ancient in its origin as his own, but to subdue the British church, through his own authority, to Rome. This was indeed an odd outlook from the point of view of the British church, which was evidently as old in its foundation as that of Rome.

Pope Eleutherus' contemporary St Irenaeus, who corresponded with

---

[12] Bede, book 1, ch. 25.
[13] Ibid., book 1, ch. 27.

him as an equal, had written *c.* 180: 'The speeches of the world are many and diverse but the force of our tradition is one and the same. The churches in Germany have no other faith; no other tradition than that which is found in Spain, among the Celts ... in Egypt, or in the mid part of the earth.' Origen was to write *c.* 230: 'The divine goodness of Our Lord and Saviour is equally diffused among the Britons, the Africans and other nations of the world.' Likewise Anobius wrote *c.* 300: 'His Word is concealed neither from the Indians in the East, nor from the Britons in the West.'

The reason why pope Gregory advised St Augustine to defer to the authority of the bishop of Arles in Gaul, whom he called 'our fellow bishop' despite the different traditions of the church in Gaul, was almost certainly because of the ancient foundation of Arles – the first archbishopric in France – near which lies 'Deux Maries sur Mer' where by tradition the Virgin Mary, Mary Magdalene, Joseph of Arimathea and St Philip landed from their sailing boat after being set adrift by the Sanhedrin following the crucifixion of Jesus. The tradition says that some of the party were left behind in Arles, making Gaul the senior church, while others travelled to Glastonbury, out of the reach of the Roman empire. Evidence of this is to be found not only in the Vatican archive but also in the gypsy traditions of Arles relating to St Sarah, who is said to have crept ashore for food. It has been estimated that Joseph of Arimathea's party arrived at Glastonbury around 37 – a full decade before the Roman army reached the Mendips to mine the lead. The researches of Robert Stoker have revealed clues to the existence of a line of archbishops of Caerleon-on-Dee (Chester) reaching back well before the Council of Arles in 314, at which bishop Edelfeid was probably the representative of the 'Fourth Provincia', accompanied by a 'deacon', according to Dr Mann of the University of Durham.[14]

Stoker's list of Celtic archbishops is as follows: (1) Dyfan, (2) Ffagan, (3) Elldryn, (4) Edelfeid, (5) Caewr, (6) Cynan, (7) Llan, (8) Llewyr, (9) Cyhelyn, (10) Guitelin, (11) Tremorius, (12) (in 490) Dubricius of Llandaff, (13) (in *c.* 600) St David, (14) Cenuac, (15) Eliud. This last bishop, Eliud (Elwald or Teilous – a fellow pilgrim of St David to Jerusalem) may have been the last archbishop of Caerleon-on-Dee, who moved to St David's before leaving, and is said to have returned seven years later in 596 but died in 604. Chester fell to the Saxons around 650, and in 664 St Chad became the first 'Roman' bishop of Mercia, which included the bishoprics of Chester and Coventry.

It is thought on the basis of this list that the Celtic archbishop described as facing St Augustine at the meeting of the two churches in

---

[14] See Robert B. Stoker, *The Legacy of Arthur's Chester* (Covenant Publishing, London, 1965), p. 17 (kindly purchased for me by Edward Cadwallader) and Colonel W.A. Salmon, *Churches and Royal Patronage* (D. Brown & Sons, Cowbridge, Glamorgan, 1983), p. 16.

603 was Cenuac rather than St David, but whichever it was the meeting is vividly described by Bede as a clash between two irreconcilable parties full of mutual suspicion. It was due to 'the aid of king Ethelbert', according to Bede, that 'bishops and teachers of the nearest British province' came to their first face-to-face meeting with St Augustine at the place called St Augustine's Oak, situated 'on the borders of the Hwiccas and the West Saxons'.[15] This was Lechdale.

At this meeting the British refused to change their customs without the consent of their own people – the Celts – and asked for a second conference. This took place at Chester, the seat of the British king and also of the British archbishop. The seven British bishops who were summoned to this meeting came from the cathedrals of Hereford, Llandaff, St Paterns (Cardigan), Bangor, Clwydd, Worcester and Glamorgan. Other learned men are said by Bede to have come 'mainly from the most famous monastery which the English call Bancornaburg [i.e. Bangor-is-Coed, Co. Flint], then ruled by abbot Dinoot'.

These British clergy first visited a 'wise and prudent hermit' to seek his advice as to whether they should abandon their own traditions at St Augustine's demand. He advised them that if Augustine 'rises courteously as you approach, rest assured that he is the servant of Christ and do as he asks. But if he ignores you and does not rise, then, since you are in the majority, do not comply with his demands.' The bishops adhered to this advice and it so happened that Augustine remained seated in his chair. At this the bishops became angry and refused to countenance the three-point plan that Augustine put to them. This was: 'to keep Easter at the correct time; to complete the sacrament of baptism, by which we are reborn to God; and to join with us in preaching the word of God to the English.'

Bede goes on to say of the British bishops that they 'refused these things, nor would they recognise Augustine as their archbishop'.[16] This was hardly surprising since as we have seen the British bishops already had an archbishop, Cenuac of Chester, who wore a pallium. As Bede states that the archbishop of Arles had received the pallium from early times, it seems that the pallium worn by the Celtic bishops such as Samson probably came from a similar early source. Stoker suggests that the most likely source of the British pallium was the emperor Constantine, who may have granted it as a mark of favour.[17]

The upshot of this conflict was that the kings of Britain in areas where Celtic church influences were strong declared and regarded themselves as head of the church in their kingdoms. In this way they could all preserve their differing traditions and practices, and protect the temporal

---

[15] Bede, book 2, ch. 2.
[16] Ibid.
[17] See Stoker, op. cit., p. 77.

control of their kingdoms from Rome – an uneasy stance, but one which encouraged the continuing existence of the Chapels Royal of these various kingdoms. This was also to be the stance adopted by the later Bretwaldas.

Let us now take a close look at one such kingdom's Chapel Royal – that of the court of king Edwin of Northumbria at Derwent Palace *c.* 625.

Of queen Ethelberga Bede writes that the 'Northumbrian people's acceptance of the faith of Christ came about through their king's alliance with the kings of Kent by his marriage to Ethelberga, known as Tata, a daughter of king Ethelbert'.[18] King Edwin of Northumbria sent an 'embassy of nobles' to Tata's brother, Eadbald, to request Ethelberga's hand in marriage, but Eadbald replied that the Christian faith and sacraments would be profaned by a Christian maiden's marriage to a heathen husband. King Edwin replied with the assurance that he would place no obstacles in the way of the Christian faith and 'would afford complete freedom to Ethelberga and her attendants, both men and women, priests and servants, to live in accordance with Christian belief and practice'.[19] The marriage was agreed on this basis and Ethelberga was betrothed and sent to king Edwin in 625.

Another part of the marriage agreement reveals eminently recognisable elements of what we know today as the body of priests and singers specifically attached to the sovereign – the Chapel Royal. It states that 'Paulinus, a man beloved of God, was consecrated bishop so that he could accompany the princess as her chaplain and by daily mass and instruction preserve her and her companions from corruption by their association with the heathen'.[20] Thus Paulinus was consecrated by archbishop Justus on 21 July 625 and accompanied the princess as 'her spiritual counsellor in the marriage'.

However, the following year the royal Christian court of queen Ethelberga was suddenly endangered through an attempt by the king of the West Saxons, Cuichelm, to assassinate king Edwin. The assassin, named Eumer, crossed the boundary of the river Humber and entered the Northumbrian province of king Edwin with instructions to kill him. Eumer reached king Edwin's 'royal residence of the Derwent' on Easter day. Pretending to deliver a message from king Cuichelm, Eumer was admitted to the king's presence and immediately seized the opportunity this afforded by drawing a double-edged poisoned dagger on the king. Edwin's counsellor and friend, Lilla, dashed to place his body between the assassin and the king, thereby receiving the blow intended for Edwin. Even so, Eumer's blow was delivered with such force that he wounded the king through the body of this faithful warrior. Despite being attacked

---

[18] Bede, book 2, ch. 9.
[19] Ibid.
[20] Ibid.

quickly from all sides, Eumer still managed to kill another warrior before he was overpowered.

That same night of Easter day queen Ethelberga gave birth to a daughter, and there then ensued a very odd thanksgiving ceremony. King Edwin thanked his 'gods' in the presence of bishop Paulinus, the queen's chaplain, while Paulinus gave thanks to Christ. King Edwin was impressed with Paulinus' prayers and 'greatly pleased at his words', and promised that if God would grant him a good recovery from his wounds and a victory over the king of the West Saxons he would renounce his idols and serve Christ. As a token that he would keep his word he gave his new baby daughter to Paulinus to undergo Christian baptism. According to Bede this took place on the Feast of Pentecost, the child being christened Eanfled – together with 'twelve others of her household'. The royal Christian court of queen Ethelberga and her chaplain had thus become firmly established under the king's protection. Furthermore king Edwin made a good recovery and led a campaign against the West Saxons which ended in the latter's crushing defeat.

King Edwin asked the queen's chaplain for a full course of instruction in Christianity before receiving the sacrament. He finally accepted Christianity in 627: 'the king granted blessed Paulinus full permission to preach, renounced idolatry, and professed his acceptance of the faith of Christ.'[21] Moreover, the chief priest Crifi destroyed the pagan temples he had dedicated. 'The site where these idols once stood is still shown, not far east of York, beyond the river Derwent, and is known as Goodmanham.'[22]

The bloodthirsty rebellion of king Cadwalla, accompanied by the warrior Penda of the Mercian royal house, resulted in the death of king Edwin and his sons Osfrid and Eadfrid, and the destruction of his entire army. So the remnants of the Northumbrian royal Christian court fled south, with the exception of the queen's chaplain's deacon, James (more of him later) in an attempt to shelter with the Christian king of Kent, Eadbald. Details of this flight reveal an insight into the attempt to preserve the sacred vessels – forerunners of those among the crown jewels – for posterity.

The details are as follows. In 633 Paulinus took queen Ethelberga to a ship together with her daughter Eanfled, Edwin's son Wuscfrea and Yffi, Edwin's grandson by Osfrid. Among the 'precious things belonging to king Edwin' that Paulinus rescued and brought with him were 'a great cross of gold and a golden chalice hallowed for the use of the altar'. Bede goes on to say that 'these are still preserved and can be seen in the church at Canterbury'.[23] Paulinus was then invited to take over the see of

---

[21] Ibid., book 2, ch. 13.
[22] Ibid.
[23] Ibid., book 2, ch. 20.

Rochester, vacant after the drowning of Romanus at sea off the coast of Italy.

Returning for a moment to the deacon, James, who remained at York, Bede writes that he 'had a wide knowledge of church music; and when peace was at last restored to the province, and the number of believers increased, he began to teach many people to sing music of the church after the uses of Rome and Canterbury'.[24] Music would, therefore, have been an important element in the worship of the royal Christian court of the Northumbrians.

Let us now look south to the courts of the Kentish and East Anglian peoples. Bede writes that king Ethelbert, who had welcomed Augustine in 597, 'was the third English king to hold sway over all the provinces south of the Humber, but he was the first to enter the kingdom of heaven'.[25] This statement omits any reference to the earlier Christian kings Lucius and Caratacus, but Bede does also mention queen Bertha's church: 'on the east side of the city [Canterbury] stood an old church, built in honour of St Martin during the Roman occupation of Britain, where the Christian queen of whom I have spoken went to pray.'[26]

King Ethelbert's conversion and growth in the Christian faith is well chronicled, and he later gave Augustine freedom to 'restore churches everywhere'. Undoubtedly church buildings still survived from earlier days, although in ruins because of the Saxon invasions, indicating an earlier spread of Christianity harking back to the days of the Roman occupation and the courts of Lucius and Caratacus. The church at Bosham, near Chichester, built in the fourth century and containing just outside the chancel arch the remains of a daughter of king Canute, pre-dates St Martin's. Its chancel was founded on a Roman court house or basilica, and Roman pillar supports and herring-bone tiles are to be seen in the chancel walls.[27]

Returning to St Martin's in the seventh century, it is recorded that Augustine and his monks assembled to 'sing the psalms, to pray, to say mass, to preach, and to baptise'. The musical aspect of the church liturgy now developed apace in Kent under Ethelbert's personal protection, and in East Anglia under Sigbert. Seventy years later in 709, the 'famous singer named Maban' is credited with having 'been trained in vocal music by the successors of blessed pope Gregory's disciples in Kent'.[28] Maban was invited by bishop Acca of Hexham to instruct him and his clergy. Maban stayed at Hexham for twelve years 'to teach them whatever church music they did not know, and also to restore to their original form

---

[24] Ibid.
[25] Ibid., book 2, ch. 5.
[26] Ibid., book 1, ch. 26.
[27] See A.S. Cooke, *Off the Beaten Track in Sussex* (Combridge, Sussex, 1911), p. 164.
[28] Bede, book 5, ch. 20.

any familiar chants that had become imperfect through lapse of time or neglect; for the bishop himself was a singer of great experience'.[29]

The north-east seems to have been particularly well blessed with enthusiasts for liturgical music and chant. One of the signatories to the Synod of Hatfield in 680 was the Venerable John, arch-cantor of the church of the Holy Apostle Peter and abbot of the monastery of St Martin of Tours. He was brought to England from Rome via Tours by abbot Benedict, founder of the monastery at Monkwearmouth, which had actually been built with the 'approval and grant' of king Egfrid, son of queen Eanfled and king Oswy. He instructed the monks there in the chant for the liturgical year as it was sung in St Peter's, Rome. He also taught the cantors of the monastery the theory and practice of singing and reading aloud, and he put into writing all that was necessary for the proper observance of festivals throughout the year. This document is described by Bede in 731 as still preserved at Monkwearmouth, with the added comment that many copies were made for other places. Furthermore, John instructed men who were proficient singers from 'nearly all the monasteries of the province' who came to hear him, and he also received many invitations to teach elsewhere. Sadly, John died after crossing the English Channel on a journey to Rome to give the pope a copy of the findings of the Synod of Hatfield. He was buried at Tours *c*. 680/1.

It is interesting to note that king Oswy of the Northumbrians, husband of Eanfled and father of Egfrid, was a friend of king Sigbert the Good of the East Saxons, who often used to visit him in the province of the Northumbrians. It was through his evangelism that Sigbert became a Christian, being baptised in the 'king's village of At-Wall' (Hadrian's wall) twelve miles inland from the east coast in 653, thereby re-establishing Christianity in the East Saxon royal court, who had had nobody to minister to them after bishop Mellitus was driven out.

We have already noted the part played by deacon James in promoting church music after the flight of the Northumbrian royal family to the south in 633. Bede states that in 629 'the knowledge of sacred music, hitherto limited to Kent, now began to spread to all the churches of the English'.[30] Eddie, known as Stephen, is described as the 'first singing-master in the Northumbrian churches'. He was invited from Kent by bishop Wilfrid to teach the English churches the Catholic way of life.

Within two years of the flight of queen Ethelberga and her court to Kent, another important event in the history of the Chapel Royal took place. In 635 on the coast of East Anglia, at a village called Dunwich, king Sigbert of the East Angles founded 'a school for the education of boys in the study of letters'. The king was aided in this project by bishop Felix, who had come from Kent with 'teachers and masters according to the

[29] Ibid.
[30] Ibid., book 4, ch. 2.

13

practice of Canterbury'.[31] Dunwich School was a royal foundation by direct edict and would most certainly have educated king Sigbert's choristers. It could thus fairly be regarded as the first school for the education of the Chapel Royal of the king of the East Angles.

The inspiration behind its foundation lay in Gaul. Sigbert had been an exile in Gaul while Redwald, and later his brother Earpwald, ruled the East Angles, and had undergone Christian baptism in Gaul during this exile. On returning to the East Angles as king on the death of Earpwald, Sigbert 'wished to copy what he had seen well contrived in Gaul' in the form of provision of places of learning for youngsters. Bishop Felix had been brought up and educated in Burgundy and asked archbishop Honorius to send him to the East Angles. There he helped Sigbert with his school project and established his see at Dunwich, remaining its bishop for seventeen years until his death.

The next reference we have to the education of Chapel Royal pupils is not to be found until Edward II's writ of 7 July 1316 mentioning the education of 'twelve other children of our Chapel' in residence at Cambridge (according to Walter Ullman, at King's Hall), where Johan de Baggeshote appears to have been the first Warden. More of this later.

The prospect of discovering exactly where this royal school at Dunwich stood is, sadly, remote. A tremendous storm in January 1326 moved a million tons of sand and shingle and banked it across the harbour mouth of the river Blyth, cutting it off from the sea and diverting it northwards. This killed Dunwich's trade and its citizens abandoned the village. The sea took its toll until by 1677 the waves had reached the market place. Now a solitary gravestone, the remains of a leper chapel and the archways of a mediaeval friary are all that are left of Old Dunwich. Any remains of Sigbert's royal school thus lie under the sea.

During Sigbert's reign the holy Fursey came to preach from Ireland, was received by Sigbert, and built a monastery on land given to him by the king within Burgh Castle, Yarmouth. Later Fursey was to sail to Gaul where he was received by king Clovis III and his chamberlain, Earconwald. He built a monastery at Lagny on the Marne and was buried at Earconwald's church at Peronne. Fursey's mission in Gaul and his royal patronage illustrate the close contacts that existed between royal families in Britain and Gaul and the consequent interchange of Christian practices that had to be resolved in the various Chapels Royal.

Turning for a moment to the court of queen Eanfled of the Northumbrians and the Chapel Royal there, we can see many of these Christian practices conflicting in the church calendar as observed by the royal court. Bede states that 'Queen Eanfled and her court, having a

---

[31] Ibid., book 3, ch. 18. It is thought that the 'practice of Canterbury' is a reference to the schools probably founded by St Augustine which were the predecessors of those established by Theodore.

Kentish priest named Romanus who followed the Catholic practice, observed the customs she had seen in Kent'.[32] This shows that the queen, and not her chaplain, determined the customs to be observed in court. In those days king Oswy of Northumbria, who had been baptised by the Scots and had 'a complete grasp of their language' observed the Celtic practice of Easter while his wife, queen Eanfled, observed the Roman practice. The confusion was great and led to some very odd results. For example, 'Easter was sometimes kept twice in one year, so that when the king had ended Lent and was keeping Easter, the queen and her attendants were still fasting and keeping Palm Sunday'.[33] This particular issue was of course settled at the synod at the monastery of Streanaeshalch (Bay of the Beacons) in 644 (now always referred to as the Synod of Whitby).

There was indeed much interchange of Christian practices and observances between the various Saxon royal courts – and in particular between the royal chaplains of these courts. Queen Eanfled's daughter, Aelfled, became a 'royal nun' at Hartlepool (founded by king Oswy in thanks for his victory over Penda) and later the first novice at Streanaeshalch. Queen Eanfled later helped to run Streanaeshalch. Trumhere, a near relative of king Oswy, became the Mercian king Wulfhere's first bishop, having been abbot of Gilling near Richmond.

The Synod of Whitby had to tackle the question of the interchange of Christian practices and observances at the level of the royal households, for the various Saxon kings still 'protected' the church within their kingdoms just as their predecessors had from the time of Caratacus; that is to say from before the elevation of the pope in Rome to a position of supremacy.

The Synod saw the meeting of king Oswy of the Northumbrians, king Alchfrid his son, the Irish bishop Colman leading the Scots clergy, bishop Agilbert of the West Saxons with the priests Agatho and Wilfrid (founder of Ripon) of the Roman persuasion, deacon James and queen Eanfled's chaplain Romanus who supported Agilbert, and abbess Hilda and bishop Cedd (founder of the chapel at Bradwell Juxta Mare, made from the stone and bricks of the Roman fort of Othona) who both supported the Scots. There were many such occasions which brought the chaplains of the various royal households together.

Let us now look at the pre-Conquest period of development of the Chapel Royal as Britain became a more unified kingdom under the later Anglo-Saxon kings. It was William Say, dean of the Chapel Royal and rector of Sutton Courtney in Berkshire, who in 1449 stated in his introduction to the *Liber Regie Capelle* that 'the Constitution or Ordinance of the Chapel Royal' enjoyed 'its proper authority and

---

[32] Ibid., book 3, ch. 25.
[33] Ibid.

jurisdiction ... by ancient and enduring custom lawfully established and continued down many wheeling centuries throughout the diverse reigns of kings, both before and after the Conquest'.

The Ely Chronicle, probably written by the monk Richard (sub-prior of Ely and then prior from 1177 until about 1194), contains a passage about the royal chancery in the Anglo-Saxon king Edgar's reign (959-975) which is of immense importance to the history of the Chapel Royal:

> [King Edgar] ordained and granted that the church of Ely henceforth and forever should exercise the office of chancellor in the king's court [an office also conceded to other churches, i.e. St Augustine's and Glastonbury], together with the administration of the sanctuaries and the rest of the ornaments of the altar.

The chronicler goes on to specify exactly who should exercise the office of chancellor:

> The abbots of these houses were to divide the year into three parts, taking over in turn at the appointed times. The abbot of Ely always entered upon his period of administration on the day of the purification, at the beginning of February, and the abbot himself or whichever of the brethren he chose, for a period of the four months allocated to him, that is a third of a year, fulfilled this office reverently and diligently. Then the others whom we named completed the rest of the year at the time assigned to them.

The point to note is that the administration of the king's chapel and its relics, etc. in the tenth century was a duty combined with that of chancellor's oversight of the Chapel Royal. While the *Constitutio Domus Regis* of 1136 specified the office of keeper of the king's chapel and relics, by the time of Thomas Becket the question of 'oversight' of the Chapel Royal had separated and come under the wing of the king's chancellor. This we learn from the life of Thomas Becket by William FitzStephen, who mentioned that 'depositio et cura' of the Chapel Royal lay with the chancellor. This remained so for a short while until the office of dean of the Chapel Royal was created, but then only gradually did the dean take over the king's chancellor's jurisdiction. Indeed for at least a year the jurisdiction of the two offices existed simultaneously – perhaps as a 'running-in' measure. In 1313 the king's chancellor is described as 'chef de la chapele nostre seignur le Roi', while a year earlier in 1312 we see a mention of the dean as 'capitalis capellanus' and in 1318 as 'chief chapellin' with five chaplains and six clerks. Edward III, whose reign began in 1327, must have nurtured the new office of dean of the Chapel Royal, for in 1349 the Calendar of Patent Rolls describes John Wodeford as 'a king's clerk and dean of his chapel'. By the time dean William Say wrote the *Liber Regie Capelle* in 1449 the transition was complete. Dean Say wrote to prince Alfonso of Portugal:

1. The Origins of the Chapel Royal

The dean, of course, is principal and head over all, holding from the king power to rule and govern the Chapel, and to select, examine and appoint clerks of the Chapel and all the other persons mentioned ... This is important (sic quod): neither the steward of the household nor the treasurer, nor any other officer or servant of the household whatever, may on any account presume to correct or punish in any matter concerning the chapel or the persons formally attached to it, but only, as has been said, the dean himself or, in case of necessity, the chamberlain of our lord the king.

It is illuminating to look a little closer into the purpose of the Chapels Royal in the pre-Conquest period.

As a general observation, it is clear that the royal Christian courts of the Anglo-Saxon kingdoms operated somewhat like a family. This was largely due to the 'limited' boundaries of these kingdoms. It is clear, for instance, that in the Kent of king Ethelbert in the sixth century the court's location was more often than not at Canterbury, where Ethelbert's wife, queen Bertha, appreciated the existence of the ancient structure of St Martin's Church. In the Northumbria of king Edwin in the seventh century it is evident that the royal chaplain, Paulinus, ministered to the needs not only of the king and queen but also of their court. For instance, Bede wrote that 'Paulinus is said to have accompanied the king and queen to the royal residence at Ad-Gefrin [Yeavering in Glendale] and remained there thirty-six days constantly occupied in instructing and baptising'.[34] Bede also tells us that in the province of Deira 'Paulinus often stayed with the king' (Edwin) and baptised in the river Swale near Catterick, that 'a basilica was built at the royal residence of Campodonum' (possibly Doncaster or Slack near Huddersfield). Favourite residences, then, were usually provided with a chapel where the chaplain could minister to the needs of king and court.

However, with the advent of the first Bretwalda, king Egbert, who held sway over most of England in c. 829, the king had of necessity to adopt a system of 'progresses' to ensure that his authority carried to all parts of his kingdom. The king and his court moved on as dictated by the seasonal food supplies and thus, in the case of the later Bretwaldas, the Chapel Royal had to become 'portable'.

In this context it is more than probable that when the Ramsey Chronicle describes how the decrees of the Council of Rheims (1049) were carefully preserved in the royal treasury 'by Hugolinus the chamberlain', and says that one piece of the triple indenture was deposited with the relics in the royal chapel (the two other parts being kept by Ramsey Abbey and the earl of Hereford), the 'royal chapel' referred to was the 'portable' household Chapel Royal which carried its own relics with it at all times together with vessels and robes on its own pack horses.

Certainly the Norman kings had progressively more and more of

---

[34] Ibid., book 2, ch. 14.

17

Britain to govern as they extended their boundaries. 'Progresses' were now essential. In a set of clerical petitions of 1295 the English prelates asked certain questions about jurisdiction in king's chapels. The petition runs thus:

> Since there are at least fourteen chapels of the king of England – namely his portable chapel [i.e. Chapel Royal], Waltham, Wolverhampton, Tettenham, Penkridge, Stafford, Bridgnorth, Derby, Shrewsbury, Wimborne Minster, Bosham, St George's in the Castle of Oxford, and also, it is said, the chapel of Dover, where there is now a priory, and the church of St Martin-le-Grand London, which is not by ancient standing one of these chapels but was granted by prelates to William Rufus, son of the Conqueror – the clergy petition that the truth should be inquired about these chapels and that justice should be done to the prelates concerning their jurisdiction in them.

The point of significance here is that the Chapel Royal was the 'portable chapel' mentioned in this petition. J.H. Denton put it most succinctly when he wrote of the 1295 petition that 'the Chapel Royal in England was not a place' and that 'as part of the household it was necessarily ambulatory'. Perhaps, though, the point is clinched on perusal of the *Liber Regie Capelle* of dean William Say in 1449 which nowhere mentions a building for the Chapel Royal but, on the contrary, devotes chapter 12 to the subject 'Of the portable altar, and of the celebration of Mass in any suitable place'. The chapter consists of one sentence which runs thus, as translated by the former Queen's Chaplain Gordon Dunstan:

> All members of the King's Chapel, furthermore, and all his servants, enjoy the right by apostolic privilege to hear mass and to conduct all other divine service in any suitable place, and to set up an altar, even in the open air if necessary, and at it to consecrate the Lord's Body and to administer the Sacraments as the occasion demands, so long as any member of the King's Chapel or any other of his servants is present in that place.

As the Norman, Angevin and Plantagenet kings devoted much time to campaigning there are, as one might imagine, many records relating to the travels of the Chapel Royal overseas to minister to the spiritual and diplomatic needs of the king during his military exploits. Perhaps the best documented are the arrangements made for the Chapel Royal to join Henry V and remain in France with him from 1417-21. There are, however, several earlier instances of the Chapel Royal going 'overseas' with the king in equally exciting circumstances, as we shall see in Chapter 2.

2

The Chapel Royal Overseas:
The Old World and the New

At the beginning of the eleventh century king Ethelred proclaimed that the English church should be independent in outlook: 'The king must be regarded not only as head of the church but also as vicar of Christ among Christian folk'. What was to happen after the successful invasion of William duke of Normandy following the battle of Hastings in 1066? Would the Chapel Royal remain under the wing of the king or would it become subject to the decree of the pope in Rome?

Initially William continued the efforts he had been making on the continent to 'reform' the church and bring it into ever closer line with the papacy. But this was to change when in 1073 Hildebrand (archdeacon of Rome) became pope with the title Gregory VII. Hildebrand's intention was to establish himself as absolute ruler over all Christendom, introducing considerable reforms. At first William was in agreement with this, but he soon became alarmed at the political consequences of increased papal power over his new kingdom. These fears were borne out when in 1076 Hildebrand demanded that William do him homage and accept the position of pope's vassal. William flatly refused and made it clear that he would continue the tradition of the English king as head of the church in England. Fortunately for William, his archbishop, Lanfranc, supported him in this stance. The English Chapel Royal's peculiar position thus remained protected from papal authority.

William had his own Chapel Royal in Normandy, as we learn from Ordericus Vitalis. His chaplain was Samson of Bayeux. William offered Samson the bishopric of Le Mans, but he refused, recommending instead another colleague from William's Chapel Royal, who accepted. Samson is recorded as saying, 'Look in your Chapel, for there is a certain poor priest but noble and of great integrity – it is he rather than I who should be offered the bishopric'.

Quite what happened to the 'personnel' of the existing English Chapel Royal after the Conquest is not clear. It is however known that at William's request papal legates unseated five English bishops in 1070. They were replaced by men from the continent of whom Lanfranc was one. From 1070 onwards whenever an English bishop or abbot died he

19

was replaced by a Norman. By 1096 there was not a single bishopric or important abbey in 'English' hands. The English church was now governed by a French-speaking aristocracy. It seems likely therefore that William's Chapel Royal would quickly have metamorphosed into a chapel of 'Norman' clerks.

There exists a remarkable record written during Henry I's reign in 1135, just sixty-nine years after the Norman Conquest, which gives an astonishingly detailed picture of the Chapel Royal. In this record, called the *Liber Rubeus Scacarii*, the particulars relating to the Chapel Royal appear in the tables of household regulations entitled 'Haec est constitutio Domus Regis de procurationibus', and deserve quotation here in full:[1]

> Keeper of the Chapel and relics and food for two men; and four servants of the Chapel, to each of whom double rations; and two sumpter horses of the Chapel, for each one a penny a day; and 1d for serving at the table and for work in the month. For service in the Chapel, two wax tapers on Wednesdays and two on Saturdays; and at night each to have one wax taper to place before the relics; and thirty inferior candles; and one gallon of white wine to be sent to them; and one sixth part of the best wine for the day of Absolution, for use at the altar. On Easter day for communion one sixth measure of white wine and one of the most expensive. The priest's expenses for bread and wine, 2s per day, and salted cumin and one sixth part of the best wine, and one wax taper, and twenty-four inferior candles.

Thus we know that at the very least the Chapel Royal in 1135 comprised two gentlemen, four vestry officials and two sumpter-horses. The horses would have been used as transport for the sacramental items and plate which were strapped on by the four vestry officials. The Chapel Royal was thus a mobile body.

It is clear that William wanted a fortress of substantial proportions to provide a good royal residence. Thus bishop Gundulph began the construction of the White Tower in what we know today as the Royal Palace and Fortress of the Tower of London. It was designed with a chapel building in mind – hence the apse-shaped protrusion of the south-east corner tower (unlike the other three); and this we can still see today. It is dedicated to St John the Evangelist. We know how bishop Gundulph's chapel looked a little later from Stow's record of redecoration during Henry III's reign:

> And that ye cause the whole chapel of St John the Evangelist to be whited. And that ye cause three glass windows in the same chapel to be made; to wit, one on the north side, with a certain little Mary holding her Child; the other on the south part, with the image of the Trinity; and the third, of St

---

[1] The *Liber Rubeus Scacarii* has been edited by Hubert Hall, and forms no. 99 of the *Rolls Series*. These details of the Chapel Royal are to be found in vol. 3, p. 807.

John the Apostle and Evangelist in the south part. And that ye cause the cross and the beam beyond the altar of the said chapel to be painted well, and with good colours. And that ye cause to be made and painted two fair images where more conveniently and decently they may be done in the said chapel; one of St Edward, holding a ring, and reaching it out to St John the Evangelist.

Meanwhile, other locations were provided with facilities for the use of the Chapel Royal in areas where the king was wont to make his regular progresses. The route of the king's progress was more often than not known in advance. The Anglo-Saxon Chronicle is quite specific in stating that William the Conqueror wore his crown three times a year: Easter at Winchester, Whitsuntide at Westminster, and Christmas at Gloucester. This practice was continued by William II and Henry I until at least 1135. Thereafter variations were introduced. So, in accordance with his movements at these major Christian festivals, William the Conqueror evicted the monks of Winchester Minster (where Alfred's dynasty were buried) and twelve burgesses from land at the south side of the High Street in order to build a new palace. This was duly noted in Domesday Book. The palace stood from 1070 until 1140, when it was destroyed by incendiary missiles from defenders at Wolvesley Castle against Matilda's army. The palace consisted of a great hall and a chapel for the use of the Chapel Royal – the site of which is now under the church of St Laurence. The king's chaplains were housed in a chamber in Winchester Castle, which was further specially enlarged for them by Henry III in 1235, by which time the Chapel Royal was housed and sang within the castle in the chapel of St Thomas, where also were kept the sacramental plate and relics of the Chapel Royal when the king was in residence or nearby. The statues, wall-paintings and stained glass of this chapel must have been familiar to gentlemen of the Chapel Royal, Willemus de Wintonia, who in 1221 was termed 'clericus domus regis de capella sua', Henry de Burneval, who in 1229/30 was described as 'capellanus domini regis', and Thomas de Brampton, who was serjeant of the vestry of the Chapel Royal in 1252.

Provision was also made for chapel buildings to be incorporated into the king's hunting lodges as the Chapel Royal and court followed him around the realm, for huge quantities of venison had to be hunted down and killed for the use of the fleet, court and chapel. For example, although king John spent Maundy at Knaresborough in 1210 and at Rochester in 1213, he stayed at Odiham Manor twenty-four times during his reign in order to hunt in the royal park and forests of Alice Holt, Woolmer and Pamber. He even set out from there to sign Magna Carta in 1215. In order to hunt in these same forests in 1285 Edward I built the hunting lodge of Bramshott Manor to include a chapel, and in that same year the royal lodge at Lyndhurst is mentioned as having a king's chapel. Edward II had a lodge at Kingsley built with a chapel. Elements of the Chapel Royal were present from time to time for worship at these establishments while the king used them for the hunt.

In London, in so far as there was a 'base' for the Chapel Royal in early Norman times, the chapel structure at the Tower of London could be construed as constituting it. By 1298 it appears that the 'base' had moved upstream, as we can surmise from an account of building works and alterations undertaken at the archbishop of York's house at Westminster for the year 1298/9 which contains references to making a wardrobe for the king's chaplains. But, as we shall now see, the Chapel Royal's 'portable' nature was by far the most important element, at least until the Eltham Palace Ordinances of 1526.

We learn that the Chapel Royal was overseas with the king in 1254 from an entry in the Calendar of Patent Rolls relating to Henry III's presence at 'Meilham' on 12 May 1254. The entry reads thus: 'Bond to Th. de Brampton, Serjeant of the King's Chapel, in 8 marks for a horse which the King took from him at Meilham, and gave to Oliver de Ingeham for a horse which he lost in the King's service; with promise to pay the same when the Treasurer comes from England.'[2]

In view of the importance of horses in transporting the Chapel Royal plate, vestments and relics, this seizure by the king of the serjeant of the vestry's horse would in all probability have been a rather disabling blow to the Chapel. It is not clear how the serjeant coped without his transport, but the importance of this horse is seen from the king's provision to reimburse the serjeant eight marks at the earliest opportunity.

The Chapel Royal accompanied Richard II to Ireland in 1394, but not, it seems, the entire personnel. The Wardrobe Accounts of 1393 give the names of eleven chaplains and clerks, among them William Excestre and the dean, John Boor. Only six of these clerks, among them a certain 'J. Excestre', together with the dean accompanied Richard to Ireland, according to the Patent Rolls.[3]

William Excestre has been credited with compositions in the early fifteenth-century choirbook of the Chapel Royal now known as the Old Hall manuscript. However, one of the three constituent parts is marked J. Excestre, not W. Excestre. William Excestre was a member of the Chapel Royal from 1392-1402. If he composed part of the Old Hall manuscript he may well have done so from a fascinating background, for he was in all probability the same William Excestre who was one of the clerks in the duke of Lancaster's (John of Gaunt's) household chapel in 1383. John Excestre came from a different background and is recorded as being connected with the Chapel Royal from 1374-96, according to the Patent Rolls of that time. He it was who accompanied Richard II to Ireland in 1394.

---

[2] Cal. Pat. Rolls 1247-58, p. 290.
[3] Cal. Pat. Rolls 1394.

2. The Chapel Royal Overseas: The Old World and the New

This Irish venture would prove momentous for the Chapel Royal. Careful preparations were made: at Hereford on 20 August the king ordered Baldwin of Radyington, comptroller of the king's household, and John de Stanley 'to arrest in England as many fishermen with their vessels, boats, nets, etc., as will suffice for catching fish at sea for the use of the household during the present expedition to Ireland, and put them in the king's service at his charges'.[4]

As we know, a quota of the Chapel Royal accompanied the king, but it was the return journey that was to prove eventful. We learn from a Patent Roll of 19 November 1400 in connection with the customary delivery by indenture to John Boor's successor as dean of the Chapel Royal, Richard Kyngeston, and the keeper of the great wardrobe, William Loueney, of 'all the jewels, vestments and other things pertaining to the chapel', that there were 'exceptions' in the list of items to be handed on. These were 'certain jewels, vestments and ornaments which were seized at Penbrok and within the Lordship of Gower in Wales at the last coming of Richard II from Ireland, of which he [John Boor] had delivered two schedules to them for full information to sue for their full recovery'. This disaster must have proved somewhat of an embarrassment for the vestry officials of the Chapel Royal who would have accompanied the expedition, having loaded the gold and silver onto the Chapel horses. We also know from a Patent Roll that in 1398 and 1399 a certain Richard Sewall was described as 'one of the yeomen-carters of the king's Chapel'. As these vestry officials were holding office certainly as soon as six or seven years after Richard's Irish expedition, we can perhaps presume that it was they who had to cope with the immediate problem of the theft at 'Penbrok' on the expedition's return.

The 'exceptions' described in the Patent Roll of 19 November 1400 give us a tantalising glimpse of what the Chapel Royal gold and silver plate consisted of at that time. They included:

> a little censer with a little ship and a spoon of silver gilt, granted to William Courteney, late archbishop of Canterbury, one whole vestment with its apparel of gold cloth of gold starred with red, and a silver gilt censer weighing six pounds late of the goods of the king's uncle the duke of Gloucester, deceased, a golden chalice weighing two pounds and eight ounces, two silver gilt candlesticks weighing ten pounds and a little frontal granted to Peter de Bosco, ambassador of Rome, and one whole vestment with trimming of cloth of gold granted to the cathedral church of Salisbury.

If these were the 'exceptions' to the handing-on process, we can imagine how splendid were the items belonging to, and used by, the Chapel Royal

---

[4] Cal. Pat. Rolls 1394, p. 523.

in the fourteenth and fifteenth centuries!

In the first year of Henry V's reign in 1413 there were in the Chapel Royal a total of twenty-seven chaplains and clerks – an increase of nine since 1402 when Richard Prentys, formerly a clerk, is recorded as being dean over eighteen chaplains and clerks. Four of the Chapel Royal members in 1413 were composers – John Burrell, John Cook, Thomas Damett and Nicholas Sturgeon.

On 11 August 1415 Henry V sailed from Southampton aboard the *Trinity* together with a fleet of 1,550 ships carrying an army of about 10,000 archers and the Chapel Royal. Landing on the Normandy coast at the Clefs du Caus, Henry beseiged Harfleur, which surrendered on 22 September. He then set off on 5 October with 6,000 men and the Chapel Royal towards Calais, 160 miles away. Shortly after crossing the Somme Henry found his way blocked at Agincourt. He believed, wrongly, that most of the French army was at Verdun, 150 miles from Calais. Henry

Illumination depicting the battle of Agincourt, before which the Chapel Royal sang mass on the battlefield. (MS 6, fol. 243, reproduced by courtesy of His Grace the Archbishop of Canterbury and the Trustees of Lambeth Palace Library)

had intended to cross the Somme at the tidal cattle ford near its mouth, as Edward III had done on his way to Crécy. He was only six miles from the ford when, on taking a Gascon prisoner, he discovered that the ford was defended by the French under marshal Boncicaut. So Henry turned to follow the west bank of the Somme, seeking an alternative crossing-place.

He crossed the river on 19 October at the fords of Beltencourt and Voyennes after destroying houses to repair the causeways across the swamps. Crossing the river Temoise at Blangy and climbing the hill opposite Henry saw, as he approached the village of Maisoncelles, the whole French army only a mile away on the plain ahead. The battle of Agincourt was to be fought in fields sown with winter wheat, with woods surrounding the villages of Agincourt and Tramecourt.

The battle took place on 25 October 1415, the feast of St Crispin and Crispinian. The night before was cold and wet and Henry was up at dawn to hear mass sung by the Chapel Royal. The English victory was resounding, Henry himself wearing the royal surcoat embroidered with the three leopards of England and the three gold fleurs-de-lys of France and wearing a magnificent crown on top of his basinet. The French lost 6,000 men and the English 400, including the duke of York and the earl of Suffolk. Nearly three weeks later Henry was back in England with the Chapel Royal.

The contemporary 'Agincourt Song' beginning 'Deo gracias, Anglia ...' incorporates a complicated counterpoint; a feature which leads John Stevens[5] to suggest that it was composed after the battle but in time for Henry's triumphal return to England when musical celebrations greeted him at every step. It is very probable that the composer of this song was from the Chapel Royal. After all, the Chapel Royal was present at the battle itself.

The next overseas journey of the Chapel Royal was to be just two years later in 1417 – this time to claim the whole of France, or at least the Angevin lands. Henry had broken with the previous traditions of the Hundred Years' War, for he now set out to conquer in an effort to establish permanent English rule. He decided to establish his first bridgehead at Caen, which had to be secured if he was to conquer lower Normandy.

On 15 August 1416 Henry's brother, Bedford, led an English fleet which engaged the French off Harfleur, defeating them and lifting the blockade at the mouth of the Seine. June 1417 saw another naval engagement when the earl of Huntingdon defeated a fleet of twenty-six Genoese and Biscayan ships after a three-hour battle in which he captured four Genoese carracks and dispersed the rest of the fleet. Not until these naval victories were won could Henry's invasion proceed.

---

[5] John Stevens, *Music and Poetry in the Early Tudor Court* (CUP, Cambridge, 1979).

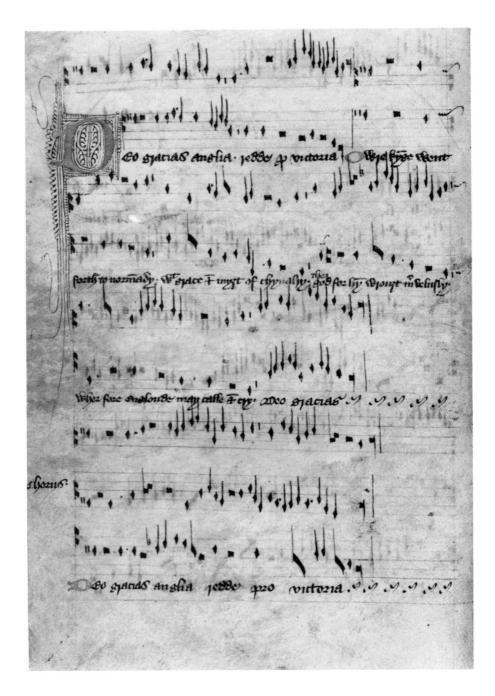

The 'Agincourt Song'. (MS Arch Sheld 13, 26, fol. 17v, reproduced by courtesy of the Bodleian Library, Oxford)

26

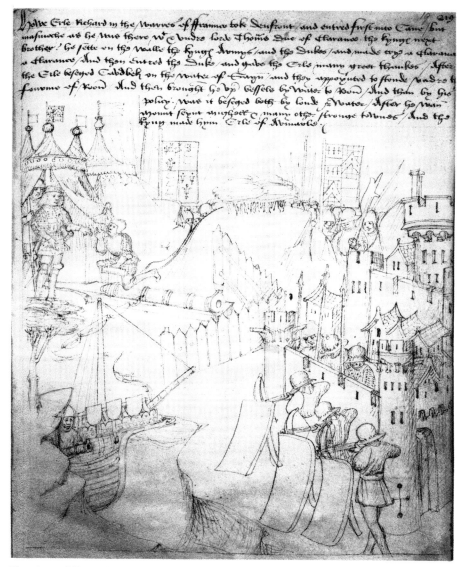

The siege of Caen, August 1417. (MS Cotton Julius EIV, fol. 19, reproduced by courtesy of the British Library)

It appears that the English fleet which sailed on 30 July 1417 and landed at Tonques contained at least some of the Chapel Royal – but certainly not all. The rest sailed about four months later after Henry had captured Caen, secured lower Normandy, made truces with Anjou, Maine and Brittany and returned to Caen in December 1417. We know that some of the Chapel Royal – if only the chaplains – were aboard the main

27

The Abbaye-aux-Dames was one of the two Norman abbeys occupied by Henry V and Clarence before their assault on Caen in 1417. It is likely that the Chapel Royal said or sung mass inside these abbeys before the main assault. (For these photographs I am indebted to Dr Michel Drieu and Timothy Voakes)

English fleet that sailed on 30 July, for at the siege of Caen three masses were said, one after the other, at dawn on 4 September before the general assault.

Ironically, the weakness of Caen lay in the two Norman abbeys on the outskirts of the city which had been re-founded by William the Conqueror and queen Matilda to commemorate William's victory at Hastings in 1066. The English needed to take them to gain the necessary elevation to fire over the city walls into Caen, and duke Clarence in fact captured both abbeys with an advance party of a thousand knights. It is said that the city burghers refused to allow the French soldiers to demolish the abbeys using explosives. The soldiers, ignoring this decision, secretly began to mine the abbeys. A monk saw this and found his way to Clarence, pleading with him to save his abbey. Clarence's forces were shown a secret way into the abbey and the next morning the English flag was flying from its walls. Henry V turned up two days later, having forced the mouth of the Orne with a flotilla of ships loaded with artillery.

Significantly, from the Chapel Royal point of view, Henry and Clarence made the two abbeys their headquarters. It is very likely therefore that the quota of Chapel Royal present – such as it was – sang or said mass there before the main assault on Caen. The resultant sacking of the city was brutal and bloodthirsty, but its notoriety meant that Henry did not have to storm another city in his Normandy campaign.

The next we hear of the Chapel Royal's activities coincides with Henry's return to Caen from December 1417 till May 1418 before his conquest of upper Normandy, which culminated in the successful siege of Rouen from late July 1418 to 19 January 1419. The Calendar of Patent Rolls and the Proceedings of the Privy Council record the 'Commission to John Colles, clerk, servant of the vestry of the king's Chapel within the household, and John Water, one of the king's clerks, to take carriage for the ornaments, jewels, books, vessels and other gear of the Chapel to the town of Southampton'.[6] But it seems that the Chapel Royal did not actually embark until two months later, in February 1418, by which time John Kyngman was added to the commission to help Colles and Water with their vestry tasks. This revised order reads as follows: 'Commission to John Colles, John Kyngman and John Water to take horses, carts and other carriage for the jewels, ornaments and other gear of the king's Chapel to the town of Southampton'.[7] We can conclude therefore that the Chapel Royal either joined the Rouen campaign, or waited in Caen for Rouen to fall in January 1419.

Upon capturing Rouen Henry established his court there, but as time went by the Chapel Royal began to experience recruitment problems from operating in France. These came to a head in 1420. Henry acted

---

[6] Cal. Pat. Rolls 4 December 1417, p. 127.
[7] Cal. Pat. Rolls 12 February 1418, p. 132.

decisively, arranging for a 'Commission to John Pyamour, one of the clerks of the Chapel of the household, to take boys for the said Chapel and bring them to the king's presence in his duchy of Normandy'. The Commission was dated 14 January 1420 and recorded at Westminster.[8] Pyamour remained with the Chapel Royal until 1421. In this period he seems to have acted as master of the children.

From the subject of their musical compositions it is clear that John Cook, Thomas Damett and Nicholas Sturgeon may have been among those clerks of the Chapel Royal who accompanied Henry on his French campaigns. Texts of two motets refer directly to Henry V's campaigns, and had to be composed before the Chapel Royal's return to England in 1421.

One of these motets was composed by John Cook, who was in the Chapel Royal from 1413. It is the 'Alma proles regia – Christi miles inclite' on the tenor 'Ab inimicis defende nos Christe' and is taken from the litany for rogation days in time of war, invoking Jesus, the Virgin Mary and St George for the welfare of the state and protection from its enemies.

The other motet was by Thomas Damett, who was in the Chapel Royal from 1413-31 and then a canon at Windsor. His 'Salvatoris mater pia – Sancti Georgi' on the tenor 'Benedictus Mariae filius qui re', from the Mary-trope of the Benedictus, has a prayer for king Henry in both texts, while the text of the 'duplum' invokes St George, 'gloriosa spes Anglorum', to bring victory and peace. This motet forms a pair with Nicholas Sturgeon's 'Salve mater Domini – Salve templum gratiae' on the tenor 'it in nomine Domini', in praise of the Virgin Mary. Sturgeon's tenor is a direct continuation of Thomas Damett's. It even continues on from where Damett's left off in the middle of the word 'venit' – with the letter 'n', as Bukofzer observes, getting 'lost in the shuffle'![9] Sturgeon, then, would seem to be among those composing on campaign for the Chapel Royal. He was later granted a prebend in Windsor in 1442.

The Chapel Royal returned to England from Rouen between 11 and 18 January 1421. The Proceedings of the Privy Council record the provision on 27 February 1422 for payment to the executors of the late treasurer of the household, John Rothendale, for expenses incurred in arranging for the dean and clerks of the Chapel Royal to return from Rouen to England in 1421. This would have involved the return to England of the children of the Chapel Royal impressed by John Pyamour for service with the Chapel Royal in Normandy in 1420.

It is more than likely that that the Chapel Royal had also accompanied Henry V to his great triumph of the treaty of Troyes, ratified in the

---

[8] Cal. Pat. Rolls 14 January 1420, p. 272.
[9] See also F. Harrison, *Music in Medieval Britain* (Routledge & Kegan Paul, London, 1958) p. 247.

The dean of the Chapel Royal played a crucial role in the making of diplomatic treaties. Here Richard Beauchamp, earl of Warwick, is at the French court taking part in the negotiations for the treaty of Troyes, ratified in the cathedral of Troyes on 21 May 1420. The dean is probably one of the three figures in the foreground, one of whom is holding a chalice. (MS Cotton Julius EIV, Art 6, fol. 6v, reproduced by courtesy of the British Library)

cathedral of Troyes in Champagne on 21 May 1420. The negotiations for the treaty with the French would certainly have involved the dean of the Chapel Royal. A fascinating sketch exists in the British Library depicting Richard Beauchamp, earl of Warwick, negotiating the terms of the treaty at the French court, in a building whose architecture suggests a royal chapel, in the company of senior clergy, one of whom is holding an elaborate chalice. It is a matter for speculation whether one of the three clergy depicted was the dean of the English Chapel Royal. It would certainly not be in the least surprising.

To reach Troyes the English marched in fighting order close under the eastern walls of Paris with archers in company to deter the Armagnac threat. After minor resistance Henry and his army reached Troyes where he was met by the duke of Burgundy. Henry then paid his respects to Charles VI, and on 21 May rode to the cathedral to ratify the treaty. Henry walked down the nave with queen Isabeau and then climbed to the high altar where the articles of the treaty were read. He then sealed the treaty with the 1360 Bretigny seal. Later that same day he was solemnly betrothed to the princess Katherine. It is scarcely conceivable that no members of the Chapel Royal were present for this climax to Henry's campaigns. Twelve days later came the wedding, and Henry, king of England, became heir and regent of France.

Two days later Henry rode out of Troyes to continue his campaigning by defeating the Armagnacs south-east of Paris. After bloody sieges and capitulations he secured the lands south of Paris and prepared for his ceremonial entrance into the city. This turned out to be an affair of great pomp and colour. Priests even brought relics for the kings, Henry and Charles, to kiss. Te Deums were sung. On the next day queen Katherine arrived. Henry did not stay in Paris for long, but he did spend Christmas there. So, probably, did the Chapel Royal, or some of it, but Henry, his brothers and his queen left for Rouen and spent a month there putting Henry's Norman territories in good order before embarking for England towards the end of January 1421. The records relating to the return of the Chapel Royal to England from 11-18 January 1421 form part of the details concerning the royal court's return to England with the king.

Soon after his return Katherine was crowned queen, and they both set off on a royal tour around England. Again, there is every reason to suppose that the Chapel Royal accompanied them. However, as the royal progress approached Beverley news was brought that the dauphin had won a great victory over Clarence's forces at Baugé, just north of the Loire between Angers and Tours. Henry knew he had to return to campaign in France. He set sail for Calais on 10 June 1421 with 4,000 fresh men, fought a brilliant campaign, but then fell ill, probably with dysentery, and died at his favourite castle of Vincennes on 31 August 1422.

Henry VI thus became king of England at the age of nine months in September 1422. A few weeks later his maternal grandfather Charles VI died, and he became king of France as well. He was crowned king of England in Westminster Abbey on 6 November 1429 and in April 1430 was taken to France by his governors, the duke of Bedford and the earl of Warwick. The Chapel Royal accompanied him to France and was present at his coronation as king of France in Notre Dame, Paris, by cardinal Beaufort, bishop of Worcester, on 16 December 1431.

The French National Archives possess several copies of the processional antiphon and a copy for the choir of the entire plainsong for Henry VI's coronation service at Notre Dame. Interestingly, these show that two changes were made in the traditional plainsong of the English

Paris in the fifteenth century, from Froissart's *Chronicles*. (Reproduced by courtesy of the Bibliothèque Nationale, Paris)

coronation ritual. These revolved around the influence of Joan of Arc and St Remigius.

Henry's journey to Paris for his coronation had not been without incident. It was to be his only journey overseas and not a happy one. First he was held up at Calais for three months because of the uncertain military situation. Then he found himself lodging in the same castle in Rouen and at the same time as Joan of Arc, just nineteen years old and facing her trial and execution.

This irony had its influence on the coronation music. The antiphon 'Firmatur manus tuas' for the entrance into the church was replaced by the respond 'Ecce mitto angelum', it seems with the visions of Joan of Arc in mind! During the procession carrying the holy oil, as it entered from

34

the vestry, a respond of St Remigius, patron saint of Rheims, where Charles VII had been crowned king of France in Joan of Arc's presence on 17 July 1429, was sung. The holy oil ceremony during Henry's coronation was conducted by the English nobles and the French bishops of Beauvais and Noyon. Also taking part were the canons of Notre Dame and the English clerks of the Chapel Royal. There was an unseemly argument between them at the offering of the wine. It is Frank Harrison's surmise that if Henry VI's Chapel Royal or the duke of Bedford's chapel sang polyphony at the service it is possible that John Dunstable's motet 'Veni Sancte Spiritus – Veni Creator Spiritus' and his Credo and Sanctus on 'Da gaudiorum praemia' were written especially for this occasion. It is thought that these may perhaps be the surviving movements of a complete polyphonic ordinary. John Dunstable was a member of the chapel of the duke of Gloucester's brother, John, duke of Bedford, in Paris, when Bedford was regent of France from 1423 to 1429, and in Rouen when he was governor of Normandy from 1429 until 1435.

Henry VI's coronation took place on 16 December 1431 in Paris, and he was hurried away at the end of that same month, landing at Dover on 9 February 1432. He had been overseas for nearly two years. Journeying via Canterbury and Blackheath, Henry eventually arrived at Deptford where he was met by a concourse of clergy. He then travelled to Southwark and thence to St Paul's Cathedral for a thanksgiving service. If subsequent similar thanksgiving services are any indication, it is almost certain that the Chapel Royal sang there for that occasion. Henry VI was never to travel overseas again.

Proceedings of the Privy Council of 30 April 1430 authorised reimbursement of cardinal Beaufort and the household treasurer for expenditure on the Chapel Royal 'ad opem Regis ultra mare'. Warrants exist for expenses of Richard Praty and John Carpenter, chaplains to the king, and John Walden, confessor, who accompanied cardinal Beaufort to France.

Sadly, the occasion for a 'reunion' between John Pyamour and his old friends among the clerks of the Chapel Royal who had come to France for the coronation may have been missed. Pyamour had apparently left the Chapel Royal in 1421 but went to France again with Bedford when the duke returned to France after his visit to England in 1427. Pyamour continued to compose and sing in the duke's chapel in France until he died sometime before 4 July 1431. The duke of Bedford's chapel was at Henry VI's coronation in Notre Dame in December 1431, after Pyamour's death. However, the Chapel Royal was in France from April 1430, so Pyamour may have been able to meet old friends before his demise.

The composer Robert Chirbury had joined the Chapel Royal by 1421 and remained with it until 1447, becoming in the meantime dean of St Mary's, Warwick, on 4 May 1443. He would therefore most likely have accompanied Henry VI at his coronation at Westminster in 1429 and

Notre Dame in 1431.

It seems that Henry V himself composed. The Rev. George F. Tull writes of Henry VI: 'It is not certain whether the king's musical talents extended to composition, since the Gloria and Sanctus in the Old Hall manuscript which have been ascribed to him are now regarded as more probably the work of his father.'[10] The true quality of Henry V's chapel music was celebrated in a poem of the time, which ran thus:

> Psallit plena Deo cantoribus ampla capella:
> Carmine sidereo laudabilis est ea cella.[11]

> (With choristers in sumptuous chapel psalms of David singing,
> The music of the stars of heaven through that sanctuary is ringing.)

Certainly Henry V's regard for the Chapel Royal was revealed in the terms of his will, in which he left £200 to the clerks of his chapel. No steps were taken until Henry VI's return from his coronation at Notre Dame ten years later to distribute this sum 'to the clerks of the chapel of the household before they separate' and in 1433 the decision was to be made to decide the proportion to be paid to each member.

During Henry VI's minority the number of members of the Chapel Royal was 'run down' so that from the last year of Henry V's reign (1421/2) when there were sixteen choristers in the Chapel Royal the number fell to just six within a year. In 1436 the Great Wardrobe Accounts show that there were just seven members of the Chapel Royal, but things were to change when a year later, in 1437, Henry VI assumed the rule of his kingdom and his household.

In the course of the year 1437 Henry VI lost both his grandmother, queen Joan of Navarre, and his mother, queen Katherine of Navarre. Henry was now almost sixteen years old and the regency and king's minority had come to an end. He now took charge of his household and one of the first visits he made as king was in 1439 to a lazar house for lepers – the hospital of St James by Westminster. Here he stayed for ten days from 18 to 28 March 1439. The hospital is mentioned in a Patent Roll dated 29 September 1265 as being under the king's protection. The then king, Henry III, had granted:

> Simple Protection, until Easter, for the following:
> Sibyl late the wife of Geoffrey Bainard.
> The master, brethren and sisters of the hospital of St James Westminster.
> Robert de London.

Just one year after the experience of visiting the hospital, Henry VI in

---

[10] The Rev. George F. Tull, *Henry of Windsor – The Scholar King* (Henry VI Society, n.d.).
[11] Quoted in Harrison, *Music in Medieval Britain*, p. 22.

1440 publicly declared his intention to found two colleges to provide a good Christian education for the rising generation. The first of these was to be sited just across the river Thames from Windsor in the parish of Eton; Henry laid the foundation stone in person on 5 July 1441. In 1450, seven years after the completion of Eton College, Henry granted the college the perpetual custody of the hospital of St James by Westminster. Eighty-one years later, in 1531, Henry VIII bought the hospital from the provost of Eton. He had the site and surrounding land at his disposal from December 1531, and, although the last of the inmates was not pensioned off until 1536, set about building a new palace for his illegitimate son Henry Fitzroy, duke of Richmond, whom he contemplated recognising as his heir. The name of the old hospital was perpetuated in the title of the palace – St James's. All that now remains of the original hospital buildings are the stone supporting arches in the 'tunnel' between colour court and ambassadors' court and the collection of 'slip tiles' found in situ during an archaeological dig in colour court in 1923 and now displayed in the vestibule of the chapel.

Before returning to the journeyings of the Chapel Royal overseas, mention should also be made of another significant foundation in relation to the Chapel Royal as we now experience it. This was the founding of the City of London School in 1442 by the town clerk of the City of London and executor of Dick Whittington's will, John Carpenter. Whether it was the same John Carpenter, or a relation of his, who travelled as king's chaplain, together with the king's chaplain Richard Praty and king's confessor John Walden, with Henry VI to France for the coronation in 1431, is not clear. Certainly the town clerk John Carpenter had his own chapel within his own house, and a domestic chaplain, Sir William Taillour. The chapel itself contained 'a great missale', 'a best silver gilt cup', 'a silver gilt paxarium [chalice cover]', 'two phials or cruets of silver' and a 'casula [chasuble] of white damask, with all its trimming'. His bed had a cover with the IHS symbolism and roses, and there was a 'litill cloth with an image of Our Lady and Seynt John Baptist over the chamber door'. We know too that he was a lay brother of the Charterhouse and also of the Fraternity of the Sixty Priests of London.

Whatever the connection may or may not be with the Chapel Royal John Carpenter, it is clear that just under 500 years later this same City of London School was asked to educate, and indeed still does, the boys who comprise the children of H.M. Chapel Royal at St James's Palace.

On his death in 1442 John Carpenter bequeathed in his will a number of estates to the City of London 'for the finding and bringing up of foure poore men's children with meate, drinke, apparell, and learning at the schooles and universities, etc., until they be preferred, and then others in their places for ever'. These four boys were choristers at the Guildhall chapel certainly from 1446, when the chapel was required by the sheriff to hand over two small copes to be used for the choristers of St Stephen's

Wallbrook, until the 'college' was dissolved by Henry VIII in 1536. Stow refers to the Guildhall chapel in his 1598 *Survey of London* stating that 'this chapel or college had a custos, seven chaplains, three clerks, and four choristers'. These boys were the 'Carpenter children'. There is no evidence that they were exempt from impressment by the Chapel Royal, as were Westminster Abbey, St George's Windsor and certain other establishments. Thus we are left with the intriguing possibility that some of the Carpenter children may have sung for the Chapel Royal 500 years before it was made an official arrangement in 1923.

The scholarly Henry VI, on assuming full power, soon took charge of his household, and accordingly in 1440 a Patent Roll records that the dean of the Chapel Royal, John Croucher, was commissioned to impress choristers. Wardrobe Accounts show that in 1441 there were twenty-six members of the Chapel Royal. In this year a most significant event occurred, for John Plummer was granted £10 – it seems for instructing and supervising the children of the Chapel Royal. This was to be the precursor of the office of master of the children. Four years later in 1444 the same John Plummer was granted forty marks a year for the exhibition of eight boys of the Chapel Royal and for his services in this respect.

The circumstances of Henry VI's death in 1471 have some relevance to the history of the Chapel Royal building within the White Tower of the Tower of London – the chapel of St John the Evangelist. While at his devotions in the small oratory in the Wakefield tower 'on a Tuesday night 21st May betwixt XI and XII of the clock, the Duke of Gloster being then at the Tower and many others', according to Fabyan's Chronicles, the king was 'stikked with a dagger by the hands of Richard of Gloster [later Richard III]'. Henry's body, 'full of deadly holes', was laid in the chapel of St John. In the morning he was brought from the Tower via Cornhill to St Paul's Cathedral in an open coffin where he bled, and then to the Dominican monastery at Blackfriars where he bled again, this being taken as a sure sign that he had been murdered, and finally transported by river to the abbey church of Chertsey where he was interred in the lady chapel.

The Chapel Royal's story now turns overseas. Edward IV was determined to re-conquer France and in July 1475 sailed for Calais with a force of 10,000 men – the largest and best equipped army ever to be led into France by an English king. His ally Charles, duke of Burgundy, however, arrived without any troops at all. He had left the Burgundian army far away at Nantes in another campaign backed by the Holy Roman Emperor. Edward's other ally Francis, duke of Brittany, deserted him. The eventual confrontation, fraught with danger, saw the dean of the Chapel Royal, William Dudley, play a crucial and leading role on the potential battlefield in an effort to secure terms for peace. A Patent Roll of 1476 describes this tense moment in extraordinarily vivid detail: 'the king being in his field beside the village called Seyncre within Vermondose a little from Peron ... [the] dean of the King's Chapel ... being with him ... upon certain offers made by the French king for a truce charged Lord Howard, the master of the rolls, the dean of the Chapel and Thomas Selynger to go to the French king ... to conclude as follows ... .' The terms involved an enormous sum of money and a stipulation that the French king 'will marry his son the dauphin at his charge to the first or second of the king's [Edward IV's] daughters ...'. These terms were accepted and the French then entertained the entire English army to a feast at Amiens.

How many of the Chapel Royal went with Edward IV on his 1475 French campaign? If the numbers of Chapel Royal establishment as recorded by William Say in 1449 in his *Liber Regie Capelle*[12] are any indication, then a maximum total of forty-nine Chapel Royal members may have accompanied the king. On this basis the campaign of 1475 would have included dean William Dudley, thirty established chapel clerks (cantores electi) of whom half were priests, one priest for the lady mass and reading the gospel, a clerk to read the epistle, ten boys 'trained to sing', one song master to train the boys in 'plain chant and harmony', one serjeant of the vestry 'with charge of the plate, books, vestments and other ornaments pertaining to the Chapel' together with one yeoman and two grooms, one grammar master to 'teach the science of grammar to the young noblemen brought up in the king's court and the boys of the Chapel as they grow older'.

However, just five years later a complete list of the king's 'honeurable household' in 1454, to be found among the Acts of the Privy Council, put the numbers in the Chapel Royal at twenty chaplains and clerks and seven children, while a year later, in 1455, at the granting of the mastership to Henry Abyngdon to take effect from Michaelmas 1456, the number of children is given as ten. Abyngdon held the mastership until 1475, when Gilbert Banester was appointed. August 1456 saw the Chapel Royal priests and clerks petition the Privy Council 'to consider their just labour because their number was less than formerley'. They appealed for twenty-four gentlemen singers, and for the 'poor priest' William Stevyns to read the gospel, say the daily lady mass and keep the vestry, and for another to read the epistle. As we know, Stevyns was confirmed in his post, and an epistler was appointed. This decision reveals a reduction in numbers, at least temporarily, as under Say's *Liber Regie Capelle* of 1449 there was a separate person designated to fill the office of priest for the

---

[12] See p. 2 of Gordon Dunstan's English translation of the *Liber Regie Capelle*, made 'In the train, London-Zurich-London, June 1971', and now lodged at the Chapel Royal, of the Latin original written by dean William Say in 1449, published by the Henry Bradshaw Society in 1961, and edited by Walter Ullmann. Say wrote this *Constitution or Ordinance of the Chapel of the Most Illustrious and Christian Prince, Henry VI, King of England and France and Lord of Ireland* for the interest of Alfonso, king of Portugal.

lady mass and gospel, the epistle clerk, and there was also a serjeant, yeoman and two grooms to look after the vestry. The 'Stevyns' compromise apparently led to the loss of four 'jobs'. There may therefore have been fewer than the forty-nine members of Say's time when the Chapel Royal went overseas with Edward IV.

We do, however, have firm details in the Calendar of Patent Rolls about the Chapel Royal eight years after this campaign, in 1483, when Edward IV incorporated the 'Royal Free Chapel of the Household'.[13] This re-organised the Chapel Royal's constitution to give it not only a dean (John Gunthorpe), but also three canons who were to act as sub-dean (Nicholas Hewys), treasurer (Richard Surland), and precentor (John Chirche). The endowments of the chapel of St Peter within the Tower of London were given to the Royal Free Chapel of the Household, i.e. the Chapel Royal. It must be said that the 'Royal Free Chapel of the Household' was in no sense a separate entity from its predecessor – the Chapel Royal had merely acquired a new name and a few more 'chiefs' between whom the increasing burdens of the dean's duties could be spread. Edward IV's ordinances for his household reveal that in 1483 his chapel had twenty-four chaplains and 'gentylmen clerkes'. It appears that the latter may well have been permitted to be lay-clerks and not necessarily required to be in holy orders even as deacons. Their qualifications were clearly defined. They had to be 'endewed with vertuose morall and speculatiff as of theyre musike, shewing in descant, clene voysed, well relysed and pronouncinge, eloquent in Reding, sufficiaunt in organes pleying'. There were two 'pistellers groweing from the children of the Chapell by succession of age and after that their voices change', and eight children under a master who was chosen by the dean from the members of the Chapel Royal to teach them 'as well in the schoole of facett as in songe, organes and such other vertuous thinges'. If there was no place for a child of the chapel on his reaching eighteen years of age, and his voice had changed, then a special provision was made for this eventuality: 'the King assineth every suche child to a college of Oxenford or Cambrigge of the King's foundation, there to be in finding and study sufficiauntly, tyll the Kinge otherwise list to advance him'.

In 1484, one year after the incorporation of the Chapel Royal, John Meylonek, 'one of the gentilmen of our Chapell', received a licence to recruit men and boys from other religious establishments for service in the Chapel Royal. The licence reads thus:

> To all and every our subjects, as well spirituall as temporell, these letters hering or seeing, greeting. We let you wite, that for the confidence and trust we have in our wellbeloved servant, John Meylonek, one of the gentilmen of

---

[13] A memorial board bearing the names of fifty-eight musicians from the time of the incorporation, including all the organists, is mounted in the vestibule of the present Chapel Royal building at St James's Palace.

our Chapell and knowing also his expert habilitie and connyng in the science of musique, have licensed him, and by these presents licence and give him auctoritie, that within all places of this our realme, as well Cathedral-Churches, colleges, chappells, houses of religion, and all other franchised and exempt places, as elliswhere, our Colege Roil at Wyndesor reserved and except, may take and sease for us and in our name all such singing men and children, being expart in the said science of musique, as he can finde, and thinke sufficient and able to do us service.

As the master of the children in 1484 was Gilbert Banester, who it appears held this office from 1475-87, it is clear that such impressment of men and boys was not always the task of the master, for John Meylonek did not hold this post. It must at the same time be concluded that certainly in 1484 and, no doubt, for some years previously and perhaps stretching back to the 1475 French campaign, the Chapel Royal was under-strength and in need of rejuvenation. This it certainly got.

The story of the Chapel Royal overseas is dramatically resumed in Henry VIII's reign at the siege of the French city of Therouanne in 1513. It was Henry's intention to prove himself worthy of his illustrious warlike predecessors and leave no doubt as to his stature as a monarch. His campaign in fact had the official status of a crusade, as pope Julius II's anger at the French king caused him to issue a papal brief taking the French kingdom away from France and giving it to Henry, this to take effect as soon as Henry had conquered the French.

There is a work known as the 'Henry VIII manuscript', on folio 1 of which an old hand has written 'henricus dei gracia res anglie'. It is a book of songs and carols by, among others, Henry VIII, Fayrfax, Cornish, Kemp, Rysbye, Farthing, Daggere, Dunstable, Pygote, Cooper and Lloyd (Flude). Of interest are the scribbles at the end, which read: 'Sir John Leed in the parish of Benyngden' and 'Syr John Berde in the parish of Benenden'. It appears that the manuscript arrived in Benenden in Kent because the comptroller of the household, Sir Henry Guildford, had his seat there and probably commissioned it. Sir Henry had been knighted in 1512 and was to be created a 'knight-banneret' on the fall of the city of Tournai – which tells of his presence on the 1513 French campaign. As master of the revels he celebrated the victory of Tournai with an interlude in which he himself played before the king. As for the Henry VIII manuscript, it has been thought that it was made for the king to sing from. Be that as it may, the songs themselves tell an adventurous story in which the Chapel Royal was to find itself an important participant. Song H 96 from the manuscript runs as follows:

Englond, be glad! Pluk up thy lusty hart!
Help now thi kyng, thi kyng, and take his part!
Ageynst the Frenchmen in the feld to fyght
In the quarell of the church and in the ryght,

With spers and sheldys on goodly horses lyght,
Bowys and arows to put them all to flyght:
Help now thi king [and take his part!]

Another song, H 97, reads thus:

Pray we to God that all may gyde
That for our kynge so to provid,
To send hym power to hys corage
He may acheffe this gret viage:
   Now let us sing this rownd all thre;
   Sent George, graunt hym the victory!

The words of both these songs were composed in the context of Henry's French campaign. The huge fleet left English shores in June 1513 and disembarked at Calais in early July. Henry's army marched out of English-held Calais in late July and made its way in a south-easterly direction towards the city of Therouanne. The artillery, which included minions, lizards and demi-culverins, was carried in the van and set the pace for the rest of the army. Next came the king's household guard under the banner of the Trinity, the duke of Buckingham together with his 400 soldiers, three ecclesiastical corps under the bishops of Durham and Winchester and Thomas Wolsey, the king's almoner. Under Henry's own banner marched a guard of 600 men, followed by the Chapel Royal priests and singers, secretaries, kitchen staff, bedchamber staff and the king's lutanist. In the rear the lord chamberlain and the earl of Northumberland led another large force.

There was only one mishap of 'ecclesiastical' note before Henry's army reached the walls of Therouanne. This concerned the bishop of Winchester, who was kicked by a mule en route! Henry's Hapsburg ally, the emperor Maximilian, arrived with a band of Burgundians shortly after Henry had begun the siege and offered to put them at Henry's disposal in return for a suitable payment. After a siege of about three weeks Henry took possession of the town with a magnificent ceremonial entry and handed it over to Maximilian, who ordered every building with the exception of the old church to be destroyed. The Chapel Royal almost certainly celebrated the victory in that church. Before going on to besiege the city of Tournai Henry stopped for several weeks of feasting and entertainment at the court of the regent of Flanders.

Tournai held out for only eight days, and this time Henry kept it for himself. Having made his point by capturing two cities, a shipload of French prisoners for ransom, and the standards and spurs of the French, Henry decided to return to England. Leaving Tournai with the Chapel Royal, he again stopped off at the court of the regent of Flanders for entertainment before returning to Calais.

We have a good idea of exactly who the members of the Chapel Royal were that accompanied Henry on this French campaign. Our information comes from a document in the lord chamberlain's records of 1511 detailing the gentlemen of the Chapel Royal for whom livery was issued for the funeral of prince Henry, who died aged only seven weeks:[14]

Mr Doctor Farefax	William Crane	William Dawbeney
Edward John	John Pende	Henry Prentisshe
Mr John Lloidd	Thomas Sexten	Thomas Farthyng
John Sidborough	John Wever	John Gyles
William Browne	John Fissher	Robert Hawkins
William Cornysh	Robert Pende	John Petwyn
William Sturton	Henry Stevenson	Davey Burten

A couple of lists survive relating to the funeral of Henry VII two years earlier in 1509, which mention the names of the children of the Chapel Royal, at least some of whom would still have been singing in the choir just four years later when it accompanied Henry to France.[15]

William Colman	Arthur Lovekyn
William Maxe	Nicholas Ive
William Alderson	John Graunger
Henry Merell	Edward Coke
John Williams	Henry Andrewe

In addition to these names, a list to be found among the state papers of Henry VIII[16] includes the name James Curteys.

The dean who accompanied the Chapel Royal on the campaign was William Atwater. He would most certainly have been present at the ratification of the treaty between Henry VIII and the emperor Maximilian on 3 July 1513 in St Mary's Church, Calais, before Henry began his campaign.

The year 1513 saw Richard Norton replace John Kyte as sub-dean. We know, too, who held the vestry offices during this campaign. The serjeant of the vestry was William Tebbe. A 'warrant to the Great Wardrobe to deliver to Wm. Tebbe, Serjeant of the Vestry, for the use of our chapell', vestments etc., is dated 28 January 1510, while another requires the great wardrobe to deliver 'half a yard of purpure velvet for our palm' to William Tebbe as serjeant of the vestry as part of the Chapel Royal's preparations for Passiontide. This warrant is dated 19 March 1510 at Greenwich. Another dated 10 June 1512 at Greenwich records the order to the great wardrobe to provide Tebbe with 'stuff to repair vestments'. The campaign of 1513 then occupies his attention before he is again

---

[14] LC vol. 550, fol. 170d, PRO.
[15] LC vol. 424, fols 202d, 203.
[16] *Letters and Papers Foreign and Domestic*, ed. J.S. Brewer, R.H. Brodie and J. Gairdner (21 vols, London, 1862-1910) vol. 1, part 1, 1509-13, p. 18.

mentioned in a warrant dated 31 October 1514 at Greenwich as the recipient of '30 surplices for men and 10 for children, albs etc.'.

As for the other vestry officials, a warrant of 1511 mentions 'Five persons of the Revestiary: Wm. Tebbe, Serjeant, Wm. Colman, John Buntyng, Nic Hunclyff, Geoffry Wright.' We learn from an earlier record of members of the 'the King's Chappell' among Henry's state papers of 'John Buntyng, yeoman, Nic. Hunclyff, Rob. Hawkyns, pysteler, Geffrey groom of the vestry'.[17] Some or all of these vestry officials, vital to the portable capability of the Chapel Royal, would have gone on the 1513 campaign.

The master of the children, William Cornish, won great acclaim for himself through the excellent quality of the singing of the Chapel Royal on this French campaign. Cornish had succeeded William Newark in 1509 as master of the children. Newark had held the post since 1493. Cornish is thought to have had some association with the poet Skelton, arch-critic of Wolsey. It is thought that this association may well have resulted in collaboration from time to time and in treasonable satire. Certainly Cornish was sent to the Fleet Prison in 1504, where he wrote 'a treatise betweene Trouthe and Enformation', notable for its use of musical terminology, arguing that his imprisonment was due to false witness. Cornish was a remarkably versatile composer. Although the Fayrfax manuscript, written about 1500, and the Henry VIII manuscript, written about 1515, contain many works by Cornish (he contributed twelve pieces to the Henry VIII manuscript, for example), sadly several of his major compositions, including masses, have been lost while only fragments of others have survived. Among these lost compositions are a Pater noster and the carol 'Pleasure it is', both of which are printed in the *XX Songes* of 1530 where only the fragmentary bass part survives. Some of the compositions of the Fayrfax manuscript may have been sung on the 1513 campaign, and Cornish's reputation was certainly greatly enhanced by the Chapel Royal's performance.

A notable name in the 1509 and 1511 lists of members of the Chapel Royal cited above is that of William Crane. He was involved, together with Cornish, the sub-dean and others, as well as the children of the Chapel Royal, in the revels that accompanied prince Henry's New Year birth. 'The Golldyn Arber in the Archeyard of Plesyer' was a pageant in which 'without un the syds were viii mynstrells with strange instrements, and befoor un the steps stood dyvers persoons dysgysyd, as Master Sub Deen, Master Kornyche, Master K[r]aan and other, and on top wer the chylldryn of the Chappell syngyng so that oon thys pagent was xxx persons, weche was marvelus wyghty to remoef and Kany, as yt dyd bothe up and down the hall and turnyd round'. The Henry VIII manuscript records this pageant (as H 68) in the words of a song:

[17] Ibid.

Adew, adew, le company,
I trust we shall mete oftener.
Vive le Katerine et noble Henry!
Vive le prince, le infant Rosary!!

Whether part or all of this song-book as we now know it was taken abroad on the 1513 French campaign remains conjecture, but it is a strong likelihood.

William Crane was to succeed William Cornish as master of the children of the Chapel Royal in 1523. Crane, together with Thomas Heywood, was entitled to wear a coat-of-arms, unlike Dr Fayrfax who, although fourth son of a knight, attained only the rank of 'poor knight of Windsor'. Oddly, no musical compositions by Crane have survived, but we do know that he was a wool-exporter, wine merchant and 'water-bailiff of the town and port of Dertmouth',[18] and that, together with his fellow Chapel Royal gentleman William Browne, he shared the king's pastime of archery:

> Item the same daye paide to William Browne for so moche money as he and the other being matched with him wanne of the King's grace and of his matche at the pryckes, and by bettes in Elthem parke divers and sundrye tymes as apperith by his bille subscribed with his hande the somme of ... £132-15s.[19]

Crane won just £7 2s 6d, but he was evidently a very rich man who was twice in a position to lend a huge sum equivalent to £30,000 today. Perhaps not surprisingly he was able to be the furnisher or outfitter of three ships and galleys to the king in 1528. The Household Book of 1530 has an 'Item, to Mr Crane for playing before the King's majestie with the Children of the Chappell, in rewarde, vj xiijs iiijd'.

Of such characters, then, was the Chapel Royal comprised on its overseas campaign in 1513.

Sagudino's letter to the Signory of Venice describing the reception of the Venetian ambassadors in 1515 indicates the continued excellence of Henry's Chapel Royal. The king invited the ambassadors and their retinue to hear mass and dine with him at Richmond Palace:

> so they went to church, and after a grand procession had been made, high mass was sung by the king's choristers, whose voices are more divine then human; non cantavano ma guibilavano; and as to the counter-bass voices, they probably have not their equal in the world.[20]

A letter written by the dean of the St Paul's, Richard Pace, to Wolsey

---

[18] See warrant in Cal. Pat. Rolls 3 June 1509.
[19] See Stevens, *Music and Poetry in the Early Tudor Court.*
[20] *Calendar of State Papers Venetian*, vol. 2, p. 247.

on 25 March 1518 reveals the king's efforts to ensure the continued excellent quality of the singing in the Chapel Royal, and also gives an excellent picture of 'impressment' in action. Dean Pace's letter to Wolsey, with reference to 'young Robin', one of the boys in Wolsey's choir, runs thus:

> My lord, if it were not for the personal love that the king's highness doth bear unto your grace surely he would have out of your chapel not children only, but also men; for his grace had plainly shown unto Cornysche that your grace's chapel is better than his, and proved the same by this reason that if any manner of new song should be brought into both the said chapels to be sung ex improviso then the said song should be better and more surely handled by your chapel than by his grace's.

It seems that the king bearded the dean again that afternoon, for the very next day, 26 March, Pace wrote again. This time he said: 'The king has spoken to me again about the child of your chapel. He is desirous to have it without the procuring of Cornish or other.' This letter did the trick, for on 29 March Pace wrote again to Wolsey at the king's command to thank him for the child. On 1 April Pace wrote a final time to Wolsey to say that 'Cornyshe doth greatly laud and praise the child of your Chapel sent hither, not only for his sure and cleanly singing but also for his good and crafty descant and doth in like manner extol Mr Pygote for the teaching of him'.[21] Richard Pygote was later to become deputy master of the children of the Chapel Royal in *c.* 1526, as well as a gentleman of the Chapel Royal from 1524-52.

Just two years after the exchange of letters with Wolsey this excellent Chapel Royal was to travel abroad with the king to the 'Field of the Cloth of Gold' in 1520. On this occasion the comptroller of the household and master of the revels, Sir Henry Guildford, again played an important role together with the Chapel Royal. The *Calendar of State Papers* refers to the 'very beautiful silver organ, with gold ornaments' which adorned the king's chapel at the Field of the Cloth of Gold. William Cornish again acquitted himself impressively, the Chapel Royal performing with great splendour.

This was to be the last journey of the Chapel Royal overseas as a 'full' choir but for two exceptional occasions to which we shall come later. A major watershed in the history of the Chapel Royal was about to be implemented, which would ensure that only a part of the full complement of the Chapel would remain 'portable' in accordance with its ancient tradition. The rest would form a permanent establishment in London. This paved the way for permanent Chapel Royal establishments at the newly emerging Tudor palaces.

In the Eltham Palace Ordinances of 1526 Henry VIII stipulated that

---

[21] *Letters and Papers of Henry VIII*, vol. 2, pp. 1246, 1249, 1252.

only a quota of the Chapel Royal should henceforth travel with him when he was away from London 'in his castle of Windsor, his Manors of Bewlye, Richmond and Hampton Court, Greenwich, Eltham or Woodstock ... at all such tymes ... the king's noble chappell to be kept in the same place, for the administration of divine service as apperteyneth'. The ordinance goes on to give the numbers of gentlemen and officers of the Chapel Royal who were to continue to travel with the king:

> Nevertheless, forasmuch as it is goodly and honourable that there should be allwayes some divine service in the Court, whereby men might be elected unto the devotion, and that it would not only be a great annoyance but also excessive labour, travell, charge and paine to have the King's whole chappell continually attendant upon his person when his grace keepeth not his hall, and specially in rideing journeys and progresses; it is for the better administration of divine service ordeyened that the Master of the Children and six men, with some officers of the Vestry, shall give their continuall attendance in the King's Court, and dayly, in absence of the residue of the Chappell, to have a masse of our Lady before noon, and on Sundays and holydayes masse of the day besides our Lady masse and an antheme in the afternoone; for which purpose no great carriage, either of vestments or bookes shall be required: the said persons to have an allowance of board wages or bouch of court, with lodgeing in or neere to the same, and convenient carriage, as in such case hath been accustomed.[22]

We gain an insight into some aspects of the Chapel Royal from Henry VIII's Book of Payments which in 1510 records that £26 13s 4d was paid for a new organ at Richmond Palace. A year's payment to William Lewes, organmaker and keeper of the king's instruments, was made in 1514. In 1518 there is a payment to 'two men of London, for mending the organs at Woodstock, and transporting the organ of Woodstock parish church to the manor of Woodstock, and thence back again to the church'. The year 1515 saw Cornish receive a payment for 'Mr Gyles who played on the organs in the chapel'. This Mr Gyles would have been the John Gyles who is recorded as being issued with a livery to sing at the funeral of prince Henry in 1511, and may well have been the same Gyles mentioned as one of the three 'mynstrells of the Chambre' issued with liveries for Henry VII's funeral in 1509.

From further entries in the Book of Payments, we know that in 1515 a London priest was paid for composing 'an anthem of defuse museke' for the king, and that Dr Fayrfax was paid large sums of money for books of polyphonic music in 1516 (£13 6s 8d), 1517 and 1518 (both £20). Quite what form these books took is not entirely clear.

The carols of the Ritson manuscript from the west country had as their principal composer a certain Richard Smert, who was rector of Plympton

---

[22] Collection of Ordinances, 1526, p. 160.

near Exeter for neary thirty years.[23] The Ritson manuscript, probably in use at Exeter Cathedral and certainly revised and kept in use from 1470 to 1520, differs in one major respect from the Fayrfax manuscript and the Henry VIII manuscript mentioned earlier. The Ritson manuscript presents the carols in score. The voices are one above the other in triplex (treble), medius and tenor – although it has to be said that the vertical alignment is 'rough and ready'. Only the bottom part is presented separately, but all parts are on a single 'opening' of the book. Thus if the song was a long one all the performers could turn the page together, and the book was designed for singers to sing standing together at a lectern. The Fayrfax and Henry VIII manuscripts, however, are large enough for only a small group of singers if used in this way.

Quite what arrangement of musical 'score' Henry was paying Fayrfax and others for is unclear, but it seems very probable that he had it in mind to equip his royal palaces and residences with such works.

The Eltham Palace Ordinances took away from the Chapel Royal the opportunity to accompany in full the king on his progresses and, by implication, on any journeyings overseas, settling for a quota only to remain 'portable'. On the other hand, this was to give great impetus to the establishment of permanent church structures in which the Chapel Royal could sing as it became less peripatetic. Before we consider at the overseas exceptions to this, it would perhaps complete the picture to look at the contemporary wages of the Chapel Royal.

'The Book of the New Order of the Household' of Henry VIII,[24] which dates from the same year as the Eltham Ordinances, details the wages in ordinary of the Chapel Royal as follows:

The Dean to Eate with master Treasurer or Master Comptroller.
Gentlemen of ye Chapell

Master of the childen for his wages	xxx li			
And xxx Boordwages				
Gospeller for wages	xiii li	vi	s	viii d
Epistoler	xiii li	vi	s	viii d
Verger	xx li			
Yeomen of the Vestry	x li			
	x li			
	x li			
Children of the Chapel	lxvi li	xiii s	iiii d	

Although the children were given no regular wage, they were recipients of

---

[23] He may have been related to an earlier John Smert who on 30 May 1415 was granted lands by the king which were originally a 'Grant for life to the King's servant John Hunt, one of the clerkes of the king's chapel within the household, of two solars, a seld, a vacant plot, and two acres of meadow in the town of Oxford' on 23 November 1414. The 'Chapel' connection, if there is one, may explain the Ritson manuscript's survival.

[24] LC 5/12

fairly large sums on various occasions, such as birthdays of the king and other members of the royal family; they received 20s at Allhallowtide for singing 'Audivi vocem' and 40s at Christmas for singing 'Gloria in excelsis', apart from monies passed to them by the master for theatrical performances.

Looking now to the exceptions to the Eltham quota rule for the Chapel Royal accompanying the king, it is very probable that the entire Chapel accompanied Henry VIII on his visit to Calais in 1532 on his mission to meet Francis I and conclude a treaty against the Turks. Henry himself sailed in the *Swallow* from Dover, together with 140 lords and knights, forty yeomen of the guard and seven bishops. At the very least the dean of the Chapel Royal would have been required at the signing of the treaty.

There is also strong evidence that the entire Chapel Royal accompanied Henry to Calais in 1544 on his last French campaign. The king's 'great army at sea' set sail in June 1544. That the children of the Chapel Royal were present is clear from a glance at the accounts of the custodian of the wardrobe, Sir Ralph Saddler, giving the expenses of Henry's voyage to France, to be found in the Exchequer Accounts.[25] The accounts read thus:

For x singinge Chyldren	off Stoore of the greate Warderobe xiiii yardes of skowlett kersey for hoose for the said children	[sine precio]
	George Bristowe for xiii yardes of yellow kersey for hoose for them also price the yarde ii s iiii d	[xxx s] [iiii d]
	of stoore ii yardes of satten crimsin for the covering of hattes for the children sine pretio	[sine precio]
	Item of the same stoore ii yardes of yellow satten for the same cause sine pretio	[sine precio]

The main force under Norfolk and Suffolk crossed the Channel first, protected by the long-oared vessels of Henry's own design with guns placed for maximum advantage against the French galleys. Henry's force, together with the Chapel Royal, followed. The warships, with the flagship *Great Harry*, were loaded with guns, hackbuts, pikes, baggage wagons .and horse harnesses. Each ship carried hundreds of men, horses and food. Other vessels held beer-filled casks and portable grinding wheels that could be mounted on the wagons in such a way that they ground as the wheels turned. Portable ovens were carried too. In this great fleet it is perhaps not too fanciful to conjecture the presence of the 'three ships and three galleys' fitted out in 1528 for the king by William Crane, gentleman of the Chapel Royal from 1509-45 and master of the children from 1523-1545. What stories he must have told the children as they sailed to France in 1544!

[25] 433/10 PRP.

Be that as it may, Henry landed at Calais and set off behind Suffolk on 25 July 1544 'armed all at pieces' and mounted on a great courser. Mounted drummers, fifers and trumpeters preceded him, leading to the supposition that the Chapel Royal was not far behind. That night a violent thunderstorm drenched the camp, but despite his illnesses Henry carried on undaunted and actually rode the thirty miles from Calais to Boulogne in a single day. He even kept a journal. His weeks of campaigning and effort were finally rewarded with the fall of Boulogne in mid-September. The king entered the town in triumph, reliving his victories thirty years earlier at Therouanne. He stayed on for a week to celebrate his success. During these festivities the Chapel Royal must surely have been called upon to participate.

Henry decided to return to England, having proved wrong all those who said he was too feeble to fight again in the field. The campaign itself ended badly, with Norfolk having to endure mutinies and Suffolk abandoning Boulogne in the face of a vast French force. But Henry's honour was satisfied.

Two years later Henry's ulcerated leg brought on a fever. He continued to hunt, exercise and meet ambassadors as usual but decided to make his will in December 1546. He died on 28 January 1547. After three days of silence in which the Council kept the news from the people, his death was finally announced and his will read in Parliament. Henry lay in state in the Chapel Royal at Whitehall for twelve days, and subsequently at Leadenhall and St Michael's churchyard in Cornhill, and a dole of one groat apiece was distributed to 20,000 paupers of the city. Whether the royal almonry was involved in this distribution is unclear.

The funeral procession that followed Henry's corpse to Windsor for burial next to Jane Seymour was five miles long – horses and pages being dressed in black. The entire Chapel Royal were issued with special liveries for the burial and sang for that occasion. There is a curious irony here, for there is one reference in Westminster Abbey's archives to the subsequent disinterment and burning of Henry's body in Mary Tudor's reign, apparently to satisfy the Roman Catholic belief that this act would somehow atone for his 'sins' in defying Rome! Subsequently it was Mary's turn to have strange decisions taken about her mortal remains following her death, resulting in her bowels being deposited under the nave of the present Chapel Royal premises in St James's Palace and the rest of her body at Westminster Abbey.

The Chapel Royal during the Civil War and the Commonwealth

The occasion for the last 'journeying' of the Chapel Royal overseas – or to be exact certain members of it – was the English Civil War. The major battles of the Civil War began in 1642 at Edgehill, north-west of Oxford. Charles I lost the North in 1644 and the Midlands in 1645. Prince Rupert held out in the Channel Islands, but after several 'confinements' at Holdenby, Hampton Court, Carisbrooke Castle and St James's Palace, among others, Charles I was executed outside the Banqueting House at Whitehall in 1649. The Restoration of the monarchy did not take place until 1660 with the triumphant return of Charles II from overseas. Where was the Chapel Royal throughout this period of turmoil, and how did its records survive?

The last entry in the Old Cheque Book is dated 'April 1641' and is 'a warrant to the Exchequer for the discharging the Gentlemen of his majesties Chappell, and the officers Vestry, from payment of the four subsidies graunted to his Majestie in this present Parliament ...'.[26] This entry was thus made just one month before the execution of Strafford on 12 May 1641. The reference to 'this Parliament' is to the 'Long Parliament' of November 1640-60, which Charles I was compelled to call in November 1640. Just seven months after the last Old Cheque Book entry on 4 January 1642 came the king's attempt to arrest 'the five' in Parliament. We also know from the Old Cheque Book that in 1636

> Mr John Stephens, Clearke of the Check to the gentlemen of his Majesties Chappell, died the 13th of May, and Thomas Day, beeing then the Master of the Children, was chosen and sworne Clearke of the Check in his place on Whitson Even following, and Richard Jennings was sworn in Mr Steven's place, the twentieth Aprill followinge.[27]

Former master of the children, and now clerk of the cheque, Thomas Day must therefore be considered a possible preserver of the Chapel Royal records, including the Old Cheque Book, the parallel Bodleian Register, and the Chapel Royal Anthem Book of 1635 – all of which survived the Civil War and two of which are at Oxford. However, clerk of the cheque Thomas Day seems not to have survived until the Restoration in 1660, for there is no record in the Old Cheque Book of his still holding office then.

The best clue as to the likely preserver of the Chapel records during the Civil War is to be found in the Old Cheque Book beneath a crossed-out entry which reads: 'Thomas Haynes was sworn Serjeant of the Vestry, the Vth day of November 1660; the same day at the same tyme as William Williams was sworn eldest Yeoman, and Whitell sworn youngest Yeoman, and Augustine Cleavland Groom.' Williams had been appointed yeoman in 1640 and Augustine Cleveland groom in 1640. Both survived to see the Restoration and have their appointments reconfirmed in 1660, although Cleveland was tragically killed in 1662 by horses pulling a carriage at Hampton Court. Let us look first at the case for Thomas Haynes.

Although he was not appointed until the Restoration, we do know that

[26] Old Cheque Book, fol. 48.
[27] Ibid., fol. 16.

This painting by Robert Streater, commissioned by Charles II at the Restoration, depicts Whiteladies and Boscobel House in Shropshire, where Charles hid after the battle of Worcester. (Royal Collection, reproduced by gracious permission of Her Majesty The Queen)

Thomas Haynes had an archival appreciation, for he compiled a series of registers concerned with the numbers of people 'touched' by Charles II to rid them of scrofula (the king's evil). These registers covered the period 1660 to 1664, and are continued in another account kept by Thomas Dunkley, keeper of his majesty's closet, covering the period 1667 to 1682. Whether Thomas Haynes had accompanied Charles II in exile abroad is not clear, but certainly from the entries to which he was witness he had custody of the Old Cheque Book from 1660 onwards. There was, though, no sign of Haynes or any other members of the Chapel Royal during Charles II's spell at Moseley Old Hall in Staffordshire in 1651. Charles was hiding in Spring Coppice outside 'Whiteladies' beyond Kidderminster, and John Penderel, searching for a more secure hiding-place for him, by chance met someone he recognised as the chaplain in secret attendance on another local Catholic gentleman, Thomas Whitgreave of Moseley Old Hall. The chaplain was Father John Huddleston. Charles was shortly to shelter there and to meet Fr Huddleston properly for the first time. Huddleston came from a Lancashire family and served in the Royalist army during the Civil War. Charles thus observed in him a patriotic English Catholic.

Charles was installed at the hall in an upstairs bedroom with a false floor and an exit door to the brew-house chimney. 'The hole' contained a pallet, the usual incumbent of this being Fr Huddleston. On meeting

Charles, Huddleston showed him the secret chapel – 'little but neat and decent'. Charles, it is said, looked at it with its crucifix and candlesticks with respect. According to Fr Huddleston Charles commented, 'If it please God, I come to my crown, both you and all your persuasion shall have as much liberty as any of my subjects.' It was on this occasion that Fr Huddleston encouraged Charles to look at a Catholic catechism (probably Turbeville's, published at Douai) together with a tract written by a Benedictine monk entitled 'A Short and Plain Way to the Faith and the Church'. On reading this tract Charles is reported as saying, 'I have not seen anything more plain and clear upon the subject. The arguments here drawn from succession are so conclusive, I do not see how they can be denied.' This observation has been taken as evidence of Charles's early conversion to Catholicism. The Benedictine monk was Fr Huddleston's uncle.

Fr Huddleston was to be appointed on the Restoration to the Queen's Chapel at St James's to minister to Charles's wife, Catherine of Braganza, and was also the priest who administered Charles's last sacrament in 1685. On his death bed Charles is said to have cried out with pleasure at the sight of Huddleston, who had made a secret visit to his bedside on 5 February 1685 – the evening before he died – saying 'You that saved my body are now come to save my soul'. The sacrament itself was brought by one of the Portuguese priests, Fr Bento de Lomez – either from the Queen's Chapel at St James's or Somerset House chapel.

Returning, though, to Moseley Old Hall in 1651, it is known that Charles 'touched' for the king's evil while in hiding there – as a demonstration that he was still king. Thomas Haynes's personal registers of numbers and dates when the king 'touched' make no mention of this – an act which he would surely have recorded with pride had he been there. Neither does Haynes make mention of the 'touching' that it is known Charles performed at The Hague in May 1660 before his triumphant embarkation at night on 23 May 1660 to reclaim the English throne.

It could be concluded from this that Thomas Haynes was not attached to the court in exile overseas – otherwise he would most certainly have included 'touching' figures in his carefully compiled registers. The Chapel Royal archives of which he took custody on 5 November 1660 – five months after Charles's return to England – must have been kept in England, although some loyal Chapel Royal members almost certainly found their way to Charles's court in exile overseas. John Cosin, who was to be appointed to the see of Durham at the Restoration, had left England for Paris in 1643, where at the order of Charles I he was appointed chaplain to the Protestant members of queen Henrietta Maria's household. Thus ministering to court exiles he would have been a potential custodian of the Chapel Royal archives. But it seems this was not so. The most likely hiding place for the Chapel records is Oxford, which Charles left secretly in disguise in May 1646.

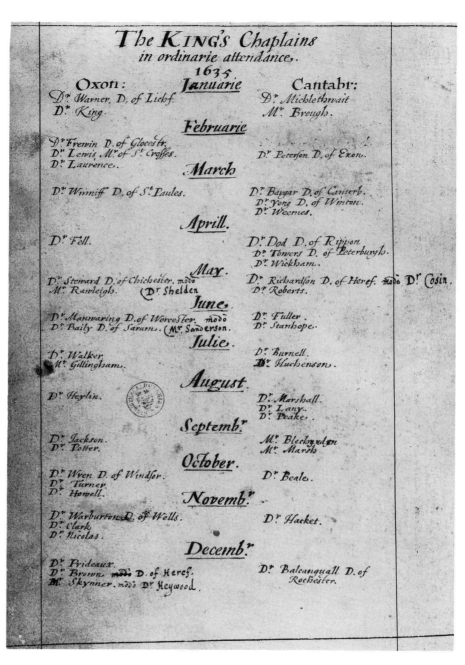

The KING'S Chaplains
in ordinarie attendance.
1635

Oxon: **Ianuarie**   **Cantabr:**

Dr Warner, D. of Lichf.   Dr Micklethwait
Dr King.   Mr Brough.

Februarie

Dr Frewin D. of Glocestr.
Dr Lewis Mr of St Crosses.   Dr Peterson D. of Exon.
Dr Laurence.

March

Dr Winniff D. of St Paules.   Dr Baggar D. of Canterb.
                         Dr Yong D. of Winton.
                         Dr Weemes.

Aprill.

Dr Fell.   Dr Dod D. of Rippon
                         Dr Towers D. of Peterburgh.
                         Dr Wickham.

May

Dr Steward D. of Chichester. modo   Dr Richardson D. of Heref. modo Dr Cosin.
Mr Rawleigh. (Dr Shelden   Dr Roberts.

June.

Dr Manwaring D. of Worcester. modo   Dr Fuller.
Dr Baily D. of Sarum. (Mr Sanderson.   Dr Stanhope.

Iulie.

Dr Walker   Dr Burnell.
Mr Gillingham.   Mr Huchenson.

August.

Dr Heylin.   Dr Marshall.
                         Dr Lany.
                         Dr Peake.

Septembr

Dr Jackson.   Mr Blechenden
Dr Potter.   Mr Marsh

October.

Dr Wren D. of Windsor.   Dr Beale.
Dr Turner.
Dr Howell.

Novembr

Dr Warburton D. of Wells.   Dr Hacket.
Dr Clark.
Dr Nicolas.

Decembr

Dr Prideaux.
Dr Brown. modo D. of Heref.   Dr Balcanquall D. of
Mr Skynner. modo Dr Heywood   Rochester.

(MS Rawl Poet 23, p. 310, reproduced by courtesy of the Bodleian Library, Oxford)

54

2. The Chapel Royal Overseas: The Old World and the New

There are other textual clues which lend weight to the Oxford theory. The Chapel Royal Anthem Book of 1635 contains the words of the anthems used by the Chapel Royal during the reign of Charles I and is preserved in the Bodleian Library as MS Rawl. Poet 23. The *Summary Catalogue of Western Manuscripts*, p. 288, describes it thus: 'A collection of words of "the full anthems" [fol. 11] and "the single anthems" used in one of the Royal Chapels in and after 1635. At the end is a list of "The King's Chaplains in ordinarie attendance, 1635", with later corrections. A letter from J. Bowack pasted on the front cover, presenting the Book to John Earl of Leicester [?], 29th April 1732, suggests that it is the volume used by Charles himself.' There are 152 'single' anthems and 65 'full' anthems. This word-book of 1635 was added to for use by the Chapel Royal following the Restoration. A version thus enlarged is in the British Library as MS Harley 6346. It contains four additional full anthems by Henry Lawes and Captain Cooke, and twenty-five additional verse anthems mostly composed by Captain Cooke. The volume ends after much blank paper with an alphabetical list of contents, and then the 'List of the King's Chaplains in ordinarie attendance' for the year 1635, with later corrections. The fact that no entries were made while Charles II was in exile abroad would seem to confirm that the Chapel Royal records were indeed hidden in England.

There is one curious riddle, though, which may serve to confirm that the Chapel Royal registers and records stayed hidden in England during the Civil War and Commonwealth period of royal exile. This clue is to be found within the covers of the 'Whitehall Register' and relates to the infant baptism of a future serjeant of the vestry, Marmaduke Alford, in 1647. The register is headed 'Chapels Royal St James's, Whitehall and Windsor. Register of Births, Baptisms, Marriages and Deaths'. All the entries are post-Restoration with the following single exception. This is our clue, and it appears on p. 3 all by itself thus: 'Marmaduke the son of Robert and Anne Alford als Oldford was baptized in the parish Church of Curry-Ryvell the tenth day of May Ano Dini 1647. Somersetshire.' This entry may well be a later interpolation, but if not then it is of great significance to our story.

The entry is important first in what it does not record – the name of the priest who performed the baptism. What we do know for sure is that Marmaduke Alford later held office with the Chapel Royal, first as yeoman of the vestry from 30 August 1675, as eldest yeoman of the vestry from 28 March 1685, and finally as serjeant of the vestry, in which office he died on 10 May 1715. If there was a Chapel Royal official present at his baptism in 1647 who wished to continue the records for posterity, it could have been William Williams who had been sworn yeoman of the Chapel Royal in 1640 before the Civil War, according to the Bodleian Register. At the Restoration William Williams was appointed eldest groom of the vestry, but died on 28 July 1665. Or it may have been John Pountney who had been appointed serjeant in 1638, according to the Bodleian Register. Other possibilities include George Witcher, younger yeoman, Augustine Cleveland who had been sworn groom of the vestry in 1640, according to the Bodleian Register, and Roger Nightingale and Henry Lawes, both mentioned as officers of the chapel in November 1660, according to the Old Cheque Book. Or it may have been Thomas Haynes, John Pountney's successor, who was appointed serjeant of the vestry on 5 November 1660, as we have seen, but who may have been associated with the Chapel Royal in some form before the Restoration. Whoever made the entry at Curry-Ryvell in Somersetshire could not have had either the Bodleian Register or the Old Cheque Book to hand, or else the entry would have been recorded therein. If Marmaduke Alford inserted his baptismal details at a later date on his acquiring custody of the Chapel Royal records, perhaps when he became serjeant, it is curious that he chose not to record his details also in the Bodleian Register or the Old Cheque Book while he was at it. One thing we can say for certain is that if the 1647 entry is contemporary, as there are no references to the Chapel Royal in exile abroad in the Whitehall Register, it never left these shores.

H.M. Chapel of the Mohawk

The year of Charles I's execution was, ironically, also the first year that the New England Company sent Anglican missionaries to the Mohawk Indians in New York State – an act of evangelism that was to result two and a half centuries later in despatch no. 333 dated 18 November 1904 from the secretary of state for the colonies to Lord Minto, the governor general of Canada, declaring Edward VII's wish that the chapel at Brantford, Ontario, be titled 'His Majesty's Chapel of the Mohawk'. The intention was not to create a new Chapel Royal beyond British shores but rather to recognise that a Chapel Royal had in practice existed on the other side of the Atlantic since 1711. Some explanation of this is needed.

Apart from the New England Company's Anglican missionaries, who ministered to the Mohawk Indians in Mohawk Valley, New York State, from 1649, the Society for the Propagation of the Gospel (SPG) had an early mission for colonists near Albany, but it seems that little was done to evanglise the Mohawk Indian settlements near at hand. Earlier, Jesuits had ministered to the Mohawks, but to little avail.

In 1711 four Mohawk chiefs visited England. On their presentation to queen Anne they declared their longing to see the 'great queen' and testified to the tedious nature of the French war in which they had taken part. The four Mohawk chiefs went on to advocate the reducing of Canada and ended with a wish that the queen send someone to the Mohawks to instruct them in a knowledge of the Saviour. As a result a limestone chapel was built at Fort Hunter on the Mohawk river, together with a parsonage. The SPG sent out the Rev. Andrews to minister to the

Mohawks. The following year in 1712 queen Anne sent a number of gifts. These included a large bible, a 'purple' altar-cloth or pulpit hanging and a seven-piece solid silver communion set. This latter consisted of two flagons, two chalices, two patens and an alms basin. Each item bore the inscription: 'The gift of Her Majesty Ann, by the Grace of God, of Great Britain, France, and Ireland and of Her Plantations in North America, Queen to her Indian Chapel of the Mohawks.'

Instructing the Mohawks in Christianity was difficult for the Rev. Andrews, largely because of the distracting influence of Dutch and English traders, together with Jesuit interference in the mission. The Mohawks withdrew their children from the mission and the Rev. Andrews became sadly discouraged. He set out to return to England, but the ship on which he sailed was lost with all hands. Another mission was sent by the SPG in 1727 in the person of the Rev. J. Milne. He worked at both Albany and Fort Hunter, but again ran across insuperable difficulties. The SPG did not despair, however, and in 1770 sent the Rev. John Stuart as a missionary with the exclusive task of ministering to the Mohawks. John Stuart's parents, who were Irish, had sailed for America in 1730, and John was born that same year in Pennsylvania. He went on to graduate at the College of Philadelphia and resolved to offer himself for the priesthood in the Church of England – a move to which his Presbyterian father took some time to consent. John sailed for England and was duly ordained. He was then immediately appointed missionary to the Mohawks at Fort Hunter. His height added weight to his arguments – he was 6 ft 4 ins tall.

John Stuart's ministry began in 1770 on Christmas day at an awkward time in America's political development. The Mohawks remained loyal to the British cause and joined the British army. The Mohawk tribe were the smallest group of the 'Six Nations of the Iroquois Confederacy'. One of their villages was close to Fort Hunter and Johnson Hall, the residence of the superintendent of Indian affairs, Sir William Johnson. The chiefs were captains John Deserontyou, Aaron and Isaac Hill, and captain Joseph Brant, called Thayendanegea by his people. Just as developments which were to culminate in the American Revolution were becoming very alarming, Sir William Johnson died suddenly in 1774. The administration of Indian affairs was then taken over by his nephew Guy Johnson and son-in-law Daniel Claus. Their instructions from England were 'that preserving the good will and affection of the Six Nations was an object they should never lose sight of '.

It was in midsummer 1775 that Guy Johnson was warned of a plot by the colonists to make him a prisoner. His reaction was to collect together over 1,000 Indians and march through the woods to Oswego, where they formed a council and decided to support the British government and protect the navigation of the St Lawrence river and the Great Lakes, and also to send a deputation of chiefs and warriors to Montreal to speak to the governor of Canada. The remainder returned to their houses in the Mohawk Valley and took part in several battles against the colonists. Their houses and property were eventually captured by the enemy in July 1777, and so under the leadership of one of their chiefs they formed the largest group of American loyalists to enter Canada. Before abandoning the Mohawk Valley, the remaining Indians buried the queen Anne silver communion set deep in the ground at midnight. It was to remain buried for seven years.

John Stuart however remained and continued to minister in the Mohawk chapel at Fort Hunter until 1781. At this time he wrote to a friend that he had only three families left as all the rest of the Mohawks had joined the king's army. But John Stuart's connection with the office of superintendent of Indian affairs made him an object of disrespect to the Whigs, who turned the Mohawk chapel into a tavern, placing a barrel of rum in the reading desk out of ridicule. It was at this point that John Stuart headed for Canada, as the Mohawk chapel at Fort Hunter was forfeited to the United States of America under the terms of the treaty of Paris in 1783. John Stuart went first to Saint John, New Brunswick, then to Montreal and finally to Kingston. He found that he was able once again to minister to the Mohawks, of whom he came across 150 settled at Tyendinaga in the bay of Quinte and 700 by the Grand river at Brantford.[28]

What events had led the Mohawks to these settlements after they left Mohawk Valley in New York State?

Late in July 1777, having left Mohawk Valley following the destruction of their houses by fire in enemy action, the large band of Mohawks headed for Canada, and under Colonel Claus finally came across a suitable spot to make a temporary settlement for the winter at Lachine. They cleared the neighbouring land for cultivation, but spent seven winters in these cramped and uncomfortable quarters, many becoming ill or dying. They were waiting for instructions from Asharegowa (i.e. General Frederick Haldimand) who had succeeded Carleton as governor and commander-in-chief at Quebec. At last they were granted in the name of the crown deeds of lands on the north shore of the bay of Quinte. This settlement was known as Tyendinaga and named after the chief, Deseronto. Captain Joseph Brant was dissatisfied with this, however, and finally secured other lands six miles wide on each side of the Grand river in the Niagara leading into lake Erie. Captain Isaac and other relatives joined Brant, and the settlement was named Brantford. Brant, moreover, asked for and received promises from Haldimand to build a sawmill, gristmill, church and school, and to supply a schoolmaster.

---

[28] John Stuart was to become the father of the Church in Upper Canada and first incumbent of what is now the cathedral church of Kingston, Ontario, having been appointed chaplain to Fort Cataraguai.

2. The Chapel Royal Overseas: The Old World and the New

The construction of chapels was begun in both settlements in 1785. John Stuart visited both settlements and preached in their chapels.

The Deseronto chapel was apparently completed by October 1791, when John Stuart wrote: '... He [John Stuart] had postponed his intended visit to the Grand River till Capt. Brant's return from Quebec ... and had actually engaged a passage in the same vessel with them, when the Society's orders respecting the Mohawk's Chapel at the Bay of Quinte arrived ... .'[29] The chapel itself was wooden with few windows and a door of deer skin. In 1798 George III gave it a triptych containing the creed, the Lord's prayer and the ten commandments, a bell and a royal coat-of-arms. The communion vessels used were, and still are, the silver queen Anne set that had been buried at Mohawk Valley on the exodus of the Mohawks in July 1777.

The communion set was recovered by a party of braves headed by John Deserontyou, who set off from lake Lachine and, returning by stealth to Mohawk Valley, dug up the silver which had been wrapped in the altar cloth for burial and returned to Canada with it. On the chalice at Deseronto is to be seen a dent made when it was struck by a shovel in the course of digging it up in Mohawk Valley. The bell presented by George III had to be hung between poles outside the chapel as it had no belfry. George III's association with this chapel at Deseronto led to its becoming known as the 'Chapel Royal'. The first permanent chaplain to be appointed to the chapel was the Rev. Saltern Givins (1830-51), during whose incumbency the stone church (Christ Church) was built in 1843 out of local limestone. The foundations of the old chapel of 1785 can still be seen beside the path leading from the rectory to the road. The stone church was struck by lightning on 12 May 1906, resulting in the destruction of the wooden coat-of-arms of George III. The triptych given by George III, which had been recovered from the first chapel and placed above the altar in Christ Church, was undamaged. Christ Church was rebuilt in 1906-7 and re-consecrated by the Rev. William Lennox Mills, bishop of Ontario, on 28 April 1907. The queen Anne silver communion set is now shared with the 'Chapel Royal' at Brantford, to which we shall now turn.

The construction of the 'Chapel Royal' at Brantford began in the summer of 1785 with the assistance of two carpenters, John Thomas and John Smith. It was completed in 1787, Daniel Claus reporting on 23 April 1787 that the new chapel 'which was built at the Expense of Governmt' was completely destitute of sacramental ornaments such as had adorned the old chapel at Fort Hunter – i.e. the queen Anne communion set. Interestingly Claus mentions that there had been two communion tables at Fort Hunter. These it seems were saved from the ravages of the American Revolution by the Rev. John Stuart and later given to the Brantford Chapel.

[29] Public Archives of Canada, SPG Journals, vol. 25, pp. 425-6.

On Sunday 21 May 1972, at 10.30 am, an historical plaque commemorating Christ Church, Tyendinaga, was unveiled at the Tyendinaga Reservation, two miles west of Deseronto. The plaque was one of a series erected throughout the province by the Archives of Ontario, acting on the advice of the Archaeological and Historic Sites Board of Ontario. Participants in the ceremony shown left to right included: Mr Leslie Claus, who gave the historical background; Mr Garnet B. Maracle, Rector's Warden, Christ Church, who acted as programme chairman; Mr Lee Grills, M.P. (Hastings); Mr Carmen Gibson, Warden of Hastings County; Mr and Mrs Joseph Doreen, who unveiled the plaque; Prof. Sydney Wise, representing the province's Historic Sites Board; Mr Earl Hill, Chief of the Bay of Quinte Mohawks; Mr Clifford M. Maracle, Warden of the Corporation of the Parish of Tyendinaga; Mr Clarke T. Rollins, M.P.P. (Hastings).

In a letter written by John Stuart to the SPG dated 2 July 1788 he describes a visit to the Mohawk village at Brantford thus:

> ... The Mohawk Village is pleasantly situated on a small but deep river – the Church about 60 feet in length and 45 in breadth, – built with squared logs and boarded on the outside and painted – with a handsome steeple and bell, a pulpit, reading desk, and Communion-table, with convenient pews. That the Church furniture lately given by Government not having arrived he took with him the plate and furniture which formerly belonged to their church at Fort Hunter – a small organ was employed in the service.[30]

[30] Public Archives of Canada, SPG Journals, vol. 35, pp. 120-1.

2. The Chapel Royal Overseas: The Old World and the New

The queen Anne communion set was in fact divided for use between the two Mohawk settlements – one of each piece going to the two chapels, but with Brantford keeping the alms basin because of the numerical superiority of the tribal members at Brantford as compared with Deseronto.

The Mohawk chapel at Brantford has survived intact since its construction in 1785. Its first incumbent episcopal minister was appointed in 1826 and it was officially consecrated as an Anglican chapel in 1830 following the petition of the Mohawk chiefs to bishop Stewart.[31] Most significantly, on 20 October 1904 Lord Minto, governor general of Canada, received a request from the incumbent of the church and superintendent of the six nations that the Mohawk chapel should in future be called 'His Majesty's Chapel of the Mohawks'. Lord Minto forwarded this request to the secretary of state for the colonies.[32] On 18 November 1904 William Lyttleton, the colonial secretary for Canada, sent a despatch to the officer administering the government of Canada (Lord Minto having left for England on 16 November 1904), the subject of which was the Mohawk chapel at Brantford. The draft of the despatch survives and reads thus:

> Gov. Canada
> 37121
>   04   IND   NOV 04.
> My Ld,
>   I have the hon. to ack. the receipt of yr. Exy's desp. No 317 of the 20th Oct, forwarding and recommending the request of the incumbent of the Mohawk Church at Brantford & the Supt. of the Six Nations, that the Church should be given the title of 'H.M.'s Chapel of the Mohawk'.
>   2. I have submitted this request to H.M., who has been pleased to approve.

This despatch has been interpreted universally in Canada as declaring H.M. Chapel of the Mohawk a Chapel Royal. It certainly falls within that definition as it now misleadingly applies to certain church buildings in England – namely the chapel buildings at St James's Palace, Hampton Court Palace and the Tower of London, and erroneously in some quarters also to the Queen's Chapel of the Savoy and St George's chapel, Windsor. At first sight, applying the correct and ancient definition of what constitutes the Chapel Royal, namely the body of priests and choir appointed to minister to the spiritual needs of the sovereign and his household, it would seem that H.M. Chapel of the Mohawk does not meet this requirement. But it does – for it was the personal meeting of the four chiefs of the Mohawks with queen Anne in 1711 that was the origin of

---

[31] Public Archives of Ontario, Strachan Papers, 1830.
[32] Public Archives of Canada, Register of Despatches to the Secretary of State for the Colonies RG7,G9, vol. 160, p. 82, no. 317.

their adoption of the Christian faith. It was queen Anne who provided a chaplain and sacramental vessels for their use, and it would therefore be expected that they would serve the British monarch's spiritual interest through prayer and any temporal interests in Canada as expressed through the governor general who represented the monarch, just as if the monarch were there in person. That is the principle of 'representation'. The personal interest of the monarch was continued by George III, as we have seen, in very tangible form.

Some mention of its choral tradition is perhaps of interest in this respect. The services at Deseronto are conducted in English, with one hymn being sung in the Mohawk tongue as a link with its past. Delegates are sent regularly to Synod. The 'Chapel Royal' at Christ Church Deseronto, although not specifically mentioned by name in the Edward VII despatch, has the older 'royal' association, and it is interesting to observe that the choir and clergy wear red cassocks and the incumbent holds the title of chaplain. Although well removed from the jurisdiction of the lord chamberlain's office of the royal household, it would seem reasonable to hope that one day the chaplains at H.M. Chapel of the Mohawk will form a strong bond with the college of chaplains headed by the clerk of the closet established in England in 1912.

3

The House of Richmond

In contemporary correspondence and foreign chronicles the family of monarchs who ruled England and Wales from 1485-1603 (now always referred to as the Tudors) was usually described as the house of Richmond, after the title conferred by Henry VI on the 'founder' of the dynasty, Edmund ap Meredith ap Tydier, whose son was to occupy the throne from 1485 as Henry VII. This title of duke of Richmond was to play a most significant part in the reason why the Chapel Royal sings and conducts divine worship today at St James's Palace.

After the birth of prince Henry, who lived for only seven weeks, in 1510/11, a pretty young girl entered Henry VIII's court. Bessie Blount was the niece of Lord Mountjoy and became one of queen Katherine's maids of honour. She became 'Bessie' to the king and the gentlemen of the court after only a short while, and an especial favourite of Charles Brandon – the king's trusted friend. The Chapel Royal must have been familiar with her presence at court masques and revels at which they sang, for Bessie's beauty was put to use as a dancer and, as she sang extraordinarily well, as a singer too.

The singers of the Chapel Royal often took part in such pageants. For example, in the royal 'May-Game' of 1515 large numbers of courtiers and servants were issued with special clothing to take the roles of Robin Hood, Friar Tuck, Maid Marian, Lady May 'and her four ladies', and many others. On this occasion there was a banquet in a bower for which music and songs were performed, after which the king's procession set off to return home escorting a 'triumphal car full of singers and musicians drawn by griffins with human faces'. It was met by a chariot bearing Lady May and her four ladies on horseback, who 'saluted the kyng with divers goodly songes and so brought hym to Grenewych'. This account is from the chronicler Halle's account of the revels, but we learn further vital details from the account of it by the Venetian ambassador, Sagudino, who noted that 'in this wood were certain bowers filled purposely with singing birds' and that 'singers and musicians ... played on an organ and lute and flutes', while the accountant Richard Gibson recorded the making of 'six ladies' garments from the king's old store, for six children of the Chapel'. The gentlemen of the chapel are known for the year 1511

View of 'Placentia' (Greenwich) from 'One Tree Hill', by an anonymous artist, showing on the left the small 'fort' where Henry VIII housed his mistresses Mary Boleyn and Bessie Blount. It was here, too, that Elizabeth I imprisoned Leicester on discovering his secret marriage to the countess of Essex. The Flamsteed Observatory was later built on the same site. The palace can be seen to the right at the foot of the hill on the banks of the Thames. (Reproduced by courtesy of the National Maritime Museum, Greenwich)

and undoubtedly include a considerable quota of those chosen to participate in this particular revel four years later.[1]

Bessie Blount almost certainly took part in this 'Maying' revel along with the Chapel Royal. She remained the king's mistress for several years and in 1519 bore him a son. She left queen Katherine's service when the signs of her pregnancy became an outrage to the queen, who knew who the father was!

Bessie left for a monastery to give birth to the baby, who was christened Henry with the honorific surname 'Fitzroy'. The sixteenth-century chronicler Stow recorded: 'He was born (we are told) in the mannor place of Blackamore in Essex: it was the prior's house of Blackamore.' This is Blackmore, about seven miles from Chelmsford. In fact the prior's house occupied the north side of the churchyard and was part of the priory of Blackmore of Augustinian canons. It was a small monastery, later dissolved by Wolsey in 1525 for the foundation of his colleges. Morant's *History of Essex* of 1768 states: 'This is reported to have been one of King Henry VIII's Houses of Pleasure; and disguised by the name of Jericho.' The name 'Jericho' evidently survived the dissolution of the religious foundation.

Bessie was henceforth known at court by the unofficial title of 'mother

[1] The gentlemen of the chapel for 1511 and the children of the chapel for 1509 are listed on p. 43 above.

of the king's son'. The king arranged for her to marry a gentleman of substance, Sir Gilbert Talboys. The king ceased any further relationship with Bessie, now Lady Talboys, on young Henry Fitzroy's birth, but to Katherine's shame both Lady Talboys and Henry Fitzroy were regarded almost as if they had become part of the royal line – even though princess Mary had been born three years earlier in 1516. This was despite the 1518 proxy wedding of the infant princess Mary to the French dauphin resulting in the treaty sworn to by England and France at the high altar of St Paul's Cathedral. In case Katherine could not produce a son for him, the king bestowed a series of most significant titles on Henry Fitzroy.

The impetus behind this bestowal of titles, which were shortly to become of such significance to the Chapel Royal's presence at St James's Palace, may have lain as much in a cassetnet full of jousting lance splinters and a ditch of water as in queen Katherine's inability to produce a male heir.

It was in the spring of 1524 that Henry experienced a sharp warning of the need to sort out the issue of his heir. He had invented a new design of jousting armour 'made of his own device and fashion' and wore it in a joust against his close friend Charles Brandon. As the two galloped full-tilt towards one another, the crowd suddenly noticed that Henry had forgotten to lower his visor, but it was too late to attract his or Brandon's attention. Brandon naturally had his view restricted by his properly fastened helmet which allowed him to see only what was directly in front of him. He did not spot the crowd signalling the danger. As his jousting lance made contact it struck the king's head-piece at its weakest point – the cassetnet on the forehead, which was meant to be covered by the visor. The lance shattered on impact, sending splinters flying into the king's face. Remarkably no splinter pierced his eye, or instant death would have resulted. The king removed his mangled head-piece and walked around briskly reassuring the crowd and the distressed Brandon that he was uninjured. An idea of the impact such a jousting lance would have made can be gained by visiting the Tudor gallery of the White Tower at the National Museum of Arms and Armour in the Tower of London, where Henry's and Charles Brandon's surviving jousting lances are still preserved.

The second accident occurred within a matter of months while the king was hawking. Henry was on the wrong side of a ditch from his hawk. In an effort to follow his hawk he tried to swing across the ditch, which was full of water, using a pole. The pole suddenly snapped under his weight and he fell head first into the ditch. Had it not been for the quick initiative of his footman, Edmund Moody, who saw what had happened and leaped into the stream to prise the king's head from the mud, Henry would have drowned.

Having suffered these two near-fatal accidents, the king decided that he should take steps to provide for his heir. The conventional view of

It was at a joust against his friend Charles Brandon in the spring of 1524 that Henry VIII was nearly killed as a result of an accident. This sharp reminder of his mortality caused Henry to turn his mind seriously to the matter of his succession. This detail from the Westminster Tournament Roll depicts an earlier joust in 1511. The king's lance can be seen breaking on contact with the challenger's helmet, as queen Katherine looks on. Charles Brandon is the second challenger on the right awaiting his turn. (Reproduced by courtesy of the College of Arms)

modern historians that this question obsessed Henry to the extent that he went to extraordinary lengths to form marriages that would give him a legitimate son and heir is correct as far as it goes but is nevertheless inadequate as a satisfactory explanation of his motives and actions as interpreted by his own courtiers. If Henry could not sire a legitimate male heir, he had to find a way of elevating one of his illegitimate sons through court circles to a position where he could be recognised as heir to the throne.

At Bridewell Palace on 25 June 1525 Henry invested his illegitimate son, Henry Fitzroy, as a knight of the Order of the Garter. He was but six years old. Seven days earlier, on 18 June 1525, he was created earl of Nottingham and duke of Richmond and Somerset. These were traditionally the titles of a royal prince. The title of earl of Richmond had been held by John of Gaunt, the fourth son of Edward III, and by John duke of Bedford, the younger son of Henry IV. It was conferred by Henry VI on his half-brother Edmund ap Meredith ap Tydier, the father of Henry VII. Henry VII in turn was usually designated by the title of Richmond before his accession to the throne, while his mother held the title dowager countess of Richmond.

That the title of Richmond was designed to prepare the path by which Henry VIII could recognise Henry Fitzroy as heir to the throne is revealed

3. The House of Richmond

This miniature by Lucas Horenbout of Henry Fitzroy, Henry VIII's illegitimate son by his mistress Bessie Blount, shows him with the title 'Henry Dvck off Richemod'. This title was conferred upon him by his father at Bridewell Palace on 18 June 1525. (Royal Collection, reproduced by gracious permission of Her Majesty The Queen)

in a letter from Lee, a royal courtier, to Wolsey dated 17 April 1527. The letter consists of conjecture as to who would occupy the throne if princess Mary married abroad. Lee wrote that the king can 'be content to bestow the duke of Richmond and Somerset, who is near of his blood, and of excellent qualities, and is already furnished to keep the state of a great prince, and yet may easily be by the king's means exalted to higher things, to some noble princess of his near blood, to the more strength of amity between them.'[2]

As for the other titles bestowed upon Fitzroy, Somerset was the title that designated John of Gaunt's legitimated heirs, while that of earl of Nottingham had belonged to Richard duke of York, younger son of Edward IV. The point of conferring these titles, and in particular that of duke of Richmond, upon Henry Fitzroy was to give him precedence over every other noble at court. An unpublished Patent Roll, classified as no. 204, granted Henry Fitzroy as duke of Richmond precedence before all other dukes, except the legitimate sons of the king and his heirs. (The Latin used for this exception is 'personis de corpore nostro seu heredum vel successum nostrum duntaxit exceptis' etc.) It will be seen later that

[2] This letter is quoted at length, together with a discussion of its significance, in *Inventories of the Wardrobes, Plate, Chapel stuff, etc., of Henry Fitzroy, Duke of Richmond*, ed. J.G. Nichols, Camden series no. 61 (London, 1854).

This map of 1585 is one of the two earliest maps of London based on a detailed survey. At the bottom right are the royal mews or stables at Charing Cross, where at one time the king's falcons were caged or 'mewed'. North of this is some of the 160 acres bordering the High Road from Charing Cross that Henry VIII purchased along with the hospital of St James in 1531. He also acquired 'Cunditt Meadows' to the left of the map in order to gain control of the water conduits for the use of the new palaces at St James's and Whitehall. (Reproduced by courtesy of the Public Record Office)

3. The House of Richmond

the Act of Succession of 1536, which placed both Mary and Elizabeth on the same level of illegitimacy as the duke of Richmond, but without the precedence granted to him, was passed fifteen months before the birth of prince Edward and must therefore have been designed to allow Henry Fitzroy precedence as a claimant to the throne over Henry's other issue. Note that he gave his other illegitimate son, Henry Carey, no such interesting precedence.

Queen Katherine was furious at Henry's action in conferring these titles upon a bastard whom he was thereby elevating to a position of rivalry with her legitimate daughter, princess Mary. Henry, in turn, was so angry at Katherine's objections that he dismissed from court the three ladies in whom Katherine most often confided. Although very much hurt, Katherine said nothing more on the subject.

Like Mary, Henry Fitzroy had a little throne and canopy of estate made with cloth of gold and fringed with red silk. He could ride a pony and handle a bow, and in 1525 killed his first buck in a royal hunting park. He learned Latin and Greek from his tutor, Richard Croke, and by the time he was eight could translate Caesar unaided. The king made him lord high admiral, lord warden of the Marches and lord of Ireland. There was even talk of his being made king of Ireland. His household had four chaplains, but the exact number of singers in his chapel is not known. The books of his chapel comprised 'a booke prykked with keryes' and 'a grete Booke of masse, prykked'.[3]

The outbreak of sweating sickness in 1529 saw Henry taking particular care for the well-being of Henry Fitzroy. Fitzroy had his court at Pontefract Castle, but six people in the neighbouring parish died of the sweating sickness, for which there was no cure and which resulted in death, sometimes within hours. Henry had an almost paranoid fear of this disease and ordered Fitzroy to be moved from the castle. He was concerned that there was no doctor near at hand to look after the boy and personally compounded medical preventives for Fitzroy and his court. When the epidemic had died down Fitzroy wrote to his father: 'Thanks be to God and to your said highness I have passed this last summer without any peril or danger of the ragious sweat that hath reigned in these parts and other, with the help of such preservatives as your highness did send to me, whereof most humble and lowly I thank the same.'[4]

Two years later, in October 1531, the provost of Eton College made over the hospital of St James at Westminster to Henry, at the dissolution of which an annual pension of £6 13s 4d was assigned by the king to each of the occupying four sisters, three of whom were widows. Although it was not until 1536 that the last of the 'inmates' was pensioned off, the

---

[3] *Camden Miscellany* 3, pp. xxiv, 14. See also J.G. Nichols's introduction to *Inventories ... of Henry Fitzroy, Duke of Richmond*, and Harrison, *Music in Medieval Britain*, p. 174.

[4] Quoted in Carolly Erickson, *Bloody Mary* (Dent, London, 1978), p. 83.

buildings, together with the surrounding land, were at the king's disposal from 1531. Here he built a new palace – but for whom? What exactly were the king's intentions in 1531?

There was little need to build a palace for the king's successive wives – they would be expected to live with him. And even after they fell from favour, Henry did not contemplate building palaces for his rejected wives, as events were to show.

For a clue to the mystery, it is necessary to look forward a little to the Act of Succession and the state opening of parliament in June 1536 – and to the architectural clues preserved in the buildings at St James's Palace. By 1536 all the king's children had become bastards. Fitzroy had been born one, Mary declared one by the Act of Succession of 1534, and Elizabeth became one when archbishop Thomas Cranmer pronounced Henry's marriage to Anne Boleyn invalid in May 1536. The Act of Succession of 1536 recognised that there was no legitimate heir but then took an unusual twist. Instead of declaring that the heir would come from the as yet unborn children of the king and Jane Seymour, it took the unique step of giving Henry the right to name any heir he chose. Henry could now without hesitation name Fitzroy, seventeen years old by this time, as his heir without waiting for Jane to produce a son. The earl of Sussex, Robert Ratcliffe, was heard to remark in the king's presence at a council meeting that as both Fitzroy and Mary were now bastards 'it was advisable to prefer the male to the female for the succession to the crown'. It is not clear what Henry's personal thoughts were on this matter, but Fitzroy was certainly given a prominent place in the formal opening of parliament in June 1536, walking as he did just in front of the king in the procession bearing the cap of maintenance. He was thus given greater precedence than the earl of Sussex, who carried the royal sword, and the earl of Oxford, who carried the king's train. Fitzroy was married to Mary Howard, the duke of Norfolk's only daughter, thereby completing his preparation for the throne. He was also prominent among the spectators at Anne Boleyn's execution at the Tower of London.

Although there seems to be no formal grant extant of St James's to Fitzroy, he certainly died there of tuberculosis in July 1536. Henry arranged an obscure burial for him with no public mourning or funeral procession. Instead the sealed coffin was loaded onto a wagon, covered with straw, and eventually buried at Framlingham, where his tomb can still be seen.

Several conclusions may be drawn from this story. First, unlike the queen, the heir to the throne would require a palace in which to establish himself and his court in London as time went on. Secondly, as Henry Fitzroy died at St James's Palace in 1536 we may assume that his household was with him. Thirdly, as St James's Palace was the place where Fitzroy died, some of the palace buildings at least must have been ready for habitation, and indeed have been occupied for some time

Queen Isabella and her army at Hereford in 1326. In the background can be seen the gruesome execution of Hugh Despenser the Younger. (Reproduced by courtesy of the British Library)

beforehand. The building we now know as the Chapel Royal at St James's Palace came into being at this time, and may well have seen its first services conducted by the household chapel of the duke of Richmond.

We are on surer ground, however, when we look at the architecture of this chapel building in the context of the accounts of building expenses relating to the construction of the palace, and in relation to exactly which buildings stood there when the king acquired the site in 1531. We know that the master of the hospital of St James at Westminster in 1384, Thomas Orgrave, with the consent of the treasurer, let to Elizabeth, Lady le Despenser for the duration of her life, at a rent of ten marks, nearly the whole hospital. The Despenser family had been Marcher lords who came to the aid of Edward II following his catastrophic defeat at Bannockburn in 1314 at the hands of Robert Bruce, and during the open defiance of Thomas of Lancaster before 1318. They were handsomely rewarded with with gifts of estates, but in 1321 were forced into exile by jealous fellow barons and Lancaster. The Despensers returned following Edward's successful invasion of the Welsh Marcher lands in 1322. He dealt with Lancaster, who had indulged in the 'treacherous' act of seeking Robert

These two massive stone arches in the 'tunnel' between ambassadors' court and colour court at St James's Palace almost certainly supported the 'stone tower' mentioned in the Despenser arrangements of 1384 and still visible in the Wyngaerde sketches of 1543 and 1558. This would thus correspond to the 'long entrance before the door of the principal hall of the hospital' mentioned in 1384. It would also confirm that this principal hall stood in what is now colour court, and that the north wall of a building uncovered in the 1925 archaeological dig in colour court was part of the hall structure. Two surviving 'Richmond' angled buttresses built in the 1530s are still visible at either end of the stone arches. Sir Robert Smirke uncovered and removed stone mullions and other masonry above these arches in 1838 in the course of rebuilding the south end of the Chapel, which lies immediately to the right, confirming the medieval date of this structure. It is, however, unlikely that the masonry uncovered was 'Norman', as described by those present in 1838, although Titus in the Cottonian Manuscripts records that the lazar house here was visited by the abbot of Westminster, Giselbertus, in 1100.

Bruce's aid, defeating Lancaster's private army at Boroughbridge and having his head hacked off. But the Despensers incurred the displeasure of queen Isabella, who was plotting to invade her husband's kingdom from abroad. When Isabella's army, which included mercenaries from Hainault, landed in Suffolk, the king and his supporters retreated – the Despensers being slowly picked off and killed. The king himself was captured on 16 November 1326 and cruelly executed with a red-hot poker in the dungeon of Berkeley Castle, his guards having failed to starve him to death. Somehow strands of the Despenser family survived and fifty-eight years later, in 1384, 'Elizabeth late the wife of Edward, Lord le Despenser' was permitted to rent nearly the whole hospital of St James.

3. The House of Richmond

This drawing of St James's Palace from 'Cunditt Meadows' has been dated to the mid-fifteenth century. This is very unlikely, however, not least because of the design of the Conduit House in the foreground. St James's Palace is on the right, with the gatehouse as a prominent feature. There is no 'stone tower' as described in 1384, apart from the gatehouse. This would indicate a date for the drawing that is post 1558 – the last possible recording of the 'stone tower' being in a Wyngaerde sketch of that year. It is in fact most probably early seventeenth-century. A curious feature is the outline of the Chapel, situated immediately to the right of the gatehouse and forming a corner of the palace. It does not seem to show much width, certainly when compared to Hollar's etching showing the same view in 1660. The rather less refined appearance of the palace in this drawing would suggest a date before 1660. (Crace Collection, reproduced by courtesy of the Trustees of the British Museum)

The buildings of the hospital detailed in the Despenser agreement of 1384 are preserved in a Patent Roll which reads thus:

> all the houses and buildings in the said hospital within the gate of the long entrance before the door of the principal hall of the hospital, as well the said hall and upper and lower chambers at each end of the hall and the stone tower as the chamber over the said entrance, the kitchen and bakery and all the other houses and buildings within the gate assigned for the master's abode with all the gardens, areas and stews within the said gate, with free ingress and egress, excepting only a cellar newly constructed ...

A papal relaxation granted in 1393 indicates that the hospital chapel was being re-built.

The theft in 1403 of a bay-horse worth 30s by an Irishman, Nicholas Cusak, 'from a man unknown at Woxebrigge' provides more vital detail about the hospital chapel. Cusak rode to London, entered the hospital and took refuge in the chapel. The coroner positioned Thomas Cotysham, John Grene and John Squier, 'constables within the liberty of the abbey

73

A VIEW OF St JAMES'S PALACE and WESTMINSTER ABBEY.

From the Village of Charing.

Hollar's view of St James's Palace and Westminster Abbey, published by Jeffery in 1806. (Reproduced by courtesy of the Guildhall Library, City of London)

in the town of Westminster', to watch the entrance of the chapel, but one of the hospital chaplains, William Cave, told the constables that no officer of the king should guard any fugitive from the law claiming the right of sanctuary under penalty of excommunication. This chaplain then threw the constables out of the precincts and 'made fast the gates of the hospital and the doors of the church' against them. Furthermore, he allowed the horse-thief to escape. It seems therefore that there must have been something in the nature of a 'back door' to the hospital precincts.

In the reign of Henry VII there were two chaplains of the hospital. In the undervalued procurations compiled by Wolsey in 1524 the hospital was valued at £50, but its property gives an idea of its rather greater wealth: 160 acres bordering the high road from Charing Cross to Aye-hill, eighteen acres in Knightsbridge, land in Chelsea and Fulham, a tenement called the White Bear in the parishes of St Mary Magdalen and All Saints, in Westcheap and Bread Street, together with lands called 'Chalcotes' and 'Wyldes' in the parishes of Hendon, Finchley and Hampstead.

These then were the buildings and lands associated with the hospital of St James at Westminster, originally founded for leprous women after the Norman invasion of 1066, which Henry VIII acquired in 1531 in order to

74

build, it seems, a palace for Henry Fitzroy, duke of Richmond, the son he had in mind as the heir to the throne.

Very few records appear to have survived with regard to the building of St James's Palace. The indenture transferring the land to Henry VIII is dated 5 September 1531[5] and must be seen in the context of a much larger building programme Henry had in mind at that time for the newly acquired buildings and lands of York Place – formerly cardinal Wolsey's great residence at Whitehall. Henry has been credited with the design of certain buildings in the expansion of York Place as the new Whitehall Palace. There is every reason to suppose, therefore, that he took a similar interest and had a hand in the design or re-design of the buildings of the hospital of St James that were to become the buildings of St James's Palace. The building records that have survived tell a very interesting, if hazy, story about the origins of the structure we know today as the Chapel Royal. Is it on the old site of the hospital chapel? Depending upon the date of its construction, who were the first choir and priests to use it?

We have listed the hospital buildings, including the chapel, that seem to have been acquired by Henry VIII in September 1531, along with the site. What happened to these buildings, and in particular the hospital chapel? Apart from a manuscript in the British Library relating to preliminary building works in 1532, the earliest set of accounts that have survived from the 'Henrician' St James's seem to relate to works effected soon after 1536, as the document also summarises work done at a house in Chelsea which was not acquired by Henry until 1536. The document forms part of the Whitehall accounts but contains a summary of expenditure at 'Sent James'. The heading of the account is missing so its exact date is uncertain, but the summary does give us some clues from which we can make fairly certain deductions. It gives only the total number of workmen of each trade and the quantities of materials purchased for the work at St James's. There were seven freemasons, thirteen carpenters, twenty-two bricklayers, five plasterers and forty-three labourers to bricklayers and diggers of foundations. The materials purchased included 70,000 bricks, 23 loads of lime, 110 loads of sand, 1,000 plain tiles, three packs of cow hair, four bundles of osiers for 'the Erber', and a quantity of charcoal 'for the galleries' for drying out the plaster.

The first observation to be made is that the quantity of bricks purchased in 1536 was comparatively small – just 70,000. These would have been barely enough to build a structure the size of the present gatehouse facing up St James's Street! As the records of 1537 are extant and were made by the then paymaster of the works at Whitehall, Sir Anthony Denny, we know that little work was done at St James's immediately following the death of the duke of Richmond there in 1536.

---

[5] PRO C.66/659 m27.

In 1537 Sir Anthony Denny received only £2,000 from the augmentations for building and repairs at Whitehall, St James's, Chelsea and Hackney. Evidence of this expenditure at St James's was revealed in 1822 when a fireplace discovered in the guard room of the state apartments was found to bear the date 1538. Unfortunately no accounts have survived for Sir Anthony Denny's expenditures at St James's in the period 1538-41, although it is known from the declarations of his expenditures from 1541-47 that £765 was spent on St James's. This represents an average of only £126 per year and indicates that very little maintenance was done at St James's in the last years of Henry VIII's reign. Thus it would seem that the palace was largely built in the ten years 1531-41, but chiefly before 1536.

There are some curious irregularities in the architecture and layout of the 'Richmond' buildings which cast doubt on the theory that the present Chapel Royal structure is built on the site of the old hospital chapel. For a start, the present chapel building faces north. It is extremely unlikely that the old hospital chapel similarly faced north. There is every reason to suppose that it faced east as was, and still is, the symbolic convention. The discovery in 1925 of foundations of a north wall of a building together with six patterned and coloured 'medieval' tiles[6] during an archaeological dig in colour court – the centre of the 'Henrician' quadrangular palace – points to the hospital chapel having occupied at least part of what is now colour court. An order of 1320 confining the sisters to their rooms except for the adjoining cloister or to go to church reveals the existence of a cloister in the hospital complex, presumably adjoining the chapel at some point.

Close examination of the patterns on these colour court slip tiles reveals some fascinating links. At the top of the frame are two tiles of fleurs-de-lys in gold on a red background, between which is to be seen a red tile with a gold dragon. It was in 1337 that Edward III laid claim to the kingdom of France and adopted the gold fleurs-de-lys on a blue field in his arms. There would seem to be a link here, from the point of view of tile manufacture, with the Cistercian abbey of Bindon in Dorset, where there are tiles displaying the royal arms as well as other mythological creatures. Furthermore, like Bindon Abbey, the colour court collection also has tiles of a quadrant pattern with roundels, revealing a shared French influence, which form the bottom tiles at the centre and left in the colour court frame. One of the two colour court quadrant tiles is identical both in pattern and size with some early fourteenth-century tiles found in 1960 at Clifton House at King's Lynn in Norfolk, formerly a merchant's house. The latter have a pale inlay on a bluish ground, while the colour court quadrant tiles are gold on red. As for the colour court dragon, a very similar but larger one has been found in London, known as Penn

---

[6] Now displayed on the wall in the vestibule of the Chapel Royal.

(Buckinghamshire) style.[7]

Let us assume for the moment that the hospital chapel faced east. We know from the horse-thief incident of 1403 that the hospital chaplain enforced the privilege of sanctuary to protect the horse-thief by locking the gates of both the hospital and the chapel. It could reasonably be presumed that the hospital structure described in 1384 as the chamber over the entrance was a gatehouse. It may well be that the two surviving substantial stone arches in the 'tunnel' between what are now ambassadors' court and colour court once formed the entrance of this hospital gatehouse. Certainly it seems unlikely that stone was used for no obvious load-bearing purpose. Stone was at a premium and was not in local supply, as is known from the fact that some of the stone used in the construction of Whitehall Palace in the 1530s came all the way from Wolsey's old college at Ipswich. The old hospital buildings at St James's were stone structures, as we know from the 1384 description of a stone tower there. It may be that this still lies within the later brick walls of the present 'Henrician' gatehouse, just as the remains of parts of Whitehall Palace were discovered within the later walls of what is now the Cabinet Office in Whitehall. Two sixteenth-century stone doorways are still to be found in the present practice room of the Chapel Royal in the gatehouse above the vestry. But, on the other hand, perhaps the stone of the old hospital at St James's was itself plundered for the Whitehall project. Where did the stone go? Certainly no stone tower is visible now at St James's – but it may be that one of the two halls of the hospital is still extant and lies within the walls of what we know now as the Chapel Royal. This is conjecture, but we can learn yet more from the present chapel itself.

The spectacular painted motif ceiling of the present chapel displays the date 1540 in many places. The lower structure of the present chapel must therefore have been built before this – but when? There are two possibilities. The roof is copper, and copper is not among the materials mentioned in 1536 and would have been too expensive to be accounted for in the £2,000 shared between Whitehall, St James's, Chelsea and Hackney in 1537. This would have left barely two years to build the entire chapel from scratch, which is unlikely. It is much more likely that the present chapel incorporates an older hospital structure – probably one of the halls – which may explain why it faces north and not east. If so its 'construction/conversion' must be confined largely to the years 1531-36. It would therefore have been largely ready – and certainly weather-proof enough – for the court painter Holbein, or another of the king's painters, to consider how best to decorate the ceiling. Certainly the ceiling structure and roof would have been completed before the ceiling was

---

[7] See J.A. Wright, *Medieval Floor Tiles: their design and distribution in Britain* (A.&C. Black, London, n.d.) esp. pp. 53, 128.

decorated, and probably by 1536.

This decoration, as can still be seen, takes the form of a geometrical tessellation. In fact the pattern of ribs owes its design directly to a plate in the fourth book of Serlio's *Regoli Generali di Architectura*, published in Venice in 1537.[8] The motif paintings bordered by this ribbing are traditionally attributed to Holbein but there is no sure evidence of this, although the attribution goes back to the seventeenth century. The emblems depicted are all either Christian symbols or the family arms, designs and mottoes of Henry VIII and Anne of Cleves, with a liberal smattering of the date 1540. But there is one major exception to be found tucked away in the north-west corner. This is the coat-of-arms of Henry's next wife, Katherine Howard, whom he married also in 1540 after

Anthony van den Wyngaerde drew the earliest existing panoramic view of London in pen and ink in 1543, although buildings of a later date are also included. It is known that he was in London again in 1558 and probably made the additions then. The magnified detail above shows St James's Palace, standing by itself across the fields from Whitehall, as it apparently looked in 1543. It is therefore the only surviving record of the palace still undergoing conversion from its former role as a hospital. Henry Fitzroy, duke of Richmond, for whom it seems to have been intended, had died there only seven years previously. Among these 'Richmond' buildings a tower with a steeple is a prominent feature – perhaps the 'stone tower' mentioned in the Despenser arrangements of 1384, which on this basis was not dismantled until after 1543 or perhaps even 1558. (Reproduced by courtesy of the Ashmolean Museum, Oxford)

[8] See H.M. Colvin and John Summerson, *History of the King's Works*, vol. 4: 1485-1660, part 2 (HMSO, 1982), p. 242.

divorcing Anne of Cleves. As Anne Boleyn was beheaded on 19 May 1536, but the letters H&A are still to be seen in the fireplaces of the armoury and tapestry rooms of the state apartments of St James's Palace, it could perhaps be reasonably assumed that this gatehouse structure and its integral dovetailing to the Chapel Royal were near enough complete by May 1536.[9] We may presume therefore that the duke of Richmond, who died at St James's later in 1536, had heard his own chapel priests and choir conduct divine service in the 'Chapel Royal' structure before his death.

Contrary to the observations of some previous writers, the monograms above the side doors of the great gatehouse at St James's Palace are not H&A (Henry VIII and Anne Boleyn). They are in fact HR (Henricus Rex) surmounted by the king's crown. The only H&A monograms extant are to be found on the iron fireplaces in the armoury and tapestry rooms of the state apartments, as we have seen, and upon the ceiling of the Chapel Royal building in colour court. While the H&As on the fireplaces may be associated with either Anne Boleyn or Anne of Cleves, the Chapel Royal ceiling is known to refer to Anne of Cleves and accordingly bears the date 1540 in several places. This does not mean that the palace was built either for Anne Boleyn or Anne of Cleves. It could not have been built for the latter, for Henry had purchased the site nine years before, while increased expenditure on Greenwich Palace in preparation for Anne Boleyn's delivery would suggest that Henry had a different purpose in mind for St James's Palace.

St James's was recognised at the time as the king's manor or palace, not the queen's – hence the HR monograms. Thus Nichols in his *Progresses of Queen Elizabeth* recorded that Anne Boleyn withdrew from Westminster Hall after her coronation and went to Whitehall. Thence, later, she 'went in her barge secretly to the King in his mannor of Westminster [St James's] where she rested that night'. There is no suggestion here that St James's was Anne Boleyn's.

Anne Boleyn was almost six months pregnant at her coronation and is known from the *Calendar of Spanish Papers* to have spent her ninth and last month of pregnancy at Greenwich Palace in 'confinement' while Henry argued with her and enjoyed the company of other women. During this time lavish expenditure was directed at Greenwich Palace in preparation for the new birth; Henry's favourite bed was even installed there.

The presence of H&As with a true lovers' knot, Tudor rose, fleur-de-lys, portcullis and crowned initial H, decorating the fireplace in the tapestry room of the state apartments, presents a problem only if they are taken to represent Henry's true emotions. For this would mean that the building in which the fireplace is to be found would have to have been habitable

---

[9] Though H&A could also refer to Anne of Cleves: see below.

Christina of Milan, whom Henry VIII intended to marry on the basis of this beautiful painting executed in Brussels by Holbein in 1538 on Henry's instructions. (Reproduced by courtesy of the National Gallery, London)

before September 1533, when Henry fell out of love with Anne Boleyn, on the birth of their daughter Elizabeth, and transferred his favour to Jane Seymour. This would imply that the palace was completed in the space of just two years. It is far more likely that the convention of marking a building with the initials of the reigning king and queen applied despite Henry's matrimonial difficulties. This would allow until Anne Boleyn's execution in 1536 for the palace to be virtually completed – a far more realistic timescale.

After Jane Seymour died in 1537, having given birth to Henry's son Edward, the king toyed with the idea of marrying Christina of Milan, a pretty sixteen-year-old widow. In 1538 he duly sent Holbein to paint a true likeness of her, only to find the prospect of marriage impossibly impaled upon the need for a papal dispensation. Henry later relied much upon Holbein's painting from life of Anne of Cleves and her sister in making his decision to marry Anne in January 1540. We can assume that the court artist Holbein, or another of the king's painters, set to work quickly in January 1540 to decorate the ceiling of the chapel at St James's in honour of the expected alliance between England and Cleves. The painting must have been all but completed by the spring of 1540 when the

3. The House of Richmond

This miniature by Holbein of Anne of Cleves is a copy he made of the famous portrait he painted for Henry, on the basis of which the king agreed to marry her. Upon this decision Holbein or his colleagues began in January 1540 to paint on the Chapel ceiling a tribute to the forthcoming alliance, only to find that Henry had divorced Anne by the summer of that year. (Reproduced by courtesy of the Board of Trustees of the V & A)

king, who had taken an immediate dislike to Anne's physical appearance upon first setting eyes on her at Rochester below the castle where she disembarked from the river Medway, began to seek seriously to divorce her. This he did at the earliest opportunity and promptly married Katherine Howard in July that year. Holbein must have wondered what to do with the ceiling of the chapel at St James's, for politics were changing his commissions quicker than he could paint them! The king's glazier, Mr Hone, later experienced similar problems at Rochester royal manor where he had inserted 'Two armys of the king's and queene's sett uppe within the lodgyngs' and thirteen 'baggs [badges] of the king's and queene's', the queen in question being Katherine Howard. Following her execution in 1542 a local glazier was employed in 'taking owte of the Lady Haywards armys'![10] It would be interesting to know if there had been any earlier attempt to paint the ceiling of the chapel at St James's during Jane Seymour's marriage to Henry.

Towards the centre of the Holbein ceiling, and again at the north end, there is a panel displaying a coat-of-arms which may indicate an unfulfilled intention of Henry VIII's. The arms in question consist of the prince of Wales feathers in white, together with the inscription 'Ich Dien',

---

[10] Bodleian MS Rawl. D785: 'Building Account of the Royal Manor of Rochester, 19 February-14 May 1542', compiled by James Needham.

flanked on either side by the letters P and E in gold, painted within a blue and red half-moon, in turn surrounded by a sun-burst of gold. The P almost certainly stands for 'Princeps' as it still does today in relation to the prince of Wales, and the E for 'Edwardus'. If so, then this would seem to pay tribute to the future king Edward VI, who had been born in October 1537. But the mystery is that Henry VIII never conferred the title of prince of Wales upon Edward. As he was just three years old when Holbein was painting the Chapel Royal ceiling in 1540, it may well be that Holbein was assuming that Edward would be made prince of Wales as his father was before him, or else was making Henry's intention to further the cause of his offspring by Jane Seymour clearly visible at a time when he was about to marry again. If so, then this coat-of-arms constitutes a statement of great political magnitude.

Prince Henry's room, built in 1610-11, retains its original ceiling displaying an almost identical prince of Wales emblem upon a sun-burst background but with the letters P and H either side of the feathers, denoting 'Princeps Henricus'. Unlike the two examples of PE at the Chapel Royal which are richly painted, the PH in prince Henry's room is moulded in plaster.

The ceiling of the Tudor Chapel Royal at the south end, over the royal or holyday closet, consisted of an elaborate pattern with hanging pendants. The closet itself extended on pillars as far north as the present 'angel' rib across the ceiling, and the hanging pendants covered this area. Surviving accounts for the year 1635/6 mention works relating to an elaborate Tudor ceiling with pendants in 'the Closett by the Chapel'. The two craftsmen, Matthew Goodrich and John Brocas, who had worked on the interior of the Queen's Chapel, effected some works in the royal closet of the Chapel Royal in 1635/6 to restore the ceiling, but sadly whatever they did was destroyed beyond recognition by the alterations carried out by Sir Robert Smirke in 1836-37. It could be surmised that the Serlio geometrical patterning of the chapel ceiling once extended towards the south end to provide the ceiling for the royal closet, but upon the reduction in the size of the royal closet following the removal of the supporting pillars the ceiling too was redecorated to honour king William and queen Adelaide.

But to return to its Tudor form, it was from this royal closet, according to the Old Cheque Book of the Chapel Royal, that on Easter day, 15 April 1593, queen Elizabeth, after hearing the gospel read, 'came down into her Majestes Travess' before receiving communion. Following this she is described as 'retourninge to her sayd Travess their devoutly stayed the end of prayers, which done her Majestie Royally ascended the way and stayrs into her presence, whom the Lord blesse for ever and ever'.[11] By 'presence' must be meant her presence chamber, which was situated

---

[11] Old Cheque Book, fol. 14b.

This watercolour drawing of the Chamber of the House of Lords undergoing demolition in 1823 clearly shows the 'borrowed' Serlio Chapel Royal ceiling pattern. (PRO Works 29/17, reproduced by courtesy of the Public Records Office)

behind the royal closet in the state apartments in what is now termed the tapestry room.

The geometrical pattern of the Chapel Royal ceiling was to be the inspiration behind the oldest surviving example of 'blackwork' embroidery, dated *c.* 1700 and displayed at Levens Hall in Cumbria, for the master of Levens Hall, Colonel Graham, was an official of the privy purse who would therefore have known the chapel at St James's Palace well.[12]

[12] For knowledge of the 'blackwork' embroidery at Levens Hall I am indebted to Mrs Smith.

Apparently a later sketch made in 1558 specifically of Whitehall, this was intended by Wyngaerde to be inserted into the 'gap' in his panoramic sketch of 1543. Fortunately it also includes an 'updated' depiction of St James's Palace from that shown in 1543. In this magnified detail the palace is seen at the top right across the park. The present gatehouse is clearly recognisable on the far right of the range. To its left is a rather indistinct structure on top of which are three stacks. This structure must therefore be the 'new' Chapel within which we still worship today. The tower at the left of this range, nearest us and at the south end of the Chapel, may be the last view of the Despenser 'stone tower' mentioned in 1384, for it does not appear in the later Hollar etchings. (Reproduced by courtesy of the Ashmolean Museum, Oxford)

This pattern, itself copied from that at St Constanza's in Rome, which dates from AD 350, also provided the inspiration for the 1623 alteration to the original high gabled ceiling of the mediaeval chamber of the House of Lords. The alteration took the form of a barrel-vault roof along the lines of the Inigo Jones ceiling at the Queen's Chapel of 1623, but decorated with the Serlio Chapel Royal geometrical pattern. The Lords continued to meet in this chamber until they moved to the former court of requests in 1801. A water-colour drawing by Sir John Soane of this chamber being demolished in 1823 is reproduced on p. 83.

Following the death of Henry VIII in 1547, Edward VI's accounts[13]

[13] See Colvin and Summerson, *History of the King's Works*, vol. 4, part 2, p. 235.

Detail from a British Library manuscript showing the serjeant of the vestry, children and gentlemen of the Chapel Royal in 1603 at Elizabeth I's funeral procession. Note the 'rich coapes' worn by the gentlemen, as described in the Old Cheque Book account of the queen's attendance at the celebration of Easter at St James's Chapel in 1593. The children depicted here would have acted at the Chapel Royal theatre in Blackfriars as well as sung with the Chapel Royal. (BL Add. MS 35324, fol. 20v, reproduced by courtesy of the British Library)

show that expenditure on the Chapel Royal at St James's accounted for by his surveyor of works averaged less than £20 per annum. Under queen Mary (whose bowels lie beneath the chapel floor) it rose to just over £100 per annum. Under Elizabeth I the year 1581 was the only significant year of expenditure, when the queen's lodgings and those of the lord treasurer and others were redecorated and the ponds cleaned, apparently for the reception of the court in connection with the entertainment of the duke of Alençon in November 1581.

The plaster royal coat-of-arms of queen Elizabeth which now hangs above the king William door at the south end of the chapel, displaying the 'Tudor' dragon of Cadwallader as a supporter, is the only other remaining 'Tudor' item still visible in the chapel, with the notable exception of the Old Cheque Book manuscript, whose earliest entry bears the date 1560, and which is still kept in the chapel. In the wall behind the altar at the north end of the chapel, but filled in, a curious low arch was revealed in May 1971 during redecoration. It was the barrow-way through which materials were brought into and out of the chapel during construction. It may date from the sixteenth century, for a similar feature is present at Hampton Court chapel.

A glimpse of what the chapel looked like in queen Elizabeth's reign can be had from the account in the Old Cheque Book headed: 'The Princelye comminge of her Majestie to the Holy Communion at Estre' and bearing the date '15 Aprill Eastreday 1593':

The moste sacred Queene Elizabethe upon Eastre day, after the Holy Gospell was redd in the Chaple at St James's, came down into her Majestes Travess: beffore her highnes came the gentlemen pencioners, then the Barons, the Bushopps, London and Landaffe, the Erls, and the ho. Councell in their Colors of State, the Harolds of Arms, the Lord Keeper bearinge the sword beffore her Majestie. Then her Majesties Royal person came most chearfully, having as noble supporters the Right Honorable the Erle of Essex, Master of her Majesties Horse, on the right hande, and the Right Hon. the Lord Admyral on the lefte hande, the Lord Chamberlain to her Majestie (also nexte beffore her Majestie) attendante al the while.

The chapel was equipped with an organ, for we learn from the same passage that 'Dr. Bull was at the organ playinge the Offertorye'. When the queen came to kneel before the table to 'offer the golden obeysant', it was the 'Bushop the hon. Father of Worcester holdinge the golden bason, the Subdean and Epistler in riche coaps assistante to the sayd Bushop' who took the offertory, conducted the service and administered the sacraments. A 'stately stoole and Qwissins [cushions]' were provided for the queen to kneel upon to receive the sacraments, which she did after the bishop, sub-dean, gospeller and epistler – 'in the kyndes of bred and wyne, according to the laws established by her Majestie and Godly laws in Parliament'. The 'bread beinge waffer bread of some thicker substance' which the bishop administered to her, Elizabeth 'toke of the Lord Bushop in her naked right hand'. Then Elizabeth 'toke the ffoote of the golden and now sacred cuppe' to drink with 'a lynned clothe layd on her cushion pillowe' and held at each corner by the earls of Hereford, Essex, Worcester and Oxford. This description gives us a first-hand account, written by the sub-dean, Anthony Anderson, of St James's chapel in use in 1593, with Dr Bull playing the organ.

These were eventful times. Just two years earlier, in 1591, Thomas Tomkins's brother, who had been expelled from the choir of St David's Cathedral and joined the navy, died a heroic death in the last stand of the *Revenge*, when fifty-three Spanish ships fought the *Revenge* and only at the last did 5,000 Spanish overwhelm the 150 English. Thomas's half-brother, John, became organist of the Chapel Royal in 1625, while Thomas himself had become organist of the Chapel Royal in 1621. As for Dr Bull who played the organ at the Easter day service in the presence of the queen in 1593, the Old Cheque Book tells us that in 1613 he 'went beyond the seas without licence and was admitted into the Archduke's service, and entered into paie there about Michaelmas'.

Dr Bull had joined the Chapel Royal in 1585 at a time of mounting concern for the safety of the realm. Three years later, in 1588, Elizabeth stayed at St James's Palace before facing perhaps the greatest threat to the rule of the house of Richmond – the daunting fleet of 130 ships carrying 50,000 men bent on the invasion of England, known as the Spanish Armada. Great 'camps' were formed for the enrolment of a kind of home guard ready to repulse any of the Armada who might escape the English ships under the command of Lord Howard of Effingham, Francis Drake, Martin Frobisher, and others too numerous to mention. The greatest of all these camps was formed at Tilbury with about 1,000 men. Elizabeth determined to go there in person to encourage those who had

This portrait of John Bull, gentleman of the Chapel Royal from 1585 and organist from 1591 until 1613 when he 'went beyond the seas without licence', shows him in the habit of a bachelor of music. On his left is the date 1589, on his right a reminder of mortality in the form of an hour-glass surmounted by a skull. Around the edges of the painting, which is on board, are the words: 'The Bull by force In field doth Raigne But Bull by Skill Good will doth Gayne.' (Reproduced by courtesy of the Heather Professor of Music, Oxford University)

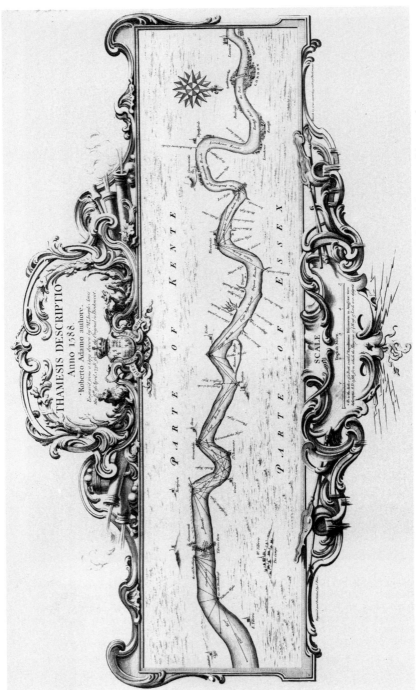

This 1738 engraving of a parchment map of the Thames made in 1588 by Robert Adams, architect and surveyor of the queen's buildings, shows the Armada defences of booms and guns with their lines of fire. There was a boom across Blackwall Reach and at Tilbury. The latter was made from 120 masts, 40 anchors, and cables 9 inches thick. Its construction was supervised by Peter Pett and Richard Chapman, but it had come adrift just before the queen decided to visit the camp. 'The Campe' at West Tilbury is at the bottom left. (Reproduced by courtesy of the National Maritime Museum, Greenwich)

made the decision to offer themselves for the defence of her realm.

It had been more than two weeks since the first sighting of the Spanish fleet. The only news that had reached the 'royal camp' at Tilbury was that Drake had seized a galleass, one of the greatships had sunk and two Spanish carracks had been captured by the ships of Flushing and Zeeland. The Armada was sailing inexorably on around Scotland, only to be wrecked on Irish shores. The great boom of ships' masts and chains that had been built across the mouth of the Thames had given way, leaving London dangerously exposed to a possible 'late' invasion by the duke of Parma's army from Flanders.

Elizabeth determined to raise morale and go in person to Tilbury. To prepare for this she stayed at St James's Palace. The queen would almost certainly have heard holy communion in the chapel before setting off for Tilbury. A contemporary poem described her movements thus:

And on the eight of August,[14] she
From fair St James's took her way
With many lords of high degree
In princely robes and rich array ...

Even allowing for poetic licence, it is clear that the queen would have been accompanied by her senior courtiers. If holy communion had been heard in the Chapel they would certainly have attended too. After rousing the assembled 'volunteers' at Tilbury Elizabeth dined there with the captains and the lieutenant general in his tent. She returned by barge to London where she attended a further review of a large company of horse and foot, rousing them in similar vein.

On the defeat and dispersal of the Spanish Armada the sense of national relief was expressed when Elizabeth attended a thanksgiving service at St Paul's Cathedral in full state on 24 November 1588. The Chapel Royal would in all probability have been present at St Paul's for this major event.

For those old enough to remember, this must have brought back mixed memories of singing in company with Philip of Spain's famous 'Capilla flamenca', whose seven boys, six tenors and four basses, including Philip de Monte, accompanied by many distinguished musicians including the brothers Cabezon, joined forces with the English Chapel Royal and St Paul's choir on 2 December 1554 – one year after Mary Tudor ascended the throne, and just five months after her marriage to Philip on 25 July 1554 at Winchester. This high mass had seen Philip

[14] In 1588 England was still using the 'old style' Julian calendar, which was ten days behind the Gregorian calendar adopted by Spain and the Catholic Netherlands six years previously in 1582. As several surviving logs from Spanish Armada vessels reveal that they were off the west coast of Scotland on 18 August 1588, Elizabeth must have made her speech in the knowledge that the remaining threat was from Parma's army.

The national thanksgiving service for the defeat of the Spanish Armada, held at St Paul's Cathedral on 24 November 1588. (Reproduced by courtesy of the Mansell Collection Ltd.)

accompanied 'by 400 of the Gard, 100 English, 100 Germans, 100 Spaniards and 100 Swiss'.

The head chorister at St Paul's in 1554 was a certain William Byrd, who was born about 1538. His name comes at the head of the choir school petition of 1554 for the restoration of obits and benefactions that had been seized under the Act of Suppression of Colleges and Hospitals in Edward VI's reign. A Roman Catholic by leaning, William Byrd nevertheless conformed, at least outwardly, to the established church in Elizabeth's reign, becoming in due time organist of Lincoln Cathedral. On the death of Robert Parsons in 1569, who, as we learn from the Old Cheque Book, had 'drowned at Newark uppon Trent on 25th January', William Byrd was 'sworne gentleman in his place at the first the 22nd of February followinge [from] Lincolne'.[15] He was apparently the son of

[15] Old Cheque Book, fol. 5. Also reprinted in Edward F. Rimbault, *The Old Cheque Book, or Book of Remembrance, of the Chapel Royal from 1561 to 1744* (Camden History Society, 1872; repr. in facsimile by Da Capo Press, New York, 1966), p. 5.

Thomas Bird, who had been 'Clarke of the Cheque' of the Chapel Royal but died in February 1561. William joined the Chapel Royal in 1569 and remained a member of it until he died on 4 July 1623 at the age of about eighty-five.

As head chorister of St Paul's Cathedral choir in 1554 William would most likely have been introduced to Philip de Monte, and in 1583 de Monte sent an eight-part setting of part of the psalm 'Super flumina' to him. William in turn replied with 'Quomodo cantabimus'.[16] It has been observed by Kerman that Byrd's 'Quomodo' contains a *double entendre*, for he rearranged the verses deliberately to allude to the 'Babylonish captivity' to which the Roman Catholic recusant families compared their circumstances. Byrd's wife was cited for recusancy in 1577 and William himself in 1587 – just one year before he would have been required to sing at St Paul's Cathedral on 24 November 1588 to celebrate the defeat of the Spanish Armada. He must have had very mixed feelings on that occasion.

Byrd's two collections of *Cantiones sacrae* of 1589 and 1591 reveal his politico-religious position very clearly. He had appeared back in 1589 on a list of places frequented by recusants in the following entry: 'William Byrd of the Chappel, at his house in p'rshe of Harlington, in com Midds.' In another entry he is described as a friend or abettor of those beyond the sea, and was residing 'with Mr Lister, over against St Dunstans, or at the Lord Padgette's house in Draighton'.[17]

Among other members of the Chapel Royal who would also have attended both the 'Spanish' Catholic service of welcome of 1554 and the thanksgiving for deliverance from the Spanish in 1588 was William Hunnis, master of the children of the Chapel Royal.

According to an entry of 1566 in the Old Cheque Book, 'Rich. Edwards died, Mr. of the Children, the last [day of] October and Wm. Hunnis was made Master of the Children the 15th of November, A 8'. He died on 6 June 1597. It was Hunnis who contributed a 'devise' and a collection of verses to the 'Princelie Pleasures' at Kenilworth Castle in 1575, at which no doubt the Chapel Royal children acted in the interludes he provided for the occasion.

The clock on the gatehouse of Kenilworth Castle was deliberately stopped at 12 o'clock as Elizabeth rode in her carriage across the moat speckled with artificial islands adorned with silver-clad young girls dressed as fairies. The clock stayed at 12 until the queen left and all the while crowds watched from the far banks of the moat. The young William Shakespeare may well have been brought as a child to watch the fantastic spectacle, and it has been conjectured that it was the inspiration for *A Midsummer Night's Dream*.

A William Hunnis is mentioned as 'Supervisor and Keeper of the greate

[16] See David Wulstan, *Tudor Music* (Dent, London, 1985), p. 309.
[17] Cited among Rimbault's comments in the Da Capo edition of *The Old Cheque Book*, p. 190.

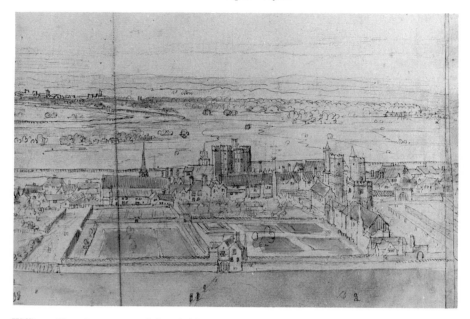

William Hunnis, master of the children of the Chapel Royal, was also 'Supervisor and Keeper of the greate gardens and orchardes at Greenwich', which can be seen here in Wyngaerde's view of Greenwich Palace drawn in 1588. (Reproduced by courtesy of the Ashmolean Museum, Oxford)

gardens and orchardes at Greenwich'.[18] As our William Hunnis called his famous translation of the Book of Genesis into English rhyme 'A Hive full of Honey' and his blessings out of Deuteronomy, prayers to Christ, Athanasius' creed and meditations in metre 'A Handful of Honeysuckles', it seems that the Kenilworth and Greenwich Hunnises may have been one and the same. Certainly Mr Cunningham thought these garden images suggestive of the gardens at Greenwich.[19] If so, then Hunnis's hard work in the gardens and orchards can be appreciated from Wyngaerde's contemporary drawing of them in his view of Greenwich Palace (Placentia) from the hill, a favourite palace of the house of Richmond.

[18] See Mrs C.C. Stopes, 'William Hunnis and the Revels of the Chapel Royal' in vol. 29 of Bang's *Materialien* series (1910).
[19] Peter Cunningham, *Extracts from the Accounts of the Revels at Court ...* (Shakespeare Society, London, 1842), book 3.

4

Favourite Palaces

Greenwich Palace (Placentia)

At the back of the Bodleian Register (MS Rawlinson D318), and upside down in relation to the rest of the manuscript, is a series of entries relating to the movements of the Chapel Royal from one favourite palace of the sovereign to another. It provides a most fascinating insight into the arrangements that had to be made to effect these moves. One such entry (fols 46-45), entitled 'A President when ther is two Removes in a moneth', is dated 1633 and reads thus:

	childres	Remoovings	Myles
	xvs	ffrom Grinwich to windsor	xxv
		Summa ... iiii li xs xd	
xvd	vis	ffrom windsor to hampton court	xi
		Summa ... xls vd	
	ixs	ffrom windsor to Richmount	xiiii
		Summa ... lis viiid	
xvd	vis	ffrom Richmount to Grinwich	xi
		Summa ... xls vd	
	ixs	ffrom Grinwich to hampton court	xv
		Summa ... liiiis vid	
iis vid	vis	ffrom hampton court to Whithall	xii
		summa ... xliiiis vid	
	iiis	ffrom whitehall to Grinwich	v
		Summa ... xviiis iid	
iis vid	iiis	ffrom whitehall to richmount	vi
		Summa ... xxvi iiiid	
	iiis	ffrom hampton court to Richmount	iiii
		Summa ... xvs iiiid	
	xiis	ffrom whitehall to windsor	xx
		Summa ... iii li xiis viiid	

when it doth happen that the remove is a-11-6-7 or -12 myles or the lyke, the odde pence to the Children and yeomen, are the Clarke of the Checks fee, as for example, llooke one the margent of the other syde.

... The xii Children for board wagis have xd apeece per diem viz xs per diem. The gent of the Chappell, the Gospeller, the Epistler, the Sergeant of the

93

Vestuarie, to each of them, haue at every remoove for Beveridge a penny a myle. The yeomen and Groome of the vestuarie haue to each of them for every fyve myles iiid – And if there be any odd myle more or lesse they haue a penny a peece for the same, As for example, they haue for remooving fower mile iiid, for six miles iiiid.

'Remooving' to the sovereign's favourite palaces was clearly a major upheaval for the Chapel Royal. Fortunately most of the palaces were situated along the Thames, making it possible to use boats to transport the necessary people and items.[1]

Let us now try to picture the buildings in which the Chapel Royal found themselves singing in the sixteenth century. We have already had a glimpse of the gardens of honeysuckle at the Greenwich Palace of Placentia in the days of the master of the children William Hunnis – so let us look there first, for it held many secrets of great import to the history of the Chapel Royal.

The chroniclers Wriothesley and Stow agree that in 1500 or 1501 Henry VII 'repayred his place at greenwich, with muche new buyldinge'. W. Lambarde's *A Perambulation of Kent*, written in 1570, remarks that Henry 'beautified the house with the addition of the brick front toward the water side'. In fact both of these statements are confirmed by the Chamber Accounts, which reveal that in 1499 brickmakers were paid for making 600,000 bricks for Greenwich Palace. This number is very much larger than the 70,000 bricks purchased in 1536 for building the 'new' palace at St James's. This would lend credence to the idea that the bricks ordered for St James's were for specific buildings rather than an entire palace. Back at Greenwich, we know that the master mason who built the chapel at the palace was Robert Vertu. He and 'his felowes' received £900 for works undertaken between March 1500 and July 1504. The master carpenter who worked on the chapel was Thomas Benks, to whom payments at the same time as those to Vertu were made for, among other things, 'the chapel, gallery and two closets at greenwich'. Robert Vertu's payments are said to have been 'for the same chapel, gallery and closets', so it is clear that these carpenters and masons worked together on the chapel. There is, though, one reference to the demolition of the old chapel in an account of the clerk of the king's works, Thomas Warley, covering the years 1500-02. So how much, if any, of these materials or fixings was re-used in the new chapel under construction until 1504 is not clear.

The result of this building work can be appreciated from Wyngaerde's view of Greenwich Palace in 1558, in which the north side (i.e. riverside) of the chapel is clearly seen as the building at the left-hand end of the range. This was the building in which the Chapel Royal sang when the Tudor court was in residence at Greenwich – as it was for extensive

---

[1] See Chapter 5, p. 117, where details of boat hire for 1573 are given.

4. Favourite Palaces

Greenachio

'Placentia' (Greenwich Palace) from the Thames. This drawing, now at the Ashmolean Museum, Oxford, was made by Wyngaerde in 1588, and shows the 'fort' with its flagpole at the top of the hill behind the palace. Elizabeth I wrote of Placentia, through whose windows she had watched Frobisher set out on his voyage to find the North-West Passage, and passing which Drake fired a salute as he returned from having sailed around the world, that 'sure the home, garden and walks may compare with any delicat place in Italy'. The Chapel Royal premises are to be seen at the left of the palace range along the riverside. (Reproduced by courtesy of the Ashmolean Museum, Oxford)

periods throughout the sixteenth century. The gardens of honeysuckle in which it seems William Hunnis worked as keeper of gardens and orchards, and in which he found his inspiration for his writings and plays in which the Chapel Royal children acted during Elizabeth's reign, were also largely laid out at this time. In 1503-04 Robert Vertu built 'two brick walls which together cost £100, which enclosed the Garden'. In 1505 another payment of £100 was made for 'a bryckewall at Greenwich enclosed to the backside of the place'. These, then, were the very walls up which the honeysuckle tended by William Hunnis had climbed to become the great source of nectar for the honey bees.

Returning to the chapel, in Henry VIII's reign it seems that, because of the newness of the structure, little needed to be done to it for some time – and what was done was confined to the interior. In 1534 'the Cardenall's [i.e. Wolsey's] armies' on 'the grette organes in the Chappell' were painted

95

out and replaced by the arms of Anne Boleyn,[2] and in 1540 the organs themselves were repaired by William Bitton, his son William, and Roger Emerson.[3]

Other references to Henrician works in the chapel relate to the annual St George's day service when mass was sung before Henry VIII 'in his robes'.[4] Both the king and the queen had what was described as a 'holy day closet', and chapters of the order of the garter were held in the chapel.

James Nedeham's surveyorship saw little done to the chapel, but there is one item that he had to see to – a painful reminder of the hawking incident in which Henry fell into a ditch head-first and nearly drowned, and which prompted him to think seriously of who should become his heir – for in 1542 Nedeham was required to construct timber bridges at strategic crossing points in nearby Woolwich marshes 'for the King's grace to ryde over dyches an hawkyng and a huntyng safflye'.

We learn little more of the chapel structure until a reference to James I 'in his clossett above', and the 'rayles which inclosed the Font', in the records of the baptism of princess Mary in 1605. The organ was still operational, for we learn too that the 'Organest begine and continew playinge' during this service. Sometime between 1567 and 1570 John Guyllam had repaired the chapel organ, while Nicholas Ushaw put the clocks in order.

Let us now look at the events concerning the Chapel Royal which took place in this chapel building at Greenwich Palace, revealing its role not only in the sacraments of baptism, churching, marriage and the eucharist, but also in state diplomacy.

The treaty of Universal Peace between England and France was sealed in September 1518 by a proxy marriage of princess Mary (Henry VIII's daughter by Katherine of Aragon) to the French dauphin – intended to be consummated when the dauphin reached fourteen years of age. In mid-September the French ambassadors from the French royal court arrived and the treaty arrangements were sworn before the high altar at St Paul's Cathedral by both parties. On 5 October 1518, at 8 o'clock in the morning, the betrothed parties met in a hall at Greenwich Palace where Mary received a ring that contained a present of a diamond from Wolsey but which was slid symbolically over the second joint of her fourth finger by admiral Bonnivet on behalf of the dauphin. They then adjourned to the chapel at Greenwich Palace for a celebratory mass conducted by the Chapel Royal.

The role of the Chapel Royal in such state diplomacy was central to the Tudor constitution. Mere reception of ambassadors involved a 'diplomatic' mass, as had been the case, for instance, on 6 June 1515 when

[2] Bodleian Library MS Rawlinson D777, fol. 172v.
[3] Bodleian Library MS Foljambe.
[4] Bodleian Library MS Rawlinson D777, fol. 199.

Henry VIII received the Venetian ambassadors at Richmond Palace and invited them to mass conducted by the Chapel Royal.

It seems likely that the same routine may have been employed at the reception by queen Mary of the first-ever Russian ambassador to England in 1557. A similar but slightly different format was followed in re-affirmations of league treaties, such as that between Spain and England in August 1604, and between France and England in January 1611, both of which were effectively conducted by the Chapel Royal in the presence of the king and the ambassadors concerned.[5]

Regarding the more usual sacraments, 'the Chapell at Greenewytche' provided the venue for the marriage of Sir William Drewery to Mrs Elizabeth Stafford in 1579, for which the fee was 'one buck and xls'.[6]

An appointment was made on 25 January 1594/5 which is remarkable for the procedure used. There was at this time during Elizabeth I's reign an interregnum of deans of the Chapel Royal – a matter to which we shall turn our attention later (see pp. 233-4). So the lord chamberlain commanded the sub-dean Leonard Davies 'at Greenwich' to swear Richard Hemmyngwaye 'extraordinary Groome of her Majesties Vestrie upon the recommendation of her Majesties chiefe apothecaries'. The appointment was commanded by the lord chamberlain to be entered 'in this booke of remembrance',[7] i.e. the Old Cheque Book.

On 19 May 1603 the Chapel Royal gathered to swear the oath to James I 'at a Chapter holden at Greenwich by the Sub-Dean and gentlemen of the Kinges Chappell ther assembled in the vestrie', and at the same time submitted themselves as was the custom 'to the check and punishment which the Dean or Sub-Dean shall thinke meete to impose upon him or them, or any of them, for suche as their absence, disobedience, or want of indeavoure'.[8] Forty-one members of the Chapel Royal set their hand to witness this agreement.

On 19 July 1618 we can glimpse this disciplinary procedure in action, for the chapter was called by the sub-dean, Mr Davies, by order of the dean, the bishop of Winton, to caution the serjeant of the vestry, Cuthbert Joyner, 'for sundrie contemptes made against the said Lord Deane and his commaundments (to whom he is sworn to obey)'.[9] The serjeant had evidently enjoyed something of a field day. He was cited 'for bringinge false messages to the Subdeane as from the Lord Deane', for 'great negligences used in the service', for his 'daily absence from his place of attendance', and 'for conveyinge certaine parcels of his Majtes goodes out of his storehouse at Greenwich, and imploying them to suche as he

---

[5] See Old Cheque Book, fols 69b and 70, for the details of these ceremonies.
[6] Ibid, fol. 16b.
[7] Ibid.
[8] Ibid., fol. 34.
[9] Ibid., fol. 35b.

pleased, without the leave or knowledge of the Lord Deane'. For committing all these offences he was 'checked the some of forty shillinges', for 'the like offence hathe never bin formerly committed by any Sergeaunt'!

Other uniquely domestic Chapel Royal matters included, on 3 June 1632, 'a Chapter holden at Grinwich by Stephen Boughton [sub-dean] and the Gentlemen of the Company there assembled togeather in the vestry beeing twenty in number', the purpose of which was to choose the 'Stuards of the Chappell Feast'. The spelling of 'Grinwich' matches exactly that used at the back of the Bodleian Register,[10] to which we had cause to refer at the beginning of this chapter. In all likelihood the same scribe was therefore responsible for entries at this time both in the Bodleian Register and the Old Cheque Book.

The only significant record of structural work on the chapel at Greenwich Palace during the early part of James I's reign relates to the construction in 1604-05 of cant windows in the great closet from which the king and queen could look into the chapel.

The next major new scheme for the chapel at Greenwich coincided, and purposely so, with preparations for prince Charles to marry the Spanish infanta. Construction of the Queen's Chapel at St James's was begun in 1623, the Spanish ambassador, Gondomar, laying the foundation stone, specifically to provide a building for Roman Catholic worship. But with such a potentially 'unpopular' development in the eyes of Protestants it seems to have been thought that a gesture ought to be made to forestall accusations of royal Catholic sympathy. Considerable work was therefore also carried out on the chapel at Greenwich, which was to remain solidly Protestant.

The carver Maximilian Colt was given the task of 'carving a greate new wyndowe in the Chappell with five columes uppon pedescales with pendantes under them with the kinges armes over heade borne by two boyes with victories on each side of them'. The five columns and five great pendants were turned in wood by John Hooker. It seems that the new window was not an exterior one but rather the partition between the chapel and the great closet at the west end adjoining the main range of the palace water frontage, thus replacing the cant windows installed in 1604-05. This is confirmed by the fact that the sergeant painter, John de Critz, specified in the 1622-23 refurbishment of the chapel the architectural mural painting to be effected upon the two sides and east end of the chapel, but there is no mention of the west end in this context. The painting of the window is specified elsewhere.

The walls of the chapel were specially plastered in preparation for the mural paintings: 'diverse times oylinge, prymeinge and stopping the two sides and east ende of the chappell and for paintinge and garnishing yt

---

[10] Bodleian Library MS Rawlinson D318.

with sondry workes of architecture and diverse compartementes and columnes, the capitalles and pedestralles beinge guilte with fyne golde and sundry boyes paynted in stone coular.'[11]

Specifications for the ceiling included

> washing the roof of the Chapel, picking out ground with fair blewe, mending the antique, painting xviij boyes in proper colurs in the ceiling, picking out the ground round about them, new laying with blewe and other colours the arms and for new gilding the garters to the arms and for new painting two boyes over the window of the King's closet in the proper colours holding the King's and Prince's arms richly gilt with fine gold and for new priming and gilding xxxi new pendantes in the roof.

The boys holding shields had gilt hair, selectively gilded drapery, and palms and garlands 'being silver and glassed with faire greens'. Although the new window was painted white, the carved decoration of the five columns was picked out in gold, similar to the 'fower great pannels wrot with Antique works' which would seem to have been situated between the five pedestals. As prince Charles's plans to marry the Spanish infanta fell through and he married Henrietta Maria instead, the work on the Protestant chapel at Greenwich continued along with that on the Roman Catholic Queen's Chapel at St James's.

We have some intriguing evidence of how the chapel at Greenwich progressed under Inigo Jones's surveyorship. The grand scheme was nearing completion in 1624-25, well before the 'completion' of the Queen's Chapel at St James's. The glimpses we get of Greenwich chapel strongly suggest that, despite its Protestant status, it was being used by Inigo Jones as a sort of 'pace setter' for the work at the Roman Catholic Queen's Chapel at St James's.

In 1624-25 John de Critz was finishing the decorative work at Greenwich chapel by painting and gilding forty-eight 'antiques', sixteen of them being 'new moulded', decorating forty-eight pilasters and painting 'Dieu et Mon Droit' in the cornice 'over the said Antiques and Pillausters'. Maximilian Colt made three moulds for ornaments and shields in the frieze. The forty-eight pilasters and 'antiques' would have had to fit into a relatively small chapel measuring 52 ft 10 in by 27 ft 8 in according to one drawing,[12] or 100 ft in length according to another plan,[13] which may perhaps have been accounted for by the great closet at the west end. Either way it was fairly small. The 'antiques' would have been statues, possibly classical caryatids. We know that a year later in 1625-26 John de Critz was responsible for gilding and painting the figure of a 'Prophett as bigg as the life at the upper end of the Chappell'. This

---

[11] PRO E351/3257 – task work John de Critz.

[12] *Drawings Collection: Jones and Webb* (RIBA, London, 1972) p. 24, no. 121.

[13] Royal Naval Museum Greenwich, Wren Society, vol. 6, pl. 10.

This German engraving is of the ratification of the proposed marriage treaty between prince Charles and the Spanish infanta at the Chapel Royal, Whitehall, on 20 July 1623. Part of the agreement required that a Chapel be built for the Roman Catholic worship of the infanta. Construction of the Queen's Chapel at St James's Palace was accordingly begun – in fact a month before the ratification pictured above – although nothing came of that proposed marriage. (Reproduced by courtesy of the British Library)

may give us a clue as to the nature of the other 'antiques', but this must remain speculative.

Outside the chapel major shoring-up work was undertaken in 1634-35 with the construction of three huge buttresses of brick on stone supports and stone offsets built on foundations of rammed rag-stone. Two of these buttresses faced onto the Thames. Supported by these massive buttresses the chapel outlasted the rest of the palace buildings at Greenwich and is still shown on a site plan of 1695. Sadly it survived only a few years longer, for as the authors of the *History of the King's Works* observed, it was 'the first example in England of a classical interior conceived partly in terms of painted relief and partly in the round: an idea which goes back to Peruzzi's Farnesina Palace',[14] and in this pre-dates the interior conception of the Queen's Chapel at St James's Palace.

[14] Colvin and Summerson, *History of the King's Works*, volume entitled *The King's Houses 1485-1660*, p. 118 (Greenwich).

4. Favourite Palaces

Whitehall Palace

The Chapel Royal's premises in Whitehall Palace were situated adjoining the east side of the great hall. The only illustration of the inside of the chapel is a somewhat stylised depiction of the ratification of the fruitless Spanish marriage treaty in the chapel on 20 July 1623 (see opposite). In it can be seen the high altar, an altar in an alcove, the organ in a gallery and a triptych over the high altar. The usual traverse and canopy set up for such treaties in accordance with the Chapel Royal's role in state diplomacy can be seen in the centre forefront of the picture, with the chief protagonists in situ. The treaty paved the way for the ultimately abortive mission of Charles to Spain to woo and marry the Spanish infanta. Somewhere in the document being signed on the table in front of the altar is the proviso that the infanta shall have a place of Roman Catholic worship to herself. This led directly to the construction of the Queen's Chapel at St James's.

The Stukeley plan of the Whitehall chapel (1718) and other plans of 1670, before the fire of 1698, are not entirely consistent. Stukeley's plan shows the dimensions of the chapel as 28 ft by 40 ft. The 1670 plans, however, show it as 75 ft long. They also show two vestries. The chapel itself lay on a north/south orientation. Presumably the altar was at the north end (a door is shown at the south), as at the chapel in colour court at St James's Palace. The two vestries were positioned either side of the chapel at the north end. The west 'outer' vestry was connected to the great hall. There was also the king's closet in a gallery and a series of rooms beyond the south end which connected to the great hall and made possible passage to the riverside vestry on the east side, which itself could also be entered from the high altar end of the chapel.

A document in the Public Record Office[15] tells us of 'Coullering and guilding with fine gold the Lead of five Cazements on both sides in the windowe in the King's Clozett that looketh into the Chappell'. Stowe adds the further information:

> That on the Left hand Our Closset shall sit the Ladyes of the Bedchamber to Our Dearest Consort the Queene in the First Seat as it is now divided. That Our Servants that are to attend upon Us to Chappell shall sitt on the Left Hand Our Closet behinde the Ladyes of the Bedchamber ... That on the Right Hand our Clossett shall sitt the Lady of the Sweet Coffer, Ladyes of the Privy Chamber, and Mayds of Honour on the First Forme, and Mother; the Dressers on the Second Forme; Mayds of Honour and Dressers to our dearest Sister the Dutchess of Yorke on the Third Forme.[16]

[15] PRO E351/3268, 1634-35.
[16] British Library MS Stowe 562.

101

In 1660 Samuel Pepys, attending a service there on 14 October, observed 'how the Duke of York and Mrs Palmer did talk to one another very wantonly through the hangings that parts the King's Closet and the closset where the ladies sit'. The Spanish ambassador was invited to watch the admission of new members of the Order of the Garter in 1615 and 'had his place for sight of divine Service and Offering in the King's Closet'.[17]

According to the Stukeley plan, the chapel had four bays with triple-light mullioned windows, which probably had traceried heads containing diamond panes of stained glass. At each end was a four-light window. At the altar (i.e. north) end, which would still have been called 'east' (i.e. liturgical east) according to church tradition, there was evidently a fine stained-glass window. We know this from the receipts of one John Rutland who, following the 1643/4 parliamentary ruling requiring the 'demolishing of all superstitious Pictures and monuments in Whitehall', was paid £7 'for 241 feet of new white glass set up in the East window of the King's Chapel at Whitehall'. There were also receipts for 'taking down the cross at Whitehall and for colouring the boards from which the carpenter had planed off the pictures', for 'cutting down the stem of the cross over the Chapel at Whitehall', for 'work done in the Chapel at Whitehall about defacing pictures and plastering the walls' and 'for taking down the organ at Whitehall'. This organ was in fact acquired by Magdalen College, Oxford but proved too small for their requirements and was bought by Sir Thomas Cave in 1649 or 1650. It was installed in the church of St Nicholas, Stanford-on-Avon, Northamptonshire, where it can still be seen.

In 1646 the altar plate was melted down to provide domestic utensils for Charles I's use in 'confinement' at Holdenby, with the notable exception of the fine silver-gilt chalice and paten presented to the Chapel Royal for use at the Tower of London in 1629, and another chalice and paten presented respectively in 1637 and 1638, also for use there. These were engraved with the royal monogram CR, and are still in use today. The chalices are older than their dates of presentation, one bearing the date mark for 1559 and the other that for 1617. The 1502 alms dish also survived, but the rest of the pre-Restoration Chapel Royal plate did not escape the great melting-down.

At Whitehall chapel the roof was of good pitch and covered with lead. It seems to have been divided into panels by moulded ribs with carved bosses at the intersections. The exterior of the chapel was faced in stone contemporary with the neighbouring great hall. The parapet was originally decorated with carved figures on high pedestals, as can be seen in Morden and Lea's view of Whitehall in 1682.

The Whitehall chapel was at the centre of the Miles Sindercombe plot

---

[17] *Finetti Philoxenis*, p. 25.

to assassinate Oliver Cromwell in 1656. Sindercombe had tried, and failed, to assassinate Cromwell in Hammersmith earlier that year. He then hatched a plot to set fire to the chapel at a time when he knew Cromwell was lodging in the neighbouring great hall. We know from a tract entitled 'The Triall of Miles Sindercombe', published in 1658, that the conspirators

> cut a hole in one of the doors of the Chappel, and so unbolting it, they … went in and placed the materials for firing, which were discovered about nine a Clock that night, for in one of the Seats was found upon the Floor a Basket filled with a strange composition of combustible stuff, and two lighted matches, aptly placed, which matches had been rub'd over with gunpowder, on purpose to keep them surely burning, and by length of time, it was conceived they would have given fire to the Basket about one a Clock in the morning.

We learn from Samuel Pepys that a new organ was installed at the Restoration, for he writes in June 1660: 'The Seventeenth, his majesty's chapell att whitehall was fitted with organs and all other things fitt for his majesty, which was the first day that his majesty was att his devocetion theire.'[18] In July he writes: 'To Whitehall Chapel … Here I heard very good music, the first time that ever I remember to have heard the organs and singing-men in surplices in my life.'

Christopher Wren was commissioned on 20 August 1663 to 'erect a large organ loft … in the place where formerly the great Double-Organ stood'.[19] According to the *Domestic State Papers* of 1676/7, Bernard Smith was ordered by the king to make 'half a note lower the organ in the Chapel' for which he was paid £100 by the lord treasurer on the petition of John Hingeston, 'keeper of his Majesty's organs and harpsichords'.

James II largely abandoned the chapel in favour of building a new but Roman Catholic chapel at Whitehall. The great court artist, Benedetto Gennari the Younger, who had painted so many masterpieces for the Queen's Chapel at St James's, one of which is still to be seen displayed at the Birmingham Art Gallery, was also paid £590 for providing pictures for the new Roman Catholic chapel at Whitehall, one of which depicted the Nativity and was placed over the high altar, its frame being carved by Grinling Gibbons.

The only member of the royal family to continue attending the Chapel Royal at Whitehall in James II's reign was the Protestant princess Anne. An order was issued announcing that:

> It is his Majesty's pleasure that Her Royal Highness Princess Anne of Denmark Doe sit in His Majesty's Closett at His Chappell Royall at

[18] British Library Add. MS 10116, fol. 103.
[19] LC 5/137, p. 292

103

This watercolour drawing of the ruins of the Chapel Royal and the Great Hall at Whitehall after the great fire of 1698 was in the Wren Collection in the library of All Souls' College, Oxford, but cannot now be traced. The point of view appears to be the middle of queen Mary's terrace. (Photography kindly undertaken by Royal Collection photographer, Stephen Chapman)

> Whitehall, upon one side of ye Kings Chaire, which must remaine in its place not turned: And that Noe man of what degree or quality soever, presume to come into ye clossett when Her Royal Highness is there, except ye Clerke of ye Clossett, or his Deputy to officiate there, And the Lord Chamberlayne and Mr. Vice Chamberlayne of His Majesty's Household to stand behind ye Kings chaire.[20]

At Anne's request the chapel was repaired and decorated.

It is unclear to what extent the chapel was affected by the great fire at Whitehall in 1698. There was in the library at All Souls College, Oxford, an undated (*c.* 1698) water-colour drawing showing the ruins of the Chapel Royal and the great hall drawn from queen Mary's terrace. Loftie even argued that the chapel was not burnt but simply fell into ruin![21] Be that as it may, there exists a letter from Sir John Stanley to Sir Christopher Wren dated 28 November 1701 stating that 'My Lord Chamberlaine has

[20] LC 5/147, p. 224.
[21] William John Loftie, *Whitehall* (Seeley, 1895).

directed me to acquaint you that he has given leave to Sir William Forrester to sett up butts for shooting with Bowes and Arrowes in the place where the old Chappell stood in Whitehall and to open a Door into it through the old Vestry'.

A year later, in 1702, queen Anne moved the choral establishment from its temporary quarters in the Banqueting House to St James's Palace, where it has remained to this day.

Hampton Court

On 11 January 1514 the Knights Hospitallers of St John leased their 'Camera' of Hampton, which they had occupied since 1236, to Thomas Wolsey with permission to alter or rebuild the 'howses, walles, mmotes, diches, workis'. There was already a chapel on the site, as we learn from the 1514 inventory drawn up at the time of the lease to Wolsey. This reads:

> First, a chalesse of silver, a pix of copur for the sacrament, ij alter clothes, a corporaxe, ij candlestikes of laton, a masse-book, a porteux, a pewterbotil for wine, a crewet of pewter, a crosse of tynne, a paxbrede of tree, an alter clothe of whyte and blue lyke unto armyn, an ymage of saint John, an ymage of saint Nicholas, an ymage of the crosse paynted on a borde, ij alte clothes, ij pewes with a chest of wynscott, an holy waterstok of laton with a stryngel of laton, ij bells in the towre, one of them broken.

Accounts of Wolsey's building works for the year 1515 have survived, from which it is not at all certain that he decided to start afresh and build a new chapel straight away on the site of this old one. Mention is made in an entry dated 26 March 1515 of 'a key to the Chappell Dore', on 8 October 1515 of 'one gret hoke for the stone dore into the Chappell', and of payment to the smith, Garet Herryson, for 'standards and staybarres for the Chappell Dore'. It seems likely therefore that the existing chapel of the Knights of St John was used for some time. It is clear, however, that Wolsey did re-build the chapel sometime before 1525.

The cloister was also constructed under Wolsey's tenure, and all was at an advanced stage of construction by 1525 when Wolsey deemed it expedient to offer the 'palace' to the king, although he remained there on sufferance until 1529. The poet Skelton wrote at this time:

> Why come ye not to Court?
> To whyche Court?
> To the Kynges Court,
> or to Hampton Court?
> Nay to the Kynges Court
> Should have the excellence
> But Hampton Court
> Hath the preemynence.

Henry VIII answered this provocative rhetoric by inducing Wolsey to surrender Hampton Court to him, and by 1529 the king exercised full control over the building works as Wolsey fell from favour. Works were carried out at Wolsey's expense until 1527. The pay-books of 1529-38 contain no references at all to the construction of walls or roof, as opposed to ceiling, of the chapel, so we can presume that it was a complete structure before Wolsey's fall from grace. There is, however, structural evidence in the shape of straight joints in the brick cloister opposite, beyond the west end of the chapel, to suggest that a full nave was in Wolsey's mind. There is also evidence that the cloister was quadrangular.

Henry VIII evidently took steps to embellish the chapel from 1535 onwards. At Sonning in Berkshire a team of carpenters worked under the master-carver Edmund More of Kingston to build a magnificent timber vaulted ceiling with pendants hanging from fan-vaulted segments. It was built in parts to be assembled later on site. Sonning Manor was the property of the bishopric of Salisbury from 1524, but on cardinal Campeggio's deprivation it came into the king's hands. It was surrounded by mature timber and bordered the Thames – thus making it a very efficient workshop with a means of transport. Campeggio had allowed Wolsey to fell trees there in 1528-29 to build his college at Oxford. As Wolsey spent a large sum of money in Sonning on the 'newe making and carving of the vaute of the church Rouff of the said Colleage' at Oxford, and as this church was never finished, it appears that the timber intended for it was diverted or re-used in 1535 for the Hampton Court chapel project. Part of the vault was committed to barge and floated down the Thames in August 1535, followed by other sections in September and December. Once there the carpenters set it all in position under the roof, and the painters 'John Hethe and Harry Blankston of London' painted and gilded it.

By now the master-carver at Sonning was one Henry Corant. He replaced More who had become ill and died in September 1536. It was Corant who now set about 'cutting, carving, joining, framing, setting up and finishing' one side of the stalls in the chapel. The other side was the work of one Richard Ridge. For their work each was paid £112 – a sum agreed by the masters Moulton, Clement and Dickinson. The chapel was completed by the insertion of glass in the double east window in 1536 – now obscured by the Wren reredos behind the altar but 'discovered' in 1980. This window replaced an earlier one which had incurred Henry's displeasure because it reminded him of Anne Boleyn (the original window bore a sixteen-foot-high image of St Anne and St Thomas). In fact as early as 1531 the master glazier, Galyon Hone, had been ordered by the king to re-glaze the chapel, probably because the 'original' windows displayed the arms of Thomas Wolsey together with his motto 'Dominus mihi adjutor', and Henry wished to have no reminder of him either. The new windows bore the arms of the king together with the 'Tudor' emblems of portcullis and rose. The organ loft was constructed in 1536, the organ itself being shipped upstream from Bridewell in May 1538 and installed by the maker John Lytton and his men. The floor was decorated with 3,000 paving tiles purchased from Thomas Nortrage of Chertsey in July 1536. Parts of this chequer-board design have survived under the staircase despite the renewing of the floor in 1711.

Finally, either side of the west doorway two stone panels bear the arms of Jane Seymour, but present something of a puzzle. The only reference to them in the building accounts in the period 1529-38 concerns the commissioning of William Reynolds to carve two crowns in freestone to set above the arms. But the supporters to the arms are neither the Beaufort greyhound nor the dragon of Cadwallader – in other words neither of the king's or queen's beasts. Rather, the supporters are cherubs – a device repeated below Wolsey's arms, still extant on the great clock. We can presume, then, that Wolsey's arms would have been changed in the first instance to those of Anne Boleyn, and then to those of Jane Seymour!

The 'holyday closets' in the gallery were supported by 'four grete postes' which were painted with 'blisse [i.e. pale blue], and fyne coloures'. The closets themselves were 'painted and gilded with fine gold', while the furniture comprised kneeling desks, and a 'Crusyfyx with Mary and John', and communion tables which were placed on the rush matting that covered the floors.

This was the building in which the Chapel Royal found itself from time to time, and we have a vivid account of its presence there at the christening of prince Edward (later Edward VI) in October 1537. The procession marshalled in the prince's lodgings on the north side of Hampton Court, near Tennis Court Lane. First in the procession were eighty gentlemen, squires and knights, in twos, bearing unlit wax candles. Then came the children of the Chapel Royal, followed by the gentlemen and ministers of the chapel, with the dean and chaplains in surplices and copes, the king's council, bishops and lords, the comptroller and treasurer of the household, ambassadors, the chamberlains to the king and queen, the lord high chamberlain, lord privy seal, lord chancellor, duke of Norfolk, and the archbishop of Canterbury, and then the royal party itself.

Authorities differ as to whether Jane Seymour was present, for she was dangerously ill.[22] Some say that she was brought on a state pallet to the service, while others say that Henry stayed with her in her room, thereby missing the service. What is certain is that she died on 25 October. Prince

---

[22] For more information and an excellent account of the history of the chapel at Hampton Court, see *The Chapel Royal at Hampton Court* (Borough of Twickenham Local History Society, September 1969), for a copy of which I am indebted to Jesse Daniel, verger at the Chapel Royal, Hampton Court.

Edward was presented at the font by his sister, Lady Mary, while the four-year-old Elizabeth, carrying chrism, was carried in the arms of Jane Seymour's brother, the future protector. The Chapel Royal sang the Te Deum during the service. After the christening the candles and torches were lit and fanfares were sounded by heralds.

On 1 November 1541, All Saints day, Henry VIII and his queen, Katherine Howard, went to the chapel where the king knelt before the altar in his holyday closet, raised his eyes to heaven and is recorded as having said aloud: 'I render thanks to Thee, O Lord, that after so many strange accidents that have befallen my marriages, Thou hast been pleased to give me a wife so entirely conformed to my inclinations as I now have.' But the very next day archbishop Cranmer approached the king at his private devotions in the holyday closet, slipping him a piece of paper with details of the queen's alleged former dalliance with Francis Dereham when living at the house of her grandmother, the duchess of Norfolk. Strickland in *Queens of England* mentions the tradition that Katherine, confined to her room, attempted to see the king when he was at mass in his holyday closet. She broke out of her room but was finally restrained and carried back, her screams clearly heard by all those in the chapel. Two years later Henry married Katherine Parr on 12 July 1543 'in an upper oratory called the Quynes Pryvey Closet' (i.e. holyday closet). The service was conducted by the bishop of Winchester, Stephen Gardiner.

Shortly before his accession to the throne prince Edward, who lived at Chapel Court, kept Christmas at Hampton Court. He made offerings at masses on the feasts of St Stephen, St John and Childermass (Holy Innocents). At the latter mass the prince gave the children of the Chapel Royal forty shillings for singing the 'Gloria in excelsis' on Christmas day.

In 1551 Edward VI received the order of St Michael from the king of France and invited the French ambassador to Hampton Court chapel for Michaelmas day. The royal arms and the emblem for the order of St Michael were displayed together while the ambassador attended communion 'where he saw the King reverently with us of his Council communicate the Sacrament, wherein, we perceive, he seeth and understandeth the great difference between our reverence in our religion and the slanders thereof usually spread by evil men'.

Four years later in 1555 queen Mary and Philip of Spain kept Easter at Hampton Court, and on St George's day (23 April) 'a grand High Mass in the Chapel Royal' was held when Philip, as sovereign of the Order of the Garter, processed around the cloisters and the courts, 'clerks and priests all in copes of cloth of gold and tissue' singing 'Salve festa dies' with the queen looking down on them from her bedchamber window. In the same year Elizabeth was brought as a prisoner to Hampton Court but given liberty after persuading Mary of her loyalty. It was on this occasion that Elizabeth was recorded as saying in reply to Mary, who was questioning her about her belief in transsubstantiation:

Christ was the Word that spake it.
He took the bread and brake it;
And what His words did make it,
That I believe and take it.

It was at this time, too, that we learn of the insertion of the four great turned pillars supporting two carved timbers and connected to twenty-four balusters, whose purpose seems to have been to form a screen for the royal pew. Also in 1555, on the feast of Corpus Christi, the members of the Chapel Royal witnessed an extraordinary exhibition of anti-Spanish feeling. A large number of Spanish noblemen and others were forming up to process into the chapel when they were set upon by a gathering of Englishmen who, for once, outnumbered them. The ensuing fracas was described by the ambassador as a 'vesper-service like that of Sicily', referring to the Sicilian Vespers massacre of 1282; he added that only 'with great difficulty was their wrath mitigated by some of the rioters less daring and indiscreet than the rest'. King Philip tried to calm feelings by ordering that the first Spaniard who dared to use a weapon would have his hand cut off!

An account of the splendour of the chapel interior, written in 1584 by the Pomeranian traveller Leopold Von Wedel, paints a detailed picture of it in Elizabeth I's reign: 'As it was Sunday, we went to the Church or Chapel in the Palace. This Chapel is richly decorated, and has a fine silver and gilt Organ, with many silver pipes, large and small ... Both sides of the gallery along which the Queen walked to the Chapel were lined by the guard bearing arms.' The queen's bodyguard of the yeomen of the guard were there as well as the Chapel Royal, for Von Wedel observed that 'before the Queen marched her Bodyguard, several score of them all chosen men, strong and tall. They bore gilt halberts, red coats faced with black velvet; in front and on the back they bore the Queen's arms silver gilt.' On this occasion 'as the day was almost ended there was no sermon, only singing and prayers'.

Paul Hentzner, visiting Hampton Court in 1598, remarked that 'the Chapel was most splendid, in which the Queen's closet is quite transparent, having its windows of crystal'.

The Hampton Court conference, by which James I intended to isolate the Puritan position, was convened in January 1604. It was held in the privy chamber, though members would have attended services in the chapel. One outcome of the conference was the emergence of the Authorised Version of the Bible.

Works reports of 1619-21 mention major repairs to the chapel roof; the west end was uncovered and protected from the elements by canvas while new joists were inserted.

In 1644 the Puritan Sir Richard Harley removed the organ and stained glass from the chapel, but the windows were re-glazed and the chapel continued to be used for Independent worship. Although Hampton Court was offered to him by parliament as a reward for winning the battle of Worcester in 1651, Cromwell at that time refused the offer. However, upon becoming lord protector in 1653, he was offered it again by parliament and this time accepted. Services of an Independent nature continued to be conducted there, as we gather from a manuscript of the duke of Sutherland giving an account of a sermon preached in the chapel there before him in August 1655 by the vicar of Hampton – the 'intruder' James Thompson, who took as the text of his sermon Proverbs 29:2: 'When the righteous are in authority, the people rejoice; but when the wicked beareth rule, the people mourn.' The original manuscript of this sermon has been presented to the Chapel Royal at Hampton Court and is among its records there.

Oliver Cromwell's daughter Mary was married to Viscount Falconbridge with full Anglican rites in the chapel at Hampton Court on 17 November 1657. Cromwell himself loved organ music, and accordingly had two organs installed in the great hall. One of these came from Magdalen College, Oxford. As we have seen, the organ which was removed from Whitehall chapel and installed in Magdalen College in 1649/50 was subsequently bought by Sir Thomas Cave and installed at the church of St Nicholas in Stanford-on-Avon in 1650, so it would seem that the organ Cromwell had installed in Hampton Court great hall was none other than the successor to the Whitehall Chapel Royal organ at Magdalen College. Even more ironic was the fact that Cromwell re-appointed the Chapel Royal organist, John Hingeston, to play the organs now installed in the great hall.

Prevented from being sold again by the action of the commander-in-chief of the Irish army, Ludlow, Hampton Court was offered to general Monk in 1660. He declined it but accepted office as 'steward of the manor'.

Samuel Pepys followed Charles II to chapel there and heard a good sermon in 1665. William III intended Christopher Wren to demolish the chapel to make way for a new west wing of the palace, but died before it could be started. Prince William was christened in the chapel in 1689, but later died at Windsor aged eleven. Cartwright's *Hampton Court* states that when Anne ascended the throne 'she restored the Chapel after the taste of the day, adorning it with fine oak panellings and carvings by Grinling Gibbons, and a royal pew with a painted ceiling'.

In 1846 the Hon. Gerald Wellesley, chaplain at Hampton Court, wrote to the Board of Works enclosing a letter from his deputy he Rev. H.J. Lloyd objecting to 'the very inefficient manner in which the singing and Choral portions of Divine Service are performed in the Chapel Royal at Hampton Court' and adding that this was because of the 'occasional absence of persons who voluntarily act as choristers and the incapability of the Congregation to unite in Psalms without having a Conductor'. Eventually, after a protracted wrangle, the choir at Hampton Court became permanently established in 1868. The Chapel Royal, with the headquarters of its choral establishment still at St James's Palace, has recently revived its old link with the chapel at Hampton Court by combining with the permanent 'Chapel Royal' choir stationed there once a year to sing evensong. The faithful followers of the Chapel Royal are today always assured of a warm welcome by the chaplain, verger and choir of Hampton Court – a far cry from the duty of the verger appointed in 1844, whose specific orders were to keep the public out of the chapel! It was not until 1886 that visitors to Hampton Court were allowed to participate in the services held in the chapel.

Lastly, mention should be made of the bell that for over 500 years has been a familiar sound to the Chapel Royal at Hampton Court. Forged in 1480 by Thomas Harris, it bears the inscription 'stella Maria maris succurre piissima nobis' (holy Mary star of the sea come to our aid). It is evidently one of the two bells belonging to the Knights Hospitallers from whom Wolsey took the lease in 1514. Such a maritime inscription points to and reflects their role in protecting the seaways to the holy land.

5

The Chapel Royal Theatre

There is another building at Greenwich to which we should turn our attention, for it was to host two people who were to have an immense influence upon the history of the Chapel Royal. This little building can be seen in Wyngaerde's view of Greenwich Palace from the river Thames. It is the little 'fort' with a flagpole situated on the hill behind the palace. It was here that Henry VIII kept at least two of his mistresses – in all probability Bessie Blount before her marriage, and Mary Boleyn, sister to Anne.

As we have seen, Henry's son by Bessie Blount was to become the duke of Richmond and be accorded the status of prince and heir to the throne, thereby prompting the construction of St James's Palace and its chapel for his residence. But Henry also had another son, by Mary Boleyn.

Mary Boleyn had accompanied queen Katherine to the Field of Cloth of Gold in 1520, having entered the English court in the summer of that year. She succeeded Bessie Blount as Henry's mistress and, to oblige Henry, was married to a minor courtier, William Carey. Mary reached the height of her relationship with the king in 1522, symbolised in 1523 by the addition of the name *Mary Boleyn* to the list of royal ships to join the *Katherine Pleasance*. Mary bore the king a son and called him Henry after his father. Henry Carey was kept very much in the background and was brought up at the monastery of Syon. Mary Carey's husband died in 1528. Her father Thomas Boleyn was reluctant to help Mary in her destitute state, so her sister Anne re-introduced her to court briefly in the summer of 1534. But Mary was soon discovered to be pregnant, much to Anne's and the king's fury, and she was dismissed from court at once.

Henry Carey, however, as Lord Hunsdon became in due time lord chamberlain to queen Elizabeth, his first cousin. Lord Hunsdon was the driving force behind the formation of the 'Lord Chamberlain's Men' – the theatre company which was to challenge the supremacy of the children of the Chapel Royal who acted at Blackfriars and which later moved to the Globe theatre with Shakespeare, Burbage and others. We shall hear more of the play-acting later, but for now the Chapel Royal's intricate connection with Shakespeare takes another turn.

Henry Carey, Lord Hunsdon, acquired a mistress in 1588, Armada year, when he was transferred away from the Scottish border where he had been lord warden of the East Marches, to come south and command the queen's bodyguard at this dangerous time. His mistress was an eighteen-year-old Italian girl, Emilia Bassani. Nine years later, on 17 May 1597, she came to consult a medical practitioner and astrologer, Simon Forman, concerning a suit her husband, William Lanier, had in hand before he had, in Forman's words, 'gone to sea with the Earl of Essex in hope to be knighted – though there was little cause why he should'. Emilia was now twenty-seven. Simon Forman noted that 'she hath had hard fortune in her youth. Her father died when she was young: the wealth of her father failed before he died and he began to be miserable in his estate. She was paramour to my old Lord Hunsdon that was Lord Chamberlain and was maintained in great pride. Being with child she was for colour married to a minstrel.'[1] On 3 June 1597 Emilia Lanier again visited Simon Forman, from whom we learn that 'she was brought up in the county of Kent, and hath been married four years'. So we know that Emilia and William had married in 1593, and that William had been a 'minstrel'. Emilia had had a son by the lord chamberlain, for we learn from Forman that 'she hath a son, Henry', named after the true father Henry Carey. Emilia's husband William still had not returned from Essex's voyage by 2 September 1597 when we learn from Forman, who had meanwhile formed a sexual relationship with Emilia, that 'she hath been favoured much of her Majesty and of many noblemen, hath had great gifts and been made much of – a nobleman that is dead hath loved her well and kept her' but that 'her husband hath dealt hardly with her, hath spent and consumed her goods'. We know that 'she hath £40 a year and was wealthy to him that married her'.[2] Forman was still seeing Emilia as late as 1600. But let us look more closely at her life with her husband William Lanier.

Emilia's father was the Italian musician Baptist Bassani. The Bassani family had been recruited to Henry VIII's court from Venice. Baptist was accorded the privilege of being issued with a livery to wear when playing at Edward VI's coronation, providing musical accompaniment along with his colleagues from the Chapel Royal. He is not described in the category of 'the king majesty's musicians' on this occasion but seems to have been regarded as a member, along with others, of the Chapel Royal complement. Also in 1547/8 he is found again under the title of 'Musytyans', along with four other Bassanis, at the burial service of Henry VIII.[3] He is issued with a further livery in 1555 near the start of queen Mary's reign, along with other members of the Bassani family (Anthonie, Jasper, John and Augustine), again under the heading

---

[1] A.L. Rowse, *Shakespeare the Man* (Macmillan, London, 1973), pp. 106-7.
[2] Ibid.
[3] LC vol. 551.

'musicians'.[4] Warrants for liveries for Baptist and other Bassanis are again found for 1558 for June[5] and Michaelmas, and for the coronation of queen Elizabeth. For this coronation Ludovike Bassani joined the other Bassanis under the heading 'musicians'.[6] Baptist appears again in a warrant for livery in July 1559,[7] Michaelmas 1560,[8] 1561, 1562, 1563 and 1564. This last date, 1564, is the last mention of Baptist in the lord chamberlain's archives. We do know that Baptist Bassani and Margaret Johnson lived as man and wife and that Emilia was their daughter.[9] Baptist died and was buried on 11 May 1576 in the parish of St Botolph, Bishopsgate when Emilia was just six years old. Emilia's mother died on 7 July 1587, leaving her to fend for herself at the age of seventeen. As we have seen, she became the lord chamberlain's mistress. (He had a large family and a natural son, Valentine Carey, who was to become bishop of Exeter.)

Lord Hunsdon had in fact formed his own company of players as early as 1564, the year of William Shakespeare's birth. Among them was James Burbage, builder of the theatre at Shoreditch, whose son Richard was to become the star of the 'Lord Chamberlain's Company' founded by Lord Hunsdon in 1594, and to strike up a friendship with William Shakespeare, who also joined the company. Lord Hunsdon was appointed lord chamberlain in 1585 and was thus a very desirable 'catch' for Emilia on their meeting in 1588. Hunsdon, when not at his manor in Sevenoaks, lived at Somerset House and leased property at Blackfriars – later converted into a theatre and used by Burbage and Shakespeare with Henry Wriothesley, the earl of Southampton, giving Shakespeare the money needed to buy his share. More of this later.

William Shakespeare had first made the acquaintance of the man who was to become his patron, the young earl of Southampton, in the winter of 1591/2. Southampton had secretly joined the earl of Essex across the Channel in January or February 1591 and offered his services to Essex in Dieppe in March 1591. We know what happened next due largely to the research of A.L. Rowse. It appears that towards the end of 1592 Shakespeare also struck up an acquaintance with Emilia Bassani, the lord chamberlain having finished with her 'services'. She became Shakespeare's mistress after he had pleaded with the young earl of Southampton to 'open negotiations' by writing to her on his behalf.[10] However, Emilia later transferred her affections to the earl himself. It is not entirely surprising that she should regard him as a better 'catch':

[4] LC vol. 811, p. 260.
[5] LC vol. 811, p. 108, and vol. 1.
[6] LC vol. 3.
[7] LC vol. 811, p. 121.
[8] LC vol. 4.
[9] Rowse, *Shakespeare the Man*, p. 106.
[10] Ibid., p. 87.

Southampton was three years younger than she, while the actor-poet Shakespeare was six years her senior and had a wife and family.

These connections are revealed in Shakespeare's sonnets. The poet's relationship to his patron Southampton is described in sonnets 34-42, while sonnets 127 to the end deal with his affair with Emilia, beginning with his emotions of pity, advancing to his sexual fascination, and ending with her discarding him.

Sonnets 40, 41 and 42 show that Southampton had now taken Emilia as his mistress. Shakespeare was in an awkward spot. His career depended upon Southampton, for it was not until the formation of Hunsdon's theatre company in 1594 that his career was secured. So, in the meantime, he had to stand by while his patron took his mistress. Although later in the sequence, sonnets 127 to the end reveal the earlier relationship between Emilia and Shakespeare. Emilia was Shakespeare's Dark Lady. The sonnets tell us that she was very dark in complexion with raven-black eyes, black hair, eyebrows and eyelashes – features also ascribed to Rosaline in *Love's Labour's Lost* (1593). She was also accomplished on the virginals. On seeing her in 1597, Forman noticed that 'she hath a wart or mole in the pit of the throat or near it',[11] and mentioned that 'she was very brown in youth'.[12]

The rivalry for Emilia's favours seems to have quietened down somewhat on the formation of the 'Lord Chamberlain's Men' by Lord Hunsdon in 1594. The company formed an indoor theatre at Blackfriars in the buildings originally leased by Lord Hunsdon, and later moved across the Thames to the Globe theatre in 1598, dismantling their old Shoreditch theatre in order to use its timbers for the Globe and shipping them across the river.

The Chapel Royal was intimately bound up in these precarious developments in the theatre's early history. In the 1580s the children of the Chapel Royal were acting in the old frater at Blackfriars, where Lyly produced his plays for the earl of Oxford. In the 1590s Lord Hunsdon leased the premises. After his death in 1596 he was succeeded as lord chamberlain by his son, who continued to lease the theatre and also favoured play-acting. We know the name of at least one child of the Chapel Royal who was acting there in 1597 – Thomas Clifton (see p. 120 below). In 1600 the children of the Chapel Royal were still play-acting there and later, in 1608, the partners in the Globe – formerly the 'Lord Chamberlain's Men' but now the 'King's Men' – took over these premises as a winter playhouse – the Globe was open-air.

The children of the Chapel Royal were not strangers to theatrical performances. One hundred years earlier, in 1483, the *Liber Niger Domus Regis* clearly states that 'the King hathe a songe before hym in his hall or

---

[11] MS Ashmole 354.
[12] Quoted in Rowse, *Shakespeare the Man*, p. 106.

Elevation of the Blackfriars theatre as it was five years before its demolition in 1655. Today Playhouse Yard occupies part of the site. The theatre was built within the walls of the old Blackfriars monastery. Shakespeare and his colleagues bought back the lease from the Chapel Royal in 1608, and on 11 March 1612 Shakespeare bought the neighbouring gatehouse of the monastery adjoining what is now Ireland Yard. This pencil drawing is at the Guildhall Library, as also is the mortgage deed relating to Shakespeare's purchase of the monastery gatehouse. (Reproduced by courtesy of the Guildhall Library, City of London)

chambre uppon All-hallowen day at the latter graces, by some of these clerkes and children of chappel in remembrance of Christmasse thorowaute. But after the songe on All-hallowen day is done, the Steward and Treasaurer of household shall be warned where it liketh the King to kepe his Christmasse.' This would entail a 'removing' of the Chapel Royal to accompany the king to whichever palace he chose. By Elizabeth I's reign such traditions of singing at major religious festival times, in particular upon Shrovetide, had developed into courtly masques and plays of considerable complexity, for which major rehearsals were often necessary.

The Office Books of the masters and yeomen in Elizabeth I's reign were extensively researched by Peter Cunningham and extracts from them published in London for the Shakespeare Society in 1842. They give us vivid glimpses of the boat-hire arrangements necessary to transport child actors to and from the queen's presence to perform their plays and masques. There were, of course, several companies with child actors, such as St Paul's, Windsor, Westminster School and Merchant Taylors, apart from the children of the Chapel Royal.

We know from Peter Cunningham's extracts from the period October 1573 until March 1574 that at least two player companies were at Hampton Court Palace at the same time for Shrove Monday and Tuesday. The extracts show that 'Philemon and Philecia' were played by the 'Earl of Lecesters men on Shrove Mundaye nighte' and 'Percius and Anthomiris' by 'Munkestrs Children on Shrovetewsdaye at Nighte'. Under the item 'Diett for Children Maskers before Shrovetide' we see that the companies of children had to cope with complicated parts. Witness in particular the passage reading 'for dietts and lodging of dyvers children at Saint Jones whiles they Learned theier pts and Jestures meete for the Mask in which ix of them did serve at Hampton Coorte. xxxiiis. iiiid.'

The ferryman's arrangements for these occasions have survived and make interesting reading. They revolve around a certain Mr Bruton of Paul's wharf, which was situated adjacent to the east wall of Baynard's Castle, thereby serving the area of Blackfriars and St Paul's. The passage reads: 'To Bruton of Powles Wharf for a Bardge and vi ores with ii tylt Whirreys that caryed the Masking geare and Children with theier tutors and an Italian woman ... to dresse their heads as also the Taylers, ppty makers and haberdashers. xxiiiis.' It would be fascinating to know who the 'tutors' were – could they have been associates of Burbage, Shakespeare, Jonson, Hunnis or Farrant?

Similar arrangements applied during Shrovetide at Kingston, presumably therefore at a date later than 1573. This we learn from other extracts telling of 'expenses at Kingston' for 'lodging, ffyer, and vittells for the Children and Women who wayted tattyer [sic] them with others who were appointed to stay till the Mask were showen and for their dynners

Engraving of Bruton's Wharf below St Paul's Cathedral before 1561, in the Conway Collection. (Reproduced by courtesy of the Courtauld Institute of Art)

the nexte daye being Shrovetewsdaye there xiiiis viiid.' Arrangements were made with 'the Barber for trymming the Children on Shrovetwisday xiid', and for 'Mother Sparo for the children's lodgings with ffyer and ffoode that nighte and in the Morning whiles they staied for botes xiis.' The bargee or ferryman, Mr Bruton, was again employed as we learn from an item entitled 'Bardge and Botehier from the Coorte'. This man enjoyed what seems to have been something in the nature of a royal warrant for his river services and can be regarded as one of the first

118

recorded royal bargemasters. The item continues: 'To Bruton for his Bardge and ii whirreyes to cary the children and stuff back to London and for his wayting daie and nighte to cary the children betwene the Coorte and Kington xxvs vid.' A further item entitled 'Expenses at the black ffryers on ash Wednesdaie' completes the 'removing' picture. It reads: 'To Thomas Totnall for ffyer and vittells for the children when they landed some of them being sick and colde and hungry vis vid.' It is possible that these 'children' were children of the Chapel Royal, for the last item to which we will refer on this subject of river transport of child players is 'To the Nine Children that served at the Coorte ixs'. There is, too, the shadowy figure of 'the Italian woman and her dawters for Lending the heaves etc. and for their service and attendaunce xxxiiis iiiid.' It is certainly possible that this lady was from one of the well known families of Italian musicians to the queen – perhaps the Bassanis?

The Chapel Royal's connection with Blackfriars began when Richard Farrant, deputy master of the children from 1569-81, and William Hunnis, master of the children from 1566-97, founded the theatre at Blackfriars in 1576. It was a candlelit indoor theatre sited within the precincts of the old monastery at Blackfriars – the remains of which are still to be seen at Blackfriars near St Andrew-by-the-Wardrobe. The latter church took its name from a house built by Sir John Beauchamp nearby, upon whose death it was bought from his executor by Edward IV as a storehouse for the great wardrobe of royal garments until the great fire of 1666 (after which it moved to Beauchamp Street in the Strand). The serjeant of the vestry was accustomed to go there in order to kit out the Chapel Royal choir of gentlemen and children – and almost certainly too for their playhouse. The Chapel Royal theatre within the old monastery was a kind of private theatre to entertain visitors from the court circles.

Among playwrights who wrote for the children of the Chapel Royal at this time were Middleton, Fletcher, Marston, Chapman, Lyly and Ben Jonson. We know the name of at least one of the children of the Chapel Royal who would have acted there in its early days in the 1580s – John Pitcher, whose career in the Chapel Royal extended from 1583 to 1589. He would thus have just missed the joint performance of the Chapel Royal and St Paul's boys at court in 1582, but he would have given long service at a momentous time in the development of the theatre. When he had to leave the Chapel Royal because his voice had broken, Elizabeth I wrote in a letter dated 18 March 1589 to the dean and chapter of Wells:

Whereas John Pitcher, sometime a chorister of your Church of Wells, was from thence brought hither to serve us in the room of a child of our Chapel, in which place he hath remained nigh this six years ... till now that his voice beginneth to change, he is become not so fit for our service. And herewith understanding that there is a singing man's room void in the said church, we have thought it meet to recommend him unto you, to be placed in the same with our express commandment that according to the order of your house, ye do admit and place him, the said John Pitcher, into the room of a singing man in the said Church.[13]

An incident involving the imprisonment of a boy, Thomas Clifton, gives us an insight into the life of the child actors at work in the Chapel Royal theatre. On 13 December 1600 he was on his way from his house in Great Bartholomew's to his grammar school at Christ Church. What happened next is described in vivid detail by his father in a petition of complaint addressed to the queen for 'the better furnisheing of your Chappell Royall with well singing children', and brought before Star Chamber on 5 December 1601.

It seems that Thomas was carried off to the Chapel Royal theatre in Blackfriars 'to exercyse the base trade of a mercynary enterlude player, to his utter losse of tyme, ruyne, and disparagment'. Thomas's father soon caught up with him at Blackfriars and discovered Thomas 'amongst a companie of lewde and dissolute mercenary players' and immediately protested. Nathaniel Giles, master of the children, and his associates Robinson and Evans replied that 'yf the Queene woulde not beare them furth in that accion, she should gett another to execute her commission for them' as 'they had aucthoritie sufficient soe to take any noble mans sonne in this land' and went on to say that 'were yt not for the benefitt they made by sayd play howse, who would, should serve the chappell with children for them'. Young Thomas was then handed over to Evans in front of his father under threat of a whipping. Thomas was given 'in moste scornfull, disdaynful and dispightfull manner, a scrolle of paper, conteyning parte of one of theire sayd playes or enterludes, and him, the sayd Thomas Clifton, comaunded to learne the same by harte'. His father Henry Clifton, esquire of Toftrees, Norfolk, had no option but to accept the circumstances at that time, but in the course of the year drew up the complaint to Star Chamber based not only upon his son's impressment but also of others who he claimed were impressed solely for the playhouse rather than to sing for the Chapel Royal. Henry Clifton accused 'one James Robinson, Henry Evans and others' of running a playhouse for their own profit at Blackfriars by taking boys 'noe way hable or fitt for singing, nor by anie the sayd confederates endevoured to be taught to singe' for the Chapel Royal. Other boys he claims were impressed for this purpose were: 'John Chappell, a gramer schole scholler of one Mr Spyke schole neere Cripplegate, London; John Motteram, a gramer scholler in the free schole at Westminster; Nathen Ffield, a scholler of a gramer schole in London, kepte by one Mr Monkaster; Alvery Trussel, an

---

[13] Quoted in *Calendar of the Manuscripts of the Dean and Chapter of Wells*, ed. W.P. Baildon (London, 1914), vol. 2, p. 314. Also *Royal Musical Association Research Chronicle* no. 5 (1965), p. 46.

apprentice to one Thomas Gyles; one Phillip Pykman and Thomas Grymes, apprentices to Richard and Georg Chambers, Salmon Pavey, apprentice to one Peerce.'[14] There was also a curious report that the dowager countess of Leicester had married 'one of the playing boyes of the chappell' in *c.* 1602.[15]

The children of the Chapel Royal were certainly in William Shakespeare's mind when he wrote *Hamlet* in 1600/1. The passage to which we shall refer was written in answer to Ben Jonson's *Cynthia's Revels*, which ridiculed the 'common stages' and 'common players'. Two of the actors in *Cynthia's Revels* and, come to that, Jonson's *Poetaster* as well, were Salalthiel Pavy and his fellow chorister in the Chapel Royal and future playwright, Nathan Field. Pavy died at the age of thirteen in 1602, either of consumption or of the plague, and Ben Jonson wrote a touching epitaph to him which reads thus:

Weepe with me all you that read
This little storie:
And know, for whom a teare you shed,
Death's self is sorry.
'Twas a child that so did thrive
In grace and feature,
As heaven and nature seem'd to strive
Which owned the creature.
Yeares he numbered scarce thirteene
When fates turn'd cruell,
Yet three fill'd Zodiakes had he beene
The stage's jewell;
And did act (what now we mone)
Old men so duely,
As, sooth, the Parcae thought him one,
He play'd so truely.
So, by error, to his fate
They all consented,
But viewing him since, (alas too late),
They have repented.
And have sought (to give new birth)
In bathes to steepe him,
But, being so much too good for earth,
Heaven vows to keepe him.

In *Hamlet* Shakespeare comments on the hostility between Jonson, who was writing at the time for the children of the Chapel Royal, and Marston and Dekker (whose answer in *Satiromastix* was perfomed by the 'Lord Chamberlain's Men' in 1601) with whom he had found cause to quarrel: 'Faith, there has been much to do on both sides ... There was for a while

[14] See C.W. Wallace, *The Evolution of the English Drama* (Berlin, 1912), p. 209.
[15] See Linda Austern, *Music in English Choirboy Drama 1597-1613* (extract deposited at Chapel Royal, n.d.), ch. 30.

no money bid for argument, unless the poet and the player went to cuffs in the question ... O, there has been much throwing about of brains.' Shakespeare goes on to refer to the children of the Chapel Royal – who still up-staged the adults of the 'Lord Chamberlain's Men' and other companies through their excellence: 'There is, sir, an eyrie of children, little eyases, that cry out on the top of the question and are most tyrannically clapped for it. These are now the fashion, and so berattle the common stages – so they call them – that many wearing rapiers are afraid of goose quills and dare scarce come hither.' Shakespeare cannot resist a swipe at the children who had so successfully dominated the theatre world for twenty-five years: 'What, are they children? Who maintains 'em?'

We know the answer to this: William Hunnis until 1597 and thereafter Nathaniel Giles, who succeeded him as master of the children of the Chapel Royal. Ultimately, of course, the answer was the sovereign, for the sovereign's consent was required for the children of the Chapel Royal to perform plays. Hunnis had pleaded in 1583 for an increase in the monies available to the master of the children, for

> although it may be objected that hir Majesties allowance is no whitt less then hir Majesties father of famous memorie therefore allowed, yet considering the pryces of thinges present to the tyme past, and what annuities the Mr. then hadd out of sundrie abbies within this realme, besydes sundrie giftes from the King and dyvers particular fees besides for the better maintenance of the sayd children and office, and besides also there hath been withdrawne from the sayd children synce hir Majesties comming to the crowne twelvepence by the daye which was allowed for theyr breakfast.

In 1585 Hunnis was duly awarded lands by the queen to augment his income. Until 1597 the children of the Chapel Royal were maintained by income from the mill and watercourse in the hamlet of Bradway at Norton in Derbyshire, from lands in Essex formerly belonging to the monastery of Manor, from lands at Sextonsfield near Barking at Great Ilford, from lands at Riple marsh and Bedfords marsh in the parish of Barking, a parcel called 'Little Paradise' in Waving Mead in the East Mersh [sic] of Dakenham, from Owens Croft in Wavering, from lands at Bury in Suffolk formerly belonging to the monastery of Barking and called 'Longbrake', from land at Teynter Croft in Wakering, from lands amounting to over forty-four acres at Stratford Langthorne in Harlow, including the tenement in Church Street Westham, from the income of all tenements in the tenure of the bailiff of the manor at Watford in Hertfordshire, from a parcel of land at Sawbridgeworth, and from twenty-seven acres of arable land and eight acres of meadow at Hampton in Middlesex in the honour of Hampton Court. All these and more were the sources of income granted by the queen to William Hunnis thereby

Unattributed portrait of Nathan (Nid) Field, who acted at the theatre in the old frater at Blackfriars as a child of the Chapel Royal. He was to become one of the 26 'Principall Actors' of Shakespeare's plays listed in the First Folio. (Reproduced by permission of the Governors of Dulwich Picture Gallery)

enabling him to maintain the theatre where the children acted at Blackfriars. Shakespeare was indeed treading on dangerous ground with his veiled question.

Shakespeare went on to ask: 'Will they pursue the quality no longer than they can sing? Will they not say afterwards – as it is most like, if their means are no better – their writers do them wrong to make them exclaim against their own succession?' But the children of the Chapel Royal continued to be very successful at Blackfriars in the private theatre, and Shakespeare gives them due credit: 'Do the boys carry it away?' – 'Ay, that they do ... Heracles and his load too' – this was a direct admission of the dominance of the Chapel Royal children over the 'Lord Chamberlain's Men', for the signboard of the new Globe theatre was a globe carried by Hercules. The 'Lord Chamberlain's Men' would have to do something to topple the supremacy of the children of the Chapel Royal.

On 24 March 1603 Elizabeth I died. Essex had been executed and

This illustration details the provisional arrangements for Elizabeth I's funeral and mentions 'The Sergeant of the Vestry, Children and Gentlemen of the Chapell in Copes 4 & 4'. (MS Vincent 151, vol II, reproduced by courtesy of the College of Arms)

Southampton imprisoned in the Tower of London – but with James I's accession to the throne Essex's colleagues were back in favour. Southampton was released from the Tower to be granted the positions of keeper of the Isle of Wight for life, keeper of the king's game in Hampshire, joint lieutenant of the county of Hampshire with the young Pembroke, the monopoly of sweet wines, and knight of the Garter. The 'Lord Chamberlain's Men' were to be rewarded too, with James heading them as patron, and they became the 'King's Men'. As such they were at

124

last acknowledged to be the premier company. The leaders of the 'King's Men' were sworn officers of the royal household. They were appointed grooms of the chamber in ordinary. In this capacity Shakespeare and his colleagues received livery of 4½ yards each of scarlet cloth to walk in the procession on the city's reception of James I. The next summer, 1604, they again attended in their royal household capacity the Spanish plenipotentiaries in London who ended the long hostilities with an affirmation of peace.

In 1608 the 'King's Men' finally 'reclaimed' the private indoor theatre at Blackfriars, which had been the stage for the children of the Chapel Royal, as a winter playhouse. The Burbages pointed out that their father had purchased the Blackfriars property 'at extreme rates and made it into a playhouse with great charge and trouble'. It had in fact been leased to one Thomas Evans who directed the children of the Chapel Royal there – 'the boys daily wearing out'. Some became 'King's Men'. The Burbages now bought back the lease as a group of seven including Evans, Shakespeare, Heming, Condell and William Sly, each paying a rent of £5 14s 4d per year. Shakespeare in fact bought a house there in 1613. The children of the Chapel Royal had had a triumphant era on stage, but this was soon to end.

A puritan pamphleteer was certainly forthright in his condemnation of the Chapel Royal children's activities in 'theatre', voicing his views in a work entitled *The Children of the Chapel Stript and Whipt*, published in 1596. The author wrote:

> Plays will never be suppressed, while her Majesty's unfledged minions flaunt it in silks and satins. They had as well be at their popish service, in the Devil's garments. Even in her Majesty's Chapel do these pretty, upstart youths profane the Lord's Day by the lascivious writhing of their tender limbs, and gorgeous decking of their apparel in feigning bawdy fables gathered from the idolatrous heathen poets ...[16]

We can see the Chapel Royal theatre in operation at Blackfriars in 1602 when the duke of Stettin-Pomerania attended a choirboy play preceded by a feast of music:

> The queen keeps a number of young boys, who are taught to sing and to play on all sorts of musical instruments – they are also expected to continue their school studies at the same time. These boys have special instructors in the various arts, and especially in music. As part of their education in courtly manners they are required to put on a play once a week and for this purpose the queen has provided them with a theatre and with a great deal of rich apparel. Those who wish to see one of the performances must pay as much as eight shillings of our Pomeranian money. Yet there are always a good

[16] Quoted in P. Le Hurray, *Music and the Reformation in England, 1549-1660* (CUP, Cambridge, 1978), p. 220.

many people present, including ladies of the highest repute, since the plots are always well developed and of a suitably elevated character. All the performances are by candlelight and the effect is indeed spectacular. For a whole hour before the play begins there is a concert of music for organs, lutes, pandoras, citterns, viols and recorders. When we were there a boy 'cum voce tremula' sang so charmingly to the accompaniment of a bass viol that with the possible exception of the nuns at Milan, we had heard nothing to equal him anywhere.[17]

Twenty-four years later the triumphant reign of the Chapel Royal theatre had come to an end – a victim of the Puritan movement. Thus a commission of impressment of boys for service with the Chapel Royal to Dr N. Giles, dated 26 August 1626, reads:

Provided always, and we straightly charge and command, that none of the said Choristers or Children of the Chappell, soe to be taken by force of this Commission, shall be used or imployed as Comedians, or Stage Players, or to exercise or acte any stage plaies, Interludes, Comedies, or Tragedies; for that it is not fitt or desent that such as should sing the praises of God Almighty should be trained or imployed in such lascivious and prophane exercises.[18]

[17] G. von Bulow, *The Diary of Philip Julius, Duke of Stettin-Pomerania*, translation for the Royal Historical Society, VI, 1892.
[18] *The King's Musick: a transcript of records relating to music and musicians, 1460-1700*, edited by H.C. De Lafontaine (Novello, London, 1909).

6

Francis Bacon and the Queen's Chapel

James I seems to have been of the opinion that the Palatinate could only be recovered if he could somehow arrange for his son Charles to become engaged to the Spanish infanta, and thereby feel entitled to ask for his wife's country back as part of the marriage settlement. The Spanish king seemed happy with the idea of the betrothal, for he saw a chance of placing a condition on prince Charles – that he become a Roman Catholic.

Charles and Buckingham left secretly for Spain without James I's knowledge, disguised with false beards. This is odd because James apparently wanted him to go there anyway. The explanation seems to point to an attempt at a sort of 'publicity stunt' to enable James to distance himself from the Protestant rage that would surely ensue if the marriage proposal succeeded.

Prince Charles was indeed received with cordiality upon his arrival in Spain, but his conversion to Catholicism was made a condition of the proposed marriage. There was a terrifying incident in which he nearly drowned in a rowing boat when the sea turned choppy, and the Spanish venture ended in bitterness.

In England the relief was immense. On his return Charles was greeted with bonfires and rejoicing – as much for the abandonment of the Spanish match as for the prince's own safety. In 1624 a book was published at Luneburg in Germany, with the text in Latin, entitled *Cryptomenytices et Cryptographiae*. Although nominally written by August II, duke of Braunschweig-Luneburg, it is evident that it was based on the work of an Englishman, probably Francis Bacon, glad to see the prince safely back home, having failed to marry the Spanish infanta. Jean Overton Fuller has identified the cryptographic dedication of the book to prince Charles.[1] We shall return to this later, for the role of Francis Bacon, together with that of William Shakespeare, in the activities of the children of the Chapel Royal and their master are not to be missed.

The 'birth' of the Queen's Chapel can be witnessed in a print depicting the signing of the Spanish marriage contract on 20 July 1623 in the Chapel Royal building at Whitehall Palace. The actual document

---

[1] See Jean Overton Fuller, *Sir Francis Bacon: a biography* (East-West Publications, London & The Hague, 1981), p. 323.

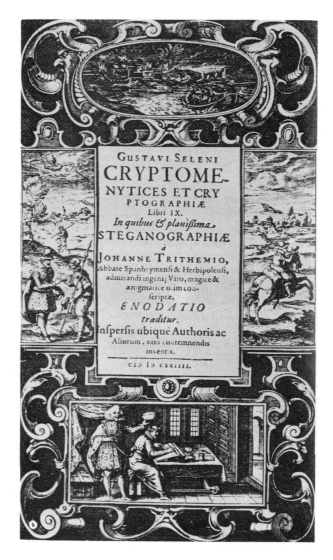

The oval entablature at the top of this title-page to *Cryptomenytices*, probably written by Francis Bacon and published in 1624 at Luneburg, shows prince Charles as a passenger in the rowing boat off the Spanish coast in which he nearly drowned while unsuccessfully courting the Spanish infanta. The entablature is 'signed' with 'Bacon lights', which can just be seen glowing in the distance by a depiction of the Globe theatre and the twin peaks of Mount Parnassus, to reveal the authorship of the book. The other cryptic pictures show, at the bottom, Bacon writing at his desk with Shakespeare attached like a dog on a lead standing behind him, holding a crown over his head to show to whom the glory is really due. The picture centre left shows Bacon giving a play to Shakespeare who goes off to the circular Globe theatre, shown in the background. On the right Shakespeare is riding off with a horn to publicise the plays. (Photography kindly undertaken by Royal Collection photographer, Stephen Chapman)

128

stipulating the necessity to provide a chapel structure in which the infanta, when married, could practise her Roman Catholic worship in England can be seen in this print, lying on the table in front of the altar.

Building works in connection with the Queen's Chapel had already begun. Prince Charles had left England in February 1623 and in March the question of which palace should be the future couple's royal residence was discussed, Inigo Jones favouring Somerset House over St James's Palace. In the end it was decided that both houses should be prepared and plans were submitted to the Spanish ambassador, Gondomar, in April 1623. He inspected the plans and demanded alterations, at the same time explaining the necessity for a Roman Catholic chapel in each. Inigo Jones was then ordered 'to have them don out of hand, and yet with great state and costlines'.[2] This would imply that there had been no provision in the plans for Roman Catholic chapels at either Somerset House or St James's Palace before Gondomar's demands of April 1623. Yet on 14 May secretary Calvert was in a position to send to Spain a copy of Inigo Jones's St James's plan.[3] Just two days later, on 16 May 1623, the Spanish ambassador laid the foundation stone of the Queen's Chapel in an inaugural ceremony:

> On May 16th, 1623, was the first foundation [stone laid] of the new Chapel at St James's for the Lady Mary of Spain, in the afternoon. The Spanish Ambassador made a cross on the first stone, laid it in mortar, made a prayer in French, that God would dispose of that foundation to His glory, and the good of His Church, and the universal good of all Christians, and gave £80 to the workmen; his son laid the second stone, and also gave them £80.[4]

Although these marriage plans did not come to fruition, the building of the Queen's Chapel continued. As it so happened, a year later in November 1624 the marriage contract with another Roman Catholic, Henrietta Maria, was signed. The same stipulation was made with regard to the necessity to provide a chapel for the Roman Catholic worship of the future queen consort. Charles came to the throne in March 1625 and married Henrietta Maria by proxy on 1 May 1625. Just a month later, on 5 June 1625, a visitor noted that 'the chapel ... is making very fyne against the Queen's cominge'.[5] The chapel was complete in nearly all respects by this time, for the declared accounts for 1622/3 mention the provision of candlesticks 5 feet 6 inches high 'for the clergymen' and eighteen 'pinnes to hang their cloakes and hates on'.[6] These items were provided by the turner, John Hooker. The urgency of the building

---

[2] Spanish Papers 14/144 no. 11, PRO; and Colvin and Summerson, *History of the King's Works*, vol. 4, 1485-1660, part 2, p. 248.
[3] Spanish Papers 14/144 no. 42.
[4] Thomas Birch, *The Court and Times of Charles I* (Colburn, London, 1848), vol. 2, p. 394.
[5] Historical Manuscripts Commission, Rutland, i, p. 473.
[6] E351/3258.

Exterior of the Queen's Chapel from the north west. (Reproduced by courtesy of the Royal Commission on Historic Monuments)

operations is revealed in the fact that the building accounts were held over for four years and written into those of 1626/7. That they were interpolated into the latter year's accounts as a kind of addendum is indicated by their position in the account roll. The total cost was £4,027 0s 4d.

Interior of the Queen's Chapel, looking west. In the west wall, with access via two panels, are the 'Gondomar' consecration crosses. (Reproduced by courtesy of the Royal Commission on Historic Monuments)

Inigo Jones's draft design for the chimneypiece in the royal closet or gallery of the Queen's Chapel, held at the RIBA, bears his own scribbled note: 'Chimneypeice in her Majesties Chappell Closett at St. Jameses', and includes its projected dimensions. This photograph of the extant chimney piece shows the later 'Braganzan' arms with crown added by Grinling Gibbons. (Reproduced by courtesy of the Royal Commission on Historic Monuments)

132

6. Francis Bacon and the Queen's Chapel

The original elliptical coffered ceiling and cornice are still to be seen and correspond perfectly with Inigo Jones's plan to gild twenty-eight coffers only over the sanctuary of the vaulted ceiling. The gilding was executed by Matthew Goodrich, who in 1626/7 works accounts was paid 'for painting and guilding xxviii squares in the roofs of the Chappell being carved with eggs and darts and carved work'. There is also mention of the 'adjoining' premises – now the sub-dean's residence – in these payments for 'the greate staires leading to the upper roomes with the pendants and roses on the roofe all'.

Other original items still to be seen include the joinery in the three western windows and two of the original consecration crosses, hidden now behind the small doors in the panelling of the west wall either side of the west door. It is possible that one or both of these corresponds to the account of Gondomar's having 'made a cross on the first stone' and subsequently laying it in mortar. We can safely assume that the mortar would not be poured directly onto the earth – it would have had a proper foundation or plinth support under it, and the presence of 'workmen' at this ceremony implies prior preparation for the foundation stones. This allows the possibility that the stones upon which the primitive crosses are painted, originally in red, but later in black as they appear now, a few feet off ground level, are in fact Gondomar's foundation stones. Gondomar's son laid the second stone – perhaps the other consecration cross stone. This may well be the reason why no further consecration crosses have ever been found in the structure.

Above the west end is the royal closet. It now lacks its screen, which was of Corinthian pilasters and festoons, but retains its Inigo Jones chimney-piece of Reigate stone for which Jones's drawings still exist.[7]

The Queen's Chapel was not the first building in Palladian style at St James's Palace. The clue to this lies in the Smythson collection at the RIBA. In it is a drawing entitled 'The Newe Building at Sant Jeames 1619', drawn by John Smythson of Bolsover who visited London that year. It is in fact a drawing of the prince's buttery, built between 1617 and 1619. This was a two-storey brick building designed to accommodate barrels on the ground floor, which was paved with Purbeck marble for this purpose, lodgings on the first floor, and a dormered garret in the roof.[8] This building was originally executed under under the eye of the principal bricklayer, Simon Wise, but a year later Francis Norfolk was employed in 'perfecting the bricklayers work'. There were two cornices and at the level of the eaves a 'great casement', apparently with an architrave. There were thirteen principal windows 7ft high by 4½ feet wide, all with architraves, together with three square and three round windows. Of particular importance to the subsequent architecture of the

---

[7] *Drawings Collection: Jones and Webb* (RIBA, London, 1972) fig. 24.
[8] E341/3252 (1617-18), and A01/2422/49 (1618-19).

Queen's Chapel, constructed just five years later, is the fact that there were three arches facing the street. Their design derived directly from a Roman bridge in Palladio's *Quatro Libri*. Here also Inigo Jones seems to have first introduced his special round-headed window of a type he was to use again just five years later in the west wall of the Queen's Chapel.

It is interesting to picture the Palladian-style buttery, facing onto what is now Cleveland Row, standing without equal in its classical innovation for five years before it was joined by the Queen's Chapel, whose architecture benefited so much from Inigo Jones's experiments with the buttery.

Returning to the interior of the Queen's Chapel, we should also note that the original cornice to the left of the royal closet's central window is made of red pine. In the 1620s the royal closet or gallery was painted with sky-blue smalt in a white lead base. Smalt is a glass pigment reflecting a rich blue colour because of its cobalt content. The glass particles were ground to form a powder. Smalt was commercially produced in England at the start of the seventeenth century and is typically Jacobean. It was used by artists and decorators alike. This decoration would have lasted quite some time, but all subsequent painting has been either buff or biscuit-colour. The north door of the closet, to the left of the chimney-piece, was covered over in the post-war repairs of 1948. There is now no sign of the staircase that hugged the south-west corner of the chapel below the closet, allowing access from the chapel to the closet and emerging at the centre window of the closet, as shown on a map of *c.* 1730.

Cosmo, duke of Tuscany, visited the Queen's Chapel in 1669, by which time the damage it sustained under Cromwell and the Commonwealth, despite the presence of general Monk, who lived at St James's for a while in that period, had been made good. Cosmo noted in his diary of travels that on entering the Queen's Chapel there were two lateral chapels in the ante-chapel (i.e. under the royal closet): one to the Virgin Mary on the right where the queen said her rosary, and the other on the left. He noted, too, that Catherine of Braganza's Capuchin friars sang in the upper choir. This would have been the eastern domed choir constructed in the 1660s.

In this apse John Turner, joiner, made fourteen new stalls in *c.* 1683, 'wrought circular with a cornish', and '2 stalls made to open in the choir', and a large one against a door. They were all provided with segmental wooden kneeling hassocks. In the centre was a revolving lectern. Access to the apse was by a door centrally situated under the Venetian window of the east wall of the chapel (i.e. the altar end). Coming from the apse into the chapel meant going through this door and then negotiating a tiny narrow passage running north-south behind the altar reredos with two doors at either end of it. These are still there and provide access to the rear of the altar.

The friary in the east of the apse was originally built to be occupied by the monks of the Order of St Peter of Alcantara, who inhabited it from

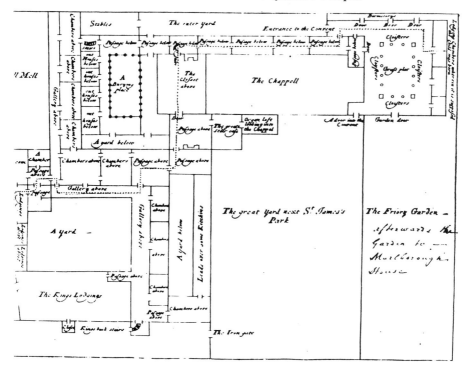

This detail of a plan dated 1689, showing the Queen's Chapel and its environs, records the buildings comprising the friary situated immediately to the east of the Chapel as they were a few months after the Benedictines left in 1688. Note that there was a burial ground beyond the west doors of the Chapel situated underneath what is today Marlborough Road.

1667-75. The interior was described by Samuel Pepys in his diary entry of 22 January 1666/7:

> Away, and my Lord Brouncker and I walking into the park, I did observe the new buildings, and my Lord, seeing I had a desire to see them, they being the place for the priests and fryers, he took me back to my Lord Almoner, and he took us quite through the whole house and chapel, and the new monastery, showing me most excellent pieces in wax work, a crucifix given by a Pope to Mary Queen of Scots, where a piece of the cross is, two bits set in the manner of a cross in the foot of the crucifix; several fine pictures, but especially very good prints of holy pictures. I saw the dortoire, and the cells of the priests, and we went into one, a very pretty little room, very clean, hung with pictures, set with books. The priest was in his cell, with his hair clothes to his skin, bare legged, with a sandal only on, and his little bed without sheets, and no feather bed, but yet, I thought, soft enough. His cord about his middle, but in so good company, living with ease, I thought it a very good life. A pretty library they have, and it was in the refectoire, where every man his napkin, knife, cup of earth and basin of the

135

The Queen's Chapel at St James's in 1687. (From an engraving in the Pepys Library, Magdalene College, Cambridge, photographed in 1971 by permission of the librarian)

same, and a place for one to sit and read, while the rest are at meals. And into the kitchen I went, where a good neck of mutton at the fire, and other victuals boiling. I do not think they fared very hard. Their windows all looking into a fine garden and the park, and mighty pretty rooms all. I wished myself one of the Capuchins.

These buildings were let by December 1688, and the supplement to the *Gazette* of 18 April 1709 records their demolition thus: 'Her Majesty, having been pleased to grant to His Grace the Duke of Marlborough the Friary next St. James' Palace ... the same is pulling down in order to rebuild the house for His Grace.'

The north transept door that once communicated with the friary is now blocked up. There is still an arched recess above it, although the window that was once there disappeared sometime after 1816. In 1685-87 a side altar and great altar were installed, together with two tabernacles. Above the high altar hung Huysman's painting of the 'Madonna and Child' which was subsequently removed in 1689 when James II fled to the continent. Also in the refurbishment between 1682 and 1684 the altar reredos and the organ gallery were built and fashioned by Grinling Gibbons. Gibbons also made the flying angels with 'two great festoons' supporting the combined arms of England and Portugal over the arch of the Venetian window. The Gibbons west screen has not survived.

The contract for this work was signed on 10 June 1682: 'To Grinling Gibbons Carver for carving the Altar in her Majestie's Chappell accordinge to a design approved of by her Majestie, Vizt. one large picture frame with ornaments on the topp, festoons on the sides relating thereto: 2 figures over the doorway next the wall: 2 ornaments over the doors: 2 suitable ornaments over the neeches ... .' Gibbons also made a 'modell for the altar piece', for which he was paid £1 17s. This model cannot now be traced. The works which Gibbons executed were painted and gilded by Robert Streater, who was also paid 'for guilding the Queen's armes & the festoons over the great frames ... etc.' It is possible that the first painted altarpiece to fit within the 'large picture frame with ornaments on topp' was that painted by Jacob Huysman which is known to have hung there until 1689. Another artist, Parry Walton, received £15 15s 'for 5 Altar peices and 3 peices putt in each picture'. There was thus a kind of pictorial barrier at the east end over and above the altar.

Of the collection of around twenty-five paintings by the court artist Benedetto Gennari the younger, made between 1675 and 1688 specifically for the queens consort to hang in the Queen's Chapel, or for its staff to hang in their quarters there, four particularly spectacular paintings can still be seen in various collections. From his own list of paintings Benedetto Gennari records that he painted one of these spectacular oils in 1674, describing it thus:

The east end of the Queen's Chapel, showing from top to bottom: the Inigo Jones/Matthew Goodrich ceiling of the 1620s, the great east window beyond which stood the domed apse for the friars between 1682 and 1707, and the 1682 Grinling Gibbons/Robert Streater reredos, still containing the two doors which led to the domed apse. This apse was remodelled in 1938 to incorporate the painting by Annibale Caracci of 'The Virgin and Child with SS Joseph, John the Baptist, and Catherine' from the collection of Charles I (see p. 405), but originally paintings by Benedetto Gennari, Jacob Huysman and Ramberg hung there. (Reproduced by courtesy of the Royal Commission on Historic Monuments)

6. Francis Bacon and the Queen's Chapel

A painting of the same size depicting the Annunciation to the Blessed Virgin Mary by the Angel with above some bright beams, the Holy Spirit and cherubim and seraphim and this as well commissioned by her Majesty the Queen for use at her altar on the feast of the Annunciation (and all other festivals of the Virgin Mary that there are in the year).

This painting is now in the Collezione della Cassa di Rispario, and measures 238.7 × 147.4 cm.[9]

Another work executed by Gennari for the Queen's Chapel was 'La Sacra Famiglia'. Now at the Birmingham City Museums and Art Gallery, this beautiful oil painting, made in 1682, measures 213 × 168 cm. Gennari describes it thus under item 81 of his London list:

A painting for the altar depicting the Virgin Mary, St Joseph and the Holy Child pretending that the Saint has woken him from his sleep in the cradle and the Child wanting to be offered milk from the breast of the Virgin Mary. In the upper part stands a host of angels playing musical instruments and singing to wake up the Baby Jesus. This painting was commissioned by the Duchess of York who put it in her private chapel at St James's.

Was this painting intended to fill the 'large picture frame with ornaments on the topp' that Grinling Gibbons was commissioned to carve upon signing his contract on 10 June 1682? Certainly the coincidence of the date 1682 for both the Gennari painting and the Gibbons contract would suggest a degree of coordination here. We could perhaps assume that the painting by Gennari was in a sense part of the refurbishment arrangements. If so, it hung over the altar before the Huysman painting. As the latter was removed in 1688 we could suggest that this Gennari hung in the Queen's Chapel over the altar from 1682 until sometime before 1688. At any rate we can be certain that it hung somewhere in the chapel between those dates, even if not over the altar.

A further painting Gennari was commissioned to execute for the Queen's Chapel was painted in 1685 for James II's queen consort, Mary of Modena, and listed by him as item 103 thus:

A large painting commissioned by her Majesty Queen Maria to put in her chapel at St James's depicting the Blessed Virgin Mary sitting with the

[9] Benedetto Gennari's own list of his paintings has been published in Prisco Bagni's *Benedetto Gennari e la Bottega del Guercino* (Nuova Alfa Editoriale, 1987). This particular painting is described in item 11 of Gennari's 'Nota dei quadri fatti in Londra principiando dall'anno 1674 alli 8 ottobre (A di 24 settembre 1674 in giorno di lunedi arrivassimo in Londra), which covers the period 1674-88. I wish here to record my grateful thanks to the Surveyor Emeritus of the Queen's Pictures, Sir Oliver Millar, and Miss Caroline Crichton Stuart, who initially generously lent me a rare copy of the Gennari list at Bologna, and later lent me Prisco Bagni's book upon its publication. My thanks also go to Charles Noble and Cazzy Neville for their help in locating Gennari paintings, and to Laura Marulli of the Central Chancery of the Orders of Knighthood for her assistance in translating the Italian inventory.

Benedetto Gennari's 'La Sacra Famiglia', now at the Birmingham City Art Gallery, was painted in 1682 apparently specifically to be incorporated into the new reredos at the Queen's Chapel which was being constructed by Grinling Gibbons. (Reproduced by courtesy of Birmingham Museums and Art Gallery)

child in her arms and St Joseph who gives him a book to read, and in the upper part a host of angels.

This oil painting, measuring 242 × 190 cm, found its way into the duke of Pembroke's (1656-1732) collection at Wilton House in Wiltshire after its removal from the Queen's Chapel, and subsequently ended up in the hands of cardinal Joseph Fesch (1763-1839), afterwards cardinal to Napoleon, who took it to Rome where he died in 1839.[10]

One of the last paintings Gennari executed for the Queen's Chapel was the 'Busto della Vergine', painted in 1688. Gennari describes it thus as item 134 in his London list: 'Another little picture of the Virgin Mary to accompany the aforementioned for the same sacristy.'[11] It was thus painted to hang in the sacristy of Mary of Modena's Queen's Chapel. It is curious, however, that it is an exact copy of the face and physical position of the Virgin Mary as she appears in Gennari's earlier 'La Famiglia Sacra', painted to hang in the Queen's Chapel of Catherine of Braganza in 1682.

Benedetto Gennari's lists are of significance too in another connection. He mentions the names of three chaplains who served at the Queen's Chapel because they themselves commissioned paintings from him in their personal capacities. They were Don Emmanuelle Dias, Don Giovanni Battista Draghi, and Don Giacomo Ronchi. Thus item 26 reads: 'An oval painting depicting St Joseph with Baby Jesus who is studying a book. This painting for Sig. Emmanuelle Dias treasurer of the Queen's Chapel.' In item 51 and 101 he is described further as the Portuguese almoner of the Queen's Chapel: '[51] A portrait in an oval of Sig. Dom Emmanuelle Dias the Portuguese Almoner of the Queen's Chapel. [101] A little oval painting showing the Baby Christ and St John the Baptist with the lamb & this for almoner Emmanuelle Dias of the Queen's Chapel.' Item 75 describes one Signor Giovanni Battista Draghi as 'maestro di capella della Regina': 'A half-figure painting showing the Christ Child and St John the Baptist. Christ is in the act of embracing the Cross and St John is in the act of giving water to the lamb. This for Sig. John Baptist Draghi, head of the Queen's Chapel.' Item 110 mentions 'signor Don Giacomo Ronchi tesoriere della capella della regina': 'A half-figure of St Geronimo in the act of writing and this I did for sig. Don Giacomo Ronchi treasurer of the Queen's Chapel.'

Other entries in Gennari's London list which record paintings he executed for the Queen's Chapel or its staff include the following:

10. A little painting depicting St John the Baptist in the act of stroking the lamb and this I brought with me a long time back to England making it a present at my arrival to Queen Catherine.

45. A large painting commissioned by the Queen of the Conception as a unique subject to put in the Chapel (at St James's) and in this Conception of

[10] Its Fesch Collection inventory number is 852-1-75.

[11] This oil painting, measuring 59 × 45.5 cm, was sold as lot no. 85 by Sotheby's on 6 December 1972.

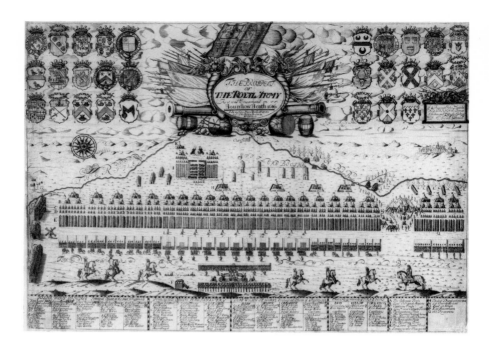

'The Prospect of the Royal Army as it was encamp'd on Hounslow Heath 1686.' To the centre right of the picture can be seen a structure labelled 'The King's Chappel'. This was a field chapel with fixed wheels built on James II's instructions to be conveyed wherever he went, being fitted up for his private masses. It remained on Hounslow Heath until after the Glorious Revolution of 1688 when it was removed and placed near the north end of Old Bond Street. It was used as a Chapel by the local inhabitants until 1716 when it was demolished and Trinity Chapel erected in its place. (Reproduced by courtesy of the Guildhall Library, City of London)

St Mary she under her feet the moon, the world, & the serpent and on the upper part some little angels & a seraph in a splendid halo of glory.

52. A small painting of St Catherine who is staring at the sky as she is crowned with roses by a little angel from the glorious heaven, and this the painting of the late sig. Dias.

82. A picture of St Francis de Sales to put in the Chapel.

83. Another painting of the same size showing St Francis Xavier and they are hung in this same Chapel one on the right hand side of the big painting and the other on the left.

90. A picture copied from mine (I mean St Francis de Sales) for a lady-in-waiting to the Duchess of Modena (from one that I had done for the Chapel of the Duchess of York).

114. A painting for the Altar for Queen Mary showing Christ Crucified, the Virgin Mary limp with exhaustion, St John crying, and Mary Magdalene at the foot of the Cross with tears in her eyes and this for the Chapel of St James to be displayed every year in passiontide.

142

6. Francis Bacon and the Queen's Chapel

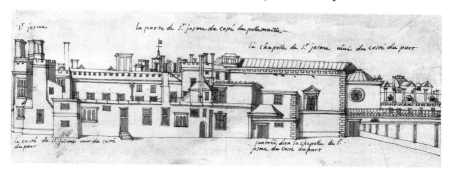

Attributed to François Gasselin and drawn in c. 1690, this view of the Queen's Chapel at St James's shows the Wren apse, demolished in 1707, and at the right of the picture the chimneys and other details of the monastery erected in 1666 for the use of Catherine of Braganza's thirteen Franciscan chaplains of the Order of St Peter of Alcantara (Arrabidoes) from 1667-75, when they were expelled by Charles II along with other Benedictine friars living elsewhere in the palace. The monastery was subsequently re-occupied by Benedictine friars under James II from 1685-88, when they fled abroad to St Germain to attend the Stuart court in exile. Of these Benedictine friars, William Cuthbert Wall had been implicated in the Titus Oates plot as a letter courier, and Henry Joseph Johnston was given James II's cipher in 1691 as a Jacobite and was allegedly implicated in the Lancaster plot as a gun-runner and in the Turnham Green plot as a convener of assassins. Abbot John Knightley, who had been at the monastery at St James's with Wall and Johnston, intervened successfully with the Orange court to save Johnston's life. (Crowle Pennant IV, no. 165, reproduced by courtesy of the Trustees of the British Museum)

118. A picture of the whole figure of St James commissioned by Queen Mary and this painting she had hung in one of the little side altars of her Chapel at St James.[12]

With regard to other decorative features of the Queen's Chapel, mention should be made of Thomas Bagley, master glazier, who inserted stained glass into the window above the high altar, depicting a crucifix and two coats-of-arms. The great architrave window of the chapel had festoons and scrolls inside and out, and a cherub's head on its keystone. It was built by master mason Thomas Wise. The cornice and pediment have been destroyed, but the external details remain. In 1699 the organ was removed to St Anne's, Soho. It should also be noted that the sacristy and vestries in the Stuart Queen's Chapel were situated along the exterior of the north wall of the chapel, containing presses for altar cloths and 'the great chest of drawers'.

On the death of Charles II in 1685 Catherine of Braganza moved to Somerset House and Mary of Modena, James II's queen consort, put in hand many alterations at the chapel, including a curved altar rail, and in 1686 a 'great niche' which was 'cutt out of the maine wall' of the chapel 'to set the font in'. This was the font in which prince Charles Edward (bonnie

[12] This reference to the side altar confirms Cosmo duke of Tuscany's observation that there were two side chapels located either side of the nave underneath the royal gallery, and gives us our only idea of what they looked like inside.

143

prince Charlie) was baptised on 15 October 1688. By the way of a postscript, in 1938 a plastered niche was revealed behind panelling on the north side of the ante-chapel (i.e. under the royal closet) immediately to the west of the pillar supports at the north end of the gallery, but this does not seem to have been the same size as the 1686 niche, which measured 8 feet high and 6 feet wide. On the other hand its position on the north side of the chapel would be customary for a baptistry. Whatever the case, a photograph of this niche exists in the archive of English Heritage at the Department of the Environment.

Mary of Modena was buried at Saint Germain-en-Laye in France, but her remains were disinterred during the French Revolution, her coffin plate being roughly wrenched off. By courtesy of the British Museum, and at the instigation of the previous sub-dean, canon James Mansel, this is now displayed on the south wall of the ante-chapel under the royal closet.

In 1702/3 queen Anne gave a new altar table, reading desk and altar rail for use by the French and Dutch Protestants, whom she permitted to worship at the Queen's Chapel. The altar rail was carved by Charles Hopson. The Accounts Ordinary and Extraordinary for 1702/3 state:[13]

> To Charles Hopson joyner
> Works done in the French Chappell at St James's. For 25 foot 3 ins of Altar Raile and Ballister at ? per foot ... £15 03s 00d.
> February 1703.

The eighteenth century saw some odd measures taken in the chapel. After 1703 it was painted red and buff, the paint pigment coming from the Forest of Dean and East Whitney in Oxfordshire.[14] Even the altar rail was painted red, perhaps for a special event. It then reverted later in the century to a less striking buff or cream colour. In 1781 the ceiling in the royal closet was partitioned for the organist's quarters, hence the marks on the Inigo Jones chimney-piece. The reredos was renewed during 1938, and the tabernacle removed.

This completes our look at the structure of the Queen's Chapel, but we should perhaps note lastly that the Portuguese Roman Catholic chaplain/almoner of the Queen's Chapel in the late seventeenth century, Signor Emmanuelle Dias, whom we have had cause to mention in connection with Gennari, actually lived in rooms adjoining the Queen's Chapel. We learn this from accounts in 1679/80 detailing the painting by Robert Streater of the 'Chappell Clossett and Mr Deas Rooms a chimnie in the withdrawing room and to the Chappell Closett the rooms next the Queen's rooms a litle clositt next the organ loft the passage from the park

---

[13] PRO 5/53.

[14] See Pamela Lewis, 'A study of the interior paints and decorative treatment of the Queen's Chapel, Marlborough House 1982', report commissioned by the lord chamberlain's office.

to the Chappell ... etc.' These are now the quarters occupied by the sub-dean of Her Majesty's Chapel Royal.

Augustus Hare in his *Walks of London* observed that the colours taken from James II at the Battle of the Boyne were hung up in the Queen's Chapel, together with the standards and other spoils, after Mary ordered them to be carried in a procession to celebrate the victory. One of James II's old comrades, Sir Robert Strange, wrote the following:

On Seeing the Colours Hung in St James's Chapel

Walking the Park, I, to my horror, there
Saw what from kindest hearts might force a tear,
The trophies of a monarch openly
Displayed in scorn before each vulgar eye
A crime which Absalom did never do.
Did ever he to every cobbler show
The relics of his father's overthrow?

Watercolour of the Queen's Chapel, entitled at the bottom right 'St James's Palace', with two stained ring marks. The view is from the old friary garden. (Reproduced by courtesy of the Guildhall Library, City of London)

7

Hell's Bells:
Sixteenth-Century Liturgical Music

The Henrician Reformation was to present the Chapel Royal with liturgical and musical challenges to which it not only rose but in which it took the lead. The Act of Supremacy of November 1534 declared Henry VIII 'the only supreme head in earth of the Church of England'. This was to elevate the power of the crown over the church in England at the expense of that of the pope. It had, too, the consequences of elevating the role of the Chapel Royal as the king's vehicle for showing how he meant the church and the liturgy to develop.

Although the daily offices of the church continued to be sung and said in Latin throughout the Henrician Reformation, Henry VIII saw to it that the services were made more intelligible to the laity. Thus item 7 of the first set of Royal Injunctions of 1536 required all parish churches to acquire and display a copy of the newly authorised English bible, and from 1543 onwards lessons at matins and evensong had to be read in English.

An English liturgy became a distinct possibility in late 1537 and early 1538 as Henry seriously considered the idea of an alliance with the Lutherans. A Lutheran delegation came to London, and Cranmer and Cromwell began to draft a new liturgy. Nothing came of it, however. Oddly, there followed a pause on the brink of a squarely Protestant stance as certain Protestant books, such as Coverdale's *Goostly psalmes*, were prohibited and burned. But this was short-lived. Probably a contributory factor in the resumption of the Protestant trend was the king's hostilities against France and Scotland in 1544. It seems that Henry thought divine help necessary to ensure success in these wars, and thus requested Cranmer to order litany processions throughout the province of Canterbury. Henry took the major and significant step of requiring an English form of wording for the litany procession, recognising that 'foreasmuch as heretofore the people, partly for lack of good instruction and calling, partly for that they understood no part of such prayers or suffrages, as were used to be sung and said, have used to come very slackly to the procession ...'.[1]

[1] See Le Hurray, *Music and the Reformation in England, 1549-1660*, p. 5.

The diarist Wriothesley noted meanwhile that an English version of the Te Deum had been sung by a group of progressives in London. It was common knowledge, too, that an English form of mass had been celebrated at least twice in small villages north of London. Cranmer was wrestling not only with the problem of formulating an English liturgy but also with the inseparable question of how to set the emerging new English services to music. He committed his thoughts on possible music to accompany the new English litany procession to paper in a letter to Henry VIII which deserves quotation because it shows the 'downgrading' in importance of elaborate church music in favour of a simpler role:

in mine opinion, the song that shall be made thereunto would not be full of notes, but, as near as may be for every syllable a note; so that it may be sung distinctly and devoutly, as be in Matins and Evensong Venite, the hymns Te Deum, Benedictus, Magnificat, Nunc dimittis, and all the Psalms and Versicles; and in the mass Gloria in excelsis, Gloria Patri, the Creed, the Preface, the Pater noster and some of the Sanctus and Agnus. As concerning the Salve festa dies, the Latin note, as I think, is sober and distinct enough; wherefore I have travailed to make the verses in English, and have put the Latin note unto the same. Nevertheless, they that be cunning in singing can make a much more solemn note thereto. I make them only for a proof, to see how English would do in song. But because my English verses lack the grace and facility I would wish they had, your majesty may cause some other to make them again, that they can do the same in more pleasant English and phrase ...

Despite Cranmer's efforts to revise the Latin breviary and write English versions of the Latin processions accompanied by his own 'plainsong' compositions, it appears that nothing more came of these.

However, on Henry VIII's death on 28 January 1547, the liturgical and musical reformation advanced yet further under Edward VI and the protectors Somerset and Northumberland. The Chapel Royal was in the forefront of all this activity, for as the king's own personal chapel it had to 'show the way'.

Less than two months after Edward VI's coronation at Westminster according to the Latin rite, the Chapel Royal sang an English form of compline. The dean of the Chapel Royal, Richard Sampson, would have smiled on this development. Appointed dean in 1516, he had taken the canons of Windsor by surprise when he supported the Bill of Supremacy in 1534, although he was subsequently imprisoned for alleged reactionary activities for a short while in 1540. He fully regained his standing at court by 1544 – in time to see the introduction of the English forms of service that the king wished his people to experience. Two extant motets of dean Sampson's attest to his skilful musicianship. He was to hold the office of dean of the Chapel Royal until *c.* 1554, when he was replaced by monsignor Hutchenson under queen Mary's Roman Catholic rule.

To return to 1547 and the Protestant ascendancy, the opening of the new sessions of parliament and convocation saw part of the customary service in Westminster Abbey sung in English. These parts included the Gloria, Creed, Sanctus, Benedictus qui venit, and Agnus Dei, while in the following year, 1548, an English supplement to the Latin mass was published. Shortly after this the choir of St Paul's Cathedral tried out English forms of the daily offices. The question was, until the 'Somerset' English Prayer Book was ready for publication, how any sort of liturgical and musical uniformity was to be achieved throughout the realm, with so many officially approved innovations coming thick and fast? The only universal guidance available in these years of flux was the 'Order of Communion', issued in 1548. But there was a solution to 'showing the way' – and the Chapel Royal was the chosen vehicle.

That this was so, and that it had for some time played this role, is evident from a letter the protector Somerset wrote to the vice-chancellor of Cambridge University on 4 September 1548, in which he stated that 'until such time as an order be taken and prescribed by his Highness to be universally kept throughout the whole realm ... you and every of you in your colleges, chapels or other churches use one uniform order, rite and ceremonies [*sic*] in the mass, matins and even-song and all other divine service in the same to be said or sung, such as is presently used in the king's majesty's chapel, and none other ...'. These forms of service administered by the Chapel Royal are unfortunately no longer extant.

When the first Book of Common Prayer eventually surfaced in 1549, so too did the question of what music should accompany it. The question had to be faced, for the first Act of Uniformity, ratified by parliament on 21 January 1549, gave just four months for 'the booke of common prayer and administracion of the sacraments' to replace all existing Latin service books. Cranmer was evidently one of the anonymous compilers of this new Prayer Book – certainly the litany to be found between its covers was his English procession of 1544. The services of baptism, confirmation, marriage, purification and burial were near enough straight translations from their Latin counterparts, but of the hitherto existing eight office hours, terce, sext and none were scrapped, while matins, lauds, prime, vespers and compline were absorbed into the English matins and evensong. The number of feast days recognised was reduced to twenty-seven of which only six were deemed of major importance: Christmas, Epiphany, Easter, Ascension, Pentecost and Trinity Sunday. This was, then, a far cry from the Sarum rites in which one day in every three was a feast of some sort, with a gradation of music based upon polyphony for festal days and plainsong for ferials.

The 1549 English Prayer Book provided just about everything the clergy needed to know to administer the sacraments, but the singing clerks and organists were left wondering what their role was now to be. The new rubric had apparently very little to say to them. For instance, in matins the Venite had rather vaguely to be 'said' or 'sung', but there were no other instructions to be found, while in evensong the only mention of the 'clerks' in the rubric ran as follows: 'Then the suffrages before assigned at Matins, the Clerks kneeling likewise, with three collects ... .' It was not clear from reading the Prayer Book whether music was to be encouraged or not. It was certainly permitted, as is clear from the communion rubric, but many might be forgiven for wondering if it was welcome. There is no doubt, though, that the first service using the new English Prayer Book would have been conducted by the Chapel Royal, and it is scarcely conceivable that Edward VI would have been absent from this momentous event.

Whatever music was sung on this occasion, the question of what music should be used was evidently a matter still to be tackled properly. Guidance was at last forthcoming from the press of the king's printer, Richard Grafton, in the form of John Merbecke's *Booke of Common praier noted*. This comprised uncomplicated 'plainsong'-type music for morning prayer, evening prayer, communion, and for the important occasional services. *The psalter or Psalms of David, corrected and pointed as they shall be sung in Churches after the translation of the Great Bible*, published in 1549, was helpful too but provided no pointing other than a simple colon dividing every verse into two! Thus pointing and chants must have varied between religious establishments, although the Chapel Royal renditions must again have 'led the way'. Merbecke's book did not go beyond a first edition, and the public's adjustment to the 'liturgical reformation' took a while. Evidence of this includes the confusion surrounding the abandonment of the observance of Corpus Christi day on 20 June 1549 as a public holiday. Apparently half the population of London observed this feast as a public holiday despite instructions to the contrary.

It seems, too, and this is most significant, that Edward VI could not trust Westminster Abbey to accord with his wishes. This elevated still further the position of the Chapel Royal as leader by example. For instance, Edward VI's royal visitation to ensure the end of 'popish' practices began within six months of his coronation. This took the form of limiting the number of candles at mass to two, restricting bells to being rung before the start of the service and not during it (thereby signalling a change in emphasis to a consubstantial view of the sacraments, for no bell would now be rung at the elevation of the host as had been the practice hitherto), monkish habits being discarded, cathedral musicians abandoning their tonsured appearance, and increased emphasis on preaching. The dean and chapter of Westminster Abbey, however, defied the king and refused to introduce the new English Prayer Book for quite some time. After a visit to Cranmer at Lambeth Palace in the summer of 1549, Martin Bucer, regius professor of Divinity at Cambridge, and Paul Fagius observed in a letter to friends at Strasbourg that Cranmer had allowed some liturgical concessions 'out of respect for ancient customs' but that 'they are only to be kept for a short while, lest the people, not yet having learned Christ, should be deterred from embracing his religion by sudden and extensive innovations'. Here, then, was evidence that a full-scale liturgical reformation was the objective. What this would have heralded for the fate of church music, and indeed the Chapel Royal, had not Mary Tudor ascended the throne in 1553 is fascinating to conjecture. Certainly the archbishop of York and the bishops of London and Worcester (Holgate, Ridley and Hooper) were of the distinct opinion that music was irrelevant to the conduct of divine service. They therefore moved to stifle it where they could.

Evidence of this is plentiful. The Royal Injunctions for St George's Chapel, Windsor, dated 8 February and 20 October 1550, reduced the number of choristers and ended the appointment of new organists. In 1552 archbishop Holgate ordered York Minster to stop the playing of the organ for both solo and musical accompaniment – 'the said playing to utterly cease and be left the time of Divine Service within the said church' – while the choristers' music was to consist only of 'square note plain' and there was to be 'none other note sung or used in the said church at any service'. At the same time Cranmer arranged for Ridley to silence the organs at St Paul's Cathedral. On 4 September 1552 the dean of St Paul's was ordered by the archbishop of Canterbury that 'he should leave the playing of the organs at the Divine service, and so left it'. Peter le Hurray observes that 'By the summer of 1553, the future of the English choral tradition was certainly in question. Is it too fanciful to see, in the succession of a Catholic monarch, its ultimate salvation?'[2] If so, it is perhaps fitting that Mary Tudor's bowels rest under the floor of the Chapel Royal building at St James's Palace!

The Chapel Royal had to make yet further adjustments in accordance with the second Act of Uniformity in early 1552, as a result of Cranmer's embracing an almost Calvinist or Zwinglian view of the sacraments. With emphasis now clearly on the memorial rather than the sacrificial aspect of the eucharist, the term 'altar' was dropped in favour of 'table', and this was placed in a central position rather than at the east end of the church. Vestments were curtailed to avoid any suggestion of 'popery' at the communion. Music, too, was to be edged out as far as possible. This is evident from a comparison of the 1549 Prayer Book with that of 1552. For example, the 1549 Prayer Book provided for 'the clerks' to sing in English the Introit and Kyrie, and the major parts of the Gloria, Creed, Offertory, Sanctus, Agnus Dei and post-communion. On the other hand, the only provision for singing in the 1552 Prayer Book seems to have been the Gloria after the communion. The Creed was to be said, and the Introit was scrapped altogether along with the sung parts of the Agnus Dei and

---

[2] Ibid., p. 29.

post-communion. The Second Act of Uniformity was passed by parliament in April 1552, but then the liturgical and musical pendulum swung to the other extreme with the accession of Mary Tudor to the throne and the return to full communion with Rome.

To say that the Edwardian reformation must have provided the Chapel Royal with successive problems of adjustment both liturgically and musically cannot be an exaggeration. As it had to 'lead by example', every official innovation must have demanded new compositions and extensive alterations to old favourites.

A glimpse of the problem faced by the Chapel Royal can be had by looking at the Wanley manuscript part-books[3] which contain music for the 1549 English Prayer Book and curious texts based either on the English Primers of 1535 (Marshall's) and 1539 (Hilsey's) or on works by Cranmer before the form of the 1549 Prayer Book was agreed. The Wanley part-books also comprise adaptations of masses in English by Taverner, among others. It is thought that these particular works were undertaken before 1548 when the Lincoln Injunction confined composition to 'a playn and distinct note, for every syllable one'. Christopher Tye, who was born around 1500 and sang as a gentleman of the Chapel Royal from about 1537 until about 1572, had early on turned his hand to the problem of composing for the liturgy in English. The text of his Nunc dimittis beginning 'Lord, let thy servant now depart in peace', for example, is the version of the 1535 and 1539 Primers and not the 'King's Primer' of 1545 which superseded these earlier ones which were then suppressed.[4]

There are among the Wanley communion settings some that appear to date from 1547, when a draft translation appeared, but with the oddity that the 'King's Primer' version (1545) of the Apostles' Creed is used rather than the Nicene Creed. It is Wulstan's opinion that this was because the Nicene Creed was not as yet available in English.

John Sheppard, who was probably born around 1515, was 'informator choristarum' at Magdalen College from 1543 to 1548, and subsequently joined the Chapel Royal in 1553.[5] He, too, turned his hand to the problems produced by Edward VI's liturgical reformation. His second service for communion contains the same Apostles' Creed oddity that we saw in Christopher Tye's – suggesting a date of composition between 1547 and 1549 – although the text otherwise corresponds with that of the 1549 Prayer Book. It is thought that Sheppard's settings of the Te Deum, Magnificat and Nunc dimittis date from that time when the English canticles were authorised to be used in the breviary services of matins, evensong and compline. Sheppard, it seems, was trying hard to keep pace

[3] Bodleian Library Wanley MS Mus. Sch. e. 420-2.
[4] See Wulstan, *Tudor Music*, p. 284.
[5] Stowe MS 571 fol. 36v and Exchequer Rolls 434, 5-10.

with the liturgical innovations and may well have fallen into the trap of predicting that metrical psalms would be included in the new services of the 1549 Prayer Book under preparation. The part-book BL Add. MS 15166, for instance, contains forty-one metrical psalms by Sheppard with the texts found in Sternhold's *Certayne Psalmes* of 1549. However, with the exception of Psalm 128 and its alternative Psalm 67, which were appointed to be used for the solemnisation of matrimony, metrical psalms were excluded from the liturgy authorised by the 1549 Prayer Book.

Christopher Tye composed a setting of Psalm 128 following the prose text, while the Wanley manuscript setting is from the metrical version and is specifically marked 'Weddings'. The earliest version of Tye's setting of Psalm 67 'O God be merciful' is to be found in the 'Lumley' part-books,[6] which contain text predating the 1549 Prayer Book. This particular work throws up a problem that had to be faced by his colleagues too – the task of dealing with the short syllables of English that were not a trait of Latin – for the words 'be it' in 'O God be merciful' are set to one note. Thomas Tallis, gentleman of the Chapel Royal from 1542 to 1586, had a similar problem with the word 'toward' in his 'Hear the voice and prayer'.

The frequent liturgical variations in English caused another problem quite apart from the technical difficulty of composing for a 'new' language. This was a problem that even the Chapel Royal could not solve. It is to be seen in many of the compositions in the Lumley and Wanley part-books and in such works as Tallis's 'If ye love me' and 'Hear the voice and prayer', and Sheppard's 'I give you a new commandment' – they were all composed for men's voices. What about the boys? It is hazarded by Wulstan that 'the four-part texture (as opposed to the three voices of many Henrician carols) suggests that boys' voices may have been omitted because of lack of rehearsal time for the music of the new rites'.[7]

It appears that even the Chapel Royal boys, whom these gentlemen of the Chapel – Tye, Tallis and Sheppard – would normally have expected to sing their works, were simply not capable of keeping up with the frequent liturgical and musical changes. Certainly a parallel situation was recorded over a century later by Matthew Locke in *The Present Practice of Music Vindicated* (1673), when he wrote: 'For above a year after the opening of His Majesty's Chappell the orderers of the musick there were necessitated to supply the superior parts of their musick with cornets and men's feigned voices, there being not one lad for all that time capable of singing his part readily.'

According to Paul Doe,[8] Christopher Tye's 'Euge Bone' contains a hidden allusion to the protectors Somerset and Northumberland in Edward VI's reign, for some of its contents relate to his setting of the

[6] British Library MS Roy. App. 74-6.
[7] Wulstan, *Tudor Music*, p. 286.
[8] *Early English Music* (1962), no. 24.

'Quaesumus omnipotens' prayer including the phrase 'famulos tuos'. It is clear that Tye had especially close relations with royalty. His work entitled *Actes of the Apostles*, printed in 1553, contained an elaborate dedication to Edward VI – although its quality is, as they say, 'something else', being described by Wulstan as 'an excruciating rendition into verse of the first fourteen chapters of the Acts of the Apostles' and a 'sub-species of anthem'.[9] But other works are much better, such as his 'Christ rising again', a setting of the 1552 Prayer Book Easter anthems but excluding the Alleluia provided for in the 1549 Prayer Book. Tye was thus doing his best to compose for every new turn in the Edwardian liturgical reformation, so keen was he to support his king's stance. He is even depicted in a play published in 1605 in which as tutor to Edward VI he actually admonishes the king and subjects him to a beating by proxy, the pain of which was thus borne by another youth. Tye continued his royal friendships after his service with the Chapel Royal ended in 1560 until his death in *c.* 1572 – he is known to have played the organ for Elizabeth I: 'but little delight to the ear; she would send the verger to tell him he played out of tune; whereupon he sent word that her ears were out of tune'![10]

Tye's daughter, Ellen, married another great composer, Robert White, who in fact succeeded Tye as organist of Ely Cathedral, moving later to Chester and finally to Westminster Abbey. Influenced initially by the works of Taverner, White soon developed his own style, very evident in his cantus firmus antiphons composed while he was at Trinity College, Cambridge, from 1554-62. Like his father-in-law, White struggled to rescue ecclesiastical music but was mainly preoccupied with psalm settings. He died of plague, along with his entire family, in 1574.

Sheppard, too, seems to have nurtured a close relationship with royalty. He presented a roll of songs to queen Mary on New Year's day 1557. He lived long enough to sing as a gentleman of the Chapel Royal at Elizabeth I's coronation in January 1559, but must have died shortly afterwards, for the Old Cheque Book which records deaths and resignations from 1560 onwards makes no mention of him.

Thomas Tallis, too, was sensitive to the affairs of his sovereigns. He is thought by Jeremy Noble to have composed 'Suscipe quaesco' in recognition of cardinal Reginald Pole's 'absolution' of the realm on 29 November 1554. It was set for the same voices as his 'Puer natus' mass, which was sung at Christmas 1554 – echoing the belief that queen Mary was with child.

Other works of Tallis and Sheppard composed at this time do, in fact, show some evidence of the difficulties of readjusting yet again to the old Sarum rites as the Protestant developments of the Edwardian

---

[9] Wulstan, *Tudor Music*, p. 287.
[10] Anthony à Wood quoted in *Athenae Oxoniensis*, edited by Bliss (London, 1813-20).

reformation were swept aside on Edward's death and the accession of the Roman Catholic Mary. There was no question that Mary would waver from her religious stance. Cardinal Pole, who had been a candidate for marriage to her, was now back from Edwardian exile under the supremacy of the pope.

To many composers in the Chapel Royal it must have seemed as if a new 'stable' era had dawned – at least from the musical standpoint. But Sheppard and Tallis had to cope with the fact that the Edwardian reformation had lasted long enough for the generation of children of the Chapel Royal who had sung Sarum rites at the end of Henry VIII's reign to have departed, their voices having broken. There was certainly an initial difficulty in trying to teach a set of boys virtually untrained in the Sarum liturgy and its polyphony.

This is duly reflected in the Gyffard part-books, which contain mostly works by Sheppard and Tallis and which seem to have been composed for All Saints day (1 November) 1553 and the celebration of Easter in 1554. They contain two settings of 'Audivi' for 1 November – Sheppard transposes his setting down an octave, which seems to have been composed for boys judging by the voice ranges, so that the boys' part could be sung by the gentlemen. The Chapel Royal evidently had some difficulty in building up its repertoire of elaborate compositions with boys' voices, with the ultimate objective of restoring the 'high treble' style. Stow records that in November 1554 a sermon was preached while beforehand was sung 'Ne timeas Maria' and afterward 'Te Deum' and 'Salve festa dies'. It is thought that Sheppard's mass 'Be not afraid' for men's voices was composed for this occasion. There is, too, the theory that if Sheppard's 'Salve festa dies' was used on this occasion then it may well be that the 'Te Deum' attributed to Taverner was actually Sheppard's and in fact completed a trilogy of pieces composed or transposed deliberately for men's voices, before the boys were sufficiently accomplished to attempt such works. Meanwhile, Tallis's 'Hodie ... gloria in excelsis' was composed for men's voices, thereby confirming the difficulties evidently experienced in training up the boys.

However, it seems that the boys of the Chapel Royal had reached a high enough standard to sing elaborate compositions in company with king Philip of Spain's 'Capilla Flamenca', which itself contained seven boys, and the choir of St Paul's Cathedral, for the celebration of mass on 2 December and Christmas day 1554. Redford, Parsons, Mundy, Tallis and Sheppard developed the Chapel Royal repertoire in a collection of polyphonic responds and hymns culminating in 'Gaude, gaude, gaude' by Sheppard and 'Videte miraculum' by Tallis, composed for Candlemas. The latter work was composed so as to place the musical emphasis on the word 'Maria', thereby paying tribute to the sovereign, while Tallis's 'Gaude gloriosa' may have been written especially for Mary, for as Wulstan points out, 'the doggerel text may be interpreted as a reference to the restoration of the 'true' church':

Gaude Virgo Maria, quam dignam laude celebrat ecclesia
quae Christi doctrinis illustra te matrem glorificat.

Sheppard's votive antiphon 'Gaude virgo christiphera' and Tallis's 'Gaude gloriosa', which appear to have prompted Mundy's splendid 'Vox patris coelestis', were perhaps the climax of the Maryan elaborate antiphonal style.

The death of Mary and accession of Elizabeth soon resulted in a liturgical compromise between Protestant and Roman Catholic in the form of the 1559 Prayer Book. Tallis, however, never hid his leanings and it has been suggested that his great composition 'Spem in alium' was written especially for the Roman Catholic duke of Norfolk, and indeed performed for him during his short period of freedom in 1571. Although Latin polyphony was not outlawed by Elizabeth, the times nevertheless required that Tallis and Byrd's 1575 collection be called *Cantiones quae ab argumento sacra vocantur*, thereby implying that the choice of sacred words was no more than coincidence. Tallis, though, never went as far as Byrd in his outward support of recusancy.

The Elizabethan settlement enshrined in the 1559 Prayer Book was at first influenced to a great extent by the Protestant elements. Outwardly the 1559 Prayer Book was merely the Edwardian 1552 Prayer Book in disguise. Tallis's work 'O Lord, give thy holy spirit' exhibits similar constraints, for it is no more elaborate than the works he composed during the Edwardian reformation. However, his five-part Te Deum shows flashes of the Elizabethan choral renaissance that was to burst forth from the hands of Sheppard, Mundy and Parsons. Unfortunately Parsons, who had joined the Chapel Royal in 1563 and composed among other works a service in five parts, was according to an entry of 1569 in the Old Cheque Book 'drowned at Newark uppon Trent the 25th January, and Wm. Bird was sworne gentleman in his place at the first the 22nd of February followinge, [illegible] Lincoln'. Mundy composed a Magnificat and Nunc dimittis to complete Parsons's five-part service. Sheppard meanwhile composed service music for the Elizabethan Prayer Book but for high treble voices once more. Thus emerged his Magnificat and Nunc dimittis 'for trebles', and Mundy's evening service 'In medio chori' together with a morning service. Matthew Parker's Psalter of 1567 provided directions for 'The Rectors', 'The Quier' and 'The Meane', and as Elizabeth's reign progressed, so a stable liturgy and musical composition of all kinds began to flow freely from the hands of the Chapel Royal composers.

The atmosphere of royal favour in which the Chapel Royal now basked was in part due to the fact that the dean of the Chapel Royal from 1558 until 1572 was none other than Elizabeth's old chaplain when she was princess – Dr George Carew. He is said to have been the only clergyman prepared to celebrate mass according to the queen's wishes at her coronation. This act of loyalty was rewarded with the deanery of the Chapel Royal. Carew was succeeded by William Day in 1572, although the New Year presents list still recorded Carew as dean of the Chapel Royal in 1578/9. According to Stow, the deanery was vacant for eight years before the appointment of James Montague in 1603. During this period the office of acting dean devolved upon the lord chamberlain of the day. Perhaps it was just as well that the children of the Chapel Royal were under the eyes of one less clergyman as their acting talents flourished upon stage at Blackfriars.

Details of the day-to-day conditions under which the children of the Chapel Royal sang during a considerable part of Elizabeth's reign may be gleaned from the petition of William Hunnis, master of the children of the Chapel Royal, to the queen in 1583, which laments the shortage of monies now forthcoming to look after their needs compared to the situation before the dissolution of the monasteries by her father. It is so descriptive that it deserves quotation at some length:

> May it please your honors, William Hunnis, master of the children of her highness Chapel, most humble beseecheth to consider of these few lines. First, her majesty alloweth for the diet of twelve children of her said Chapel daily six pence a piece by the day, and forty pounds by the year for their apparel and all other furniture. Again there is no fee allowed neither for the master of the said children nor for his usher, and yet nevertheless he is constrained, over and besides the usher still to keep both a man servant to attend upon them and likewise a woman servant to wash and keep them clean. Also there is no allowance for the lodging of the said children, such time as they attend upon the court, but the master to his great charge is driven to hire chambers both for himself, his usher, children, and servants. Also there is no allowance for riding journeys when occasion serveth the master to travel or send into such sundry parts within this realm, to take up and bring such children as be thought meet to be trained for the service of her majesty. Also there is no allowance nor other consideration for those children whose voices be changed, who only do depend upon the charge of the said master until such time as he may prefer the same with clothing and other furniture unto his no small charge.

Comparison with the provisions made for the children a hundred years earlier as detailed in the *Liber Niger Domus Regis* of Edward IV shows there to have been a decline in conditions but an increase in opportunities for the boys. Of their conditions in Edward IV's reign (1461-83) the *Liber Niger* had this to say:

> Children of the Chapell VIII founden by the Kinge Jewelhouse for all thing that belongith to thayre apparayle, by the hand or oversight of the deane, or by the master of the song, assigned to teche them, whiche maister is apoynted by the seyd deane, and chosen out of the numbyr of the felashippe

of Chapell, and he to draw thees children, all as well in the Scoole, of facet as in song, organes, or suche other vertuose thinge. Thees children, etyn in the hall, dayly at the chapell bourde, next the yomen of vestiary, taking amonge them in lyverey, for all daye, brekfaste and at night II loaves, I messe of greete mete, II gallons of ale, and for wynter season, iiii Candille pic, III tal and litt for their beddis, of the Sgeaunt usher, and carriage at the Kinge cost, for their compotent bedding be oversight of the countroller, and amonge them all, to have one servant in to this court, to trusse, and bere theyre harneys, and to set theyre harneys in Court. And such dayes as the Kynge chapell requireth, any thes children, then present, receveth iiiid. at the grene seald of the countinghouse, for horse hyre dayly, as long as they be journaying, and whan any of thes children be syke, they take lyvery as withe the syke yoman of household. Also when they be growen to the age of xviii yere, and then theyre voyce changed, they cannot be preferyd in this chapell, nor within this courte, the number beyng full, then they will absent, the King assigneth every such childe, to a college of Oxinford, or Cambrige, of the Kinge fundacon, there to be in fynding, and study, sufficiauntly, tyll the King othir wise list to avaunce him.

This passage is quoted in an undated manuscript entitled 'Concerninge the Chapel Royal' which has on the cover the words: 'Mrs Clarke begs Dr Wesley's Acceptance of the enclosed Booke.' It is in the possession of the Chapel Royal.

Henry VIII is known to have paid for the university education of children of the Chapel Royal whose active singing career had ended, or to have looked after their interests in other ways. Sometime between Henry's death and the early years of Elizabeth's reign this long-established practice was abandoned. Hunnis was at pains to point this out and tackle the question of maintenance of the children later on in his 1583 petition:

although it may be objected that her majesty's allowance is no whit less than her majesty's father of famous memory therefore allowed: yet considering the prices of things present to the time past and what annuities the master then had out of sundry abbeys within this realm, besides sundry gifts from the king, and divers particular fees besides, for the better maintenance of the said children and office: and besides also there hath been withdrawn from the said children since her majesty's coming to crown twelve pence by the day which was allowed for their breakfasts as may appear by the treasurer of the chamber his account for the time being, with other allowances incident to the office as appeareth by the ancient accounts in the said office which I here omit. The burden hereof hath from time to time so hindered the masters of the children viz. Master Bower, Master Edwardes, myself and Master Farrant: that notwithstanding some good helps otherwise some of them died in so poor case, and so deeply indebted that they have not left scarcely wherewith to bury them. In tender consideration whereof, might it please your honors that the said allowance of six pence a day apiece for the children's diet might be reserved in her majesty's coffers during the time of their attendance. And in lieu thereof they be allowed meat and drink within this honourable household for that I am not able upon so small allowance any longer to bear so heavy a burden. Or otherwise to be considered as shall seem best unto your honorable wisdoms.

In Hunnis's case the problem of money for maintenance was solved through the grant to him of crown lands in 1585 at Great Ilford and elsewhere. James I restored the custom of placement at university in 1604 by authorising the master of the children to send any boy who had served three years or over with the Chapel Royal and whose voice breaking was the reason for his having to leave, to be placed in any college of the royal foundation in Oxford, Cambridge or elsewhere, where he should be entitled to the honour of a 'scholar of the foundation'. Charles I also followed precedent in 1629 by granting a request from a child of the Chapel Royal for a recommendation to a choral place in Salisbury Cathedral, but some of the boys are recorded merely as having 'gone off'.

These, then, were the conditions of service under which the children of the Chapel Royal found themselves serving while having to cope with the unprecedented liturgical and musical changes thrust upon them by the reformation in the sixteenth century.

8

Sea-Dog Almoners and Deans of the Chapel Royal

On 20 June 1596 the English navy was sighted off Cadiz. The Spanish had captured Calais from the French, and Philip of Spain had agents in Ireland sounding the coastline for suitable anchorages for a large fleet. Faced with this Elizabeth I had decided that the best form of defence was attack. Thus it was that the combined English and Dutch fleet sailed over the horizon, described by a watching Spaniard as 'the most beautiful fleet that ever was seen'.

The lord admiral and the dashing young earl of Essex were joint admirals of the naval forces and joint generals of the 7,000 troops carried aboard. Lord Thomas Howard as vice-admiral and Sir Walter Raleigh as rear admiral both commanded squadrons. Among the gentlemen volunteers was one John Donne, future dean of St Paul's Cathedral, who was yet to be ordained. Elsewhere in the fleet there sailed nine chaplains. Essex had four, the lord admiral had two (an indication of the supremacy of the 'puritan' faction?), while Howard, Sussex and Raleigh had one each. Among the four assigned to Essex was one George Montaigne (or Mountain).

George Montaigne was a Yorkshireman, fellow of Queens' College, Cambridge and lecturer in divinity at Gresham College, who became in time master of the Savoy, dean of Westminster Abbey in 1610, and then successively bishop of Lincoln in 1617, London in 1622, and Durham in 1628. He eventually became archbishop of York in 1628, thereby allowing William Laud to take the see of London and the deanery of the Chapel Royal, into which he had been sworn at Whitehall on 6 October 1626 when bishop of Bath and Wells (as we learn from the Old Cheque Book).

George Montaigne appears in the Old Cheque Book in a series of entries relating to 'The Continuance of the Lord Amoner's benevolence to the Chappell' – namely the 'benevolence yearelye from the Lord Amoner to the Gentlemen of the Chappell on Maundye Thursdaye'. Montaigne's entries stretch from 1621-28, and he is described as 'Dr Mountaine B. of Lincolne for the Maundy, and afterwards of London 1622'. He was in fact lord high almoner from 1619-28.

In 1596, with the navy off Cadiz, events took a strange twist. The

George Montaigne (Mountain), lord high almoner 1619-28, had earlier seen service with the Royal Navy as chaplain to the earl of Essex in the 1596 raid on Cadiz. (Reproduced by courtesy of Hammersmith and Fulham Archives)

Spanish, seeing the English fleet, took the precaution of burning their own ships in the inner harbour to deprive the English of any ransom opportunities. So the English landed and sacked the city – though with moderation. They took over Cadiz Cathedral, removed all its 'popish' symbols, and on Sunday 27 June 'divine service was had, and a learned sermon was there made in the afternoone, by one Mr Hopkins the Right Honourable the Earl of Essex's preacher, a man of singular good giftes'.[1] Hakluyt mentions his 'sweet utterance'. Of the two other clergy accompanying Montaigne, William Alabaster and Leonel Sharp, it is interesting to note that the former's experience at Cadiz caused his brief conversion to Roman Catholicism before he recanted to become a prebendary at St Paul's Cathedral and rector of Therfield in Hertfordshire, while Leonel Sharp had been with Essex at Tilbury camp

---

[1] British Library Sloane MS, quoted in Gordon Taylor, *The Sea Chaplains: a history of the chaplains of the Royal Navy* (Oxford Illustrated Press, 1978), p. 54.

in 1588 when Elizabeth I came so dramatically from St James's Palace to raise their spirits. It was Sharp who was chosen to repeat the queen's speech to the whole army assembled there.

As for Montaigne, Fuller records that at Cadiz he 'showed such personal valour that out of his gown he would turn his back on no man'.[2] Although A. Tindal Hart says that Montaigne was 'something of a buffoon', he nevertheless had an excellent sense of humour and this was said to have worked in his favour when he was appointed archbishop of York. Lastly, perhaps, we should also mention that he was a strong supporter of the dean of the Chapel Royal, William Laud.

Considering Montaigne's participation in the Cadiz naval enterprise, it is strangely apt that his appointment to the office of lord high almoner entitled him to use the emblem of a ship, the design of which was based upon the great three-masted ship built in 1512 by Wolsey and presented by him to Henry VIII. It was while Wolsey was the king's almoner from 1509-14 that he had this ship in full sail represented upon a seal which he used in connection with almonry matters, although the association of the almonry with a ship can be traced back to the seal of Stephen Payne, almoner to Henry V from 1414-19, which pictures the almoner standing under a canopy but holding in his arms a model ship on wheels. It may be of interest, too, to note that the ship *Sampson* of Henry VIII's navy, accompanied by the new *Mary Guildford*, which sailed from London in June 1527 with 'divers cunnyng men to seek straunge Regions', was almost certainly named after dean Sampson of the Chapel Royal, who held office from 1516-54.

There were to be at least two further bishops associated with the Chapel Royal whose seafaring exploits deserve mention.

In late 1681 a certain Lancelot Blackburne, newly ordained, left English shores aboard a ship bound for the West Indies. He joined a crew of buccaneers aboard a pirate ship, acting as their chaplain and sharing the plunder that came their way. He eventually returned to England, becoming a prebendary at Exeter in 1691, sub-dean of Exeter in 1695 and rector of Calstock in 1696. It appears that he was then forced to resign as sub-dean in 1702 because of rumours and accusations concerning his buccaneering past. He was, curiously to those not 'in the know', re-installed in 1704, becoming dean of Exeter, archdeacon of Cornwall, bishop of Exeter in 1717, and finally archbishop of York from 1724-43. But his greatest length of service was as lord high almoner with the Chapel Royal – a service he performed for twenty years from 1723-43.

Horace Walpole wrote of 'the jolly old archbishop of York, who had all the manners of a man of quality, though he had been a buccaneer, and was a clergyman. But he retained nothing of his first profession except his seraglio.' There was a famous joke about a pirate who, upon reaching

---

[2] Thomas Fuller, *The Holy State and the Profane State* (1841).

British shores, asked what had become of his old mate Blackburne, to which the reply came that he was archbishop of York!

If one looks closely, however, there are aspects of Blackburne's career that do not tie in with his buccaneering past. Not least of these is the fact that he was invited to preach three sermons before queen Anne, one to the House of Commons and one to Convocation. Moreover, it seems almost incredible that he should have been appointed to Calstock, a duchy of Cornwall living, in 1696.

The real story behind Blackburne's career is altogether more interesting and explains his ultimate appointment as lord high almoner with the Chapel Royal. He was in fact working for the king's secret service, and was deliberately sent to the West Indies to glean information about pirate activities. In the records entitled 'Moneys Received and Paid for Secret Services 1679-1688' Blackburne's name appears under the heading 'Payments and allowances to private persons for services rendered to the Crown' where he is detailed as having been paid £20 'for his transportation to Antego'. For obvious reasons the nature of his mission is not stated. Preferment to a 'royal' living must have been a kind of reward for services rendered, as was his re-instatement as sub-dean at Exeter after the 'rumours' about his past surfaced to force his resignation. He was obviously not permitted to answer his critics and was duly rewarded for his loyalty to the crown by his appointment as lord high almoner over the heads of those who had been only too ready to criticise him, being ignorant of the true purpose of his mission to the West Indies. He did, however, answer his critics in an oblique way by publishing a sermon in 1708 entitled 'Blessedness of Suffering Persecution for Righteousness Sake' – a veiled justification for his activities. Blackburn served as lord high almoner until his death in 1743. He was buried in St Margaret's, Westminster, and his sword is to be found at Christ Church, Oxford.

It is interesting to speculate as to what Blackburne's religious activities as chaplain aboard a pirate ship would have entailed. One can only hope that the report of events on a contemporary pirate ship is no indication of how he may have conducted a service. The Jesuit priest, père Labat, an authority on the buccaneers of the time, recalled a pirate, captain Daniel, who kidnapped a local priest in the Saintes – a group of tiny islands lying to the south of Hispaniola – in order that mass could be celebrated aboard ship for the benefit of the crew. The mass was accompanied by salvoes and the firing of cannons at the sanctus, elevation, benediction and exaudiat. The service ended with prayers for the king of France, but not before the captain had shot a crew member through the head for adopting an indecent posture during the service. The service ended, his body was committed to the deep and the priest was rewarded with a negro slave for his efforts.

More recently another bishop associated with the Chapel Royal was involved in Royal Navy operations – this time during the Second World War in 1941. On this occasion the clergyman in question was Gerald Ellison (RNVR) who later became dean of the Chapel Royal.

The theatre of operations was Crete, where the Royal Navy had been trying to prevent the Germans from carrying out a seaborne invasion. The decision to evacuate the 32,000 soldiers fighting on the island was taken on 27 May, involving naval evacuations from Heraklion and other small harbours on the south and east coasts, and the cruisers *Orion, Ajax* and *Dido* sailed to Heraklion to put this into effect. The future dean of the Chapel Royal was at this time chaplain of the *Orion*. The three cruisers evacuated the garrison of 4,000 from Heraklion and were subjected to air attacks in which the *Orion* and *Dido* were hit and badly damaged with loss of life. Aboard the *Orion* one bomb killed 260 and wounded 280 when it exploded in the messdecks, the bridge was machine-gunned killing the captain and wounding the admiral, the 'A' turret was hit, and for a while the ship was not only on fire but also out of control. Eventually it reached Alexandria displaying a heavy list.

In February 1945 Gerald Ellison visited HMS *Rodney* at Scapa Flow. He was accompanying the archbishop of York, Dr Garbett, having resumed his duties as the archbishop's senior chaplain at York. HMS *Rodney* had a chapel with stained glass covering the scuttles and a brocade altar-frontal made from hangings used at the coronation at Westminster Abbey in 1937, which had therefore formed part of the splendid surroundings in which the Chapel Royal sang at that service.

Gerald Ellison subsequently became dean of the Chapel Royal from 1972 until 1981 and, fittingly as such, led the prayers and service along with the Chapel Royal at the annual Service of Remembrance for the War Dead. The Second World War dates on the Cenotaph, executed in 1946, were carved by the recently retired keeper of the closet of H.M. Chapel Royal, John Lake, whose distinguished fifty-two years of service to the crown included at that time the post of monumental mason at the Ministry of Works.

Many unsung seafarers, soldiers and airmen have made great contributions to the life of the Chapel Royal either as members or supporters, some making the ultimate sacrifice for their sovereign and country. Let us, though, go back to the early seventeenth century and look at the efforts of one Dr John Layfield, the result of whose labours has affected everyone connected with the Chapel Royal since 1611.

The Authorised Version of the Bible, published in 1611 and appointed to be read in the Chapel Royal from that moment, contains from Genesis to the end of the Second Book of Kings the results of the work of Dr John Layfield. Layfield had accompanied the privateer George Clifford, earl of Cumberland, as his chaplain on the last of ten privateering voyages Cumberland led between 1586 and 1598. This last voyage saw Cumberland and Layfield sail in the 'merchant' ship *Scourge of Malice* on

Portrait by Nicholas Hilliard of George Clifford, earl of Cumberland, under whose command John Layfield sailed as chaplain on the privateering voyage of 1598 to Dominica. (Reproduced by courtesy of the National Maritime Museum, Greenwich)

6 March 1598. The fleet crossed the Atlantic to Dominica where Cumberland attacked Puerto Rico in a brilliantly executed operation. The fleet returned in October 1598 with treasure valued at 400,000 crowns. Layfield was a very observant man with a particular interest in architecture, and he noted down the details of the cathedral at Puerto Rico while the city was being sacked:

> faire and handsome; two rows of proportionate pillars, make two allies besides the middle walke, and this all along up to the high Altar. It is darker then commonly Countrie Churches in England. For the windows are few and little, and those indeed without glasse (whereof there is none to be found in all the towne) but covered with Canvas, so that the most of the light is received by the doores.

These acute architectural observations while participating in the sacking of a city were evidently a major factor in Layfield's favour when he was chosen to join the company of those at Westminster who were revising the Bible prior to publishing it by authority of the king as the 'Authorised Version' thirteen years after these privateering exploits. He seems to have been deliberately assigned to that part of the Bible which included the details and proportions of the temple of Solomon at Jerusalem. Few others at that time could have mastered this technical and intricate task, but Layfield had proved himself eminently qualified.

This was of the greatest significance for the Chapel Royal, for this segment of the Authorised Version of the Bible was to provide many 'texts' for sacred and liturgical music subsequently produced by the Chapel Royal composers. Let us choose as an example perhaps the finest piece of music ever to flow from the hands of the Chapel Royal composer G.F. Handel – the oratorio *Israel in Egypt*, composed in 1738.

The final section of this oratorio begins with the words 'Sing ye to the Lord for He hath triumphed gloriously' and is rendered by unaccompanied soprano solo. This is followed by full orchestra and chorus singing the words 'The Lord shall reign for ever and ever', 'The horse and his rider He hath thrown into the sea', and the choral 'For he hath triumphed gloriously'. Handel tells us where he found the words: 'Moses' Song, Exodus, chapter xv'. The words he chose were thus those written by Dr John Layfield in the Authorised Version of the Bible. Layfield translated the Hebrew thus: 'I will sing unto the Lord, for he hath triumphed gloriously: the horse and his rider hath he thrown into the sea',[3] and 'The Lord shall reign for ever and ever'.[4]

The authors of the Authorised Version, perhaps rather better known as the King James Bible, including of course Dr Layfield, submitted their completed efforts to James 'King of Great Britain, France and Ireland' in

---

[3] Exodus 25:1.
[4] Exodus 25:18.

This manuscript page of Handel's Oratorio *Israel in Egypt*, composed in 1738, displays the text: 'Sing ye to the Lord for He hath triumphed gloriously. The Lord shall reign for ever and ever.' These words, from Exodus 25, vv. 1 and 18, were taken from Dr John Layfield's translation for the Authorised Version of the Bible commissioned by James I and published in 1611. (RM 20 h.3, fol. 72v, reproduced by courtesy of the British Library)

a letter still to be found at the front of all these Bibles. Reference is made to contemporary events such as 'the setting of that bright Occidental Star, Queen Elizabeth, of most happy memory', but mostly to praise of James I for commissioning this great revision, for he had shown himself to be 'every day at home, by religious and learned discourse, by frequenting the house of God, by hearing the Word preached, by cherishing the teachers thereof, by caring for the Church, as a most tender and loving nursing father'. The authors noted how the King 'had once, out of deep judgement, apprehended how convenient it was, that, out of the original sacred Tongues, together with comparing of the labours, both in our own and other foreign languages, of many worthy men who went before us, there should be one more exact translation of the Holy Scriptures into the English Tongue'. They craved that 'it may receive approbation and patronage from so learned and judicious a Prince as Your Highness'. It did receive his approbation and was accordingly 'appointed to be read in Churches'.[5]

The Biblical textual skeleton provides the backbone to 'sacred' music, including anthems, and to some extent determines the parameters within which the music finds itself 'constrained'. The work of men such as Dr Layfield is therefore vital to a full appreciation of the development of music by the Chapel Royal.

[5] I am indebted to my mother-in-law, Mrs Jessie Smith, for the loan of her splendid Scottish edition of the King James Bible.

9

The English Chapel Royal in Scotland

The Scottish Chapel Royal established by James IV of Scotland in 1501 comprised sixteen canons, nine prebendaries and six boys. The Scottish Reformation severely curtailed church music, but despite this Mary queen of Scots tried to encourage the choral tradition. On her arrival in Scotland from France in 1561 sung mass was celebrated at the seat of her Chapel Royal, Stirling Castle, as well as at her chapel at Holyrood House. This, however, provoked considerable hostility, leading on both occasions to 'broken heads and bloody ears'. It seems that the attack on church musical accompaniment and perhaps also on unaccompanied choral works took its toll within the next ten years or so, for in 1571 the organ at Stirling Castle was dismantled by order of the captain of the castle.

In the 1580s an attempt was made to revive the choral and musical tradition, for in 1586 there was an effort to 'search and try out the old foundation'. The birth of prince Henry necessitated a royal baptism, and for this a new chapel was constructed at Stirling Castle in 1594 to replace the old ruinous building. A contemporary observer noted that 'the provost and prebends ... did sing the twenty-first psalm of David according to the art of music, to the great delectation of the noble auditory'. Although it was evidently the intention of James VI of Scotland to restore much of the grandeur of the Scottish Chapel Royal, it seems that on leaving Scotland in 1603 to be crowned James I of England he had to entrust responsibility for this to James Gibb, who had been one of the grooms of the bedchamber.

King James however remained determined to break the power of the Scottish Kirk – and even more so when he experienced what he regarded as the delights of the established Church of England. Accordingly he invited eight Scottish ministers, led by Andrew Melville, to London to discuss the situation with him. James took the opportunity this presented to commit Melville to the Tower of London for three years and forbid him ever to return to Scotland. James's views on Scottish Presbyterianism were clearly stated at the Hampton Court Conference of 1604 when he said: 'A Scotish Presbytery ... agreeth as well with a monarch as God and the Devil.' He went on to yell at one Scottish delegation: 'I give not a turd for your preaching!' He now set about trying

William Laud, archbishop of Canterbury. As dean of the Chapel Royal he accompanied Charles I to Scotland overland in 1633, while others of the English Chapel Royal sailed to Edinburgh from Tilbury. (Reproduced by courtesy of Hammersmith and Fulham Archives)

to anglicanise the Kirk, and the Scottish Chapel Royal was to be his instrument.

It was in these circumstances that the custody of the Scottish Chapel Royal was eased from the hands of James Gibb by bishop Cowper and preparations were set afoot at the chapel of Holyrood Palace to prepare for a royal visit by the king. Stalls for prebendaries and choir were decorated with carved and gilded angels and a new altar was dressed with ornate candlesticks. An organ was installed by Mr Dallam, who was paid £133 6s 8d for it, while Inigo Jones was commissioned to design its case.

James eventually arrived in Edinburgh on 16 May 1617, accompanied by William Laud, king's chaplain and future dean of the English Chapel Royal. It seems that at this time Laud was both dean of Gloucester Cathedral and king's chaplain. Nowadays a queen's chaplain is prohibited from holding office on preferment to the status of dean, but this example shows that it was not ever thus. The dean of the English Chapel Royal at this time was James Montague, bishop of Bath and Wells, who received for the use of the Chapel Royal £400 and a well-furnished ship, aboard which some or all of the Chapel Royal sailed to the Firth of Forth.

The day after his arrival James attended a choral service in the Holyrood Palace chapel, and on Whitsunday he went to communion celebrated by a number of the Scottish bishops. Before leaving Edinburgh he issued specific instructions that choral services should continue. This dean Cowper of the Scottish Chapel Royal successfully achieved, for we learn from a letter he wrote to the king in September 1618 that 'the organs and musicians, four on every part, men and boys, agreed in pleasant harmony, to the contentment of all, because they understood what was sung'. The general populace of Edinburgh however remained very distrustful of these developments.

Dean Lamb held office for two years in succession to dean Cowper, and then the office of dean was attached to the bishopric of Dunblane. Dean John Bellenden continued the efforts to further the musical excellence of the Scottish Chapel Royal, suggesting the appropriation of 'prebendaries, chaplainries and altarages'. James agreed to this request, but it aroused so much opposition that on his death Charles I had to reverse the decision.

Charles I thus faced a delicate situation in Scotland. He directed William Laud to revise the services along the lines of those conducted by the English Chapel Royal. As he was dean of the English Chapel Royal from 1626-33 Laud was in a particularly good position to achieve results. Court attendance with the Scottish Chapel Royal at Holyrood Palace chapel was tightened up by an order requiring members of the Scottish Council and other departments of state to attend communion there – the administration of communion itself being conducted to the sound of trumpets at the king's command.

A key man was appointed to a prebend of the Scottish Chapel Royal, becoming as well director of music and receiver of revenues. This man, Edward Kelly, had been servant to the high chancellor of Scotland (the viscount of Diplene) but was now to play a crucial role in advancing the cause of music, both instrumental and choral, in the Scottish Chapel Royal.

In 1630 Kelly came to London to visit the Chapel Royal in order to learn at first hand how services were conducted by them. He ended up by seeing to the copying out of 'twelve great books, gilded, and twelve small ones with an organ book' from those used by the English Chapel Royal, which took five months. He also engaged an organist, 'two men for playing on the cornets and sackbutts, and two boys for singing divisions in the verses'. This supplemented his existing Scottish Chapel Royal to the extent that it now comprised at least sixteen men, six boys and one organist. Kelly was able to write to the king in a report dated 24 January 1631/2 that the boys now practised daily in a room especially set aside for them, and that they were joined by the men for a full rehearsal twice weekly. When singing in the chapel the men wore black gowns and the boys 'sad-coloured coats'. It is known that the choir was seated antiphonally as in London and that before the sermon was preached the Scottish Chapel Royal sang a full anthem and afterwards 'an anthem alone in verses with the organ'.

This was the situation on the eve of Charles I's intended visit to Scotland for his crowning as king of Scotland in 1633. The king set off by land for Scotland accompanied by William Laud. A large portion of the English Chapel Royal, consisting of sixteen gentlemen, eight children of the Chapel, two organists and officers of the vestry, sailed to Scotland from Tilbury aboard the *Dreadnought*. Their names are detailed in the lord chamberlain's papers and were entered as follows:

1633 May

List of those appointed to wayte on his Majesty in his Scottish journey, 1633, as it was signed by his Majesty 1632:–

Trumpeters

Sergeant Broome	Peter Jones
Robert Ramsey	Richard Stocke
Randolph Floyd	Edward Juxe
George Porter	William Ramsey

The Chappell
Bases

Thomas Piers, Senior	John Frost, Junior
Ezechell Waade	Ralph Amner
Roger Nightingale	Thomas Rayment

Tenors

George Cooke	John Frost, Senior
John Clarke	Walter Porter

Contratenors

Thomas Day	Richard Sandy
Thomas Pierse	Thomas Laughton
Henry Lawes	Nathaniel Pownell

Organists

John Tomkins	Giles Tomkins
Eight Children of the Chappell[1]	

---

[1] LC vol. 738 (at end of volume).

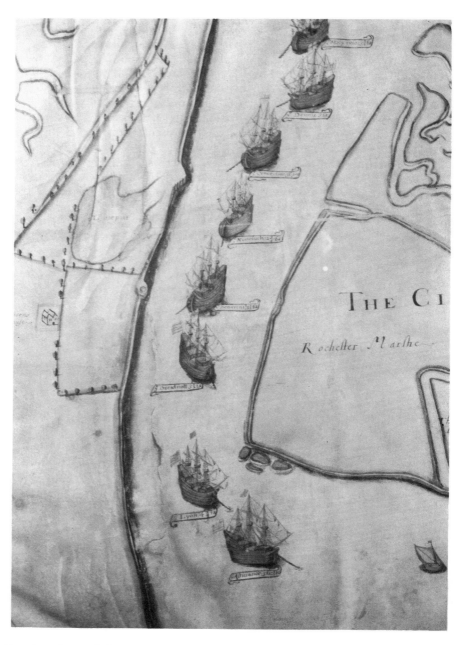

Dreadnought, sixth from the top, as depicted on a map showing the fleet at anchor off Rochester Marsh in 1633. (Courtesy of the Duke of Northumberland and reproduced with his Grace's permission)

9. The English Chapel Royal in Scotland

The details of the transport arrangements for the Chapel Royal on Charles I's progress into Scotland in May 1633 are to be found in the Bodleian Register on folios 42 and 42b. We learn from this entry that 'a petition was delivered to his Majesty for foure hundred pownds, for a shipp to carry the Gentlemen, and their goods'. We learn, too, that not all this sum was immediately forthcoming, for 'three hundred pounds were graunted, which they had by privy seale out of the exchequer' but 'A shipp was granted allso', and an additional £53 was acquired by a different route – 'procured by Mr Secretary Cooke being one of the Commissioners appoynted for the orderinge of the progress'. This additional money was directed to 'Sir Sampson Dowell victuler of the Navie' from the exchequer. Sir Sampson then delivered the money to 'Mr Sidenham the captaine of the shipp called the Dreadnought, where in the gentlemen of the chappell and officers of the Vestry were with the stuff, and allso the Children of the Chappell'. The £300 was then distributed.

> There went into Scotland of the gentlemen of the Chappell 19, they had 12 li a peece which came viz in toto to 228 li ... There went of the Children of the Chappell eight they had amongst them delivered to their Master a great part viz – 12 li. The Serjaunt of the Vestry had a great part viz – 12 li. One Yeoman and the groome of the vestry then goinge had vi li a peece in toto – 12 li. The two servants of the Chappell and vestry had 40 s a peece viz – 4 li. The remainder of the 300 li was left remayninge in the Deane of the Chappells hands which was distributed amongst such gentlemen of the Chappell as he thought best deserved in that journey of which the Sub-dean had v li and divers of the gent. 20 s a peece and i think the serjaunt of the vestry had 20 s.

This last comment tells us that the author of the entry was almost certainly neither the sub-dean nor the serjeant of the vestry, but most likely the clerk of the cheque of the Chapel Royal.

We also know of the boarding arrangements for the start of the voyage. The passage concerned runs thus: 'The Lord Chamberlain then gave his warrant to the Master of the Kinges Barge for barges and lighters to carry the gentlemen and the rest with their stuff, copes, surplesses etc. from Whitehall to the shipp which lay then at Tilbury hope neare Graves End.'[2]

As we saw in Chapter 5, in 1573 the task of 'Bergehier and Botehier to Hampton Court' necessary for transporting the companies of child players, including the children of the Chapel Royal, was given 'to Bruton of Powles wharf' who then had at his disposal at least 'a bardge and vi ores with ii Tylt whirreyes' large enough to carry 'Masking geare and children with their tutors and an Italian woman'. The waterman, Mr Bruton, could perhaps be regarded as the predecessor of the 'Master of

---

[2] Bodleian Register fol. 41b.

173

The battle off Dunnose, Isle of Wight, was one of the actions in which *Dreadnought* took part during the defeat of the Spanish Armada in 1588. This illustration is from a contemporary tapestry. (Reproduced by courtesy of the National Maritime Museum, Greenwich)

Kinges Barge' of 1633 who had 'barges and lighters' at his disposal to take the Chapel Royal from Whitehall to the *Dreadnought* anchored off Gravesend.

Dreadnought had seen much action since her construction and launch at Deptford on 10 November 1573 as a 400-ton royal naval 'great ship' of forty-one guns. She measured 80 feet in length, 30 feet in beam, and 16 feet in depth. In April 1587 she played a leading role in the sinking and capture of thirty-seven ships in the Bay of Cadiz, an expedition which Drake described as having 'singed the King of Spain's beard'. While returning from this she participated in the capture of the *San Felipe*[3] and subsequently distinguished herself in the defeat of the Spanish Armada of 1588, taking part in action off Lyme Regis on 23 July, off Dunnose Point on the Isle of Wight on Thursday 25 July, and off Gravelines on Monday 29 July. In 1589 under vice-admiral Thomas Fenner she took part in Francis Drake's expedition which resulted in the capture of

---

[3] Papers found on board the *San Felipe* revealed the enormous profits the Spanish were harvesting from the East Indies, and this led directly to the foundation of the East India Company of London.

Corunna shortly before low tide at midnight on 24/25 April.[4] She was re-built in 1592, joining the fleet again at the capture of Brest in 1594 and Cadiz in 1597. The future lord high almoner with the Chapel Royal, but in 1597 only one of the ship's chaplains to Essex, George Mountain, took part in this attack upon Cadiz.[5] *Dreadnought* subsequently took part in the 1597 expedition to the Azores and the attack on Coimbra in 1602. She was re-built yet again in 1613, classed as a third-rate vessel, and took part in another expedition to Cadiz in 1625.

In 1633, in her sixtieth year, *Dreadnought* was made available to the Chapel Royal for their journey to Scotland for Charles I's coronation at Edinburgh as king of Scotland. While his numerous retinue sailed up the coast, the king made his own journey to Scotland by land, accompanied by the dean of the Chapel Royal.

On 31 May 1633 the king and his retinue stayed a night with the bishop of Durham at Aukland Castle, making a ceremonial entry into Durham on 1 June where he was met by the high sheriff and gentlemen of the county. He went straight to the cathedral, where elaborate preparations had been made for him, including a specially bound and embroidered folio Prayer Book as a gift for his use, and new copes for the clergy.[6] Charles, after saying the Lord's prayer at the north door, processed under a canopy of state held by eight prebendaries in surplices to a chair in the second bay of the choir, near the font, on the south side. He listened to an address of welcome from dean Hunt, and prayers were said for the success of his journey to Scotland. Following the singing of the Te Deum Charles then went to see the tombs of St Cuthbert at the east end and the Venerable Bede in the Galilee chapel at the west end. He was presented with a gift of a splendid rich cope, which he handed to William Laud for use with the English Chapel Royal. If it was one of the series made specially for Charles's visit to Durham then it may well have looked like the one the cathedral still possesses. Having received a petition requesting confirmation of the ancient rights of the cathedral, the king retired to Durham Castle.

The next morning the king attended matins in the cathedral, taking the dean of the English Chapel Royal with him, and we know that 'none were admitted save his nobles, the clergy and the choir'.[7] The sermon was preached by the bishop. After the service the king went to dine at the deanery, although at the bishop's expense, and then attended evensong before returning to the castle where he 'touched' several people to rid them of the king's evil. Entertaining the king, the dean of the Chapel

---

[4] The preliminary planning chart for this attack at Corunna in 1589 has been discovered and identified by my brother, Robert Baldwin, Curator of Cartography and Hydrography at the National Maritime Museum, Greenwich.

[5] See Chapter 8.

[6] One of these copes is still in the cathedral's possession.

[7] *The Correspondence of John Cosin* (Surtees Society, 1868), p. 212.

A globe chalice similar to the one shown here may well have been used aboard the *Dreadnought* on the Chapel Royal's voyage to Scotland in 1633. This example takes the form of a gilt brass celestial globe, hallmarked for Frankfurt-am-Main in 1589. (Reproduced by courtesy of the National Maritime Museum, Greenwich)

Royal and others of the retinue cost the bishop of Durham £1,500 a day!

Meanwhile the rest of the English Chapel Royal had been sailing up the North Sea, and we can speculate as to what form of services were held on board the *Dreadnought* on this voyage. In a letter dated 21 June 1623 from the secretary of the privy council to the earl of Rutland just ten years before this voyage mention is made of the 'Inferior officers and mariners when they have been at common prayer and Singing of Psalms, which is the ancient custom of relieving and setting of watches' and goes on to impart the king's command for 'all the captayns and officers of ships to be very carefull that noe scandalous words nor actions be offered, especially when the ship's company shall be at either prayers or at the singing of the psalmes'.[8] If the king's command was obeyed on the 1633 voyage the Chapel Royal would either have augmented or participated in this naval routine or conducted separate services themselves. We learn further from the surveyor at Chatham in 1624, Joshua Downing, that the 'Common prayers allowed by his Matie. [were] namely ... the Lord's prayer the belief & the ten Commandmts'.[9] It is very likely that the *Dreadnought* would have followed these normal practices, and she may

[8] *Calendar of State Papers Domestic, James I, 1619-1623*, vol. 147, p. 28.
[9] *Calendar of State Papers Domestic, James I, 1623-1625*, vol. 182, p. 29.

well have possessed a globe chalice for administering the eucharist.

Charles I met the English Chapel Royal at Edinburgh on 15 June 1633. He was duly crowned king of Scotland with full Anglican rites in the abbey church at Holyrood with great ceremony and much music. He had brought with him the six state trumpeters listed above in case of shortage of instruments or players in Scotland. A suspicious observer at the coronation noted the English and Scottish Chapel Royal choirs, the surplices and the music, and went on to write:

> There was a four-cornered table in the manner of an altar standing within the kirk having thereupon two books, with two waxed chandeliers and two waxed candles which were unlighted, and a basin wherein there was nothing. At the back of this altar there was a rich tapestry wherein the crucifix was curiously wrought; and as these bishops who were in service passed by this crucifix, they were seen to bow their knee and beck, which bred great fear of in-bringing of popery![10]

The bishops in fact wore blue copes with gold embroidery.

The repercussions of Charles's Scottish visit were not as he would have hoped. He had thought that the splendour of the English Chapel Royal would help to capture the imagination of the Scots and attract them to the Anglican rites. This task was entrusted to William Laud, who was elevated from dean of the Chapel Royal to archbishop of Canterbury after the Scottish visit.

Within two months of the court's return from Scotland, the king wrote to dean Bellenden of the Scottish Chapel Royal requiring that services be sung twice daily 'with the choir, as well in our absences as otherwise'. Archbishop Laud now required that the Scottish clergy wear gowns or surplices, and, apparently as a reward for his efforts with the Scottish Chapel Royal, in October 1633 a certificate was issued 'that Mr Edward Kelly is sworn Master of His Majesty's Chappell in Scotland'.[11]

Things certainly did not go the way Charles intended, for it was not long before dean Bellenden wrote to Laud to explain that there was a lack of money resulting in the gentleman of the choir being paid at irregular intervals and becoming very poorly off. Laud promised relief but apparently did nothing. There was some suspicion that Mr Kelly was embezzling Chapel Royal funds. Although this was not proven, Kelly was replaced as master by Edward Miller in 1635. However, Miller's chances of success were curtailed by Charles's intention to foist a new prayer book on the Scots. Realising that the English Book of Common Prayer would be unwelcome, he ordered a commission to prepare a 'Revised Prayer Book' for Scotland, which was read for the first time in St Giles's Church, Edinburgh on 23 July 1637. The reaction was violent. Hardly had Dr

---

[10] Quoted in T. Steel, *Scotland's Story* (Collins, London, 1984), p. 100.
[11] LC vol. 738.

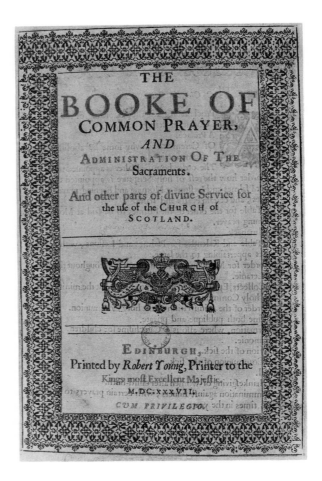

Title page of Charles I's 'Revised Prayer Book' for Scotland which caused a riot when read for the first time at St Giles's Church, Edinburgh, on 23 July 1637. (Reproduced by courtesy of the Trustees of the National Library of Scotland)

Hanna, the dean, begun the service before there was a riot in the church. Armed guards expelled the rioters, but the Scottish privy council had to take refuge inside Holyrood Palace while the public rioted and demonstrated in Edinburgh and other Scottish towns.

Holyrood chapel was badly damaged. The minister for Kilwinning, Robert Baillie, noted in his *Letters and Journals* that 'Almost all our nobility and gentry of both sexes count that book little better than the Mass'. Opposition to Charles was soon organised and on 28 February 1638 the 'National Covenant' was signed, declaring that the king's church reforms 'tend to the re-establishment of the Popish religion and tyranny, and to the subversion of the true reformed religion, and of our liberties,

178

laws and estates'. No less than 150 nobles signed the original document, and subsequent days saw many more sign copies, culminating in the entire Edinburgh congregation in March 1638.

War loomed, and Charles told his council that he would have to raise an army against 'this small cloud in the North'. He was advised by the duke of Northumberland in the following terms: 'I think there is reason to fear that a great part of them will be readier to join with the Scots than to draw their swords in the King's service ... God send us a good end of this troublesome business, for to my apprehension no foreign enemies could threaten so much danger to this Kingdom as doth now this beggardly nation.'

The king's two efforts to force the submission of the Covenanters by an army ended in humiliating defeat for his own forces, while the cost of it all forced him to summon Parliament. The English Parliament then took up arms to defend its rights in opposition to the despotic behaviour and demands of the king. While Charles ordered repairs to the Holyrood chapel, the Scottish Parliament excommunicated Bellenden and Wedderburn. Civil war broke out in England too and in 1642 Charles raised his standard at Nottingham while the English Parliament sought help from the Scottish Covenanters. This was forthcoming in the shape of the 'Solemn League and Covenant' signed by Argyll and the English Parliamentarians in 1643.

As we have seen, the Chapel Royal played an important role in the origins of this discontent. It was partly the sight of divine service conducted by the English Chapel Royal in Edinburgh according to the king's wishes and its emulation, enforced or otherwise, by the Scottish Chapel Royal, that provided the first-hand 'evidence' of the king's intention to inflict Anglicanism on the Presbyterian stronghold of Scotland – at least in the eyes of the Scots. The visit of the English Chapel Royal to Scotland in 1633 must have been an abiding memory in the minds of those who saw it or heard about it. Indeed the presence of the *Dreadnought* in the Firth of Forth would have been a dramatic sight in itself.

It was to the Scottish at Newark that Charles surrendered in May 1646. He refused to accept the Covenant and was therefore handed over to the English Parliamentarians. The Covenanters were to offer the king a last-minute escape, sending a representative group to the Isle of Wight to talk to him at Carisbrooke Castle. He still refused their terms and therefore any hope of military support. Charles I thus faced death on the scaffold outside the Banqueting House in Whitehall on 30 January 1649.

There were, however, some strange twists in the story of the Chapel Royal and the Civil War which could have, and very nearly did, result in a very different outcome, as we shall see in Chapter 10.

179

10

Hammond: King's Chaplain or Cromwell's Spy?

A gale-force wind was blowing and rain was pelting down on Hampton Court as Charles I made his escape from the palace at the dead of night on 11 November 1647. He made his way to Thames Ditton, having rendezvoused with one of the grooms of the bedchamber, colonel William Legge. There he met colonel John Ashburnham and Sir John Berkeley, who were waiting with horses. The royal party now set off for Bishops Sutton in Hampshire, where a change of horses was waiting for them, with the king as guide. He had estimated they would reach it about three hours before dawn broke, but the foul weather caused the king to lose his way in Windsor forest to the west of his planned route. Dawn broke as they reached Farnham and it was daylight by the time they finally reached Bishops Sutton. The servant providing the change of horses there at the inn had to make his way out of the inn and warn the royal party against their rendezvous there, as the county committee was meeting on Parliamentary business. The change of horses was accomplished secretly despite this, but the party clearly had to press on. The king ordered them to dismount and walk the horses down the hill, while he apparently considered what to do next.

Colonel Berkeley suggested he make for the west country, but the king rejected the idea and said he had decided to try the Isle of Wight. He then declared that he and colonel Legge would ride to the earl of Southampton's house at Tichfield, on Southampton Water, while colonel Ashburnham and Sir John Berkeley would lay a false trail by riding further on to Lymington, crossing to Yarmouth at the west tip of the Isle of Wight, and then ride east nine miles to Carisbrooke to talk with colonel Hammond, the newly appointed governor of the Isle of Wight, in the hope that he would not be unfavourable to the king's presence.

As it happened, gale-force winds and rough seas in the Solent prevented Ashburnham and Berkeley from crossing to Yarmouth from Lymington, where they had arrived on the evening of Friday 12 November. They crossed first thing on Saturday morning and rode to Carisbrooke Castle, reaching it just after 10 o'clock. They arried to find they had just missed Hammond who had left for Newport, the capital,

180

with militia officers and some gentlemen. Newport was barely a mile from the castle, and Ashburnham and Berkeley managed to overtake Hammond on the road.

Berkeley, acting as spokesman, asked Hammond if he knew who was near him. Hammond replied he did not, to which Berkeley added 'Even good King Charles who is come from Hampton Court for fear of being murder'd privately'. Hammond's reaction, according to Berkeley, was that 'he grew so pale, and fell into such a trembling, that I did really believe he would have fallen off his horse'. The outcome, however, was that Hammond agreed to act as nothing more than a man of honour and honesty but would do what he could, for he had to observe his 'Trust to the Army' too. Hammond finally suggested that they all set off to see the king, and this was agreed. So the party headed off for Cowes, where the commander of Cowes Castle, captain Basket, was asked to join them by Hammond. They then sailed up Southampton Water and landed at Tichfield. Only then did Ashburnham tell Hammond that the king was at the earl of Southampton's house.

The earl was strongly royalist. We know from the Old Cheque Book that he had been christened at a Chapel Royal service: 'James, the sonne and heire of the right honorable the Earll of Southampton, was baptized in the Chappell in the third yeare of his Maj. raigne, when was payd to the Gentlemen of the Chappell for fees 5 li.' A marginal note reads: 'Baptized in March the 26 daye 1605 ... The Deanes fee 10 li.'

Ashburnham went ahead of the party to let the king know of Hammond's presence, and found him waiting nervously for news from Southampton of a boat that could take him to France – apparently unaware that all the ports were closed. After half an hour's private deliberation the king eventually invited Hammond into his room. Hammond and Basket kissed his hand on entering his presence – a fact worth noting, as we shall see. Hammond told the king that he would do all he could to meet the king's demands in relation to the orders and directions of Parliament. Charles understood this and agreed to go along with him. About two hours later the royal party sailed for the Isle of Wight, arriving at Cowes where the king was accommodated for the night, not in the small Henrician castle but in the local inn, the Plume of Feathers. Meanwhile Hammond worked through the night and wrote a letter informing Parliament that the king was now on the Isle of Wight. That Sunday morning the king and his escort left Cowes and reached Carisbrooke Castle. This was to be his 'home' until events forced his return to London.

But why the Isle of Wight, and how did the king escape from Hampton Court Palace in the first place? Behind all this there is a story of intrigue in which a member of the Chapel Royal played a key role. The first clue to this surrounds colonel Hammond's appointment as governor of the Isle of Wight.

A contemporary pamphlet entitled 'His Majesties Demands to Colonel Hammond' contained this illustration on the title page showing Charles I and Robert Hammond, governor of Carisbrooke Castle on the Isle of Wight. Colonel Hammond was J. Meade Faulkner's inspiration for the character John Mohune (Blackbeard) in *Moonfleet*. (Thomason Tracts E446(24), reproduced by courtesy of the British Library)

Robert Hammond was twenty-six years old on his appointment. Under Parliament he had risen to the command of an infantry regiment in the New Model Army. He was commissioned as a captain in July 1642, became a colonel in 1645 and governor of Exeter in 1646, and was very influential in the formulation of army objectives in 1647. But during that year his views changed from those of a militant Independent defying Parliament's request that the army be disbanded and refusing to go to Ireland, to a much more conservative and moderate stance. The reason was the rise of the Levellers, of whom Hammond soon openly disapproved. Cromwell was later to write to Hammond recalling that he had 'through dissatisfaction ... desired retirement from the army, and thought of quiet in the Isle of Wight'. Ashburnham was to recall a conversation with Hammond as the royal party headed for the Isle of Wight 'upon the Highway near Kingston, and found him not very averse to his Majesty'. Hammond told Ashburnham that 'hee was going downe to his Government because hee found the Armie was resolv'd to breake all promises with the King, and that hee would have nothing to doe with such perfidious actions'.

The method of appointment of Robert Hammond to the governorship of the Isle of Wight is curious. The usual practice was for governors to be appointed by royal patent, but with the removal of the royalist earl of Portland in 1642, Parliament made the appointment of his successor, the earl of Pembroke. Pembroke governed the island through the entire course of the Civil War, mainly through his deputy, colonel Carne. On 1 September 1647 general Fairfax wrote to the speaker of the House of Lords that the earl of Pembroke was satisfied in the 'disposall of the Government of the Isle of Wight to Colonel Robert Hammond'. On 3 September Pembroke himself told the House of Lords that general Fairfax required colonel Hammond's appointment as governor – 'he being a person looked upon by the General as a fit Person for that Trust'. That day the Lords drafted his appointment, which was then accepted by Parliament. On 18 September colonel Hammond was elected and sworn a burgess of Newport, and on 1 October he was made vice-admiral of the county of Hampshire and the Isle of Wight. Pembroke in fact had to be edged out of the post on the pretext of 'crimes against the state', according to a Venetian source in London. This suggests rapid preparation for some purpose.

Clarendon observed that 'Hammond himself left the Army but two or three days before the King's remove, and went to the Isle of Wight at a season when there was no visible occasion to draw him thither'. Sir John Oglander of Nunwell House wrote: 'Hammond was made Commander of the Isle of Wight purposely to be King Charles's Keeper'. Rumours were rife that Cromwell had to move Charles out of reach of the army Levellers who threatened to kill him, and therefore put his moderate colleague, Hammond, on the island, allowed the king to escape from Hampton Court Palace, and forced his hand to choose the Isle of Wight option. This may seem fantastic, but it was widely believed at the time.

A shadowy series of backstairs manoeuvres by a king's chaplain of the Chapel Royal had played a key role in these events. The Rev. Henry Hammond (1605-1660) was educated at Eton and Magdalen College, Oxford. He became a fellow and gained his MA in 1625, after which he was appointed incumbent of Penshurst in 1633, earned his DD in 1639, and became archdeacon of Chichester in 1643. His *Practical Catechism* brought him to the notice of the king in 1644, after which he became a canon of Christ Church and public orator at Oxford in 1645, as well as serving as chaplain to the royal commissioners at Uxbridge in 1645. He was finally appointed a royal chaplain to the king in 1647. He was later to find himself deprived and imprisoned, but afterwards he was permitted to live with Sir Philip Warwick and Sir John Packington. He published his *Paraphrase and Annotations on the New Testament* in 1653. He was in fact colonel Robert Hammond's uncle.

During September 1647 Robert Hammond was met by his uncle, who took him to see the king at Hampton Court Palace. Robert Hammond was brought before the king and 'recommended to him as a penitent convert ... which his Majesty taking it well, he gave him his hand to kiss'. There is no reason to doubt this account, for one of the criticisms of the Levellers was that Cromwell and other officials were visiting the king and 'kneele and kiss and fawn upon him'.[1] The kissing of the hand was, as we have seen, repeated at the earl of Southampton's house when Robert Hammond accompanied Berkeley and Ashburnham to see the king in hiding there.

The last recorded visit to Charles I at Hampton Court was on the day before his escape by none other than the earl of Southampton. If Henry Hammond, the king's chaplain, had a key role to play apart from introducing Charles to his future captor, then it was to 'square off' the escape route with the earl of Southampton. He may even have played a double agent's role if, as has been speculated, he was actually working as a spy and agent of Cromwell.

Henry Hammond continued to visit the king at Carisbrooke, where his nephew was now captain of the castle, along with other chaplains to the king on the strength of the Chapel Royal, until they were prohibited from the castle at the end of December 1647. The king then refused the services of the Parliamentary chaplains. Up to that time, though, the king maintained a 'public' profile of divine status by 'touching' a continual stream of loyal subjects at the castle to rid them of the king's evil. In early July 1648 Lord Rich was given a permit to visit the king to be touched for the king's evil, but the secretary of the spy-breaking Derby House committee wrote to colonel Hammond privately on 6 July to warn him that Rich's real intentions were to consult the king about the Royalist revolt in Surrey.

On the night of 20 March 1648 Charles was frustrated in his attempt at a well-planned escape from the castle when he became wedged while attempting to escape through his iron-barred windows. He eventually managed to climb back inside his room, but Osborne and Worsley's waiting horses and boat had to vanish quietly as it became clear that the escape had failed.

The king's morale was raised at the news of the well-executed escape of his son, the fourteen-year-old James, duke of York, from house-arrest at St James's Palace on 21 April 1648. The duke of York, marquis of Worcester and princess Elizabeth were all at this time confined at St James's Palace under the eye of the duke of Northumberland. Nevertheless, agents of the emigré court that had settled in Holland managed to establish some sort of contact with the young duke of York and an escape was planned. Thus on that Friday evening, under the guise of a game of

---

[1] See J.D. Jones, *The Royal Prisoner* (Lutterworth Press, Guildford & London, 1965) p. 28.

Charles I imprisoned at Carisbrooke Castle, as depicted in a contemporary cartoon. (Thomason Tracts E422(29), reproduced by courtesy of the British Library)

hide-and-seek, James slipped through a door in the park into the helping hands of a colonel Bampfield. They stopped at a 'safe-house' for James to put on girl's clothes and then slipped down the Thames in a skiff to rendezvous with a large boat which took them safely to Holland.

Charles's last hope had been to agree to the terms of the Scottish Commissioners who visited Carisbrooke Castle in December 1647. He initially signed a treaty at the castle, and a copy was secretly buried in a garden on the island to be retrieved later by agents. However, he could not bring himself to recognise the Solemn League and Covenant by which Scotland had revolted against the imposition of the rule of bishops and the trappings of the English church, especially as he would have had to allow the establishment of Presbyterianism for three years in England as part of the agreement. The treaty of Newport collapsed, and on 1 December 1648 Charles was brought to Hurst Castle on the banks of the Solent, observing at the time that he was leaving the best castle in England for the worst. Following Pride's Purge of the House of Commons, after which the army officially seized power, the king was taken to Windsor Castle and then to St James's Palace, where he spent his last few days before his execution as a 'tyrant, traitor, murderer, and public enemy to the good people of this nation'.

This drawing of Carisbrooke Castle was made by John Livesay in 1798 and shows the window through which Charles I tried to escape in March 1648. The king's window was the lowest of the set of four beneath the high gabled building to the right of the drawing. The windows were re-modelled in 1856. (Reproduced by courtesy of the Trustees, Carisbrooke Castle Museum)

The details of his last days are well chronicled. From the Chapel Royal's point of view it is interesting that the king had mass celebrated according to the rites of the Church of England either in his sleeping quarters or in the king's chapel, colour court, on the morning of his execution. He was beheaded at about two o'clock in the afternoon on Tuesday 30 January 1649 outside the Banqueting House. The reason for the delay in his execution that day was that a curious constitutional crisis had developed. It was suddenly realised that the House of Commons had omitted to pass a measure actually abolishing the monarchy and that the execution of Charles would merely result in the automatic succession of his son to the throne. A measure was therefore hurriedly passed in the course of the morning 'that no person whatsoever should presume to declare Charles Stewart (son of the late Charles) commonly called the Prince of Wales, or any other person, to be King, or chief magistrate, of England and Ireland ...'. In fact the monarchy was not officially abolished until six weeks after the execution of the king.

Charles's execution found its way into the Chapel Royal's liturgy soon after the Restoration. In 1662 a form of liturgy was devised to commemorate his martyrdom which is still used by the Chapel Royal today, while the Restoration paten of Charles II, and the alms dish and candlesticks of James, duke of York, Charles I's two sons, adorn the altar. The liturgical choices available include reference to 'our gracious

10. Hammond: King's Chaplain or Cromwell's Spy?

Sovereign King Charles the First' who was 'taken away by the hands of cruel and bloody men', and to the 'anointed and blessed King Charles the First' who was caused to 'fall into the hands of violent and blood-thirsty men, and barbarously to be murdered by them, yet thou didst not leave us for ever, as sheep without shepherd; but by thy gracious providence didst miraculously preserve the undoubted Heir of his Crowns our then gracious Sovereign King Charles the Second, from his bloody enemies, hiding him under the shadow of thy wings, until their tyranny was overpast; and didst bring him back, in thy good appointed time, to sit upon the throne of his father; and together with the Royal Family didst restore to us our ancient Government in Church and State.'

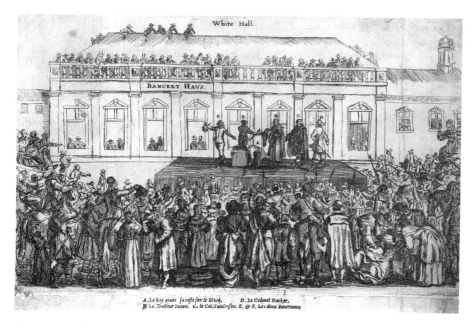

The regicide of Charles I outside the Banqueting House on 30 January 1649, as depicted in a contemporary illustration. The former dean of the Chapel Royal, bishop Juxon (marked B) is shown accompanying the king. (Reproduced by courtesy of the Guildhall Library, City of London)

187

11

The Restoration Chapel

The Chapel Royal buildings were not well treated under Cromwell and the Commonwealth, as the records of the destruction of the fabric at Whitehall chapel under Cromwell show. Shortly after 1644 the east window of stained glass was destroyed, for John Rutland was paid £7 'for 241 feet of new white glass set up in the East window of the King's Chapel at Whitehall'. There was, too, a 'receipt for ... taking down the cross at Whitehall and for colouring the boards from which the carpenter had planed off the pictures'; a 'receipt ... for cutting down the stem of the cross over the chapel at Whitehall'; and a 'receipt ... for work done in the Chapel of Whitehall about defacing pictures and plastering the walls'.

The year 1644 also saw the organ removed from the chapel at Whitehall, but the building seems to have retained its consecrated status as Cromwell's own daughters, Frances and Mary, seem to have been married there to Robert Rich, grandson of the earl of Warwick, and Thomas Belasyse, viscount Fauconberg. Clarendon mentions that 'the marriages were performed in public view' – suggesting the Chapel Royal building – and that they occurred on 11 and 19 November 1657 'at Whitehall, with all imaginable pomp and lustre'.[1] Indeed, an account of the wedding feast of Frances and Robert Rich mentions that there were '48 violins and 50 trumpets, and much mirth with frolics, besides mixt dancing (a thing heretofore accounted profane) till 5 of the clock' on the next morning.[2] Robert Rich died only a few months later on 16 February 1658 'in his apartments in Whitehall'. Cromwell was fortunate that both he and the chapel building were around at all to host these marriages, for the building had been the scene of an assassination attempt upon him by Miles Sindercombe in 1656, which, if successful, would have destroyed the chapel by fire.[3]

Four years later Cromwell was dead and Charles II set about restoring the Chapel Royal in grand style, as we shall see.

---

[1] *History of the Rebellion*, ch. 25, p. 510.

[2] Letter written by William Dugdale, dated 14 November 1657, reproduced in Historic Monuments Commission, Appendix to 5th Report, p. 177.

[3] The details are to be found in a tract published in 1658 entitled 'The Triall of Miles Sindercombe'. See p. 103 above.

This organ stood in the Chapel Royal, Whitehall Palace, until Oliver Cromwell ordered it to be stripped out. It was acquired by Magdalen College, Oxford, and shortly afterwards sold to Sir Thomas Cave who placed it in St Nicholas's Church, Stanford-on-Avon, Northamptonshire, in 1649/50, where it has been ever since. This photograph was taken by the sub-dean of the Chapel Royal in 1985.

A document of the lord chamberlain's office dated 2 July 1660 records that John Hingeston, 'tuner and repairer of organs, virginalls and wind instruments', was sworn into office. He set to work quickly to instal an old organ at Whitehall chapel. However, Samuel Pepys wrote in his diary on 17 June 1660: 'This day the organs did begin to play at White Hall before the King'. It was only nineteen days since Charles's triumphant arrival in London after nine years of poverty and exile. A British Museum manuscript contains an entry which reads: 'June, 1660. The Seventeenth, his majesty's Chapell att whitehall was fitted with organs and all other things fitt for his majesty, which was the first day that his majesty was at his devocetion theire.'[4] This confirms Pepys's observation. This organ evidently lasted two years, for on 10 December 1662 Hingeston was paid £200 of £900 owed him for further work done installing a new organ at the Whitehall chapel. A warrant at the Public Record Office describes this new organ as a 'fair double organ for Whitehall Chapel'. Freeman writes that there is little doubt that this organ was the first built by Father Smith.[5] On 19 April 1664 Hingeston was paid a further £300 of the sum owed, with the final £400 paid on 22 November 1664. He did a good job and no repairs were necessary there until 1668, at which time he was owed £100 for repairs he made to it.[6] The money owed for this was finally paid on 27 November 1668. Further 'regulating and repairing' was necessary the next year in 1669, for which Hingeston was paid £130, and after this no further repairs were needed until 1681.

On 7 October 1662 Hingeston was described as 'keeper of His Majesty's organs', a post which included the task of ordering the 'curtain of crimson damaske 12 yards in breadth and 2 yards in depth for the organ loft and gallery of his Majesty's Chappell Royall at Whitehall'.[7] In a warrant dated 20 August 1663 there is a directive

> to the surveyor general to make and erect a large organ loft by his Majesty's Chappell at Whitehall, in the place where formerley the great double organ stood, and to rebuild the rooms over the bellowes roome, two stories high, as it was formerley, the lower story for the subdeane of his Majesty's Chappell, and the upper storey with two rooms, one of them for the organist in wayting and the other for the keeper and repayrer of his majesty's organs, harpsicords, virginalls, and other instruments, each room to have a chymney, and boxes and shelves for keeping the materials belonging to the organ, and the organ books.[8]

Hingeston, whom we know from this document to have lived in quarters above the sub-dean at Whitehall chapel, was busy too at the other chapels customarily used by the Chapel Royal. Thus a warrant of 1 April 1663 talks of a payment of £67 11s to Hingeston for 'removing and setting up an organ in her Majesty's Chappell at St James', for removing another organ from Whitehall to St James' for the French musick, and for the portage of a large organ from Mr Nicoe's to St James, and setting it up there'.[9] Hingeston was shortly afterwards paid £83 15s 'for taking down the organ in her Majesty's Chappell at St James's, and remounting the

---

[4] British Library Add. MS 10116, fol. 103.
[5] A.J. Freeman, *Father Smith* (Musical Opinion, London, 1926).
[6] See Andrew Ashbee, *Lists of Payments to the King's Musick in the Reign of Charles II (1660-1685)* (Andrew Ashbee, 1981), pp. 2, 5, 6, 10, 12.
[7] LC vol. 817, pp. 332, 367.
[8] LC vol. 741, p. 292.
[9] LC vol. 741, p. 420.

same in the new musique room'.[10] These records all refer to works effected at the building we still know as the Queen's Chapel in Marlborough Gate – hence the terminology of the warrants, which refer to '*her* Majesty's Chapel'.

Hingeston also worked at 'the King's Chappell at Hampton Court' repairing the organ and harpsicord, for which he was paid £155 on 19 April 1662,[11] and a month later received a crimson taffeta curtain for the loft.

Meanwhile a bill dated Lady Day 1664 mentions shoes 'for the three children of the Queen's Chappell',[12] and a warrant for 20 July 1664 provides 'for three liveries to be delivered to Mr Ferdinando for the three children of the Queen's Chappell'[13] at the same time as the liveries for the 'twelve Chapel Royal children were to be delivered to Captain Henry Cooke', the master of the children. The following warrant, dated 17 September 1661, shows the inventory of uniform items that were now to be worn by the children of the Chapel Royal following the king's wishes at the Restoration:

> Warrant to deliver to Henry Cooke, master of the twelve children of the Chappell Royall, the following materials for their liveries: For each of them one cloak of bastard cloth lyned with velvett, one suit and coat of the same cloth made up and trimmed with silver and silk lace after the manner of our footmen's liveries, and also to the said suit three shirts, three half shirts, three pair of shoes, three pair of thigh stockings, whereof one pair of silk and two pair of worsted, two hats with bands, six bands and six pairs of cuffs, whereof two laced and four plain, three handkerchiefs, three pairs of gloves and two pieces and a half of rebon for trimming garters and shoestrings. And at Easter for their summer liveries, for each boy one cloak of bastard scarlett lined with sattin and one doublet of sattin with bastard scarlett trunk hose made and trimmed up as aforesaid, with three shirts, three half shirts, three pairs of shoes, three pair of thigh stockings, whereof one pair of silk and two pairs of worsted, two hats with bands etc.[14]

A year earlier, on 3 December 1660, the livery provision includes that of the gentlemen and also the musicians appointed to serve the Chapel Royal: 'Warrant to provide three score and four surplices of fine holland cloth for the gentlemen of the Chappell and twelve surplices for the musicians and thirty-four surplices of the like fine holland cloth for the Children of the Chappell.'[15] The wearing of surplices continued alongside the new colourful liveries of the children, as subsequent warrants show.

[10] LC vol. 742, pp. 96, 97.
[11] LC vol. 741, p. 209.
[12] LC papers, bundle 5.
[13] LC papers, bundle 8.
[14] LC vol. 814, p. 106.
[15] LC vol. 802, p. 5.

Services were held at Whitehall 'every Sunday and Holy Day' with musical accompaniment consisting of 'double curtolls' (a kind of bassoon) played by Robert and Edward Strong, and 'violls' played by Thomas Bates and William Gregory.[16]

With regard to the 'decking out' of the Chapel Royal buildings and the provision of sacramental items, books, etc., an entry in the Old Cheque book gives us an invaluable insight into the practicalities. The entry records a letter dated 4 May 1663 from Charles II to his cousin Edward, earl of Sandwich, who was master of the great wardrobe, ordering items to be delivered to the serjeant of the vestry, Thomas Haynes, 'immediately upon sight hereof', and it deserves quotation at least in part:

> Item, twenty ells of diaper for foure cloaths for the Communion table, in the body of the sayd Chappell.
> Item, twenty ells of broad cloath for six towells for the Communion.
> Item, seven ells of broad canvas and foure yards of greene cloathe.
> Item, three Bibles of the great volume.
> Item, four Communion bookes and 34 psalter bookes.
> Item, one denny carpit of Turky worke to lay before the Communion table, and one other Turky carpit of a lesser size to lay upon the alter.
> Item, one grosse of silke points for the coapes.
> Item, three standards, whereof one is for the song books of our sayd Chapell, being two setts more than formerly have bin.
> Item, two bare hydes of oxe leather.
> Item, three thousand of tenterhookes, three hamers, one fire shovel, one pare of tongs, three black jacks, three gispins, two brushes, one perfuming pan of iron, six houre glasses, and a paire of strong iron andirons.[17]

Meanwhile a warrant dated 15 January 1663 talks of delivery to Henry Cooke, master of the children, of 'thirteen Common Prayer Books in octavo, for the said children to doe their service in his Majesty's Chappell'.[18] These books would have been the first, for which we have evidence, of the new 1662 Books of Common Prayer authorised by Charles II, supplied for the use of his Chapel Royal. This version is still used today.

As for the children of the Chapel Royal, they were once again billeted with certain of the gentlemen and the master, who received extra payments for their keep and also taught them to play musical instruments. The children were, as before the Civil War, once again 'impressed' from other cathedrals and choral establishments for service with the Chapel Royal.

The sub-dean also had a crucial role to play in the early days of the

[16] LC vol. 741, p. 352.
[17] Old Cheque Book, fol. 50b.
[18] LC vol. 817, p. 401.

restoration of the Chapel Royal. This we learn from the Pipe Office Accounts of the treasurer of the chamber, one of which reads: 'Dr Walter Jones, Sub-Dean of his Majesty's Chappell Royall, for Paper and books and for pricking Services and Anthems for his Majesty's Service in the said Chappell from May 1662 to the end of December 1668, by Warrant dated the 31st December 1669: £73.'[19] This valuable work was continued by his successor, as we learn from a later Pipe Office Account of 1676:[20]

To Doctor William Holder, subdeane of his Majesty's Chappell, for transcribing into bookes of His majesty's Chappell Royall severall Anthems and Services in the space of 6 years ending at midsummer 1676, as may appear by the bill annexed:

A Catalogue of Severall Services & Anthems that have beene transcribed into the Books of His Maties Chappell Royall since Anno 1670 to Midsumer 1676:

Farrants High service	£2
Mr Humphryes service	£2
Mr Blowes service in A	£2
Mr Blowes service in G	£2
Mr Blowes Benedicite	£2
His Te Deum to ye Benedicite	£0. 10s.
Mr Tuckers Benedicite service	£2
Dr Childs Benedicite service	£2
Dr Childs evening service in G	£1
Mr Ferraboscos Evening service	£1
Dr Rogers service in E	£2
Dr Rogers Sharpe service in D	£2
Dr Childs Te Deum to his Benedicite	£0. 10s.
Dr Rogers service in G	£2
Dr Rogers evening service in A	£1
Mr Wises service	£2
Mr Hen: Alldrigs service	£2
Dr Childs service in E Flatt	£2
Dr Childs service in A re	£2

Anthems

Turne thou us O good Lord	Jo: Blow
In thee O Lord	Jefferies
O God ye proud	Bird
I will magnifie Thee	Hooper
O prayse God in his Holynesse	White
O Give thanks	Mr Tucker
Heare my prayer O God	Battens
Teach mee O Lord	Dr Rogers

[19] Ashbee, *Lists of Payments ... (1660-1685)*, p. 83.
[20] LC 5/141, pp. 431-3.

O prayse the Lord	Dr Child
O prayse God in his Holynesse	Gregory
Behold how good &c	Blow
Blessed is he that Considereth ye poore	Wise
Prepare ye the way	Wise
Awake	Wise
How long	Dr Gibbons
Thou O god	Dr Holder
Have pitty	Wise
Oh prayse our God	Dr Holder
By the waters of Babylon	Ferrabosco
The Lord said unto my Lord	Wise
I beheld & loe a great	Dr Rogers
O clap yor hands	Dr Rogers
O pray for ye peace of Jerusalem	Dr Child
O clap your hands	Mr Tucker
I was Glad	Mr Tucker
Praise ye Lord ye servants	Mr Tucker
O Lord I have sined	Mr Blow
Lord how are they increased	Mr Blow
Lord How long	Mr Tucker
Wherewithall	Mr Tucker
This is the day	Mr Tucker
My heart is fixed	Mr Tucker
Unto thee O Lord	Mr Tucker
Comfort yee my people	Mr Tucker
Have mercy upon mee O God	Mr Humfryes
How are the Mighty fallen	Mr Wise
I will magnifie thee O God my King	Mr Tucker
O prayse God in his Holinesse	Mr Wise
By the waters of Babilon	Mr Wise
The earth is ye Lords	Dr Child
O be joyfull	Mr Humfryes
Not unto us O Lord	Mr Lock
The Lord is my shepherd	Mr Wise
Thou art my king O God	Dr Child
The prodigall	Mr Wise
O lett my mouth be filled	Dr Child
Behold how good and joyfull	Dr Child
Lett God arise	Dr Child
O sing unto ye Lord	Dr Child
O Lord our Governor	Mr Isaac Blackwell
Christ riseing	Mr Wise
Lord what is man	Mr Wm. Turner
O Lord God of hosts	Mr Turner
If the Lord himselfe	Mr Hen: Alldridg
O how amiable	Mr Blow
God is our hope & strength	Mr Blow
O God wherefore art thou absent	Mr Blow
Save mee O God	Mr Blow
Lord teach us to number our Dayes	Mr Humfryes
Heare O Heavens	Mr Humphryes

194

O Lord thou has searched mee out	Mr Blow
Lord thou has been our Refuge	Mr Turner
Like as the hart &c	Mr Humphryes
O Lord my God	Mr Humphryes
O Lord Rebuke mee not	Dr Child

[each anthem is priced at 10s]

This was followed later by a warrant to pay Dr William Holder, sub-dean, for the copying of anthems and services into the books belonging to his majesty's Chapel Royal, for the period 12 February 1676/7 to 25 December 1680, itemised thus:[21]

For two Bookes & Ruled pap. for ye Children	£1. 15s.
For Mr Wises creed in Elami	15s.
for Mr Wises creed in F faut	15s.
Dr. Gibbons evening Service wth verses	15s.
Mr Albertus Brynes Service wth verses	£2.
O give thankes vers Mr Lock	10s.
O be Joyfull Mr Lock	10s.
I will hearken Mr Lock	10s.
Why doe ye Heathen id.	10s.
Lord thou hast been gracious id	10s.
Awake up my Glory id	10s.
Teach mee O Lord Dr Gibbons	10s.

these written in ye Childrens bookes torne out:
O Lord Our governour
Christ riseing
Lord what is man
I beheld and loe
O Lord God of hosts

part of Dr blowes service	[the group] 10s.

[second column]
Anthems written in the Childrens books which were torne out &c
O Lord I have sined
I was glad
Prayse ye Lord
Lord How long
O clap yor hands

where wth all	[the group] 10s.

My heart is fixed
unto ye Lord
Comfort yee my people
How are ye Mighty
Have mercy upon mee

I will Magnifie yee	[the group] 10s.

[21] LC 5/144, p. 40; 5/121.

O praise God in his holinesse
By ye Waters of Babilon
The Earth is ye Lords
O be Joyfull in ye Lord
Not unto us O Lord
The Lord is my shepheard   [the group] 10s.

Thou art my King
The prodigall child
O lett my mouth
Behold how Good
Lett God arise
O sing unto ye Lord   [the group] 10s.

The whole sume is £12. 00. 00.
Will: Holder   Subdean

The provision of musicians for the Chapel Royal's services was the responsibility of the master of his majesty's musick. At the Restoration Nicholas Lanier was re-sworn master and in 1661 a certificate[22] was sent to

all his Maties Musicians in generall that Nicholas Lanier is sworn Master of his Maties Musick, and hath power to order and Convocate the same at fitt time of practize and service as is expressed in his privy seale given him by his late Majesty when he was Prince of Wales, and that if any amongst them refuse to wayte at such convenient tymes of practize and service as he shall appoint, and for such Instruments, voyces and musick as he in reason shall thinke them fittest to serve in, upon his just Complaint I shall punish them either in their persons or their Wages as I shall thinke the offence deserves.

But it seems that attendance of these musicians at the Chapel Royal services became irregular after a few years, and under the mastership of Louis Grabu this state of affairs had to be corrected by an order of 22 May 1665:[23]

Whereas his Majesty hath appoynted the Musitians for the Wind Instruments to give theire Attendance in his Majesty's Chappell Royall and yet some of them have neglected theire Duty, I doe therefore Order that if any one of them shall absent himselfe from ye service of his Majesty's Chapel, that person for Neglecting his service and Duty shall (by ye Appoyntmt of ye Mast. of his Majesty's Musique) give such an allowance to ye rest of his followers that attend as ye Master of ye Musique shall request.

[22] LC 5/137, p. 316.
[23] LC 5/138, p. 417.

11. The Restoration Chapel

The Civil War and Commonwealth had resulted in the loss or destruction of much of the Chapel Royal sacramental plate. Ironically the sacramental vessels used at the Whitehall chapel were melted down in 1646 on Cromwell's orders and sent to Charles I for use at Holdenby where he was imprisoned.[24] We shall see what was done to re-equip the Chapel Royal in Chapter 12.

[24] See F. Peck (ed.), *Desiderata Curiosa: or a collection of divers, scarce and curious places relating chiefly to matters of English history* (London, 1732), p. 373.

12

Chapel Royal Sacramental Plate

Over 400 years before the destruction of most of the Chapel Royal sacramental plate during the Interregnum, another great loss was suffered by the crown.

Low water in the Wash on 12 October 1216 was at about noon. The highest spring tide was only two days away. The local phenomenon of 'stolen tide', i.e. a tide occurring as much as two hours earlier than expected, was a distinct possibility. It was in these conditions that king John set off from King's Lynn with his baggage train, including the Chapel Royal with its silver and gold plate and relics, to cross the Wash at the Wellstream. What happened next is best described by Abbot Ralph of Coggeshall in his *Chronicon Anglicanum*, written between 1207 and 1218:

> Moreover, the greatest distress troubled him, because on that journey he had lost his chapel with its relics, and some of his packhorses with divers household effects at the Wellstream, and many members of his household were submerged in the waters of the sea, and sucked into the quicksand there, because they had set out incautiously and hastily before the tide had receded.

According to the account of the chronicler Roger of Wendover in his *Flores Historiarum*, written some time before his death in 1234, the king, 'barely escaping with his army, spent the following night at the Abbey called Swineshead'. But it is known that the king spent at least part of the disastrous 12 October 1216 at Wisbech before travelling on to Swineshead. Furthermore, contemporary Patent Rolls show that while at Wisbech he arranged for eight mariners with their ships to transport his 'goods and merchandise' on to Grimsby. This would have been a hasty arrangement to transport the surviving items now that his packhorses had drowned in the Wellstream.

The Patent Rolls reveal that for the ten months prior to October 1216 king John had been gathering a vast quantity of jewels and precious vessels from their usual places of repose at monasteries, and it is thought that he had a considerable proportion of these items with him at the time.

Archaeologists have found quicksand at mediaeval levels a few miles

The coronation of Edward I, from the 'Merton' *Flores Historiarum*, depicting him holding a sceptre surmounted by a dove in his right hand. It was buried with him, and when his tomb was opened for the first time in 1774 he was found to be holding it between the two forefingers and thumb of his left hand. (Reproduced by permission of the Provost and Fellows of Eton College)

north of Wisbech near the line of a natural causeway, and it is possible that this is the location of the Wellstream disaster and therefore the lost Chapel Royal plate and relics. The 'King John chalice' was rescued and can still be seen at the Guildhall in King's Lynn. It can be regarded as the earliest item of Chapel Royal sacramental plate to have come down to us today.

Apart from the Chapel Royal items, those thought to have been lost at the Wellstream include the coronation regalia, consisting of the great crown, purple robes, the sword of Tristram, and a golden sceptre with a dove. The last item, however, seems to have survived for it clearly appears in a depiction of the coronation of Edward I in 1272 and was buried with his body at Westminster Abbey in 1307. This rod of just over five feet in length, displaying oak leaves of green enamel and surmounted by a ball with a dove perched on top, did not see the light of day until it

199

This silver-gilt great alms dish, made in 1660 by Wolfgang Howzer, adorned the high altar at Westminster Abbey on the occasion of Charles II's coronation on 23 April 1661. The King Charles spaniel represents the Restoration of the monarchy. (HM Chapel Royal, reproduced by gracious permission of Her Majesty The Queen)

The Aukland dish, made by Wolfgang Howzer between 1659 and 1662. (Reproduced by courtesy of the Dean and Chapter, Durham Cathedral)

Charles II's coronation in Westminster Abbey on 23 April 1661 from Ogilby's *Entertainment of Charles II* shows the Chapel Royal's great alms dish forming the centrepiece on the high altar. (Reproduced by courtesy of the Guildhall Library, City of London)

was dug up along with Edward I's body clothed in full regalia in 1774.[1]

Such regalia was not available to Charles II, who had to start largely from scratch. A major factor in the delay of the date for his coronation was the need to make the necessary regalia, most which had been destroyed during the Interregnum. Silversmiths and goldsmiths were suddenly in great demand as the king's wishes became known, and the Chapel Royal was to benefit accordingly.

There was a pressing need to furnish the Chapel Royal with sufficient splendid gold and silver-gilt vessels and other sacramental plate, the originals having been melted down in 1646, as we have seen. The need to replace these items with the utmost speed became evident when Charles began to attend the chapel at Whitehall just nineteen days after his triumphant arrival in London. Although a complete inventory of plate used by the Chapel Royal was not recorded accurately until 1721,[2] nevertheless items made for use with the Chapel Royal can still be clearly identified using other methods.

---

[1] See Joseph Ayloffe, 'An account of the body of king Edward the first, as it appeared on opening his tomb in the year 1774' in *Archaeologia* 3 (1775), p. 384, and also Antonia Gransden, *Historical Writing in England, c. 550 to 1307* (Routledge & Kegan Paul, London, 1974), p. 458 and plate XIIb.

[2] PRO, Treasury Papers, vol. 235.

Large alms dish depicting the Last Supper, made by John Cooqus in 1664 and at present displayed at the jewel house in the Tower of London. (Crown copyright)

Perhaps the most magnificent item of all is the great alms dish. It has a diameter of 37½ inches and depicts the Last Supper in the centre in high relief. The only clearly distinguishable mark on this dish is the London date-letter for 1660. For the key as to who made it we have to transfer our gaze to a 21-inch diameter dish made for bishop John Cosin, now at Aukland Castle in Co. Durham. Cosin was Bishop of Durham from 1660-72. The Aukland dish was fashioned by an immigrant craftsman by the name of Wolfgang Howzer sometime between 1659 and 1662. Like the great Chapel Royal dish it too depicts the Last Supper and also repeats the tight 'mollusc-like' scroll-work around the border. We can conclude from this that Wolfgang Howzer was the craftsman who fashioned the great dish for the Chapel Royal in 1660.

The purpose of this dish was to adorn the altar at the east end of the chapel at Whitehall in place of the cross and stained-glass window that had stood there before 1644. It was also used to adorn the high altar of Westminster Abbey at Charles II's coronation on 23 April 1661 and is, in fact, clearly shown on the high altar in a contemporary print. It is still used today by the Chapel Royal to mark major festivals of the church.

Similar dishes, evidently made by the same craftsman, are to be found

202

The 'animal dish', made in 1660. (Crown copyright)

The Maundy dish, made in 1660. (Reproduced by courtesy of the Controller of Her Majesty's Stationery Office)

Pair of feathered flagons, dated 1660. (Reproduced by courtesy of the Controller of Her Majesty's Stationery Office)

elsewhere. An almost identical twin can be seen at the jewel house in the Tower of London, made four years later in 1664. This dish has been used as the centrepiece of the high altar at Westminster Abbey for coronations ever since that of James II. The maker's initials on this one are 'HG'. It may be that the 'H' still stood for Howzer. The 'G' is a mystery, but it could perhaps stand for another craftsman who helped him. There are in fact two more dishes, although smaller at 28½ inches in diameter, evidently also made by Wolfgang Howzer. One depicts a different representation of the Last Supper, and the other Christ washing his disciples' feet. These are to be found at St George's chapel, Windsor. The 'HG' mark appears also on plate of the Mercer's Company from 1650-63, on plate at Bermondsey church, and in the Imperial Collection at Moscow.

Other plate made in 1660 for the Chapel Royal included a silver-gilt alms dish 24 inches in diameter with the maker's mark 'HG' with a crescent above and cinquefoil between two pellets below, depicting around the rim a horse, stag, boar and cow. The centre of this dish was refashioned later to display the AR monogram of queen Anne with a rose and crown in the centre.

Pair of feathered flagons made by Robert Smithier in 1664. (Crown copyright)

The need for a large dish for the Maundy distribution (the number of recipients corresponding to the sovereign's age) was also filled in 1660. Although it displays the cyphers of king William and queen Mary, this is a later refashioning. It is in the 'no Scottish' style, as is revealed by the presence of two Irish harps and no Scottish lion. This Maundy dish is still used today and is at present augmented at Royal Maundy by the use of two 'fish dishes' dating from *c.* 1685 which depict on the one 'fresh water' fish, and on the other 'sea water' fish. These two, however, are said to be of continental origin.

There was obviously a need for flagons to hold the communion wine before its consecration in chalices. One pair at least of 'feathered flagons' was made in 1660 and another probably in 1664. A fine pair of silver-gilt chalices, together with covers, was also made. One of the covers has a date-letter for 1660 and displays a tiny Charles II crown, while the other betrays evidence of a slightly more laboured technique in the fashioning of the chased decoration and a tiny 'Orange' crown, suggesting that the silversmith was copying the earlier original. The two chalices bear only the maker's mark of a heart containing the letters 'IN' with a bird below,

The 1660/1 coronation service, now displayed in the jewel house at the Tower of London. (Crown copyright)

and the latter additional engraving of the arms and cyphers of William and Mary. The letters 'IN' in a heart, but with a star rather than a bird beneath, occur on a plate belonging to Chester Cathedral dated 1662, and also on later plate there. However, a tankard of 1663 with the letters 'IN' with a bird beneath has been identified and belongs to the Barber Surgeons Company. It is reasonable to assume therefore that the chalices and cover sets belonging to the Chapel Royal were made between 1660 and 1663. They are still in constant use with the Chapel Royal at St James's today.

Two patens 'accompany' these chalice and cover sets, again with later William and Mary engraving. One bears the maker's mark 'IA' in script, and the clue to their date is to be found in another beautiful object of sacramental plate – a plain communion chalice with finger-ring cover paten of 1664. This piece also bears the 'IA' mark. It may have been used for 'private' services, but appears later in the Kensington Palace chapel

206

inventory of 1832. Today it is used by the Chapel Royal at St James's for the early morning communion on Sundays and at weekday saints' days. This small chalice stands just under 9 inches high and is very light in weight.

In addition to this Restoration plate of the Chapel Royal, mention must also be made of the five gold communion vessels consisting of two chalices and three patens, which were made for Charles II's coronation on 23 April 1661 and used for the first time at that service. Two of the gold patens are similar, measuring 7 inches and 6 inches in diameter respectively, but the third is 7¼ inches in diameter and of sexafoil design. The two accompanying chalices differ in many respects – not least in the relief decoration around the stems and the shape of the sexafoil bases. One chalice stands 10⅝ inches high, the other is 10 inches. The two chalices bear two makers' marks side by side, but display different initials. One of these marks occurs on a plate of 1646 at the 'Charles church' in Plymouth which was evidently fashioned fifteen years earlier at the height of Cromwell's successes, and it is possible that a similar story lies behind the Charles II vessels.[3]

The final significant group of Chapel Royal Restoration communion plate we shall look at is that made specifically for Charles II's brother James, duke of York, in about 1661. As James was at this time officially in residence at St James's Palace, it is likely that these were regularly in use there at the king's chapel in colour court.

The group is identified by the 'DL' monogram surmounted by a royal ducal coronet and flanked by crossed feathers or palms tied in a bow. It is known that these pieces were made for the duke of York because he was

---

[3] See Wilfred Cropps's private letter published in Edgar Sheppard, *Memorials of St James's Palace* (Longmans, Green & Co., London, 1894) vol. 1, p. 266.

The duke of York alms dish displaying, at bottom, the 'DL' monogram. (HM Chapel Royal, reproduced by gracious permission of Her Majesty The Queen)

the only prince entitled to this form of coronet, as specified by the royal warrant of 1661. This is supported by the presence of the monogram on bookbindings in Windsor and the British Museum, and also by letters, one of which, from James to his niece, the countess of Lichfield, contains the monogram on a seal. The 'D' stands for Dux and the 'L' is in fact a 'J' upside down – i.e. Dux Jacobus. James's cousin Louis XIV adopted a similar upside-down encryption for his monogram. It is possible that the origin of James's encrypted monogram lies in his experiences as a prisoner at St James's Palace. He had been captured by the Parliamentarians following the fall of Oxford and confined at the palace, his birthplace. It was at this time that James devised a plan of escape which involved smuggling out letters written with the use of a secret cypher. James himself recalled in his memoirs[4] hiding the cypher with which he used to encode these letters. When one of these letters was intercepted,

There came to him a committee of both Houses, two Lords and four Commoners, who were sent to examine him. They began by showing him the letter, which he could not deny to be his own handwriting; and they

[4] Later published as *The Life of James II, collected out of memoirs writ with his own hand.*

asked him for the cypher, to which he answered 'that he had burnt it'. They pressed him exceedingly to discover who had been assisting him to escape, but found him so very reserved that he would acknowledge nothing, though they urged the danger he ran of being sent to the Tower; but when they saw that none of their artifices could prevail they left him.

This incident evidently left a lasting impression upon James. He made his successful escape in 1648, but it may well be that the practice of encoding which had saved his life then was later 'enshrined' in the form of his upside-down encoded monogram which appears on his communion plate.

The only fully hallmarked pieces in this group are the altar candlesticks, which bear the date-letter for 1661 and a maker's mark of a greyhound sejant. This mark also appears on the two flagons of the group. The group itself comprises a pair of 22-inch candlesticks, a pair of flagons, a chalice with a cagework calyx, a paten, a 10-inch chalice and a cover, three chalices at the private chapel at Windsor Castle, and an alms dish.

It was not until 1970 that the identity of the maker's mark 'S', common to nearly all these items, was revealed by Charles Oman in his *Caroline Silver*. It is the mark of Robert Smithier, not Charles Shelley to whom it had previously been attributed. Smithier's mark is found on the alms dish and three Windsor chalices with cover patens standing on incurved hexafoil feet. He was also the maker of the 'feather flagons' of 1664 mentioned earlier, but not in this group.

However, the cagework calyx chalice with the 'DL' monogram was, it now seems clear, fashioned by the silversmith John Cooqus. P.A.S. Phillips argued that this was so on the basis of its decoration and style, which shows the influence of the Dutch silversmith Van Vianen, and the fact that it has a 'movable ornament' apparently non-existent at the time in examples of established Church of England vessels. This feature was not uncommon in Roman Catholic circles, but at that time was only made by foreign craftsmen. Phillips argues that even if the chalice was made and given to the Chapel Royal for use in Whitehall, the 'additional ornament' must have been fashioned by a craftsman in the Continental tradition, such as John Cooqus.

Phillips also attributes the two 'fish dishes' now used at Royal Maundy, and dated *c.* 1685, to John Cooqus. If this is so, then we may have a clue to the circumstances in which they were made in the list of 'Moneys received and paid for secret services of Charles II and James II from March 1679 to 25th December 1688', printed by the Camden History Society in 1851:

	li. s. d.
[p. 144] Account of 31st December 1686:	
To John Coquus, by advance, to provide plate	
for the Chappell in Whitehall	300 0 0

Saltwater fish dish, used to supplement the Maundy dish. (Reproduced by permission of the Controller of Her Majesty's Stationery Office)

Freshwater fish dish, used to supplement the Maundy dish. (Reproduced by permission of the Controller of Her Majesty's Stationery Office)

12. Chapel Royal Sacramental Plate

[p. 154] Account of 22nd March 1686:
To John Coquus, in full, for silver works by
him p'formed and furnished in the Chappell in Whitehall   487 7 0
[p. 160] Account of 24th June 1687:
To John Coquus (as is supposed), for several
silver provisions by him made and supplies to the said
Chappell [at Dublin Castle]   54 1 7
[p. 179] Account of 10th January 1687:
To John Coquus, viz. 335li 9s 11½d., for silver
works made and provided for the Chappell at Whitehall,
and 6li 14s 6d for provisions for the Chapel at Windsor.

It is very probable that the 'fish dishes' were among the 'plate' or 'silver' provided for the 'Chappell in Whitehall'. Moreover, if by this chapel is meant not the Chapel Royal premises but rather James II's 'new' Roman Catholic Chapel at Whitehall then the reason why these entries appear in the 'secret' accounts becomes clear. On the other hand the concept of altar alms dishes was essentially a Protestant notion conceived as a replacement for images of the cross. Whichever chapel premises these silver-gilt fish dishes were meant for, they were certainly regarded as part of the collection of Chapel Royal plate soon after they were made, if not immediately.

John Cooqus was a Fleming who had settled in London certainly by 1664, for he received the royal patronage of queen Catherine of Braganza in that year – a fact we know from a petition 'of John Cassen and John Cooqus Silversmiths, and Foreigners' to the king, dated 1679, in which they write 'That your petitioners are sworn servants to your majesty's Royall Consort in theire said art and for the best part of fifteen yeares'. This petition also gives a clue as to why Cooqus's maker's mark did not appear in the Goldsmiths Company's records, for 'your petitioners way of working is different from that practis'd by the silversmiths in London ... the Company of Goldsmiths in London taking offence do very much molest and threaten to ruin your petitioners'. Evidently the Goldsmiths Company's jealousy was directed at a silversmith/goldsmith who enjoyed royal favour, but it is clear from the secret accounts quoted above from the 1680s that their bid to ostracise Cooqus failed.

John Cooqus is known from the poor-rate books to have lived in a house on the north side of Pall Mall (alias Catherine Street, after the queen) from 1672 until his death and burial in St James's Church, Westminster, in 1697. Charles II's mistress Nell Gwyn also lived in Pall Mall, and Cooqus actually made her bedstead. The bill has survived and reads thus:

Work done for the righte Honourable Madame Guinne. John Cooqus, silversmyth his bill. 1674. Delivered the head of the bedstead weighing 885 onces 12 lb, and i have received 636 onces 15 dweight so that their is over and above of me owne silver two hundred forty eight onces 17 dweight at 7s 11d par once (the silver being at d't worse par once according the reste)

211

Pair of silver-gilt candlesticks, dated *c*. 1662. (Crown copyright)

which comes to £98 10s 2d. For making of the 636 onces 15d't at 2s 11d par once comes to £92 17s 3d.

Before leaving the sacramental plate made for the Restoration Chapel Royal, mention should also be made of the *c*. 1662 pair of silver-gilt 'standard' candlesticks, maker's mark 'IN' and 37 inches high.

On his return to London in 1660 Charles II told the treasury that he intended to marry a Spanish princess, and that he would need a font in which his offspring could be christened. In the event he married a Portuguese but retained the font. He is said to have had some of his thirteen illegitimate children christened in it.

Exactly how all this Restoration plate was employed in Chapel Royal services is revealed in vivid detail by an entry in the Whitehall Register of the Chapel Royal dated 1676. Many of the pieces of sacramental plate we have looked at are clearly recognisable from the description:

Font and altar dish commissioned for Charles II. Some of his thirteen illegitimate children were christened in the font. (Crown copyright)

The Attyre of the Altar

On Holy day Eves and Holy days the Altar is to be covered with a Carpet partly Velvet, and partly white Gold flower'd Sattin: an Altar-piece of the same hung up. A great Charger set on, three Basons, one bigger and two less, two great ffeathered flagons, and two less of the same work, two fflaggons with chac'd work, two Candlesticks with Tapers, A rich Bible in two parts, Three Common Prayer books, two at the West end and one at the East, on a velvet cushion.

For the Communion, two Patins, two chalices with covers.

On ordinary dayes the Altar Peice and Carpet to be taken away and return'd to the Standard; All the Plate (except the Candlesticks and the bigger of the three Basons, which are to remain on the Altar) to be return'd to the Jewell-House; and the Altar to be cover'd with a clean Diaper.[5]

[5] This entry is to be found in the Whitehall Register of the Chapel Royal, now deposited at the Public Record Office, before an entry dated October 1676, on fols 12 and 13.

The lily font, commissioned by Queen Victoria. (Crown copyright)

The sacramental plate was saved from damage or dispersed in 1688 on the flight of James II to the Continent, for according to Macaulay's *History of England* the 'rich plate of the Chapel Royal was deposited at Wild House, near Lincoln's Inn Fields, the residence of the Spanish Ambassador, Ronquillo'. Somehow, too, it survived the Whitehall fire of 1698 which is said to have destroyed the Chapel Royal building there, but this may have been because most of the items were, as we have seen, stored in the jewel house and collected and returned by the serjeant of the vestry for use in the services of the Chapel Royal. This practice, too, is revealed in action in two entries from serjeant William Lovegrove's private manuscript book which are of interest also because they show the continuity of the practices detailed a hundred years earlier in the 1676 Whitehall Chapel account. Serjeant Lovegrove's account reads thus:

214

12. Chapel Royal Sacramental Plate

On Tuesday the 8th Day of September 1761, His Majesty King George The Third was Married in the Royal Chapel at St James's between the hours of 9 and 12 o'clock at Evening ... The following Plate was new gilt, and the Altar Decked with the same upon the occasion, viz.:–

1. One large Gilt Bason for the Altar
2. Two large Candlesticks for the Altar
3. Three basons
4. Two Feather Potts
5. Two Feather Flaggons
6. Two Chaced Flaggons
7. Two Chalices, Two pattons, and Two Covers
8. Two Gold Chalices, Two Covers, and one Patton
9. One Virgers Rod Gilt.

All the above mentioned Plate was in the Serjeant's Care and Custody, and a Receipt for the same is given and signed in the Books at the Jewel Office.

Wm. Lovegrove, Serjeant.

This account appears on fol. 127 of William Lovegrove's manuscript and is followed by a description of the interior fittings, furniture, etc. in the chapel at St James's Palace in 1762 and later in 1767 (fols 128-9). The second Lovegrove entry concerning the Chapel Royal plate which is of interest to us reads thus:

The 2nd May 1768

Sir,
It has been Customary to have the following Plate new clean'd and gilt against Whitsunday Yearly, viz:–

2 Large Candlesticks at the Altar
3 Basons, 2 Chalices & Covers, 2 Pattens.
2 Chaced Flaggons.

The following Plate has not been clean'd & Gilt since the Marriage of his present Majesty. And it is now become necessary to have something done to it, being very much tarnished
viz:–

1 Large Gilt Bason for the Altar
2 Feather Potts
2 Feather Flaggons
2 Gold Chalices & Covers and one Patten.
1 Virgers Rod

To Sir William Wilmot
        I am
            Sir
            Your Most Obedient Servt.
            Wm. Lovegrove, Serjeant.

One of a pair of alms dishes, probably made in 1660, and used by the Chapel Royal at weddings, christenings and major feasts. (HM Chapel Royal, reproduced by gracious permission of Her Majesty The Queen)

These accounts are of great importance to the history of certain items of Chapel Royal plate, sometimes as much for what they do not say as for what they do. The first mention of the silver-gilt virger's rod still carried by the serjeant of the vestry today appears in the account of silver made by serjeant Lovegrove in 1761. There is mention in both the 1761 and 1768 Lovegrove accounts of 'two large Candlesticks for the Altar' and '2 Large Candlesticks at the Altar', but these are likely to have been the fairly large 'duke of York' altar candlesticks rather than the 'standards' of 1662 or 1717 designed to sit on the sanctuary steps. It therefore seems likely that the 'standard' silver-gilt candlesticks made by Benjamin Pyne in 1717 (apparently to match an earlier pair made for Windsor Castle chapel) and still used by the Chapel Royal today, were not yet in use at St James's in the 1760s.

The pair of candlesticks which now adorn the altar of the Queen's Chapel during the week are from a set of six given in memory of Harold Douglas Caesar, priest, by the parishioners of St Luke's Southampton where he was vicar from 1923-59. At that time the opportunity was taken to silver the high altar brass cross and add the figure of the crucified Christ. This figure was carved by the man who played St John in 1890 and Joseph of Arimathea in the 1900 and 1910 Oberammergau passion

12. Chapel Royal Sacramental Plate

Chapel Royal silver-gilt plate as used for a major festival. At the centre is the Howzer 1660 coronation dish of Charles II; to its left and right two smaller restoration alms dishes of *c.* 1660; two candlesticks with 'DL' monograms of 1661; two large chalices of *c.* 1660 displaying later William & Mary monograms, and two chalice covers – one still displaying a Stuart crown but with later William & Mary monograms; two patens of *c.* 1660 displaying later William & Mary monograms but again one retaining a Stuart crown; and a ring-top chalice of 1664.

plays. This cross accompanies the two candlesticks on the altar during the week by the kindness of the present sub-dean who recovered these items in memory of his father.

13

Handel: Composer Extraordinary

On 25 February 1723 G.F. Handel was appointed 'Composer of Musick for his Majesty's Chappel Royal'. This title was carefully constructed to allow Handel to contribute to the musical development of the Chapel Royal without actually being a member of it. He could not be a member because he was still a German citizen. According to Donald Burrows, his functions 'seem to have been concerned with the provision of instrumentally accompanied ceremonial anthems for occasional royal services'.[1]

Handel eventually became a naturalised British subject on 20 February 1727. Later that same year, on 11 June, George I suddenly died

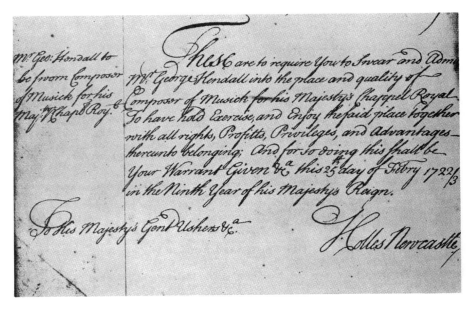

This Warrant appointing 'Mr George Hendall' as 'Composer of Musick for his Majesty's Chapel Royal' is dated 25 February 1722/3, and was discovered by Donald Burrows at the Public Record Office.

[1] D. Burrows, 'Handel and the 1727 coronation', *Musical Times* 118 (1977), p. 469ff.

Portrait of William Croft, *c.* 1690, by an unknown artist. (Reg. no. 1192, reproduced by courtesy of the National Portrait Gallery, London)

in a coach on the high road to Osnabruck. On the very day he died, uttering the words 'Drive on, drive on', a hand was writing the entry into the New Cheque Book recording the names of the gentlemen of the Chapel Royal. This record is of crucial importance in relation to the notes made by Handel on his autograph manuscripts of music for the forthcoming coronation. The names are as follows:

William Turner	John Weldon, Composer.
John Church	George Laye
Thomas Jennings	Samuel Weely
Thomas Edwards	Thomas Gething
John Freeman	Peter Randall
William Croft Dr. of Musick, Organist.	James Chelsum
William Croft Dr. of Musick, Composer.	Talbot Young
John Mason	Thomas Ball
Bernard Gates	Jonathan Smith
Francis Hughes	Clerk of the Cheque
John Weldon, Organist.	William Perry

Shortly after this list was written, William Croft, organist and composer, died on 18 August at Bath. The bishop of Salisbury recommended that the post be filled by Maurice Green, 'the greatest Music Genius we have'. Accordingly Green was appointed organist and composer of the Chapel Royal on 4 September 1727. His appointment brought the Chapel Royal complement back up to two organists and composers – the other being John Weldon. It seems, however, that George II did not want Dr Green to compose for his coronation. We gather this from a manuscript interpolation in a copy of John Mainwaring's *Memoirs of the Life of the Late George Frederic Handel* in the possession of the Royal Library. The handwriting is in fact remarkably similar to that of George III. We learn from it of:

> That wretched little crooked ill-natured insignificant writer, Player and Musician, the late Dr. Green, organist and composer to King George II who forbad his composing the Anthems of his Coronation October 22nd 1727, and ordered that G.F. Handel should not only have that great honour, but, except for the 1st choose his own words. He had but four weeks for doing this wonderful work which seems scarcely credible, as to the first Zadok the Priest it is probably the most perfect if possible of all His superb compositions.[2]

The king's choice of Handel instead of the resident Chapel Royal organists and composers was confirmed at the beginning of September 1727 by the *Norwich Mercury*, which stated that 'Mr. Hendel, the famous composer to the Opera, is appointed by the King to compose the Anthem

---

[2] Sir Walter Newman Flower, *George Frideric Handel* (Cassel, London, 1959).

G.F. Handel by Philippe Mercier, *c.* 1735/6. (Reproduced by courtesy of The Viscount FitzHarris Collection)

at the Coronation which is to be sung in Westminster Abbey at the Grand Ceremony'.[3] As soon as this decision was made Burney records that 'At the Coronation ... Handel had the words sent to him, by the bishops, for

[3] Quoted in O.E. Deutsch, *Handel: a documentary biography* (London, 1955), p. 213.

the anthems; at which he murmured, and took offence, as he thought it implied his ignorance of the Holy Scriptures'.[4] By 'bishops' Burney meant the archbishops of Canterbury and York. Handel replied to their initiative by saying 'I have read my Bible very well, and shall choose for myself'. He did.

Time was short, and we learn from the *Parker's Penny Post* issue of 4 October 1727 that Handel was employing 'Italian Voices, with above a Hundred of the best Musicians', and from the *Norwich Gazette* of 14 October 1727 that 'Yesterday there was a Rehearsal of the Coronation Anthem in Westminster Abbey, set to Musick by the famous Mr Hendell: There being 40 voices, and about 160 Violins, Trumpets, Hautboys, Kettle-Drums, Bass's proportionable; besides an Organ, which was erected behind the Altar; And both the Musick and Performers, were the admiration of all the Audience.' There had, though, evidently been a previous rehearsal of sorts, for ten days earlier *Parker's Penny Post* said of the coronation music: 'The Whole is allowed by those Judges in Musick who have already heard it, to exceed any Thing heretofore of the same kind.'

On the day of the coronation itself, which had been postponed from 4 October to 11 October 1727, the huge orchestra and chorus were arranged amphitheatrically. As part of the chorus the Chapel Royal numbered ten children and twenty-six gentlemen. 'Five of the ten Chapel Royal boys had gone from the choir with broken voices in June and the pluralism amongst the Gentlemen was such that only one member of the Westminster Abbey choir was not accounted for from the ranks of the Chapel Royal.'[5]

Damien Cranmer, editor of the edition of Handel's autograph manuscripts for Ernst Eulenburg, now in the British Library, observed that: 'At the beginning of "The King Shall Rejoice" the composer has written against the voice parts "C12, H et 6, Freem et 6, Church et 6, Wheely et 6, Gates et 6". This information is repeated four times in the said anthem, though not in any other.'[6] We know from the New Cheque Book record cited above that the letter 'H' must have stood for Hughes, 'Freem' for Freeman, and 'C' for Canto. If the New Cheque Book list followed precedent and listed the gentlemen of the Chapel Royal in order of seniority, then we can observe that this was not the basis for Handel's choice of 'heads' to lead groups of six gentlemen. His choice must have reflected their choral expertise. We know from Handel's annotations that there were in all thirty-five male singers and twelve boys.

It seems that all did not go smoothly on the coronation day itself, for the

---

[4] Burney's 'Sketch of the Life of Handel' in *An Account of the Musical Performance* (1785), p. 34.

[5] Burrows, op. cit., p. 471.

[6] See H.C. Robbins-Landon, *Handel and His World* (Weidenfeld & Nicolson, London, 1984), p. 116.

Caricature of Handel by J. Goupy entitled 'The Charming Brute', published 21 March 1754.
Verses accompanying the cartoon read as follows:

The Figure's odd – yet who wou'd think?
(Within this Tunn of Meat & Drink)
There dwells the Soul of Soft Desires
And all that HARMONY inspires:

Can Contrast such as this be found?
Upon the Globe's extensive Round;
There can – yon Hogshead in his seat,
His sole devotion is – to Eat.

(Reproduced by courtesy of the Fotomas Index)

223

Westminster Abbey Chapter Minutes of 14 November 1727 hint at an awkward start to the day caused by a gentleman of the Chapel Royal, Francis Hughes, who was one of the aforementioned heads chosen by Handel to lead a group of six. The Minutes read: 'Order'd. That an Action be brought agaist hues in the name of the Dean for assaulting and refusing his Lordship Entrance into the Choir the day of the performance of Musick there against their majesties Coronation.'

The members and players of the King's Musick provided many instrumentalists, including trumpeters and the kettle-drum player. Liveries for the coronation were supplied to the master and thirty-three musicians, twenty-four of whom were entitled to wear coronation medals. The lord chamberlain's records show Bernard Gates to have been paid 42 guineas for additional female and male singers, while Christopher Smith was paid for fifty-seven 'supernumerary' instrumentalists at 3 guineas each.

The end product of all this on the day was variously judged. William Wake, archbishop of Canterbury, perhaps still a little irritated at Handel's rebuff over the choice of anthem texts, wrote in his order of service: 'The Anthem in Confusion: all irregular in the Music', against 'My heart is inditing'. In fairness to the archbishop, however, it may well be that the Chapel Royal choir was not as good in this period as it had been in others, for at the prince of Wales's marriage to the princess of Saxe Gotha at the Chapel Royal building in colour court, St James's Palace, on 27 April 1736, the earl of Egmont commented that 'an anthem composed by Handel for the occasion was wretchedly sung'.[7] Furthermore, at the funeral service for queen Caroline on 27 December 1737, the duke of Chandos wrote to his nephew that Handel's anthem 'was exceeding fine ... but I can't say so much of the performance'.[8]

Whatever the quality of the performance, however, Handel's four anthems for the 1727 coronation were spectacularly popular, with the result that they have been used at every coronation since.

---

[7] Deutsch, op. cit., p. 443.
[8] Ibid.

14

Deans of the Chapel Royal

It is clear that the transfer of power and authority over the Chapel Royal from the king's chancellor to the dean – a post evidently created to receive this authority – was completed by 1318 when the Chapel Royal consisted of the 'chief chapellin', five chaplains and six other clerks, together with the boy choristers and vestry officials. By 1349 the dean's office was firmly established, John Wodeford being described as 'a king's clerk and dean of his chapel'.

The status and authority of the dean of the Chapel Royal was great, and was reflected in the concurrent offices granted by the king. Thus dean Thomas de Lynton also held the treasurership of the church of Wells in 1380, and the king issued instructions to 'arrest and bring before the King and council' those who had attempted to 'disturb' Thomas in his possession of this treasurership. In 1391 dean John Boor was granted 'a messuage and two virgates of land and meadow with appurtenances in Chapelashtoun, Co. Wilts', and in 1397 was made a prebendary of Myddleton in the Winchester conventual church of Wherewell. On 10 May 1399 the king conferred a 'Grant, for ten years, to Richard Kyngeston, dean of the King's Chapel, and Richard Louney, keeper of the Great Wardrobe, of all swans not marked flying within the River Thames and all other rivers running into or out of it between Graveshende and the Bridge of Oxford'.[1] This was a most valuable grant – swans were considered a delicacy fit only for the sovereign, except in the countryside – and also reveals, incidentally, that a system of marking the sovereign's swans was operating in 1399, thus constituting firm evidence for the 'swan-upping' ceremony still performed today.

Nearly a century later in 1475 we find the dean of the Chapel Royal, William Dudley, named as one of the three beneficiaries of a grant from the king – the other two being the queen consort and the bishop of Salisbury. If the dean of the Chapel Royal could be considered worthy of this company, then so were the terms of his grant equally grand. It reads:

Grant to the king's consort Elizabeth, queen of England, Richard, bishop of Salisbury, and Master William Dudley, dean of the Chapel of the household,

[1] Warrant in Cal. Pat. Rolls 10 May 1399.

Dean of the Chapel Royal, the Rt Rev. and Rt Hon. Graham Leonard MA, DD, bishop of London (right) and the sub-dean of the Chapel Royal, the Rev. Canon Anthony Caesar LVO, MA, MusB, FRCO, in 1990.

of the custody of all castles, lordships, manors, lands, rents, possessions and hereditaments in England, Ireland, Wales and the Marches of the same late of John, late earl of Shrewsbury ... with the exception of the castle of Goderych and Irchynfeld ....[2]

Just a year later in 1476 William Dudley played a key role on the battlefield at the direct request of the king. His part in the negotiation of the truce has been described in Chapter 2.[3] A truce being a form of temporary treaty, the dean of the Chapel Royal would have been required for any oath-swearing that might conclude the terms of the truce. The

[2] Warrant in Cal. Pat. Rolls 1475.
[3] See p. 32 above.

dean was thus wearing his 'hat' of state diplomacy, discharging a vital responsibility acquired through holding office as 'dean of the chapel of the household'. It can be assumed that a quota of the Chapel Royal accompanied the dean and the English king on this occasion.

Returning for a moment to the beginning of the fifteenth century, we can trace the growing status and authority of the deans of the Chapel Royal under deliberate royal patronage. It was the king who granted a licence to confirm the papal bull of 1406 giving to dean of the Chapel Royal, Richard Prentys, a canonry and prebend in the cathedral church of Lincoln – but only after making it clear to the pope that this was the king's wish, or else the pope's 'trespass' would have been disallowed.[4] There also exists a licence, dated 1412, 'for the king's Clerk Richard Prentys, dean of the king's chapel within the household, canon of the Cathedral Church of Dublin and prebendary of Swerdes in the same in Ireland, to dwell in England and receive all fruits of his prebend for ten years, notwithstanding any statute or ordinance against absentees from Ireland'.[5] In 1416 dean Edmund Lacy was granted by the king the 'temporalities of the bishopric of Hereford during its vacancy',[6] and in 1425 the king granted dean Robert Gilbert the 'treasurership of the cathedral church of York, in the king's gift by reason of the temporalities being in his hands'.[7]

Aside from these royal grants and mandates, the accumulated wealth of the Chapel Royal was enjoyed by the dean and passed on to his successors. Thus we learn on 18 April 1414 of the

> Acquittance of the king's clerk Richard Prentys, late dean of the chapel of Henry IV within the household, who received divers jewels, vestments and other ornaments and goods for the chapel from Richard Kyngeston, late dean, by indenture, and has delivered them to the king's clerk, Edmund Lacy, now dean of the king's chapel within the household, by the king's command except certain things which he has delivered to divers persons by the king's command.[8]

A glance at the sheer variety and quantity of these excepted 'certain things' which must have been a minor portion of the whole, reveals what a vast accumulation of wealth was evidently passed from a dean of the Chapel Royal to his successor:

> In primis Johanne regine Anglie vii ymages dor de saint Michell sur un pee garnis ove vi bal' vii saphirs xiii troches chacun de iii perles un escu ove un graund bal' et viii grosses perles un croys ove un rubie et iiii perles un

[4] Cal. Pat. Rolls 10 November 1406.
[5] Cal. Pat. Rolls 1412.
[6] Cal. Pat. Rolls 4 January 1416, Westminster.
[7] Cal. Pat. Rolls 16 July 1425, Westminster.
[8] Cal. Pat. Rolls 18 April 1414, Westminster.

chapelet ove un rubie poisant de troie v marcs vii unces iii quartrons.

Item a Piers Luyk, ambassatour Denmark, un ymage dargent enore al gise dun erchevesque pour sire Johan de Beverle portant en sa mayn un tabernacle de bevill pur reliques poisant mesme le pois xvi libres.

Item al chapell de Wodestoke un vestiment convenable cestassavoir un aube, un chesible, un front, un contrefront drapp dor de nethelx, i parure, ii ridelx, i stoll, un phanon, i amyte, i surplys.

Item a monsieur Johan fitz du Roy un vestiment blank drapp dor de cypres nomez ffernez cont' iii amytz, iii aubes, ii stoles, iii phanons, un chesible, un frontell, i contrefront, ii tuniclez, un cas pour un corporas, i pilwe, ii ridelx de tartaryn, i chalice dargent ennore poisant ii libres et ii unces et ii creuttes dargent ennore de mesme le pois i libre.

Item a William de Burton un vestiment velvet oeuvrez dor raiez diverses colours dont un chesible, un aube, un amyte, i stoll, i phanon, un front, un contrefront, i frontell ove tuayll dun suyt.

Item a Arnold Hulkere i chesible rouge de bocasyn, i aube, i amyte, i stoll, i phanon, i chalice dargent ennore ove un cros sur la paten poisant de troye, un libre, xi unces, i corporas, ove le cas et ii tuailles et i parure.

Item a Lichfield i vestiment velvet enbr' deglez dor le cypres dont i chasible, ii tunicles, iii aubes, iii amites dont falt, i drapp pour i amyte, iii frontelles donnt deux sont degles et lautre et xi capes dune suyt et i veille drapp dragmas pour sauf garde des biens avaunditz.

Item a sire de Gray un vestiment blank de hyndes dor, i chesible, iii aubes, iii amytes, ii stolez, ii tuniclez, ii auterclodes, un frontell ove tuaill et iii cappes.

Et a labbay de Dowre i vestiment drapp dor blank raiez, i chesible, ii tunicles, iii aubes, iii amytes, ii stoles, iii phanons, iii auterclodes, un frontell, ove tuaill et iii cappes dune suyt.

Et a William de Burton vii capes de velvet raiez dor.

Et a Willaim Lovenay garderober i bacyn dargent ennore brusez poisant, iii libres et iii unces, i crucifix dargent ennore ove Marie and Johan sur deux branches brusez poisant iiii libres iii unces, un bastons dargent poisant viii unces.

Et a sire de Sparre i vestiment drapp dor rouge raiez, ii chesibles, ii tunicles, iii aubes, iii amitez, ii stoles, iii phanons, iii auterclodes, un frontell ove tuaille, v capes dune suyt et i drapp dor ragmas bloy colour.

Et a Sire Hugh Ducheman un tablet dargent ennore ove reliques dedeins sur deux pees poisant vi libres et viii unces.

Et a luniversitie Doxenford un crois dargent ennore poisant xviii libres et i unce.

Item a N. Bubbewyth, nadgairs evesque de Sarebirs, pour la rouge un ymage de sainte Katerine dor eisn' blank garni ove ii grandes bal', ii saphirs, xiii autres bal', xi troches chacun de iii perles et sur la corone vi perles poisant vi marcs et v unces.

Et a mesme levesque un myter couchez ove perri garni ove diverses peres ove un cros dargent ove lassumption en la somment.

Et a Henry Bowet, evesque iadys de Bathe, i libre pontificall.

Item al priour de Pomfet i vestiment velvet enbr' ove cerfs, i chesible, ii tunicles, iii aubes, iii amites, ii stoles, iii phanons, ii auterclodes, ii pety frountell, iiii capes velvet rouge et i cape de la suyt de vestiment avantdib et un bevill garni dargent ennore ove un croune et i crucifix poisant ii libres et vii unces.

Item a lospitall in Smythfeld iiii draps dor dragmas dount ii rouge i vert et i bloy.

Item a Wauter Burton i frount, i countr' i tuaill ove parure, i cape, i aube, i amyte ove perulez, stoll et phanon, tout drapp soy bloy ove pynnapples et orfr' de rouge velvet enbr' dor.

Item a Henry Fouler ii tunicles rouge velvet enbr' ove fiollez, ii aubez, ii amytes, ii stolles et ii phanons.

Item a hospitall de Sainte Eleyn de Colchestre i vestiment drapp blank satyn contre i front, i contrefr', i frontell, i chesible, iii aubes, iii amytes, ii stolles, iii phanons, iii capes, ii tunicles, ii ridelx, i cas pour un corporas.

Et a chappell de Newenton un vestiment drapp dor de Luyk ove angelx dor et archangelx, rouge contre i front ii contrefr', i chesible, ii tunicles, iii aubes, iii amitez, ii stoles, iii phanons, et iii capes dune suyt.

Item al feretre de saint Thomas de Canterbris ii chandelers dor poisant de trois xviii marez.

Et a la tumbe de Richard, nadgairs roy, iiii drapps dor dragmas. Et a Nicoll Ervisby ii drapps dragmas blank.

Item a tabbe de Percheaur i vestiment velvet rouge ove flures dor i chesible, ii tunicles, iii aubes, iii amitez, ii stoles iii phanons i frount, i contrefr', un frontell ove vi capes de mesme la suyt.[9]

Edmund Lacy's successor, Robert Gilbert, travelled overseas to deliver personally a similar list of articles of exception that were not destined to be passed on to his successor. Thus we read in a 'Mandate by Assent of the Council [dated 1425], that Master Robert Gilbert, late dean of the Chapel of the king's father, be discharged at the exchequer relative to gifts delivered by him to certain churches of France, pursuant to the testament of the said late king'.[10]

This kind of 'inherited' wealth, passed down from dean to dean of the Chapel Royal, could be enjoyed by the dean but not be realised or disposed of for personal gain. Indeed the dean was personally responsible to the king for its custody and safe-keeping for future generations.

The dean did, however, also have a huge personal income for his own disposal, and he enjoyed great status. This is clear from dean Say's *Liber Regie Capelle* of 1449 which states proudly and categorically in a chapter entitled 'Of the Dean's Income' that: 'on every day of the year unless it be a double or solemn feast the king and the queen offer gold' consisting of a five nobles' weight talent of gold from the king and a similar one from the queen. The former 'is redeemed by the king every day for seven pence sterling and these the dean receives at the hands of the clerk of the king's jewels and purse'. The queen's talent was similarly redeemed for four pence, which the dean also received.[11]

[9] Cal. Pat. Rolls 1414, p. 226.

[10] Cal. Pat. Rolls 1425, pp. 289 and 292.

[11] One one side of the king's talent was engraved a figure of the Trinity, with a superscription in the margin reading: 'Receive, O Holy Trinity, this oblation which I offer in thine honour.' The other side of the talent was engraved with the Annunciation of the Blessed Virgin Mary, the margin inscription reading: 'And to the blessed Mary and all thy Saints.'

This then was the dean's regular source of income, but it was grandly augmented by different arrangements on major feast days of the church. On these occasions the king and queen offered a noble of gold instead of the talent, while the prince, dukes and duchesses offered half a noble each, earls and countesses a quarter of gold, barons and baronesses a silver groat, and knights, squires and nobles a penny each. When one considers that on the six feasts of Christmas, Good Friday, Easter, Whitsun, Trinity Sunday and All Saints 'every one in the king's house and household is bound to make an offering', and that the household numbered '1,200 persons whose names are always written in the exchequer roll of the royal household', then one can begin to appreciate the enormous value of the dean's income when these pieces were redeemed.

'Taper talents' were also offered on the feast of the Purification of the Blessed Virgin Mary, when the king, queen, prince and 'all others of the king's court ... offer gold or silver pieces fixed into their tapers or candles'. The king and queen offered five nobles each, the prince, dukes, duchesses and marquesses five golden crowns each, earls and countesses five golden quarters, viscounts and barons five silver groats, knights and nobles five pennies, esquires and squires one penny each.

Lastly, on Good Friday rings of silver and gold together with other precious jewels were offered by the 'king in person in the chapel to the fragment of the most holy cross which remains continually in the dean's keeping in the vestry'. As Gordon Dunstan discovered, dean Say wrote, in relation to touching for the king's evil, that the rings 'are evidently consecrated by the touch of the king's hand, as the healing of various sicknesses effected by those rings frequently proves'.[12] The dean received a hundred marks on their redemption, although the king kept the actual right of disposal of the rings to himself. The queen, prince and other lords and courtiers also offered silver and gold in a similar manner to that heretofore described.

Dean Say concluded that at the time he was writing (1449), 'the oblations, regular income and other emoluments of the dean's office, over and above his right of vesture and service, and table allowance and dining rights for himself and his servants within the court, amounted to six hundred nobles, that is, one thousand two hundred ducats a year'.[13]

Dean Say tells us that the dean received every year for his livery twelve yards of scarlet or other fine cloth dyed in grain for his gown, tunic and under-tunic – or else eight marks in cash. We also learn that 'within the king's court he holds the status of a baron, having with him in the court itself 5 servants with him at table and an expense allowance from the

[12] *Liber Regie Capelle*, ch. 8.
[13] Ibid.

king as the other barons have'.[14]

The *Liber Niger Domus Regis* of *c.* 1483 gives us further information about the dean's rights. We hear that he had 'in the court a chapeleyn under him which he may assign to be by his power Confessor of the household'. For his quarters both day and night the dean was entitled to have three loaves, two measures of 'greete meat', half a pitcher of wine, two gallons of ale, and in the winter one torch and candles. To the dean also went all the wax used in the king's chapel on Candlemas day. Bedding and harness were provided for him, as were rushes all year round by the sergeant usher of the hall and chamber. The dean was also assigned 'loggin sufficiaunt for his horses'. If the dean was away from court then his personal yeoman was entitled to 'ete in the hall at the Chamberlain's bourde'. The other servants had to be provided for out of the dean's own pocket. The office of the vestiary was in his gift. We also learn from the *Liber Niger* that 'this Deane was determyned by King Henry V for ever to be a bachelor of divinity or a doctor'.

What of the dean's duties and functions in the fifteenth century? The *Liber Regie Capelle* states that the dean has 'in himself and by deputy, authority and power to order and administer all the sacraments and all sacramental rites within the chapel'. He had power to hear confessions and to absolve and dispense in all cases 'except those reserved to the Holy See'. But the dean also exercised 'the original jurisdiction of an archdeacon and the secondary jurisdiction of a bishop in criminal causes and the proving of wills'. The dean 'recognises no superior in spirituals except the archbishop of Canterbury for the time being'. As a final parting shot William Say clearly states that the 'jurisdiction and power of the dean extends over all the servants and household of the king and queen, of whatever dignity, estate or condition they may be'.[15] In his chapter entitled 'Of the Office of the Dean' Say describes it as the dean's duty to conduct the king and queen into the chapel for divine service, 'walking ahead of them in surplice and almuce'. On every major feast day the dean celebrated high mass and all other divine offices of the day both morning and evening, 'unless a bishop happens to be present'. Furthermore, 'the king is wont to wear his crown at least six times in the year, that is on Christmas day, the Epiphany, Easter day, Whit Sunday, All Saints day and on both feasts of St Edward'. On these occasions it was the dean's duty to carry the sceptres of the king and queen 'solemnly' to the chapel before mass, and there to kiss them and place them on the altar. The dean then carried the sceptres to the king and queen just before the procession and sprinkling of the holy water – the king and queen 'sitting in state beneath their canopies'. The king had meanwhile, before the procession, entered 'the choir of the chapel' wearing his crown,

[14] Ibid.
[15] Ibid., ch. 2.

and then went to 'the principal stall on the right of the choir, furnished with carpets and curtains of gold, and beneath a golden canopy'. After waiting there in 'royal apparel' surrounded by his lords, also in their 'distinctive apparels', until the procession moved down, the king then followed the procession out of the choir, a baron carrying the sword in front of the king, a duke or earl carrying his birretum, and the lord chamberlain following behind holding up the hem of the king's mantle. The dean was required to lead the queen, who was also crowned on these days, into her oratory, where she was accompanied by her lords, ladies and others. As the procession left the chapel the queen followed the king at a respectful distance and 'with features modestly composed'. The procession over, the king and queen returned 'until the offertory' to their oratory which was hung 'with hangings of gold and arras'.

It would have been during these great processions that the children of the Chapel Royal spotted the forbidden wearing of spurs in the chapel and challenged the wearer after the service to claim the fee due for this infringement of the Chapel Royal rules. Today, the Offering of The Queen's Gifts of gold, frankincense and myrrh is still an integral part of the service at the feast of the Epiphany on 6 January every year. The gifts are offered at the 'offertory' by two gentlemen ushers, representing the sovereign and sitting in the royal pew (i.e. gallery) in the chapel at St James's Palace. The nave and transept are lined by a detachment of yeomen of the guard in state uniform, while the gentlemen ushers process to the altar with the sovereign's gifts placed on two salvers,[16] which are received first by the sub-dean at the step to the sanctuary and then in turn from the sub-dean by the dean at the altar, who then elevates them in offering to God. Before the death of princess Caroline in 1758 the king offered these gifts in person, with the heralds present rather then the yeomen. Exactly what happened on the feast of Epiphany in 1758 is described in the New Cheque Book of the Chapel Royal on fol. 121:

Memorandum:-
The 6th January, 1758, On Account of the Princess Caroline's death (she being buried but the night before) His Majesty deputed His Grace the Duke of Devonshire Lord Chamberlain, to make the offering.

His Grace came into the Closet a little after 12 o'clock. The Carpet and Stool, and Velvet Carpet on the Communion Rails being placed (without the Cloth of Tissue) and the Nicene Creed ended – His Grace came down, and proceeded directly to the Altar (attended by the Hon. Mr Pelham, his Secretary, with the Box and Purses) took the purses and put them into the Gold Bason (held by the Sub-Dean) and returned back to the Closet.

N.B. The Yeomen of the Guard stood on each side of the passage to the Altar instead of the Heralds etc., etc.

---

[16] Dated 1821 and made by William Eaton, these once formed part of the collection of Chapel Royal plate at Brighton.

The ancient customs surrounding the crown-wearing ceremonies detailed by Say in 1449 have thus survived in very recognisable form. The dean still performs much the same function during the feast of the Epiphany as detailed in the description of 1449, while the youngest child of the Chapel Royal still receives 'spur money' from one of the gentlemen ushers upon challenging him (he wears spurs as a deliberate infringement, thus subjecting himself to the possibility of challenge) in the vestibule at the end of the service – the fee being conditional upon successful rendition of the gamut by the challenging chorister.

Returning briefly to the fifteenth-century duties of the dean, we learn some intimate details concerning the choral organisation under his eye from the *Liber Niger Domus Regis*, where it is clearly stated that 'the Dean makithe the said Rules of the parsones, clerkys, and all theire ceremonies, in this chappell', and that 'he assigneth the Subdeane and all the chaunters to guyde kepe and to Rule all the quere in stedfast service and honourable demeaning to oversee their service and song'. More specifically 'he assigneth also the order how any preest or clark shall take his rome aftir othir; hym ordereth every fryday to ... Rehearse the fautes [i.e. FA-UT]'.

In matters of discipline the dean's responsibility was 'to appoynt the remedis, and such as be defectiff or disobedient'. If it was decided to punish an offender, it was the prerogative of 'the deane or his deputie to send to the countinghouse to put hym out of wage as ofte as hym thynkith nedefull', according to the *Liber Niger*. The Old Cheque Book of the Chapel Royal contains many instances of such actions by the dean in the sixteenth and seventeenth centuries. Perhaps the most spectacular was the suspension of yeoman of the vestry, Henry Eveseed, on 29 September 1620 at a chapter held at Hampton Court 'under my Lord Deanes hand', for, among other misdemeanours, assaulting Mr Orlando Gibbons. Eveseed was given until All Saints following to reform his behaviour. He continued to misbehave, and at Whitehall on 3 March 1621 'his Lordship ... did then in Chapter ... pronounce his place to be utterly voyd'.[17]

We have already told the story of deans and their actions and responsibilities in the previous century under the house of Richmond (the Tudors),[18] but we should look at a most curious interregnum which occurred in the succession of deans during Elizabeth I's reign.

Dean George Carew's term of office ended in 1572. He had been appointed, as we have already seen, at the start of Elizabeth's reign in 1558. His term of office spanned almost exactly the same period as that of the lord chamberlain, Lord Howard of Effingham. The year 1572 saw the appointment of William Day as dean of the Chapel Royal while he was also dean of Windsor. There is some doubt as to whether his term of office

[17] See Chapter 23 for further details and other incidents involving Henry Eveseed.
[18] See Chapter 3.

as dean stretched as far as 1595. It appears that his term coincided with that of the lord chamberlain, the earl of Essex, who held office from 1572 until 1585, when he was succeeded by Henry Carey, 1st Lord Hunsdon.

An entry in the Old Cheque Book of the Chapel Royal dated 2 November 1608 refers to the calling of a chapter by the dean, James Montague, who had been appointed on Christmas day 1603, in which 'the said Deane examininge howe that office had byn used in tymes tofore, he founde that whiles syxe Lord Chamberlaines had the government of the Chappell (in the vacancy of a Deane) that the Subdeane and Gentlemen did injoye in the vestery those privileges which officers now would abridge them of.'[19] There is one earlier reference to this interregnum of deans in the Old Cheque Book, and this relates to 1593, when the sub-dean ruled that the gentlemen guilty of a third offence should 'by the said Subdeane be dismissed of his surplice and service in the Chapple or vestrye tyll he cann get relieff at the hand of the Deane, and, for the present of the Right Honorable the Lord Chamberlayne, our Cheefe Governor, under her Sacred Majestie'.[20] As the parallel cheque book of the Chapel Royal (or Bodleian Register, as I have for clarity termed it, held at the Bodleian Library but probably written by the sub-deans at the same time as the Old Cheque Book of the Chapel Royal held at St James's was written by the clerk of the cheque and serjeant of the vestry) mentions the office of dean in an item written under the year 1580, we can now see that sometime between 1580 and 1593 the office of dean of the Chapel Royal was relinquished by William Day in favour of the lord chamberlain. It would seem reasonable to assume, therefore, that the date of this transfer occurred in 1585 when Henry Carey was appointed lord chamberlain. If this was so then we can now understand why no further deans were appointed until Elizabeth's death in 1603 – for a dean might have wished to exercise his power to stop the children of the Chapel Royal acting on stage. It seems probable that in order to prevent the possible obstruction of a dean, Elizabeth I, Lord Hunsdon and his son George moved to prevent any such appointment. Certainly their love of theatre cannot be underestimated. John Stow in later editions of his *Survey of London* mentions the reign of six lord chamberlains over the Chapel Royal – exaggeration but not without a basis of truth.

The succession of deans of the Chapel Royal resumed with James Montague's appointment on Christmas day 1603. We know from the Old Cheque Book that the dean of the Chapel Royal presided over the wedding of Sir Phillipp Harbert and Susanna de Vere, daughter of the earl of Oxford, 'in the Chappell at Whitehaule, 1604, wher was payd for fees to Mr Deane of the Chappell xli, and to the gentlemen of the sayd Chappell vli'. The Dean is recorded too as having presided at the

---

[19] Old Cheque Book of the Chapel Royal, fol. 35.
[20] Ibid., fol. 2.

marriage of the 'young Earl of Essex ... to Frances Howard, daughter of the Earl of Suffolk, Lord Chamberlaine, in the Kinges Chappell at Whitehall, the 5th or 6th January 1605 (the Kinges Majestie giving her in maryage) wher was paid for fees to the Dean of the Chappell, he maryinge them, 10 li, and the gentlemen of the Chappell then her attendyinge 5 li'. Similarly, 6 January 1606 saw the wedding of Lord James Haye to Honor, the daughter of Lord Dennie, 'the Kinges Majestie giving her in marriage', and 'Doctor Mountague, Deane of the Chappell, marryinge them, had for his fee 10 li. And the Gentlemen for their extraordinary service and attendance 5 li as before had byn payd them and for the lyke service'.[21] The same fees applied to the wedding of Lord Haddington to Elizabeth, eldest daughter of the earl of Sussex ('the Kinges Majestie giving her in maryage') at the king's chapel at Whitehall on 9 February 1607.

These fees had become established about 1580, for before this, at marriages in both Westminster and Greenwich chapels used by the Chapel Royal in 1571, 1573, 1578 and 1579, the fee had been 'one bucke and xls'. Whether the dean received the 'bucke' or the money is not mentioned.

However, we do hear more of the dean's role in the wedding of Frederick Prince Elector Count Palatine of Reine and Lady Elizabeth, daughter of the king, in 'his Majestes Chappell at Whithale' on Sunday 14 February 1612, when although the archbishop of Canterbury performed the marriage ceremony, and 'uppon the sides of the Chappell from the stales up to the Communion Table weare a duble rowe of seates made for the Gentlemen of the Chappell, arayed with tapestry very comely', the 'Bishopp of Bathe and Welles, Deane of His Maj. Chappell, went into the pulpitt, which stood at the foote of the stepp before the Communion table, and preached uppon the Second of St John, the marriage of Canaa of Galilee: the sermon beinge ended, which continued not muche above halfe an hower, the Quier began another Anthem ...'.

At subsequent marriages in 1613 in the Whitehall chapel and 1617 at Hampton Court chapel there is no mention of the dean; only the gentlemen receiving 'five poundes' for their fee 'as before had been'. It is probable, however, that the dean did preside over these weddings and receive his fees.

The deans of the Chapel Royal had a very special role in state diplomacy. It was the dean's duty to hold a large Vulgate Bible at the swearing of oaths by the king and foreign ambassadors, within the sanctified precincts of the Chapel Royal buildings, signifying the 'maintenance and continuance' of treaties and leagues between England and foreign powers. The seventeenth century saw the dean performing much the same diplomatic role as his predecessors had done on the

---

[21] Ibid., fol. 76b.

battlefield – such as the concluding of terms for the truce between England and France at Vermondose in 1476 – only on a more refined indoor basis after the terms had been agreed.

Thus the Old Cheque Book records that in August 1604 'came an Embassador out of Spaine to take the Kinges othe for the maintenance and continuance of the League between them ...'. We are told then of 'his Majestie cominge into the Chappell, on his righte hand went the Constable of Spayne, and on his left the Spanishe lidger Embassador, and so they went up to the Communion table together'. The 'Lattin Bible of the Vulgar translacon' was 'held by the Dean of the Chappell in a Coape all the while the Oath was reade'. The assembled company eventually dismissed to the sound of 'organs playinge'. A similar 'manner and forme' of ceremony and oath-swearing is recorded in 1610, when the French ambassador and John Beaumanoir, Lord of Laverdin, took 'his Highnes Oath for the maintenance and continuance of the League between them' on 27 January, 'the Byble beinge held by the Bishopp of Bathe and Welles Deane of the Chappell, in a Coape, all the while the Oath was read'. A seventeenth-century engraving of the dean performing his role in state diplomacy has survived at the British Museum.[22] It depicts the ratification of the proposed marriage treaty between prince Charles and the Spanish infanta at the Chapel Royal, Whitehall, on 20 July 1623, and shows dean Launcelot Andrewes at the high altar.

We have already looked at many of the seventeenth-century deans in Chapter 8. Of importance to the royal succession is the information we learn from the principal baille to the Presbytery of Irvine that the marriage between 'the Lady Mary', eldest daughter of Charles I, with count William of Nassau, eldest son of Henry, prince of Orange, took place on 2 May 1641 and that 'Good Bishop Wren made the marriage'. Matthew Wren had been dean of the Chapel Royal since 1636. The only child of this marriage was the future William III.

The future dean of the Chapel Royal, Henry Compton, who was only ten years old at the outbreak of the Civil War, was for safety brought into the royalist camp at Edgehill and was therefore present at the first major battle between king and parliament. His father was killed at the battle of Hopton Heath 'refusing to give or take quarter'. Henry Compton was later to join a regiment of horse (in fact the future Life Guards) under Aubrey de Vere, earl of Oxford, serving until he was thirty years old, at which time he left the army for ordination. This army backround served him well as matters came to a head in the Glorious Revolution of 1688, culminating in the flight of James II by royal barge from Whitehall to Gravesend en route to Rochester and exile abroad. Learning of princess Anne's fear of her father's anger, especially towards her husband, George of Denmark, who had defected to William of Orange, Compton's reaction

---

[22] Reproduced on p. 100 above.

was to escort the princess from Bishop's House in Aldersgate Street to his country house at Castle Ashby via Epping Forest, preceding her in buff-coat and jack-boots, and armed with a sword and pistols.

Compton succeeded Walter Blandford as dean of the Chapel Royal. He was advanced to bishop of London from Oxford in 1675. Having been entrusted by Charles II with the education of his nieces – the princesses Anne and Mary – he found himself officiating at the marriage of Mary to William, Prince of Orange, on 4 November 1677 at Anne's private apartments at St James's Palace at 9 o'clock at night. The archbishop of Canterbury, for whom dean Compton was deputising, had fallen victim to the plague. The Chapel Royal Register of Marriages also records the marriage of Sir Christopher Wren and Jane Fitz-William on 24 February 1676. Wren, who at this time was supervising the beginning of the construction of St Paul's Cathedral to his own design, was to find himself barely a decade later refurbishing the Queen's Chapel at St James's. In 1683 dean Compton officiated at princess Anne's wedding to prince George of Denmark at 10 o'clock at night in the Chapel Royal building at St James's Palace. Charles II gave his niece away in the presence of queen Catherine of Braganza and the duke and duchess of York, among others.

Dean Compton's adherence to Protestantism did not go down well with the Roman Catholic James II, whose accession to the throne was marked by the necessity to alter the coronation service, as he refused to receive communion according to the rites of the Church of England. It was to be a different matter on William III's accession, when Henry Compton was required to conduct the service. He later recalled that part of the service which required the offering of thirty pieces of silver by the sovereign. These could not be found and had to be hastily produced by one of the peers! However, the year 1689 saw Henry Compton appointed dean of the Chapel Royal for the second time, in succession to to Nathaniel Crewe of Durham, to be succeeded in turn in 1713 by another soldier, John Robinson. Robinson had accompanied Charles XII of Sweden in his war against Denmark, Poland and Russia, returning to England in 1709 to be appointed dean of Windsor.

A series of plans of St James's Palace, known as William Dickinson's Notebook,[23] has only two names written on it. On one sketch 'Bishop of Salisbury' is written within the confines of a building which then occupied the area which is now the guardroom in engine court. Within another area towards the east end of the south range, later destroyed in the palace fire of 1809, occupying what is now an apartment in the south-west corner of friary court, is written 'Dolben'. This was the name of the sub-dean of the Chapel Royal from 1712-17. The bishop of Salisbury, Dr William Talbot, was appointed dean of the Chapel Royal by

---

[23] Dickinson had been assistant to Sir Christopher Wren. The Notebook is now at the Bodleian Library, MS Gough misc. antiq. 17.

This view of 'St James's House' from the south west, drawn by Kip in 1705 and published in *Britannia Illustrata* in 1708, shows both the dean's and the sub-dean's quarters. In 1717 dean William Talbot occupied the building towards the left side of the picture in front of and below the great gatehouse, facing onto the pump court with a low wall running in front of the house and adjoining an abutment onto the north-south range of state apartments. A cellar and secret tunnel still survive. Also in 1717 sub-dean Dolben occupied the area of the second 'bay' facing onto the palace gardens on the centre right of the picture. (Reproduced by courtesy of the Guildhall Library, City of London)

George I on 15 March 1717. This therefore dates the sketch exactly to 1717.

The dean's house can be seen in a sketch drawn in 1705 by Kip and subsequently published in his *Britannia Illustrata* in 1708. The cellar of the dean's house still survives beneath the present 'modern' guardroom in engine court, as does a tunnel lined with brick, evidently built as a secret passage, leading south under what is now bottle arch, parallel to the quarters of the gentlemen-at-arms, before running off at an angle south-eastwards under the north/south range of state apartments.

The marriage of princess Anne, the princess royal and eldest daughter of George II, to prince William of Nassau and Orange was conducted by the dean of the Chapel Royal, Edmund Gibson, who had succeeded William Talbot in 1717. The wedding took place in the Lutheran chapel (i.e. Queen's Chapel, Marlborough Gate) on 14 March 1734. The elaborate decorations made especially for this event can be appreciated from the etching by Kent now in the print room of the British Library. Anne is said to have had a thirst for power and to have remarked to her father, upon hearing his warning of William's unattractive appearance, 'I would marry

The secret tunnel at St James's Palace as it is today.

him even if he were a baboon'! In fact she grew very fond of him. The anthem sung at this marriage was composed by Handel who four months before the wedding had conducted a rehearsal of it in front of 'their Majesties and the Royal Family at St James's'. According to the heralds' office records, 'at this marriage the prince made no endowment or gift of gold or silver, the Bishop of London acquainting Garter that that form had long been discontinued'. We learn also that 'the officers of arms had a supper provided for them at the Gloucester Tavern in Pall Mall, by order of the Board of Green Cloth, and wine from his Majesty's cellars'. Dean Gibson also conducted the wedding of Frederick, prince of Wales, eldest son of George II and the princess Augusta, youngest daughter of the duke of Saxe-Gotha, in the Chapel Royal building at St James's Palace on 27 April 1736. The Precedent Book of the lord chamberlain's office stated

The marriage of Anne, eldest daughter of George II, and William, prince of Nassau and Orange, in the Queen's Chapel, St James's Palace (then the French and Dutch Chapel), on 14 March 1733/4. (Photographed from the print by William Kent at the Guildhall Library)

240

that 'the marriage service was read by the Bishop of London (Dr. Edmund Gibson), Dean of the Chapel Royal, and after the same was over a fine Anthem was performed by a great number of voices and instruments'.

Edmund Gibson was not, however, called upon to celebrate the marriage of princess Mary, fourth daughter of George II, to Frederick, hereditary prince of Hesse Cassel for whom the duke of Northumberland stood proxy, which took place on 8 May 1740 in the Chapel Royal building at St James's Palace. The Precedence Book records that the ceremony was conducted by the archbishop of Canterbury, and that after the benediction 'an Anthem, composed and set to music by Mr Handel was sung'. Nor was Thomas Sherlock's successor as dean of the Chapel Royal, Thomas Hayter, called upon to conduct the marriage of George II to princess Charlotte of Mecklenburg-Strelitz on 8 September 1761, although it took place at the 'German chapel' (i.e. Queen's Chapel, Marlborough Gate) at 10 o'clock in the morning. The service was conducted by Dr Secker, archbishop of Canterbury. Dr Boyce, at this time composer with the Chapel Royal, composed a grand anthem specifically for this occasion, entitled 'The King Shall Rejoice'. Garter king of arms noted that 'Over the Altar were the organ, and gallery for the music and Choir, the lower part of the walls being hung with crimson velvet, the upper part with tapestry, the floor covered with cloth, and the Haut Pas before the Altar with silver tissue. The King and Queen sat under a canopy of Crimson velvet laced and fringed with gold, and lined with silver tissue.'[24]

At the Chapel Royal in St James's Palace, George Augustus Frederick, prince of Wales and duke of Cornwall, eldest son of George III, married princess Caroline Amelia Elizabeth, daughter of the duke of Brunswick-Lunenburg on 8 April 1795. Again the marriage was conducted by the archbishop of Canterbury rather than the dean of the Chapel Royal. We know from Sir Stephen Cottrell's account of this service that there was a 'Closet of the Maids of Honour in the Chapel Royal at St James's' which was used on this occasion for foreign ministers and their ladies.

Two years later, on 18 May 1797, the prince of Württemberg married the princess royal, eldest daughter of George III, at the Chapel Royal, St James's, and we can see from the details of this marriage that the power of the dean of the Chapel Royal had diminished little since Henry Compton deputised for the archbishop of Canterbury in 1677 and conducted William III's coronation in 1689. Certainly it was the archbishop of Canterbury who conducted this marriage in 1797, but we learn from the Old Cheque Book that the guests were 'admitted by permission of the Dean of the Chapel Royal'. He issued the tickets and allotted himself twenty, the lord chamberlain twenty, and the sub-dean six in the chapel and twelve behind the orchestra. There was no question

---

[24] See Sheppard, *Memorials of St James's Palace*, vol. 2, p. 81.

of the lord chamberlain assuming responsibility for the seating arrangements. The prince and princess of Orange were allotted the royal gallery (closet), as had been done at the prince of Wales's wedding.

No further royal weddings took place at this chapel for forty-three years, until queen Victoria married prince Albert in 1840, and so nothing further can be gleaned from such occasions concerning the responsibilities of the dean of the Chapel Royal during that period.

In 1770 Richard Terrick, dean of the Chapel Royal, gained possession of 32 St James's Square. It was to become a base for successive bishops of London as deans of the Chapel Royal, and would have provided an ideal location from which to attend the services at the Chapel Royal, St James's. Thus deans Lowth, Beilby Porteous and Randolph used it, and dean Howley rebuilt it in his term of office as bishop of London between 1814 and 1828. Dean Blomfield's son was to write in his memoirs of his father: 'Of the two episcopal residences the Bishop always regarded London House in St James's Square as little more than an official place of business ... Obliged to spend the season in London, he returned to Fulham in the summer ... .'

Following dean Archibald Tait's translation to Canterbury as archbishop in 1868, it seems that subsequent bishops of London rather abandoned London House, as no. 32 had come to be known, in favour of Fulham Palace.[25] Dasent remarked that no. 32 was empty at the time he was writing 'save on those occasions when it is galvanized into temporary usefulness for the purposes of a charity bazaar or a missionary meeting'.[26] It was dean Mandell Creighton who revived London House in 1897. The seventeen bedrooms at no. 32 were completely renovated, as was the room that was to become a chapel. Dean Winnington Ingram managed to keep London House afloat until 1921, when the Caledonian Club took a lease on it, eventually buying it in 1939. The dean was thus no longer able to stay within a short walk of the Chapel Royal, but subsequent deans have admirably maintained their duties to the Chapel Royal despite this disadvantage.

Although the dean had enormous power at his disposal, he had nevertheless to keep a tight rein on the Chapel Royal to prevent abuses going on behind his back. A case in point was the unseemly sacramental wine dispute of 1762, which was eventually settled at 'Bishops House' in Frith Street, Soho, where the confessor to the household, Dr Morgan, and the serjeant of the vestry, William Lovegrove, were ordered to be present. There dean Osbaldeston 'severely reprimanded Mr Morgan for Consecrating above a pint of Wine more than was necessary for the Congregation that Received the Sacrament, on purpose to have the overplus for his own use, which he ordered to be set by for himself. The

[25] See Denys Forrest, *St James's Square* (Quiller Press, London, 1986)
[26] A.I. Dasent, *History of St James's Square* (Macmillan, London, 1895).

Bishop told him, if he heard of any such practice again he wou'd suspend him.'[27] The dean ruled that the serjeant of the vestry was clearly in the right according to past precedent for 'the Serjeant was in the Situation and Place of a Church Warden, and that the care of the Wine belonged to him, and not to the Curate'.[28] Appeal to the Old Cheque Book confirmed this in every respect. The extensive correspondence relating to this dispute is also interesting for quite a different reason, for we gain from it some idea of the numbers of communicants at the Chapel Royal services at this time. In one letter of April 1762 Mr Morgan stated that 'there were not above two or three and twenty Communicants'.[29] We learn too that 'formerly six Bottles were allow'd, very lately but three'.

Dean Thomas Sherlock (1748-61) had a delicate matter to settle with regard to accusations that he was starving the seventy-year-old groom of the vestry, Richard Norton (1730-56), and in particular that he had 'taken away his bread and given it to another'. Norton had in fact abused his position over a number of years. It began when dean Edmund Gibson (bishop of Lincoln) first allowed the groom of the vestry 'to place Ladies in the vestry, and to take to his own use the Fees and Perquisites arising from thence'.[30] This resulted in the groom taking care 'to fill it so full, that the Bishops and Preachers have found great difficulty in passing to and from the Vestry',[31] and dean Sherlock himself wrote on 15 May 1756 that 'so long ago as the year 1752 I thought it necessary to take off a passage from the inner Vestry into the Chapel, for the Vestry was generally so full of Company, and Hassocks, that it was very difficult to get by them, and I have been forced myself to go into the open Court, where the Footmen wait, in my Habit, to get round by the other Door to my Seat'.[32] Serjeant Lovegrove elaborates that this latter door was by the 'great door', that is to say the gatehouse door, and was thus the door still used on occasions today at the back of what is now the sub-dean's vestry and in which there is a small observation grille. But to avoid this necessity, 'a small slip of the Vestry has been set apart from the rest and inclosed (by your Lordship's Order) for the free passage of the Bishops and Preacher to and from their Places in the Chapel'.

Groom Norton retaliated by stirring up the ladies to support his cause. He allowed them to block the 'slip' passage against the serjeant's instructions and accused the dean of taking his bread away and giving it instead to another servant. He then managed to get his case represented (to the princess Caroline) 'in a deplorable but unfair light which was however productive of a letter from Dr Couryare to Mrs Sherlock'. Dean

---

[27] Serjeant William Lovegrove's private manuscript, fol. 147.
[28] Ibid.
[29] Ibid., fol. 143.
[30] Ibid., fol. 96.
[31] Ibid.
[32] Ibid. fol. 99.

Sherlock had finally had enough. He wrote in reply that he did indeed 'straiten the room for the Ladies, and consequently Mr Norton's Perquisites' which led to 'indifferent language upon that account' but, as we have seen, out of necessity. As for the bread incident 'it is true in neither part', for it should have been distributed, according to Chapel Royal custom recorded in the Old Cheque Book, to all the officers of the vestry. The groom had in fact been procuring it all to himself and the dean had only restored the former practice in which the groom got a share anyway. Dean Sherlock noted that he had 'borne with him for eight years, till at last he thought himself under no Control, and claimed the Governing of the Vestry, and behaved with so much insolence and rudeness, that I thought it necessary to put an end to his Attendance there, and to order him to his own Duty as Groom of the Vestry'. It was made clear that 'as to the rank in which these officers [serjeant, yeoman and groom] have one amongst another, the Serjeant is the First and as he is the proper person to convey the Orders of the Dean to others, they are to obey and observe his directions'.[33] Thus the matter was finally settled.

By and large the deans enjoyed a good reputation, although dean Sherlock, upon appointing William Lovegrove as serjeant of the vestry in 1752, appeared at the same time to have fleeced him by making him 'pay dearly for his Place' with 'Saddle Bonds', concerning which Lovegrove states: 'I have and must pay up to Lady Day 1777 which will amount to upwards of £1,800.' But although Lovegrove writes that 'I imagine this point of Saddle Bonds will be continued by the Deans of the Chapel Royal', he pointedly excludes the dean from the later advice he gives to his future successors as serjeant of the vestry: 'Act cautiously, but firmly, the whole Body (excepting the Dean) are Leeches, and the Serjeant's Mortal Enemies; they wou'd strip him to his shirt if they could.'[34]

Sub-dean Aspinwall was singled out for particular criticism by Lovegrove for apparently adding the duty 'to keep the Altar' to the serjeant's duties after dean Gibson had signed the new order for duties. Lovegrove thus describes the sub-dean as 'the Serjeant's Mortal Enemy'. Lovegrove claimed, perhaps rather fancifully, that the serjeant 'never did Sweep and Dust the Altar for he received no allowance for mops, brooms, dusters etc.'

However, deans seem to have been well thought of by most Chapel Royal gentlemen and officials despite their role as ultimate judge in matters of discipline.

Serjeant Lovegrove was to be proved right over the question of 'Saddle Bonds', however, as is recorded in serjeant Roe's diary, kept between 1807 and 1812. Roe was house steward to Beilby Porteous, bishop of London and dean of the Chapel Royal, and evidently thought the bishop

33 Ibid., fol. 100.
34 Ibid., fol. 151.

To The Right Reverend The Lord Bishop of London.

My Lord /

In compliance with your Lordship's desire, I lay before you the following, respecting the Old Surplices at The Chapel Royal.

After I had seen your Lordship on Monday at Fulham Palace, I called at Chelsea on Mr. Smith, The Father of the Chapel, and I had the following plain statement from him, which he says has been handed down from time immemorial, Viz: That New Surplices were provided every Three years, and that as a matter of course, The Gentlemen, and Children, took the Old ones as their perquisites, at the same time paying Mr. Dix, the then Sergeant of the Vestry, Two shillings and sixpence each, as a remuneration for his trouble, in placing every month in our Cupboards, Clean Surplices, and removing the dirty ones. It cannot however be thought that the trifling sum of half a Crown so paid, could have been given as the Value of the Surplices, but for some supposed extra trouble. It should also here be mentioned that the Sergeant of the Vestry, has a Salary of 40£ a year for getting the Surplices washed: and also that the Gentlemen continue to this day the same sum of half a Crown to Mrs. Rose for keeping their Vestry clean.

After Mr. Dix died, Mr. Rowe was appointed Sergeant, and it was agreed to pay him 5⁄ each for his trouble. During the war with America the Surplices were sent to the various Hospitals, to make bandages &c. on the termination thereof, they were not sent away, and on New Surplices being again provided, Mr. Rowe demanded 10.6. this Mrs. Smith declares was always

---

Written sometime before April 1833, this letter requesting the perquisite of disposing of old surplices previously worn by gentlemen of the Chapel, written by one of the gentlemen, Richard Clark, reveals that 'During the war with America the surplices were sent to the various Hospitals, to make bandages'. This would have been the Anglo-American war of 1812-14.

prone to some sharp practice with regard to questions of patronage. Thus in an entry relating to the year 1805 Roe writes:

> the Master of the Boys at the Chapel Royal has died the previous morning having also held the post of Lutinist at £41 a year on sinecure (not being required to perform any duties). Two applicants by the names of Page and Evans have been after his place, and the Bishop ought to give it to his Servants, but I fear unless he is the gainer by it he will give it from them. I have a pretty good experience of this for it is certain I should never have been Serjeant of the King's Chapel had not the Bishop been interested in it, for I paid to his order £1,000. I hope the world will know it.

The 'Master of the Boys at the Chapel Royal' to whom Roe referred was the late Edmund Ayrton, whose place was in the event given neither to Page nor Evans but to John Stafford Smith. However, we could perhaps add 'Saddle Bonds' to the sources of regular income of the deans of the Chapel Royal, certainly in the eighteenth century.

For at least the last 220 years it has been the custom for the dean of Westminster Abbey to preach at the Chapel Royal on Good Friday. He has done so by a form of standing royal command. This was made clear by dean Stanley, describing the circumstances of the appointment of Dr John Thomas to the deanery of Westminster Abbey in 1768:[35]

> The King was heard to say, upon his appointment, 'I am glad to prefer Dr Thomas who has so much merit. We shall now be sure of a good sermon on Good Friday.' This alludes to the long-established custom by which the Dean of Westminster (probably from the convenience of his being in town at that season) preaches always in the Chapel Royal on that day.

Along with the lord high almoner when not a bishop, and the sub-almoner when not a royal chaplain, the dean of Westminster was until at least 1900 robed in a black Geneva gown and bands when preaching at the Chapel Royal, as he was not on the list of royal chaplains. The Preachers Books at the Chapel Royal, dating from 1780, record that in addition to preaching upon Good Friday the dean of Westminster preached upon Easter day at the Chapel Royal on two occasions during the Napoleonic War, in 1804 and 1805. As it is traditional for the Chapel Royal not to wear surplices on Good Friday, the dean of Westminster may well not have been aware that that the surplices of holland cloth worn by the clergy and gentlemen of the Chapel Royal for all other services were donated for hospital use to support the war with America between

[35] Dean Stanley, *Memorials of Westminster Abbey*, p. 511, quoted in Sheppard, *Memorials of St James's Palace*, vol. 2, p. 309n.

1812-14, during which the White House was burnt and many casualties resulted. The national memorial to major general Robert Ross, who successfully led that attack, is located over the crypt door at St Paul's Cathedral – the seat of the bishop of London, who has held simultaneously the office of dean of the Chapel Royal since 1748.

15

Sub-Deans of the Chapel Royal

The origins of the office of sub-dean of the Chapel Royal evidently extend back further than the formal establishment of that office in 1483 as a result of the formation of the royal free household chapel in that year.

Say's *Liber Regie Capelle* of 1449 makes mention in the chapter entitled 'Duties in the Chapel' of 'decani aut eius substituti' (the dean or his substitute) in relation to the conduct of matins every morning at the summons of a bell rung by one of the children of the Chapel at 7 o'clock. Later, in the chapter entitled 'Of the Office of the Dean', it is stated to be the duty of the dean himself, or his deputy, to conduct the king and queen into the chapel at the due and accustomed hours for divine service. The Latin used reads: 'Ad officium insuper decani pertinet per se aut suum depatutum.' The Latin for sub-dean, 'sub-decanus', is apparently deliberately not employed – merely the word 'deputatum'. Certainly no special arrangements are mentioned in relation to the income of the dean's 'deputy'. We can therefore presume that although the dean occasionally found need for a deputy this role was not officially recognised until the formation of the royal free household chapel in 1483, as a result of which one Nicholas Hewys was appointed officially to discharge the function of 'sub-dean'.

The origins of the sub-dean's office may not be as simple as this, however, for there is a curiosity which still points to a pre-1483 date for the establishment of the office. This is to be found in Edward IV's *Liber Niger Domus Regis*. Woodfill suggests that this work was written about 1478.[1] If so, then its remarks with regard to the sub-dean are of especial significance. The chapter on the dean's office contains a passage which reads: 'he assigneth the Sub-Dean and the Chaunters to guyde kepe and to Rule all the quere in stedfast service and honourable demeaning ... .' Moreover should any of the singing clerks be disobedient or 'defectiff' in his rendition of the 'Fa-uts' (i.e. Gamut) which were rehearsed every Friday, then 'the Dean or his deputie to send to the countinghouse to put hym out of wage as ofte as hym thynkith nedeful'. From this account, therefore, one could presume that a sub-dean held office at least from

---

[1] W.L. Woodfill, *Musicians in English Society from Elizabeth to Charles I* (Da Capo Press, New York, 1969), p. 161.

1478. But if Woodfull is mistaken and the Chapel Royal entry in the *Liber Niger Domus Regis* was not written until five years later, then 1483 would indeed fit neatly as the date when the office of sub-dean was formally established, and consequently described in Edward's IV's Household Ordinances of that year. One certain observation can be made from all these accounts, and this is that the sub-dean and/or his predecessors had the specific task of ensuring the continued high standard of musical training and performance. For this reason the sub-dean had to be a musician of good standing and it was thus natural that he was chosen at first by the gentlemen clerks of the Chapel Royal from among their numbers.

The formation of the royal free household chapel in 1483 formalised the following hierarchy: the dean and three canons who were to act as sub-dean, treasurer and precentor, together with twenty-four chaplains and gentlemen clerks, as well as the children and vestry officials of the chapel.

The actual responsibilities of the sub-dean were to choose the music and anthems to be sung, authorise absences and prescribe penalties for minor offences that could be dealt with without recourse to the adjudication of the dean. The sub-dean, being chosen from among the 'Worshipfull Companye of Gentlemen', is almost invariably found subscribing his name first to the rules and ordinances adopted by the gentlemen or required by the dean.

The 1592 oath sworn by the sub-dean survived in the same form, with minor changes to the sovereign's name and title, under Stuart and Hanoverian monarchs, requiring the sub-dean 'not to conceal or kepe secrete anye treasons committed or spoken againste her Highness [Queen Elizabeth I] or anye her successors' but to reveal such 'within 24 hours' to the 'Councell' or to the nearest justice of the peace. He had, too, to recognise the sovereign as 'the only supreme Governor of this Realme and all other her Highnes dominions and contreys, as well in all spirituall and ecclesiasticall things and causes as temporall'.

Rules with regard to absentees were first recorded in the Old Cheque Book from the year 1593, while the choice of services and anthems was first recorded in 1604. Of interest is the period 1630 to 1640, during which the standing orders were signed by the dean himself rather than the sub-dean. But if the choice of service and anthems was the task of the sub-dean, there were other duties with regard to the conduct of services which were not his prerogative.

For example, one of the gentlemen clerks elected from among their company was elected a 'recorder of songs'. At the time of James I's funeral a certain John Steephens held that office and was accorded the same extra provision of black cloth as the master of the children, clerk of the cheque and the senior organist. This gives some indication of the importance of the post. Elsewhere in the Old Cheque Book, we learn that

The Chapel Royal

in 1623, following the death of William Byrd and before the admission of John Crocker, the wages were disposed of in the meantime in the following manner: 'To Mr Steephens the xxix May ... parte for pricking of a sett of bookes for the ... iii li iiis. To him the Third of December ... for pricking in the bookes iii li xiis. Item, for li quire of ruled [paper]. Item paid for a reame of ordinary paper vs. Item, Mr Stephens the third of May 1627 for paper, pricking 20 smale bookes for the Chappell iii li iis.' The task of actually providing the music required by the sub-dean was the responsibility of the recorder of songs.

The exception to this was in the period following the Restoration in the latter half of the seventeenth century when numerous entries are to be found regarding the pricking of songs by the sub-dean, acting as 'recorder of songs'. These, though, were exceptional circumstances and matters returned to normal. Today there is still a music librarian elected from among the gentlemen of the Chapel Royal who performs the ancient task of the recorder of songs. This office, though, does not necessarily combine with that of senior gentleman by length of service. Nor is it to be confused with the curatorial duty of the serjeant of the vestry to maintain the Chapel Royal's manuscripts and books.

An entry in the Old Cheque Book dated 1603/4 reveals that the sub-deans had evidently from time to time chosen music too difficult for the children of the Chapel to sing:

it was ordered at the same Chapter that the whole service and the songes to be performed in the Chappell shall be appoynted by Mr Dean or by the Sub-Deane of the Chappell at all tymes, and in their absence by the substitute, yet not without the advice of the Master of the Children, for suche songes as are to be performed by the Children of the Chappell.

Alan Smith writes of the Bodleian Register – the parallel manuscript to the Old Cheque Book – that it may have been kept by a member of the Chapel, 'perhaps the sub-dean, who was in charge of the day-to-day administration of the Choir'.[2] The Register conflicts in some entries with the record of the Old Cheque Book, which was probably the 'official' record of Chapel Royal affairs.

The death of a sub-dean would on occasion require special provision for his funeral, in that his burial wishes could involve travel to the chosen place. Thus the Old Cheque Book records that on the death of sub-dean Davies in 1623, the dean provided 'for the charge of the gentlemen and children for iii choches [coaches] and boat hire from Westminster to Harmonsworth to the funerall of Subdean Davies ...'.

Sub-deans generally enjoyed the respect and, often, the affection of the gentlemen clerks and were thus crucial in encouraging the gentlemen to

2 'The Gentlemen and Children of the Chapel Royal of Elizabeth I: an annotated register', *Royal Musical Association Research Chronicle* 5 (1965), pp. 13-46.

perform their best. This is still the case today – the present sub-dean being a musician of high standing and a co-editor of the *New English Hymnal*, published in 1987, which the Chapel Royal have warmly adopted.

The sub-dean's role in the eighteenth century was summarised clearly by serjeant William Lovegrove in his record of the affairs of the Chapel Royal written between 1752 and 1777:[3]

> To the Sub-dean it belongeth to supply the absence of the Dean, and to be as frequently at the Chapel as he can: to take care that everything therein be conducted with decency and regularity; More especially upon Sundays and Holy Days, when it is the Duty of his Office to go up to the Altar, and to read the Second Service. On certain days the Subdean goes into the Desk, and Reads the whole service, Viz: Upon Christmas Day, Easter Day, WhitSunday, Ash Wednesday, Good Friday; and on all other days appointed, as Days of Thanksgiving, and Fasting. The Subdean Swears and admits all persons into their Places and Offices, by Virtue of a warrant from the Dean, To him directed for that purpose ...

At this time the sub-dean's residence was in Middle Scotland Yard, but this building was demolished along with other houses in 1819. Dr Bailey was the last sub-dean to reside there, and he died in 1792. His successor, Dr Pearce, 'finding the house in a dilapidated state' obtained in 1794 a grant of £30 per annum in lieu of the house. On his succession by Dr Holmes an application for the same allowance in 1803 was at first refused by the treasury on the basis that it had been a 'personal' claim of Dr Pearce. But finally, in 1819, the treasury reconsidered their view and paid an allowance of £60 per annum. This was confirmed by a treasury warrant of 8 January 1834 which provided for the allowance 'as a compensation for the loss of the Official house lately attached to the situation of the Sub Dean of the Chapel Royal'.

The early nineteenth century saw little or no change in the sub-dean's duties. The dean's rules of 20 May 1831 for example state clearly that 'the Sub-Dean shall be constant in his attendance, and shall take care that every thing be conducted with decency and regularity'. This was no inconsiderable commitment, as we also learn that 'Divine Service is performed in the Chapel Royal, Morning and Evening, throughout the Year'.

Thirty years later, in 1860, the Chapel Royal commissioners produced a report, the details of which were recorded in the New Cheque Book of the Chapel Royal. They claimed to have looked carefully into the roles of the various members and officials of the Chapel Royal, with a brief to streamline their duties. The Chapel Royal 'Rules for the performance of Divine Worship in the Chapel Royal' determined by the dean in a chapter

---

[3] Lovegrove manuscript, fol. 50.

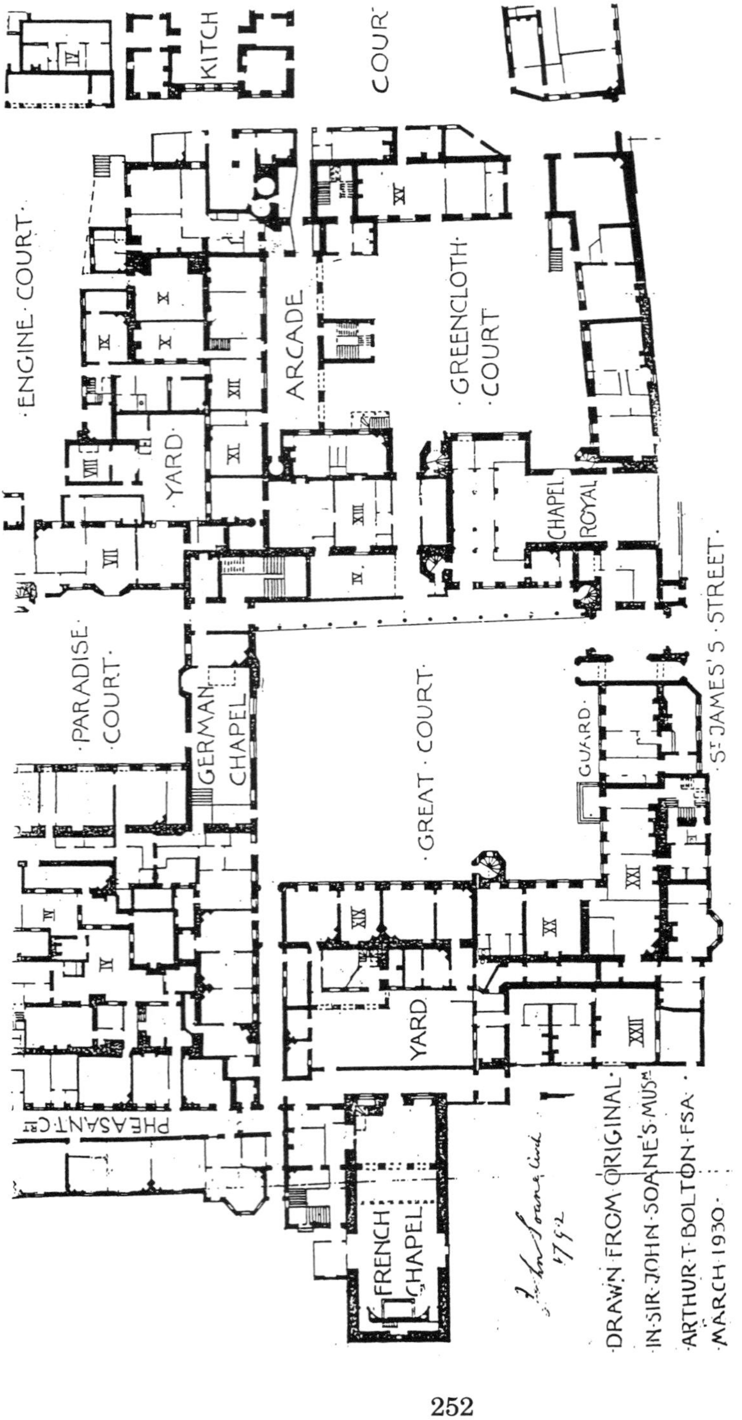

The Sloane Plan of 1792.

Labels visible on plan:

KITCH
COURT
ENGINE·COURT·
·YARD·
·X·
·IX·
·XII·
·XI·
·VIII·
·VII·
ARCADE
·XV·
·GREENCLOTH·
·COURT·
·XIII·
·IX·
CHAPEL ROYAL
·PARADISE·
·COURT·
GERMAN CHAPEL
·GREAT·COURT·
GUARD·
·IV·
·IX·
·XIX·
·XX·
·XXI·
·YARD·
·XXII·
·PHEASANT·C.T·
FRENCH CHAPEL
St·JAMES'S·STREET·

·DRAWN·FROM·ORIGINAL·
·IN·SIR·JOHN·SOANE'S·MUSM·
·ARTHUR·T·BOLTON·FSA·
·MARCH·1930·

252

held in the dean's vestry in the Chapel Royal at St James's Palace in 1792, specifically detailed the sub-dean to 'regularly examine the Cheque, and shall deliver the same to the dean every Sunday Morning when he is present, and send it to him when he is absent'. By the 'Cheque' was meant the attendance roll of the gentlemen of the Chapel, for 'All the priests and Gentlemen of the Chapel shall wait in their turns in their persons, according to the waitings last appointed and if leave of absence should in future be wanted through illness or any other urgent case, application shall be made to the Subdean and by him reported to the Dean'. These specific duties of the sub-dean were reaffirmed in the dean's rules of 1823 issued from 'London House in St James's Square', and again in the dean's rules of April 1831.

The report and recommendations of the Chapel Royal commissioners of 1860 were supposedly based upon a thorough appraisal of the duties hitherto performed by members and officers of the Chapel Royal. In fact it was woefully lacking in its historical appreciation. For instance, the commissioners stated of the sub-dean's office that 'constant attendance does not seem to have been required of the Sub-Dean previous to the appointment of the late Dr Wesley, who having been originally Chaplain to the Household at St James's Palace eventually held the 3 appointments of a Chaplain in Ordinary to the Queen, Chaplain to the Household, and Subdean of the Chapel Royal'. This observation was wrong, for the dean's rules of 1792 stated clearly that 'the Subdean shall attend the Chapel Service daily as long as health will permit, particularly on Sundays and Holy days, and shall take care that everything therein be conducted with Decency and Regularity'. Moreover the dean's rules of 1823 stated that 'The Subdean shall be constant in his attendance, and shall take care that everything be conducted with decency and regularity'. The dean's rules of 1831 use the same wording. Dr Wesley was appointed sub-dean in 1847, so the commissioners were wildly adrift in their knowledge of the true workings and constitution of the Chapel Royal. They made many other mistakes in their historical summing-up, but eventually ended by recommending that the sub-dean do in fact, and apparently unknown to them, what his predecessors always had done, namely:

> be responsible under the Dean's direction for the due regulation of the whole service, and for the musical arrangements, and that he be required to preach, in the absence of the Chaplain-in-Ordinary in Waiting … hold himself in readiness when called upon to do any duty required in Her Majesty's private Chapel … be responsible for the Pastoral care of the families resident within the precincts of St James's Palace … matters connected with the discipline of the Chapel … keep the Registry, and Cheque Book of Attendances of the officers of the Chapel Royal and of the Ceremonies which take place there … that his duties be principally confined to the Chapel Royal at St James's Palace.

The sub-dean was also to retain jurisdiction over the German chapel at St James's, the French chapel, the Whitehall chapel and, curiously and mistakenly, the Savoy chapel. For all this the commissioners recommended that the he be paid a salary of £300 per annum together with £60 from the office of works in lieu of the house in Middle Scotland Yard formerly belonging to the office of sub-dean.

Although the Chapel Royal commissioners produced their report in 1860, their subsequent continued presence led to some confusion. There exists a letter written by the lord chamberlain's office to the sub-dean, and kept in the Chapel Royal archive on the premises, which reads: 'Dr Holden's appointment is not held under the commission – It is a private arrangement which is made with their sanction.'

One of the first matters dealt with by the sub-dean after the commission report was the vexed question of moustaches! This was apparently of rather worrying concern to queen Victoria. It culminated in an instruction from the dean to the sub-dean dated 15 February 1862: 'I have received from the Lord Chamberlain an intimation that her Majesty the Queen has given him authority to prevent the wearing of moustaches by clergymen holding appointments and officiating at her Majesty's Chapels Royal, as a household and Court regulation. I have therefore to request you to see that this regulation is carried out.'

While the lord chamberlain's office was tightening its grip on surviving moustaches, a year later the sub-dean, Edgar Sheppard, was pursuing more conventional lines of duty – acting on behalf of the dean in minor matters of discipline and regulation. An attendance list, or 'cheque', was enforced for the clergy and gentlemen of the choir because 'certain difficulties have been found to arise in securing the attendance of the required number ...'. So from 5 October 1863 there was by order of the dean 'suspended on each Sunday Morning in the passage leading to the Chapel a complete list of the Clergy and Gentlemen of the Choir who are appointed to officiate at each service on the Sunday next following'. The sub-dean had a specific duty under these orders, for the list was 'to be signed by the Sub-Dean and no change shall be allowed ... except by formal leave obtained in writing by the Dean, or the Sub-Dean, and such a list shall remain hung up until after the Sunday of which it regulates when it will be sent to the Dean with a Certificate from the Sub-Dean that it has been fully complied with'. Although this order was issued from London House on 25 August 1863 it was merely one more in a series of such orders issued from time to time through the centuries when attendance broke down.

The sub-dean's traditional role of maintaining the high standard of musical accompaniment to divine service is clearly reflected in his memorandum of 1890 requiring 'the Organist to practice the Boys of the Chapel Royal daily for the space of one full hour in the Chapel Royal – the hours, to avoid any confusion, to be fixed every week with the Master of the Boys and Mr Organist'. The name 'Jekyll' is here crossed out, thereby suggesting a long-lasting rule for the future rather than a temporary memorandum. Also in this memorandum of 1890 is the requirement for 'the Organist to attend full rehearsal (Boys and Gentlemen) every Saturday Afternoon'.

The latter half of the nineteenth century and the early twentieth century were curiously characterised by a disturbing ignorance with regard to the Chapel Royal and its distinguished history. There were directives from the lord chamberlain's office that were evidently based upon the misconception that the Chapel Royal was a building, or series of buildings. This led to an awkward moment when the Whitehall chapel was discontinued as a building to be used by the Chapel Royal on 29 October 1890. The lord high almoner, writing from '6 Grays Court', decided that in future Royal Maundy would be held at Westminster Abbey and that the services of the Chapel Royal would thus no longer be required – the choir of Westminster Abbey would provide the necessary choral accompaniment. This, of course, totally misunderstood the position of the Chapel Royal, whose task and purpose it had always been to accompany the sovereign on major occasions of a religious and state nature, and to minister to the personal spiritual welfare of the sovereign wherever the sovereign might be. For this reason sub-deans of the Chapel Royal have often been also sub-almoners of the royal almonry. The matter was eventually settled in favour of the Chapel Royal, though not without a struggle, for it had to be appreciated that although the sovereign had not actually made a distribution of Royal Maundy in person since 1685, and in fact was not to do so again until George V made one of the distributions in person in 1932, the lord high almoner or sub-almoner made the distribution as the sovereign's representative.

There was to be a curious decision in the 1920s to abolish the office of sub-dean and instead make him 'precentor'. It is doubtful whether this decision was based on the knowledge that the only precedent for establishing such an office within the Chapel Royal was in the reorganisation of the Chapel Royal under the title of the 'Royal Free Household Chapel' in 1483. This curious decision was borne by 'sub-dean' Percival and 'sub-dean' Elliott, but by 1945 it had become quite impossible to discharge the necessary functions sensibly under the title 'precentor'. 'Precentor' Elliott therefore made a 'Humble Submission' in 1945 making the point 'that, since the title of Precentor is misleading and carries with it no authority (as is well recognized), the Precentor be given again the title (Sub-Dean) of all his predecessors but one (Prebendary Percival). This is a question of need, not of dignity.' The office of sub-dean was restored in 1946. Interestingly, sub-dean Elliott also requested at the same time 'that consideration be given to the original status of the Chapel Royal as a body rather than as a Building. The future of the Chapel Royal might well depend upon that status.' Its distinguished past certainly has, as previous sub-deans have taken pains to record.

The origins of the misconception of regarding the Chapel Royal as a building lay in the 'power struggle' between the earl marshal and the lord chamberlain. Ceremonial 'proceedings' to St Paul's Cathedral and the 'Chapel Royal' had originally been the province of the earl marshal, who was a domestic officer of the royal household. His position was gradually developed into a great office of state, and so the heralds, his ministers, found themselves removed from court by the distance between the City and Westminster and Kensington. They began to be summoned to those ceremonies which were formal and public in character. The thanksgiving service in 1588 for the defeat of the Spanish Armada at which the Chapel Royal were present was just such an occasion. The 'Rouge Croix' of the College of Heralds, Mr Brookesmouth, had given a false name (Brooke) when admitted to the College and also had his tabard confiscated by the earl of Leicester, deputy to the earl marshal, for misleading secretary Walsingham into giving him the position of 'Rouge Croix' by describing it as 'a Messengers place in Ordinary who commonly called themselves Pursuivants'. After Leicester's death Mr Brookesmouth without any permission took his tabard again to take part in the queen's thanksgiving service in 1588 at St Paul's Cathedral. He was in fact subsequently committed by the lord chamberlain to the porter's lodge at Whitehall for uttering unseemly words at Garter on Easter day. He was later released by Garter 'without leave or warrant from my lord Chamberlain' and he 'putt on his coat and wayted with the rest of the Herauldes before the knightes unto the Chappell'. The earl marshal had won this round, but his prerogative to order proceedings to and ceremonials at St Paul's Cathedral was soon to be undermined by the lord chamberlain.

By an ingenious contrivance in 1702, when queen Anne went, according to custom, to St Paul's Cathedral to give thanks for her accession, the earl marshal's jurisdiction over ceremonial was ousted by an order in privy council declaring the cathedral the queen's Chapel Royal for that day! There was more to come. In 1714 the College of Arms had actually drafted the ceremonial for George I's procession to St Paul's Cathedral to give thanks upon his accession, and laid it before the king in council. The vice-chamberlain then stepped in to assert that because in queen Anne's time St Paul's Cathedral was declared her majesty's private chapel, she had therefore transferred the formulation of this ceremonial from the earl marshal to the lord chamberlain. The truth was that the presence of the Chapel Royal in accordance with its own duty to accompany the sovereign was used as a tool by the lord chamberlain through the privy council to wrench the ordering of the ceremonial from the earl marshal and College of Arms. The vice-chamberlain's claim in 1714 again therefore had to use the presence of the Chapel Royal as the excuse for excluding the earl marshal from any jurisdiction over the ordering of the ceremonial procession. This led to an inevitable treading on toes in the cathedral itself, for if the thanksgiving was to be regarded as a 'private' service because the king's household Chapel Royal was present, then who was to conduct the service – the dean and chapter of the cathedral or the dean and college of the Chapel Royal?

The account in the Old Cheque Book of the Chapel Royal gives us the answer. It was written by the sub-dean of the Chapel Royal, John Dolben, and reads thus:[4]

> January 20th, 1714. Memorandum. That on the day of the date above written (beinge a day of publick thanksgiving) I read prayers at St Paul's Church, as beinge the King's Chappell upon this occasion, that I appointed those who read the Lessons and Litany, and likewise in the absence of the Dean of the Chappell (by whose especiall order, confirmed by the Vice-Chamberlain, I officiated) that I read the Communion Service, being preceded by the Serjeant of the Vestry, and attended by the Gentlemen of the Chappell Royal. And this I thought might be proper to insert in the Check Book in order to prevent any contest or difference which upon the like occasion might possibly hereafter arise between the officers of the Chappells Royall and the Church of St Paul. S. Dolben, Subdean.

Dolben had already inadvertently fallen into the lord chamberlain's 'trap'. He had no need to justify his presence on this occasion, for the Chapel Royal had a perfect right to be there anyway as the body of priests and singers appointed to serve the monarch at his command wherever that might be.

The poaching of the earl marshal's prerogative by the lord chamberlain advanced yet further in July 1717 in the arrangements for the christening of prince William, when the lord chamberlain asked the heralds through his secretary to furnish him with precedents. Leake said of this: 'It would have been for their interest indeed to have come under the Lord Chamberlain, but they acted with more Justice and honour to the Earl Marshal than he to them, usurping upon all Occasions upon their rights and priviledges, tho' he had not in his power to serve them.' The chapter of the College of Heralds decided on 15 October 1717 to resolve to send the following answer to the lord chamberlain: 'that the same interfering with the rights and priviledges of the Earl Marshal to whom (under the King's Majesty) they were subordinate and conceiving that the Earl Marshal was Jure officii the only proper officer that should receive his Majesty's pleasure touching the ceremonials required, they therefore hoped his Grace would permit them first to Communicate the Letter to the Lord Marshal to receive his Lordship's Command.' There was, significantly, no reply to this letter by the lord chamberlain. It was evidently ignored, for it was arranged for the christening to take place in private. This was certainly not in accordance with precedent prior to 1717

---

[4] Old Cheque Book, fol. 54.

as, for example, we learn from an entry in the Old Cheque Book relating to the christening at Greenwich of 'Marye the daughter of the Mightie Kinge, James etc. the fyfte of Maye, Anno 1605' during which, directly following the anthem after the naming of the child at baptism at the font in which 'The Arch Bishop baptised with great reverence (beinge still in his rich cope), who was assisted in the administration of the Sacrament by the Deane of the Chappell (he also beinge in his cope)', the 'herolds put on their coates, and Garter the Kinge of Heroldes standinge neere the rayales which inclosed the Font, and turninge his face towards the Kinges Majestie, did with a loud voyce proclayme what was his dutie to do'. This was the accustomed practice, but the contrived and successful usurpations by the lord chamberlain in the thanksgivings of 1702 and 1714, together with the christening of 1717, changed all that. An entirely new precedent had been contrived that 'used' the presence of the Chapel Royal at these events to indicate somehow that they were 'private' occasions, and therefore came under the control of the lord chamberlain rather than the earl marshal! This was the reason underlying the unprecedented declaration of St Paul's Cathedral as a 'Chapel Royal' for the day in 1702 and 1714.

A description of the duties of the sub-dean of the Chapel Royal would not be complete without a reminder of the privileges to which he was entitled. Sub-dean Aspinwall recorded on 1 January 1728/9 in the Old Cheque Book that he had received the degree of doctor of divinity from the king on 25 April 1728 at Cambridge University, for the 'Sub Dean of the Chappell had a peculiar title to be set down in the list for the Degree of Doctor of Divnity' by historical precedent. Sub-dean Battell had obtained his degree in the same way by favour of queen Anne when she visited Cambridge. Sub-dean Aspinwall thought fit to record this so that 'my successors ... may not hereafter be depriv'd of a claim and privilege due to them on such occasions'.[5] The Old Cheque Book also records that this applies to the sovereign's visit to Oxford University as well.

Nowadays such academic and other honours are invariably hard won and indicate a genuine, sustained and valuable contribution. Sub-deans have been appointed who reflect such demanding standards. Thus, for example, Canon J.S.D. Mansel MA, FSA, appointed Extra Chaplain to The Queen following his retirement as sub-dean in 1979, was awarded the MVO in 1972 and the KCVO in 1979. The present sub-dean, Canon Anthony Caesar, MA, BMus, Fellow of the Royal College of Organists, was awarded the LVO in 1988. Indeed a glance at the academic and other achievements of those who have been appointed sub-dean since the formal creation of that office in 1483 shows a remarkably high standard of attainment in the fields of theology and music.

[5] Ibid. fol. 55b.

Chapel Royal staff, October 1977. *Front row:* Giles Stockton, John Coutts, Robert Sawdy, Michael Hughes. *2nd row:* Frederic Hodgson, Norman Cooper, Timothy Farrel, Rev. James Mansel, Peter Goldspink, Richard Edwards. *3rd row:* Mark Thomas, Neil Thomas, Bruce Trathen, Gavin Kibble, Richard Cave, Colin Campbell. *Back row:* Graham Trew, John Watts, Matthew Graham, Colin Scull, John Lake, Richard Lewis.

Sub-dean Anthony Caesar's published works

1948	unison song	The Echoing Green	Year Book Press (A&C Black)
1949	part song	The Deserter's Meditation	Year Book Press (A&C Black)
1986	joint editor	*The New English Hymnal*	Canterbury Press
	hymn tune	Newtown St Luke (Child of the stable's secret birth)	
	hymn tune	Dome Alley (God is love: let heav'n adore him)	
	descant to	Wessex (Brightest and best of the sons of the morning)	
	descant to	Cornwall (O Love divine how blest thou art)	
1986	carol	Child of the stable's secret birth (extended version of the hymn above)	Royal School of Church Music
1988	anthem	Soul of my Saviour	Roger Dean Publishing Company
1989	anthem	O for a closer walk with God	Roger Dean Publishing Company
1989	anthem	O Love Divine	Roger Dean Publishing Company
1989	mass	Missa Brevis Capella Regalis (dedicated to Richard Popplewell and the children and gentlemen of H.M. Chapel Royal, St James's Palace)	Stainer & Bell
1990	piano duet	Tango for Two	Stainer & Bell

16

Chaplains in Ordinary and Priests in Ordinary

Chaplains in ordinary

The existence of the chaplains in ordinary is a true reminder of the origins of the Chapel Royal, for in a very real sense they deserve to be recognised as holding the oldest office of all within the Chapel Royal.

We have seen how the chaplains themselves from the first century AD constituted what has now become the formalised Chapel Royal. The Christian British and Anglo-Saxon kings and queens had chaplains appointed to serve their needs and those of their courts. These chaplains conducted divine service, chanted and sang. Occasionally their singing and musical efforts were augmented by the arrival or visit of expert musicians, priests and monks from elsewhere, sometimes Rome. Gradually 'singing clerkes' were appointed to achieve a more professional effect. The Chapel Royal as we now know it was taking shape fast. The sway of the Bretwaldas advanced the process, reducing the number of independent kingdoms and thus the number of Chapels Royal. The Chapel Royal was now the body of priests and singers serving a single monarch whose realm covered most of the country. This process was advanced still further by the Norman conquest of 1066.

Although the *Liber Regie Capelle* of Dean Say, written in 1449, talks in rather vague terms of 'one dean and thirty established chapel clerks of whom a half are normally priests', together with the gospeller – 'one priest' – for the lady mass, and elsewhere talks of the clerks of the Chapel Royal 'with the other ministers of the Chapel' being summoned at 7 o'clock every morning by a chorister ringing a bell, we gain a much clearer picture of the chaplains in ordinary at work in the *Liber Niger Domus Regis* of 1483, which talks of the 'Chapleyns and Clerkis of Chapell xxvi, by the Kinge choyce', and the provision that 'every chapleyn hath in to this court, whiles he is present, i honest servant ... and lyvery sufficiaunt for theyre horses'. We learn too that 'the statute of noble Edward the III, apoynted the numbyr of vi cunyng preeste, tyll they were avaunced, to take vii½ a day'.

In all this a distinction can be seen between those priests who are quite obviously the predecessors of today's chaplains in ordinary in the form of the chaplains to the court entitled to servants, livery and horses, and those who are the predecessors of today's priests in ordinary in the form of the 'vi cunyng preeste'. The situation is made a little clearer when the *Liber Niger* makes mention of the 'Clerke of the Closett' who 'etith in the hall with the Serjeant of the Vestyary by the gentilmen and taketh for his lyvery at night ½ gallon of ale ...'. He was paid 'dayly for his wage in court by chekkyr Roll iiii½ a day'. From a glance at this wage it could be argued that the 'Clerke of the Closett' was actually the vestry official later known as the keeper of the closet – for this wage is the same as that earned by the serjeant of the vestry. However, he may well have been a 'Chapleyn' who earned 4½d over and above his daily wage as a priest for performing extra duties as 'Clerke of the Closett'. What is certain is that the chaplains in ordinary were involved in what he did, for the *Liber Niger* states that he 'kepith the stuff of the closett, he preparith all thing for the stuff of the aulters to be redy and taking up the travers, leying the quysshyns and carpette and he settith all other thing necessary ffor the King and Chappleyns'. It is noted, too, that 'then he helpith the Chapleyns to sey masse'.

We know that before the formation of the 'College of Chaplains' in 1912, the forty-eight chaplains in ordinary still each had an annual allowance in lieu of board wages – i.e. for court residence. We can certainly conclude from this historical remnant of their board wages that their predecessors were the 'chapleyns' mentioned as 'other ministers of the chapel' in the *Liber Regie Capelle*.

It is known that a 'chaplain' had to be present at court for the ceremony of the touching for the king's evil. This was administered by the sovereign in person from the reign of Edward the Confessor until that of George I. The rubric for this 'service' in the time of Henry VII was printed two centuries later in 1686 by Henry Hills, 'printer to the King's most excellent Majesty, for his Household and Chapel'. It reads at several points: 'the Chaplain, kneeling before the King, having a stole about his neck, shall answer and say ... .' The 'chaplain' read the gospel from the 16th chapter of St Mark, beginning at the 14th verse. While 'the King is handling the sick person' the chaplain repeats the clause 'Super aegros etc.', and 'in the time of the repeating the aforesaid words, the Clerk of

Angel token of Charles I, pierced for use as a touch-piece in the service for the curing of the king's evil. (Reproduced by courtesy of Spink & Son Ltd)

Knight harbinger
Mr Henry Wroughton.

Chaplaines that waite monethly

January.
- Dr Heath
- Dr Wittm Brough.
- Dr Humph. Peak
- Dr Peter Heylin

July.
- Dr Joseph Crofton
- Dr [illegible] Gardiner
- Dr Lauren Burnell
- Dr Coo. Dillingham.

February.
- Dr Wittm Lewis
- Dr Tho: Laurence
- Dr Peterson D. of [illegible]
- Dr Lancy D. of [illegible]

August
- Dr Wittm Watts
- Dr Hamlet Marshall
- Dr [illegible]
- Dr Robert Crofts D. of Hereford.

March.
- Dr young D. of Winton
- Dr Potter D. of Worcest.
- [illegible]
- Dr Samuell Baker
- Dr Cuthbert D. Poldon

Sept.
- Mr Thomas Poske
- [illegible]
- Dr Richard Marsh D. of yorke:
- Dr Matthias Styles
- Dr Tho: Borkin D[illegible]

Aprill
- Dr Richard Osborne
- Dr Thomas Soll
- Dr [illegible] Nicholas D. Bristoll
- Dr Hell D. of Chch.

October
- Dr Wren D. of Windsor
- Dr [illegible] D. of Chichest
- Dr Wittm Beale
- Dr Tho: Turner.

May
- Dr Edward Burton
- Dr [illegible] Goldsworth
- Dr John Cosins
- Dr Raleigh D. of [illegible]

Novemb.r
- Dr John Hacket
- Dr Wittm Paull
- Dr [illegible]
- Dr Tho: Wood
- Dr Henry Fferne

June
- [illegible]
- Dr Tho: Walker
- Dr Ffuller D. of Ely
- Dr Wayly D. of Sarum.
- Dr Croston [illegible] D. of Litch.

December
- [illegible]
- Dr Wittm Heywood
- Dr Balcanquall D. of Durham
- Dr John Oliver
- Dr Stephen Goffe

Chaplains in ordinary and extraordinary in 1641. (Reproduced by courtesy of the Public Record Office)

Chaplaines Extraordinary

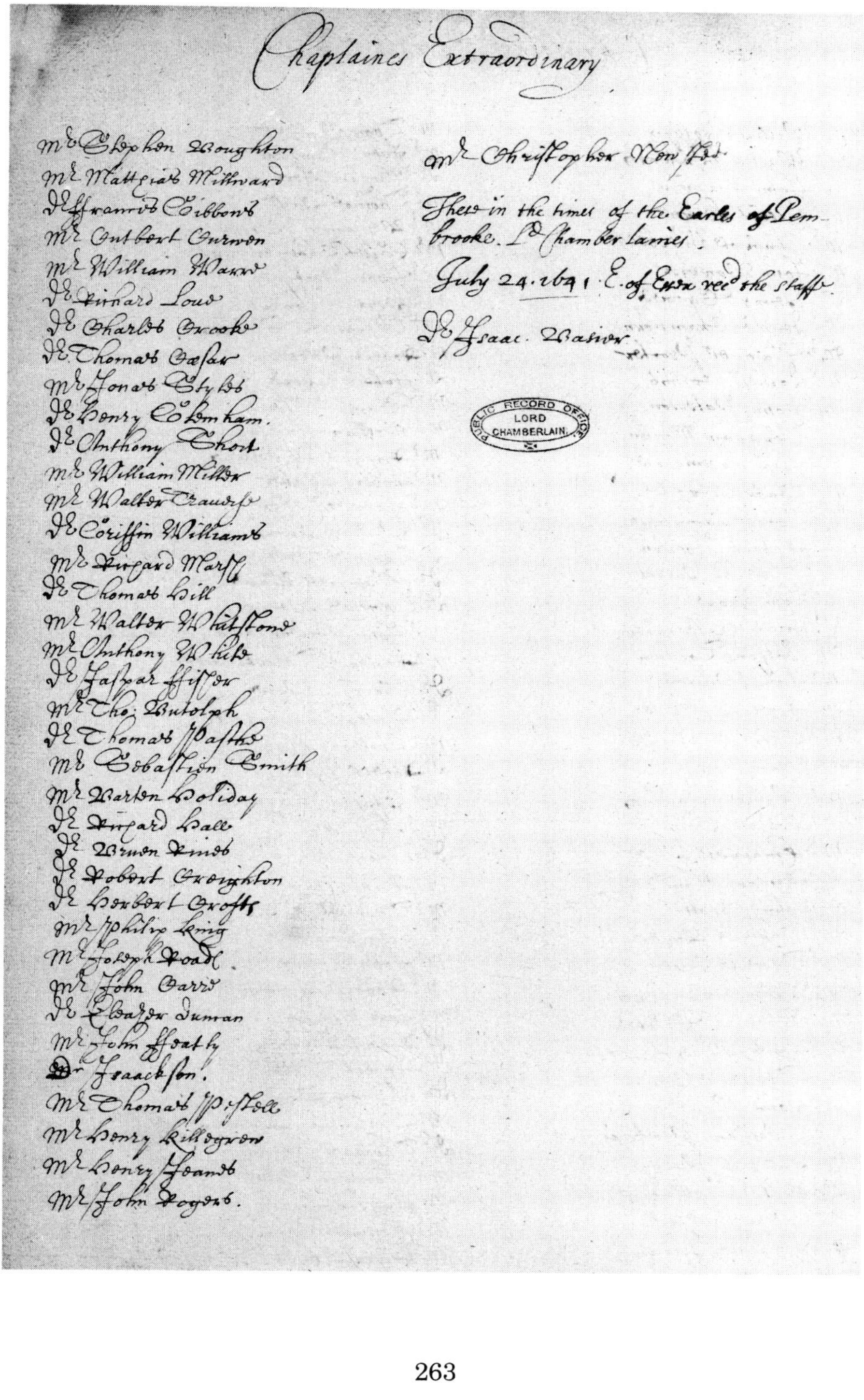

Mr Stephen Boughton
Mr Matthias Milward
Dr ffrancis Gibbons
Mr Cutbert Curwen
Mr William Warre
Dr Richard Love
Dr Charles Crooke
Dr Thomas Cæsar
Mr Jonas Styles
Dr Henry Cookham.
Dr Anthony Short
Mr William Miller
Mr Walter Travers
Dr Griffin Williams
Mr Richard Marsh
Dr Thomas Hill
Mr Walter Whatstone
Mr Anthony White
Dr Jaspar ffisher
Mr Tho: Butolph
Dr Thomas Paske
Mr Sebastian Smith
Mr Barten Holiday
Dr Richard Hall
Dr Bruen Rives
Dr Robert Creighton
Dr Herbert Crofts
Mr Philip King
Mr Joseph Hoad
Mr John Carre
Dr Eleazer Duncan
Mr John ffeatly
Dr Isaackson.
Mr Thomas Pistell
Mr Henry Killegrew
Mr Henry Jeames
Mr John Rogers.

Mr Christopher Newsted

These in the times of the Earles of Pembrooke. Ld Chamberlaines.

July 24. 1641. E. of Essex recd the staff.

Dr Isaac Basier

the Closet shall kneel before the King, having the sick person upon the right hand'. The king having laid 'his hand upon the sore of the sick person', and the chaplain having ended the gospel, the sick person was then led from the king's presence by the 'chirurgeon'. After a few responses between king and chaplain the latter then read another gospel lesson and again the clerk of the closet knelt before the king with the sick person on his right while the 'Lux vera', was repeated 'so long as the King shall be crossing the sore of the sick person with an angel noble: and the sick person to have the same angel noble hanged about his neck and to wear it until he be full whole'. The chaplain then finished the gospel, and after responses and prayers the service ended. The format of this service remained much the same until it was abolished, or rather simply excluded from the rubrics to be found in the Book of Common Prayer by George I. Lancing College possesses a queen Anne Prayer Book, with the original blue binding and royal cypher thought by Bart Peerless to have belonged to the Chapel Royal at St James's Palace, which contains the rubric for 'touching'.[1]

An entry relating to 'touching' in the Privy Purse Expenses of Henry VIII dated January 1530 reveals that this 'service' had taken place at the new Whitehall Palace, for it reads: 'it'm the same [xxvii] daye paied to iiii pouer people that the Kinges grace heled of ther diseases at Yorke place xxxs.' Latterly this 'service' took place more often than not in the presence chamber at St James's Palace. Possibly connected with this particular event is another item also dated 1530 but the month before, reading: 'It'm to the clerc of the Kinges Closet for his botehire for fetching of certen stuf from grenewiche to yorke place, iis.'

There is a manuscript at the Bodleian Library[2] consisting of a collection of words of 'full anthems' and 'single anthems' sung by the Chapel Royal in and after 1635, with later corrections. It is thought, from the letter pasted on the front cover from J. Bowack presenting the book to John, earl of Leicester, on 29 April 1732, that it was the volume used by Charles II himself. Its interest for our story is that it contains at the end a list headed 'The King's Chaplains in ordinarie attendance, 1635', with later corrections. As we have seen, one of these royal chaplains in ordinary (curiously not entered among the later corrections), the Rev. H. Hammond, played a secret role in the circumstances of Charles I's 'imprisonment' in Carisbrooke Castle in the Isle of Wight.[3] The recent research of Mr L. Fisher into his ancestor, the Rev. Thomas Pestell, has revealed a complete list of the king's household in the year 1641 which shows the later amendments to the 1635 royal chaplains in ordinary list

---

[1] See Lancing College Magazine, vol. 76-5 (December 1986), pp. 32-5.
[2] MS Rawl. Poet 23.
[3] See Chapter 10.

'Chaplains having dignities', detail from Ogilby's *Entertainment of Charles II*, 1662. This illustration shows the king's chaplains riding in procession at Charles II's coronation in 1661. (Reproduced by courtesy of the Guildhall Library, City of London)

to be selective and incomplete, for Thomas Pestell is mentioned twice in the 1641 list as both one of the serving chaplains in ordinary and also as a chaplain extraordinary. He is known to have preached before the king and also before the council at York in 1640, and to have resigned his living at Packington to his son Thomas in 1644, and thereafter complained twice during the early days of the Civil War of being robbed five times and of theft of his goods and cattle. It was these royal 'chaplains in ordinarie' who during Charles I's illness offered up prayers constantly for him in the royal chapels – the chaplains relieving each other every quarter of an hour. At the restoration Charles II saw to it that 'the dinner which was prepared daily for the Royal Chaplains at St James's Palace was reprieved from suspension by an effort of wit'. Charles II had appointed a day for dining with his chaplains. On these occasions it was Dr South's custom to say grace, and the form of it ran thus: 'God save the King, and bless the dinner.' Dr South cleverly re-arranged the wording so as to say: 'God bless the King, and save the dinner'! The king replied 'It shall be saved', and it was. As Charles was habitually accustomed to fall fast asleep during Chapel Royal sermons, usually being woken towards the conclusion of the sermon by Harry Bennet, earl of Arlington, this was a truly magnanimous gesture.

Swift's *Journal to Stella* records on 6 October 1711 that 'I never dined with the Chaplains till to-day. It is the worst provided table at Court, we ate in pewter. Every Chaplain, when he is made a Dean, gives a piece of Plate, and so they have got a little, some of it very old. One who was made Dean of Peterborow (a small deanery) said he would give no Plate, "he was only Dean of Peterborow".'

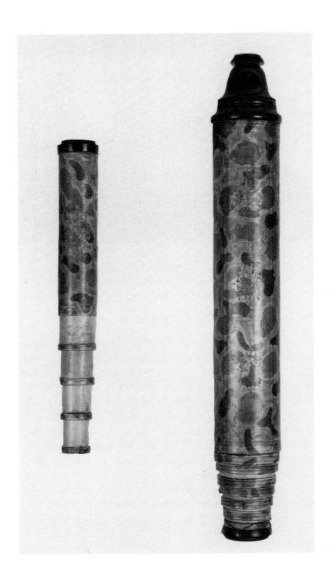

This telescope, probably made in Italy, is one of two belonging to the Rev. Ralph Taylor, king's chaplain, who went into exile with James II and after leaving St Germain lived for a time at Rotterdam. (Reproduced by courtesy of the National Maritime Museum, Greenwich)

However, in 1727 George II decreed that henceforth any chaplain in ordinary advanced to the dignity of dean had to cease to be a chaplain in ordinary. Furthermore, chaplains in ordinary were never to attend upon him as king or upon the queen in her closet. This order was confirmed by queen Victoria in 1865. The Clerk of the Closet has in fact always been a

Some of the king's chaplains in the robes in which they appeared at the coronation of Edward VII and queen Alexandra on 9 August 1902. *Front row:* Rev. Canon Ainger, Rev. Prebendary Gibson, Rev. Canon Teignmouth Shore, Rev. Edgar Sheppard (sub-dean), Rev. Canon Hervey, Rev. Hon. L. Tyrwhitt, Rev. Canon Clement Smith. *Back row:* Rev. J.W. Adams, Rev. J.H. Ellison, Rev. Canon Moberly. (HM Chapel Royal, reproduced by gracious permission of Her Majesty The Queen)

bishop since 1714 and so in 1727 became the only cleric to have a 'constitutional' duty to attend the sovereign as king or queen in his or her own closet. Thus ended the practice of at least 1,500 years of lowly royal chaplains ministering to the personal needs of the sovereign. The decisions of 1727 and 1865 paved the way for a newly defined role for the chaplains in ordinary.

In 1860 the Chapel Royal commissioners recommended that the number of chaplains with a salary be reduced from forty-eight to thirty-six. They should continue to preach their sermons in the Chapel Royal, be ready to officiate at the private chapel at Buckingham Palace and assist in the service at the Chapel Royal, St James's. In 1881 it was suggested that eight 'honorary chaplains' should succeed to paid appointments as vacancies occurred. Their duty was to preach only when there were five Sundays in a month. Otherwise the sub-dean was to preach at the first Sunday in every month, and the thirty-six chaplains, each preaching once, would fill the rest of the Sundays throughout the year. These recommendations seem to have been partly carried through,

267

GROUP OF THE CHAPLAINS OF KING GEORGE V.
IN THE ROBES IN WHICH THEY APPEARED AT THEIR MAJESTIES CORONATION
JUNE 22ND 1911

Rev F.A.S.Ffolkes M.V.O. M.A.   Rev Canon Hon.L.Tyrwhitt M.V.O. M.A.   Rev Canon C Smith M.V.O. M.A.   Ven Arch Deacon Wood D.D.
Rev. M.E.Kennedy M.V.O. M.A.   Rev Canon Duckworth C.V.O. M.A.   Rev.H.Gee D.D.
Rev Canon Sandey D.D.   Rev J.H.Ellison M.A.   Rev Canon T.T.Shore M.A.
Ven Arch Deacon Westcott D.D.   Rev Canon Edgar Sheppard C.V.O. D.D.   Rev F.P.Farrar M.V.O. M.A.
(SUB DEAN)

(HM Chapel Royal, reproduced by gracious permission of Her Majesty The Queen)

for in 1894 there were thirty-seven 'chaplains in ordinary' and eleven 'honorary chaplains', according to sub-dean Edgar Sheppard.

The year 1912 saw the completion of the metamorphosis of the chaplains in ordinary, headed by the clerk of the closet, then bishop Boyd Carpenter (previously of Ripon). In March 1918 a rearrangement of the College of Chaplains was approved by the king so that in future it should consist of one 'Clerk of the Closet', one 'Deputy Clerk of the Closet' and thirty-six 'Chaplains to the King'. These thirty-six chaplains would replace the existing eight chaplains in ordinary and honorary chaplains, and all were to wear the gold badge until then only worn by the chaplains

268

Members of Her Majesty's Ecclesiastical and Medical Households following attendance at choral evensong in the Queen's Chapel on 2 May 1989 are pictured here in the state apartments at St James's Place. The Queen's gifts of frankincense and myrrh offered at the Feast of The Epiphany are still provided by the Apothecary to The Queen.

269

in ordinary.[4] This badge dates from 1906, when Edward VII approved that it should replace the embroidered scarf worn hitherto and bearing the royal crown and cypher.

The recently retired clerk of the closet, the Rt Rev. John Bickersteth, formerly bishop of Bath and Wells, has written that 'the Chaplains in Ordinary were all part of the Chapel Royal Establishment', but 'as the separation of the College from the Chapel Royal was in 1912, you could say that in this year of grace 1986 we are in the 75th year of our existence'. The duty of each Chaplain to The Queen is still, though, to preach one sermon a year at the Chapel Royal, for which a fee is received. The sub-dean of the Chapel Royal also holds the office of deputy clerk of the closet, thereby maintaining the Chapel Royal's close relationship with the College of Chaplains to The Queen, and thus a special relationship which stretches back to the very origins of the Chapel Royal itself. It is therefore doubly appropriate that upon the retirement of the sub-dean, The Queen should appoint him 'Extra Chaplain to The Queen', an office held at present by Canon James Mansel, along with the Ven. Ted Ward.

Priests in ordinary

As we have seen, the *Liber Regie Capelle* mentions thirty chapel clerks of whom half were normally priests, and the *Liber Niger Domus Regis* talks of twenty-six chaplains and chapel clerks sitting together in the Hall 'at the deanes bourde, and logging together within the courte in one chamber'. The Old Cheque Book states that 'whosoever shall be admitted into a priest's place in the Chapel Royal shall sweare to take on him the office of a Deacon, the next ordination, and to do the service thereunto belonging'.

Before 1860 the priests in ordinary numbered ten. They were divided into two groups of five, each group being in waiting every alternate month. Every Sunday one priest from each group was assigned duty at the Chapel Royal. Their turns were arranged by the senior priest of the month. They also had one authorised deputy, and so we find the Old Cheque Book recording that in 1742 'The Revd. Mr Smith, belonging to the Cathedral of Worcester, is, on account of performing extraordinary service in singing before the Royal Family, allowed to wait three months only – namely February, April and May. The other three months – November, December and January – are supplied by a Deputy.'

In 1860 the number of priests in ordinary was reduced from ten to eight. As a result of this one priest was required to be constantly in waiting to the sub-dean throughout the day. The waiting of these eight priests was arranged every year among themselves with the approval of

---

[4] Memorandum (lord chamberlain's office), March 1918, held in the Chapel Royal Archive.

the sub-dean, with the result that each priest took two months of waiting every alternate year, or six weeks at a time.

In 1901 it was decided to reduce the number of priests in ordinary from eight to four. The four chosen from among the eight were H.A. Sheringham, A. Tahourdin, H.D. Macnamara and H.G. Daniell Bainbridge. The other four remaining priests were made 'honorary' priests in ordinary. A stipulation was added for the future that the 'four' should undertake three months of duty each in the course of a year, and that they should be resident in London. Should any move to the 'suburbs' or 'country' they must resign.

Today the number of priests in ordinary stands at three (William Booth, Adam Ford and Gordon Watkins), and there is also a deputy priest in ordinary (Hugh Mead).

17

The Society of Gentlemen and Organists

My intention in this chapter is not to chronicle the lives of the gentlemen singers of the Chapel Royal – so comprehensively tackled by Grove[1] – but rather to look at their conditions of service.

The singing clerks of the various royal courts of the Saxon kings should rightly be regarded as the predecessors of the post-Conquest singing clerks of the Chapel Royal, for the Chapel Royal is defined by its purpose to serve the spiritual needs and state politics of the monarch (see Chapter 1 above).

It is known that Edward I had five clerks in his Chapel Royal in 1279, but the conditions of service for the mediaeval singing clerks only start to become clear in the reign of Henry III, who had a particular liking for the royal laudes (Christi vincit, etc.). Between the years 1227 and 1241 he required the gentlemen clerks of the Chapel Royal to chant the laudes before him on all important Christian festivals, for which three, and from time to time four, clerks of the Chapel Royal were paid twenty-five shillings each, and later £5 a year. In Edward III's reign John Wodeford is described in the Calendar of Patent Rolls for 1349 as 'a king's clerk and dean of his chapel'. The number of chaplains and clerks of the Chapel Royal is recorded as eleven in the Wardrobe Accounts of 1393.

Whether these singing clerks were also required to play the organ is not clear. The Westminster Abbey archives contain a reference to 'a certain Nicholas' who was paid 26s 8d for playing 'ad organa' in 1387-88. He also appears in the Chapel Royal accounts but was apparently at that time a child of the Chapel Royal.

There were certainly enough clerks of the Chapel Royal to provide an organist in Henry IV's reign. The year 1402 saw eighteen chaplains and clerks with a former clerk, Richard Prentys, as dean. The number had grown to twenty-seven by 1413 in the reign of Henry V. These included the composers Burrell, Cook, Damett and Sturgeon. The entire number of clerks travelled to Normandy to serve Henry V abroad on campaign from 1417 to 1420. While in Normandy the clerk John Pyamour was given

---

[1] *Grove's Dictionary of Music and Musicians* (Macmillan, London).

the task of 'impressing' choristers for service with the English Chapel Royal in Normandy. This was to be the start of the office of master of the children, and subsequently nearly all masters, with a couple of notable exceptions including Captain Cooke, were chosen from the society of gentlemen of the Chapel Royal. Although the year 1440 saw the task of 'impressing' exercised by the dean, this was only a temporary reversion, for the following year, 1441, saw the clerk John Plummer again taking over the role that was to be exercised by the master of the children until the twentieth century. (See Chapter 19 for further details of this office.)

By far the clearest picture we have of the conditions of service enjoyed by the society of gentlemen at this time is to be found in the *Liber Regie Capelle* of 1449 which says of the gentlemen clerks: 'In the said Chapel there are continually in the service of God and the king one dean and thirty established chapel clerks (*cantores electi*) of whom a half are usually priests.'

It was the dean's prerogative 'to select and appoint the clerks of the Chapel', but there was also an element of 'protection' that went with them and indeed every member of the Chapel Royal, for 'neither the steward of the household, nor the treasurer, nor any other officer or servant of the household whatever, may on any account presume to correct or punish in any matter concerning the Chapel or the persons formally attached to it, but only, as has been said, the dean himself'.[2]

The daily routine of the gentlemen clerks made for a very full day. Clad 'in their surplices' and 'under the supervision of the dean or his deputy' – suggesting that the office of sub-dean preceded the 1483 reorganisation of the Chapel Royal – the gentlemen clerks were summoned by a bell rung by one of the boys at seven o'clock 'every morning of the year', and sang as a body matins and lauds. At ten o'clock they sang high mass, and vespers at four o'clock in the evening, followed by compline 'all in a mode and measure changing and varying, in song, in reading, in the colours of the vestments and other ornaments … according to the varying solemnity of the festivals'.[3] The Chapel Royal followed at this time the 'use or custom of the Cathedral Church of Salisbury', but had 'variants of its own, however, in the music and in many ceremonies, as befits the honour and dignity of the Chapel'.

Furthermore at 'every night in the year', except for the three nights before Easter, the gentlemen clerks sang three solemn memorials of the Trinity, St George and the Blessed Virgin Mary immediately after compline. This was followed by the psalm 'De profundis' for the dead, and the saying of the lesser litany, and then 'in a quiet voice two by two' they said the psalm 'Miserere mei deus' and the officiating priest ended by saying aloud 'Lord, we beseech thee graciously to behold thy servant our

[2] *Liber Regie Capelle*, ch. 3.
[3] Ibid., ch. 4.

King, and this thy household for which our Lord Jesus Christ ... who with God the Father ... etc.' Only when all this had been accomplished could the clerks retire 'in peace'.

This format was followed throughout the year except on Trinity Sunday, Corpus Christi, St John Baptist, SS Peter and Paul, St Thomas Archbishop and Martyr, the English Feast of Relics, and the patronal festival of the church if it should fall within this period. We are told that the Chapel Royal held the Trinity 'especially in honour'. Perhaps if the Chapel Royal had a dedicatory festival as a body of priests and singers then it should be the Trinity. Dean William Say is quite specific about this, writing of 'Trinity Sunday (which is the local festival in the King of England's Chapel)'.[4]

With regard to these seven great festivals, at the beginning of matins the 'rectors of the choir' sang a solemn invitatory with the psalm 'Venite', but matins was sung after vespers at dusk on the eve of the festival day 'just as, on the three days before Easter, matins is sung in a protracted and doleful mode at tenebrae' in memory of the Passion.

In addition 'general and solemn litanies' were sung on St Mark's day and at Rogation-tide before Ascension day. While these processions occurred only once a year, two special processions were made with the cross and taperers 'every week in the year', except for the festivals of Christmas, Easter and Whitsun, for the good estate of the king and queen and for the peace of the kingdom. These processions occurred on Wednesdays and Fridays and were preceded by antiphons and psalms. Dean Say notes: 'The king is sometimes present, the queen is seldom absent; a great part of the household joins in.' On the return of the procession to the Chapel the gentlemen clerks sing the antiphon 'From our enemies defend us, O Christ' 'on the way through the Chapel'. After the prayer of All Saints is said 'the rectors of the choir begin the mass of the day, in which the whole choir joins'.[5]

Finally it was customary, according to Say, for a 'community obit day' to be observed four times a year for the ancestors and progenitors of the kings and queens. For this the 'Chapel and its altars are arrayed in black, and the rectors of the choir and the other ministers wear black copes and vestments, with cloth of gold or black velvet'. The royal family wore black, too, while the 'exequies and the mass are sung to a lengthy and mournful setting'.

On six feasts in the year (Christmas, Good Friday, Easter, Whitsun, Trinity Sunday and All Saints) 'every one in the king's house and household is bound to make an offering'. After the king and queen, the prince and 'all the other lords and ladies and nobles ... have made their offerings at the step before the high altar in the Chapel (on which step

[4] Ibid., ch. 3.
[5] Ibid., ch. 5.

these oblations are always made, by custom), first the rectors of the choir, then the other members of the Chapel (in the copes which they always wear on major festivals during the whole of the procession and the mass so far as the third Agnus dei) come up to make their offerings in due order.'[6]

The gentlemen clerks had, too, a role to perform in the 'Manner of Baptising the Illustrious Son or Daughter of His Serene Highness the King of England and France and Lord of Ireland'. This would be a rare occasion but a splendid one. The chapel was festooned with cloth of gold and arras tapestries while the floor was covered with 'beautifully patterned carpets'. The specific role of the gentlemen clerks was to go out and meet the child in the great hall 'in their almuces and surplices or copes' but with 'no music or singing'. Then a procession was formed which included two hundred squires or esquires with torches, as yet unlit, and the kings of arms and heralds with their arms and tabards taking their place between the Chapel Royal and squires. The procession then moved to the 'outer gate' of the church when it met a procession that had come from within the church 'but still without song or sound'. At this point the archbishop made the child a catechumen while the serjeant of the king's pantry held the 'golden salt cellar filled with the finest salt in the best cloth of Raines'. After the catechising the child was then undressed and taken to the font in the crossing of the church by the godmother. After baptism the child was taken to the high altar and a candle was lit 'super altare', which was the sign for all 200 torches held by squires to be lit. The archbishop began the Te Deum and, at last, the gentlemen clerks sang, 'the Chapel Royal taking up the hymn in full solemnity with organ'. The recession to the queen's chamber saw 'the Chapel leading and singing a responsory of thanksgiving to the Holy and Undivided Trinity, as in the Processional Book'.[7] The Chapel Royal gentlemen clerks also had a role in the churching of the queen, and the obsequies of the king when the archbishop, bishops and suffragans, 'together with the Chapel Royal, execute the whole office for the dead' with the archbishop in his seat, the bishops in the higher stalls and 'the Chapel Royal in the lower stalls'.[8]

These then were the singing commitments of the gentlemen clerks of the Chapel Royal in the fifteenth century, but what of their other conditions of service?

The first thing to be said is that all members of the Chapel Royal were excused residence in any benefice which they held and 'even from major dignities in cathedral churches for which residence is prescribed and required',[9] so long as they remained in attendance upon the sovereign. Dean Say goes on to be more specific about the gentlemen: 'As for the priests and the choral clerks in the king's Chapel, they enjoy in the court

---

[6] Ibid., ch. 8.
[7] Ibid., ch. 13.
[8] Ibid., ch. 16.
[9] Ibid., ch. 11.

the status of gentlemen'. We can see this in action vividly at the banquet on St George's day at Windsor in Henry VIII's reign, when the king's antiquary, Leland, records that there were four tables. The king had a table to himself while at the right-hand table sat all the knights of the Garter and 'a littill byneith them ... on both sides of the table, the Dean, the Chanoignes [Canons] and Por Knyghts of the College, in ther Mantells, and byneith theym the residue of that Quere [i.e. gentlemen clerks of Windsor]'. At the centre table sat various lords 'and a lytill byneith theym satt the King's Chapell'.[10] Also in the same year at another Windsor feast it is recorded that 'at the table in the Medell of the Hall sat the Dean and thoos of the King's Chapell'.[11]

Say mentions that 'in addition to the allowances, table rights and service due to them as to other gentlemen of the court', the gentlemen of the Chapel Royal also received payment for themselves and for one servant: 'For their wages each of these chapel clerks receives seven pence ha'penny a day, which amounts to fifty six ducats a year', and the lesser clerks and officers of the vestry receive 4½d a day. There was also a livery or clothing allowance of 'four yards of fine cloth, dyed in grain, or twelve ducats instead thereof'. They also expected to receive on certain festivals in the year gifts from the king of 'one hundred marks or one hundred pounds to be divided amongst themselves, as it shall please his royal majesty'.[12]

The *Liber Niger Domus Regis* of c. 1483 tells us much more about the practical everyday living conditions of the gentlemen clerks than the *Liber Regie Capelle*.

For instance, it tells us, albeit in tortuous grammar, that there were 'Chapleyns and Clerkis of Chapell xxvi' who had to be 'men of worship, endewed with vertuose, morall, speculatiff, as of theyre musike, shewing in descant, clene voysed, well relysed, and pronouncing, eloquent in Reding, sufficiaunt in organes pleying, and modestiall in all other maner of behaving'. The *Liber Niger* conjures up a vivid picture by adding 'all thees sitting together in the hall at the deanes bourde, and logging together within the courte in one chamber'. It confirms that 'every which hath dayly alowed in the Chekker Roll vii½d'. Each gentleman clerk was allowed 40s for clothing from the 'greete Warderobe of household'. They also had 'to theyre chamber at night, amongst them all' two loaves, one pitcher of wine, six gallons of ale, and from All-Hallow tide until Easter two wax candles, twelve peric candles, and eight talshields. We gather that 'they pay for theyre own cariage of bedding and other harneys', but on the other hand they have all the year round 'litter and Rushes off the

---

[10] John Leland, *De Rebus Britannicis Collectanae*, ed. T. Hearne (2nd ed., 6 vols, 1770), vol. 4, p. 240.
[11] Ibid., p. 237.
[12] *Liber Regie Capelle*, ch. 10.

Serjeant Ussher of the hall, or chambre'. Moreover for every two gentlemen clerks there was 'one honest servant', and they were provided with stabling 'sufficaunt for theyre horses'. When the Chapel sang matins at night – 'black mattyns', or a solemn dirge for the king's father or mother – then there was allowed to the singing clerks 'spice and wyne'.

Promotion was a matter for the king, for he 'avaunceth these priests and clerkes by prebendaries [churches of his patrimony], or by his letters recomendatory', according to the *Liber Niger*. Examples of promotion or advancement by gift of prebend from the king abound under previous reigns too. At times it led to some awkward moments. A case in point was the gift in 1406 to Richard Prentys of a prebend associated with Lincoln Cathedral which nearly led to a fracas with the pope:

> Whereas the pope has made a provision to the king's clerk, Richard Prentys, dean of the king's chapel within the household, of a canonry and prebend in the Cathedral Church of Lincoln, the king pardons the trespass in this and grants licence for the execution of the bull.[13]

In case it is thought that such prebendal advancement relied on prodding from the pope, this was most certainly not the case. Advancement at the king's pleasure was an accepted procedure stretching back to Willemus de Wintonia in 1221 who, described as 'clericus domini regis de capella sua', was rewarded 'with letters of presentation to the church of Wirlingham, which is vacant and in the gift of our lord the king'.[14]

Straightforward prebendal advancement was indeed a commonplace reward for the gentlemen clerks of the Chapel Royal. For example, we learn in 1419 of the 'presentation of Thomas Gyles, clerk of the chapel of the household, to the prebend which John Cook, late clerk of the chapel of the household, lately had within the free chapel of Hastynges'.[15] John Cook in fact had also been presented with the church of Althorpe in the diocese of Lincoln. Robert Lywer was rewarded in 1420 with the prebend of the cathedral church of St Peter at Exeter.[16] Henry Hawnshard, 'chaplain' and 'one of the clerks of the king's chapel within his household', was given the prebend in 1426 which the chaplain John Newark held before his death of the chapel of St Mary and Holy Angels adjoining the cathedral church of St Peter, York.[17] Gerard Hesyll was given the prebend in the cathedral church of Aukland, replacing Robert Neville who had been consecrated bishop of Salisbury. John Couper, 'king's clerk' and 'one of the chaplains of the king's chapel within the household', was

---

[13] Cal. Pat. Rolls (1405-08), November 1406, Westminster.
[14] Cal. Pat. Rolls (1216-25), 1221, p. 300.
[15] Cal. Pat. Rolls (1417-20), 1419, p. 219.
[16] Ibid., p. 282.
[17] Cal. Pat. Rolls (1422-29), 1426, p. 319.

presented in 1417 with the prebend of 'Woetlyng, Hoo and Nenfeld in the free chapel of Hastings'.[18]

Rewards often took other forms too. For instance, John Hunt, 'one of the clerks of the king's chapel within the household' was, in 1414, granted for life 'two solars, a field, a vacant plot and two acres of meadow in the town of Oxford', although he later surrendered these to John Smert in 1415. Edmund Lacy, dean of the Chapel Royal, was in 1416 granted the temporalities of the bishopric of Hereford during its vacancy. Stephen Peynton, 'one of the clerks of the chapel within the household', was granted in 1415 the 'chantry within the king's manor of Clypeston with the wardenship of the free chapel of St Edwin within the forest of Shirwode'.[19]

These are merely a few examples of the advancement process for the gentleman clerks of the Chapel Royal depending upon the king's pleasure.

Returning to the *Liber Niger*, provision was also made in cases of a gentleman clerk's sickness or blood-letting, in which eventuality the sick clerk was to withdraw into the town 'taking dayly two loaves, one messe of greete meete, one messe of roast and one gallon of ale'. Certainly a good regimen for eating one's way out of illness!

The wages of the gentlemen clerks remained static as time went on. In 1544, nearly a hundred years after the *Liber Regie Capelle* was written, they were still paid 7½d a day, but board wages of one shilling a day were also paid to them in lieu of dinner and supper in kind. As Elizabeth I's reign wore on, and inflation gathered pace with the influx of gold from the New World, the wages of the gentlemen clerks of the Chapel Royal still obstinately remained at 7½d a day and one shilling board, making a total of £29 13s 1½d a year. So it is perhaps not surprising that in 1596 the gentlemen clerks banded together to conduct a suit, through the offices of 'one Mr Hills, of London, gentleman', to the queen for 'some gift or grant ... for the yearly increase of [their] livings'. Eight years later in 1604, 'after a long and chargeable suit', the gentlemen clerks won an increase of £10 a year 'to every man, so increasing their stipends from thirty to forty pounds ...'. Much rejoicing was had at this and it was thought fit that the 'King's bounty ... should be recorded' in the Cheque Book 'to be had ever in remembrance'. The names of the gentlemen and vestrymen living at the time of this 'victory' are listed below. They are the gentlemen and others of the Chapel who were present at James I's coronation in 1603. This list is to be found at the end of the Old Cheque Book as a result of rebinding at some later date.

---

[18] Cal. Pat. Rolls (1417-20), 1417, p. 63.
[19] Cal. Pat. Rolls (1413-16), 1415, p. 63.

17. The Society of Gentlemen and Organists

A note of the names of the Subdeane, Gentlemen and others of the Chappell, at the tyme of the Coronation of Kynge James the First.

Anno Domini
1603.

Leonard Davies, Subdeane.

Bartholomew Mason.	Stephen Boughton.	
Anthony Harrison.	Williaam Lawes.	Mynisters.
William Barnes.	Anthony Kirckbye.	
Robert Stuckley.		

Nathanaell Gyles, Master of the Children.
Thomas Sampson, Clerke of the Check.
Jo. Bull, Doctor in Musicke.

Robert Stone.	William Randall.	James Davies.
William Birde.	Robert Allison.	William Lawrence.
Richard Granwall.	Jo. Stevens.	Jo. Amery.
Crue Sharpe.	Jo. Hewlett.	Jo. Baldwine.
Edmond Browne.	Richard Plumley,	Francis Wyborough.
Tho. Wooddeson.	Tho. Goulde.	Arthur Cocke.
Henry Eveseede.	Peter Wright.	George Wooddeson.
		Jo. Wooddeson.

Gentlemen

Ralphe Fletcher, Sergant.	
Jo. Patten, Yeoman.	Officers of the Vestry.
Robert Hewes, Yeoman.	
Henry Allred, Groome.	

[f.87.]

The sixteenth century saw some of the traditional perquisites of the gentlemen clerks either lost or replaced by provision of a different nature, but the gentlemen remained a close band of friends. Thus Robert Penne, who had been master of the children at Westminster Abbey until 1500, and a friend of the laureate John Skelton, was admitted a gentleman of the Chapel Royal in 1515. He was subsequently awarded the annuity of twenty marks from the Lordship of Denbigh in North Wales. He died in 1538 and left a will, dated 26 September, in which he desired, 'that Mr Subdean of the Kynge Chapell with all my ffellows have every man a penny that ys at my dirige or at my masse to drynk and to say god have mercy on my soule'.[20]

Another insight into the friendship of the gentlemen is enshrined in the 'Tudor' oath, sworn by the gentlemen of the Chapel Royal in 1592. It is recorded in the Old Cheque Book and survived with just the sovereign's name and title altered in Stuart and Hanoverian times. Apart from recognising Elizabeth I as 'by the word of God the only supreme Governor of thys Realme ... as well in all spirituall or ecclesiastical thinges or causes as temporall', the gentlemen swore 'to be obedyente to the Deane

---

[20] Quoted in Edward Pine, *The Westminster Abbey Singers* (Dennis Dobson, London, 1953).

and Sub-Dean ... and unto all such lawdable orders as are or shall bee by them and the whole bodye of this Companye thought meete and convenient to bee devysed for quyetnes'.

Clothing continued to be supplied in liberal quantity. While state trumpeters were supplied with 'cassocks' and 'sea-slops' emblazoned with the house of Richmond colours of green and white, the gentlemen clerks of the Chapel Royal found themselves well provided for when it came to great occasions such as the Field of Cloth of Gold in 1520. Typically lavish examples are to be found in the Wardrobe Accounts of Henry VIII which contain a warrant providing Thomas Sexten, one of the genetlemen of the Chapel Royal, with a gown costing £11 18s. William Crane was equipped with a gown costing £9 12s. Gowns provided for three other gentlemen cost £26 13s 3d. What the gentlemen did with the 'gowns' was a different matter! A century later in 1632, we find that the dean of the Chapel Royal, William Laud, had to reprimand the gentlemen in a chapter meeting for their slackness of attire, decreeing that 'the Gentlemen of the Chappell shall (at all tymes as they doe attend that service) come in decent manner in their gownes and surplyses, and not in cloakes and surplyses, nor with bootes and spurres'. This apparently went largely unheeded, for five years later at another chapter held on 5 April 1637 in the vestry at Whitehall, the sub-dean was required to enforce 'the due observation' of the 1632 order 'against wearinge of cloakes or cominge in with great boots and spurs under there surplices, and if any transgresse to checke them as if they were absente'.

The wearing of spurs by the gentlemen indicates that provision was no longer made to billet the singing clerks in the palace where the court was residing with the sovereign, unlike the previous arrangement detailed in the *Liber Niger* of *c.* 1483. It is a good surmise that this transition took place around 1544 when the decision was taken to pay each gentleman clerk £29 13s 1½d a year instead of dinner and supper in kind, which would have meant communal dining and implied that prior to this they were billeted at court. A century later in 1663 we learn of an instruction at a chapter meeting held in the Whitehall vestry that 'all the Gentlemen of his Majesties Chappell shall have their habitations within or near the City of London, to be ready to attend at all times when the Deane or Sub Deane shall summon them'. Furthermore, all members of the Chapel Royal had to give 'a note to the Sub Deane of the place of their abode'.[21] They did, however, retain their right to a servant, for the 1664 orders state 'that the servant to the Gentlemen of his Maj. Chappell shall attend as well as the servant of the Vestry to help put on the gowns, as well as the other surplusses, befor service begins'.[22]

If the transition from palace residence of the gentlemen to their own

[21] Old Cheque Book, fol. 45b.
[22] Ibid.

Chalk drawing of Henry Purcell, attributed to J. Closterman. (National Portrait Gallery, London)

private dwellings took place around 1544, the vestiges of court residence evidently still remained to plague the serjeant of the vestry. Thus on 8 November 1608 the serjeant of the vestry and other officers of the vestry petitioned the dean to insist that neither the sub-dean 'nor any of the gentlemen should have eyther bed or trunk to stand in the vestery, but to have the place private unto themselves'. Twelve years later in 1620 we hear that the yeoman of the vestry, Henry Eveseed, who 'did violently and sodenly without cause runne uppon Mr Gibbons and took him up and threw him downe uppon a standard' was also 'infected with a fowle disease of his groine, to the great offence of all, but chiefly to those that were constrained by means of their service to lye neere him, uppon which the late Lord Deane thought him unfitt to serve his Majestie in his progresse into Scotland'.[23] It seems that Henry Eveseed made a nuisance

23 Ibid., fol. 37.

of himself even on those occasions when the gentlemen did find themselves eating together at court, for he is recorded as having 'vomited in a dishe of pottage which Mr Harrison and others were eatinge of', and at Greenwich of 'continuall late cominge in drounke, at which tymes he takes occasion to quarrel and beate the servauntes'.

The problem faced by the gentlemen of finding suitable accommodation in London was craftily solved by Henry Purcell, who lived in 'a suite of apartments in St James's Palace, access to which was obtained by a winding staircase in the clock-tower'.[24] The poet Dryden used to take refuge with him in these apartments for weeks on end when in debt after being deprived of the laureateship in 1689 until Purcell's death in 1695 so as to avoid the clutches of persistent creditors. Henry Purcell's residence at St James's Palace must have been as a result of, or later than, his first appointment to office with the Chapel Royal as one of its organists in 1682, although he had entered the Chapel Royal singing as a child under Captain Cooke shortly after his sixth birthday. Orlando Gibbons, however, chose to live at the Whitehall end of the Chapel Royal's operations in the Long Wool-Staple, on the site of the present Bridge Street, outside the north wall and gate of New Palace Yard, on the north side adjoining which was Canon Row. He had entered the Chapel Royal first as a gentleman in 1604/5.

So much, then, for the living conditions of the gentlemen of the Chapel Royal in the sixteenth and seventeenth centuries. Let us now take a look at their 'working' lives over this period. We shall see that the daily routine was not quite as demanding in terms of hours as that experienced by their forebears in the fifteenth century, so vividly described in the *Liber Regie Capelle* and *Liber Niger*. More emphasis was placed upon the role of the organ in choral compositions, with the result that the gentleman were soon faced with mastering this 'ally grown large'.

We know from the Westminster Abbey archives that in 1387/8 'a certain Nicholas' was paid 26s 8d for playing 'ad organa'. As he also appears in the Chapel Royal accounts it may be that he performed a similar service for the Chapel Royal.

The *Liber Niger*, talking of the necessary talents of gentlemen clerks of the Chapel Royal, mentions that they should be 'sufficiant in organes pleying'. It is clear that at this time the duty of playing the organ was shared out among the complement of gentlemen clerks.

In 1498 Arnold Jeffrey is named as an organist at the court of Henry VII,[25] but, significantly, his name does not appear in the Chapel Royal lists. As a chamber organ could easily be used for such court entertainment as 'Maying', it is likely that Arnold's duties were in no way

[24] H.B. Wheatley, *Round About Pall Mall* (Smith, Elder, London, 1870), p. 294.
[25] Privy Purse Expenses of Henry VII, 20 July 1498, quoted in *Excerpta Historica*, ed. S. Bentley (1831).

ecclesiastical.

As the great organists of Henry VIII's court, Dionisius Memo and Benedictus de Opitiis, apparently had nothing to do with the Chapel Royal, we can presume that Chapel Royal organ duties were still performed by the gentlemen clerks as the occasion arose. This would have been the case at the Field of Cloth of Gold in 1520 where the English Chapel Royal was equipped with a silver chamber organ. However, with the development of the verse service and anthem the duty of playing the Chapel Royal organ became more difficult and demanding, as well as time-consuming, and the practice soon arose of appointing gentlemen to the Chapel Royal specifically for their ability to play the organ. Leach and Harris have pointed to the fact that the ability to teach organ playing to choristers was more in demand after 1535 than before.

We know for certain that Thomas Tallis and William Byrd described themselves on the title page of the *Cantiones quae ab argumento sacrae vocantur*, which they published in 1575, as 'generosis et organistis'. Tallis had joined the Chapel Royal as a gentlemen clerk in about 1540 and Byrd in 1570. On Tallis's death in 1585 William Blitheman is said to have become organist of the Chapel Royal until his death in 1591. There is an epitaph to him recorded in later editions of Stow's *Survey of London* which runs thus:

Here Blitheman lies, a worthy wight who feared God above;
A friend to all, a foe to none whom rich and poor did love.
Of prince's Chapel, Gentleman, unto his dying day,
Whom all took great delight to hear him on the organs play,
Whose passing skill in music's art a scholar left behind,
John Bull (by name) his master's vein expressing in each kind.
But nothing here continues long, nor resting place can have,
His soul departed hence to heaven, his body here in grave.

1592 sees the first record in the Old Cheque Book of a specific title of organist, applied to John Bull who had been a gentlemen clerk since 1586. The Cheque Book reference to him as an 'organiste' is almost in passing, for it appears in the context of admitting Phelps of Tewkesbury into the appointment of gentlemen extraordinary for the latter's kindness in coming to Dr Bull's aid when 'robbed in those parts'. This reference is dated 29 May 1592 and runs: 'William Phelps of Tewkesbury, in the Countye of Glocester, trayned up in the noble science of musick, for his care kindes to Mr Bull, Organiste in her Majestes chappell ... .' There is a portrait of Dr Bull at the music school at Oxford, painted on a board and representing him in the robes of a bachelor of music (see p. 87 above).

There is evidence, too, of William Randall, from Exeter, who had been epistler with the Chapel Royal from 1584, sharing duties with Dr Bull, for he signs himself twice in the Old Cheque Book, on 10 and 15 July 1592, as 'organist'. In 1604 Edmund Hooper was elected in Randall's place and signs himself 'organist' on 2 November 1615. But on 3 March 1600, before Hooper succeeded Randall, a certain 'Arter Cocke' was sworn 'gentlemen in ordinary and organiste (without pay) in her Majestes saide chapple, until an organiste place shalbe come voyde, and the said Arter Cocke (by his Honor's appointment) [there being no dean, at this time the lord chamberlain was acting-dean] to geve his attendaunce, and to supply the wantes of organistes which may be throughe sickness or other urgent causes ...'.[26]

'Arter Cocke' in fact replaced George Waterhouse, who had joined the Chapel Royal as a gentleman in 1588 but died in February 1602. Waterhouse, therefore, was probably an 'organiste'. In January 1606, when Cocke died, he was replaced by Orlando Gibbons, who signed himself later as 'organist' on 2 November 1615. Hooper was succeeded by Thomas Tomkins in 1621 and Tomkins is accordingly listed as 'organist' at the time of the coronation of Charles I. There is a reference to John Tomkins in 1626 being sworn for the next organist's place that should fall vacant, and, as he filled the place occupied by John Wilborow who had been epistler in 1599 but died at Ely in 1626, we can presume that Wilborow, too, was 'organist'. Thomas Warwick succeeded Orlando Gibbons in 1625, and Richard Portman succeeded John Tomkins in 1638.

The tuning of the organs in the various buildings occupied from time to time by the Chapel Royal was carried out from 5 November 1615 by William Ward who was sworn, according to the Old Cheque Book, 'Groome of his Majestes Vestery Extraordinarie, for the tuninge and mendinge of his Majestes organes when he shallbe thereunto required by those that have the charge thereof ...'.

The transition from the appointment of specific 'organists' from among the gentlemen clerks to appointment as 'organist' in their own right looks, therefore, as though it took the following form:

	Thomas Tallis	1584	William Randall
	William Byrd	1604	Edmund Hooper
	William Blitheman	1621	Thomas Tomkins
1586	John Bull		
1588	George Waterhouse	1599	John Wilborow
1600	Arter Cocke	1626	John Tomkins
1606	Orlando Gibbons	1638	Richard Portman
1625	Thomas Warwick		

(The date indicates the probable year of appointment as organist. Up to four held office simultaneously. The columns indicate direct succession.)

---

[26] Old Cheque Book, fol. 24b.

17. The Society of Gentlemen and Organists

The position of 'organist' held great status. This is revealed by the fact that they often received the large quantity of cloth for livery to which the 'mynister' gentlemen clerks were entitled. At Elizabeth I's funeral in 1603 John Bull and the 'mynisters' received nine yards of cloth as compared with seven yards for the other gentlemen clerks. Again for James I's funeral Orlando Gibbons received nine yards. Gibbons's successor, Thomas Warwick, though, ran into trouble, being checked in 1630 'of his whole paye for the Moneth of March because he presumed to playe verses on the organ at service tyme, beinge formerly inhibited by the Deane for doinge the same by reason of his insufficiency for that solemn service'.[27]

Concerning John Bull who, as the Old Cheque Book records, 'went beyond the seas without licence, and was admitted into the Archduke's Service' in 1613, it is interesting to note a letter dated 30 May 1614 from Mr Trumbull to James I concerning the reception of Dr Bull, 'the King's Organist', by the archduke without permission.[28] Dr Bull went on to succeed Rumold Waelrant as organist of Notre Dame at Antwerp in 1617. He lived in a house adjoining the cathedral on the site of the Place Verte. He died on 12 or 13 March 1628 and was buried on 15 March in the cathedral.

It is also worth noting that Orlando Gibbons married Elizabeth Patten, daughter of John Patten who was yeoman of the vestry of the Chapel Royal at the time of the coronation of James I in 1603. It had been John Patten's duty to arrange for all the accoutrements of Elizabeth I's Chapel Royal to be packed up and transported with her as she moved from place to place.[29]

Before turning to the tasks of the other gentlemen clerks of the Chapel Royal we should look at the rota arrangements devised for these gentlemen 'organists'.

A 'controversie between Organistes' arose in 1615 which gives us a valuable glimpse of the 'manner of their waytinge at principall feastes', as the Old Cheque Book describes it. The dean adjudicated and decided that 'alwaies heerafter the auncient custom should be observed, which was, and still must be, that the most auncient organist shall serve the eeve and daye of every principall feast'. These were Christmas, Easter, St George and Whitsun. It was the 'next Organist in place to serve the second day' and 'the third to the third daie if ther be so many Organistes'. As for all other festival days in the year, these were performed by the organists 'as they shall fall out in their severall wekes of waytinge'. We learn, too, that aside from the feasts, 'he that did or shoulde begin the Saterdaie before shall finish up the same weeke,

---

[27] Ibid., fol. 40b.
[28] BL Add. MS 6194.
[29] Old Cheque Book, fol. 23.

accordinge to former custom'. The other organist(s) then followed. The exception to this rule was Christmas, 'for then they change every daye, as the quier dothe duringe the whole twelve days'.[30]

The words 'auncient custom' and 'former custom' used by the dean in this 1615 chapter ruling suggest that this was the practice under the Tudor monarchs, the last of whom had died just twelve years before this adjudication. Thus we may have here the only glimpse so far into the practice followed by the gentlemen 'sufficiaunt in organes pleying' who preceded the appointment of specific organists to their company.

There is an undated entry in the Old Cheque Book entitled 'Orders for the Attendance of the Gentlemen of His Majestes Chappell', signed by the bishop of Bath and Wells. It was therefore made by the dean, James Montague, who held this bishopric and the deanery of the Chapel Royal together for the years 1603-19. The orders state: 'If there be above two Organistes at once, two shall allwaies attend; if ther be but two in all, then they shall wayte by course, one after another, weekly or monthly, as they shall agree betwixt themselves.' They had to inform the sub-dean and clerk of the check of 'their waytinge' arrangements and submit to 'such checks in the same manner as the other gentlemen are'.[31]

Let us now turn to the arrangements concerning the other gentlemen of the Chapel Royal. These same orders made between 1603 and 1619 give us further details as to how the rota was drawn up: 'Every yeare within the twelve dayes of Christmas a liste or rowle to be made new and drawne by the Subdeane and three or more of the gentlemen.' These three gentlemen were chosen by the 'major parte' of the 'fellowshippe' in a special chapter called to determine them. The three gentlemen chosen at this, together with the sub-dean, did then 'dispose of theyre wayting in the Chappell by a monthely course' so that 'a competent number' of gentlemen was appointed to attend services upon 'the workinge dayes throughout the yeare (except in the accustomed tymes and weekes of libertye called playing weeks)' under penalty of 'a checke for every one absence from any in his appointed monthe'.[32] There was also a gradation of fines for lateness.[33]

The 'antient tymes of lyberty and playinge weekes' were the 'quarter of liberty' of St Peter's day to Michaelmas. If the gentlemen were commanded to wait during this quarter they did so only on Sundays and holy days. The 'playinge weekes' were the week before Christmas and the weeks after Twelfthtide, Candlemas, Easter, St George, and all 'removinge' weeks. This list, entered sometime in the period 1603-19, also included the following entries scored through: the weeks after

[30] Ibid., fol. 33b.
[31] Ibid., fol. 39b.
[32] Ibid.
[33] See p. 296 below for details of these fines.

Allhallowtide, Shrove Monday and Tuesday, a week after the Rogation week, a week after Whitsuntide, and 'at all tymes when the Kinges Majestie is from a standinge house'. Their attempted erasure suggests the withdrawal of these privileges.

How many gentlemen made up the complement of singing clerks in the Chapel Royal from which the monthly 'rowle' was made?

By the middle of the sixteenth century the regular number of Chapel Royal members had settled at thirty-two. The Old Cheque Book list for the coronation of James I lists the gentlemen in order of seniority. First comes the sub-dean, followed by seven 'mynisters' in order of seniority, then the master of the children, the clerk of the check, 'Jo Bull, doctor in music', followed by twenty-two 'gentlemen' also in order of seniority, and four officers of the vestry. There is a curiosity in the Calendar of State Papers for 1604 which contains a draft of a warrant to increase the numbers, as it specifies thirty-eight gentlemen. There are even 'misleading' entries in the Old Cheque Book. For example, a list of 1603 detailing those attending a chapter at Greenwich 'in the first yeare of the raigne of our Soveraigne Lord Kinge James' shows forty signatories, nineteen of whom only became gentlemen in ordinary after this chapter. Perhaps the 'extras' were indeed 'extraordinary' members, for these were appointed 'gentlemen extraordinary' for special reasons. We have seen that William Phelps was appointed 'extraordinary' for helping Dr Bull on the latter being robbed near Tewkesbury in 1592. William West was likewise made a gentleman extraordinary 'the rather for that he did attend by the space of eighte dayes at the great solemnitye of the league of Spayne to his great charge'. Often, though, this category of membership was 'used' by the holder to wheedle his way into a paid or even unpaid 'ordinary' position. Strict conditions were often attached to their appointment to prevent this, although they did receive liveries for special occasions, such as the 'blacks' for the funerals of Elizabeth I and James I. Indeed a 'perpetuall decrye' was made 'in a Chapter holden at Greenwich by Anthonye Anderson, Substitute for the presente of her Majestes Chappell Royall, and the reste of the Worshippful Companye of the gentlemen thereof there assembled in the vestrye, the 18 of June 1592', which specified that 'no persons, of what qualitie, deserte, or place soever, shallbe admitted by our consentes into our said companye extraordinarye hereafter at any tyme but in and by the common consente by voyces in the chapter where and whensoever the Courte shall then be ...'. The successful applicant would then have to pay £5 to the clerk of the check 'for the use of the said companye'.[34]

Whether these extraordinaries were included in the 'list or rowle' of monthly waits of the gentlemen in ordinary is not clear. We do, however, know that 'all that shall be in the aforesaid list or rowle of daylie wayters,

---

[34] Ibid., fol. 19.

'Gentlemen of the Chapel Royal, in number 12' (though only eight are depicted), as they appear in an illustration from Sandford's *Coronation of James II*. (Reproduced by courtesy of the Dean and Chapter of Westminster)

as well out of their appoynted moneth as in it, shall attend [the services] uppon Sondayes, Principall tymes at Christmas, Easter, and Whitsuntide, uppon holy dayes at bothe services, uppon festivall and offerynge daye eves, at evening prayer, uppon sermon dayes at morning prayer',[35] at any rate in the 1603-19 period.

If this regime was much the same or stricter in early Tudor days then it must have been a very busy life. For with the master, William Cornish, the gentlemen acted in plays and masques for Henry VIII under the title 'Players of the Chapel' – as distinct from the 'Players of Interludes'. The children, of course, took part as well, receiving a gratuity of £6 13s 4d for each dramatic performance under Cornish. On one occasion Cornish received £200 for a performance, which would have been divided among the gentlemen who took part. Similar entries applied to William Crane's mastership.

Other 'offices' held by gentlemen included the crucial role of clerk of the check. This office was much valued for its dignity and privileges and accordingly was filled by vote of the gentlemen in a vestry meeting. It combined the roles of secretary, accountant and treasurer, and it was thus the clerk of the check who often recorded the actual entries in the Old and New Cheque Books of the Chapel Royal, along with the serjeant of the vestry.

[35] Ibid., fol. 39b.

Thomas Barrow, who sang solo soprano in Handel's *Esther* in 1732 as a child of the Chapel Royal. He later became a gentleman of the Chapel Royal (alto) from 1746-89, and was also a member of the choir of Westminster Abbey, where he is buried. (HM Chapel Royal, reproduced by gracious permission of Her Majesty The Queen)

One more crucial office was filled from among the gentlemen, the 'recorder of songs' or, in effect, music librarian. It was held by John Steephens under the sub-deanship of Stephen Boughton from at least 1625. This office is still in existence and is at present discharged by the gentleman of the Chapel Royal, Richard Edwards, by common consent of the gentlemen assembled under the senior gentleman, Norman Cooper.

In a chapter held on 29 April 1632 the dean, William Laud, tightened up the slackness that he had identified in clothing and uniforms, ordering that 'the gentlemen of the Chappell shall (at all such tymes as they doe attend that service) come in decent manner in their gownes and surplyses, and not in cloakes and surplyses, nor with bootes and spurres'.[36]

A few of the Gentlemen survived the ravages of the English Civil War and Commonwealth to return and participate in the splendour of the

[36] Ibid. fol. 41b.

Stylised depiction of the Chapel Royal from John Church's anthem book of 1712 entitled *Divine Harmony: a collection of anthems used at Her Majesty's Chapel Royal*. (Reproduced by courtesy of the British Library, Music Library H820)

Restoration Chapel Royal under Charles II. They continued to base their choral foundation for most of the time at the Tudor Whitehall chapel building which had survived the Miles Sindercombe fire plot against Cromwell's life, but which eventually succumbed to the Whitehall Palace fire of 1698. Although the choral foundation then moved to base themselves at the Banqueting House, queen Anne's decision to transfer her court on a permanent basis to St James's Palace in 1702 resulted in a parallel move by the Chapel Royal to occupy the chapel in colour court of St James's. This has ever since been the nearest thing to a 'home' for the Chapel Royal.

Serjeant of the vestry William Lovegrove had this to say of the gentlemen of the Chapel Royal in 1752: 'In order that so much of the Public Service as is directed to be sung, may be performed with greater decency and exactness, there are a certain number of Laymen, Vocal performers, appointed. The present Establishment are Sixteen, who are to attend Eight in each Month Alternately the Daily Service both Morning and Evening at Eleven and Five of the Clock.'[37] Serjeant Lovegrove goes on to give further details relating to the musical accompaniment during the services sung by the gentlemen in 1752: 'That Musick may be performed in the Chapel Royal in the best and most Solemn manner, there are appointed a certain number of Instrumental performers in the Organ Loft.' These were detailed as lutenist, violist, organist and composer, and organ blower.[38]

Exactly what duties the traditional offices of 'composer' and 'organist' in the Chapel Royal entailed at this time is difficult to determine, but we do get some idea from a passage in the Old Cheque Book dated 1736, which reads:

> Whereas the Right Reverend the Lord Bishop of London, Dean of His Majesty's Chapels Royal, has appointed William Boyce to be Composer, and Jonathan Martin to be organist of the said chapels; and whereas the place of Organist has much more duty and attendance belonging to it than the place of Composer (both which were enjoyed by Mr Weldon lately deceas'd, during whose long indisposition the two places were joyntly supply'd by the two persons aforesaid), I the said William Boyce do promise and agree that so long as I shall continue in the place of Composer, I will perform one third part of the duty and attendance belonging to the Organist, provided that I am allow'd one third part of the travelling charges belonging to the place. And I Jonathan Martin promise to compose Anthems or Services for the use of His Majesty's Chapel whenever required by the Sub-Dean for the time being ... .[39]

---

[37] William Lovegrove manuscript, p. 59.
[38] Ibid., p. 62.
[39] Old Cheque Book, fol. 58.

St James's Palace, July 1819, by C. Wilde, published by A. Dry for Pyne's *Royal Residences*, vol. 2. (Royal Library, Windsor Castle, reproduced by gracious permission of Her Majesty The Queen). S.S. Wesley was a child of the Chapel Royal from 1817-1826.

Serjeant Lovegrove also writes of the senior gentleman's privileges in 1765: 'Whereas by Antient Custom and Constitution of the Chapel has been that the Senior Member, either Priest or Gentleman, is excused from all attendance both in Person or by Deputy, as Father of the Chapel Royal.' Consequently the serjeant 'never makes any surplices nor allows any book to the Father of the Chapel'. We learn that 'Mr Mason was Father of the Chapel in my time, and never had either surplice or book. Mr Bernard Gates succeeded Mr Mason, and never has had surplice or Book as Father of the Chapel.'[40] Indeed the Old Cheque Book described William Byrd as a 'Father of Musick' at his death in 1623 – perhaps for this particular reason.

The report of the Royal Commission of 3 July 1860 recommended a reorganisation of gentlemen of the Chapel Royal which resulted in their numbers being reduced by half. The commissioners observed:

[40] Lovegrove manuscript, p. 173.

The Chapel Royal choir, winter 1957. *Front row:* John Murray, Richard Onslow, Eugene Danks, Brian Ward, John Clargo. *2nd row:* Colin Knight, Charles Hawkins, Harry Gabb, Rev. Maurice Foxell, Stanley Riley. *Back row:* Peter Knight, Malcolm Chatwin, Stanley Silcock, Colin Scull, Roy Wellington, Roger Overington, Alan Cross, William Buckle.

The Gentlemen of the Chapel Royal are 16 in number who appear in two divisions, one division of 8 taking each alternate month's service. Their salary is £58 a year. In both divisions the voices are two altos, three tenors and three basses. [The Commissioners recommended that] certain of the Gentlemen who have now served a long time, and are getting into years, shall retire with part of their previous salary, retaining also their rank as well as their Entree to the Chapel Royal, and their membership with the Corps, and whatever privileges pecuniary or otherwise may be therein involved until their number is reduced to 8 who shall be constantly required to attend the Chapel morning and evening, being forbidden to assist or accept any singing engagements at any other Choir on Sundays or holydays – leave of absence to be obtained from the Sub-Dean in writing.[41]

In an undated note sub-dean Edgar Sheppard recorded the precise mechanics of this time of change:

Subject to the proper arrangements of the voices present selected at the discretion of the Dean – Senior Members of the Choir shall retire with the

[41] Recorded in New Cheque Book, fol. 230.

honorary rank of Gentlemen of the Chapel Royal at a pension of £36 p.a. The 8 Gentlemen of the Chapel Royal who do not retire shall be required to perform the which of the Duty being present each Sunday and receiving a salary of £80. The Anthem and Service of the Sunday shall be rehearsed each Saturday by the Gentlemen and Children of the Chapel ... .[42]

The salaries were in fact £80 for those on the 'active list' and £40 on the 'retired list'. These new arrangements were to be carried out 'as soon as vacancies will permit'. This duly happened and can be chronicled in the Royal Kalender over a period of fifteen years or so.

Subsequent re-arrangements concerning the gentlemen of the Chapel Royal are dealt with in Chapter 26 below.

Compositions of Richard Popplewell, organist, choirmaster and composer of HM Chapel Royal

Piano/violin

Idyll (violin solo and piano)
Lyric Aria (violin solo and piano)
String Quartet Movement
Three Preludes for 2nd May (piano solo)

Organ

Suite (O.U.P.) (in three movements)
Puck's Shadow (O.U.P.)
Cantilene
Elegy (Banks) in Memoriam H.E.D.
Jubilee March
Prelude Under One Note
Prelude On 'Pange Lingua'
Prelude On 'Easter Hymn' (O.U.P.)
Prelude On 'Down Ampney' (Banks)
Prelude On 'St Columba'
Aria 'The Time of the Singing ...'
Two Trio Sonatas in D (three movements)
Romance (Roger Dean U.S.A.)
Variations on a New Year's Carol
Variations on 'Away in a Manger'
Variations on A Theme by Kreisler
Chants d'Oiseaux, des Poules, des Moutons et des Vaches (pour la main gauche et pédale) from A Garland for D.G.A.F. (Weinberger)

---

[42] Loose letter kept with the Chapel Royal archive.

17. The Society of Gentlemen and Organists

Organ & full orchestra

Concerto No. 1 in D (three movements)
Concerto No. 2 in F (four movements)
National Anthem dedicated by gracious permission to H.M. Queen Elizabeth II
In Praise of Giving (for 250th Anniversary of Royal Society of Musicians) (choir & orchestra)
Magnificat in E – S.S. Wesley (orchestrated by Richard Popplewell)

Vocal

Royal Christening Anthems
   (1) Prince Michael of Kent's Son, Frederick
   (2) H.R.H. Prince William of Wales
   (3) H.R.H. Princess Beatrice of York
Two Final Amens (Banks) 8-Part
Carol 'It came upon a midnight clear' (SATB)
Carol 'There is no rose' (SS AA TT BB)
Wassail Carol (M.V.)
Jubilate (M.V.) in C
Psalm 23 The Lord is my shepherd (SATB) (for choir of St Michael's Cornhill)
Psalm 23 Chant (SS AA TT BB)

Solo songs

The Solitary Reaper (tenor and piano)
To Daffodils (bass and piano)
Everyone Suddenly Burst Out Singing (duet S.S. and piano)

Baroque lute

Variations on 'Brigg Fair'
A Lament

18

Clerks of the Cheque

The duty of the clerk of the cheque has evidently always been to keep a list of attendance of the priests, gentlemen and officers of the vestry, and to note any shortcomings in the efforts of those who were required to attend according to the 'list or rowle to be made new and drawne by the Sub-Dean and three or more of the Gentlemen' every year 'within the twelve days of Christmas'.[1] As we know from the same orders the gentlemen with the sub-dean did 'dispose of theyre wayting in the Chappell by a monethly course, that a competent number of the Gentlemen be appointed to attend the service upon the workinge dayes throughout the yeare'.

Should any of the gentlemen fail to attend his appointed services, the clerk of the cheque administered 'the penalty of a check for every one absence from any in his appointed monethe'. 'Check' or 'cheque' meant 'fine' and it is perhaps easier to understand the title 'clerk of the cheque' as 'clerk of fines'. In the early seventeenth century the check for 'absence from morning prayers, holy dayes, festivall tymes, and sermon dayes, shalbe 4d, from evening prayer uppon such dayes and their festivall eves 3d, for absence from morninge prayer uppon workynge dayes 3d, from eveninge prayer 2d'. Moreover, 'the check for latecominge, viz. after the first gloria patri 1d, after the first lesson 2d, after the second as for absence from the whole service'. There were, of course, exceptions to 'checking' such as sickness, when the sub-dean appointed someone from the 'contrary month' to fill the place – again under penalty of check for absence if he, too, failed – and when 'any of the gentlemen in his appointed moneth shall have any urgent business or any impediment to be approved by the Sub-Dean, his absence shall be tolerated', as long as a deputy of a 'contrary month' fills his place.

We know, too, that in the early seventeenth century 'all the checks shall monethly be divided amongst those of the gentlemen that have been most diligent in wayting that moneth, by the judgement of the Sub-Dean of the moneth's wayters'.[2] It was the task of the clerk of the cheque to

---

[1] Early seventeenth-century orders of the dean, the bishop of Bath and Wells, in Old Cheque Book, fol. 39, entered sometime between 1603 and 1619.
[2] Old Cheque Book, fol. 39b.

Chapel Royal. St. James's Palace.

Fines incurred by Officials of Her Majesty's Chapel
Royal, St. James's Palace, for non-attendance or unpunctuality.

	£	s.	d.
The appointed Preacher at 12 o'clock for not Preaching	4	4	0
The Chaplain in Waiting for not appearing to Read the Gospel when another Preacher is appointed	1	1	0
The Priest in Waiting for non-attendance at 12 o'clock	4	4	0
At 10 a.m. for do.	2	2	0
At 5.30 p.m. for do.	2	2	0
Organist for non-attendance at 12 o'clock	1	1	0
At 10 a.m. for do.	0	10	0
At 5.30 p.m. for do.	0	10	0
Gentlemen of the Chapel Royal for lapses at 12 o'clock	0	10	0
At 10 a.m for do.	0	5	0
At 5.30 p.m. for do.	0	5	0
Any Official for arriving late	0	5	0

Signed,

J. LONDON,

1878. *Dean.*

administer the distribution of these fines.

The level of fines or checks rose as time went on, and the Chapel went through occasional periods of slackness in attendance. Thus we find that in 1878 the dean also signed an order stating that 'the appointed Fine for non-attendance on the part of the Gentlemen of the Chapel Royal will henceforth be exacted (excepting sudden cases of indisposition) when leave of absence has not been asked for, sufficiently early, to give time for considering the application'.

It would be misleading to confine the clerk of the cheque's ambit to the gentlemen in their singing capacity, for the early seventeenth-century orders of the dean, promulgated sometime between 1603 and 1619, also charge the clerk of the cheque with the duty to watch and check the organists' rota of waits. Thus the organists were required to give notice to the 'Clerk of the Check how they do dispose of their waytinge … and they shalbe subject to such orders, and to such checks, in the same manner as

[3] Ibid.

297

the other gentlemen are'.[3]

The office of clerk of the cheque was respected as a high responsibility, reflected in the Old Cheque Book 'Note of the names of the sub-dean, gentlemen, and others of the Chapel, at the time of the Coronation of King James the First' in which the sub-dean is listed first, then the seven 'mynisters' in order of seniority, then the master of the children, followed by the clerk of the cheque, 'Jo Bull Doctor in Music', the twenty-two gentlemen and, lastly, the four officers of the vestry.

The office of clerk of the cheque is perhaps most clearly defined in William Lovegrove's account of *c*. 1752-77, where he states that 'the duty of the Clerk of the Cheque, is to keep an Account of the Daily Attendance, and the Absence of the priests and Gentlemen of the Chapel Royal, in order to lay them before the Dean or Sub-Dean, the beginning of every month'. Furthermore he 'should attend at every Admission of a Priest, Gentleman, and officer of the Chapels Royal when sworn in, and to enter his name in the Cheque Book and to sign it after the Sub-dean'. For this duty the Clerk of the Cheque 'has ten shillings and Sixpence, from the Members of the Royal Chapel'. He received also 'from every member of Whitehall, French, Dutch, and Lutheran Chapels, One Guinea' and 'at the Readmission and Swearing in of every Member, upon Accession of a new King, Half the above Named Fees'. Although there was no salary as such for his office he did receive two guineas for the first week and one guinea for each subsequent week, as long as the king and court resided at Kensington, Hampton Court or Windsor, for his travelling wages in the same way as the priests and gentlemen of the Chapel Royal.

The first name of a clerk of the cheque that has come down to us is that of Thomas Byrd, who served as a gentlemen of the Chapel Royal from 1526-61, Robert Morecock succeeding him upon his death in February 1561. It is possible that the parallel manuscript to the Old Cheque Book held by the Bodleian, which also starts its account in 1560,[4] may have been started and kept by the clerk of the cheque.

Next to an entry for 1615 the Old Cheque Book records that 'Thomas Sampson, Clark of the Check, was drowned on 24th of April and John Myners was sworne in his place the 4th daye of June followinge; and John Hewlett havinge executed the place of Clark of the Check for Mr Sampson above eight years, was allowed to be Clarke of the Check by our Lord Deane and consent of the company'. This decision was questioned five years later but settled in a specially convened vestry meeting on 20 June 1620 'and there by a scrutiny he was ellected and allowed to be clerk of the check by the major part of the gentlemen, beinge then 25 in number'. John Stephens, clerk of the cheque, died on 13 May 1636, to be succeeded in that office by Thomas Day, who was sworn on 20 April 1637. The last entry to be found in the Bodleian Register before the outbreak of the Civil

[4] MS Rawl. D318.

War is dated November 1643 and thus post-dates the last entry in the Old Cheque Book, which resumes at the Restoration in 1660. As Thomas Day does not seem to have survived until the Restoration, a strong candidate for having hidden and preserved both the Old Cheque Book and the Bodleian Register, together with the Chapel Royal Anthem book, is Henry Lawes, who had been clerk of the cheque in 1625. He died two years after the Restoration on 21 October 1662.

The principle of election from the ranks of the gentlemen by common consent in vestry was abandoned in 1720 when the then serjeant of the vestry, Jonathan Smith, 'by vertue of a warrant from the Rt. Revd. the Lord Bishop of Sarum, Dean of His Majesty's Royal Chapels ... was sworn Clark of the Cheque ... on 4th day of Aprill 1720, by me Edw. Aspinwall, Subdean'.[5]

Serjeant of the vestry Francis Lingard was the last person to hold the ancient office of clerk of the cheque, for in 1860 the Chapel Royal commissioners recommended that 'the duties of the Clerk of the Cheque ... henceforth be performed by the Sub-Dean, and the office may therefore on the next vacancy be abolished'. Today, therefore, the office of clerk of the cheque no longer exists. Although the commissioners said that the duties of this office should be performed by the sub-dean, and this was stated to be the case by Edward Rimbault in 1966, in his Introduction to his edited version of the Old Cheque Book, one might argue that the specialised accounting techniques developed by clerks of the cheque to levy and distribute the proceeds of fines, etc., are today more clearly to be seen in the duties of the honorary treasurer of the Chapel Royal.

[5] Old Cheque Book, fol. 30.

19

Masters of the Children

The earliest detailed description of the role of the master of the children is to be found in Say's *Liber Regie Capelle* of 1449, which has this to say: 'There is a also one Song Master, or Master of Music, whose duty it is to teach these boys and duly to instruct them in both plain chant and harmony'. (The Latin reads 'in cantu plane et organico', which, as Gordon Dunstan points out, may mean 'plain chant and polyphony'.) As this passage also mentions that there are 'ten boys trained to sing and to read', we know that the master's duty was to look after ten children and teach them the art of music – both choral and instrumental.

We can go back earlier and find reference to the master at work with the Chapel Royal, but with no such detailed job-description. Thus in 1420 the composer John Pyamour, who was termed merely 'one of the clerks of the Chapel of the household' in a Patent Roll,[1] was commissioned 'to take boys for the said Chapel and bring them to the King's presence in his duchy of Normandy', where his household Chapel (i.e. the Chapel Royal) had been with Henry V since 1417. It is known that in the year 1421/2 the number of children of the Chapel Royal was sixteen, but within the space of one year the number had dwindled to just six.[2]

In 1440 Henry VI commissioned not a clerk, but rather the dean himself to impress choristers for service with the Chapel Royal. The commission read as follows: 'to the King's clerk Master John Croucher, dean of the Chapel within the household, to take throughout England such and so many boys as he or his deputies shall see fit and able to serve God and the king in the said royal chapel.'[3] A year later, in 1441, the priest, clerk, composer, ex-verger at Windsor and now 'one of the clerks of the king's chapel', John Plummer, was granted the sum of ten pounds. It is thought that this was for instructing the boys in choral music as well as for supervising them. It appears therefore that the dean handed the 'impressed' boys over to Plummer for instruction, so we can tentatively regard John Plummer as the master of the children from at least 1441.

---

[1] Cal. Pat. Rolls 14 January 1420 (p. 272 in printed edition).
[2] See Chapter 20 below.
[3] Cal. Pat. Rolls 12 July 1440 at Eashampstead Manor (p. 452 in printed edition).

More definite evidence of his activities appears in a grant dated 1444 'for the exhibition of eight boys of the Chapel and for his reward, of 40 marks yearly from Michaelmas last so long as he have the keeping of the said boys or others in their place, from the ulnage of woollen cloth for sale and from a moiety of the forfeiture thereof in the town and suburbs of Bristol'. This grant was repeated in 1446,[4] but a rather more explicit grant of 1445 reads: 'during good behaviour, to the King's Serjeant John Plummer, one of the clerks of the Chapel, for his daily labours in the teaching and rule of the King's boys of the Chapel, of the said teaching, rule and governance.'[5]

Although Say's *Liber Regie Capelle* states the number of boys as ten, it is known from a list of the king's 'honeurable household' that there were only seven children just five years later in 1454,[6] with the number rising to ten again according to the grant of the mastership of the children to the priest Henry Abyngdon in Michaelmas 1455, 'to whom the king committed the instruction and governance of the ten boys of the Chapel of the household, of 40 marks yearly from Michaelmas last, the date of his appointment ... so long as he shall have the said instruction and governance; so that he act by advice and survey of the dean of the Chapel'. This grant was made on 16 March 1456. Similar grants to Henry Abyngdon were repeated in 1465 and 1471, and this leads to a conundrum, for a Patent Roll dated 24 March 1465 refers to the 'Master of song', Robert Bunnock, who received a grant 'for his good services in the instruction of boys in the art of music to sing in the king's Chapel, of a yearly rent of 10 marks'. The wording of this grant suggests that Robert Bunnock received a commission as Master of Song from one year to the next, and yet throughout this period it has hitherto generally been assumed that Henry Abyngdon held that office. It is possible that as Abyngdon earned '40 marks yearly' and Bunnock only 'a yearly rent of 10 marks', Bunnock may have acted as Abyngdon's deputy. But this is by no means certain, and the Patent Rolls are clearly contradictory on the face of it.

The *Liber Niger Domus Regis* of Edward IV, which was probably written in 1483, sheds much more light on the master's role with the Chapel Royal and also gives us fascinating glimpses of the everyday routine experienced by the children. The master of the children from 1478-86 was Gilbert Benester. The *Liber Niger*, talking of the 'Children of Chapell viii,' goes on to specify the duties of the 'Master of Song, assigned to teche them, whiche maister is apoynted by the seyd deane, and chosen one of the numbyr of the felashippe of Chapelle, and he to draw theese children, all as well in the Scoole, of facet as in song, organes, or suche

[4] Cal. Pat. Rolls 30 May 1446 (p. 455 in printed edition).
[5] Cal. Pat. Rolls 24 February 1445 at Westminster (p. 333 in printed edition).
[6] Acts of the Privy Council, vol. 6, p. 223.

other vertuouse thinge'. The master and children of the Chapel Royal were boarded and lodged in the royal palace in which the court happened to be residing. The Chapel Royal accompanied the king when he went 'journeying', and provision was made for 'horse hyre dayly' for the children. The master or the dean had to oversee the issue of 'apparyl' for the boys.

The priest Lawrence Squire held the mastership from 1486 to 1493 and was succeeded by William Newark who held it until 1509. William Cornish served as his deputy master from 1508 and succeeded him to hold the mastership until 1523. The high point of Cornish's mastership must surely have been at the Field of Cloth of Gold in 1520 when he was given the task of devising the pageants on the Sunday night. The Calendar of State Papers contains details headed: 'A memorial of things to be done at the meeting and interview of the King's highness and the emperor Charles at Gravelines.' Under this heading is the reference to Cornish: 'The garnishing of the church is committed to the Dean of the Chapel, the devising of pageants at the banquets to Cornish, and the mummery is referred to the King's pleasure.' Special arrangements had been made in advance for Cornish's pageants as is clear from the Calendar directive regarding vestments given to Westminster Abbey by Henry VIII's father: 'The rich copes with the Vestments given to the monastery by the late King are to be borrowed for this voyage, and afterwards returned. The Clerk to the Closet is to warn ten Chaplains to accompany the King, and provide the Closet with the best hangings, travers, jewels, images, altar cloths etc. that the King has.' Elsewhere there are other items giving Cornish's salary and also the figure 28s 8d for board and wages for the children. Cornish had his hands full during sea passages when the children of the Chapel Royal were aboard ship. There is a Calendar entry 'for diets for 10 of the Children during the King's voyage to Calais 62 days at 2d'.

A deputy appointment similar to that which had originally been held by Cornish was made in 1526 when Richard Pygote was appointed deputy master to William Crane, who had held the mastership from 1523 and was to serve in this capacity until 1545. Pygote in fact never succeeded Crane, (Crane's replacement as master was Richard Bower), despite the fact that Pygote continued to serve with the Chapel Royal until 1552.

The idea of appointing a deputy master was, however, evidently a success, for Richard Edwards served as deputy master from 1560-61 under Richard Bower, succeeding him as master in 1561 and continuing in the post until 1566. Richard Edwards's contribution to the office of master of the children cannot be overestimated. He was not only a priest but also a poet and playwright of great talent. He wrote many plays for the children of the Chapel Royal to act and could be said to have sown the seed of the children's involvement in the formation of the Chapel Royal theatre under the future masters Farrant and Hunnis, which was continued under Nathaniel Giles until 1626.[7]

Edwards's fame was of sufficient magnitude to impress William Shakespeare, that great critic of choirboy actors, for in *Romeo and Juliet*[8] Shakespeare quotes from one of Edwards's songs 'When griping griefs'. Claude de Sainlien wrote of Edwards in his dialogue published in 1573:

Roland:	I should not bee a singing man except I shold drinke well …
Guest:	There is a good songe. I do marvell who hath made it.
Host:	It is the maister of the children of the Queenes Chappell.
Guest:	What is his name?
Host:	Maister Edward.
Guest:	Is hee alive?
Host:	I heard say that hee was dead.
Roland:	It is already a good while ago: it is at the least five yeares and a halfe.
Host:	Truly, it is a pitie: he was a man of good wit, and a good poet: and a great player of playes.[9]

Richard Edwards's successor, William Hunnis, served as master from 1566 until 1597, during much of which time he, too, had a deputy – Richard Farrant – who served in that capacity from 1569-81. However, the close of the Tudor era saw the end of the office of deputy master of the children, and all the responsibilities were again vested in one individual – the master.

We learn much about the daily duties and occasional responsibilities of the master of the children from warrants granted to captain Henry Cooke, who was the first master appointed at the Restoration in 1660 and had earned his rank of captain in the Royalist Army during the Civil War. His predecessor, Thomas Day, who had succeeded Nathaniel Giles, served from 1633 until 1654. The dispersed Chapel Royal thus had no master for at least six years prior to the Restoration, for an order of 9 May 1661 talks of 'Henry Cooke, Master of His Majesty's Chappell Royall, in the place of Thomas Day … 1660'.[10]

Henry Cooke's responsibilities were the same as those of his predecessors, so we find quarterly payments of £10 each paid to him for keeping and teaching two choristers of the Chapel Royal from 1660-72, in which year he was succeeded by Pelham Humphrey. Cooke took great pains to ensure that the boys were always well turned out. Thus we find a bill for the period ending Michaelmas 1661 showing provision by Cooke of shoes and gloves for the children of the Chapel Royal.[11] He travelled to cathedrals to spot talented boys for impressment to the Chapel Royal, for

---

[7] For details of the activities of these masters, see Chapter 5 above.
[8] Act 4, scene 5.
[9] Quoted and discussed in Wulstan, *Tudor Music*, p. 81.
[10] LC vol. 181, p. 55.
[11] LC bundle 21, 9/378.

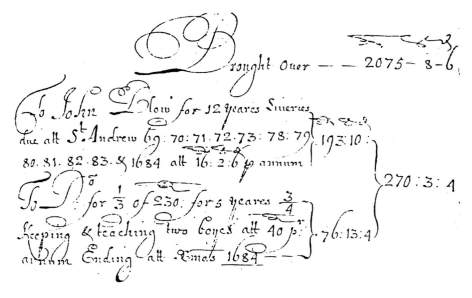

Transcript of a warrant to the Great Wardrobe detailing payment to the master of the children of the Chapel Royal, John Blow (1674-1708), for 'Keeping & teaching two boyes'. This entry is contained in a volume of warrants, formerly the property of Sir Charles Graham of Netherby Hall, Cumbria, sold by Sotheby's on 10/11 July 1986.

there is a warrant as early as 4 July 1661 for payment of £23 16s 9d to Cooke 'master of the children of the Chappell, for fetching five boys from Newarke and Lincolne for his Majesty's Service'.

Charles II's coronation meant much practice and hard choral work as well as travelling and so we find a payment of 16 September 1661 to Cooke of £19 10s 'being extraordinary charges for himself and 12 Children, commanded to attend upon his Majesty at Windsor for the space of six days, at the rate of 5s a day to each, and £2 16s for torches and lights for practising the musick against his Majesty's Coronation'.[12]

The 'scarlet cloth' uniforms of the boys trimmed with silver and silk lace 'after the manner of footmen's liveries' were delivered to Cooke in his capacity as master of the children.[13] A payment of £45 to Cooke detailed in a warrant of 24 March 1661 reveals that he paid 'masters for teaching the said children to write and learne to speake latine'. This indicates that the education of the children in matters of grammar was undertaken by a professional but arranged by the master. Similar entries are to be found throughout Cooke's mastership.

Cooke was evidently a busy man, for apart from holding the office of

---

[12] LC vol. 741, p. 85.
[13] LC vol. 814, p. 106.

View of St James's Palace in 1753, by T. Bowles. The windows of the Chapel Royal building can be seen to the right of the gatehouse. (Reproduced by courtesy of the Guildhall Library, City of London)

master he also was admitted on 9 November 1660 to 'his Majesty's private musick in ordinary'. Initially he took 'the place of Mons Du Vall for a lute and voyce, £60 per annum, and £20 per annum for strings. Also £24 per annum for breeding a boy for vocall musick which Thomas Day lately enjoyed.'[14] In this connection he came under the direction of Nicholas Lanier, 'master of his Majesty's musique', and is mentioned along with others in the arrangements for 'hiring of two large rooms for the practice of musique and for keeping the instruments in, for one year from 24th June 1660 to 24th June 1661'.[15] This hiring of rooms continued year by year. They had yearly liveries issued at the feast of St Andrew. A number of members of the king's 'musique in ordinary' were appended to the Chapel Royal to provide instrumental accompaniment for their services. Thus we find, for example, a warrant for payment of £30 to William Saunders, 'musician in ordinary', for, among other things, 'a double sackbutt for His Majesty's Chappell Royall' in September 1661. The instruments themselves were kept in 'three very large trunkes barrd strong and bound round with iron, the locks, handles and squires of the best and lined with fine bayes'.[16] To be one of the 'Musicians that do service in the Chappell Royall' could be a very great commitment. Thus,

[14] LC vols 180 and 477.
[15] LC vol. 472, p. 76.
[16] LC bundle 10.

for example, 'Robert Strong and Edward Strong are to attend with their double curlotts in his Majesty's Chappell Royall at Whitehall, and Thomas Bates and William Gregory with their violls, every Sunday and Holy day, all the rest to wayte their turnes', according to a warrant of 1662.[17]

Cooke's responsibilities as master of the children of the Chapel Royal did not extend to providing for the three children of the 'Queen's Chapel' who sang in the Inigo Jones chapel at St James's Palace, providing a choral element to the Roman Catholic worship there. Mr Ferdinando saw to the needs of the children separately recruited and involved there. Thus we read of a warrant in 1664 'to deliver to Captain Henry Cooke materials for liveries for the children of the King's Chappell, and to Mr Ferdinando the same for the three children of the Queen's Chappell'.

The wide range of responsibilities of the master with the post-Restoration Chapel Royal in the seventeenth century is encapsulated in the following record of payment dated 23 May 1671:

> The sum of £167-17s-4d. to be paid to Capt. Cook, master of the children of his Majesty's Chappell Royall, for learning the children on the organ, on the lute and theorbo, for fire and strings in the musique room in the Chappell, for doctors, nurses, and for looking to severall of the children when they were sick; for going to Westchester, Litchfield, Canterbury and Rochester to look for boyes, and for other service for one year from Lady Day 1670, to Lady Day 1671.

This is a fairly typical analysis of a year's duties for the master in the seventeenth century. A hundred years later the tasks of the master had not changed all that much. Serjeant of the vestry William Lovegrove compiled between the years 1752 and 1777 a personal notebook of events and officials associated with the Chapel Royal. He had this to say of the duties of the Master before listing (with a couple of minor inaccuracies concerning dates) the names of masters from 1563 to 1757:

> The Master of the Children hath generally (tho' not always) been chosen out of the Organists or Gentlemen of the Chapel. In the following list there is one instance to the contrary, viz. Capt. Henry Cook, all the rest have been either Organists or Gentlemen of the Chapel Royal.
>
> By the present Establishment, the Children are ten in Number, they wear the King's Livery, which is provided them Annually out of the King's Wardrobe. The Master's Duty is to teach them to sing, to play upon the Harpsicord or Organ, Writing Arithmetick, and compose.
>
> They are to attend the Service of the Chapel Daily throughout the Year, where his Majesty Resides, Kensington excepted.
>
> When their voices break and they become unfit for the Chapel, His

[17] LC vol. 741, p. 352.

Dr Edmund Ayrton, master of the children of the Chapel Royal 1780-1805, as painted in 1786 by former child of the Chapel, John Hoppner RA. (Reproduced by courtesy of Leger Galleries Ltd., London)

Majesty gives thirty pounds to the Parents or friends of each Boy, to place him out Apprentice.

If they behave well, and their Voices turn out usefull; they are frequently admitted Gentlemen of the Chapel Royal.

The only significant difference from a century beforehand appears to be the teaching of 'Writing Arithmetick', apparently now the duty of the master rather than an 'outside' teacher.

There is a fascinating letter[18] from Richard Clark (gentleman 1820-58) to the dean of the Chapel Royal concerning the perquisites to which the master of the children was entitled:

> I have seen the following Document, in possession of Mr Hawes, dated 1757, written by B. Gates the Master of the Children at that time, viz. Received as Master of the Children, 4 Old Prayer Books, and 10 Bibles as my Perquisites. Mr Ayrton also (son of Dr Ayrton one of the Gentlemen in 1764) positively asserts, that his Father had two surplices, as perquisites, and that he has now two Prayerbooks, and several Bibles which he received, after he became Master of the Children in 1780.

As we enter the middle of the nineteenth century we find that the master's role and duties continued to be the same as those described four hundred years earlier in Say's *Liber Regie Capelle* – the only significant difference being the increased opportunity for causing mischief afforded the children of the Chapel Royal by 'modern' Victorian life, and the consequent challenges presented to the master. I recently had the pleasure of meeting Don Helmore, direct descendant of the master of the children of the Chapel Royal, Thomas Helmore, who had held the office of master from 1846 until 1886. Mr Helmore had in his possession a book written by Thomas Helmore's brother, Fred, entitled *Memoir of the Rev. Thomas Helmore – Late Priest in Ordinary and Master of the Children of her Majesty's Chapels Royal; Precentor of St Mary's College Chelsea; Hon. Precentor of the Motet Choir, and of the London Gregorian Choral Association.*[19] This book is full of detail about the everyday lives of the master and children of the Chapel Royal in his charge.

Thomas Helmore was priest-vicar at Lichfield Cathedral and curate of St Michael's before he took up the post of vice-principal and precentor of St Mark's Training College for Schoolmasters at Chelsea. This college was in the process of foundation, and its object was to raise the standard of schoolmasters. The man selected to be principal was the Rev. Derwent Coleridge, son of the poet. Portraits of both Helmore and Coleridge are still to be seen there. The dean of the Chapel Royal, Dr Blomfield, took a keen interest in the college, hoping that it would become the means to revive the ancient office in the church of sub-deacon, so that the ordained schoolmasters could have more influence over the older schoolchildren. Moreover he placed great importance on the value of musical training and the duties of choirmasters.

It was from this background that Thomas Helmore was in 1846 appointed to the mastership of the children of the Chapel Royal, vacant

---

[18] Written at no. 46 Strand sometime between 1820 and 1833.
[19] Published by J. Masters and Co., London, 1891.

after the death of Mr Hawes. In the meantime Thomas had married Kate Pridham at St Andrew's Plymouth on 11 January 1844. She was to play a great role in looking after the children of the Chapel Royal.

We know from the letters of Frederick Walker of St Paul's Cathedral, who mentions in one that he himself 'entered the Chapel Royal on September 5th 1844', that in 1846 'the boys went from Adelphi Terrace, Strand, to live with Mr Helmore, at Robert Street, Chelsea'.[20]

Thomas Helmore had inherited a problem of discipline, or rather the total lack of it, among the children of the Chapel Royal – the entire company of whom now stayed with him. The actual acts of 'dreadful cruelties practised on the junior boys by their seniors' are detailed in Chapter 20 below. Suffice it to say here that upon the death of the former master of the children, Mr Hawes, 'it was not long before Mr Helmore realized the degraded state of brutality to which the boys intrusted to his care had sunk'. Helmore promptly abolished the existing 'fagging' system until the troublesome senior boys had left and then re-established it:

> Each boy, as formerly, in the senior division had a junior, for whose conduct, cleanliness, attention to his singing, and preparation of other lessons, he was responsible. If, as was frequently the case, they had to attend concerts, rehearsals, or any other engagements in London or elsewhere, each senior had to take charge of his fag and bring him home safely. In return for these attentions the juniors had certain duties to perform for their Masters in the same way as Eton fags have to work for theirs.[21]

The new system 'was perfectly successful' for Thomas Helmore carefully watched for abuses. Frederick Walker summed up the results: 'Everything was done by Mr and Mrs Helmore to bring about a different tone amongst the boys, who soon responded with such gentle influence.' Mr Walker wrote much about the moral change brought about in the boys by the 'refining influnce of his [Helmore's] talented and judicious wife'. The behaviour of the boys rapidly improved under this influence: 'Ladies in particular were wont to say that the Chapel Royal boys were thorough little gentlemen.' Some of the credit too, though, must go to the first 'boy's-maid' who began service with them at Robert Street, Chelsea – Sarah Adams (*née* Sumpster).

The boys lived at Robert Street, Chelsea, until some of the houses in Onslow Square were built. When no. 1 Onslow Square was completed, Thomas Helmore and the children of the Chapel Royal moved there.

In the past masters had earned a good income from hiring out the children of the Chapel Royal to concerts and other musical engagements – often with no church connection. This changed under Thomas Helmore, who adopted the policy of letting them go only to special functions

[20] Quoted in *Memoir of the Rev. Thomas Helmore*, p. 52.
[21] Frederick Walker, quoted in ibid., p. 54.

No. 6 Cheyne Walk.

'consistent with their position as choristers of the Chapel Royal'. He saw to it that the children attended the Motet Society and the Madrigal Society. On certain special occasions they also attended the rehearsals and performances of the Sacred Harmonic Society. Frederick Walker records that some of the former Chapel Royal choristers 'are now living witnesses of Mendelssohn's reading of his own work "Elijah". For, having rehearsed under his baton, they are able to correct some of the false readings of more modern conductors.' Mr Walker adds that 'there being no regular daily service at St James's, it was an advantage to the boys to be taken to St Mark's, the precentorship of which Mr Helmore still retained'.[22]

[22] Ibid.

The boys, then, soon adapted to a much more suitable routine than in previous years. But the question of accommodation still cropped up from time to time. From no. 1 Onslow Square Thomas Helmore, his family and the Chapel Royal boys moved to no. 6 Cheyne Walk on Lady Day 1854. This house, now a grade II starred listed building, was built in 1718 within the great garden of Henry VIII's manor house. This manor was owned by Lord Cheyne, from whom Cheyne Walk took its name, towards the end of the seventeenth century. In 1712 Sir Hans Sloane bought the manor and sold the building leases for what are today nos 1-8 Cheyne Walk. No. 6 is the largest with a ⅓-acre garden. Originally the house was approached from Flood Street, rather than the Riverside as later on, so its north front is consequently as impressive as the present south front. Indeed, the old horse mounting-steps can still be seen at the base of the steps leading up to the garden door.

The first occupant of the house was Joseph Danvers, MP for Boroughbridge, Bamber and Totnes. His family owned the house until 1764 at which date the lease was taken over by the Venetian nobleman, Dr Bartholomew de Dominicetti, who converted the house to include 'fumigatory' baths and built three further apartments in the garden. Of these, only the garden cottage still survives. Among his 'patients' was the then duke of York. Later in the eighteenth century the house became a fashionable school. It was this format which Thomas Helmore inherited on his occupation in 1854. There is still original panelling to be found in the house on the second floor, believed to date from the sixteenth and seventeenth centuries and to have come from Henry VIII's manor house when Sir Hans Sloane sold the materials from it to the builders of the Cheyne Walk houses.

When Thomas Helmore occupied it there was a row of splendid old elm trees on the river side of the road, propped up against which were often to be seen oars and masts used by the watermen who touted for customers to use their wherries. Brightly coloured lighters and barges with their brown sails floated there at high water or rested on the mud at low water. Across the river from no. 6 could be seen the glittering roof of the Crystal Palace. Hot-air ballons would occasionally ascend from nearby Cremorne Gardens in the daytime, and fireworks at night.

Less then three weeks after the removal to Cheyne Walk, Arthur Sullivan was appointed one of the children of the Chapel Royal on 12 April 1854. It was the organist, Sir George Smart, who had recognised his potential and suggested to young Arthur, 'Now you must go and see Mr Helmore.' He nearly didn't! He was taken to Onslow Square which Helmore had just vacated. Undaunted, however, Arthur is recorded as saying: 'They must have eaten when they were here; let us ask at the butcher's shop.' This they did and were directed to Cheyne Walk, where Thomas Helmore heard Arthur sing 'With verdure clad' and play his own accompaniment. He was accepted on the basis of this by letter two days later and was appointed to sing in the Chapel Royal the day before Maundy Thursday, when the Chapel Royal was due to attend the queen at Whitehall. Arthur duly made his debut on that occasion singing in the duet of Nares's anthem: 'Blessed is he that considereth the poor and needy.'

Arthur Sullivan found the circumstances at Cheyne Walk ideally suited to his musical talents, for Thomas Helmore held 'musical matinees' in the drawing room at no. 6, which was almost purpose-built for such occasions, measuring 50 feet long and spanning the width of the house on the first floor. Arthur was chief accompanist at these performances at which professional artists, amateurs and the children of the Chapel Royal took part. Mendelssohn wrote a letter, which Arthur framed, thanking him for 'his lovely singing' on one of these occasions. Charles Lockey was a frequent attender – he was the tenor who sang the 'Obadiah' solos in *Elijah* on its first performance in England. Close neighbours included Carlyle at no. 10 Cheyne Walk, and John Goss, organist of St Paul's Cathedral, at no. 5.

Thomas Helmore's brother, Frederick, was an accomplished choir-master, and Thomas often arranged for the children of the Chapel Royal to join Fred on his 'tours' of various parts of the country, and many times to Withyam – a favourite spot with the boys (see pp. 333-4 below). An observer was quoted as saying that there had not been 'such singing in Withyam since – since – since – since the Flood'.

Another highlight of the children's time with Thomas Helmore was the marriage of the prince of Wales on 10 March 1863 at St George's Chapel, Windsor Castle. For this Thomas and Fred Helmore and a few selected singers, among whom was Jenny Lind, together with the children of the Chapel Royal, occupied the rood-loft on the south side of the organ.

Like his predecessors, Thomas Helmore found that his income could not adequately provide for the needs of the boys in his charge. In a letter to Frederick Walker dated 8 September 1851 from Onslow Square, Thomas wrote: 'In starting my new vocation as Master of the Chapel Royal boys I have already sunk £1,000 and the income derivable from the Chapel has been less than my annual expenditure by about £150 every year.' How reminiscent this is of the letter of appeal by master William Hunnis to Elizabeth I nearly three hundred years earlier!

Thomas Helmore died on 1 July 1886 and his burial service was held at St Saviour's Church, St George's Square, Pimlico, on 9 July. The sub-dean, priests in ordinary, gentlemen and children of the Chapel Royal sang the office.

Thomas was greatly missed, but his successors also did a fine job in difficult circumstances. Today, one hundred years on, the office of master is combined with that of organist, choirmaster and composer in the person of Richard Popplewell. The first combined organist, choirmaster and composer of the Chapel Royal was Harry Gabb from 1953-74.

20

Children of the Chapel Royal

The Calendar of Patent Rolls for the year 1303, in the reign of Edward I, states that 'Richard of Nottingham and Thomas Duns, choirboys of the Chapel Royal, were sent to Oxford'. Later, from a writ of Edward II to the sheriff of Cambridge, dated 7 July 1316, we learn that at least some of the children of the Chapel Royal were educated at Cambridge University in those days. In this writ the king mentions a clerk and 'twelve other children of our chapel' in residence at Cambridge. The sheriff is required by the writ to pay their arrears of allowances. The following passage in French speaks of John de Baggeshote in connection with these children: 'Come nous eions envoiez noz chs. clerc Johande Baggeshote et douze autres einfaunz de notre chapelle a luniv'site de Cantabrg a demorer y en estodez (a noz coustages) pour profiter ... .'[1] He was apparently the first warden of the 'Aula Scholarium Regis', that is to say the King's Hall, which was founded for the purposes of educating members of the royal household. It was one of the two foundations which later formed Trinity College, Cambridge.

We can try to picture the scene of the children of the Chapel Royal at study there in the fourteenth century, for there is still evidence to be seen of the buildings in which they played, studied, slept and ate together.

In 1336, twenty years after Edward II's writ, Edward III set about enlarging King's Hall by purchasing the house of Robert de Croyland which gave accommodation for an additional thirty-two scholars. This was a large house with an internal quadrangle and adjoined what is now King's Hall Lane and King Edward's Gate. In 1338/9 the king opened negotiations to purchase land and tenements adjoining the High Street. Among these was the house and garden of Edmund de Walsingham, which was repaired in 1346/7. Money was also spent on buying utensils, lead and other items for a brewery. The warden and scholars proceeded to acquire without licence, but with the nod of the king, part of the land adjoining St John's. All these purchases were effected in 1347. These are the buildings that would have been familiar to the dean of the Chapel Royal, John Wodeford, who held that office certainly in 1349, as we

---

[1] In *Documents relating to the University and Colleges of Cambridge* (Queen's Commissioners, London, 1852), vol. 1, p. 66.

The bowling green front, King's Hall (Trinity College), Cambridge, where Chapel Royal boys received their education from 1316. (This photograph and the following four illustrations come from *King's Hostel, Trinity College, Cambridge ... An Examination of the History of King's Hall with Special Reference to the Ancient Buildings Recently Disclosed* by W.D. Caroe, printed for the Cambridge Antiquarian Society in 1909, and for the Master and Fellows of Trinity College, Cambridge, by whose courtesy these illustrations of fourteenth- and fifteenth-century remains of King's Hall, revealed in 1905, are reproduced)

gather from the Patent Rolls. In 1376 William Atte Conduit's house, which occupied the area near to the Great Gate, was purchased. This acquisition completed the bid for land necessary for the enlargement of the college.

Richard Rouhale was warden in 1375 when new building on this land began – in the new 'perpendicular' style. A new hall and chambers were slowly built and completed in the wardenship of Thomas Hethersete. The master of the King's Hall lived in a chamber which has been identified as the third room on the first floor of the west range, counting from the St John's boundary. The years 1386-87 saw the timbering for the new kitchen in the east range being prepared and a lardary built on its east side. The new kitchen was completed in 1395 when the chimney stack was constructed. A solar was built on the west side of the kitchen and subsequently became the squire's chamber.

Quite what the scholars and children of the Chapel Royal had been

314

getting up to in annoying the master and brethren of adjoining St John's College is not clear, but it resulted in an agreement whereby glazed windows of obscured glass were placed in the boundary wall between King's Hall and St John's, stretching 115 feet from the north end of the kitchen towards the river. If the glass was broken for any reason it had to be repaired within one month under penalty of 40d. This was evidently to protect the master and brethren of St John's from the intrusive eyes and pranks of King's Hall. This wall agreement also mentions the existence of a library at King's Hall. A new one was later built and completed in 1422, to which the bishop of Rochester, Richard Young, had contributed £20 in 1416. This was a year before the Chapel Royal went abroad on campaign in Normandy in 1417, where they were to stay for three years, and a year after the great victory of Agincourt at which the Chapel Royal had also been present to sing mass before battle. What stories must have been told among the children of the Chapel Royal who continued their education at the university but who had been present at these momentous events!

Among other buildings erected at this time were the wooden chapel and cloister in 1418/19. The chapel had wooden angle posts, wooden windows, and 204 lbs of ironwork in stanchions and saddlebars. In 1422/3 the oratory was decorated with painted hangings costing 28s 8d. Wood for the altar in this chapel had already been bought and all was in position for Henry VI's visit in 1425. Under the heading 'Expense extravgantes' in the college library building and bursarial accounts is to be found provision of an organ for the king's visit: 'Pro i pari organum pro missa regia xcs.' Entries for the year 1452/3 show that the college chapel roof had to be repaired. A new chapel was begun in 1465 but was not completed until 1485. Thus the old wooden chapel continued in use and was from time to time repaired. For this reason painters were employed in 1469-70 and in 1471 much work was done on the organ. The roof was again repaired – which was perhaps just as well for the organ. Although the new college chapel was eventually completed in 1485 it was not consecrated until 1498/9. Later in 1556/7 the Marian chapel we now see replaced the previous one.

Just two years after Henry IV ascended the throne in 1399, he engaged a chaplain, John Bugby, to teach grammar to the boys of the Chapel Royal. According to a Household Account found by my predecessor Colin Scull, Henry IV appointed 'John Bugby our chaplain retained three years ago pur apprendre et enformer les enfants de notre chapelle en la science de gramaire at 100/- p.a. nothing yet paid, £15 due'. He can be regarded as the first master of the grammar of the Chapel Royal, and probably taught the Chapel Royal children at court rather than at King's Hall.

We have observed that in 1421/2, the last year of Henry V's reign, there were sixteen children, but the numbers had dwindled to just six by the following year. The names of these six together with other details concerning their clothing and bedding were recorded in an Act of the

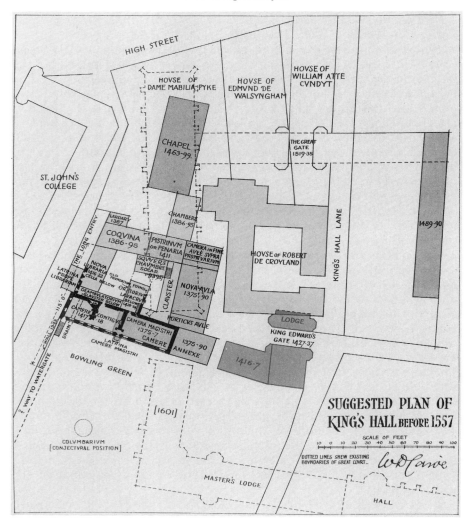

Twelve children of the Chapel Royal whose voices had broken were educated at King's Hall in 1316 by command of Edward II. This practice was reflected over a century later when the dean of the Chapel Royal, Robert Ayscogh, simultaneously held the office of warden of King's Hall in 1448.

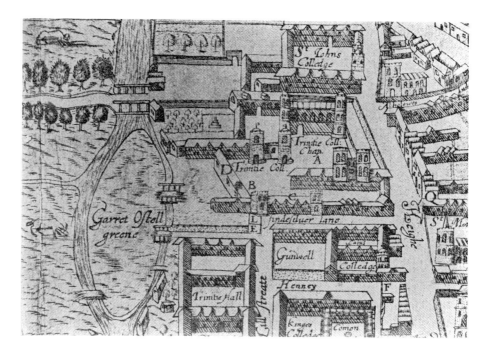

King's Hall (Trinity College) as it appeared in Lyne's map of Cambridge in 1574.

Privy Council dated 15 June 1423 which reads as follows:

> Thys ben ye necessary thynges that be rythe nedful for ye schyldern of the schapel – of which ye namys be,
> Thomas Myldevale
> John Brampton
> John Maydeston
> John Grymmesby
> Nicolas Hyll
> Stephnus Howell
> In primis every schyld i gowne, i hode, i doublat, ii payre of linnen clothys and ii payr of hosyn and iii payr of schon. In bedyng ii schylder, i contour testour, i payr blankets, ii payr schetys, i paylet, i canvas
> Lra inde fuit facta apud Westm. xxiii die Junii
> anno primo.[2]

The appointment of John Bugby indicates that a distinction must be made between the children of the Chapel Royal singing and being educated at court, and those whose voices had broken and who subsequently went to Oxford or Cambridge to continue their studies

---

[2] The original of this is catalogued as British Library Add. MS. 4603, art 130.

Fifteenth-century doors to the cloister, King's Hall, Cambridge.

while awaiting preferment at court.

In this connection I have unearthed a Patent Roll dated 1448 which not only reveals the intimate connection between King's Hall and the Chapel Royal but also makes this distinction quite clear. In this Patent Roll the dean of the Chapel Royal, Robert Ayscogh, is described as 'warden of the king's scholars, Cambridge, and of the 32 scholars herein, of the foundation of Edward III and of the king's patronage'.

If we now look at the *Liber Regie Capelle*, written in 1449 by Robert Ayscogh's successor as dean, William Say, we learn that the master of the children, or 'master of the music' as he terms him, had the duty towards the ten boys of the Chapel Royal 'to teach these boys and duly to instruct them in both plain chant and harmony',[3] and elsewhere in the same book 'to teach them chant and descant, and to govern and rule them and provide them with all things necessary. To this master is assigned for the needs of each boy, sixteen ducats a year, as well as table rights and allowances, at the charges of the king, within the Court; and he is under the dean's supervision.'[4] We can glimpse the master of the music at work from a passage stating that it is the specific duty and practice of the

[3] *Liber Regie Capelle*, ch. 3.
[4] Ibid.

Fifteenth-century door, King's Hall, Cambridge.

Chapel to sing the mass of the Blessed Mary: 'Twice a week at least, that is to say on Wednesdays and Saturdays, this mass is sung solemnly by the boys of the Chapel, supervised and assisted by their schoolmaster; and at this mass, too, the king is often present, when he is so pleased. The queen, again, hardly ever misses it.'[5]

The master of the grammar had a different teaching role to that of the master of the music, for Say writes: 'There is also one grammar master appointed to teach the science of grammar to the young noblemen brought up in the king's court and the boys of the Chapel as they grow older.'[6] Although it is tempting to place this grammar master at university it is obvious that one such grammar master could not be in more than one place at the same time, so it is clear that he was not

[5] Ibid., ch. 6.
[6] Ibid., ch. 3.

319

involved at the university end of their education as they left the choir and awaited preferment. It looks as though the master of the grammar must have worked alongside the master of the children at court.

The university end of their education is, however, dealt with in the *Liber Niger Domus Regis* of Edward IV, written about 1483. It goes some way to clearing up the mystery by showing that university education was, at least by then, something only available to those who had left the Chapel Royal choir rather than to those who still sang in it. Interestingly, as the voice of a child in those days would often survive intact until he was about eighteen years old, a child of the Chapel Royal who subsequently went to university would be very much older than his fellow colleagues at college who had come from other walks of life. The relevant passage in the *Liber Niger* reads as follows: 'When they be growen to the age of XVIII yere, and then theyre voyce be chunged, he cannot be pferryd in this chapell, nor within this courte, the numbyr beyng full, than if they wull assent, the King assigneth every such childe, to a college of Oxinford, or Cambrige, of the Kinge fundacon, there to be in fynding, and study, suficiauntly, tyll the king othir wise list to avaunce hym.'

It was probably twelve Chapel Royal children in these circumstances for whom Edward II had made provision in his writ of 1316, a century and a half earlier. These boys who opted for university after their voices broke would therefore have been familiar with the buildings of King's Hall as I have described them, certainly until Henry VIII's reign. Exactly which other colleges of Oxford and Cambridge the Chapel Royal boys were permitted to join apart from King's Hall in this period is not clear. Certainly the 1303 Patent Roll mentions two 'choirboys of the Chapel Royal' at Oxford, but it could perhaps be said that the university link was cemented by the dean of the Chapel Royal's also holding the position of warden of King's Hall, Cambridge, in the mid-fifteenth century.

Let us now turn to the everyday life of the children of the Chapel Royal at court in the latter half of the fifteenth century at the time of the incorporation of the royal free chapel of the household in 1483. This event holds the key to the date of the *Liber Niger Domus Regis*, for the incorporation re-arranged the officials of the Chapel Royal so as to create the hierarchy of a dean supported in his duties by three canons, who were to act as sub-dean, treasurer and precentor, and sharing with them the endowments of the chapel of St Peter ad Vincula in the Tower of London.[7] The *Liber Niger* contains a passage which, talking of the dean's duties, says also: 'he assigneth the subdean and the chaunters to gyde kepe and to rule all the quere ... .' So the lively and detailed account of the children of the Chapel Royal contained in the *Liber Niger* would seem, on the basis of its reference to the sub-dean's newly created office, to recreate the scene as it was in about 1483.

[7] Cal. Pat. Rolls 1483.

From it we see that there were 'children of chapell viii' who went to 'the Kinge Jewelhouse for all thing that belongeth to thayre apparayle', which was issued 'by the hand or oversight of the deane, or by the master of song'. This master of song, who was 'apoynted by the seyd deane, and chosen one of the numbyr of the felashippe of Chapelle', had the task 'to draw theese children, all as well in the Scoole, of facet as in song, organes, or suche other vertuouse thinge'. We learn, too, that 'thees children, etyn in the hall, dayly at the Chapell bourde, next the yomen of vestiary, taking among them in lyverey, for all daye, brekfast and at night ii loves, i messe of greete mete, ii gallons of ale, and for wynter season, iiii candille peric, iii tal and litt for their beddis'. This matter was the responsibility of the 'comptroller' of the household. The children also had a servant 'among them all' in court 'to trusse, and to bere theyre harneys, and to sett theyre harneys in Court'. They enjoyed 'carriage at the Kinge cost' for 'such dayes as the Kynge Chapell removeth, eny of thes children, than present, receiveth iiiid. at the grene [cloth] seald of the countinghouse, for horse hyre dayly, as long as they be journaying'. When any of the children became sick 'they taken lyvery as with the syke yomen of household'.

Some of the children of the Chapel Royal, though, were boarded out and taught various musical arts by the senior members of the Chapel Royal 'society' (i.e. gentlemen). Let us look for a moment at the names of the children of the Chapel Royal as they appear in the issue of liveries for the household on the occasion of the funeral of Henry VII in 1509:

William Colman	Arthur Lovekyn
William Maxe	Henry Andrewe
William Alderson	Nicholas Ivy (Ive)
Henry Meryll (Merell)	Edward Cooke (Coke)
John Williams	James Curteys[8]
John Graunger	

In connection with these children we know that the gentleman of the Chapel Royal, Robert Fayrfax (later created a knight of Windsor in 1514), was paid the sum of 1s per week for boarding William Aderton (Alderson) and Arthur Lovkyn, as well as 46s 8d 'for their learning' throughout the year. Similar entries for Fayrfax occur in the King's Book of Payments dated December 1511 and December 1513. William Cornish is also mentioned as providing the same services for boys in April 1514. Interestingly this 'system' still operated even after a child's voice broke if he was retained at court (usually as epistler with the Chapel Royal), for Cornish was paid in April 1517 for 'finding and teaching' William Saunders 'late child of the Chapel'.[9]

---

[8] These names are to be found in several sources including LC vol. 550, fol. 131, LC vol. 424, fol. 203 (which omits the name of Curteys), and the *Calendar of State Papers Domestic*.

[9] Book of Payments, 1517.

This miniature by Lavina Teerlinc (once attributed to Nicholas Hilliard) of the Royal Maundy service of 1565 shows near the top of the painting at least seven children of the Chapel Royal, clad in long white surplices over red cassocks, while behind them stand the gentlemen of the Chapel Royal wearing copes. (Reproduced by courtesy of the Executors of the late Countess Beauchamp)

Impressment of choristers had been commonplace, as we know from the writ issued by Henry V to John Pyamour to impress choristers for service in Normandy where the Chapel Royal had been since 1417. An exchange of letters a century later, in 1518, between the dean of the Chapel Royal, Richard Pace, and cardinal Wolsey shows the process of impressment in vivid detail.[10]

Quite what effect impressment had on the child himself is hard to say, but it is known that Thomas Tusser had a sad time as a result of it. Tusser had a fine treble voice and was accordingly placed as a chorister in the collegiate chapel of Wallingford in Berkshire. He was discovered and

[10] See Chapter 2, p. 46 above for details.

'The children of His Majesty's Chapel Royal, in number twelve' (though only eight are depicted here), as they appear in an illustration from Sandford's *Coronation of James II*. (Reproduced by courtesy of the Dean and Chapter of Westminster)

'impressed' into the Chapel Royal choir of Henry VIII and/or Edward VI. He served his time there and was then admitted into the choir of St Paul's Cathedral where he came under the tuition and guidance of the master of the choristers and almoner there, John Redford – that famous composer who died *c*. 1547. He next was sent to Eton School, and, judging by the poem he wrote entitled 'The Author's Life', did not enjoy it. Thomas Tusser was the author of *Five Hundred Pointers of Good Husbandrie*.

The choir 'uniform' of the children of the Chapel Royal under the house of Richmond is known from the miniature painted by Lavina Teerlinc of Elizabeth I at the Maundy service of 1565. Although the painting is only 2¼ inches wide, over a hundred figures are clearly visible. Among them, near the top of the painting, can be seen at least seven children of the Chapel Royal clad in long white surplices worn over red cassocks, together with gentlemen of the Chapel Royal in copes. The royal colours of the house of Richmond were green and white, so there were many occasions upon which the palace chapel buildings were decked out in these colours. Black, though, remained as usual the colour for court mourning, and we see in the illustrations of the Chapel Royal in the funeral procession of Elizabeth I that black livery was worn.

The Eltham Ordinances of 1526 were an attempt, as we have seen, to reduce the numbers of Chapel Royal members 'continually attendant

Watercolour painting by an unknown artist depicting the children of the Chapel Royal crossing St James's Park in 1790, purchased from McInnes (Eastbourne) Limited in 1967. Notes on the reverse of the watercolour may give the names of the children depicted, but the list of 'addresses' presents a conundrum, for one of the names in the 'address' list is that of the master of the children, William Hawes, who was master from 1817-46, and who lived at 7 Adelphi Terrace, Strand. He had succeeded John Stafford Smith, who lived at 27 Craven Street, Charing Cross, who himself had succeeded Edmund Ayrton who was master at the time this picture was painted. The notes read as follows:

1	ADAMS	8	6	MARCHALL	11
2	BRAY	7	7	ALLCROFT	7
3	JONES	10	8	BOYE	12
4	FARNDELL	11	9	BUTTS	13
5	CARTWRIGHT	11	10	OGILVEY	14

1 Corner of Stanford Street, Blackfriars Rd.
2 Old Burlington, 16 Bond Street.
3 Good St., Tottenham Court Road, No 16.
4 Mme Burwive, Great Suffolk St., Haymarket, No 5.
5 No 11 Bread Street, Cheapside.
6 Mr Hawes.
7 No 14 Clipstone Street, Fitz Roy Sq.
8 North Westminster.
9 Warmaworth Rd.
10 North Audley Street, Oxford St.

upon his [the king's] person when his Grace keepeth not his hall, and specially in rideing journeys and progresses'. Thus it was 'ordeyned that the master of the children and six men, with some officers of the vestry, shall give their continuall attendance in the King's Court'. It would be misleading, though, to assume from this that the 'horse hyre dayly' of the *Liber Niger* of 1483 for the children's journeying had ended. This is because a document has survived dated January 1525/6 which mentions the children as well. It reads slightly differently from the Eltham Ordinance: 'It is ordered for the better administration of divine service that the Master of the Children of the King's Chapell with six of the same children and six men, with some officers of the vestry shall give their continuall attendance in the King's Court.'[11] Indeed it is clear that this latter document gives the correct position, for what would have been the point of requiring the attendance of the master of the children on journeys and progresses unless some children were to be travelling too? It is clear that six children was now the number fixed for travelling on most, but not all, occasions. Even today, although the entire number of Chapel Royal children travel on royal Maundy, often to distant cathedrals and abbeys, only the 'top six' attend the St Cecilia festival at St Sepulchre-without-Newgate in Holborn.

The life of the Chapel Royal children at the Chapel Royal theatre in Blackfriars during the reigns of Elizabeth I and James I added a wholly diverting dimension to the life of the boys, and is dealt with separately in Chapter 5 above. Also treated separately, in Chapter 9 above, is the journey of the Chapel Royal to Scotland by sea for the coronation of Charles I in 1633.

The Restoration Chapel Royal saw the continued practice of 'impressment'. Poaching from other cathedrals and choral establishments continued apace. Captain Cooke, for example, master of the children in the reign of Charles II, visited among other places 'Westchester, Litchfield, Canterbury, and Rochester' for the specific purpose of 'impressing' choristers. The scarlet silver-lined state-coat uniform of the Restoration Chapel children is described in Chapter 11 above, but there is an illustration of the children of the Chapel Royal following the serjeant of the vestry at the coronation of James II showing the children wearing surplices.

The accession of queen Anne in 1702 meant an uprooting of the Chapel Royal's choral 'headquarters building' from Whitehall to St James's Palace. The old Chapel Royal building at Whitehall that had served the Tudors and Stuarts so well had burned in the great Whitehall Palace fire of 1698. The Chapel Royal for a while afterwards 'based' itself at the Banqueting House, but this was a temporary measure – although it remained a favourite place to hold royal Maundy services.

[11] LC vol. 590, p. 50.

Illustrations exist of the children of the Chapel Royal in the eighteenth century which give a clear idea of how they looked, both in surplice and state-coat attire. There is, for example, a diagrammatic illustration and painting of the children wearing long white surplices for the 1727 coronation, for which the composer to the Chapel Royal, George Frederick Handel, wrote the anthem music by royal command. Hanging in the dean's/sub-dean's vestry of the Chapel Royal building in colour court is a water-colour painting of the ten children of the Chapel Royal in scarlet state-coats and bicorn hats crossing St James's Park with Westminster Abbey in the background. It dates from 1790 and was acquired in 1967 during the sub-deanship of canon James Mansel (see p. 324 above).

Less than a century later it was reference to these scarlet state-coats that played a vital role in enticing the young Arthur Sullivan to offer himself for audition to join the ranks of the Chapel Royal children. The incident is recorded in Fred Helmore's book on the life of his brother Thomas, master of the children. Arthur Sullivan's 'schoolmaster had told him of the gold-embroidered coats of the Queen's choristers'.[12] Arthur became more determined than ever to overcome his father's opposition to his becoming a chorister. One morning he exclaimed, in an effort at persuasion, 'Father, Purcell was an Abbey boy.' There was a long delay during which Arthur went to school in London, and then he finally induced his schoolmaster to take him to Sir George Smart. The rest of the story is recounted in Chapter 19 above. The eye-catching state-coat uniforms of the Chapel Royal children have thus had a striking part to play in the history of the Chapel Royal. The sort of everyday life Arthur Sullivan and his contemporaries lived, or endured, as children of the Chapel Royal is vividly recalled by Fred Helmore and also by Frederick Walker, who had joined the choristers in 1844.

Under the mastership of Mr Hawes, who in fairness had no idea what went on behind his back, discipline among the boys had sunk to a 'degraded state of brutality'. William Hawes himself had been a child of the Chapel Royal from 1793-1801 where he learned to play the violin and organ. During this time the dean of the Chapel Royal, Dr Beilby Porteous, issued a set of regulations on 4 April 1793 concerning the children of the Chapel Royal which gives a remarkable insight into both their education and their pastimes.

A few years before, in 1785, Reginald Spofforth, organist of Lincoln Cathedral, recorded in his *Musical Memoranda*: 'At St James's the Boys complained of Dr Ayrton and said they were starved. The parents took it up, complained by Petition to the Bishop of London and said that if he did not redress them they would go to the King. The Bishop made enquiry, and found, on Dr Ayrton's bringing the weekly accounts of meat, that they had very sufficient provisions.' The dean found Dr Ayrton blameless

[12] Fred Helmore, *Memoir of the Late Thomas Helmore ...*, p. 73.

on this occasion, but standards of education and welfare were evidently too low. Spofforth sheds light on the background to this problem by recalling the provisions made seventy years earlier:[13]

> Academy of antient music. Begun 1710 by Gentlemen, and the most eminent masters, to promote the study of vocal and instrumental music.
> A library was founded, under the direction of Dr Pepasch, assisted by Dr Green, Mr Galliard and Mr Gates, in 1710. The Boys of St Paul's and the Chapel Royal attended. About 1728 Dr Green left it and set up an Academy at the Devil Tavern, which continued a few years.
> 1734. – Mr Gates retired and took away the Chapel Royal children with him.

We gather too from a statement at the very end of the *Memoranda*:

> The Boys have no Pocket Money, except the Christmas Boxes, and what is occasionally given.
> The Christmas Boxes formerly amounted to £30, now not to £25, people saying there is now so little Choir service.
> When it was £30, after several deductions, the Senior Boys received only £2 7s each.
> They paid half a guinea to the servant for a Christmas Box, Blacking Shoes and Cleaning; four guineas a year to the Barber for Sunday dressing, which was flour and Powder, blue-salt sometimes.

In May 1804 the dean expanded the 1798 regulations considerably to deal with the deficiencies. These 1804 regulations make illuminating reading:[14]

REGULATIONS RESPECTING THE CHILDREN OF THE CHAPEL MADE BY THE DEAN MAY 2nd 1804

1. They shall have proper instructions in *singing* and *playing* for a reasonable time in every Day, four Days for singing and two for playing.

2. They shall have one good instrument to practise on, constantly kept in good Order.

3. They shall have a writing Master, as formerly *three* times a Week and to be two Hours with the Boys each time.

4. More attention shall be paid to their Moral and their religious Principles more particularly on *Sunday* when some Instructions shall be given them in the Doctrines and the Duties of Religion.

5. The Senior Boys shall not be suffered to treat the juniors cruelly, and harshly, but shall be punished if they do.

---

[13] *Musical Memoranda* (1785), p. 16.

[14] They are reproduced in Peter Jones, 'The musical education of the children of the Chapel 1820-1870' (Dissertation held at the Chapel Royal). The original regulations, now barely legible, are written on a wooden board held at the Chapel Royal.

William Hawes, master of the children 1817-46, drawn on stone in 1836 by Richard J. Lane.

6. The Boys shall not be allowed to sing at either of the play Houses and when they return home from singing at the *Oratories*, the *Antient Music* or any other Concert public or private, upon the leaving they shall have a coach to carry them home and a good Supper, and in Winter a fire at their return.

7. More attention shall be paid to the cleanliness of their persons, their clothes and the room they principally inhabit; more particularly they shall have *two Towels* and *two Shirts* a week and the Maidservant who waits upon them shall be enjoind carefully to attend to all these things.

8. The Subdean shall attend once in every Quarter at the Master's House and hear the Boys sing and play and read and repeat the Church Catechisms.

9. The Boys shall be furnished with some Bibles and prayer Books, and each a form of Prayer for their own Private use, which they shall be enjoined to use Morning and Evening.

10. A fair Copy of these Regulations shall be hung up in the School Room that they may be known to the Boys.

11. Each Boy shall have according to antient Custom a Cloak to wear in cold or wet Weather.

Chapel Royal, St. James's.

It is ordered that for the future the following Regulations be observed, with respect to the Boys of the Chapel Royal, in order to the better promotion of diligence and good behaviour amongst them.

1st.   That no boy be admitted into the Choir of the Chapel Royal, until the Sub-Dean shall have ascertained, by enquiry, the respectability of the Boy's Parents; with an especial reference to the care with which they bring up their children.

2nd.   That no boy be admitted who cannot read fluently, and write a legible hand.

3rd.   That no boy be admitted who cannot answer the questions in the Church Catechism.

4th.   That twice in every year the Boys of the Chapel Royal be examined by the Sub-Dean as to their religious knowledge, and their proficiency in the other branches of their education, and a report thereof be made to the Dean.

5th.   That twice in every year the Boys be examined by the Senior Organist and Composer; or by some Member of the Chapel named by the Sub-Dean for that purpose, as to their skill in Music, and especially in Chanting; and a report thereof made to the Sub-Dean, and by him to the Dean.

Signed,

C. J. LONDON,

Fulham, 14*th August*, 1845. *Dean.*

Before Thomas Helmore's mastership there had been a long-standing tradition that the children could undertake public engagements to earn more money both for themselves and for their master. The *Musical Memoranda* record that 'The children of the Chapel Royal (8) made Dr Nares £100 a year by going out at 10/6 each. He gave them sixpence among them for Barley Sugar. He made of their clothes £50 a year.' Nares was, however, a gifted teacher. His *Treatise on Singing*, written *c.* 1780, was used by the Chapel Royal until Helmore's arrival in 1846. The preface to this work is directed at the children: 'My intent in this short essay, is to exhibit the Different methods made use of to teach Young People and Others to sing by Notes, and to try and facilitate the practical study of Vocal Music, the Introduction to which at present is almost as various as the Names of the Masters who teach it.' He extolled the virtues of the gamut as the only sure method of 'conveying Sounds to very young minds'.

Under master John Stafford Smith the children had lived at no. 27 Craven Street, Charing Cross, but under his successor, William Hawes – at thirty-two the youngest master since Blow and Humphreys – the boys moved to no. 7 Adelphi Terrace, Strand, where they were to remain until 1846.

Mr Hawes appears, according to Peter Jones, 'to have known no way of imparting learning, or correcting delinquencies, except by means of the birch'.[15] This view is confirmed by Fred Helmore, although John Goss's recollection of life as a child of the Chapel Royal suggests that things had by no means been right under previous masters. John Goss, who had entered as a child of the Chapel Royal in 1811, recalled later in life:

> The education of chorister boys in those days, even within the shadows of the Palace of St James, was of a most happy-go-lucky description. On two days a week a parochial schoolmaster attended the house in Adelphi Terrace where the boys lived, and gave then an hour and a half's instruction. These days were appropriately termed 'slate days' because the rudiments of arithmetic occupied the greater part of the time. This constituted for a considerable period the only training 'in litteris humanioribus' of the young gentlemen of His Majesty's Chapel Royal. Nor was musical instruction, outside the usual routine work of learning necessary anthems and services, any more liberally bestowed.

Master William Hawes did occasionally stretch himself to teach the boys, as is recorded by E.J. Hopkins, a child of the Chapel Royal from 1826-33:

> Old Hawes during a fit of generosity took some older boys into his room, where his Little Organ, with pedal 'pull-downs', was kept. He gave them some hints on service playing, that is hymn playing, extemporaneous introductions and also unpremeditated interludes. He used St Anne's tune to demonstrate the points, but modulated so far out, that he could not think of a way back. Realizing this, Hawes jumped off the stool saying 'And so on, boys'. This phrase became a byword for insoluble problems.[16]

Perhaps the fact the Hawes entered into musical publishing in the 1820s, directed the performances of the English Opera at the Lyceum, and masterminded most of London's society parties, had something to do with the little time he apparently spent with the children of the Chapel Royal.

Frederick Walker, recalling his experiences in the days of Mr Hawes at no. 7 Adelphi Terrace, wrote: 'I entered the Chapel Royal on September 15th 1844 ... After I had been there a year and six months, my father

---

[15] 'The musical education of the children of the Chapel', p. 7.

[16] W. Spark, *Musical Memories* (1888), pp. 139-40, and Jones, 'The musical education of the children of the Chapel', p. 8.

thought of removing me on account of the dreadful cruelties practised on the junior boys by their seniors.' Mr Walker recalled two ghastly practices that had developed:

> Two seniors would seize a junior and hold him down on his back, whilst a third would take hold of his nose and slit upwards with a penknife! ... A junior boy was 'buried'. That is, a sort of coffin was made with bolsters, pillows, blankets etc., and tied fast with sheets, so that the air was entirely excluded: this being done, he was hoisted upon the shoulders of his school-fellows, and tumbled into a large copper, and then, after dancing on the 'coffin' for about ten minutes, they dragged him out, generally in a fainting condition; but a copious supply of cold water brought him round. This I have seen repeatedly.

It was recalled by Fred Helmore that some of those poor victims were heard to pray that they might die to avoid further cruelties. Further cruelties there undoubtedly were! One such was to turn a chorister out of the window on a frosty night with only his night-shirt, leaving him to shiver on the sills for hours with a bitter wind blowing across the Thames.[17] A 'fagging' system operated whereby each boy in the senior division had a junior 'fag'. This system had become abused and degraded and merely perpetuated further horrific cruelties.

The appointment of Thomas Helmore as master of the children in 1846 led to many changes. For a start the boys left their 'prison' in Adelphi Terrace and went to live with Mr Helmore at Robert Street, Chelsea. There he broke the ring of bullies and reformed the fagging system personally to remove any elements of or chances for cruelty, and made each senior boy responsible for the daily needs of a junior, with a duty to bring his junior 'home in safety' from concerts and rehearsals. Conditions rapidly improved and, as the bullying subsided, the opportunities for developing the children's musical talents increased under the master's enthusiastic eye. As Frederick Walker observed, 'I have seen him in tears at our describing the mode of living at Adelphi Terrace'. All this now changed, and went hand in hand with another move from Robert Street to Onslow Square, and then Cheyne Walk, which was to become such a haven of musical talent. The presence of captain Ottley, who together with Fred Helmore had patrolled Onslow Square and neighbouring streets armed with constables' staves during the Chartist Riots when Louis Napoleon (later the Emperor of France) was among the specials, undoubtedly helped to maintain a high level of discipline among the boys.

In that eventful year of 1848 the children of the Chapel Royal sang a performance of *Elijah* on the evening of 15 December at Exeter Hall. This was an extraordinary time, for under Wellington's instructions cannons were placed in position on the bridges over the Thames and no groups of

---

[17] Fred Helmore, *Memoir of the late Thomas Helmore ...*, p. 52.

To the Right Hon: & Right Rev:
The Lord Bishop Blomfield.
    Dean of Her Majesty's Chapels Royal

These are to certify that Arthur Seymour
Sullivan, one of the Children of Her Majesty's
Chapels Royal, having broken his voice, is
dismissed from the said Chapels.

    In addition to the usual commendations of
a Chorister who has fulfilled the duties of his
office to our entire satisfaction, we think it right
to mention that Arthur S. Sullivan, early in the last
year, won the Mendelssohn Scholarship, to which
he has been re-elected this year. He has in consequence,
while continuing to discharge all the duties of one
of the Children of H. M. Chapels Royal, been also
studying Music in the Royal Academy. His talent and
industry, as well as his good & amiable conduct have
won for him the esteem and affectionate regard of
all his Tutors. We therefore commend him to your
Lordship as more than usually deserving of the gratuity
ordinarily bestowed upon the Children who have served the
Chapel well. signed Thomas Helmore M. A. Master of the Children
        Countersigned Charles Wesley D.D.
            Sub Dean of the Chapels Royal.

This commendation of Arthur Sullivan, child of the Chapel Royal, by master of the children Thomas Helmore, counter-signed by the sub-dean, was written on the occasion of Arthur's voice breaking, thereby necessitating his resignation from the Chapel Royal in 1857. This document was discovered by my colleague, Robin Hobbs, with whom I had the pleasure of working at Lambeth Palace Library sorting the papers of bishop Blomfield under the direction of the archivist, Miss Melanie Barber. (Tate Papers 431, fol. 32, reproduced by courtesy of His Grace the Archbishop of Canterbury and the Trustees of Lambeth Palace Library)

more than two or three people were allowed across at any one time to prevent rioting. It must have been an exciting time for the boys, but worrying for the master.

The children's weekly routine consisted of singing the service at St James's Palace chapel on Sundays, attending St Mark's Training College for Schoolmasters of which Thomas Helmore still retained the precentorship from time to time through the week, attending the Motet and Madrigal Societies, and sometimes the Sacred Harmonic Society, ending up with attendance at Dr Iron's church, Brompton, which service Thomas Helmore conducted.[18] This was all quite apart from the regular 'musical matinees' held in Mr Helmore's drawing room at no. 6 Cheyne Walk, which Arthur Sullivan so enjoyed. Sullivan left the choir in 1857, the year of the first Handel Festival, but not before completing some impressive compositions as a child of the Chapel Royal. For example, his little madrigal 'O lady dear' was, according to a note at the top of the original manuscript which still survives, 'Written while lying outside the bed one night, undressed, and in deadly fear lest Mr Helmore should come in'.[19]

Edward Lloyd, the great tenor, wrote: 'I also met Sir Arthur Sullivan and Cellier playing at cricket. The boys of the Chapel Royal, St Paul's, and Westminster frequently opposed each other with bat and ball. Sullivan was my elder. Cellier was always the life and soul of us all at cricket, a thorough good fellow, though he did bowl me out once.'[20] Today the sporting challenge is maintained, though now between The Temple and the Chapel Royal in the form of a 'summer' football match played until recently upon Temple lawns. And last year, due to the kindness of David Rankin Hunt and the governors of the Tower of London, in the grass moat of the Tower.

From time to time Mr Helmore took the children to the country village of Withyham. Henry Wilberforce's son-in-law Dr Mill was the curate there, and it was he who came up with a brain-wave, during one of those musical extravangazas, while drinking tea at the Brasted Rectory. Thomas Helmore's brother, Frederick, also an accomplished choirmaster, was visiting his friend Mr Mill at Withyham and had been singing Latin hymns along with Mrs Mill and her husband, when one of them said: 'What a thousand pities it is we cannot utilize these glorious hymns for our own service!' Dr Mill, after a few minutes of drinking tea, suddenly shouted, 'I have it! I have it! Helmore, here's your brother coming down in a few weeks to Withyham. You must take him over and introduce him to Mason Neale. We'll bring them together! We'll make Neale translate the hymns, and your brother shall arrange the music.' This decision led to the children of the Chapel Royal, along with Thomas and Frederick Helmore

[18] Ibid., pp. 54, 64.
[19] Ibid., p. 76.
[20] Pine, *The Westminister Abbey Singers*.

and others, visiting Dr Neale at Sackville College in East Grinstead at his invitation. The 'hymnal deputation' consisted of carriages full of priests and gentlemen singers, and boys from town and country. On their way through one sleepy village on the journey to East Grinstead, the locals were startled by a carriage full of children of the Chapel Royal accompanied by an American clergyman, who had been invited by Wilberforce from East Farleigh. The boys were singing the National Anthem but noticed that the American's hat was still firmly on his head. One of the boys swung a gold-buttoned coat and connected with the offending hat worn by 'brother Jonathan', causing it to fall in the road. A chorister jumped down and retrieved it. He then climbed back and dusted it down. The clergyman is recorded as having 'looked more than astonished, but said nothing'. This was the only incident to mar an otherwise inventive and fruitful trip to Dr Neale. With the boys' help Dr Neale and Helmore began to try out various settings and words – a process culminating three years later in the first edition of the *Hymnal Noted*.

Other occasional events included royal weddings. Thus the marriage of the prince of Wales, celebrated at Windsor on 10 March 1863, was an occasion for the children of the Chapel Royal to sing from the rood loft on the south side of the organ.

Boys will be boys, though. We learn that on one occasion in Piccadilly, on their way back to Cheyne Walk, the boys noticed a man in a pyramidal sandwich-board. Spotting his vulnerable posture with his arms occupied in holding two handles inside the pyramid, the boys set upon him with feathers to tickle his nose and ears. This 'feather ordeal' occurred frequently until one night when a variant was devised – the children shoved a hot potato just out of the oven of a neighbouring stall into the man's mouth. The result was 'strong language' from the victim after he managed to eject the obstruction. The master never knew of this incident, although his brother, Frederick, was certainly told.

Another incident involving the children of the Chapel Royal did however tax Thomas Helmore's 'keen sense of the ludicrous'. It involved a fish shop, the smell of which was abhorrent to the boys. The shop was situated in a street leading into Cheyne Walk. One night on returning from a concert the children, who occupied three cabs, had prepared a plan to give the proprietor of the fish shop a 'royal salute'. As the first cab passed the shop the occupants fired a salvo of peas from shooters at the window of the shop. This had the desired effect of inducing the customers of the shop to gather at the door out of curiosity only to receive another unexpected broadside from the second passing cab! The cabs were pursued to the door of no. 6 Cheyne Walk, where the following morning the proprietor of the fish shop lodged a complaint of assault and battery. Mr Helmore sent for the boys on hearing of the 'attack' and asked for an explanation. One of the boys, Tom, replied, 'Sir, we did it by way of

Photographic copy of a painting by W.F. Yeames exhibited at the Royal Academy depicting the children of the Chapel Royal at the time of the Diamond Jubilee of queen Victoria in 1897. The names of the children were supplied in 1975 by Frank Physick: George Blacklock, Frank Physick, Leonard Rowe, Burford (?), Leyland (?).

The Chapel Royal School, Clapham, 1896. *Front row:* W.G. Physick, O.J.L. Pidwell, T.C. Minter, R.P.E. Shaugnessy (or A.G. Thorogood), S.L. Rowe, B. Gawthrop. *Back row:* A.E. Witty, F.S. Physick, H.J. May, G.T.C. Blacklock. (Copied from a photograph lent by Frank Physick, who remembered the names in January 1977 at the age of 95)

lodging a protest at the villainous stench which proceeds from the shop and often reaches the garden.' Mr Helmore demanded to see every pea-shooter in the possession of the boys, but he was rather taken aback at the consequences of his demands. For each child was something of an expert in the trajectory habits of peas, and each had a cache of at least half-a-dozen shooters of varying lengths and bore! The child who related the story to Frederick Helmore, Tom Hepworth, was one of the culprits, and he recalled that the shooters thus produced looked 'like the pipes of a young organ laid out in readiness for future erection'.

The 'musical renaissance' enjoyed by the Chapel Royal children was soon to be somewhat curtailed by the decision of a subsequent dean of the Chapel Royal to limit the musical education of the children to their school and chapel. So much could be said of the 'Choir School' of the children of the Chapel Royal; of its staff and boys alike; of its routine and the formative contribution it made to the future of these boys. My few words will be rightly deemed inadequate by those still possessing a lively memory of those days. It is good to record that Sir Thomas Armstrong, a pupil of the 'Streatham' days, still takes a lively interest in the music

336

Particulars.

The well-built Valuable Detached Main Road

FREEHOLD RESIDENCE

KNOWN AS

"Derwent Mount,"

No. 15, STREATHAM HIGH RD., S.W.

The House stands in its own Grounds, and is approached by a Carriage Sweep, through well-shrubbed and timbered fore-garden, and is entered by a flight of marble and mosaic steps.

The accommodation, which is well-arranged, comprises :—

On the TOP FLOOR—Right Front Bed Room, measuring about 21-ft. 10-in. by 17-ft. 3-in., fitted with register stove, painted mantel, tiled hearth and hanging cupboard; Left Front Bed Room, measuring about 17-ft. 3-in. by 16-ft., fitted with register stove, painted mantel, tiled hearth and hanging cupboard; Left Back Bed Room, measuring about 17-ft. 3-in. by 15-ft. 10-in., fitted with register stove, painted mantel, tiled hearth and hanging cupboard; Right Back Bed Room, measuring about 21-ft. 3-in. by 17-ft. 3-in., fitted with register stove, painted mantel, tiled hearth and hanging cupboard; Large Bath Room, fitted with bath (h. & c.), also geyser, lavatory basin (h. & c.); and housemaid's cupboard and sink; Large Linen Room, fitted with heated cupboards; Large Landing.

On the FIRST FLOOR—Right Front Principal Bed Room, measuring about 22-ft. by 16-ft. 10-in., fitted with modern stove, marble mantel, tiled hearth and jambs, leading to a Dressing Room, which is fitted with lavatory basin (h. & c.) and hanging cupboard; Left Front Bed Room, measuring about 17-ft. 3-in. by 16-ft., fitted with register stove, marble mantel, tiled hearth and jambs; Left Back Bed Room, measuring about 17-ft. 3-in. by 15-ft. 9-in., fitted with register stove, marble mantel, tiled hearth and jambs; Right Back Bed Room, measuring about 21-ft. 6-in. by 17-ft. 3-in., fitted with modern stove, marble mantel, tiled hearth and jambs, and hanging cupboard, communicating to principal Bed Room; Large Bath Room, fitted with bath (h. & c.), leading to w.c.

On the GROUND-FLOOR—Large Entrance Hall with Cloak Room, fitted with lavatory basin (h. & c.), w.c.; Morning Room, measuring about 15-ft. 10-in. by 10-ft. 10-in., fitted with register stove, marble mantel, tiled hearth and jambs, leading through French casement windows to Grounds; Spacious and artistically decorated Drawing Room, measuring about 32-ft. 9-in. by 16-ft. 10-in., fitted with modern gas stove, ornamental carved marble mantel, designed tiled hearth and jambs, leading through French casement windows on to Balcony, thence to large Conservatory and Grounds; Handsome Dining Room, measuring about 27-ft. 10-in. by 16-ft. 9-in., fitted with register stove, tiled hearth and jambs, ornamental marble mantel.

In the BASEMENT—Large Light Kitchen, fitted with double kitchener, dresser, cupboards, hot-plate oven, etc.; Large Pantry, with sink (h. & c.), cupboards, etc.; Larder, fitted with shelves and cupboards; Coal and Wine Cellars; Housemaids' cupboard; Servants' w.c. The Domestic Offices have tiled floors and walls; Tradesmen's Side Entrance, Gardener's Entrance.

Capital Detached Stabling for Three Horses, Double Coach House, with Living Rooms over.

Let on Lease to the Comptroller of the Lord Chamberlain's Department as a School for the Boys of the Chapel Royal, for a term of 21 Years from Christmas, 1911 (determinable by Lessee at end of 7th or 14th year), at

PER £130 ANN.

Lessee Repairs and pays Insurance Premium.

The Well=Laid=Out and Ornamental Grounds of about One Acre

ARE WELL-SHRUBBED AND TIMBERED,

and comprise full-sized Tennis Lawn, shaped Flower Beds and Gravelled Walks, Productive Kitchen Garden, Fruit Trees, Vinery and Double Greenhouses, Thatched Summer House, Fowl House and Run, Tool Sheds, etc.

The Lessee has, with the Vendor's permission, made alterations in the Garden for the purpose of forming a Playground, and has entered into a covenant to reinstate the Garden to its former state if he may be so required at the expiration of the Leasehold term.

The Property occupies a Valuable Main Road Site with Frontage of about 100 feet, with a considerable depth.

THE TITHE RENT CHARGE HAS BEEN REDEEMED.

'Derwent Mount' as described in 1915 by the estate agents May & Philpot.

337

sung by children of the Chapel Royal today on their attendance at the festival of St Cecilia held at St Sepulchre's-without-Newgate.

The death of Thomas Helmore in 1886 brought to an end the traditional arrangements whereby the children of the Chapel Royal were accommodated at the master's house. In 1871 Mr Helmore had reached an agreement for the children to attend the Westminster and Pimlico Commercial School as day scholars to advance their education, but he retained his responsibility for the progress of the boys and their musical education. After his death temporary arrangements were made for his successor, the Rev. H.A. Sheringham, to take the boys at his house in St George's Square until other arrangements could be made. In due course the Chapel Royal Choir School was established at Clapham Common. Photographs of the boys at this establishment have come to light, largely through the correspondence of the late serjeant of the vestry, Colin Scull, with their families.

The school, however, did not remain there. A lease was taken upon a property called Derwent Mount at no. 15 Streatham High Road, and

Chapel Royal School, Streatham, winter 1913. *Front row:* Claude Andrews Farebrother, Reginald W. Cox, Ralph S. Marriott. *Back row:* Leslie Nelson, Frank Pridmore, Frederick Alexander Naylor, John Cole, Alan Butler, Herbert Stuart Robertson, Charles J. Nethersole, Hugh Joseph Butler. (Copied from a photograph lent by John Cole in September 1976)

Claude Selfe's successor as master of the children, Percy Davis of Keble College, Oxford, saw the boys into that establishment. An excellent description of the house survives through the fortunate circumstance that the owner wished to sell in 1913. A firm of local estate agents, May and Philpot, prepared an account of the property prior to auction. In the event it never reached the reserve price and was withdrawn from the market, but the description survives (see p. 337).

At that time the Chapel Royal was permitted to advertise in appropriate quarters for auditions to fill vacancies in the choir resulting from boys' voices breaking. A schedule was issued to the parents of successful candidates which extolled the virtues of the school. We are told, for example, that the 'proximity of two large Commons, make possible an exceedingly healthy out-door life', and that the boys travel to their duty at St James's Palace via the London Brighton and South Coast Railway's electric trains from Streatham Hill Station to Victoria, making possible a journey time of thirty-five minutes door to door.

At that time the routine required the boys to leave the school on a Sunday morning at 8.30, sing at the Chapel, and return for dinner at 2.30, only to leave again at 4.30 in the afternoon to travel to the Chapel for evensong, returning to the school again at 7.30 in the evening.

Dr W.G. Alcock, sub-dean Edgar Sheppard and the children of the Chapel Royal on a river-boat outing in 1915. (Photograph from a scrapbook kindly donated to the Chapel Royal by Mr Heather in January 1990)

The Chapel Royal in the St John's day procession to Grand Priory Church outside the north of the gatehouse in Clerkenwell, as published in 1947 in the *St John's Gate Picture Book*. (For knowledge of this photograph I am indebted to the treasurer of the Chapel Royal, Richard Smith, and it is reproduced by courtesy of the Order of St John)

The master, Percy Davis, received a sum of £725 a year for the upkeep of the school. Like his predecessors, he found himself supplementing this sum from his own income. Thus in 1919 he had, despite great efforts to stay within the budget, incurred a deficit of £107 over a period of two years and nine months. This was dealt with sympathetically by the lord chamberlain's office, which not only paid off the debt but ensured that in future the annual school grant would be raised by a further £36.

Most accounts of the Choir School days paint a picture of lively happiness. The late Frank Physick recalled his cricketing days with George Blacklock, who 'was a very fast bowler. I was a very good batsman, and together we won so many matches when the odds were all against us. Always one short, all the 10 had to play, whilst our opponents such as Westminster Abbey and St George's Windsor could pick their XI from about 20 boys. The great match of the year against Westminster Abbey took place at the Crystal Palace where Alford Jackson paid all the expenses ... Marquee and sumptuous lunch and tea.'[21]

[21] From a letter written by Frank Physick held by the Chapel Royal.

20. Children of the Chapel Royal

The Chapel Royal School, Streatham, 1921-22. *Front row:* H.R. Tuffs, E.D. Harper, L.F.P. Weeks, B.M. Dean. *Back row:* G.G. Doel, F.G. Ryan, L. Newham, M.O. Witham, D.M. Collison, T.S.J. Pearson. (Given to the Chapel Royal by Mrs F.G. Ryan, March 1974)

Happy days were recalled by Elaine Butler in correspondence with the late Colin Scull about the Butler brothers (1909-15). She recalled the 'Annual day out to Beachy Head with the Madrigal Society, when the Gentlemen rode up in a brougham or similar' while the boys 'had to race to the top on foot. Also the fact that Dr Alcock had 5, I think, daughters – the grand finale – at his home was always Rice Pudding! But oh what Rice Pudding – rich and creamy such as they had never tasted before.' She also talked of Alan Butler's album, now housed with the Chapel, which not only contained all the programmes and orders of service for all occasions on which he sang from 1909-15, together with royal weddings, funerals, a royal confirmation and Madrigal Society programmes, but also two Alexandra Roses dated 1913 and 1914 and a handwritten letter from the king dated 15 October 1915 addressed to 'My Dear Boy' expressing his delight with Alan's solo in the anthem that morning! He was also given a gold watch by queen Alexandra, which is still in the family's possession.

The annual round of services included all those we still celebrate today and also other engagements, such as the annual service of the Order of St John, with its splendid procession through the streets near St John's Arch in Clerkenwell. As for the regular weekly services, provision was made from 1919 for the boys to have dinner at the Monarch's Grill opposite the Royal Mews before returning to the palace to sing evensong.

Children of the Chapel Royal, 1948. *Front row:* James Hey, Peter Goldspink, ? Martin, Ernest Linden, Christopher Green, Hugh Saddleton. *Back row:* Michael Ruddleston, Roger Tilford, David Lawson, Reginald Leeder. (HM Chapel Royal, reproduced by gracious permission of Her Majesty The Queen)

There were occasional instances of bullying, however. At the turn of the century they took ugly and brutal forms. For example, an inquiry had to be made into allegations that senior boys forced juniors to drink as much water as they could before going to sleep and then dared them to reach the toilets, hitting those who could not hold their water through the night with knotted scarves. This practice ceased upon complaints of

342

The Chapel Royal (St James's) Old Boys Association thirty-fifth annual dinner at the Café Royal, London, on Saturday 14 May 1938.

The City of London School in 1987, where the Chapel Royal choristers receive their education as The Queen's Scholars.

inexplicable bruising upon the youngsters. Instances of this sort of bullying declined as the century got under way and little is heard of such matters under the watchful eye of Percy Davis.

The Choir School survived the Great War, but in 1922 the decision was taken to close the school at Derwent Mount, Streatham, dispose of the lease, and arrange for the children to be received as day scholars at the City of London School. This came into effect on 1 May 1923. Oddly, by this time the total complement of children of the Chapel Royal had dwindled to eight. This was raised to ten upon the new arrangement coming into effect. Regulations for the future admission of boys were devised by the lord chamberlain's office in conjunction with the precentor (sub-dean) of the Chapel Royal, and the headmaster of the City of London School.

The initial change in arrangements led to a few difficulties. For example, two of the Chapel Royal boys could not commute from their parents' houses as they lived too far away. Grants of £40 per annum were initially made available to parents of Chapel Royal boys in compensation for board and lodging, but the parents of the two boys who lived far away received more to enable the boys to take lodgings in London. These difficulties, though, did not arise with future generations of boys who had not been recruited in 'Streatham' days.

Today the children of the Chapel Royal are all still The Queen's Scholars at the City of London School – a school which I myself attended.

21

Serjeants of the Vestry

Say's *Liber Regie Capelle* of 1449 states that 'in the vestry, with charge of the plate, books, vestments and other ornaments pertaining to the chapel, there are one clerk called the serjeant, one yeoman (valectus) and two other lesser officials who are called grooms (garciones)'.[1] Say also includes the following information: 'The lesser clerks of the chapel and the others in the vestry (de vestibulo) receive for wages four pence ha'penny a day, which comes to thirty-seven ducats a year, and for their livery four yards of cloth or eight ducats instead.'[2]

These are the duties and entitlements that must have been enjoyed by the 'poor priest' William Stevyns, who was appointed to 'keep the vestry' five years later in 1454, following a petition of the gentlemen of the Chapel Royal in that year on his behalf. Some of William Stevyns's predecessors as serjeants of the vestry, though, enjoyed a rather more colourful existence with very different privileges.

Serjeant of the vestry Thomas de Brampton was on service with the Chapel Royal overseas in 1254 when the king seized his horse to replace that lost by one Oliver de Ingeham. Depriving the serjeant of his horse must have dealt a crippling blow to the ability of the Chapel Royal to accompany the king on the move. This was evidently recognised and a bond of compensation was made out to Thomas de Brampton by the king at Meilham in 1254. This document still survives as a Patent Roll dated 1254. It reads: 'Bond to Thomas de Brampton, Serjeant of the King's Chapel, in 8 marks for a horse which the king took from him at Meilham, and gave to Oliver de Ingeham for a horse which he lost in the King's Service; with promise to pay the same when the treasurer comes from England.'

Two very significant points arise from the details of this bond. First, it confirms that the Chapel Royal physically accompanied the king on his travels – and sufficiently closely for him to be able to take the serjeant's horse. Secondly, the speed at which the matter was settled is indicated by the issue of the bond from the same town in which the incident occurred. The importance of the Chapel Royal in the king's eyes can thus be inferred from this quick settlement.

---

[1] *Liber Regie Capelle*, ch. 3.
[2] Ibid., ch. 10

Thirteen years later, in 1267, the king issued from Stratford a 'grant to Ebulo de Montibus of the wardship of the lands and serjeantry of the king's chapel and of the office of spigornel of the king's seal, late of Bartholomew de Capelle, deceased, who held in chief, with wards, reliefs, escheats and dowers'.[3] We could, perhaps, presume from this that Bartholomew de Capelle was the serjeant of the vestry who succeeded Thomas de Brampton, before Ebulo de Montibus was appointed to succeed Bartholomew in 1267. The fact that the king's grant to Ebulo de Montibus in 1267 included the 'serjeantry of the king's chapel' in the same mouthful as the office of 'spigornel of the king's seal' is the clue to interpreting a mandate of 22 October 1276 issued at Westminster which mentions the 'office of the king's chapel and spigornel', without being more specific, in relation to one John de Bohun. The mandate reads thus: 'Mandate to Luke de Luka, and his fellows, merchants of Lucca, to pay to John de Bohun 330 marks, in satisfaction of 500 marks in which the king is bound to him for the release of the office of the king's chapel and spigornels'.[4] We can thus presume that the same twinning of the office of serjeant of the king's chapel with the office of spigornel applied in 1276, just as it did just nine years earlier in 1267. John de Bohun can with confidence be included among those who held office as serjeant of the vestry.

A century later we learn, indirectly, more about the work of the serjeant of the vestry. It seems that he had help in his heavy manual duties, for a grant of 1398 survives which reads 'Grant, for life, to Richard Sewell, one of the yeomen-carters of the king's chapel of 100s a year from the issues of the counties of Bedford and Buckingham'.[5] Some idea of the apparently hernial tasks facing the serjeant of the vestry and his yeomen-carters when the Chapel Royal was 'on the move', can be glimpsed from the list of vestments and other items under the dean of the Chapel Royal's custody and care, which the king wished to be 'delivered to divers persons' upon dean Richard Prentys's retirement. This was by no means the majority of items under the dean's care, for that bulk was customarily passed down from dean to dean, as we learn from the 1414 'Acquittance' of Richard Prentys, 'late dean of the Chapel of Henry IV within the household, who received divers jewels, vestments and other ornaments and goods for the Chapel from Richard Kyngeston, late dean, by indenture and has delivered them to the King's clerk Edmund Lacy, now dean of the king's chapel within the household, by the king's command ...'. This staggering list of exceptions to be 'delivered to divers persons by the King's command' instead of to the new dean is quoted in full in Chapter 14 above.

Quite what Chapel Royal items it was deemed necessary to take to

[3] Cal. Pat. Rolls (1266-72), 1267, p. 40.
[4] Cal. Pat. Rolls (1272-81), 22 October 1276.
[5] Cal. Pat. Rolls (1396-1401), 1398.

Normandy to accompany Henry V remains somewhat vague, but they must have been considerable. We know this much from the commission issued at Westminster on 4 December 1417 which reads: 'Commission to John Colles, clerk, servant of the Vestry of the King's Chapel within the Household, and John Water, one of the King's clerks, to take carriage for the ornaments, jewels, books, vessels and other gear of the Chapel to the town of Southampton.'[6] A further commission issued on 12 February 1418 gives a few more details: 'Commission to John Colles, John Kyngman and John Water to take horses, carts, and other carriage for the jewels, ornaments and other gear of the King's Chapel to the town of Southampton.'[7] It is probable, but by no means certain, that Kyngeman and Water were at least acting as yeomen-carters for the serjeant, John Colles, although John Water is once described as 'one of the king's clerks' without reference to any other function.

Say's description of the duties of the serjeant of the vestry in 1449 naturally concentrated upon the 'charge of the plate, books, vestments and other ornaments pertaining to the Chapel'. The help of the yeoman and two grooms also mentioned would thus have been vital to the serjeant.

The *Liber Niger Domus Regis* of *c.* 1483 gives us some very detailed glimpses of the everyday life of the Plantagenet serjeants. We learn that the 'office of Vestyary hath in hym a serjeant preest or layman as the King by the Dean is advised semeth best according for to ward saifly and oversee all suche sacred stuf of holy churche and othyr richesse belonging to the chappell and vestiary'. Twice a year all these items are 'vewed and dewly examyned by the King's Chamberlayn and Dean'. More specifically the serjeant was charged with the duty of 'making the changes of the awlter clothes and vestymente in sewte and colors as the saynte and feste require with all other ornamente accordaunte'. He was also charged with the provision of 'bred, wyne, holy bred every Sonday a chiet loff, washing of surplyse of all the chapell, incense torches, tapers, morters, and small candille of wax, and the lynnen clothes for the sepulcre and font, which lynnen cloth of the sepulcre is aftyrward fee to this Serjeant ... .'

As to the serjeant's daily habits, we learn that 'the Serjeant of this office etith in the hall and takith lyvery for his chambre at night half a gallon of ale, and for wynter lyvery for all this office nightly in wynter season i candill peric, i candill wax talshied'. For 'his dayly wage by the Chekker Roll whiles he is present in Court iiii½d. and for clothing for the chapell wynter and sommer or xxs of the countinghouse'. He was provided with 'rushes and litter for chapell and vestiary all the yere of the Serjeant ussher'. He had at every fourth feast day in the year 'naprons of the greete Spicery, ii Ells of lynen clothe price iid, and having into this Court i

[6] Cal. Pat. Rolls (1416-22), December 1417, p. 127.
[7] Ibid., February 1418, p. 132.

honest servant, and lyvery for his horses'. He had also 'i yoman or ii as the Steward and they think nedefull eting with the Serjeant in the hall at Chapell bourde ...'. He had 'i groom' to help him, 'obedient to the Serjeant and yoman as for the King', but this groom sat in the hall beneath the yeoman 'or by the children of chapelle'. Finally we learn from the *Liber Niger* that the master of grammar sat 'with the Serjeant of the vestiary and clerk of the closett'.

The serjeant of the vestry would have played his traditional and vital role with regard to the transport of sacramental vessels, vestments etc., when the Chapel Royal went overseas to serve Henry VIII on his 1513 campaign in France, marching under Henry's personal banner and behind Henry's own guard of six hundred men, culminating in the successful sieges of Therouanne and Tournai. Again the serjeant would have accompanied the Chapel Royal on Henry VIII's 1544 Boulogne campaign.

The duties and tasks of the serjeant of the vestry in the sixteenth and seventeenth centuries as described in the Old Cheque Book of the Chapel Royal remained almost exactly the same a century and more after the details we have noted from the *Liber Niger* of *c.* 1483.

There are one or two clues to be found within the pages of the Old Cheque Book about the Chapel Royal sacramental plate in the care of the serjeant under the Tudors and Stuarts before it was melted down by Cromwell for Charles II's use in 'confinement' at Holdenby in 1646.[8] The Old Cheque Book account of 'the Princelye comminge of her Majestie to the Holy Communion at Estre' celebrated at the Chapel Royal building in St James's Palace in 1593, mentions a 'golden bason' held by the bishop of Worcester upon which was placed Elizabeth's 'golden obeysant'. At Elizabeth's own personal communion at the altar step mention is made of 'the foote of the golden and nowe sacred cuppe' which the queen 'toke up in her hande'. A cloth was held at four corners covering her cushion by four earls – one of whom, the earl of Oxford, Edward de Vere, had commanded a ship against the Spanish Armada five years earlier, put a vast sum of money towards Martin Frobisher's voyages, played the virginals for queen Elizabeth and tennis against Sir Philip Sidney (possibly at the St James's Palace tennis court sited under what is now the Rothmans building on the corner of Pall Mall and St James's Street), and whose daughter, Suzanne de Vere, was to be married at the Chapel Royal building at Whitehall Palace in 1604.

The record of prince Henry, James I's son, receiving his communion publicly on 5 April 1607, two days after his confirmation at Whitehall Palace chapel, contains a clear account of three chalices used separately on this occasion: one for the dean and assistants 'in one sort of bread and cup', another for the 'King's Majestie in bread and cupp prepared for

---

[8] See Peck, *Desiderata Curiosa*, p. 373.

himself alone', and lastly one for the 'Prince in bread and cupp prepared only for his Grace'.[9]

These records suggest a sizeable collection of Chapel Royal sacramental plate, for which the serjeant of the vestry Ralphe Fletcher (who served in that capacity from 1592 until 1608) was responsible. These vessels may have accompanied serjeant Cuthbert Joyner on the ship provided for the Chapel Royal on the Scottish venture of 1617, and later aboard the warship *Dreadnought* for Charles I's coronation in Scotland in 1633 under the care of serjeant Thomas Mellor. This sacramental plate was moreover almost certainly that melted down in 1646.

The Restoration sacramental plate, dating from 1660, was extensive, and it was all the responsibility of the serjeant of the vestry.[10] These responsibilities still remain today, although much of the Chapel Royal plate is now on loan to the jewel house in the Tower of London for the public to see. A sizeable collection is still retained for weekly use by the Chapel Royal at St James's Palace, and so the serjeant of the vestry still maintains his duty to care for its maintenance and use.

As we have seen, the serjeant of the vestry at the time of Elizabeth I's Easter communion in the chapel at St James's on 15 April 1593 was Ralphe Fletcher, who had replaced serjeant John Dison upon the latter's death in December 1592, being appointed on Christmas eve of that year. Fletcher had been eldest yeoman under Dison and now became serjeant, but this was the period of the interregnum of deans, and so Fletcher was 'by her Sacred Majestie appointed, upon the forsaid Lord Chamberlens presentinge to her Majestie (his Honour by her Majestie ordeneyed our cheefe governor havinge no other Deane) was by the Subdean likewise sworn Serjeant of the said Vestrie'. As we have seen, Fletcher arranged for one of the yeomen of the Chapel Royal, John Patten, father-in-law of Orlando Gibbons, to be saddled with the job of organising the packing and transport of items necessary for Elizabeth's Chapel Royal.

Both Fletcher, the serjeant, and Robert Hewes, yeoman, signed this order in January 1596. However, Fletcher did not always get on well with his Chapel Royal colleagues. In 1603 he chose to disrupt a chapter meeting, 'at which meetynge the Serjeant of the Vestrie did then and there to the great disturbance of the sayd companie unreverently and undutifully behave himselfe towardes the Subdean and Gentlemen present'. For this behaviour he was checked twenty shillings out of his next quarter's wages. Later, in 1608, Fletcher 'made over his place to Cuthbert Joyner the 26th June'. Fletcher had been present both at Elizabeth I's funeral and James I's coronation, and it is probable that a

---

[9] Old Cheque Book, fol. 78b.

[10] See Chapter 12 above for a full inventory and the serjeant of the vestry's responsibilities in relation to it.

The serjeant porter and the serjeant of the vestry of the Chapel Royal, from Sandford's *Coronation of James II*. (Reproduced by courtesy of the Dean and Chapter of Westminster)

surviving picture of the serjeant of the vestry and other members of the Chapel Royal at the funeral of Elizabeth I may contain a true likeness of him.

Serjeant Cuthbert Joyner had the task of loading items for use by the Chapel Royal aboard the ship provided by James I for the chapel to accompany him on his Scottish journey of 1617. A year later, however, Joyner was cautioned by the sub-dean for 'sundrie contemptes made against the Lord Deane and his commaundments',[11] for 'bringinge false messages to the Subdeane as from the Lord Deane', for 'daily absence from his place of attendance', and for 'conveyinge certaine parcells of his Majesties goodes out of his storehouse at Greenwich, and imloying them to suche uses as he pleased'. For these offences he was fined 40 shillings.

[11] Old Cheque Book, fol. 35b.

Serjeant Joyner died on 6 January 1625 and was buried at the Savoy chapel.

Thomas Mellor was sworn 'Joynt Serjeant of his Majesties Vesterie' for a while before Joyner's death, prior to succeeding him. The coronation of Charles I on Candlemas day 1625 saw the following procession:

> The Chappell followed the Knights of the Privie Counsell, who went next after the Knights of the Bath, the Serjeant Porter with his black staff and Serjeant of the Vestry with his virge goinge before them; next the Quier of Westminster, then the Chappell, who went singing through the Pallace yard and round about the Church, through the Great Sanctuarie till they came to the west dore of the Church: when all the Chappell were within the Church they began the first Anthem.[12]

Serjeant Mellor had the task of loading the Chapel Royal items aboard the veteran Armada warship *Dreadnought* for the Chapel Royal's attendance in Scotland at Charles I's coronation as king of Scotland – although many members of the Chapel Royal, including the dean, followed the king's retinue on land. The Bodleian 'parallel Register' to the Old Cheque Book, discovered by Hillebrand, gives a detailed account of these arrangements for the journey to Scotland.[13]

After Thomas Mellor's death on 25 June 1636, Thomas Walker, then eldest yeoman of the vestry, was sworn as serjeant of the vestry on Christmas day 1636. Walker, who had been the bishop of Winchester's servant, must be counted among those who may have hidden the Chapel Royal manuscripts during the Civil War.

Thomas Haynes was the first serjeant to be sworn at the Restoration. He had a great task to restore the Chapel Royal buildings and other items to their former glory.[14] The Old Cheque Book contains the information that Haynes was sworn serjeant twice in accordance with custom following the accession of a new monarch. He died on 30 June 1687. A likeness of Haynes may exist in Sandford's *Coronation of James II* depicting four children of the Chapel Royal, the serjeant porter and the serjeant of the vestry.

Serjeant Henry Parker, appointed in 1687, served both James II and, after his flight, subsequent monarchs until 1714. We learn from the first entry in the Whitehall Register that Parker's successor as serjeant, Marmaduke Alford, was baptised in the parish church of Curry Ryvell, Somersetshire, on 10 May 1647. This entry may be a later interpolation in the Whitehall Register, but if not, the Alford family too must be considered among the possible protectors of the Chapel Royal manuscripts during the Civil War and Commonwealth. Alford was buried

---

[12] Ibid., fols 71b, 72.
[13] See Chapter 9 above.
[14] See Chapters 11 and 12 above.

at St Margaret's Westminster on 14 May 1715.

Serjeant Jonathan Smith, appointed in 1715, also became clerk of the cheque on 4 April 1720. Serjeant Smith had his role to perform in the public thanksgiving service at St Paul's Cathedral on 20 January 1714, when the sub-dean 'read prayers at St Paul's Church, as beinge the King's Chappell upon this occasion ... read the Communion service, being preceded by the Serjeant of the Vestry, and attended by the Gentlemen of the Chappell in their surplices; and that all others of our Society waited there as in the Chappell Royal'.[15]

Serjeant Smith's successor in 1752, William Lovegrove, kept his own account or 'Memoranda' of the affairs of the Chapel Royal. In particular, he noted down for the future the entitlements of the serjeant of the vestry. His relations with the other members of the Chapel were in some cases, to say the least, strained – although perhaps with justification. He was at times outspoken in his comments. Thus, for example, he himself states that 'before I was sworn in Serjeant, My Lord [the dean] made all the enquiries he possibly cou'd to gain the knowledge of the Profits of the Serjeant's place; when he had accomplished this Point, he then saddled me ... with an annuity of Eighty Pounds a year, to be paid half yearly to his own servants'. He continues: 'they have made me pay dearly for my Place, as I have and must pay up to lady day 1777 which will amount to upwards of £1,800,'[16] Lovegrove talks of 'Subdean Aspinwall, the Serjeant's mortal Enemy'.[17] The groom, Mr Norton, evidently tried to wriggle out of cleaning duties, for which Lovegrove pointed out he was paid a special allowance, and 'disputed the point with Serjeant Lovegrove, as he did many other things, till at last he was turned out of the Vestry where the Ladys sit'.[18]

Lovegrove provides us with an insight into the provision of the sacramental bread and wine: two mauchetts or rolls were to be provided every Sunday and sermon-day, together with one bottle of madeira. For every first Sunday in the month were to be provided six loaves and twelve bottles of wine. Every other Sunday in the month saw one loaf and three bottles of wine provided. At Easter, Whitsunday and Christmas ten extra loaves were provided, together with twenty-four bottles of claret from the board of green cloth. Finally '6 Bottles of Red Port were allowed on the King's Accession, the Coronation, the King's Birthday, the Queen's Birthday, the Prince of Wales's Birthday, the Princess of Wales's Birthday, the Christening of the Prince of Wales and all other of the Royal Children, on the Birth of any of the Royal Family, on all Weddings of the Royal Family, on every Publick Rejoicing, when the Tower Guns are ordered to be Fired off. Also on 29th day of May.'[19]

---

[15] Old Cheque Book, fol. 87.
[16] Lovegrove manuscript, fol. 54.
[17] Ibid., fol. 25.
[18] Ibid. [19] Ibid., fol. 79.

21. Serjeants of the Vestry

We learn from Lovegrove that 'the Serjeant of the Vestry walks before the Sub-Almoner, whilst he distributes the Shoes and Stockings ... the Woolen Cloth and Linnen ... the small silver in purses' in the Maundy service at Whitehall which was held at 4 pm in Lovegrove's day (1752-77). He adds the information that 'the Serjeant ties round his waist three Ells of the cloth alllow'd him, during the Ceremony'. After the service the sub-almoner, yeoman of the almonry and serjeant of the vestry 'drink the King's Health out of Beechen cups, keep the cup, and retire into the Vestry, and there eat a bit of a roll and drink a Glass of Wine'.[20]

Relations with fellow members of the Chapel Royal staff fluctuated in Lovegrove's time from the very friendly to quite the opposite. As we have seen, it seems he did not approve of groom Richard Norton's action in taking advantage of the 1728 order allowing the groom to take care of the public vestry to sit the ladies there, in order to keep the key to it. Serjeant Smith had overcome this problem by 'placing his Majesty's Trunks, Standard and Plate in it', which meant he had to retain access to the vestry. Lovegrove tried the same approach with less success, until the vestry became so blocked with ladies at service times that the dean had to go into colour court and enter the altar end of the Chapel Royal by the 'grille' door under the arch of the great gatehouse.

The trouble had started in 1755 when groom Norton had the lock changed on the vestry door without the serjeant's knowledge. The dean reacted with an order that 'according to the Antient Constitution of the Chapel, the Serjeant is the Chief Oficer of the Vestry ... as to the Keys of the Vestry, they belong to the Serjeant to keep ... that no person has a right to Lodge in the Vestry but the Serjeant, or such person as he shall appoint'.[21] The dean pointed out in a letter dated 15 May 1756 that the 'Groom attends the Great Doors to let in people', but groom Norton had abused this. The dean lamented, 'I have borne with him for Eight years, 'till at last he thought himself under no control, and claim'd the Governing of the Vestry, and behaved with so much insolence and rudeness, that I thought it necessary to put an end to his Attendance there, and to order him to his own duty as Groom of the vestry.' Norton had in fact also used 'rude language' to the dean and serjeant, which did not exactly help his cause.

Lovegrove was frank about his fellows. 'Act cautiously,' he writes in 1761, 'but firmly, the whole body (excepting the Dean) are Leeches, and the Serjeant's Enemies; they wou'd strip him to his Shirt if they could.'[22] A letter from Lovegrove to the dean dated 28 June 1767 stated boldly 'that in Bishop Gibson's time the Ministers and Gentlemen of the Chapel were all combin'd to crush the Serjeant, and to deprive him of his just

---

[20] Ibid., fol. 86.
[21] Ibid., fol. 98.
[22] Ibid., fol. 151.

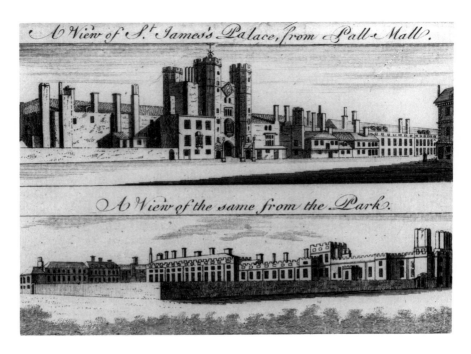

Views of St James's Palace engraved for the *Royal Magazine, c.* 1760. (Reproduced by courtesy of the Guildhall Library, City of London)

right and Perquisites, and I may say some of them have been since, and still are, and will be, if the Serjeant should lose the Support and Protection of the Dean, which hitherto he has happily enjoyed'.[23] In a letter written the following day Lovegrove declared in the course of an argument about the provision of surplices: 'Mr Pordage and Dr Allen were subdeans in my own time; and they never had but two surplices, and they attended the Service of the Chapel (when able) more strictly and duly than the present subdean does, and also came into the Chapel before service began, and that is what Dr Bayly seldom does.'[24] He went on to call Dr Bayly the 'High Priest' and ruminated that 'what the Church and Clergy were formerly (and nearly are now, whenever they have Power) may be gathered from the History of Harry's and King John's time'.[25] He declared in an entry dated 25 April 1771 that 'the Officers of the Vestry have always been considered as Members of the Chapel, and not their Servants, as one of the Gentlemen once expressed himself. The Serjeant stands upon an equal footing with any Gentlemen belonging to the Chapel, except the Dean and Subdean.'[26]

[23] Ibid., fol. 180.
[24] Ibid., fol. 183.
[25] Ibid.
[26] Ibid., fol. 226.

Of the coronation of George III in 1761 Lovegrove wrote that he 'made use of but 2½ Ells of the Cloth, for one Table Cloth and one Napkin. Those things are to be left for the Harpies of Westminster Abbey. They seize all they can lay their paws on, as their perquisite, so that I took down as little as I possibly cou'd.'[27] This was, of course, aside from the two trunks containing the 'Plate, Surplices, Mantle, Gown, Rod, and little box which held the Wine and Bread' which he reclaimed the next morning, 'but the empty Bottles staid behind with the Table Linnen for the Cormorants'.[28]

Lovegrove's 'Memoranda' are full of the most interesting information particular to the Chapel Royal's affairs at St James's Palace. In an entry on folio 231 he tells us that when he was first appointed serjeant in 1752 the dean 'advised me to have the Plate weigh'd off by the Officers of the Jewell Office at Whitehall for fear there should be any deficiency as he had no good opinion of my predecessors honesty'. A day was fixed for this when the late serjeant's son and the officers of the jewel office brought their weights to St James's to conduct the weighing exercise. Afterwards a new list was made of the Chapel Royal Plate, entered in the books of the jewel office and signed by William Lovegrove. He also mentions that the 'Christening Plate is made use of at St James's'.

It was just as well that the dean insisted on this exercise, for there was a close run thing with the gold and silver Chapel Royal plate in 1767. The Chapel Royal building in colour court, St James's Palace, was shut on 3 August 1767 to allow it to be painted, whitewashed and repaired. The dean meanwhile ordered that the services be held temporarily in 'the French chapel in the Fryery'. Lovegrove tells us that 'the French Chapel (soon after) was attempted to be broke open and robbed, upon which the King's plate which was carried there, was immediately removed again into the Serjeant's Vestry and Custody'.

Shutting the Chapel Royal building in colour court for repairs and redecoration was a fairly common event – indeed almost annual – but a particularly interesting reason for its closure is mentioned on folio 185: 'when his late Majesty was abroad (at the Battle of Dettingham) the Royal Chapel at St James's was shut up, and the service performed at the French & Dutch Chapel in the Fryery.' The 'battle of Dettingham' (i.e. Dettingen) was the last battle in which a British monarch led the army on the battlefield.

As for George III, he was 'married in the Royal Chapel at St James's between the hours of 9 and 12 o'clock at Evening'.[29] On this occasion the serjeant 'walk'd up to the Altar before the Archbishop of Canterbury and the Bishop of Winchester, Clerk of the Closet'. At the end of the service the serjeant led the bishops back to the yeoman's vestry for a bottle of

[27] Ibid., fol. 135.
[28] Ibid., fol. 136.
[29] Ibid., fol. 126.

claret and madeira and two rolls 'for their refreshment'. Elsewhere an unholy scene was taking place as the surplices issued for the gentlemen and boys for the occasion 'were all thrown down into the Chapel out of the Musick Loft'. It was not until the following morning that 'all was removed into their proper places'.

For George III's coronation in Westminster Abbey we learn from Lovegrove that 'the Serjeant, Yeoman, and Deputy, carry'd the Plate etc. from the Deanry into the Choir, and made ready the Altar'. At queen Anne's coronation the serjeant stood near the north door between the choir and St Edward's chapel. This practice was continued at George III's coronation, for the Serjeant 'stood at the North side of the Altar with Yeoman Rowling, and Deputy Mr Cain, while opposite stood, on the South side, the Serjeant Porter and Mr Martin, Chapel Keeper at Whitehall'.[30] For the coronations, a new virger's rod is allowed. Lovegrove tried to take up this prerogative, but it was not until after the event that Mr Egerton of the jewel office 'found out a Fee that had been paid to that office by my predecessor, Serjeant Smith, at the Coronation of King George the Second, for a new Virger's Rod, or a composition for one'. As Lovegrove was eventually paid six guineas 'in lieu of a new virger's Rod'[31] and a spectrographic test has shown that the present one used by the serjeant is of roughly mid-eighteenth-century date, we can perhaps conclude that the one now in use was indeed that made for serjeant Smith at George II's coronation.

As to Lovegrove's accommodation adjacent to the Chapel Royal building at St James's, we can draw a hazy picture. He tells us in 1767 that he was 'obliged to constant residence at St James's', and for this he had 'but one room, which served him for kitchen, Parlour, and Bedchamber'. On appealing to the lord chamberlain he was given 'a garret adjoining, but having no accommodation at present, and being greatly out of repair'. Lovegrove then asked the board of works 'to have a communication made' so as to 'make the Apartment useful and convenient'. The result is, in all probability, the apartment (no. 11) still appointed for the official use of the serjeant of the vestry, adjoining the chapel building in the north-west corner of what is now ambassadors' court.

Lastly, it is perhaps only right to let William Lovegrove explain in his own words the ambit of his duties: 'Sir Robert ask't me if I look upon myself as Serjeant of all the King's Chapels, as supposing His Majesty might have a Chapel at Richmond, Kew, Hampton Court, and Windsor.' Lovegrove's reply was constitutionally accurate: 'I said I was Serjeant of that Chapel or Church wherever the King went to hear Divine Service, as Sovereign, and also wherever the Dean of the Chapels Royal have any

---

30 Ibid., fol. 137.
31 Ibid., fol. 138.

Government or Authority (as Dean) in the Service of the Church or Chapel.' Thus the serjeant attends 'upon the Dean or Subdean at St Paul's on any publick Thanskgiving, at Westminster Abbey on a Coronation' and 'the Maundy at Whitehall'.[32]

I shall not draw any more from Lovegrove's 'Memoranda' out of respect for his aim to protect the rights and privileges of future serjeants of the vestry: 'My advice and caution to my successors are that they should never show this Book to the Dean, Subdean, or any Member of the Chapel ... the less others know of your affairs the better'!

Serjeant Roe was appointed to replace serjeant Dickes in 1790 by the dean, Beilby Porteous, but complained, as did serjeant Lovegrove, about the 'saddle-bonds'. Serjeant Roe wrote in his diary: 'I should never have been Serjeant of the King's Chapel had not the Bishop been interested in it, for I paid to his order £1,000. I hope the world will know it.' Serjeant Roe died in 1816, to be replaced by Richard Howse who served until Francis Lingard was appointed in 1840. The Chapel Royal commissioners supposedly looked closely at the terms of his employment as part of an overall look at the Chapel Royal with a view to reducing its numbers.

In 1860 the commissioners made recommendations concerning the office of serjeant of the vestry which were based upon a remarkable lack of appreciation of what the duties entailed: 'The offices of the Serjeant and Yeoman of the Vestry and that of Clerk of the Cheque are now held by the same person Mr Francis Lingard. In the first two named offices it is his duty to take care of the furniture, and other material appointments of the Chapel.' This is the sum total of the commissioners' observations of the duties of the serjeant of the vestry. Except in the vague wording 'other material appointments of the Chapel' there is nothing which appreciates his work looking after and maintaining the sacramental vessels, candles, altar dressings, clergy vestments, choir robes, duties in divine service, seating of congregation, packing of robes and Chapel items on journeyings, etc. However, the commissioners did go on to observe that Francis Lingard, 'the present holder of the 3 places likewise receives an allowance of £54 per annum for washing Surplices, £60 a year as Compensation in lieu of Admission Fees to the Chapel Royal, sometime since abolished, and has a small apartment attached to the Chapel'.[33] The commissioners recommended that the serjeant and yeoman's offices be 'united in one and that a Salary of £100 a year be attached to it, and that no Fees whatsoever should be taken by the holder'. This was a step backwards, for a hundred years earlier we learned from serjeant Lovegrove that he had to pay £80 per year out of his salary to the dean for the privilege of retaining his position. He must therefore have earned over and above this as an annual income. The commissioners further

[32] Ibid., fol. 169.
[33] New Cheque Book, fol. 231.

Colin Scull, gentleman in ordinary 1957-70, serjeant of the vestry 1970-84.

recommended that the expense of washing surplices should in future be paid by bill.

The reader will gain no idea at all of what the duties of the serjeant of the vestry actually entail from these inadequate and lacklustre 'observations' of the commissioners. These duties have never been better explained than in the dean's order in chapter of 28 May 1728, reproduced here:

> His daily Duty. To the Serjeant it Appertaineth to open the Door of the Vestry, where he attends as Serjeant, at the hours of Prayer. To keep that Vestry Clean and in Decent Order: To assist the Sub Dean in putting on his Surplice, To walk with his Virge before the Dean, the Bishops and Sub Dean to their Seats, To place the Candlesticks on the Communion-Table, to keep the Altar clean and in decent order, To place the Velvet Cover on the Lesson Desk, and on Litany Days on the Litany Desk, and the Bibles on the Lesson Desk.
>
> His Sunday Duty. To the Serjeant it appertains on Sunday and whenever

the Sacrament of the Lord's Supper is administered, to spread on the Communion Table a fine white Linen cover, to provide Bread and Wine for the Sacrament, to attend during the Administration of it, that he may be ready in case anything be wanting. To turn and mark the places in the Common Prayer Book for the Communion Service on Sundays, and on Holy Days. To walk with his Virge, before the Dean, Sub Dean, and others of the Priests, when they go up to officiate at the Communion Table, and before the Preacher to the Pulpit.

His Occasional Dutys. To the Serjeant it also appertains to provide New Books and Surplices, and new Furniture for the use of the Chapel, according to the direction of the Dean; to take care that the Surplices for the Use of the Chapel be duly wash'd, and kept clean and white; To provide clean Surplices for the Gentlemen once a Fortnight, when they are in daily waiting, and once a month when they wait only on Sundays and Holydays; and to provide for the Boys of the Chapel, clean Surplices every Sunday, when in daily waiting, and once a Month when they wait only on Sundays and Holydays. When new Surplices are ordered, he is to procure from the Great Wardrobe, the finest and best Holland allowed on such occasions, and cause to be made two Surplices for every Gentleman of the Chapel, each marked with the Initial letters of his Name, and to take special care that the surplices be long and large enough, and fit in the Neck.

Lastly, he is to continue within the Chapel during the time of Divine Service.[34]

---

[34] Ibid., fols 11, 12.

22

Yeomen of the Vestry

The office of yeoman of the vestry was an ancient one. The Calendar of State Papers, in entries for the years 1398 and 1399, contains a 'grant, for life, to Richard Sewell, one of the yeomen-carters of the king's chapel of 100s a year from the issues of the counties of Bedford and Buckinghamshire'.

The name of John Pritewell, 'Yeoman of the King's Chapel' survives in a grant at the beginning of the fifteenth century. Dated 18 March 1401, this grant from the king, recorded in the Patent Rolls, took the form of conferring upon John Pritewell also the 'Office of purveyor of necessaries for the works within the Palace of Westminster and the Tower of London'.

Say's *Liber Regie Capelle* of 1449 included among the vestry officials a 'valectus', or yeoman. The passage runs thus: 'there are one clerk called the serjeant, one yeoman and two other lesser officials who are called the serjeant, one yeoman and two other lesser officials who are called grooms.' These officials had 'charge of the plate, books, vestments and other ornaments pertaining to the Chapel'.[1] The *Liber Niger Domus Regis* of c. 1483 mentions 'One Yeoman or two ... eting with the Serjeant in the Hall at Chapel bourde proved trew men and diligent to kepe this office and great richesse with the Serjeant ...'.

An entry in the Old Cheque Book, apparently entered in 1558, has the heading 'Touching the Yeomen and Grome of the Vestrye'. It states that they were 'also to bee at the commaundment of the Sergeaunte of the Vestry for the tyme beinge, touching the service of her Majestie from tyme to tyme, so helpe yow God and the hole contentes of that booke'.[2]

The yeomen's duties – most of the time there were two of them – were clearly described in a chapter of 9 January 1630 detailed in the Old Cheque Book: 'That the yeomen by turnes make readdy the alter, see the books, surplices, and plate returned to the standerd, and take care that the Kinges cussions be not made common at Communions, and not to suffer woemen to be in the Chappell in seates or otherwise at Communion tymes but such as receave the Sacrament.' Thirty-five years earlier, in 1595, the Old Cheque Book contains an order stating that 'the two Yomen

[1] *Liber Regie Capelle*, ch. 3.
[2] What 'that booke' was is not certain – perhaps it meant the Bible or the Bodleian Rawlinson manuscript parallel to the Old Cheque Book?

of the Vestrie are by dewtie to see her Majesties stuffe meete for her Chappell, to be trussed upp at everye remove and sent to her highnes nexte house of waytinge'.[3] The yeomen's mediaeval duties as 'carters' for the Chapel Royal baggage train are still recognisable in this sixteenth-century order.

In 1591 yeoman John Burchall 'died at Chichester in the Queen's progresse'. This confirms that the Chapel Royal accompanied Elizabeth I on her progresses around her realm. In fact John Patten was sworn groom to fill the gap 'in the same progresse by the Gentlemen Ushers'. He had to be re-sworn by the sub-dean 'at his return' before he could receive his wages.

One Henry Eveseed was sworn yeoman of the vestry in 1615. (He is not to be confused with the gentleman Henry Eveseed, who was a 'childe of the Chappell', subsequently appointed gentlemen in 1585, and who died on 18 November 1614.) The Henry Eveseed to whom we now refer held his first office with the Chapel Royal as a groom of the vestry, to which office he was appointed in 1611, following the dismissal of Henry Alred as groom for 'suspicion of stealing 3 coapes out of his Majesty's Vestry at Greenwich'[4] and for 'drounkennes, many greate disorders, and threatning the spillage of the Sub-Dean's bloude'. Accusations of 'blasphemy' and 'whoredom'[5] one suspects could not have helped his cause. However Henry Eveseed was to go the same way, being in his turn dismissed on 3 March 1620 'for many disorders committed and proved against him'[6] after serving for five years as yeoman.

The actual nature of these 'disorders' is mind-boggling. As we saw in Chapter 9, in 1616 Eveseed had the misfortune to be 'infected with a fowle disease in his groine, to the great offence of all, but chiefly of those that were constrained by means of their service to lye neere him, upon which the late Lord deane thought him unfitt to serve his Majestie in his Progress into Scotland' in 1617. Clearly objections would have been forthcoming from the gentlemen who had to share their sleeping quarters aboard the ship provided for this voyage through the North Sea. On one occasion, 'at midnight, and in his drounkennesse, he rose out of his bed naked', tore his flesh crashing through a glass window and was thus 'not whole in a good while after'. On another occasion 'one night he came and vomitted in a dishe of pottage which Mr Harrison and others were eatinge of'.[7] On St Peter's day 1619 he 'did violently and sodenly without cause runne uppon Mr Gibbons, took him up and threw him doune upon a standard whereby he receaved such hurt that he is not yett recovered of

---

[3] Old Cheque Book, fol. 23.
[4] Ibid., fol. 3.
[5] Ibid., fol. 31b.
[6] Ibid., fol. 3.
[7] Ibid., fol. 37.

Colour court, St James's Palace, by W. Capon, 1802. The Chapel Royal building forms the range on the left-hand side. (Reproduced by courtesy of the Guildhall Library, City of London)

the same, and withall he tare his band from his neck to his prejudice and disgrace'.[8] He did not stop there, but 'proceading from Mr Gibbons mett our fellow Mr Cooke in the Chappell, where he gave him three blowes in the face', and then 'challenged the field'. He told the serjeant of the vestry that 'the Sub-Dean sate in Chapter as the knave of clubbs, and the rest of the company as knaves about him'. He was accused of being a 'blasfemer and a filthy speaker in all places', while the sub-dean and others of the vestry reported him to be 'the most negligent officer in his place that he hath knowne in his tyme'. Despite warnings, checks and suspensions Henry Eveseed persisted 'dayly in his former abuses against the Sub-dean and others of the gentlemen', and the dean 'finding no hope of reformation in him', he was dismissed.

The Chapel Royal orders for the year 1728 contained in the New Cheque Book[9] give perhaps the clearest description of the yeoman's duty to be found in any account. He had 'to open the Pew Seats within the Chapel at the Hours of Prayer', to 'have the care of setting and placing

[8] Ibid.
[9] New Cheque Book, fol. 12.

362

forms and hassocks within the Chapel', to ensure that the prayer books were 'in their proper places', to 'provide wax candles and hassocks for the use of the Chapel' and 'to place wax candles for the Winter evening service in their proper places for the benefit of light, and to light them before the Service begins'. He had the specific duty 'to keep out of the Chapel, Persons and things not fit to be there'.

A hundred and thirty-two years later, in 1860, the Chapel Royal commissioners took the decision to abolish the office of yeoman of the vestry and 'unite' it with that of serjeant of the vestry. The office thus ceased to exist with the death of the last holder, Francis Lingard, in 1868.

23

Grooms of the Vestry
and Keepers of the Closet

There have been grooms of the vestry since at least 1449, for Say's *Liber Regie Capelle* mentions among the vestry officials two 'garciones' or grooms, as well as one 'valectus' or yeoman, aside from the serjeant of the vestry.

Since the Chapel Royal constitution at that time provided for two grooms it is possible that John Webster and John Kyngman, who are described in a commission of 1418 as accompanying the serjeant of the vestry, John Colles, were clerks also acting as grooms. They were given the task of taking 'horses, carts, and other carriage for the jewels, ornaments and other gear of the king's Chapel to Southampton' before sailing for Normandy to join Henry V on campaign there. The office they held, though, must remain a matter for speculation. It may well be that they were yeomen-carters of the Chapel Royal rather than grooms.

We are, however, on much sounder ground when it comes to the duties and conditions of service of the groom of the vestry as detailed in the *Liber Niger Domus Regis* of *c.* 1483. It talks of 'one groome to kepe and to attend uppon this office diligently helping to dresse the chapel ... and trusse the stuff wayting on the carriage, fetching in the liveries'. The groom had to be 'trew proved and obedient to the Serjeant and Yoman', but he nevertheless sat 'in the hall beneath the yoman off this office at chappell bourde or by the children of chappell, taking his reward like the grooms of household, and if any groom be sent out by the power of the countinghouse, then he taketh for expense dayly 3d after the old custome'. The groom was also provided by the jewel house with 'carriage of harneys'.

The year 1558 saw an order 'Touchinge the Yeomen and Grome of the Vestrye'[1] who were to 'bee at the commandment of the Sergeaunt of the Vestry', while the appointments of grooms in the sixteenth and seventeenth centuries were often made from personal servants of the dean. For example, Roger Judd, 'servant to the Bishop of Norwich, then Deane of his Majesties Chappell, was sworne Groome, uppon Shrove Tewsday' in 1636. Earlier, in 1624, Thomas Walker, 'servant to the Lord

---

[1] Old Cheque Book, fol. 16.

Bishop of Winton, and Dean of the Chappell, was sworne Groom'.[2] Almost invariably the appointment of a new groom followed the promotion of the existing groom to fill a vacancy among the yeomen of the Chapel Royal. That this was a firmly established system of promotion is revealed in the exception to the rule in 1680 when Morice Morer was appointed to fill the place of 'eldest Yeoman of the Vestry', George Whitcher. This appointment 'was not to be a president to hinder the groome of his right for the future'.[3]

In 1770 a dispute between yeoman and groom which was settled by the dean indirectly gives us a glimpse of the groom at work: 'To prevent any dispute that may henceforward arise betwixt the Yeoman and Groom of the Vestry, in relation to the right of keeping the doors of the Chappel, I do declare that the care of the outward doors and parts of the Chappel is in the Groom and not in the Yeoman of the Vestry.' The dean gave the groom some leeway, too, by declaring that 'if there be any occasion for an assistant, the groom shall employ some person whose deportment shall give no offence to any, and who shall submissively and readily comply with the directions of the Serjeant and Yeoman'.

The clearest description of the groom's duties, though, is to be found in the New Cheque Book orders of the Chapel Royal dated 20 May 1728, which state:

> To the Groom it appertains to take care of all the Publick Doors, ie., of all Publick inlets and outlets of the Chapel, and to open them at the hours of prayer and to shut and lock them when Divine service is over. To take care that the Chapel be not crowded by letting too many persons into it, so as to hinder the passage to the Communion-Table. To hinder persons and things from entering, that are unfit to be there. To clean the Chapel, Brush the Pulpit-cloth, and keep all things clean within the Chapel. To assist the Gentlemen of the Chapel to put on their surplices, and to provide Tallow-Candles for the use of the Ante-Chapel and the Gentlemen's Vestry.

The office of groom of the vestry escaped the clutches of the Chapel Royal commissioners in their report of 1860. They declared concerning the groom's office and that of organ blower: 'Upon those of the Groom of the Vestry and Organ Blower your Majesty's Commissioners have no suggestions to make.'

The office of groom of the vestry had its quota of characters over the centuries. We have already had occasion to look at the lifestyle of Henry Alred. Appointed groom in 1593, he was cautioned by the dean in a chapter of eighteen gentlemen in 1601 for his 'many and great disorders committed'. Despite his promise on 29 June 1601 to mend his ways, he was again reprimanded in chapter on 28 March 1608 by the dean for 'his fearefull blasphemies, wicked execracons and threatnings to spill bloud'

[2] Ibid., fol. 3 and reverse.
[3] Ibid., fol. 3b.

at the service held the previous day. Later that year on 2 November 1608 he was again reprimanded for 'drounkenness ... and threatninge the spillage of the Sub-deanes bloude'. To these indications of a loose life were added the accusations of 'whoredom' and 'contemtes' in 1610. It is not entirely surprising, therefore, that Henry Alred was expelled by the dean in chapter on 21 March 1611, after eighteen years of service with the Chapel Royal.

The *Liber Regie Capelle* of 1449 mentions '2 garciones', while the *Liber Niger Domus Regis* of *c*. 1483 mentions 'one groome'. It appears that 'one groome' was the order of the day until the early years of the seventeenth century, when certain appointments of grooms overlap one another. Upon close examination it seems that almost invariably, when this is the case, one of them was appointed with the specific duty 'to attend the Prince'. Thus, while Christopher Clark was evidently the main 'groom of the vestry' from 1608-10, William Dale was also appointed on 15 May 1608 'groome of the Kinges Majesties Vestrie, to attend the Prince'. Similarly in 1614 Roberte Colman was sworn 'Groome ... to serve Prince Charles' at the same time as William Lowther was just groom of the vestry. The oath for Roberte Colman continues: 'to serve Prince Charles in that place in suche manner and sorte as Thomas Miller, next underneath writt, was sworne to serve Prince Henry.' Thomas Miller had been sworne 'Yeoman of the Kinges Majesties Vestery, and to attend the Prince', on 26 May 1607, but it seems he had performed that role for the prince when groom, for he received his oath then as 'Yeoman after the same manner and forme as he did beinge sworne Groome'.[4] After the Civil War and Restoration the task of 'attending the Prince' metamorphosed into closet-keeper, and this then appeared to go hand in hand with the yeoman's post.

After queen Anne moved the headquarters of the choral foundation of the Chapel Royal to St James's Palace from Whitehall in 1702, a closet-keeper's position had to be maintained at Whitehall chapel in the Banqueting House, where serjeant Lovegrove tells us that in the 1750s at least the choir there comprised three men and five boys. There was also a separate chaplain and other officials appointed solely to continue the services there. The ecclesiastical and choral establishment there was abolished in 1890. But the 'move' of queen Anne to St James's Palace in 1702, accompanied by her Chapel Royal, meant that a closet-keeper was required at St James's too. These two positions of closet-keeper were never held by the same person. More of this shortly.

Returning briefly to the grooms of the vestry, there were two instances of the appointment of 'Groome Extraordinarie for the Tuninge and Mendinge of His Majesties organs'. In 1615 William Wardes was thus appointed, to be followed by John Burwood in 1626.

---

[4] Ibid., fol. 28b.

Vestry officials William Buckle, Leonard Wyatt and William Collins with PC Jack Colman, winter 1960-61.

At the Restoration Augustine Cleveland was sworn groom, but two years later he 'unfortunately dyed by the violence of horses and coach running over him at Hampton Court' on 1 June 1662, and was buried in Hampton parish church on 3 June 1662.

As to keepers of the closet of the Chapel Royal, just three years after the Restoration it was deemed necessary to appoint a closet keeper at Whitehall. The man chosen for this task was one Thomas Dunkley. An entry in the Old Cheque Book, reading 'Thomas Dunkley was this day sworne Yeoman of his Majesties Vestry extraordinary, to wait Closett Keeper in ordinarye', is accompanied by a note in the margin: 'March 21, 1663 At Whitehall.'[5] He still held the post on Charles II's death and was

[5] Ibid., fol. 45.

re-sworn on James II's accession. Thomas Dunkley kept a record of the touching for the king's evil. The fact that he was keeper of the closet at Whitehall chapel confirms that Charles II performed this healing at Whitehall Palace – and almost certainly at the Chapel Royal building. Dunkley's record covers the years 1667-82, and it continues the record entered in registers kept by serjeant of the vestry Thomas Haynes from 1660-64. The first and last years of these records, 1660 and 1682, saw the greatest number 'touched' in any one year: 6,725 in 1660 and 8,577 in 1682. The total number 'touched' between these years was 92,107.[6]

Thomas Dunkley's records are a very valuable insight into a kingly practice which through its apparently successful medical results, attested by thousands of people, had the political advantage of demonstrating the truth of the notion of the 'divine right of kings', so recently challenged with the regicide of Charles I in 1649.[7] The impact of Charles II's 'touching' on the population throughout the realm cannot be underestimated. On 9 January 1683 at Whitehall the king caused a proclamation advertising the 'fit times ... necessary to be appointed for the performing of this great work of charity' to be 'read publicly in all parish churches'.

The great fire at Whitehall in 1698 largely destroyed the Chapel Royal building, and so the Banqueting House built by Inigo Jones was pressed into service for the use of the Chapel Royal. Queen Anne's decision to move the headquarters of the Chapel Royal to St James's Palace in 1702 meant that a closet keeper was then needed for both buildings. The succession of closet keepers at the Banqueting House, Whitehall continued until 1890 when it was abolished as an ecclesiastical establishment, but parallel with this succession was the appointment of a closet keeper of the Chapel Royal at St James's.

Upon the abolition of the position of closet keeper at the Banqueting House in 1890 the closet keeper there, Sir John Hassard, complained that he had now been deprived of his job without any provision having been made for his future employment. Faced with this the Chapel Royal commissioners decided to offer him the post of keeper of the closet at St James's at the next vacancy. This was accordingly offered to him upon the death of Mr Davis of the Chapel Royal at St James's in 1892. In the event Sir John then declined the offer, and Miss Jane Shackle was appointed instead.

---

[6] See A.J. Stephens, *The Book of Common Prayer with Notes* (EHS, 1850), vol. 2, p. 996.

[7] For the origins of the notion of divine right see my BA Dissertation lodged at the University of Durham entitled: 'The form in which Aristotle's Politics reached Western Christendom and the latter's reaction to it up to the time of St Thomas Aquinas' (1977).

24

Bellringers, Violists, Lutenists, Organ Blowers, Friends of the Chapel and Daily Ladies

Bellringers

The office of bellringer to the Chapel Royal, abolished following the recommendations of the Chapel Royal commissioners in 1860, had by that time become a sinecure. But its origins were far from that, and can be traced certainly as far back as the fifteenth century.

Say's *Liber Regie Capelle* of 1449 mentions in ch. 4 that the 'clerks of the Chapel in their surplices, with the dean or his deputy, at the summons of a bell rung by one of the boys, at about seven o'clock on every morning of the year, sing ...'. By the seventeenth century the office of bellringer had become more formalised and was held no longer by a boy chorister, but by an adult. Thus the Old Cheque Book records that on 23 February 1606 Robert Bicknar was sworn 'Bellringer for his Majestes householde, in the vestrie at Whitehall, by Leonard Davies, Subdean'. This, though, was at the 'comaunde' of the dean, Dr Montague, who now possessed the 'free gift' of the office of bellringer. Robert Bicknar was required to swear 'obedience to the Deane and Subdeane of the sayd Chappell, and to the Confessor of his Majestes householde for the tyme beinge, in all matters and thinges apperteyninge to his said place and service'.[1] Bicknar served until 1624 when he was succeeded by Sampson Rowden, who 'took his oathe in all respects as Robert Bicknar did'.[2] His successor in 1626, Robert Evans, was the last recorded holder of the office before the Civil War.

It is not clear exactly what happened to the office at the Restoration in 1660, but it seems that Samuel Blayton was appointed, for the Old Cheque Book records that he was 'suspended by my Lord of Winchester, Dean of his Majestes Chapell Royall, the 5th of Aprill 1666'.[3] The oath for Adam Watkyns in 1672 and his successor Henry Watkins in 1678 took the same form as that of Robert Bicknar back in 1606.

The eighteenth century saw the appointment of Isaak Ellis as bellringer in 1703, followed by Thomas Brookes in 1711 and John Herring

[1] Old Cheque Book, fol. 29b.
[2] Ibid., fol. 29.
[3] Ibid., fol. 86b.

in 1732 – he 'having first (as usual) sworn obedience to the Dean, Subdean and Confessor'. Herring resigned in 1737 and was succeeded by John Martin. Rather curiously he was in 1743 appointed 'Chapel Keeper of His Majesties Chapel at Whitehall' following the death of John Richardson. John Williams was appointed to fill the vacant bellringer's office in 1743.

We know something the bellringer's specific duties from William Lovegrove's account, written between 1752 and 1777.[4] They were 'to attend at the Chapel every stated Hour of Prayer, at present, Eight of the Clock in the Morning, Eleven, and Five o'clock of the Day. To go round a certain part of the palace with his stand bell, to give notice that the time of Divine Service is approaching.' In 1894 sub-dean Edgar Sheppard noted that 'the original hand-bell is kept in the sub-dean's vestry in the Chapel Royal',[5] although there is no sign of it today.

In the nineteenth century the office of bellringer was reduced to a sinecure. Frederick Lingard was the last person to hold the office, having been appointed in 1858.

Lutenists and violists

A *nota bene* in the Old Cheque Book dated 8 August 1715 tells us that 'there were added in King George's establishment ... A Lutenist, which place Mr John Shore was sworn and admitted into. A Violist, which place Mr Francisco Goodsens was sworn and admitted into ... by me Dolben, Subdean'.

From a later entry we learn that Goodsens died in 1741 and was succeeded as violist by Peter Gillier. He was succeeded on 10 March 1778 by John Crossdill, who earned the same sum as Giller: £40 per annum. William Lovegrove tells us that the lutenist and violist were among those 'instrumental performers in the Organ Loft'.[6] John Crossdill held the post until his death in 1825. Born in 1751, he was a pupil at Westminster School where he struck up a life-long friendship with Lord Fitzwilliam. In 1768 he became a member of the Royal Society of Musicians, studying the cello under Pierre Dupont. He played at the Gloucester Festival in 1769, becoming principal cellist at the Concert of Antient Music in 1776. As well as being violist with the Chapel Royal, Crossdill also joined the King's Private Musick. So good was he that in 1782 he was appointed chamber musician to queen Caroline and taught the cello to the prince of Wales. The Handel Festival at Westminster Abbey in 1784 saw Crossdill as principal cellist. He married a lady of wealth in 1785 and retired to live at Titchfield, although he did come out of his seclusion to play at George IV's coronation in 1821. Dance painted a portrait of Crossdill, which in

---

[4] Lovegrove manuscript, Royal Library, Windsor Castle.
[5] Edgar Sheppard, *Memorials of St James's Palace*, vol. 2, p. 326.
[6] Lovegrove manuscript, p. 62.

profile was later engraved by Daniell.

In 1825 Crossdill was succeeded as violist by G.T. Anderson, who was paid £32 per annum as a wage.

Regarding the office of lutenist, John Shore's successor was John Inmyns in 1752. George Medley held the post for ten years from 1764 until 1774. E. Ayrton appears to have held the post, worth £41 10s, being succeeded by C. Evans in *c.* 1810.

Both these offices died out in the nineteenth century.

Organ blowers

This position was generally filled from the ranks of the dean's personal servants. We learn from the Old Cheque Book that Matthew Shelley was organ blower before 1716, and that Samuel Clay, 'a servant to the Dean', was appointed to succeed him. John Ray, appointed in 1727, held office for a very long time, and was paid the sum of £20 per annum.

An organ blower was obviously needed wherever there was an organ in use. Although this may have been one of the duties of a vestry official in late mediaeval times, it became a necessary and vital task the more the organ became accepted into the format of divine service. The office of organ blower survived until this century when the application of electricity removed his raison d'être and consequently his job. The care of our electrical organ blower motor has for years been in the capable hands of a good friend to the Chapel Royal, Vic Hobbs.

Common servant to the gentlemen

This position certainly dates back as far as 1483, for the *Liber Niger Domus Regis* mentions of the 'Clerkis of Chapell xxvi' that 'for every ii gentymen clerke in to this courte' they were entitled to 'i honest servant'. One-and-a-half centuries later the position of 'honest servant' was evidently still going strong, for the Old Cheque Book states that 'William Hewes, our common servant, being often times formerly admonyshed of his ill behavior and carriage towards his said masters and himselfe' and growing 'worse and worse in dronkennes and other disoerderly behavior',[7] was dismissed on 20 June 1625. After the Restoration we learn that George Wyatt, who in 1672 was 'admitted and entertained Common Sergeant to the Gentlemen of his Majestes Chappell Royall' (not to be confused with serjeant of the vestry), had to promise to 'bind myselfe and my heires not to embezell or pawne my Badge in the sum of forty shillings, but to leave it when I dy to the Gentlemen my masters for the use of my successor'.[8] In other words the gentlemen had a badge of office

---

[7] Old Cheque Book, fol. 22.
[8] Ibid., fol. 1.

at their disposal for their servant to wear. There is now no sign of its whereabouts.

Friends of the Chapel and daily ladies

Recently, as friends of the Chapel Royal and beyond any official duties, the making, care and repair of robes, uniforms and other sacramental items have been undertaken by Mrs James Mansel, late wife of Canon James Mansel, the previous Sub-dean and now Extra Chaplain to The Queen, Eileen Scull, in the days of the late Colin Scull who was my predecessor as serjeant of the vestry, my wife Andrea, Mary Reid and Mrs Oates.

*

Latterly 'daily ladies' have played an essential part in the smooth running of the Chapel Royal. They have usually, but not always, been wives of the vestry officials or household staff, and have had the task of maintaining the cleanliness of the Chapel Royal building as well as other sacramental and clothing items.

The major contribution of the Kollman family to the upkeep of the Queen's Chapel, Marlborough Gate, in the eighteenth and nineteenth centuries should be mentioned here.

Augustus Frederic Christopher Kollman was admitted into the 'place and office of Porter of His Majesty's Lutheran Chapel St James's' on 17 September 1782, by virtue of a warrant from the dean. He replaced John Augustus Walter, who had died in office. On 9 April 1784 he was admitted into the 'place and office of Chapel-Keeper the Lutheran Chapel at St James's' in the place of Nicholas Daniel Kannmaker, who had died in office.

According to the New Cheque Book, Augustus died on 25 May 1829, at which time he was 'organist':

> George Augustus Kollman By Virtue of a Warrant from the Right Reverend Charles James Lord Bishop of London, Dean of His Majesty's Chapels Royal, was sworn and admitted into the Place and offices of Organist, Clerk and Chapel-Keeper of His Majesty's German Lutheran Chapel St. James's in the room of Augustus Frederic Kollman Deceased this Twenty Fifth day of May, One Thousand Eight Hundred and Twenty Nine.

Sub-dean Pearce died in 1802 and records seem to have lapsed between then and 1820. It is probable therefore that Kollman's appointment as organist occurred between those dates. He is described as 'Organist of His Majesty's German Chapel at St. James's' in the title-page of his *Essay on Musical Harmony*, published in 1817.

Another member of the Kollman family, Joanna Sophia Kollman, a spinster, was appointed 'Organist, Clerk and Chapel-Keeper' at 'His Majesty's German Lutheran Chapel, St. James's' on George's death on 13 May 1845. She held the post until 1849.

William Lovegrove's account, to which later additions were made after his tenancy of the office of Serjeant of the Vestry, confirms the appointment of Augustus as 'porter' on 17 September 1782 and as 'chapel-keeper' in 1784. He makes no mention of Joanna in his own book, or rather no mention is made of her in its later entries, but there is an entry for 'Frederick Weber' as 'Organist and Chapel-Keeper' in 1849 alongside the entry '£58.10'. In the New Cheque Book it is Richard Howse, who had become serjeant of the vestry in 1816, who made the entry concerning George's appointment as 'organist' on Augustus's death in 1829, and it is Lingard, who had replaced Richard Howse as serjeant in 1840 and who also held the office of clerk of the cheque, who made the entry concerning Joanna's appointment in 1845.

The German Lutheran chapel was originally built in queen Anne's reign and occupied a site in friary court (now just a courtyard) until an arrangement was made for the German Lutherans to worship in the Queen's Chapel, Marlborough Gate, as it is called now, in 1781. The Germans used this chapel until 1902. The original 'German' chapel in friary court was destroyed in a fire in 1809. Augustus's predecessor as 'porter' therefore knew the friary court chapel as the 'German' chapel, but Augustus took office just about the time of its 'removal' to the Queen's Chapel, so the Kollman family contribution was, it seems, entirely confined to the Queen's Chapel, itself built in 1623.

25

The Royal Almonry

The Chapel Royal's association with the activities of the Royal Almonry has revolved principally around the Maundy service.

Although St Augustine talked of Maundy in AD 600, the first recorded instance of the sovereign distributing 'alms' at a Maundy service is king John's provision 'for the robing of garments of poor men, sewing of garments 2s 2d; for 13 girdles, 13 knives, 13 breeches for the same poor men; the king fed 1,000 poor men, paid £4 13s 9d for food, 9s 4d for fish', at Knaresborough near Ripon in Yorkshire in 1210. An article concerning this appeared in the *Guardian* of 2 April 1985, shortly before Royal Maundy was to be celebrated at Ripon Cathedral: 'The Mayor of Knaresborough, Councillor Arnold Kellet, who discovered this information in a pipe roll in York Minster Library and among the Rotulus Misae deposited at the John Rylands Library, suggests that King John, who had been excommunicated in the year 1209, intervened to show what a good Catholic he was!'

King John also took part in the Maundy service at Rochester in 1213, perhaps at the castle, when he is recorded as distributing thirteen pence to each of thirteen men. It is known that the priest 'Thomas the Almoner' held office from 1210-11, followed by John Braz. They would have been present at the Maundy distributions made by the king.

We know something of the almoner's duties and functions from a chronicle almost certainly written by Roger the Templar, almoner to the king, recording contemporary events from 1171-77, brief notes from 1177-80 and more detailed events from 1180-92, after which date it was revised. Roger the Templar was almoner from 1177-89. The chronicle gives fascinating details of royal itineraries and regularly mentions where the king spent Christmas, as well as recording appointments to bishoprics and abbeys closely associated with the king. Roger is evidently writing about himself when he mentions that in 1177 Henry II appointed an almoner of the royal household, chosen 'with the wise counsel of his bishops and other wise men', ordered him to hear claims and to receive one-tenth of all food and drink consumed in the royal household for distribution to the poor. Roger, who was a Knight Templar, accompanied Richard I on his third crusade to the Holy Land in 1190 and recorded fascinating details of this campaign, which are also to be found in this chronicle.

25. The Royal Almonry

During the mediaeval period the almoner was almost always chosen from among the king's chaplains – affording another link with the Chapel Royal. During the thirteenth century there were sometimes two, or even three, almoners to the king holding office at the same time. For example, the Calendar of Patent Rolls for the years 1232-47 mentions John de Leuekenor and Roger de Cramfeld as almoners at the same time. One of them, probably Roger de Cramfeld, would have acted as sub-almoner.

The perquisites associated with holding office as king's almoner in the thirteenth century show that it was a major office within the royal household. Roger de Cramfeld held the 'Keepeing of the King's Hospitals' as 'King's Almoner', and an entry in the Patent Rolls dated 1253 states that 'whereas Master William de Kilkeny, Archdeacon of Coventry, at the King's great and constant instance, has undertaken the keeping of the King's hospitals which Roger, sometime the King's Almoner, had from the King, the King wills that the said William and his heirs, and the executors of his will be quit of all account and reckoning for the whole time that he shall hold the said keeping'. The 'hospitals' concerned would have included that at St James's. An order for 'simple protection until Easter' in the year 1265 includes 'the Master, brethren and sisters of the hospital of St James by Westminster', appears in a Patent Roll of 1265 and is signed by Robert de London. Also concerning the almoner in 1253 is a 'charter granting to him that he and the ministers of his household may, whenever he will, hunt with his own dogs the hare, fox, badger, and cat through all the forests of England and dig after them and take them ...'. King's almoners might also hope for further office: Edward I's almoner, Henry de Bluntesdon, described in a Patent Roll as 'King's Chaplain and Almoner', was granted the archdeaconry of Dorset on 9 June 1297, a post he retained until 1316.

While there were undoubtedly substantial perquisites, there was also hard work attached to the office of king's almoner. We learn from the anonymous author of *Fleta*,[1] in the reign of Edward I, and certainly talking of Henry de Bluntesdon, that:

The High Almoner has to collect the fragments from the Royal Table, and distribute them daily to the poor, to visit the sick, poor widows, prisoners, and other persons in distress; he reminded the King about the bestowal of his Alms, especially on Saints' Days, and was careful that the cast off robes, which were often of high price, should not be bestowed on players, minstrels or flatterers, but their value given to increase the King's Charity.[2]

Henry de Bluntesdon's successor, John de Leek, who was 'King's Clerk and Almoner' from 1306-12, found himself in 1309 acting as 'king's

[1] *Fleta*, edited with translation by H.B. Richardson and G.O. Sayles (Selden Society, London, 1955-), vol. 2, ch. 23.
[2] See *The Royal Maundy* (Buckingham Palace, 1946), p. 23.

proctor to receive the bookes, vestments, vases and other ornaments of the Chapel of St Matthew, late Bishop of Dunkeld, which by Scottish custom are the king's by reason of the bishop's death'.[3] Some idea of the great importance of the office of king's almoner in the fourteenth century can be had from the orders received by Bernard de Kirkeby, vicar of the church of Norton in Durham. He, 'King's Almoner, has by special command remained by the King's side from 3rd April in the fifth year to 25th September in the present year of his reign', and this order is dated 1313.

A century later little had changed but for one significant development: Henry IV ordered that the number of recipients at Maundy should correspond to the monarch's age in years. The almoner's prerogative had apparently been allowed to slip a little. This was quickly rectified by the king on 24 May 1421, through the appointment of 'King's Clerk, John Snell, the King's Almoner, to collect by himself and his deputies from time to time all deodands by land and sea within the realm due to the King from the day of the Coronation and expend them on the maintenance of the King's Alms; as such deodands pertain to the almoner of the household for this purpose, and for lack of such collection may have been taken by many people to their own use'.[4] John Snell was duly rewarded by the king a year later on 16 March 1422 for accomplishing this task with the grant 'of the Archdeaconry of London in the Cathedral Church of St Paul, London, in the King's gift by reason of the temporalities of the bishopric being in his hand'.[5]

John Snell's predecessor, Stephen Payne, king's almoner from 1414 until May 1419, and dean of Exeter from 1415-19, has been credited by some sources with the adoption of a ship as the badge of office of the Royal Almonry. This is based on the fact that his seal depicts the almoner standing under a canopy but holding in his arms an enormous wooden model of a ship on wheels, with a high 'castle' at the bow and stern. Indeed an alms box in the form of a ship on wheels that could be towed around has been known, but there is a much more plausible and better documented reason for the adoption of a ship by the Royal Almonry. It lies with Thomas Wolsey.

Wolsey, as king's almoner between 1509 and 1514, or 'high almoner' as the post had been known since 1476, had built a great three-masted ship which was launched in the year 1512. He subsequently presented this splendid ship to Henry VIII, and also had it represented on the seal he used for documents connected with arrangements for Royal Maundy. This three-masted ship has remained the official emblem of the Royal Almonry ever since. Indeed since 1976 the present lord high almoner has worn a medallion of it around his neck at the Royal Maundy service.

[3] Cal. Pat. Rolls (1307-13), 1309, p. 203.
[4] Cal. Pat. Rolls (1416-22), 1421, p. 363.
[5] Cal. Pat. Rolls (1422-29), 1422, p. 414.

25. The Royal Almonry

The close association of the Royal Almonry with the Chapel Royal in the sixteenth century is revealed in a manuscript in the College of Arms, evidently referring to Henry VIII, in which is detailed the 'Ordre of the Kinge goinge to the Chapell on Shere Thursday and from thens into the Hall to the Maundy'. This order instructs 'at suyche oure as shall please His Grace to appoynt at afternone a bisshopp and the deane of the Chapell to be their redy revested to wayte upon the Kynge with all the Clergy of the Chapell in their surplusses wayting in Lyckewyse'. The herald who compiled this account noted that the king went

> strayte to the hye Aulter the Chapell[ain] begynyng suyce [service] thereto belonging the Kynge and the Bysshopp and the dean to washe the Aulter and that don the Chapell[ain] the Bysshopp and the Dean to passe through ... into the Body of the Chapell the Bysshopp and these to the Aulters as before said. And this don to passe forth to the Kinge Closset and to wash the Aulter there in lycke man and from there to the Queenes Closset as before is said.

This is a most interesting passage, not least in that it provides unique details of the existence of a series of altars in the main body of the Chapel Royal building at Whitehall Palace, as well as noting the existence of the altars in the royal closets there too.

Having done this the chaplain, bishops and dean of the Chapel Royal processed in front of the king 'in to the Hal and then the King shall pause a little there'. After this the king 'goe in the Wardrop of his Robes to put on the gowne which he shall geve to some one of the pore men ... and then to retorne into the Hall ageyne and then the Chapell[ain] to begyn suyce [service] accustomed'. At this point the 'towel and the apron' were brought to the king by the 'Kynge Almoner', and the lord chamberlain or vice-chamberlain put the towel on his head so that it draped over his shoulders, and the apron around his waist. Lords and nobles then, similarly attired, went to the 'lower end of the Hall' to receive from 'officers of the Eurey and of the Amory [Almonry] basons of silver with water in them to bring to the Kynge to wasshe the pore menes fete ...'. The 'Kynge Almoner' first washed the men's feet followed by the king. The king then distributed a 'gowne and hod' to a poor man and the nobles and lords did the same. The poor men received a pair of shoes, a 'case of brede and messe of fyshe', a 'cup of wyne', a 'towel and apron', and then the treasurer of the king's chamber brought 'to the Kyng for eny pore men an halfpenny purse and as many pens [pence] in it as there be poore men in nombre'. The king then returned to his wardrobe, delivered his gown to the almoner who carried it out in front of the king again to the hall where the king gave it to a poor man. 'This done the Chapell shall begyne ageyne suyce accostomed and that done the kyng shall go to his Closset the Bisshop and Deane with all them of the Chapell and begyn suyce there. And that don the Kyng to retorne to his chamber.'

377

It is interesting that the Tudor queens consort also gave their own Maundy. Thus, in the course of his deteriorating relationship with his wife Katherine of Aragon, in 1525 Henry VIII forbade her to 'keep her Maundy'. She nevertheless defiantly declared her intention in 1536 of doing so 'in spite of the king's order last year to the contrary'. Henry could only reply with consent but qualified it by stating that 'the King is content if she does not keep it as Queen; if so she and others would be guilty of treason'. It is unlikely, though, that 'others' would have included any members of the Chapel Royal. It was quite usual at this time for nobles other than royal personages to give Maundy doles. Wolsey and the earl of Northumberland were examples. It would be interesting to know if Wolsey still retained the ship emblem in connection with his own personal Maundy doles, such as that at Peterborough Cathedral, after he was succeeded as high almoner by Richard Rawlins in 1514.

That the Chapel Royal continued to play a vital role in the Maundy distribution is seen in a contemporary account of Elizabeth I's distribution at Maundy in Greenwich Palace great hall on 19 March 1572 which mentions the role of the 'chappelan' and 'some singing and prayers made'. This was the occasion on which the queen is recorded as following Edward IV's fairer practice by redeeming her gown for red leather purses each containing 20 shillings and distributed to the Maundy recipients. This redemption money still forms part of the total received today by Maundy recipients. A stunningly detailed miniature painting by Lavina Teerlinc depicting Elizabeth I with her principal lady-in-waiting, Blanche Parry, at the Maundy distribution of 1565, also clearly shows the priests, gentlemen, officers and children of the Chapel Royal behind the 'stool and cushion of estate'. Over a hundred people are clearly depicted in a painting measuring 2¾ × 2¼ inches (see p. 322 above).

Were any Royalist members of the Chapel Royal present at York Minster in 1639 when the king did not fail to 'keep his Maundy', while heading for Scotland? The king's almoner, Doctor Curle, bishop of Winchester, was certainly 'in the Minster' on 11 April, for he gave the gifts to thirty-nine poor men 'for' the king. Later, in 1642, Christopher Hildyard noted that 'this year His Majesty kept his Maundy in the Minster upon the Seventh of April'.

At the Restoration Charles II restored the Maundy service to its full glory, but although the service on 16 April 1685 is described in the Whitehall Chapel Royal Register as 'the Service of the Church of England usuall on that occasion', 'his Majesty being present all the time', this was the last year in which the sovereign actually washed the feet in person. However, this fact can be used to date an entry in the Old Cheque Book, which contains a complete list (except for the years of unrest and Civil War from 1631 to 1659, which are simply not mentioned), of 'Certayne benevolence yearelye from the Lord Almoner to the Gentlemen of the Chappell on Maundy Thursdaye' from 1580-1715, including also benevolences to the serjeant of the vestry and the children of the Chapel Royal, and 'the Order of the Maundy'. As this 'order' states that 'His Majestie (attended by the Lord Almoner and the white staves) goes to the poore men in order, sprinkles their feet of hyssop dipt in water, wipes them and kisses them', it can be assumed that it pre-dates 1685 and post-dates 1603. It details the role of the Chapel Royal in the seventeenth century very clearly: 'The Sub-Dean begins the Exhortation, Confession, and Proper Psalm for the occasion, Psal. 41'. After the lesson from St John 13:1-18, the king performs the washing of the feet described above. Then the Chapel Royal sing the first anthem, 'Hide not Thy face from us O Lord etc.'. Shoes and stockings are then distributed by the king. Then the second anthem is sung, 'Prevent us, O Lord, in all our doings etc.', after which the king distributes the 'cloaths woolen and linen'. The Chapel Royal then sing the third anthem, 'Call to remembrance, O Lord, thy tender mercyes', after which the king distributes the purses. The fourth anthem is then sung, 'O praise the Lord all ye Heathen etc.', after which the king distributes the fish and bread. The gospel from St Matthew 25:14—end is then read, after which the last anthem is sung. After this follow the prayers and then a blessing, rounded off by the 'Lord Almoner' calling for wine to drink 'to all the poore the King's health'.

The gentlemen were customary recipients of certain hospitalities bestowed by high officials: namely the dean of the Chapel Royal upon appointment, the lord high almoner every Maundy Thursday and New Year's day, and the lord high treasurer at the New Year, as follows:

The Lord High Treasurer of England gives to the Gentlemen of the Chappell for their New Year's Gift forty shillings.

The Right Reverend the Deane of his Maj. Chappell for the time being gives to the Gentlemen of the Chappell for their New Year's Gift forty shillings.

The Right Reverend Father in God Dr Henry Compton, Lord Bishopp of Oxford and Deane of his Maj. Chappell Royall, gave to the Gentlemen of his Maj. Chappell (at his coming in to be their Deane) a buck and ten pounds in gold to drinke his Lordship's health, which was accordingly done at Windsor the 16th day of August 1675.

The Lord Allmoner for the time being giveth to the Gentlemen of the Chappell every Maundy Thursday twenty shillings, and five shillings every New Year's Day.

The Right Reverend Father in God Doctor John Robinson, Lord Bishop of London and Dean of his Majesties Chappell Royall, gave to the Gentlemen of his Majesties Chappell ten guineas to drink his Lordship's health, and (buck venison being out of season,) his Lordship was pleased to give a guinea to buy venison, which was accordingly done; and as many Gentlemen as wear in toun mett and din'd at the Bell Tavern in Westminster the 22d day of October 1719.

The Right Revd. Father in God Dr. Wm. Talbot, Lord Bishop of Sarum, upon his being made Dean of his Majesties Chappells Royall, gave a buck

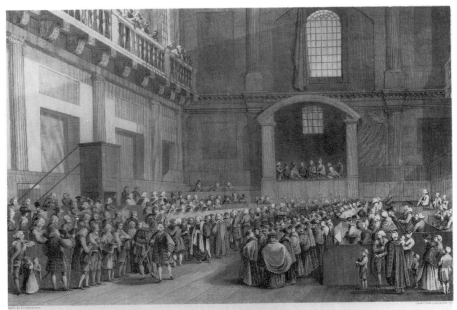

THE DISTRIBUTION OF HIS MAJESTY'S MAUNDY, BY THE SUB-ALMONER in the Chapel Royal at WHITEHALL.

From the Original Drawing, in the Possession of the Rev'd Dr RICHARD KAYE, F.R.S. Sub Almoner to his MAJESTY, and Trustee of the British Museum &c.

This engraving by James Basire of S.H. Grimm's drawing of 1773 depicts the Maundy distribution by the sub-almoner in the Chapel Royal, Banqueting House, Whitehall. This is the only known depiction of serjeant William Lovegrove, carrying the serjeant Smith virge (still used today). He displays a rather fine long wig, and wears a virger's gown slung from the shoulders. He is leading the procession, together with, on his left, a yeoman of the guard bearing a partizan. The subscription reads: 'The distribution of His Majesty's Maundy, by the Sub-Almoner in the Chapel Royal at Whitehall. From the original drawing, in the possession of the Revd. Dr. Richard Kaye FRS, Sub-Almoner to His Majesty, and Trustee of the British Museum.' Kaye, sub-almoner 1773-84, gave a quantity of Maundy money to his friend Captain James Cook, who set off on a voyage of discovery in 1776 to find the North-West Passage. Cook named 'Kaye Island' (now Kayak Island) on the Alaskan coast after the sub-almoner, and arranged for a bottle of Maundy money to be buried there on his discovery of it in 1778 and also for another bottle containing Maundy money to be buried at the north-east end of Cook Inlet. (Reproduced by courtesy of the Guildhall Library, City of London)

and tenn guineys to the Gentlemen of the said Chappell to drink his Lordship's health, which was accordingly done at the Rummer at Chearing Cross, the [?] day of August 1718.[6]

The period 1730-1890 saw the Royal Maundy service celebrated mostly at Inigo Jones's Banqueting House which was converted for the use of the Chapel Royal after the Whitehall Palace fire of 1698 had largely

[6] Old Cheque Book, fol. 74.

380

The Chapel Royal choir before the Royal Maundy service at Selby Abbey, April 1969, led by William Buckle, serjeant of the vestry.

destroyed the Chapel Royal building within Whitehall Palace. There are three particularly famous drawings of 'The Distribution of His Majesty's Maundy, by the Sub-Almoner in the Chapel Royal at Whitehall' by S.H. Grimm and dated 1773, a copy of one of which hangs in the vestry corridor at St James's, while there are general accounts of the Royal Maundy service to be found in the New Cheque Book covering this period. Of particular interest, though, is William Lovegrove's account of the details of the ceremony in which he states that in his day, 1752-77, 'the Serjeant of the Vestry walks before the Sub-Almoner, whilst he distributes the shoes and stockings ... the Woolen Cloth and Linnen ... the small silver in purses' in the Royal Maundy service at Whitehall which was held in the evening at 4 p.m. He adds that 'the Serjeant ties round his waist three Ells of the Cloth allow'd him, during the ceremony'. Today the serjeant wears his gown and carries his virge and precedes the sub-almoner as formerly, but no longer wears the cloth around his waist. Now only the lord high almoner, sub-almoner, secretary and assistant secretary of the Royal Almonry wear linen towels. The towels date back to 1883 and have been used in Maundy distributions ever since. Christopher Williams, who affixes these towels, has virged The Queen on Royal Maundy for the past twenty-three of his twenty-eight years as clerk of the domestic chapel at Buckingham Palace.

On the closure of the Whitehall chapel at the Banqueting House as an ecclesiastical establishment in 1890 and its use thereafter for the Royal United Services Institute, the Royal Maundy service was transferred to Westminster Abbey, where in 1932 George V restored the ancient custom

The Tudor Great Standing, or Queen Elizabeth's Hunting Lodge as it is commonly known, at Chingford.

of the sovereign actually participating in the Maundy distribution – a practice that had lapsed since the reign of James II. Edward VIII, before his abdication in 1936, also distributed the Maundy gifts in person. George VI continued the practice even during wartime in the years 1940, 1945, 1946 and 1948. The years 1911 and 1937 saw Royal Maundy held at St Paul's Cathedral rather than Westminster Abbey, because of the coronation preparations. This was again the case in 1953 as preparations were made for the coronation of Elizabeth II. The present reign has seen the Royal Maundy service take on a new lease of life as one element of The Queen's natural gift for taking the monarchy to her subjects. The venues for the service have included St Paul's Cathedral, Southwark, St Albans, Windsor, Rochester, Chelmsford, Canterbury, Durham, Selby, Tewkesbury, York, Salisbury, Peterborough, Hereford, Carlisle, Winchester, Worcester, St David's, Exeter, Southwell, Ripon, Chichester, Ely, Lichfield, Birmingham and Newcastle.

The Royal Maundy dish of the Chapel Royal, together with a 'fish dish' depicting either seawater or freshwater fish depending upon whether the venue is near the coast or inland, at other times displayed in the Tower of London, are used to convey the purses for distribution at the service itself. They are carried by the great friends and neighbours of the Chapel Royal, The Queen's Bodyguard of the Yeomen of the Guard. Two of the two dozen or so yeomen selected to accompany the sovereign at

382

Maundy carry the two dishes on their heads. The Chapel Royal, as we have seen, has been accustomed to accompany the sovereign for nine hundred years. Since the foundation of the king's bodyguard of the yeomen of the guard upon Henry VII's victory over Richard III in 1485 at Bosworth Field, the Chapel Royal and bodyguard have accompanied the sovereign on battlefield and within these shores – the one to assure the sovereign's spiritual safety, and the other the sovereign's physical safety.

Our picture of Maundy would be incomplete without mention of the Chapel feast. This feast, for which the food was supplied upon the direct and personal instruction of the sovereign, has ancient origins. While medieval Patent Rolls record these provisions, the Old Cheque Book contains information as to which royal forests provided the three bucks decreed necessary for the feast.

Elizabeth I ordered Sir Thomas Heneage to see to it that the three bucks be shot 'within Chynkeford Walke, within our Forreste of Waltham, in our Countye of Essex ... 2 Buckes Henald Chappell; 1 Bucke, Enfield Chase'.[7] Elizabeth's 'Great Standing' (i.e. 'Grand-Stand') as it was known in the sixteenth century, now better known as Queen Elizabeth's Hunting Lodge, still exists at Chingford. It originally had an 'open' top storey from which the hunt on the grounds below bordering on Epping Forest could be seen. It was from this Great Standing that the shooting of bucks for the Chapel Royal's feast would have been viewed.

Charles I ordered the 'Ranger, Keeper or Underkeeper of our Chase at Enfield' to provide 'one Fatt buck of this season' and the 'Keeper and Underkeeper of our Parke of Mariebone' to provide 'two fatt buckes of this season' for the Chapel feast in 1626.

The sovereign provided bucks from the royal estates until 1690, when William and Mary decided to grant a sum of money in lieu of the bucks, together with the following perquisites:

At the Salsary fine flower 1bs 1d. At the Poultry butter 36pd.
Pant Cheat fine 2doz. Coarse 2 doz.
Buttry Beer 1hhd. At the Cellar Clarrett 2gs 2ps.
At the Larder a sir loyne of beef 46pd.[8]

By 1793 the perquisites had been replaced by the following allowances:

£21 from the Board of Green Cloth in lieu of Bread, Beer and Wine.
£20 from the Lord Chamberlain's Office in lieu of two Bucks.
10s 6d from the Pantry in lieu of Flour.

However, 36 lb of butter, 50 lb of beef, and one pitcher of wine for each feast were still forthcoming. In 1814 these latter items were replaced by a

[7] Ibid., fol. 85.
[8] Ibid., fol. 84b.

monetary allowance, the board of green cloth agreeing to pay an extra £9
to increase its contribution to £30. At this time it was usual for the
numbers attending the feast to number one hundred, including the
members of the lord steward's and lord chamberlain's offices, as well as
members of the board of green cloth. But the feast received a blow in 1828
when the lord chamberlain's office withdrew its grant in lieu of bucks and
thereafter the feast was scaled down despite the valued support of the
lord steward.

The Crown and Anchor tavern was the regular venue for the feast, and
the tavern bills from 1818-33 still survive tucked into a manuscript
passed on by tradition to successive senior gentlemen of the Chapel Royal
but held at the Chapel Royal, entitled 'Papers Relating to the Ancient
Maundy Feast of the Gentlemen and Priests' covering the years
1879-1971. Also extant and passed on in the same manner are two other
manuscripts entitled 'List of Stewards for the Chapel Royal Feast, with
the dates of Admission into the Chapel – the year wherein each Steward
served the office last – and the order of those who have not served a
second time – allowing for vacancies', and 'Stewards for his Majesty's
Venison-Feast beginning with the year 1792. General Account – 1807'.
This latter manuscript lists the entire range of food and drink consumed
at the Crown and Anchor – a list of awesome proportions and variety.

Although the Chapel feast no longer takes place, the Maundy feast,
which is thirteenth-century in origin, is still held. The two feasts shared
these toasts:

Church & King
The Queen, Prince of Wales & Royal Family.
The Bishop of London
The Lord Steward of the Household
The Lord Chamberlain
The Pay Master of the Household
The Sub-Dean & Absent Brethren

The following were 'added at the venison feast':

The Choirs of St Paul's & Westminster
The Steward Elect
The Present Stewards & Thanks

The smaller Maundy feast, now held in July, was usually held on the
Thursday in Easter week. The following allowances for this feast were
forthcoming in the eighteenth century:

From the bishop of London   £1 18s
From the lord chamberlain   £1 00

Maundy fees   £1 2s

8 bottles of claret from his majesty's wine cellar

8 loaves and 12 manchets (in latter years 16 rolls of bread)

5s allowed to the person detailed to carry the bread and wine from 'St James's to the Tavern'.

Nowadays the Maundy feast is held at a venue near St James's, and the senior gentleman acts as steward.

26

The Chapel Royal Today

Upon approaching what is now the front door of the Chapel Royal across ambassadors' court, St James's Palace, one can see on the left of the door, mounted on the wall, a notice stating that Charles I took his last communion in this Chapel on the morning of his execution at Whitehall on 30 January 1649. He slept apparently in what was the marshalmen's room, now the practice room for the children of the Chapel Royal, and the marshalmen's brass plate is still to be seen fastened to the front of the door at the foot of the staircase although now, sadly, it is barely legible. It was down this staircase that Charles descended to take his last communion.

Today the martyrdom of Charles I is still commemorated by the Chapel Royal in a unique way. Apart from the missal containing the special rubric for the day, the altar with red frontal is adorned with the two cherub alms dishes commissioned by his son Charles II, while the altar candlesticks used are those commissioned by his other son, James II, whose royal ducal coronet as duke of York is to be found upon one side of the triangular legs.

In reality just an ordinary silver-gilt drinking cup, the 'chalice' from which Charles I received his last communion stands 7½ inches high, bears the London marks of 1629-30, and displays an inscription in contemporary lettering: 'King Charles the First: received the Communion in this Boule: on Tuesday the 30th of January 1649 being the day on which he was Murthered.'

According to the memoirs of Sir Thomas Herbert, Thomas Juxon, bishop of London, who administered this last communion, at the time 'had his Lodging in Sir Henry Henn's house, near St James's Gate'. The arms of Sir Henry Henn (1st baronet of Winkfield, Berkshire, who died in 1668) are engraved on the chalice, with his initials and those of his wife under the foot, so it is clear that Juxon borrowed Sir Henry's cup for this last administration and then returned it to him. Sometime before 1744 it came into the possession of the duke of Portland, and as late as the Second World War was seen by prebendary R.J.C. Lumley of Lichfield at Welbeck Abbey when he was chaplain at nearby Worksop College from 1941-45, to whom I am indebted for the knowledge of the chalice and its whereabouts.

Inside the vestibule or ante-chapel to the right is a frame containing six mediaeval slip-tiles. Unearthed in 1925 under colour court, these variously patterned tiles are almost certainly from the convent chapel that preceded the sixteenth-century Henrician palace occupied by the duke of Richmond, as the tiles were found 'inside' and within foundations that were evidently the north wall of the covent chapel. Burials were unearthed there too.

On the opposite wall of the vestibule, there is a memorial to the old boys of the Chapel Royal who gave their lives in the Great War of 1914-18. It is a marble gilded tablet with a gold cross on the left, under which is the inscription 'O.C.R.B. Requiescant in Pace'. The rest of the tablet reads thus: 'To the Glory of God and in Faithful and Devoted Memory of the Following who Were formerly Children of His Majesty's Chapel Royal Who Gave Their Lives in The Great War 1914-18: A.E. Butler, F.L. Carter, W.B. Manson, S.G. Mayor, W.E. Osborne, F. Pownall, S.C. Sanderson, R.P.E. Shaughnessy, A. Thorogood, W.I. Wright, W.G. Physick.' Perhaps I will be forgiven for taking just one to speak for them all. W.B. Manson, a great friend of Thomas Armstrong (now Sir Thomas) in the Chapel Royal, although he was two years senior to Thomas, was set for a very promising career as a gifted composer. But it was not to be, for he was killed along with so many other thousands of young soldiers in July 1916 on the first day of the Battle of the Somme.

A little further along that wall in the vestibule is a board displaying the names of organists, musicians and composers of the Chapel Royal picked from a 'short list' of 113 names, dating back to 1444. Among them are names we have come across in our story: Tallis, Byrd, Gibbons, Blow, Purcell, Greene, Boyce and Handel, to name but a few.

Opposite the king William door to the Chapel are two plaques displaying the names of all the sub-deans of the Chapel Royal since the establishment of the royal free chapel of the household in 1483.

Near the end of the vestibule and standing in a clasp attached to the high cupboard is the fine silver and crystal-glass processional cross, used for all major services and the cenotaph, made by The Queen's Silversmith, Leslie Durbin, in 1971.[1] Also Leslie Durbin's work is the silver-gilt altar cross given in 1972 to mark the silver wedding of The Queen and the Duke of Edinburgh. The credence table, given in 1973 by the honorary treasurer of the Chapel Royal, Malcolm McQueen, as a memorial to his mother, was made of walnut by Edward Barnsley.

The present altar was bought towards the end of the Second World War at the request of the then Queen by sub-dean W.H. Elliott as an

---

[1] He also made the sacramental vessels given by my father as a memorial to my grandparents at St George's Church, Beckenham.

387

Children of the Chapel Royal leaving Buckingham Palace in 1936. *Far row:* (M.C. Symons), (P.M. Blake), E.C. Wyncoll, (G. Wise), J. Beadle. *Near row:* K. Ffitch, (P.J. Windibank), A.I. Wolfenden, A.J. Robinson, D.I.B. Wheeler.

immediate replacement for the one destroyed by the Pall Mall bomb which fell at half past ten one night, destroying the original altar. The bomb hit a passing car, killing its occupants and leaving a huge crater. Guard and wardens were all killed. Sub-dean Elliott recalled that 'a phone call from the Serjeant of the Chapel brought me to the Chapel early next morning'. The bomb had burst the water mains, and sub-dean Elliott observed of the Chapel: 'It was a pitiful sight to see it. Floods of water had soaked everything. The east window was blown clean out. The Altar was smashed, with other things in the Sanctuary. The panelling was pitted everywhere with tiny spikes of glass.' The sub-dean telephoned Buckingham Palace and asked the Queen to come and advise him as to what should be done: 'Very quickly she came, and together we surveyed the damage. She agreed that a new English altar must be put up and as soon as possible.' Sub-dean Elliott therefore 'bought an altar with beautiful riddle posts outright'. It is this altar which stands in the sanctuary today.

Following this bombing sub-dean Elliott was allowed to requisition at once all the blue brocade he could 'at a certain very well-known shop near Langham Place'. He was also given the option on some gold material. He

W. FOLLAND   J. BEADLE   M.C. SYMONS   D.L.B WHEELER   BRADBRIDGE WHITE, Esq.   GRAHAM SMART, Esq   G. WISE   A.J. ROBINSON   R.B. WHITTINGTON

HATHERLEY CLARKE, Esq.   MARTIN BODDEY, Esq   PREBENDARY L J PERCIVAL, K.C.V.O.   BERTRAM MILLS, Esq.   CHARLES HAWKINS, Esq

P. M. BLAKE   P. J. WINDIBANK   K. J. SHEEDY   D.A. DANIELLI

The Chapel Royal in 1937.

arranged to place the two materials side by side in the sanctuary so that the Queen could decide which colour she wished. She came 'almost at once' and chose the blue. The sub-dean knew that to effect the necessary repairs quickly would be impossible if the usual official channels had to be approached. The Chapel would have to be closed in the meantime. After a word with the Queen the problem was quickly solved: 'Get it done, Mr Elliott' was her reply. This by-passed the maze of administrative problems that would have undoubtedly arisen. On seeing the completed works the sub-dean expressed his concern at the cost. The Queen asked to see the bill, smiled reassuringly and said, 'Give it to me, Mr Elliott, I will see that it is paid.' Sub-dean Elliott was convinced that but for the Queen's 'constant kindness nothing else could have happened but the closing of the Chapel, and that might have been for ever'.[2]

Returning to our look at the Chapel Royal, a glance at the gallery to the right of the altar, known as the 'strangers' gallery', holds another reminder of the Second World War. The domestic chapel at Buckingham Palace had been gutted in the bombing of 1940. The Queen's Chapel,

[2] Wallace Elliott, *Undiscovered Ends* (Peter Davies, London, 1951), p. 225.

Edgar Stanley Roper, master of the children of the Chapel Royal 1923-53. (HM Chapel Royal, reproduced by gracious permission of Her Majesty The Queen)

Marlborough Gate, had been so severely damaged that the cracked roof had to be held together with steel rods – and nobody was allowed to enter it. And so only the small chapel within St James's Palace was left in which to worship. The official uniformed choir of the Chapel Royal was disbanded in 1939, but despite this, divine service was conducted at the chapel without a break throughout the war. This was due in major part to Stanley Roper, the organist, who quickly gathered together around him an adult choir of volunteers. Sub-dean Elliott recalled that one was 'a well-known general from the War Office' who normally brought a friend with him. There was also 'a doctor (of Law), rarely absent – now long dead'. Apart from these there was 'a small but valiant band of ladies, who were resolved, Sunday by Sunday, to go through hell and high water (and sometimes it was that!) to keep those Services going'.[3] Sub-dean Elliott also recalled that 'high up in the Strangers' Gallery they sat together'. As the war drew to its close the small voluntary choir increased in numbers and 'they came downstairs'. Their singing reached such a point of excellence that a deputy priest in ordinary (and minor canon at Westminster) on duty at the Chapel Royal on Easter day commented at the end of the choral eucharist that 'the Abbey couldn't have done that'.

[3] Ibid., pp. 222-3.

Back Row.
C.Whitehead, J.Hatherley Clarke.Esq., Rev.W.H.Elliott(Sub.Dean), C.Hawkins.Esq., G.Armitage..Esq., C.Knight.Esq., R.Wellington.Esq.(A Henderson.Esq) absent
Front Row.
R.Johnson, K.Kilburn, P.Goldspink, R.Leeder, J.Wickens, J.Stenner, J.Bennett, J.Waddell, C.Weir, C.Beckett.

The Chapel Royal, February 1947

Sub-dean Elliott in fact petitioned for a signed appreciation of their services to the Chapel Royal through wartime, but it was 'deferred until the end of the war'. By that time it was too late. Writing in 1951, Elliott observed that 'they are dispersed, and some of them are dead'. He went on to observe that 'congregations in those days actually were small, but the Chapel Royal has always had a small but most devoted band of adherents and worshippers, who, even when things were at their very worst, still kept their ancient places'.[4]

A long lull in the bombing prompted Elliott to petition for the restoration of the uniformed Chapel Royal. Some 'excellent boys whose voices were good enough' were found 'mostly from North London' and they attended practices for an entire year without having the opportunity to sing at the services in the Chapel Royal. This, it seems, was partly because of the excellence of the wartime voluntary adult choir. The boys finally made an appearance in the Chapel Royal on Low Sunday complete with their state coats and breeches of scarlet, gold and black. Initially only a nominal quarterly wage could be paid. The dean (who later became

[4] Ibid., p. 223.

archbishop of Canterbury) backed the revival, and as Elliott recalled, 'we got it settled fairly easily in the Lord Chamberlain's Office'.

There was, however, a principle at stake too. There had been grave doubts about restoring the Chapel Royal after the First World War. George V in fact appointed a Royal Commission under archbishop Randall Davidson with the brief to decide whether or not the choral establishment should be abandoned. After long deliberation the Commission eventually decided that the choir should be restored. Sub-dean Elliott predicted a similar doubt would arise as the Second World War drew to an end. It was for this reason that 'with the strictest economy, I got a choir back into the chapel before the war ended … But for that move I assert unhesitatingly – in the light of what happened afterwards – that there would be no choir at all in the Chapel Royal today. Perhaps not even a Chapel Royal.' Although this comment seems to display a confusion between building and choral establishment, unless he meant that only the clergy of the Chapel Royal would be left, Elliott corrects any such confusion later by reasserting that 'the Chapel Royal is not a building at all, but a body of singers and musicians, who accompanied the king wherever he went'. He should, though, have added singing clerks in holy orders. It was in this context that George IV had the Chapel Royal with him at Brighton. Today we are reminded of the connection with Brighton by the use of the two 'credence stands' from the Chapel Royal premises at Brighton which are now used by the sovereign's representatives to carry The Queen's Gifts of gold sovereigns, frankincense and myrrh to the altar on the occasion of the feast of the Epiphany on 6 January every year.

Much has been said already of the spectacular service at Epiphany when The Queen's representatives, escorted by the yeomen of the guard in full state uniform and carrying partizans, offer the gifts described in the New Testament as having been given by the astronomers, by Old Testament prophecy kings of foreign lands, and foretold in Psalm 72 in the Old Testament as coming from 'Saba, Tharsis and The Isles'. It is interesting that the gum-resin from the *Boswellia caterii* tree (unusual in that it obtains all its nutrients from the air, and is therefore frequently found growing on solid rock), known more commonly as frankincense, still comes from Biblical Saba (i.e. modern-day Ethiopia and the Yemens). The feast of the Epiphany is described in detail, as we have seen, in Say's *Liber Regie Capelle* of 1449, from which we learn that it was one of the six feasts in the year for which 'the king is wont to wear his crown'. It was the duty of a certain baron to carry the sword in front of the king in procession, while a duke or earl carried the king's cap (birettum), with 'the king's chamberlain following behind to hold up the hem of the royal mantle'.[5]

---

[5] *Liber Regie Capelle*, ch. 9.

Until 1758 the sovereign always attended the feast in person as previously described, preceded by heralds, pursuivants and knights of the Garter, Thistle and Bath. It was the sad death of princess Caroline and her funeral on the eve of the Epiphany in 1758 which understandably led the king to depute his lord chamberlain to present his gifts. We learn from a footnote in the Cheque Book that because the monarch was not there in person the yeomen of the guard were in attendance instead of the heralds. In other words, the escort became from that date the responsibility of the lord chamberlain rather than the earl marshal.

The challenge of the spur money which occurs at the end of the service at the foot of the stairs to the royal closet has ancient origins but was by no means peculiar to the Chapel Royal. The earliest reference to the prohibition on the wearing of spurs when attending the Chapel Royal is in a tract of 1598, 'The Children of the Chapel stript and whipt', which we have already noted in Chapter 5. The author(s) of this tract offer the suggestion: 'We think it very necessarye that every quorister sholde bringe with him to Churche a Testament in Englishe, and turn to everie Chapter as it is daily read, or som other good and godly prayer booke, rather than spend their tyme in talk, and hunting after Spur Money, whereon they set their whole mindes and do often abuse dyvers if they doe not bestowe somewhat on them.' In the same year bishop Bancroft, on visiting St Paul's Cathedral, found that the choristers there spent 'their time in talk and hunting after spur money, even in service-time; the hallooing and hooting above in the steeple were intolerable at divers times'.[6] The identical phraseology in parts of these two accounts points the finger at bishop Bancroft as the author of the tract.

It is recorded that in 1851 the duke of Wellington, who was accustomed to attend the Chapel Royal on Sunday mornings, entered the Chapel with boots and spurs. The child of the Chapel Royal who first spotted him thus attired demanded the spur money for transgressing the 1622 ruling of the dean recorded in the Old Cheque Book thus: 'if anie Knight or other persone entituled to weare spurs, enter the Chappell in that guise he shall pay to the quoristers the accustomed fine, but if he command the youngest quorister to repeate his gammut, and he fails in so doing, the said Knight or other shall not pay the fine.' The duke, knowing this rule, immediately requested the youngest child to be summoned and required him to repeat the gamut. The little chap failed and the duke was therefore excused the fine. Nowadays the sum of the fine exacted from the gentlemen ushers transgressing the rule regarding the wearing of spurs is £5 if the youngest child of the Chapel Royal challenges and successfully repeats the gamut.

Returning again to the Chapel interior, opposite the strangers' gallery

---

[6] See also John S. Bumpus, *The Organists and Composers of St Paul's Cathedral* (London, 1891).

This Thomas Elliott organ stood in the Chapel Royal, St James's Palace, from 1819-37. It was removed from there via Milverton and shortly afterwards placed almost unaltered in St Margaret's Church, Crick, Northants in 1841. (This photograph was taken by the sub-dean of the Chapel Royal in 1985)

on the west side is sited the organ loft or gallery. Originally this gallery was positioned along the same wall but above the sanctuary. My present living room incorporates the two arches by which this gallery was entered, while the room itself seems to have been at one time the organ pipe-room. Organs sited here have included one built by Christopher Schrider in 1710 together with Father Smith. Schrider was organ-maker to George II. This organ was altered in 1785 at Dupuis's request and the pitch was lowered half a note because 'it used to strain the voices'. A 'double gamut' was added. These alterations cost £100. More alterations were made in 1802 while the choral services were discontinued from 8 August until 19 December. Again the alterations cost £100. The Schrider organ was finally removed in 1819 and bought for the episcopal chapel in Long Acre for £200. It remained there until 1866, when it was removed to the chapel of the Mercers' Hall. Thomas Elliott built the organ for the Chapel Royal at St James's which replaced the Schrider organ in 1819. The Elliott organ was itself removed in 1838 to Milverton and then to Crick, where it still remains. It was replaced at the Chapel Royal by a Hill & Davidson organ in 1838, but before its installation in 1838 the organ gallery was moved from its position over the sanctuary to its present position half way along the west wall. This organ did not prove satisfactory and was sent to Barrow-in-Furness in 1868, being replaced by another Hill & Davidson organ. This organ was improved by the incorporation of further stops from the organ made redundant at the Whitehall (Banqueting House) chapel in 1890 upon the latter's closure,

The procession of queen Victoria and prince Albert following their marriage at the Chapel Royal, through the state apartments behind the royal closet, on 10 February 1840. (Reproduced by courtesy of the Guildhall Library, City of London)

before that organ was sent to the Tower of London. Number 11 organ stop was identified as one of Father Smith's time. This improved Hill & Davidson organ remained in use until 1925 when George V gave the present organ. This is a large three-manual and pedal organ built by Hill, Norman and Beard. It was rebuilt by N.P. Mander Ltd. in 1980.

Turning back to look at the altar end of the Chapel, the 'great' window was enlarged in 1840 for the wedding of queen Victoria. Sir Robert Smirke's alterations to the Chapel Royal, costing £7,606, were completed by 1837 and it was in this restored Chapel Royal building that the queen's marriage to prince Albert took place in February 1840, for which occasion temporary galleries for spectators were erected in colour court. Total expenditure on the wedding was £5,323 5s.

In 1858 the princess royal was married in the Chapel Royal, and traced glass with a coloured border of blue and gold was inserted in that year. However, it was all blown out by the Pall Mall bomb that fell in the Second World War destroying the sanctuary of the Chapel Royal building. Such of the glass that did remain was splintered and embedded in the mahogany panels installed in 1836 by Sir Robert Smirke. The

The Chapel Royal as arranged for the marriage of the princess royal and prince Frederick of Prussia in 1858. (From the *Illustrated London News*, 23 January 1858)

The Altar as prepared for the
Marriage of T.S.H. The Prince and Princess George of Battenberg.
Wednesday, November 15th, 1916.

(Reproduced by gracious permission of Her Majesty The Queen)

previous sub-dean, Canon James Mansel, recalled this embedded glass and the beer and treacle treatment the panels received while describing to me the details of the alterations made in 1968-70 during his term of office. These later alterations included a reduction in the glass area of the 'great' window to its pre-1840 size, gilding and colouring of the Chapel, the making of colour-season sanctuary curtains, etc. In the course of these alterations a curious solid low brick arch was revealed behind the altar under the 'great' window. A similar feature occurs at Hampton Court chapel. It is in fact the barrow-way which was used to carry materials from what is now Cleveland Row into the interior of the Chapel during construction or alteration.

397

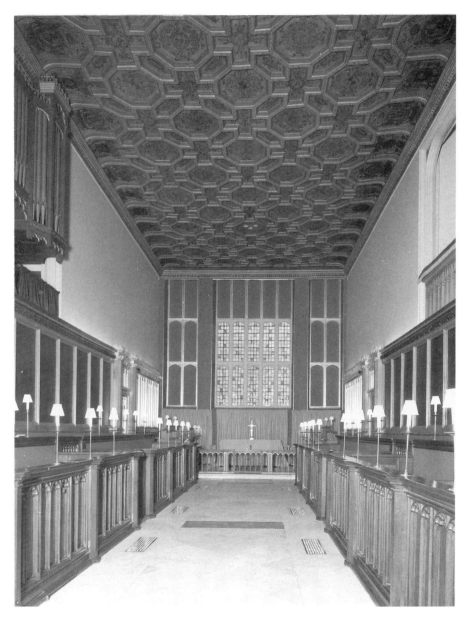

Above and right: The Chapel Royal on completion of the restoration, March 1972. (Photographed by S.W. Newbery for the Department of the Environment)

The 'barrow-way' below the altar window at the north end of the Chapel was revealed during redecoration in 1971. It would have been used to bring materials into and out of the Chapel during a period of construction or alteration.

The choir stalls were placed each side of the altar following the wedding of the duke of York (later George V) to Mary of Teck in 1893. In that year the cast-iron sanctuary rails were installed and the pulpit removed. The top step was found to be inconveniently narrow and so in 1923 the top step was removed and the altar itself thereby lowered.

Nowadays the services are regularly adorned by gifts from the royal family, members of the Chapel Royal and the congregation. These include altar frontals, copes, a fine linen altar cloth, a gilded wooden altar lectern and a silver candle-snuffer. Other 'unseen' gifts are received for use at the Chapel Royal from time to time, for which grateful thanks are recorded here.

Along the length of the Chapel are to be seen the lateral box-pews installed in 1876. Looking now at the royal closet end of the Chapel a distinct break in the ceiling painting is discernible. The 1540 'Holbein' ceiling stops at the large rib with angel supports, beyond which towards the royal closet it was continued in the same style by Sir Robert Smirke in his 1836 alterations. (Older photographs show that a pair of supporting angels existed also at the altar end of the Chapel – the destruction of which the previous treasurer of the Chapel Royal, Malcolm McQueen, remembered during the wartime bombing.) At the other end, the Smirke

The pulpit in Christ's Church, Harwood, Bolton, Lancashire, said to have been previously in the Chapel Royal, St James's Palace. Christ's Church was founded in 1840 by Robert Lomax, a cotton merchant, who collected antique furniture to embellish the church. The lettering around the base of the pulpit was added in plaster when the church was built. The Chapel Royal was enlarged and refurnished in 1837 by Sir Robert Smirke, who installed the present panelling. The pulpit of that period was removed in 1893 for the wedding of the duke of York and princess Mary of Teck (George V and queen Mary) and was not replaced afterwards. (Information and photograph kindly supplied by the Rev. Canon Arthur J. Dobbs, Vicar of Harwood, in December 1981)

ceiling displays the names and cyphers of William IV and queen Adelaide.

Sir Robert Smirke's other alterations included reducing the size of the royal closet and designing the side galleries, known as the 'peers' gallery' (west side) and 'peeresses' gallery' (east side). In the latter is a tablet fixed to the balcony structure which reads: 'Laura Seymour. Princess. Victor of Hehenlohe. From MDCCCLXII till MDCCCCXII'. It was placed there in 1919 by Lady Gleichen to commemorate the place where her mother used to sit during the services.

Below the royal closet but above the king William door are the arms of Elizabeth I, the last sovereign to adopt the Welsh 'Tudor' dragon of

PRINCESS VICTORIA WAS CONFIRMED AT THE CHAPEL ROYAL, ST. JAMES'S.

Photograph of the Chapel Royal from *V.R.I – Her Life and Empire* by the Marquess of Lorne.

Cadwallader as a supporter. These arms have survived from her day and adorn the Chapel now just as they did 400 years ago.

To the right of these arms, but somewhat hidden between the red curtains surrounding the sub-dean's stall, is to be seen the memorial plaque to sub-dean Edgar Sheppard – placed there at the express wish of the congregation in 1923. Its installation was supervised by Sir Aston Webb.

The painting in the royal closet depicts the 'Infant Christ in a Garland of Flowers'. Originally recorded by Vertue as painted by Carlo Maratta and hanging in Frederick prince of Wales's closet at Leicester House in 1750, eventually arriving at the Chapel Royal via Buckingham House (1819), and Windsor Castle (1835), this painting (no. 546) is not by Maratta, although in a 'Maratta' frame of ornately gilded wood. It has been classed as a school work by Mezzetti, and it has lately been suggested by Anthony Clark that the painter may have been Luigi Garzi.

Let us now glance briefly at the sub-dean's vestry, situated below the marshalmen's room and adjoining the sanctuary. Covered up and

HM Chapel Royal, June 1990. *Front row:* H. Leithead, A. Jayawardena, L. Robinson, Bobby Dog (*canis capellae*), A. Virr, J. Keddie, J. Rockhold. *2nd row:* N. Cooper, R. Smith, D. Baldwin, R. Popplewell, T. Prescott, sub-dean Canon Anthony Caesar, O. John, S. McGregor, priest in ordinary Rev. William Booth, Sir William Heseltine, R. Edwards. *Back row:* M. McGuire, G. Trew, L. Bruton Simmonds, G. Charlett, D. Scholes, P. Riordan, E. Cadwallader, C. Rich, R. Lewis, S. Kent. (Photograph by Mike Harvey)

therefore no longer to be seen is the original fireplace with a four-centred arch in a square head with stop-moulded jambs and spandrels carved with foliage and fleurs-de-lys. Close by are kept the manuscripts belonging to the Chapel Royal.

On Easter day and through the summer the Chapel Royal conducts divine service at the Queen's Chapel, Marlborough Gate, instead of the Chapel Royal building in colour court. This entails a procession from the vestry of the latter, through the lower corridor of the state apartments of St James's Palace, across Marlborough Road, and finally into the Queen's Chapel.

The Chapel Royal have sung in the Queen's Chapel only since 1938, at the inspiration of queen Mary. We have already touched upon its earlier history in connection with the three children who wore uniform 'like in every respect' to that worn by the children of the Chapel Royal in the seventeenth century, when the chapel was used by the queens consort to the Stuart kings.

It was William III who authorised the use of the Queen's Chapel by the Reformed denominations of the Dutch and French-speaking communities. Queen Anne later opened a German Lutheran royal chapel in a small wooden church situated in the middle of the now vanished south

The German Chapel, St James's Palace, in 1818. (Photographed from an engraving, by kind permission of the Archivist, Westminster City Libraries)

range of buildings which crossed 'friary court'. A swap of premises was arranged in 1781 when the French occupied the friary chapel and the Germans moved to the Queen's Chapel. Thereafter the Queen's Chapel was commonly called the 'German chapel'. The Germans worshipped there until 1902 when their own church was erected at Montpelier

'The Virgin and Child with SS. Joseph, John the Baptist and Catherine' by Annibale Caracci, which hangs on the altar reredos of the Queen's Chapel. If this is the same as that mentioned as no. 105 of the 1627 Gonzaga inventory then it must have had an additional border of over an inch all around added at sometime subsequent to this, for it then measured 49 x 43 inches, but now measures 50¼ x 44½ inches. (Royal Collection, reproduced by gracious permission of Her Majesty The Queen)

Square. The 'German chapel' registers were also transferred there. Meanwhile the 'French' friary chapel in friary court, or more correctly between 'paradise court' and 'great court' as they were then described on a map of the palace drawn in 1792 and still held at the John Soane Museum, was destroyed in the palace fire of 1809.

405

The Danish Lutheran community used the Queen's Chapel from 1880 until 1938 – hence the tablet on the interior of the north wall of the chapel in memory of the Danish queen Alexandra. In fact the permission granted to queen Alexandra (then princess of Wales) in 1880 by queen Victoria for the Danes to worship at the Queen's Chapel was continued by George V in 1921 at the request of the king of Denmark. This request was again approved by Edward VIII at the request of the king of Denmark, and finally in January 1937 approval was also given by queen Mary. Now that there was no longer any need to host these Danish services the king in 1938 discontinued the arrangement at the same time as arranging for the rector of St Clement Danes to host the community – a move meeting with the approval of the rector and churchwardens there.

Upon the Queen's Chapel becoming Chapel Royal premises in 1938, the altar reredos was remodelled to incorporate the painting 'The Virgin and Child with SS. Joseph, John the Baptist and Catherine' by Annibale Caracci, from Charles I's collection.

The 1760 Snetzler organ, originally at Buckingham Palace domestic chapel but given to the Lutherans by William IV in 1830, was also rebuilt in 1938. Hill, Norman and Beard had added a swell manual and pedals in

The combined choirs of Her Majesty's Chapel Royal and St Paul's Cathedral in procession at St Paul's on the occasion of the wedding of HRH The Prince of Wales and Lady Diana Spencer on 29 July 1981.

406

1862 and effected the rebuilding in 1938. Originally sited over the reredos, the organ is now sited on 'ambassadors' gallery' over the south vestry door.

The redecoration and refurnishing of the Queen's Chapel also involved the levelling of the sanctuary floor and re-arrangement of the altar rails. The sanctuary was furnished with brocaded silk and a carpet. The designs and colours of the altar furnishings and the oriental carpet in the sanctuary were selected by queen Mary with the king's approval. There was also a slight change in the position of the royal pew, with a consequent alteration of the seating and minor refashioning of the pews. The work was all completed by October 1938 and a service of dedication was held in the chapel on Sunday 30 October. A full choral evensong, to which members of the public were invited, was also held there that day.

During the Second World War the Queen's Chapel was so badly damaged that steel rods had to be used to pin the roof together. Services there were suspended. Sub-dean ('precentor') Wallace Elliott, appointed in 1941, recalled that 'there was no house for us at St James's Palace, since the house traditionally provided for the Precentor had been badly bombed and was quite out of the question'. All he could do was to put some of his furniture in there while looking for another residence (he eventually settled at Little Bookham), but another bomb fell smashing all the furniture and china in the 'precentor's' house next to the Queen's Chapel. Sub-dean Elliott did eventually occupy these quarters next to the Queen's Chapel, but writing in 1951 he had this to say: 'There is a stair, between the walls of that Chapel. I wonder if in the extensive alterations the workmen have found that secret stair. I should be interested to know.'[7]

It was queen Mary's practice to attend the 11.15 choral matins sitting in the royal closet of the Queen's Chapel above the congregation at the west end. But on Sunday, when the service was a choral eucharist, she sat in the front row of pews. She did, however, always adopt the Chapel Royal custom of following the clergy, gentlemen and children of the Chapel Royal to make her communion, often waiting until many of the congregation had taken theirs first.

Today there is one regular exception to the rule that the Queen's Chapel is only used from Easter day until the last Sunday in July, and that is to mount the carol service shortly before Christmas. Holding the service there rather than in the chapel in colour court is a recent innovation and reflects the popularity of this special service of musical delights in which it is also traditional for the lord chamberlain, a gentleman and a child of the Chapel Royal to read extracts from the Bible. Services throughout the rest of the year from October to Good Friday are held in the chapel in colour court, with the regular exceptions

[7] Elliott, *Undiscovered Ends*, p. 68.

of the Cenotaph service in Whitehall, the festival of St Cecilia at the 'musicians' church' of St Sepulchre-without-Newgate in Holborn, the Royal Maundy service, and joint evensong on occasion with the Chapel Royal Hampton Court, together with other venues by Royal Command.

The life of the Chapel Royal today is thus as vigorous as it has ever been since its inception in AD 58.

Russian Orthodox Chapels
at St James's Palace

There were two other chapels at St James's Palace, over which the Chapel Royal had no jurisdiction. These were both Russian Orthodox and located at Clarence House.

In 1866 prince Alfred, duke of Edinburgh, was granted the use of Clarence House, and in 1874 married princess Marie Alexandrovna, daughter of the Russian tsar, at St Petersburg. To minister to her needs a permanent chaplain was appointed for a short period prior to 1875 and a chapel was built before 1877 at Clarence House where she lived as duchess of Edinburgh. Then in 1879 a new Russian Orthodox chapel was completed at Clarence House. The archives of the Russian Embassy church at the PRO in Chancery Lane have been researched by protodeacon Christopher Birchall, who has discovered the following entry amongst the annual reports which the Russian Orthodox chaplain was obliged to submit to St Petersburg relating to Eugene (Evgeny) Smirnoff (chaplain from 1877-1923): 'At the desire of Her Imperial Highness, the Grand Duchess Marie Alexandrovna, Duchess of Edinburgh, I performed the rite of consecration of the new Chapel in her Highness's London palace, on 13th April 1879.' Although there is no evidence that a chaplain was permanently appointed to this new chapel, Eugene Smirnoff does report that he conducted services there on specific occasions.

The researches of protodeacon Birchall reveal that Smirnoff had in fact served for two years in New York before his appointment to London. Shortly after his arrival he became a regular visitor to Buckingham Palace and was in due course asked to conduct Russian Orthodox memorial services there for the two Russian tsars Alexander II and Alexander III. He also wrote a book on *Russian Orthodox Missions*.[1]

The duke of Edinburgh died at Rosenau near Coburg on 30 July 1900 and it appears that the duchess subsequently ceased to use both Clarence House and its Russian Orthodox chapel. She died at Zurich in 1920. The chapel structure with its tall arched triple windows at Clarence House has survived, however, although the only original decorations, by a French artist, that can still be seen are a couple of alcove paintings of abstract patterns in deep red, blue, green and gold.[2]

---

[1] I am greatly indebted to protodeacon Christopher Birchall for divulging the fruits of his research.

[2] I remain very grateful to Sir Alastair Aird, Comptroller of Her Majesty Queen Elizabeth the Queen Mother's Household, for informing me of the existence and allowing me to see the Russian Orthodox chapel at Clarence House.

Chapel Royal Personnel

Deans of the Chapel Royal

1312	'Capitalis Capellanus'	
1318	'Le Chief Chappelin'	
−1349–1350−	John Wodeford	
−1356−	John de Lek	
−1380−	Thomas de Lynton	
−1389–1399−	John Boor	
1399–1403	Richard Kyngeston	
1403–1413	Richard Prentys	
1413	Dean Prophete	
1414–1417−	Edmund Lacy	
−1425	Robert Gilbert	
−1438−	Richard Praty	
−1440−	John Croucher	
−1449	Robert Ayscogh	
1449–1468	William Say	
−1471–1476−	William Dudley	
1481−	John Gunthorpe	
1483	William Chauntre	
1489	Richard Hill	
1496	Thomas Jane	
1497–1501	Richard Nikke	
1501	Geoffrey Simeon	
1502–1514	William Atwater	
1514–1519	J. Voysey	
1519–1523	John Clark	
1523–1544	Richard Sampson	†Chichester
1544−	Dean Thirlby	
−1558	Monsignor Hutchenson	
1558–1572	George Carew	Dean of Exeter
1572–c.1585	William Day	Dean of Windsor
c.1585–1603	'6' Lord Chamberlains	
1603–1619	James Montague	†Bath and Wells
1619–1626	Launcelot Andrewes	†Winchester
1626–1633	William Laud	†Bath and Wells
1633–1636	William Juxon	
1636–1641−	Matthew Wren	†Norwich
1660–1663	Gilbert Sheldon	†London
1663–1668	George Morley	†Winchester
1668–1670	Herbert Croft	†Hereford
1671–1675	Walter Blandford	†Worcester
1675–1685	Henry Compton	†London
1686–1689	Nathaniel Crewe	†Durham

1689–1713	Henry Compton	†London
1713–1717	John Robinson	†London
1717–1721	William Talbot	†Sarum
1721–1748	Edmund Gibson	†Lincoln
1748–1761	Thomas Sherlock	†London
1761–1762	Thomas Hayter	†London
1762–1764	Richard Osbaldiston	†London
1764–1777	Richard Terrick	†London
1777–1787	Robert Lowth	†London
1787–1809	Beilby Porteous	†London
1809–1813	John Randolph	†London
1813–1828	William Hawley	†London
1828–1857	Charles Blomfield	†London
1857–1868	Archibald Tait	†London
1868–1885	John Jackson	†London
1885–1896	Frederick Temple	†London
1896–1901	Mandell Creighton	†London
1901–1939	Arthur Winnington-Ingram	†London
1939–1945	Geoffrey Fisher	†London
1945–1956	John Wand	†London
1956–1961	Henry Montgomery Campbell	†London
1961–1972	Robert Stopford	†London
1972–1981	Gerald Ellison	†London
1981–	Graham Leonard	†London

Sub-deans of the Chapel Royal

–1449–	'Deputatum'
1483–1486	Nicholas Hewys
1486–1509	Richard Surland
1509–1513	John Kyte
1513–1526	Roger Norton
1526–1546	Richard Wade MA
1546–1548	John Donne STB
1548–1557	Emery Tuckfield MA
1557–1559	Edmund Danyell STB
1559–1567	John Angell
1567–1568	John Norrice
1568–1569	William Gravesend
1569–1584	Richard Tirwitt
1584–1592	Robert Greene
1592–1593	Anthony Anderson
1593–1623	Leonard Davies
1623–	Stephen Boughton (died before the Restoration, and lodged in St Martin's-in-the-Fields, where he paid 35s ship money tax in 1636, according to a Domestic State Paper of 1636.
1661–1672	Walter Jones DD
1672–1674	Richard Colebrand DD
1674–1689	William Holder DD
1689–1712	Ralph Battell DD
1712–1717	John Dolben DD
1717–1732	Edward Aspinwall DD

1732–1746	George Carleton MA
1746–1751	Edward Pordage MA
1751–1764	Fifield Allen DD
1764–1792	Anselm Bayly DCL
1792–1803	Thomas Pearce DD
1803–1833	William Holmes MA
1833–1847	John Sleath DD
1847–1859	Charles Wesley DD
1859–1884	Francis Garden MA
1884–1922	Edgar Sheppard MA
1922–1941	Launcelot Percival MA ('Precentor')
1941–1948	Wallace Elliott MA ('Precentor')
1948–1965	Maurice Foxell MA
1965–1979	James Mansel MA
1979–	Anthony Caesar MA

Clerks of the closet, 1660–1990

[c. 1649]–1665	John Earle	Bishop of Worcester, then of Salisbury
1665–1671	Walter Blandford	Bishop of Oxford, then of Worcester
1672–1685	Nathaniel Crew (3rd Baron Crew of Stene)	Bishop of Oxford, then of Durham
1685–1689	Thomas Sprat	Bishop of Rochester
1689–1691	John Tillotson	Dean of Canterbury, then of St Paul's (Archbishop of Canterbury 1691)
1691–1695	Thomas Burnet	Master of Charterhouse
1695–1702	Hon. John Montagu	Dean of Durham (1699)
1702–1714 {	Dr William Graham	Dean of Carlisle, then of Wells
	Dr John Younger	Dean of Salisbury
	Dr Samuel Pratt	Dean of Windsor
1714–1723	Charles Trimnel	Bishop of Winchester
1723–1734	Richard Willis	Bishop of Winchester
1735–1746	Henry Egerton	Bishop of Hereford
1746–1752	Joseph Butler	Bishop of Bristol, then of Durham
1752–1757	John Gilbert	Bishop of Salisbury (Archbishop of York 1757)
1757–1781	John Thomas	Bishop of Salisbury, then of Winchester
1781–1808	Richard Hurd	Bishop of Worcester
1809–1812	[Vacant]	
1813–1815	William Jackson	Bishop of Oxford
1815–1827	Hon. George Pelham	Bishop of Exeter, then of Lincoln
1827–1837	Robert James Carr	Bishop of Chichester, then of Worcster
1837–1849	Edward Stanley	Bishop of Norwich
1849–1865	John Graham	Bishop of Chester
1866–1892	Henry Philpott	Bishop of Worcester until 1890
1891–1903	Randall Davidson	Bishop of Rochester, then of Winchester (Archbishop of Canterbury 1903)
1903–1918	William Boyd Carpenter	Bishop of Ripon until 1911
1919–1925	Hubert Murray Burge	Bishop of Oxford
1925–1937	Thomas Banks Strong	Bishop of Oxford
1937–1942	Cyril Forster Garbett	Bishop of Winchester (Archbishop of York 194?)

1942–1963	Percy Mark Herbert	Bishop of Norwich until 1959
1963–1975	Roger Wilson	Bishop of Chichester until 1974
1975–1979	William Gordon Fallows	Bishop of Sheffield
1979–1989	John Monier Bickersteth	Bishop of Bath and Wells
1989–	John Wayne	Bishop of Chelmsford

Priests in ordinary, 1743–1893

Year appointed		*Year appointed*	
1783	Thomas Pearce DD	1829	William John Hall
1743	Henry Evans MA	1833	Charles Wesley
1746	William Fitzherbert MA	1833	J.V. Povan MA
1754	Moses Wright MA	1834	John Clarke Haden MA
1761	David Walter Morgan	1845	George Herbert Repton
1771	Henry Waring MA	1847	Thomas Helmore MA
1771	William Clarke MA	1855	John Antrobus MA
1790	Henry Fly MA	1859	Francis Garden MA
1792	John Moore BA	1864	Albert Sitwell MA
1793	William Clarke MA	1869	Samuel Flood Jones MA
1795	William Holmes MA	1875	John Troutbeck MA
1795	John Pridden MA	1876	William Harrison MA
1796	Edward Cannon BA	1878	Henry Cotton MA
1797	George Hicks MA	1878	Edward Wood Kempe MA
1798	Edward James Beckwith MA	1882	Edgar Sheppard MA
1803	William Hayes MA	1884	Henry Alsager Sherringham MA
1814	John Memlen	1884	Edwin Prince MA
1816	James William Vivian MA	1889	Daniell Bainbridge MA
1820	Henry John Knapp	1891	R. Tahourdin MA
1821	Christopher Packe	1892	John Swire MA
1824	Richard Barham	1893	E. Van der Noot MA
1825	Robert William Packman		

Sources: Sub-dean Pearce MS at Chapel Royal; New Cheque Book at Chapel Royal; Edgar Sheppard, *Memorials of St James's Palace*.

Gentlemen of the Chapel Royal

This list comprises information from both primary and secondary sources in an attempt to produce as comprehensive a list as possible of all the gentlemen of the Chapel Royal.

Primary sources

I have compiled the core of this list, printed in Roman type, exclusively from the primary sources of the Chapel Royal. It lacks certain familiar dates readily obtainable from other or secondary sources but which curiously do not appear in the Chapel Royal archives. There are therefore some startling omissions. It does however include the names and dates of appointment of many gentlemen of the Chapel Royal hitherto unknown and unlisted elsewhere. It is hoped that scholars will benefit accordingly, but it should be understood that, as with many primary archive sources, conflicts of dates compared with other sources inevitably arise. This list is thus presented as a true record of names and dates as they were recorded, with occasional inaccuracies, by officials of the Chapel Royal, or authorised for publication by officials of the Lord Chamberlain's Office.

Up to 1560 the list is compiled largely from Patent Rolls, Proceedings of the Privy Council, State Papers and Lord Chamberlain's Office records. From 1560 until 1643 the information comes mostly from the Old Cheque Book of the Chapel Royal, and its parallel the Bodleian Register (Rawlinson MS D318). Quotations concerning the gentlemen in the period 1560-1727 are from the Old Cheque Book and thereafter from the New Cheque Book or Lovegrove Manuscript, unless qualified by the abbreviation 'Bod. Reg.', which indicates the Bodleian Register as the source. The period 1660 until 1744 is largely compiled from the Old Cheque Book and thereafter by the New Cheque Book, but complemented by the Lovegrove Manuscript for the period from 1708-1858. Millan's Universal Register was used for the year 1758, followed by the Royal Kalendar from 1762. Chapel Royal anthem books, its photographic archive from 1896, warrants of appointment, Chapel Royal correspondence and the Royal Maundy Feast Manuscript 1886-1990, in the care by tradition of the senior gentleman, were the sources for the more recent information. For the sake of easy reference I have included recent past organists, sub-organists and composers, since they were originally chosen from among the gentlemen in ordinary in days past.

The primary sources used to compile this list were as follows:

Proceedings of the Privy Council
State Papers Domestic
Close Rolls
Patent Rolls
Liber Regie Capelle of 1449
Liber Niger Domus Regis of 1483
Papers deposited by Lord Chamberlain's Office
Eltham Palace Ordinances of 1526
Bodleian Rawlinson Manuscript D318
Old Cheque Book of the Chapel Royal
New Cheque Book of the Chapel Royal
Lovegrove Manuscript (Royal Library)
Royal Kalendar
Chapel Royal Anthem Books
Chapel Royal Photographic Archive
Old Chapel Royal Association correspondence.
Warrants of appointment
Royal Maundy Feast Manuscript 1886-1990 (kindly lent to me by the senior gentlemen, Norman Cooper.)

Secondary sources

The secondary sources used to fill the gaps left by the primary sources held by the Chapel Royal are compiled mostly from references in *Grove's Dictionary of Music and Musicians*, 5th and 6th editions, together with a few other sources, collated for the late Colin Scull by Miss Jane Williams in 1979. They appear in the list in italic type in conjunction with the following key:

[1] = Sir George Grove, *Dictionary of Music and Musicians*, 5th edition by Eric Blom (London, Macmillan, 1954)

[1supp.] = Sir George Grove, *Dictionary of Music and Musicians*, 5th edition by Eric Blom, supplementary volume (London, Macmillan, 1961)

[1 Banaster] or [1 C.R.] = *Grove's Dictionary*, but mentioned in an entry other than under the relevant gentleman's name.

[2] = *New Oxford History of Music*, vol. 3, *Ars Nova and the Renaissance: 1300-1540*, edited by Dom Anselm Hughes & Gerald Abraham (London, OUP, 1960)

[3] = Percy Marshall Young, *Sir Arthur Sullivan* (London, J.M. Dent, 1971)

[4] = H.C.L. Stocks, *British Cathedral Organists* (London, Hinrichsen, 1949)

[5] = John Ebenezer West, *Cathedral Organists Past and Present ...*, 2nd edition (London, Novello, 1921)

[6] = François Arsène Cellier & Cunningham Bridgeman, *Gilbert, Sullivan and D'Oyly Carte*, 2nd edition (London, Pitman,1927)

[7] = William Alexander Barrett, *English Church Composers* (London, Sampson, Low & Marston, n.d.)

Abbreviations

B = bass
T = tenor
CT = counter tenor
A = alto

I apologise for any inadvertent omissions from these records.

Using the list

The left-hand column of dates gives the year of appointment to the Chapel Royal. A dash to the left of this indicates that an earlier date is to be inferred from the source used, but that the gentleman concerned was certainly a member of the Chapel Royal by the date given in the left-hand column.

A dash after the date in the left-hand column indicates that the appointment continued until the date in the right-hand column. If there is no date in the right-hand column, or indeed the left-hand column, then this is because the information is not available in the Chapel Royal Archive. A dash to the right of the date in the right-hand column indicates that the appointment seems to have continued after this date, but that the date given is the last mentioned concerning this gentlemen in the Chapel Royal Archive.

Examination of the later extensive Great Wardrobe Accounts and Lord Chamberlain's records deposited at the Public Record Office, will provide most of the 'missing' information for scholars pursuing more information on certain gentlemen prior to 1900.

1221	Willemus de Wintonia, 'clericus domus regis de capelle sua'
c.1258	*Henry Blacksmith, clerk [1, 6th ed]*
1229–1230	Henry de Burneval, 'capellanus domini regis'
1259	Richard le Rus, 'King's Clerk'
1259	Master Umbert de Coquenato, 'King's Clerk'
1305	John de Nassington, 'King's Clerk'
1305	Master Jordan Moraunt, 'King's Clerk'
1309	John de Leek (Lek), 'King's Clerk and Almoner'

1312	'Capitalis Capellanus'
1318	'Le Chief Chappelin'
–1349–1350–	Johan de Wodeford, 'Dean'
1356	John de Lek, 'Dean' and 'King's Clerk'
1361	William Rous, 'King's Clerk' and 'one of the clerks of his chapel'
–1374–1396–	J. Excestre, 'clerk'
1376–1377	*Roger Gerveys [1, 6th ed]*
1380	Thomas de Lynton, 'Dean'
1389	William Lane, 'Priest' and 'one of the clerks of the Chapel within the household' and 'his horse'
1389–1399	John Boor, 'Dean'
1393–1402	William Excestre
1399–1403	Richard Kyngeston, 'Dean'
1400	Robert Keynsham, 'one of the clerks of the King's Chapel within the Household'
1400	Prophete, 'King's Clerk' and 'Dean' for one year in 1413
1403–1412–	Richard Prentys, 'Dean'
1406/13–20	*Richard Blythe, gentleman [1 Blich]*
1413–1422–	*Alan Hert, gentleman [2 p. 129 n²]*
1413	John Burrell *1413–1421 at least [1 supp., 1 C.R.]*
1413	Thomas Damett
1413	Nicholas Sturgeon
1414–1437–	John Hunt, 'one of the clerks of the King's Chapel with the Household'
1413–1419	John Cook, 'clerk of the Chapel of the Household'
1414–1417–	Edmund Lacey, 'Dean'
1415	Stephen Peynton, 'one of the clerks of the Chapel within the Household'
1417	John Couper, 'King's Clerk' and 'one of the Chaplains of the King's Chapel within the Household'
–1417–1418–	John Colles, 'Clerk' and 'Servant of the Vestry of the King's Chapel'
1417	John Water, 'one of the King's Clerks'
–1417–1418	John Kyngman, 'one of the King's Clerks'
1419	Thomas Gyles, 'clerk of the Chapel of the Household'
1420	John Pyamour, 'one of the clerks of the Chapel of the Household'
1420	Thomas Lywer, 'clerk of the Chapel of the Household'.
1421–	Robert Chirbury
–1425	Robert Gilbert, 'Dean'
1426–1444–	Henry Hawnshard, 'Chaplain, one of the clerks of the King's Chapel within the Household'
1427–1452	Gerard Hesyll, 'one of the clerks of the King's Chapel'
1429–1455–	John Cook, 'clerk of the Chapel'
1436–1440–	William Ayscough, 'King's Clerk' and 'Chaplain within the household'
–1437–	Henry Haslop, 'one of the Chaplains of the Chapel within the household'
1437	John Caton, 'Chaplain within the Great Wardrobe'
1437	Robert Chirbury, 'one of the Chaplains of the King's Chapel within the household'
–1438	John Cardmewe
–1438	Robert Chamberlain, 'clerk of the King's Chapel' and 'good service to Henry V and the King'

–1438–1442–	John Fouler, 'one of the clerks of the King's Chapel', *clerk 1433–1467 [1 Fowler]*
1438	Richard Praty, 'King's Clerk' and 'Dean'
1440	John Croucher, 'Dean'
–1441–1445–	John Plummer, 'one of the clerks of the Chapel' and 'Serjeant' in 1445
1443	William Boston, 'clerk of the King's Chapel'
1444	Thomas Testwode, 'Serjeant ... one of the clerks of the King's Chapel'
–1445–	John Brown, 'Serjeant ... of the King's Chapel' and 'long service to Henry V and the King'
–1446–1448–	John Champayn, 'Chaplain of the King's Chapel'
–1446–1456–	John London, 'one of the clerks of the Chapel of the household'
1446–1452	*Henry Souleby [2 p. 196]*
–1448–1449	Robert Ayscogh, 'Dean'
1449–	William Say, 'Dean'
–1450–1459–	Richard Bowyer, 'Chaplain, clerk of the King's Chapel'
–1451–1454–	Thomas Normanton, 'clerk of the chapel'
1452	John Penant, 'one of the Chaplains of the Chapel of the Household'
1455	John Stevyns, 'poor priest'
1456	Thomas Donne, 'chaplain of the chapel within the household'
–1456–1471–	Henry Abyngdon, *clerk 1451–, master 1455–1478 [1 Banaster]*
1457	Thomas Eyre
1460	Philip Reynold, 'clerk of the Chapel of the household, impotent and mutilated in his right arm'
1462	John Fowler (possibly the same as 'Fouler' of 1438 above), 'one of the clerks of the Chapel within the King's Household'
1463–	*John Brown, gentleman [1, 6th ed]*
1471	William Gull, 'one of the clerks of the King's household'
–1471–1476–	William Dudley, 'Dean of the King's Chapel'
1486–1493	*Laurence Squire, dep. master 1486–1487, master 1487–1493 [1 Banaster, 1 Newark]*
1475–1486–	Gilbert Banaster (master of the children 1478–1486)
1490–	*William Cornysh, gentleman [1]*
1490s	*William Browne [1 Brown, J.]*
–1503–1509–	Edward John
–1503–1509–	William Newerk (master of the children 1493–1509)
–1503–1509?	John Sidburgh
–1503–*c*.1509	Thomas Blaydsmyth
–1503–1511–	John Penne
–1503–1509–	Henry Wilkyns
–1503–*c*.1509	John Cornysh
–1503–*c*.1509	John Prate
–1503–1511–	Robert Fairfaux, *gentleman by 1496–1521 [1, 1 Nares]*
–1503–1509–	John Petwyn
–1503–1511–	Thomas Sexten
–1503–1511–	William Sturton
–1503–1538	Robert Penne
1503–1547–	John Fyssher
–1503–*c*.1509	John Venner
–1503–*c*.1509	John Fowler *1499–1518 [1]*
–1503–1509–	William Tebbe (serjeant of the vestry 1510–1514–)

–1503–1511–	William Browne
c.1509–	William Cornysshe, *gentleman ?1496–1509 dep. master–1509 master 1509–1523 [1, 1 Burton, A., 1 Crane, 1 Jones, R., 1 Lloyd, J., 1 Nares, 1 Pygott]*
c.1509–	John Weyver
c.1509–	William Dobeney (serjeant of the vestry 1509)
c.1509–	William Crane (water bailiff of Dartmouth 1509, master 1523–1545)
c.1509–	John Smythe
1509	Henry Stevynson
c.1509–	Henry Prentyce
1510	John Loidd
1510–	Thomas Farthyng, *gentleman1508–1520, (1511–*) [1, 1 C.R., *Chorister at King's, Cam. 1477–]*
–1510–	John Gyles
–1510–	Robert Hawkins
–1510–	Davy Burten
–1512–1536	*Robert Jones, chorister, pupil of Newark, gentleman 1512–1536 [1]*
1524–1548–	Robert Phelipps
1526–1548–	Thomas Burye
1526–1548–	Richard Pigott
1526–1548–	John Allen
c.1526–1548–	Richard Stephin
1526–1548–	Robert Hockland
c.1540–1548–	Richard Barwyck
c.1540–1548–	William Poope
1520–1566	William Hychyns (first entry concerning gentlemen in the Old Cheque Book of the Chapel Royal)
1526–1561	Thomas Byrde
1526–1563	Richard Bower, *master 1545–1561 [1 Crane, 1 Edwards, 1 Tallis]*
1526–1548–	Robert Perrye
1526–1548–	William Barber
1526–1586	Robert Richemound
c.1526–1548–	Thomas Whayt
c.1540–1585	Thomas Talys
c.1540–1548–	Nicholas Mellowe
c.1540–1548–	Thomas Wrighte
1546–1548	*Robert Okeland, gentleman c. 1546–1548, sang at 1547 coronation [1, 1 supp.]*
c.1553–	Emery Tuckfield
c.1553–	Nicholas Aurchbalde, 'Priest'
c.1553–1563	William Walker, 'slaine' according to the Old Cheque Book and 'Priest'
c.1553–	Robert Chamberlayne, 'Priest'
c.1553–1569	William Gravesend, 'Priest'
c.1553–1567	John Angel, priest
c.1553–1613	Robert Stone (died aged 97)
c.1553–1592	John Benbowe
c.1553–	John Shepherd
c.1553–1583	William Mauperley
c.1553–	George Edwards
c.1553–1581	Robert Morcocke (clerk of the checke)

*c.*1553–1597	William Hunnis (master of the children 1566–97)
*c.*1553–*c.*1560	Thomas Mann (not in Old Cheque Book)
*c.*1553–1566	Richard Aylesworth
*c.*1553–1589	Thomas Pulfreyman
*c.*1553–*c.*1560	Roger Kenton (not in Old Cheque Book)
*c.*1553–*c.*1560	Lucas Cuastell (not in Old Cheque Book)
*c.*1553–1564	Richard Farrant
*c.*1553–*c.*1560	Robert Adams (not in Old Cheque Book)
*c.*1553–*c.*1560	John Singer (not in Old Cheque Book)
*c.*1553–*c.*1560	Robert Bassocke
*c.*1553–1569	Thomas Causton
*c.*1553–*c.*1560	Richard Lever (not in Old Cheque Book)
*c.*1553–1567	John Denman
*c.*1553–*c.*1560	Walter Thirley (not in Old Cheque Book)
*c.*1553–*c.*1560	Morris Tedder (not in Old Cheque Book)
*c.*1553–*c.*1560	Hugh Williams (not in Old Cheque Book)
*c.*1553–1566	Richard Edwardes (dep. master 1560–61, master 1561–66)
1558–1590	*John Blitheman [1]*
1560–1569	Mr Causter (Bod. Reg. – possibly the same as Thomas Causton who served until 1569), 'Pistler'.
1561–1596	Mr Paternoster
1561–	Mr Rawlins (sworn 27 Sept., Bod. Reg.)
–1563	Mr Merton
1563–1590	Thomas Wiles
1563–1569	Robert Parsons (sworn 8 Jan., Bod. Reg.), 'drowned at Newark Uppon Trent'
1563–1591	William Mundy
1564–1615	Thomas Sampson, 'drowned'
1566–	Nicholas Morgan (died in 1581, Bod. Reg.)
1566–1592	Robert Greene (sub-dean from 1584)
1566–	James Causter (sworn gent. on 11 Dec., Bod. Reg.)
1566–	John Ridley ('Pistler', Bod. Reg.)
1567–1578	John Addie, 'priest'
1567–1592	John Hottost, 'priest'
–1568	Mr Norris
1568–1591	William Ivett
–1569	Hugh Sullyes
1569–1571	Robert Goodale
1569–1581	Richard Farrant, 'from Windsore' (deputy master of children)
–1569	Roger Centon
1569–1591	Nicholas Beighton
–1572	*Christopher Tye, ? gentleman, ? organist ? –1572 [1, 1 C.R.]*
1569–	Nicholas Brighton (sworn pistler 25 Feb. and gent. in 1571, Bod. Reg.)
1569–1623	William Byrd, 'a Father of Musick' (organist from 1572)
–1571	Henry Alred
1571–	Richard Granwall
1571–1573	Giles Carott, 'Dominus' and 'Pistler'
1569–1581	Mr Ednye, died 'of Plague'
1573–1605	Bartholomew Mason, 'Priest' (but appointed 1575, Bod. Reg.)
–1575	John Ridley
1575–1585	William Boddinghurst ('Roddinghurst', Bod. Reg., which also describes him as 'Yeoman' since 28 Feb. 1575)

1578–1580	John Savill, 'priest' and 'slaine' (but also 'Yeoman' since 28 March 1578, Bod. Reg.)
–1579	Jo Russell
1579–1583	Richard Morrice, 'Fledd beyond the Seaes' (but also 'Yeoman' since 30 March 1579 and appointed gent. in 1580, Bod. Reg.)
1580–	William Bulman ('Gentlemen Extraordinary', Bod. Reg.)
–1580	Thomas Raulins
1580–1588	Ellis Stempe
1580–1602 or 1626	Crue Sharp (also 'Yeoman' since 9 Nov. 1580, Bod. Reg.)
1581–1598?	Anthony Todd (formerly 'Yeoman' since 26 Feb. 1581, Bod. Reg.)
–1581	Mr Morgan (died 9 May, Bod.Reg. – probably the same as Nicholas Morgan, appointed in 1566, Old Cheque Book)
1580–1623	Leonard Davies, 'Gospeller' (subsequently sub-dean)
–1582	Mr Moorcock
1582–1582	John Moore (appointed clerk of the cheque in June 1582 he died that same year on 2 Oct.)
1582–1606	Edmund Brown
1582–	Thomas Woodson
1582–1598	Robert Talluntire
1582–	Thomas Sampson ('Clerk of the Cheque', Bod. Reg.)
–1580	William Jones, 'Priest and Gospeller'
1581–1588	Salomon Compton, 'Pistler'
1583–	Anthony Harrison ('Gospeller', Bod. Reg.)
1583–1603	William Barnes, 'Gospeller'
–1584	Robert Tirwitt
1584–1603	William Randoll, 'Pistler'
1585–1591	*William Blitheman, organist [1, 1 Bull]*
1585–1614	Henry Eveseed, 'childe there'
1585–1613	John Bull, 'went beyond the seas without licence'
1586–1602	Isaak Burgis, 'drowned in cominge out of the Lowe Countrie'
1587–1593	Tymothie Greene
–1587	Mr Gooch
1588–1601	George Waterhouse
1588–1600	Edward Pearce, 'yielded up his place for the Mastership of Poules'
1589–1609	Roberte Allisone, 'sold his place'
1590–	John Steevens, sworn 'in ordinary' by lord chamberlain not dean, owing to the interregnum of deans at this time; also clerk of the cheque from 1627.
–1590	Mr Wyles
1591–1627	Jo. Hewlett (clerk of the cheque)
1591–1611	Richard Plumley
–1591	Mr Blitheman
1591–1593	Anthony Anderson (sub-dean from 1592, sworn by lord chamberlain)
1591–1608	Thomas Goolde
1592–1602	Thomas Morley
1584–1592	Robert Greene (sub-dean)
1592–	Humphreye Westerne, 'Extraordinary'
1592–	*William Phelps, gent. extra. 1592– [1 Bull]*
1592–1617	Peter Wrighte
1592–1595	Thomas Madoxe

420

1593–	William Asplend, 'Extraordinary'
1593–1606	Mr Laurence, 'died of the Plague 10 Nov.' also 'Pistler'
1593–1620	James Davies
1593–	John Marchant, 'Extraordinary'
1594–1615	Jo. Baldwin, 'tenor'
1595–1623	John Amery, 'Basse'
1596–	Roger Godbalde, 'Extraordinary'
1596–1609	Robert Stuckey
1596–	Richard Martin, 'Extraordinary'
–1597–1633	Nathaniel Giles (master of the children; organist, 1633)
1598–1626	Francis Wiborow, organist?
–1598	Nathaniel Todd
1600–1602	John Heathman
1601–	George Green, 'Extraordinary'
1601–1604	Arthur Cock
1602–	Stephan Boughton, 'minister from Herifford'
1602–	Anthony Kirckbie, 'Extraordinary' and 'from Canterbury'
1602–	Anthony Kirkby (possibly the same as Kirckbie)
1602–1605	George Woodson, made 'Extraordinary' in 1594, but a 'Thomas Woodson' sold his place in 1605 as gent. to Wm. West
1602–	William Lawes
1603–	Jo. Woodeson
–1603	Mr Bucke
1603–1607	Edmund Shergold
1603–1621	Edmund Hooper, 'Organist'
1603–	*Matthew White, gentleman 1603– [1]*
1604–	Michaell Vasco, 'Extraordinary'
1604–1625	Orlando Gibbons, *gentleman 1605–1625, organist 1605–1625 [1, 1 C.R., 1 Masque]*
1605–	Richard Coton, priest
1605–	William West, extraordinary in 1604/5
1605–	George Tucker, 'of the church of Exeter'
1606–	Randoll Tinker, 'died of the Plague the 20th Sept.'
1605–	Richard Gyles, 'Extraordinary'
1605–	Elway Bevan, 'Extraordinary', *gentleman 1605–1637, pupil of Tallis, expelled 1637 [1, 1 Masque]*
1606–1627	Luke Jones, 'Gentleman' and 'Subdeane of St Paule's London'
1605–	Nicholas Rogers, 'Extraordinary'
1606–1616	David Henley
1606–	John Lilliat, 'Extraordinary'
1606–	Edward Doughtie, 'Clerk' and 'Confessor'
1606–	John Shepperd, 'Extraordinary'
–1606/7	Mr Granwall
1606–1609	Thomas Paine, 'Extraordinary' in 1605 and 'of Isle of Wight'
1607–1608 or 1660	George Cooke, 'Childe of the Chappell'
1607–	William Becket, 'Clerk' and 'Confessor'
1608–1638	John Clarke, 'Childe of the Chappell'
1609–	George Sheffield
1609–1630	Humfrie Bache
1609–1666?	Thomas Pearce
1611–	Ezechiel Waad, 'Confessor' from 1629

1611–	Jo. Frost
1611–	Thomas Brasfield, 'Extraordinary'
1613–1614	Mathew White 'Priest' and 'Basse'
1613–1624/5	Peter Hopkins
–1613	Robert Stone
1614–	William Crosse
1614–	William Heather
1615–1615	John Miners
1615–	John Amyon, 'Extraordinary'
1615–	Thomas Day (master of the children from 1634, and clerk of the cheque from 1636)
1615–1620	Martin Otto
1616–1616	John Greene, 'for a year of probation', but 'did so misdemeane himselfe and also marryed a second wiffe (the first beinge livinge) was therefore dismissed ...'
1616–	Walter Porter, 'tenor', *gent. extra 1616–1617, gentleman (T) 1617–1644 [1]*
1617–	Edmund Nellam, 'Deacon' and 'Basse of the churche of Westminster'
1618–	Francis Sennock
1619–1661	Roger Nightingale, 'Base' and 'Confessor'
1620–1633	Thomas Peirse, 'resigned'
1621–	John Frost, 'Base' from Salisbury
1621–	Thomas Tompkins, 'Organist' and previously 'organist of Worcester'
–1621	Anthony Harrison, 'Base'
1623–1625	John Croker, 'Pistler', 'Contertenor', and served 'a yeare of probacon'
–1623–1636	Mr Steephens (choir librarian), in 1623 was paid for 'pricking of a sett of bookes'
1623–1663	Ralph Amner, 'Basse'
1623–1625	John Cooke, 'Pistler', 'Basse' and wages to end of quarter to sub-dean's widow
1623–	Stephen Boughton (sub-dean)
–1623	James Davies (possibly the same as the Davies of 1593)
–1623	Orlando Gibbons
1623–	Thomas Warwick, 'Organist'
1625–	George Woodeson, 'the Younger' and 'Gospeller'
1625–1662	Henry Lawes (clerk of the cheque)
1625–1641	Richard Boughton, 'Base'
1625–1638	John Tompkins, 'Extraordinary Gent', 'Gospeller' and 'an excellent organist' (Bod. Reg.)
1626–	Thomas Rayment, 'Basse'
1627–	Richard Sandy, 'Contra-Tenor'
1627–	Nathaniell Pownall, 'Pistler' and 'Gospeller', 'Gent' from 1633
1627–1638	Thomas Loughton, 'Gospeller', 'Gent' from 1633, dismissed 1638
1630–	George Nutbrowne, 'Pistler'
–1697	*William Child, gentleman 1660–1697, organist 1632–1643 [1, 1 C.R., 1 Pigott]*
1633–1638	Thomas Holmes (sub-dean), died at Salisbury 1638
1633/4	Thomas Day, sworn master of the children in place of Giles
1637–	Thomas Holmes, sworn 'Gent.' 12 April 1637

1637–	Thomas Day, sworn clerk of the cheque
1637–	Thomas Hazard, 'Pistler' and 'Gospeller'
1638–1684	John Hardinge, 'Pistler' and 'a counter-tenor'
1638–1697	John Cobb, 'Gospeller'
1638–	*John Cobb, referred to as organist [1]*
–1638	John Clarke, 'a tenor deceased in the plague'
1638–	Richard Portman, 'Organist', and sworn epistler on Michaelmas day)
1639–	Richard Watkine, 'probationer'
–1639	George Woodeson, 'a Countertenor', died
1639–	Matthew Pearce, 'tenor' sworn 'probationer'
1639–1642	John Ffrost (also 'Chaunter of Westminster Church … he was a base and of extraordinary sufficiency for his quality allso of honesty and good', Bod. Reg.)
1640–	William Webb, 'Tenor' sworn 'probationer'
–1640	William Kros, 'a Countertenor', died, possibly the same as William Crosse appointed in 1614
–1641	George Woodeson, 'Tenor'
1641–1643	James Try, 'tenor' sworn 'probationer', also of Westminster
1641–	Thomas Lowe, 'base of St Paules Church London'
1642–	Mr Woodcock MA from King's College Cambridge, sworn 'probationer' and 'Countertenor'
–1643	William West, ('tenor', died in November 1643. This is the last entry in the Bodleian Register before to the Civil War. The last entry made in the Old Cheque Book concerning the gentlemen before the Civil War was that of Richard Portman in 1638)
–1675	Raphael Courteville, *gentleman (CT) ?–1643, 1660–1675 [1 Wise]* *Randle Jewett, 'Singer in the King's Chappell', brother of Randolph [1]* *Randolph Jewett, in 1642 Charles I paid him 'for his service in ye Quire' when the king visited Chester [1]* *William Jewett, 'one of the Queenes Ma[jes]tes Chappell', father of Randolph [1]*
–1682	Thomas Purcell, *gentleman 1660– [1]*
–1676	Christopher Gibbons, *chorister, organist, 1660–1676, gentleman –1676 [1 Blow]*
–1704	John Goodgroome, *gentleman 1660–1704 [1]*
–1682	Edward Lowe, 'organist' *1660–1682 [1 Jeffries, Geo., 1 Purcell, H. ii]*
–1672	Captain Henry Cooke, *chorister, gentleman (B) 1660–1672, master 1660–1672 [1, 1 C.R., 1 Humfrey]*
1660–1697	*James Cob (Cobb) [1, 1 Church]*
–1660	George Cooke, 'August'
1660–1708	Edward Braddock (clerk of the cheque from 1688)
1660–	Roger Nightingale, 'Clerk' and 'Confessor' from 1660
1661–	*Matthew Locke, composer * 1661– [1, 1 supp. * comp. in ordinary to the King 'anthems for C.R.']*
1661–1673	Roger Hill
1661–	Philip Tucker (Tinker), 'Confessor'
1662–	George Yardley, 'Base' sworn at Hampton Court
–1662	George Low, 'Resigned' 1662, 're–admitted' 1663, died 1664
1662–1673	Dr John Wilson, 'Countertenor'

1662–1688	Thomas Blagrave (clerk of the cheque)
–1663	John Cave, 'about the New Exchange, was by one James Elliott, a Scott, run through the body'
1663–1678	Charles Husbands, 'probationer' and 'Countertenor'
1663–	William Wake
1663–1663	William Jackson
1663–1699	Blaze White, 'Base'
–1664	Henry Purcell
1664–1712	Thomas Richardson
1664–	William Hopwood, 'Base'
1664–1669	Andrew Carter, 'Priest'
1666–1688	Henry Smith, 'Priest'
1666–	Matthew Peniall
1666–	Thomas Hazard
1666–1674	Pelham Humphrey (master of the children from 1672)
–1669	Edward Colmon, died 'at Greenwich'
1669–	William Turner, 'Counter Tenor'
1669–1670	Edmund Slauter (Slater?)
1670–1718	James Hart, 'Base'
–1670	Gregory Thorndale, 'Base'
–1671	Durant Hunt
1671–1715	Andrew Trebeck, 'Basse'
–1661–1672	Walter Jones (sub-dean)
–1672	Captain Henry Cooke (master of the children)
1672–1679	Burges Howes
1672–1674	Richard Colebrand (sub-dean)
–1673	Philip Tynchare, 'Confessor'
1673–1697	Stephen Crispin, Student of Christ Church Oxford, 'Confessor from 1675', but refused to sign 'the association'
1673–1679	Richard Gadbury
1674–1708	John Blow (master of the children and 'Composer' from 1699), chorister from 1660–1664
1674–	William Powell, 'Tenor'
1674–1686	William Holder, sworn sub-dean by lord chamberlain on request of the dean who was absent in Bath
1675–	Michael Wise, 'Countertenor'
–1676	William Howes, *gentleman 1660–76 [1]*
1675–	John Billon La Marre
c.1676–c.1710	*William Norris, chorister, sang at 1685 coronation [1]*
1676–1681	Alphonso Marsh
1676–1687	John Chrissostome Dusharroll
1678–	Thomas Hawood
1678–	John Dowsing, 'Extraordinary'
1678–1733	John Gostling, 'Base', 'Extraordinary' and 'Priest in ordinary'. He was re-sworn in 1727 at the coronation of George II but at Canterbury where he was a minor canon because he could no longer travel owing to his great age and infirmities.
–1678	William Tucker
1679–	John Abell, 'Extraordinary'
1679–1697	Morgan Harris
1681–1717	Leonard Woodeson
1682–1695	Henry Purcell, 'Organist', succeeded Lowe

1682–1695	Josiah Boucher
1683–1702	Nathaniel Vestment
–1683	William Hopwood
1683–	Samuell Bentham, 'Extraordinary', 'Ordinary' 1693, and 'Confessor' from 1716
1683–	Thomas Browne, 'Extraordinary'
1685–	Edward Morton
1685–	William Davies, 'Extraordinary'
1685–	John Lenton, 'Extraordinary'
1688–	John James Gaches
–1689	Richard Hart
–1689	Thomas Haywood, 'resigned' in 1689, probably the same as Hawood of 1678
1689–1702	Moses Snow, 'Epistler' 1693, and 'Extraordinary'
1689–1719	Thomas Linacre, 'Epistler' 1684 and 'Gospeller' 1693
1689–1612/13	Dr Battle (sub-dean)
1690–	Alexander Damascene, *gent. extra. (A) 1690–5, gentleman 1696–1719 [1]*
1691–1708	John Howell, 'Extraordinary', 'Epistler' 1694 and 'Gospeller' in 1693
1691–	David La Count
1691–	William Battle
1691–	Symon Corbitt
–1692	Alphonso Marsh (evidently not the same as Marsh of 1676–81), *gentleman 1660– [1]*
1692–1720	Daniel Williams, 'Extraordinary', 'in Ordinary' from 1697, clerk of the cheque from 1708
1692–	Charles Greene
–1693	John Sayr
–1694	George Bettenham
1694–1699	George Hart, 'Extraordinary', 'in Ordinary' from 1697
1694–1710	Mr Barnes, 'Extraordinary'
1695–1704	Francis Piggot, 'Organist Extraordinary', and 'in Ordinary' from 1696. Replaced Dr Child as organist)
–1696	Mr Frost
1696–	John Church, *tenor, appointed gent. extra. first in 1697, in January, and then to a full place in August 1697. Also principal copyist till c. 1735. Compiled the earliest extant set of C.R. part books now in the British Library Reference Division (ref. R.M.27a1–15), and was thought to have been responsible for the C.R. anthem word book of 1712, 'Divine Harmony: a collection of anthems used at Her Majesty's Chapel Royal'. From 1729 to 1740 kept the 'Chapel Royal Subscription Book for a perpetual fund' to provide pensions for the relatives of deceased choirmen. [1]*
–1697	Dr Child, 'Organist'
1697–	Thomas Jenkins
1699–	William Washbourne, 'Extraordinary'
1699–	Thomas Adwards
1699–1716?	John Ratcliffe, confessor?
1699–1708	Humphry Griffith, 'Extraordinary'

1699–1707	Jeremiah Clarke } organists in 1704. Clarke was senior organist in
	William Croft } 1707, and master in 1708, as well as composer
	until 1727
1700–	John Freeman, *gentleman –1736 [1 Kent]*
1701–1736	John Weldon, *organist 1708–1736, composer 1715–1736 [1 Greene]*
–1702	Mr Watkins
1702–1714	Richard Elfford
1703	Mr Harper } 'Chaplains of St James' in 1703
1703	Mr Palmer }
1703	Mr Richardson
1708–	Francis Hughes, held 2 places simultaneously from 1730 because of 'his extraordinary skill in singing and his great usefulness to the choir in the performance of verse anthems'
1708–1752	John Mason
1708–c.1774/7	Bernard Gates (master of the children 1727–1757)
1710–1728	William Battell
–1711	Stephen Crespion
1711–1732	Edward Aspinwall (sub-dean from 1717/18)
1712–1765	George Laye, 'Counter tenor'
1714–	Samuel Weely, 'Base'
1714–1721	William Morley
1714–	George Carleton
1714–1745	Thomas Baker, 'Priest'
1714–1754	Samuel Chittle, 'Priest'
1715–	The Rev. Flitoff of Worcester, reader in Whitehall chapel replacing Dr Mangay)
1715–1727	*Luke Flintoft, gentleman [1]*
1716–	John Gethin
1717–1746	Peter Randall
1718–	James Chelsum
–1717/8	Dr Dolben (sub-dean)
1719–	Thomas Blennerhaysett
1719–1758	Talbot Young
1719–1743	Thomas Bell
1720	Jonathan Smith, 'Serjeant of his Majesty's Chapells and Vestryes' was sworn clerk of the cheque on 4 April 1720
1721–1777	William Perry
1723–	G.F. Handel, *composer appointed 25 Feb. 1723, but 'Greene was preferred to Handel as Organist and Composer in 1727'. Samuel Champness was listed as a chorister in 1748 under 'that great master Handel' in Magnae Britanniae Notitia, 37th ed. by Chamberlayne [1 Handel, 1 Champness]*
1727–1756	Maurice Green, 'Organist and Composer'
–1730	Thomas Edwards
–1731	Thomas Gething
1731–1758	David Cheriton
1732–1746	George Carleton (sub-dean), possibly the same as Carleton of 1714
1733–	*Walter Powell, gentleman (CT) 1733– [1]*
1736–1755	Francis Rowe
1736–	William Boyce, 'Composer' from 1736 and 'Organist' 1758–1779
1736–1737	Jonathan Martin, 'Organist' from 1736
1737–1758	John Travers, 'Organist' from 1737, replaced Martin

1740–1755	Prince Gregory
1740–1783	Nicholas Ladd
1740–1744	Anselm Bayly, 'Priest in Ordinary' 1744–64 (sub-dean 1764–94)
1743–1747	William Richardson
1743–1779	Thomas Vandernam
1744–1764	Robert Wass
1744–1753	Ben Mence
1744–1789	William Savage
1746–1789	Thomas Barrow
1747–1783	Robert Denham
1752–1762	Thomas Baildon
1753–1754	Moses Wight, priest in ordinary from 1754
1754–1764	John Buswell
1755–1764	Hugh Cox
1755–1767	William Coster
1756–1783	James Nares, 'Composer' and 'Organist' from 1756 (master of the children from 1757)
1758–1772	Ralph Cowper
1758–1816	Robert Hudson
1760s	*J. Battshill, deputy organist, 'officiated for Boyce' [1]*
1762–1786	Samuel Mence
1764–1808	Edmund Ayrton (master of the children from 1780, paid £24 p.a. for maintaining children, £80 for teaching)
1764–1779	John Reynolds
1764–1794	John Soaper
1765–1771	William Clarke, priest in ordinary from 1771
1767–1797	Philip Hayes
1771–1801	Richard Bellamy
1772–1788	John Dyne
1774–1805	George Medley, 'Lutenist' from 1764
1774–1786	David Wood
1777–1799	John Friend
1779–1810	Richard Guise
1779–1783–	James Henry Short
1779–1796	Thomas Saunders Dupuis, 'Organist' and 'Composer' from 1779
1783–1802	Samuel Arnold, 'Organist in Ordinary' 1783–1802, 'Composer in Ordinary' 1783–1802, chorister *c.* 1750–1758
1783–1820	Joseph Corfe
1783–1828	John Sale
1784–1836	John Stafford Smith, 'Organist' from 1902 (master of the children from 1805 at £320 p.a.)
1786–1789	John Christian Luther
1786–1802	Charles Knyvett, 'Organist' 1796–1822, 'Composer' 1802–1808
1788–1831	Israel Gore
1789–1840–	Stephen Heather
1789–1827	James Salmon
1789–1805	Samuel Champness, *–1803 [1 Sale, J.B.]*
1794–1843	Jonathan Nield
1803–	*Charles Smith, chorister 1796–1798, dep. org. 1803– for Knyvett and Smith, J. [1]*
1796–1838	Thomas Attwood, 'Composer' from 1796, 'Organist' from 1836, chorister 1774–1781

1797–1856	William Knyvett, 'Composer' 1808–
1799–1821	James Bartleman
1801–1810	Rev. Richard Webb MA, 'Priest in Ordinary' from 1803
1802–1848	Thomas Welch
1803–1856	J.B. Sale, 'Organist' 1838–1856
1803–1843	Thomas Vaughan
1805–1846	William Hawes (master of the children 1817–1846)
1808–1817	John Jeremiah Goss
1808–1849	Charles Evans
1816–1820	William Beale
1817–1858	William Salmon
1820–1856	Richard Clarke
1820–1838	Henry Mullinex
1821–1866	John Roberts
1822–1867	Sir George Smart, 'Organist' 1822–, 'Composer' 1838–, chorister –1791
1827–1866	William Hobbs (John), to retired list 1877
1828–1840	Henry Goulden
1831–1867	Henry Wylde, to retired list 1873
1832–1854	Frederick William Horncastle
1836–1867	Orlando Bradbury, to retired list 1873
1839–1847	Enoch Hawkins
1840–1867	Edward Chapman
1843–1867	James Bennett, to retired list 1871
1843–1867	William Machin, to retired list 1871
1846–1886	Thomas Helmore (master of the children 1846–1886)
1846–1876	Thomas Francis, to retired list 1889/90
1847–1875	Robert Barnby
1848–1867	Charles Lockey, to retired list 1891
1849–1857	George Gray
1854–1868	George Benson, to retired list 1886
1856–1877	George Cooper, 'Organist'
1856–1872	Sir John Goss, 'Composer' 1856–1872, chorister 1811–
1856–1868	Henry Whitehouse, to retired list
1856–1889/90	Thomas Lawler, to retired list 1893
1857–1867	John Foster, to retired list
1857–1889/90	Lewis William Thomas, to retired list 1895
1858–1868	Alfred Montem Smith, to retired list 1888
1865–*c.*1872	W.H. Cummings
1865–1887	William Winn
1869–1871	E. Aspa
1869–1876	J.K. Gedge
1869–1896	J. Hodges
1869–1886	R. Wilkinson, to retired list
1870–*c.*1878	E. Lloyd, also sang with C.R. at 1911 coronation

(N.B. the statutory no. of gentlemen was reduced from 16 in 1863 to 15 in 1864, 12 in 1865, 9 in 1867, 6 in 1868, but thereafter remained at 9 until 1921 when the number was again reduced to 6 and remains so today)

1873–1886	Charles Beckett, to retired list 1897
1876–1891	Charles Sherwood Jekyll, 'Organist and Composer' 1876–1891
1876–1878	W. Shakespeare

1877–1909	H. Guy
1877–1887	J.A. Birch
1878–1886	C. Abercrombie
1886–1928–	J. Gawthrop
1887–1923	David Strong
1887–1931–	D.S. Shepley
1887–1935–	W.H. Brereton
1889–1904	Frederick Bevan
1891–1901	William Creser, *organist and composer [4, 5]*
1891–1910	S. Noble
1892–1933	Ernest Taylor
1893–1931	Walter Coward, librarian
1899–1920	Charles Ackerman, military service in Persia and Mesopotamia
1902–1916	Sir Walter Galpin Alcock, 'Organist and Composer'
1902–1928–	Harold Wilde
1902–1912	Walter Ivimay
1910–	Harry May, military service from 1915
1912–1916	Stewart Gardner
–1915	Mr Hamel, still in army in 1915
1916–1919	Charles Harford Lloyd, 'Organist and Composer'
1916–1921	George Parker
1919–1953	Edgar Stanley Roper, 'Organist and Composer' 1919–53 (master of the children 1923–53)
1919–	F. Webster
1919–1924–	Felix Baker
1920–1923	Roy D. Russell
–1923–1939–	Graham Smart, librarian
1923–1939	Bertram Mills, 'guest' at Maundy Feast in 1948
1925–1968	C.E. Hawkins, librarian
–1926–1939–	F. Odell
1930–1939–	Martin Boddey, 'guest' at Maundy Feast 1969
1935–1939–	Bradbridge White
–1937–1957	J. Hatherley Clarke 'guest' at Maundy Feast 1969
1939–1948	A. Henderson, 'guest' at Maundy Feast 1969
1946–1968	Colin Knight
1948–1969	Stanley Riley
1950–1971	Stanley Silcock
–1948–1950	Mr Armitage
–1948–1969–	Roy Wellington
1953–1974	William Harry Gabb, 'Organist and Composer'
1957–1970	Colin Scull, librarian from 1968, and serjeant of the vestry 1970–1984
–1957–1974	John Birch, deputy organist
1958–1974	Mr Flemming, sub-organist
1968–1980	Peter Goldspink, librarian from 1971
1968–1973	Richard Swift
1970–1972	David Uglow
1970–1971	Christopher Tipping
1970–1971	Paul Hillier
1971–	Norman Cooper, librarian 1987–
1971–	Richard J.A. Edwards, librarian 1980–1987
1972–1976	Timothy N. Penrose

1972–1973	N.H. Darby
1973–1976	John W. New
1973–1975	E.J. Thornton
1974–1987	Peter Chase, deputy organist
1975–	Graham Trew
1974–1979	Timothy Farrell, organist and composer
1976–1980	Freddie Hodgson
1976–1976	Paul Crinon
1976–	Richard Lewis
1979–	Richard Popplewell
1980–1981	Richard Stevens
1980–1981	Timothy Wilson
1981–1985	John Halsey
1981–1982	Andrew Lawrence-King
1982–1987	Andrew Round
1985–1987	Graham Bartholomew
1987–	Simon McGregor, sub-organist
1987–	Michael McGuire
1987–	Stuart Kent

Clerks of the cheque

Year appointed		*Year appointed*	
1561	Thomas Bird	1668	Edward Braddock
1562	Robert Moorcock	1708	Daniel Williams
1581	John Moore	1720	Jonathan Smith
1605	Thomas Sampson	1752	William Lovegrove
1615	John Hewlitt	1777	William Dickes
1627	John Stephenson	1790	Joseph Roe
1636	Thomas Day	1816	Richard Howes
1661	Henry Lewis	1840	Francis Lingard
1662	Thomas Blagrave		

Sources: Old Cheque Book of the Chapel Royal; Lovegrove Manuscript; New Cheque Book of the Chapel Royal.

Masters of the children

1420	John Pyamour
1441	John Plummer
1455–1471–	Henry Abyngdon
1465	Robert Bunnock (deputy master?)
1478–1486	Gilbert Banester
1486–1493	Rev. Lawrence Squire
1493–1509	William Newark
1508/9	William Cornish (deputy master)
1509–1523	William Cornish
1523–1545	William Crane
1526	Richard Pygott (deputy master)
1545–1561	Richard Bower
1560–1561	Richard Edwards (deputy master)

1561–1566	Richard Edwards
1566–1597	William Hunnis
1569–1581	Richard Farrant (deputy master)
1597–1633	Nathaniel Giles
1633–1654	Thomas Day
1660–1672	Captain Henry Cooke
1672–1674	Pelham Humphreys
1674–1708	John Blow
1708–1727	William Croft
1727–1757	Bernard Gates
1757–1780	James Nares
1780–1805	Edmund Ayrton
1805–1817	John Stafford Smith
1817–1846	William Hawes
1846–1886	Thomas Helmore
1886–1892	Harry Alsager Sheringham
1892–1912	Claude Robert Selfe
1912–1923	Percy Frederick Davis
1923–1953	Edgar Stanley Roper
1953–1974	Harry Gabb
1974–1979	Timothy Farrell
1979–	Richard Popplewell

Children of the Chapel Royal, 1893–1990

This list was compiled by the late serjeant of the vestry, Colin S. Scull. He used the following sources:

List I from Chapel Royal concert programmes 1893–1911 (Larkhill Rise and Clapham Road).

List II from Percy Davis's manuscript book entitled 'Children of His Majesty's Chapels Royal School Records of every boy admitted during the Mastership of P.F. Davis M.A. Jan. 1912–May 1923'.[1] This covered residence at Derwent Mount, Streatham.

List III from Lord Chamberlain's Office cards, and a list supplied by the bursar of the City of London School for the period 1923–40.

List IV from Miss Weaver's register of the wartime choir, a photograph and LCO cards, covering the period 1944–47.

List V from LCO cards and Chapel Royal Magazine, covering the period 1947–1977.

List VI from current records.

---

[1] The Percy Davis Manuscript contains the following information about each of the children: name, date of birth, name and address of parent, profession of parent, previous school, previous voice training, previous choir, date of leaving, remarks on career after leaving, date of admission, remarks and reports.

LIST I

Year admitted	Year left	Name
	1893/4	C. Flinn
	1893/4	F. Jackman
	1894/5	P.G. Ranson
	1894/5	L. Ovens
1891	1894/5	J.S. Physick
	1894/5	H.E. Bullen
1892	1898	F.S. Physick
	1896/7	W.T. Stoton
	1896/7	L.T. Pidwell
	1896/7	A.F. Wareham
	1896/7	W.T. Powell
	1898–1900	G.T.C. Blacklock
1894/5	1897/8	H.J. May
1894/5	1897/8	A.G. Thorogood
1894/5	1897/8	A.E. Witty
1894/5		S.L. Rowe
1894	1896	W.G. Physick
1896/7	*c.*1902	T.C. Minter
1896/7	1898/1900	R.P.E. Shaugnessy
1896/7	1898/1900	B. Gawthrop
1896/7	1900/2	B.H. Burford
1896/7	1898/1900	O.J.L. Pidwell
1897/8	1898/1900	G.W. Leyland
1897/8	1900/2	A.G. Bounder
–	–	A.H. Pinnington
–	–	N.M. Stone
1897/8	1900/2	J. Harrington
1898/1900	1900/3	E.L. Ardley
1898/1900	1900/2	H.F. Thacker
1898/1900	1903/4	W.E. Osborne
1898/1900	1904/6	C.A. Viner
1898/1900	1900/2	W.V. Heathorne
1900/3	1903/4	W.N. Everitt
1900/2	1904/6	A.E. Ackerman
1900/3	1906/7	W.I. Wright
1900/3	1907/8	R.S.P. Thacker
1903	1907/8	F.S. Jacob
1900/3	1904/6	H.S. Rowe
1900/3	1906/7	S.C. Sanderson
1900/3	1904/6	H.C. Hadden
1903/4	1908/9	R.L. Whittle
1903/4	1907/8	S.W. Thorogood
1904/6	1908/9	D.A.R. Rawlings
1904/6	1907/8	C.B. Harvey
1904/6	1909/11	V.H. Benzon
1904/6	1909/11	S.B.E. Cutler
1906/7	1910/11	W.B. Manson
1906/7	1907/8	S.W. Latham
1907/8	1909/11	S.J. Everitt
1907/8	–	F.G.H. Pownall
1907/8	1909/11	F.L. Carter
1907/8	1908/9	N.A. Honer
1909	1911	S. Whinyates

1908	1913	T.H.W. Armstrong
1908	1913	L.J. Dancey
1909	1915	A.E. Butler
1909	1915	F.A. Naylor
1909	1914	L.F.N. Pridmore
1910	1913	R.W. Cox
1910	1914	C.A. Farebrother
1911	1914	R.S. Marriott
1911	1916	J. Cole
1911	1915	C.J. Nethersole
1913	1915	H.S. Robertson
1913	1916	H.J. Butler
1913	1917	A.J.H. Windebank
1913	1915	H. Fitch
1914	1917	H.A. Rudling
1914	1918	F.D. Alcock
1915	1918	A.T. Heather
1915	1919	R.W. Dolman
1915	1917	J.E.H. White
1915	1918	C.F. Harvey
1915	1919	R.C. Humphreys
1916	1920	E.L. Ellisdon
1916	1919	R.E. Sweny
1917	1917	D. Foot
1917	1924	M.O. Witham
1917	1917	S.H. Giggins
1918	1922	L. Newham
1917	1921	S.J. Hooker
1918	1920	A.W. Ellisdon
1918	1921	L.C. Humphreys
1918	1924	L.P.F. Weeks
1919	1924/5	E.D. Harper
1919	1920	R.S. Miles
1919	1924	B.M. Dean
1920	1924	D.M. Collinson
1920	1925	H.R. Tuffs
1921?	1925/6	G.G. Doel
1921	1923	T.S.J. Pearson
1920	1926	F.G. Ryan

1923	1924	F.A. Lake
1923	1925	S.A. Free
1923	1926	L.G. Thorne
1924	1927	P. Handover
1924	1926	J.C.H. Silcock
1924	1928	T.T. Montgomery
1925	1930	H.H. Siems
1925	1929	W.G. Hook

1925	1931	C.F.C. Mann
1925	1928	R.W. Metcalfe
1926	1928/9	F.E. Powell
1926	1932	B.A. Lock
1926	1930	E.C.N. Hutchinson
1927	1928/9	S. Charvet
1927	1933	F.J. Dobinson
1928	1934	L.D. Hubbard
1928	1932	N.F. Rowbottom
1929	1933	W.F. Snell
1929	1933	D.V. Turnpenny
1929	1932	H.A.H. Moore
1930	1935	G.L. Soul
1930	1934	J.E. Hugo
1931	1935	K.C. Hopkins
1932	1938	D.L.B. Wheeler
1932	1939	J. Beadle
1933	1935	P.L. Davies
1933	1938	M.C. Symons
1933	1937	E.C. Wyncoll
1933	1937	K. Ffitch
1934	1938	G.J. Wise
1934	1937	A.I. Wolfenden
1935	1939	A.J. Robinson
1935	1940	P.N. Blake
1935	1939	P.J. Windibank
1937	1940	R.B. Whittington
1937	1939	D.A. Danielli
1937	1940	K.J. Sheedy
1938	1940	M.T. Banks
1938	1940	P.A. Miles
1939	1940	B.E. Clark
1939	1940	M.J. Morgan
1939	1940	D.A. Moore

LIST IV

1944	1945	J.G.M. Daniels
1944	1947	J.R. Bennett
1944	1945	M. Guinery
1944	1946	G. Phillips
1944	1947	K.D. Kilburn
1944	1946	R. Kendall
1944	1947	L.C. Beckett
1944	1946	D.J. Allen
1944	1946	C.H. Whitehead
1944	1947	J. Stenner
1944	1945	K.E. Seeger
1944	1946	D.P. Paine
1944	1945	G. Brown
1944	1945	M. Newell
1944	1945	R.W. Wooton

1944	1947	J.P. Wickens
1945	1947	R. Johnson
1945	1947	J. Waddell
1945	1947	G. Weir
1947	1947	P.S. Goldspink
1946	1947	R. Leeder

LIST V

1947	1947	J.E. Stern
1947	1947	A.P. Skinner
1947	1949	H. Saddleton
1947	1948	R.J. Martin
1947	1947	M.J. Parke
1947	1949	D. Lawson
1947	1950	J.M. Hey
1947	1949	C.J.B. Greene
1947	1949	R.B. Tilford
1947	1950	P.S. Goldspink
1947	1949	R. Leeder
1947	1951	E. Lindon
1947	1949	M. Ruddlesden
1948	1953	B.D. Townsend
1948	–	M. Osbourne
1948	1955	M.E.J. Neary
1949	1952	R. Saddleton
1949	1954	R. Saunders
1949	1953	C. Chatwin
1949	1953	G. Green
1950	1954	M. Wilkinson
1950	1956	P.E. Lough
1952	1954	T. Slatter
1951	1956	C.J. North
1952	1954	C. Webster
1953	1956	H. Wilkinson
1953	1957	P. Chatwin
1954	1957	P.C. Knight
1954	1959	J.M. Chatwin
1954	1956	P. Cross
1954	1960	J.B. Murray
1955	1957	A.R. Cross
1955	1959	E. Danks
1956	1958	R.F. Overington
1956	1958	B.C. Ward
1956	1961	R.I. Onslow
1957	1962	J. Clargo
1957	1963	G.M. Pritchard
1958	1961	C. Duffell
1958	1963	H.J. Watson
1958	1964	P. Brown
1958	1964	J. Mander
1959	1963	P.S. Onslow

1959	1961	S. Owen
1960	1965	N. Reynolds
1961	1966	D. Coster
1961	1966	S. Fielding
1961	1965	D.H. Lloyd
1962	1966	D.A'Bear
1963	1967	J. Brockless
1963	1966	D. Lynch
1963	1968	J. Ashford
1964	1967	J. Baines
1964	1969	N. Pearmain
1965	1968	M. Attree
1965	1968	J. Reynolds
1966	1969	S. Ashford
1966	–	S. Montgomery
1966	1969	W. Jervois
1966	1971	R. Cordery
1967	1970	R. Hobbs
1967	1970	P. Lewis
1968	1971	M. Wills
1968	1973	M. Stockton
1968	1972	T. Shaw
1969	1972	G. Dean
1969	1972	S. Goldspink
1969	1973	S. Preece
1970	1974	S. Pearmain
1970	1972	J. Attree
1971	1975	P. Stockton
1971	1974	J. Hull
1971	1974	M. Graham
1972	1977	N. Thomas
1972	1975	D. Kottnauer
1972	1976	N. Cave
1973	1979	M. Thomas
1973	1975	R. Hester
1973	1977	G. Stockton
1974	1979	G. Kibble
1974	1979	R. Sawdy
1974	1976	C. Campbell
1975	1977	B. Trathen
1975	1977	R. Cave
1975	1980	J. Coutts
1976	1979	M. Hughes

LIST VI

1978	1979	J. Dale
1978	1979	Peter de Soissons
1978	1979	Patrick de Soissons
1978	1981	J. Poole
1978	1981	M. Groves
1979	1983	J. Edwards

1979	1982	T. Holmes
1979	1983	R. Mildren
1979	1983	N. Devaney
1979	1983	C. Sawdy
1979	1984	T. Plumtree
1980	1982	J. Atter
1980	1984	C. Edwards
1981	1983	P. Kane
1982	1984	K. Stent
1982	1986	R. Edwards
1982	1986	L. Glynn
1983	1986	R. Gough
1983	1984	D. Wood
1983	1985	R. Gardner
1983	1986	P. Riordan
1983	1987	J. Ashworth
1984	1986	L. Ainger
1984	1987	S. Funnell
1984	1987	R. Prescott
1984	1988	E. Glynn
1985	1987	K. Iino
1985	1988	T. Denford
1986	1988	D. Scholes
1986	1989	A. John
1986	1986	B. Hollington
1987	–	T. Prescott
1987	–	O. John
1987	1989	W. Mangar
1987	1990	H. Maroon
1987	–	L. Bruton-Simmonds
1987	–	C. Rich
1988	1989	B. Webb
1988	–	A. Virr
1988	–	L. Robinson
1989	–	J. Keddie
1989	–	A. Jayawardena
1990	–	H. Leithead
1990	–	J. Rockhold

Serjeants of the vestry

1254	Thomas de Brampton, present at 'Meilham'
–1267	Bartholomew de Capelle
1267–	Ebulo de Montibus, 'Serjeantry of the King's Chapel'
1276	John de Bohun
1417/18	John Colles
1417/18	John Water ⎱ co-opted to Serjeant Colles for
1417/18	John Kyngman ⎰ Southampton embarkation for Normandy
1454	John Stevyns, 'poor priest' appointed to 'keep the vestry'
–1509	William Dobney
–1509–1514–	William Tebbe
–1592	John Dison

1592–1608	Ralphe Fletcher, 'Serjeant Extraordinary' from 1608
1608–1625	Cuthbert Joyner, initially sworn 'Joynt Serjeant of his Majesties Vestrie', Bod. Reg.
1625–1636	Thomas Mellor, died 'midsommer', Bod. Reg.
1636–1638	Thomas Walker
1638–	John Pountney, sworn Serjeant 3 May – formerly 'eldest yeoman', Bod. Reg.
1660–1687	Thomas Haynes
1687–1715	Henry Parker
1715–1715	Marmaduke Alford
1715–1752	William Smith
1752–1777	William Lovegrove
1777–1790	William Dickes
1790–1816	Joseph Roe
1816–1840	Richard Howse
1840–1868	Francis Lingard
1868–1895	Samuel Chapman
1895–1910	Mr Hebblethwaite
1910–1917	W. Gale
1917–	W. Folland
–1946–1952	J.W. Saunders
1952–1956	F. Dean
1956–1970	William Buckle
1970–1984	Colin Scull
1984–	David Baldwin

Yeomen of the vestry

1398–1399	Richard Sewall, 'one of the yeomen-carters of the King's Chapel'
1401	John Pritewell, 'Yeoman of the King's Chapel'
1449	'one Valectus' from *Liber Regie Capelle*.
–1509–1510–	John Buntying, 'Yeoman'
1510	William Coleman, one of the 'five persons of the Revestiary'
1526	Eltham Palace Ordinances speak of three 'yeoman of the vestry'
1575–1577	William Roddinghurst, sworn 'Yeoman' 28 Feb.
1578–1579	John Sewell, sworn 'Yeoman' 28 March
1579	Richard Morrice, sworn 'Yeoman' 30 March
1580	Crue Sharp, sworn 'Yeoman' 9 Nov.
1580/81	Anthony Todd, sworn 'Yeoman' 26 Feb.
–1591	John Burchall, 'Eldest Yeoman'
–1593	William Pike, 'Second Yeoman'
1593–1596–	Robert Hewes, 'Younger Yeoman'
–1595–1608	John Patten, 'Eldest Yeoman' and father-in-law of Orlando Gibbons
1604–1613	William Phillipps, 1613 'Yeoman ... to serve Prince Charles as formerly he was sworn to serve Prince Henry'
1605	Rob. Hand, 'Yeoman of the Vestry'
1605	John Davies, sworn 'Yeoman of the Vestry' in the place of Hand, but then sold his place to become 'Yeoman of the Vestry Extraordinary' in 1607

1605–1615	John Nicholas, 'Youngest Yeoman of the Vestry', then 'Eldest Yeoman' after 1608
1607	Thomas Miller, 'Yeoman of the King's Majesties Vestery, and to attend the Prince'
1608	John Patten, 'Eldest Yeoman of the Vestry', made over his place to Christopher Clarke who was sworn Groom, Patten being at the same time sworn 'Yeoman Extraordinary'
1608–1611	Henry Alred, sworn 'Eldest Yeoman' in 1608, but dismissed in 1611
1611–1624	William Lowther, sworn 'Eldest Yeoman'
1615–1620	Henry Eveseed, dismissed 3 March
1620	Richard Patten, sworn 'Yeoman'
1625	Robert Colman, sworn 'Yeoman'
1625	Silvester Wilson, sworn 'Yeoman'
−1635/6	Thomas Pownell, died 'Eldest Yeoman of the Vestry'
1636	Thomas Walker, 'Eldest Yeoman'
1636	John Pountney, sworn 'Youngest Yeoman' on 12 Feb., and 'Eldest Yeoman' on 18 Feb.
1636–1640	Hugh Jenkins, sworn 'Youngest Yeoman' in 1636, and 'Eldest Yeoman' in 1638
1640–1660–	William Williams, sworn 'Yeoman' in 1640, and 'Eldest Yeoman' after the Civil War upon the Restoration in 1660
1660	Mr Whitell, sworn 'Youngest Yeoman'
1660–1680	George Whitcher, sworn 'Younger Yeoman', and then later 'Eldest Yeoman'
1663–1685–	Thomas Dunkley, sworn 'Yeoman of the Vestry Extraordinary, to waite Closet Keeper in ordinarye', and re-confirmed in post in March 1685
−1675	Captain Owen Phillips, 'Yeoman of the Vestry', died at Richmond, Surrey
1675–1714	Marmaduke Alford, 'Yeoman of the Vestry', 'Eldest Yeoman' from 1685, and serjeant of the vestry March 1715, but died May 1715
1680–1686	Morice Morer, sworn 'Youngest Yeoman', but it was 'not to be a president to hinder the groome of his right for the future'. Re-confirmed as 'Youngest Yeoman' in 1685
1714–	Jo. Hill
1722–1754	Thomas Langhorn
1754–1778	William Rowling
1778–1816	Thomas Foster
1816–1838	Henry Berry
1838–1840	Mr. Howse
1840–1868	Francis Lingard (office of yeoman of the vestry abolished upon Lingard's death

Sources: Patent Rolls; *Liber Regie Capelle* of 1449; Eltham Palace Ordinances of 1526; Bodleian Rawlinson Manuscript D318; Old Cheque Book of the Chapel Royal; New Cheque Book of the Chapel Royal; Lovegrove Manuscript (Royal Library); Royal Kalendar.

Grooms of the vestry

1449	*Liber Regie Capelle* speaks of 'two lesser officials who are called grooms', and '2 garciones' (i.e. grooms)
1483	*Liber Niger Domus Regis* speaks of 'one groom'
–1509–1510–	Geoffrey Wright, 'Groom of the Vestry'
1526	Eltham Palace Ordinances speak of 'some officers of the Vestry'
1558	Old Cheque Book speaks of the 'Grome of the Vestry'
1591–1608	John Patten
1591–1593	Robert Hewes, subsequently 'Yeoman' from 1593
1593–1611	Henry Alred
–1593	John Salisbury
1595–	Richard Hemyngwaye, 'Extraordinarie Groom'
1607–1620	Henry Eveseed the younger, 1607 'Groom of the Vestrie Extraordinarie', and in ordinary from 1611
–1607	Thomas Miller (Mellor) 'Yeoman' from 1607
1608–1610	Christopher Clark
1608–	William Dale, groom 'to attend the Prince'
1610–1611	William Lowther, became 'Yeoman' in 1611
1614–1625	Roberte Colman, groom 'to serve Prince Charles'
1615–	Richard Patten
1615–	William Wardes, 'Groom extraordinarie … for the tuninge and Mendinge of his Majesties organes'
1620–	Thomas Pannell
1624–	Thomas Walker
1625	Robert Colman and Silvester Wilson become 'joynt Yeomen of his Mayesties Vestry' having been grooms
1626–	John Burward, 'Groom of the Vestry extraordinary for Tuninge and Mendinge of his Majestes organes'
–1636	Hugh Jenkins
1636–	Roger Judd
1638–1639	Thomas Kithermister, resigned his place 1639
1639–1640	William Williams, became 'Yeoman' in 1640
1640–1662	Augustine Cleveland, 'dyed by the violence of horses and coach running over him at Hampton Court'
1662–1671	Hugh Powell
–c.1665	William Williams, 'Eldest Groom'
1665–	Owen Phillips
1671–	Richard Ouldner
1675–1695	George Ouldner, re–confirmed 1685
1695–1697	Isaac Cook
–1708	Matthew Fairles
1708–1719	John Lenton
1719–	William Duncombe
1730–1756	Richard Norton
1756–1760	Richard Wraith
1760–1768	William Smith
1768–1784	William Horn
1784–1801	Moses Jackson
1801–1814	George Stockes
1814–1855	William Sansom

1855–	Francis Lingard, 'Deputy groom' from 1840
1899–1910	W. Gale
1910–1917	W. Folland
1917–1948	E. Pearce
1948–1955	B.H. Browne
1955–1959	W. Collins
1960–1970	L.E. Wyatt
1970–1983	M.J. Watts
1983–1988	Edward Cadwallader
1988–	George Charlett

Keepers of the closet

1607–	Thomas Miller, 'Yeoman for the Princes Vestery'
1608–	William Dale, 'Groom ... to attend the Prince'
1613–	William Phillips, 'Yeoman of the King's Majesties Vestery ... to serve Prince Charles in that place'
1614–	Robert Colman, 'Groom of his Majestes Vestry ... to serve Prince Charles in that place'
1663–1685–	Thomas Dunkley, 'Yeoman of his majesties Vestry extraordinary, to wait Closett Keeper in ordinarye ... at Whitehall'
–1704	Nicholas Phipps
1704–1718	Daniel Farmer, 'Closet Keeper of Whitehall Chapel'
1718	Philip Bennet, 'Closet Keeper'
–1743	John Richardson
1743–	John Martin

Closet keepers at St James's following queen Anne's move from Whitehall to St James's Palace in 1702. [I have traced these names from 1758 until the present day, although there was almost certainly a direct and unbroken succession from queen Anne's reign as a result of the move in 1702]

1758–1786	J.N. Hart
1786–1795	Mr Cockdon
1806–1866	Mr Cockerton
1838–1866	Charles Fleet (Flett)
1866–1868	George Brinkworth
1868–1891	John Davis
1892–1914	Miss Jane Shackle
1914–1920	S. Ash
1920–	W. Smith
–1956	B.H. Browne
1948–1955	W. Collins
1955–1956	S.W. Roblou
1956–1959	L.E. Wyatt
1959–1961	J.G. Duggan
1961–1970	M.J. Watts
1971–1987	John Lake
1987–	Edward Cadwallader

Appendix II

Bellringers

1449	'one of the boys' – *Liber Regie Capelle*
1606–1624	Robert Bicknar
1624–1626	Sampson Rowden
1626–	Roger Evans
–1666	Samuell Blayton ('suspended' by dean in 1666)
1672–1678	Adam Watkyns
1678–	Henry Watkins
1703–	Isaak Ellis
1710–1732	Thomas Brookes
1732–1737	John Herring
1737–1743	John Martin
1743–1761	William Seamer, £15 p.a.
*c.*1783–*c.*1786	Thomas Leach, £20 p.a.
*c.*1786–1845	James Wynn (Wynce), £15 p.a.
1845–1858	John Husk
1858–	Frederick Lingard

Sources: *Liber Regie Capelle* of 1449; Old Cheque Book of the Chapel Royal; New Cheque Book of the Chapel Royal; Lovegrove Manuscript; Royal Kalendar.

The Chapel Royal complement, 1990

Dean	Rt Rev. Graham Leonard (Bishop of London)
Sub-dean	Rev. Canon Anthony Caesar (sub-almoner, deputy clerk of the closet, domestic chaplain)
Priests in ordinary	Rev. William Booth
	Rev. Adam Ford
	Rev. Gordon Watkins
Deputy priest in ordinary	Rev. Hugh Mead
Organist and choirmaster	Richard Popplewell (composer to the Chapel Royal)
Sub-organist	Simon McGregor
Gentlemen in ordinary	Norman Cooper (senior gentleman)
	Richard Edwards
	Graham Trew
	Richard Lewis
	Michael McGuire
	Stuart Kent
Children of the chapel	Thomas Prescott (head chorister)
	Oliver John
	Leo Bruton-Simmonds
	Christopher Rich
	Alexander Virr
	Luke Robinson
	Jamie Keddie
	Anthony Jayawardena
	Howard Leithead
	Joel Rockhold
Honorary treasurer	Richard Smith
Serjeant of the vestry	David Baldwin
Groom of the vestry	George Charlett

Chapel Royal Personnel

Keeper of the closet	Edward Cadwallader
Keeper of the closet (emeritus)	John Lake
Daily ladies	Andrea Baldwin
	Mary Reid
Crucifers (all former children of the Chapel)	Giles Stockton
	Dennis Bartlett-Arnot
	Richard Edwards
	Laurence Glynn
	Edmund Glynn
	Philip Riordan
	Richard Prescott
	Simon Funnell
	Thomas Denford
	Dominic Scholes
	Ben Webb
	Alexander John
Voluntary flower arrangers	Andrea Baldwin
	Christopher Williams
	Jessie Smith
	Marie Bayliss
Occasional red-letter days	Pamela James
	Edith Adams
	Esther Salmon
Epiphany ushers	Vernon Stockton
	Mark Stockton

Royal Almonry personnel, 1990

Lord high almoner	Rt. Rev. John Taylor, bishop of St Albans
Sub-almoner	Rev. Canon Anthony Caesar LVO
Secretary	Peter Wright CVO
Assistant secretary	Derke Waters CVO
Wandsmen	Geoffrey Button MVO (head wandsman)
	Gavin Taffs
	John Ratcliffe
	Andrew Wright
	John Taffs
	James Button
Co-opted supernumerary	Bob Brooks

Other establishments closely associated with the Chapel Royal

The Domestic Chapel, Buckingham Palace

Domestic chaplain: Rev. Canon Anthony Caesar
Clerk of the Domestic Chapel: Christopher Williams

Appendix II

The College of Chaplains

The thirty-six chaplains to The Queen who form the College are listed below along with other clergy associated with the Chapel Royal as their preachments were disposed in 1990:

JANUARY

7th	1st Sunday after Epiphany	Ven. R. Simpson, LVO, MA (chaplain)
14th	2nd Sunday after Epiphany	Canon C.J. Hill, BD, MTh, AKC (chaplain)
21st	3rd Sunday after Epiphany	Rev. R.S. Clarke, AKC (chaplain)
28th	4th Sunday after Epiphany	Canon R.H.C. Lewis, MA (chaplain)

FEBRUARY

4th	5th Sunday after Epiphany	Ven. K.S. Pound, MA (chaplain)
11th	Septuagesima	Canon G.A. Elcoat (chaplain)
18th	Sexgesima	Canon J.F. Hester, MA (chaplain)
25th	Quinquagesima	Bishop of Chelmsford (clerk of the closet)

MARCH

4th	1st Sunday in Lent	Canon J.G. Grimwade, MA (chaplain)
11th	2nd Sunday in Lent	Ven. D.N. Griffiths, RD, MA, FSA (chaplain)
18th	3rd Sunday in Lent	Canon D.C. Gray, TD, PhD, AKC (chaplain)
25th	4th Sunday in Lent	Rev. E.R. Ayerst (chaplain)

APRIL

1st	5th Sunday in Lent	Rev. J.G. Haslam, LLB (chaplain)
8th	Sunday next before Easter Palm Sunday	Canon A. Glendining, LVO (chaplain)
13th	Good Friday	Very Rev. M.C.O. Mayne, MA (dean of Westminster)
15th	Easter Day	Canon A.D. Caesar, LVO, MA, MusB, FRCO (sub-dean)
22nd	1st Sunday after Easter	Rev. K. Huxley, MA (chaplain)
29th	2nd Sunday after Easter	Canon D. Landreth, TD, MA (chaplain)

MAY

6th	3rd Sunday after Easter	Ven. E.J.G. Ward, LVO, MA (extra chaplain)
13th	4th Sunday after Easter	Rev. D.T. Tonge (chaplain)
20th	5th Sunday after Easter	Rev. M.A. Moxon, BD (chaplain)
27th	Sunday after Ascension	Rev. G.D. Watkins (priest in ordinary)

JUNE

3rd	Whitsunday	Bishop of London (dean)
10th	Trinity Sunday	Canon R.J.W. Bevan, PhD (chaplain)
17th	1st Sunday after Trinity	Canon J.S.D. Mansel, KCVO, MA, FSA (extra chaplain)
24th	St. John the Baptist	Canon R.C. Craston, BA, BD (chaplain)

JULY

1st	3rd Sunday after Trinity	Canon D.N. Hole (chaplain)
8th	4th Sunday after Trinity	Ven. D. Scott, MA (chaplain)
15th	5th Sunday after Trinity	Canon P.A. Welsby, MA, PhD (chaplain)

| 22nd | St. Mary Magdalene | Bishop of St. Albans (lord high almoner) |
| 29th | Patronal Festival of St. James the Apostle | Rev. D.J. Burgess, MA (chaplain) |

OCTOBER

7th	17th Sunday after Trinity (sub-dean)	Canon A.D. Caesar, LVO, MA, MusB, FRCO
14th	18th Sunday after Trinity	Rev.J.R.W. Scott, MA, DD (chaplain)
21st	19th Sunday after Trinity	Rev. G.S. Pedley, MA (chaplain)
28th	SS. Simon and Jude	Canon R.T.W. McDermid, MA (chaplain)

NOVEMBER

4th	21st Sunday after Trinity	Ven. P. Ashford (chaplain)
18th	23rd Sunday after Trinity	Rev. A.H.H. Harbottle, LVO, MA (chaplain)
25th	Sunday next before Advent	Canon J.V. Bean, MA (chaplain)

DECEMBER

2nd	1st Sunday in Advent	Canon G.R. Hall (chaplain)
9th	2nd Sunday in Advent	Canon N. MacDonald Ramm, MA (chaplain)
16th	3rd Sunday in Advent	Canon E.A. James, MA, BD, AKC (chaplain)
23rd	4th Sunday in Advent (ordinary)	Rev. A.H. Mead, MA, BLitt (deputy priest in
25th	Christmas Day (sub-dean)	Canon A.D. Caesar, LVO, MA, MusB, FRCO
30th	1st Sunday after Christmas (extra chaplain)	Prebendary S. Austen Williams, CVO, MA

The Lord Chamberlain's Office

Friendly oversight and help with certain aspects of the Chapel Royal and College of Chaplains has been maintained by the Lord Chamberlain and his officials. Those who exercise responsibilities in this respect are:

The Lord Chamberlain	The Earl of Airlie, KT, GCVO (lady clerk Margaret Moore)
Comptroller	Lt. Col. George West, CVO (lady clerk Sukie Hay)
Assistant comptroller	Lt. Col. Malcolm Ross, OBE (lady clerk Lucinda Pears)
Secretary	John Titman, CVO (lady clerks Helen Asprey and Juliet Marsham
Assistant secretary	Peter Hartley, MVO (lady clerk Clare Britton)
Registrar	Jonathan Spencer
Sub-dean's lady clerk	Sukie Hay
Office keepers	Patrick Carroll and Edmund Wheeler

Mention should also be made of the customary assistance of the state invitations assistant, Maj. John Leech, the yeoman of T.R.H. The Prince and Princess of Wales's Office, Sgt. Ron Lewis, livery messengers Joe Carter, Allan Higgs and David Otton, and housekeeper Gladys Bushell. The Chapel Royal also enjoys the co-operation of the Print Unit at Buckingham Palace, David Groves and Eric Williams, the Royal Gardens at Windsor Castle, and the officers of the Royal and Diplomatic Protection Group.

Bibliography

The Chapel Royal archive

This list is based upon that produced by the late serjeant of the vestry, Colin S. Scull, revised in 1985 by Mr Beric Lloyd and again in 1987 by the present author.

Chapel Royal registers etc. held at St James's Palace

St James's Palace

1 1675-1709 and 1647*
2 Baptisms 1709-1755; Marriages 1790-1754
3 Baptisms 1789-1897; Churchings 1869-1873; Confirmation 1885
4 Baptisms 1897-1905
5 Marriages 1905-the present
6 Baptisms 1906-the present
7 Marriages 1933-the present
8 Confirmations 1959-the present

Buckingham Palace

1 Baptisms 1843-1864; Marriages 1843, 1849 and 1857; Churchings 1843-1857

Kensington Palace

1 Baptisms 1721-1764 and 1789; Marriages 1721-1751, 1872 and 1889
2 Baptisms 1840-1900

Whitehall Palace

1 Marriage licences 1687-1754†
2 Baptisms 1753-1796; Marriages 1704-1754 and 1807
3 Baptisms 1817-1825, 1853-1890
4 Marriages 1824 and 1829
5 Marriages 1839-1889

Royal Register

1 Births and Baptisms 1755-1875 and 1730; Marriages 1761-1880*
2 1882-1961
3 1963-the present

Record Books of the Clerk of the Closet

Churchings, Baptisms, Confirmations, Marriages (including Privy Council Orders) of the royal family, wherever the ceremony is held. No coronations or funerals are included. Not open to public inspection.

Cheque Books

1 1561-1744 (The Old Cheque Book), transcribed by Edward Francis Rimbault and published by the Camden Society in 1872 (new series, III)

2   1721-1910 (The New Cheque Book)
The Cheque Books relate to appointments, ceremonies, customs and lists of officials etc. of the English, Dutch, French and German Lutheran Chapels Royal at St James's Palace.

Preachment Books

1727-1828	Preachers from Oxford and Cambridge Universities
1780-1810	Preachers at St James's Chapel Royal
1811-1846	Preachers at St James's Chapel Royal
1811-1841	Preachers at St James's Chapel Royal
1841-1878	Preachers
1847-1892	Preachers at St James's Chapel Royal
1843-1893	Chaplains Book
1891-1977	Preachers at St James's Chapel Royal
1837-1880	Preachers at Whitehall Chapel
1880-1890	Preachers at Whitehall Chapel

Also held by the Chapel Royal St James's Palace are miscellaneous volumes of sacrament money distributions from Whitehall, St James's and Kensington Palace Chapels, anthem books, records of benevolent contributions to widows of members of the Chapel Royal *et al.*, prayer books printed in German for use at the 'German chapel' (i.e. Queen's Chapel), and a volume of loose letters dating from the latter half of the nineteenth century.

The Registers of the Dutch, French and German Lutheran Chapels Royal are now at PRO.

*Now at PRO; copy only at St James's Palace.
†Now at PRO.

Chapel Royal registers etc. no longer held at St James's Palace

Somerset House Chapel Royal
Phillipps MS 25646 purchased by HM Treasury in 1938 and repaired. Now in the library at St Catherine's House, Kingsway, London WC2. Printed by Sir Thomas Phillipps in 1831 and reprinted by James Coleman in 1862 with notes.
1   Baptisms 1732-1775; Marriages 1714-1758, 1764, 1769, 1776; Burials 1720-1726, 1741-1758, 1770

Whitehall Palace
(now at the PRO)
323 original marriage licences bound in 3 vols:
1   1-159 (1687-1728) PRO RG8-76
2   160-313 (1729-1754) PRO RG8-77
3   1-10 (1710-1719) PRO RG8-78
A chronological table and alphabetical index to 1-313 is at the end of RG8-77. There is another bound copy in PRO at LC 5/211.

St James's Palace
Chapel Royal (now at the PRO RG8-110)
Baptisms & Births 1647, 1675, 1685, 1689, 1695-1708; Marriages 1675-1709; Deaths 1675-1685; appointments, orders, ordinations, memoranda 'in passim'.

Bibliography

Dutch Chapel Royal
(now at the PRO RG4-4574&4575)
1 Admissions, Baptisms, Marriages 1689-1743
2 Admissions 1742-1774; Baptisms 1742-1775; Marriages 1743-1754; Armen Gelt 1772-1812; Memoranda 1742-1825

(now at Guildhall Library MS 7382 & References L.19/92)
1 Baptisms, in Dutch, 1602-1857
2 Archives, printed, of the Dutch Church, 1568-1872; Baptisms, Marriages, Burials of the Dutch Reformed Church, Austin Friars, London, 1571-1874. This register was published privately by T.J.C. Moens in 1884.

French Chapel Royal (now at the PRO RG4-4640, 4539, 4540, 4541)
1 Baptisms 1738-1756; Marriages 1700-1702, 1713-1754, together with original marriage licences bound in 3 vols; Reconnaissances 1732, 1747, 1749; Temoignages 1740, 1746, 1753, published by the Huguenot Society, as *Registers of the Churches of the Chapel Royal, St. James's and Swallow Street*, edited by W. Minet & S. Minet (The Huguenot Society, Manchester, 1924). Copy held at Chapel Royal.

German Lutheran Chapel Royal
(now at the PRO RG4-4568&4569):
1 Baptisms, Births, Marriages, Deaths 1712-1760
2 Baptisms 1760-1836
(now at the German church, Montpelier Place, London SW7):
3 Baptisms and Births 1866-1914, 1922-(1985)
4 Marriages 1800-(1985)

The Roman Catholic Queen's Chapel (now at the Portuguese Embassy)
The Catholic Chapel Royal of Catherine of Braganza was at St James's Palace from 1662-1671 when she moved to Somerset House until about 1687. The registers of this chapel were afterwards used by the Embassy chapel of Portugal and are kept at the Portuguese Embassy. The Marriages have been published by the Catholic Record Society as *Catholic Record Society Registers of the Catholic Chapels Royal and of the Portuguese Embassy Chapel 1662-1829*, vol. 1, *Marriages*, edited by J. Cyril & M. Weale (London 1941). Copy held at Chapel Royal.

Additional unpublished sources and MSS in the Chapel Royal Archive

'The Chapel Royal Anthem Book of 1635', typescript notes held at Chapel Royal.
'Chaplaines that waite monethly ... Chaplaines Extraordinary ... These in the times of the Earles of Pembrooke, Ld. Chamberlaines, 1641'.
'Concerning the Chapel Royal ... Mrs. Clark begs Dr. Wesley's Acceptance of the enclosed Book', Pearce Manuscript held at Chapel Royal.
Manuscript anthem book with gold-edged paper inside dark brown leather cover embossed with queen Victoria's monogram and crown covering the years 1837-42, with the inscription: 'John Bumpus – Presented to me by John Hawes (son of William Hawes ob. 1846: Gentleman Master of the Children of the Chapel Royal and Almoner and vicar choral of St. Paul's Cathedral) shortly before his death in August 1890'.
'The Musical Education of the Children of the Chapel Royal 1820-1870 – A brief Survey', unpublished paper by Peter Jones, 1976.

Bibliography

Manuscript list of Chapel Royal old boys from 1893 compiled by Colin Scull.

'Some Historical Notes by the Precentor of the Chapels Royal', unpublished typescript notes by sub-dean Wallace Elliott, 1945.

'H.M. Chapel of the Mohawks, Brantford. Ontario', unpublished research of J. Burrant, Research and Reference Officer, Paintings, Drawings and Prints Section, Public Archives of Canada, 1977.

'Historic Tyendinaga Mission', *Ontario Churchman*, February 1908.

'Tyendinaga Rector Inducted', *Ontario Churchman*, February 1970.

'Programme for the Royal Visit 1984 to Her Majesty's Chapel of the Mohawks', H.S.M.B.C., 1984, sent to the author by his friend E.F.P. Moroney from the chapel.

S. Claus, 'Mohawks of Tyendinaga Reserve', unpublished typescript.

J. Coleman, 'A personal reminiscence re. The Queen Anne Communion Set of the Mohawks', unpublished typescript.

The Chapel Royal photographic archive
(catalogued by the serjeant of the vestry in 1987)

Envelope 1

1. Thomas Barrow, gentleman 1712-1789.
2. William Hawes, master 1825
3. Children at the Chapel Royal School, Clapham, 1896.
4. Painting by W.F. Yeames of children of the Chapel at queen Victoria's Diamond Jubilee, 1897.
5. Children at the Chapel Royal School, Streatham, 1910.
6. Children at the Chapel Royal School, Streatham, 1913.
6a. Children at the Chapel Royal School, Streatham, 1916-17.
7. Group photograph at marriage of prince Arthur, duke of Connaught to princess Alexandra, duchess of Fife, 1913.
8. Children at Chapel Royal School, Streatham, 1921-22.
9. Children and gentleman in colour court at St James's Palace, 1930.
10. Children and gentlemen leaving Buckingham Palace, July 1935.
11. 'Greek' royal wedding of princess Marina in 1934: children outside Buckingham Palace.
12. 'Greek' royal wedding of princess Marina in 1934: children inside Westminster Abbey
13. Children leaving Buckingham Palace, 1936.
14. Group photograph in colour court, 1937.
15. Group photograph in colour court, 1947.
16. Children in tunnel archway to colour court, 1948.
17. Edgar Stanley Roper, 1953.
18. Children depicted in the *Evening News*, Friday 29 May 1953.
19. Group photograph, colour court, winter 1957.
20. Group photograph, colour court, winter 1959, and photos to/from the Queen's Chapel in 1959.

Envelope 2

1. Choir leaving Buckingham Palace after prince Andrew's Baptism in April 1960.
2. Wedding of princess Margaret and Anthony Armstrong Jones, 6 May 1960.
3. Chapel officers of the vestry in tunnel archway to colour court, winter 1960/61.
4. Choir leaving Buckingham Palace after baptism of Lady Sarah Armstrong Jones, 13 July 1964.

5. Francis Skeat's stained-glass window at St Anne's Church, Rochdale, of a child of the Chapel Royal.
6. Children in colour court, July 1966.
7. Choir processing from Queen's Chapel, summer 1967.
8. Children in colour court, July 1968.
9. Royal Maundy procession at Selby Abbey, 1969.
10. Wedding of Elizabeth Mansel and Timothy Upton.
11. Choir crossing Marlborough Road, April 1970.
12. Children in colour court, July 1971, and after Confirmation at St Paul's Cathedral, 1972.
13. Fred May's cartoons of St Cecilia festival dinner, 1973.
14. Group photograph in colour court, spring 1974.
15. Group photograph in colour court, October 1977.
16. Group photograph in colour court, March 1980.
17. Group photograph in colour court, 1982.
18. Group photograph in colour court, July 1985.

Envelope 3
1. 1660 pulipt now at Christ Church, Harwood, Bolton, Lancashire.
2. Queen's Chapel, 1687.
3. Marriage of Anne (princess royal) to prince of Nassau and Orange, at 7 pm on 14 March 1733/4.
4. Chapel Royal building, colour court, sketched 10 Feb. 1816.
5. German Chapel (Queen's Chapel), 1818.
6. Chapel Royal building in 1858.
7. Chapel Royal building in 1891.
8. Chapel Royal building, Victorian interior.
9. Chapel Royal altar as dressed for marriage of prince and princess Arthur of Connaught, 15 Oct. 1913.
10. Chapel Royal altar as dressed for marriage of prince and princess George of Battenberg, Wed. 15 Nov. 1916.
11. Close-up of above.
12. Greek Orthodox marriage of the duke of Kent and princess Marina of Greece at Domestic Chapel, Buckingham Palace, following their wedding at Westminster Abbey on 29 November 1934.
13. The three crowns and holy gospel resting on the table at the domestic chapel, Buckingham Palace, for the above wedding.
14. Chapel Royal altar plate as photographed for Arthur Grimwade's article in *Connoisseur*, vol. 195, June 1977.
15. Benedetto Gennari the Younger's 'Holy Family with St Joseph, The Christ Child, The Virgin Mary and Angels' painted in 1682.
16. Mounted photos of: ambassador's court in July 1966/Christmas day 1970/barrow-way behind altar.
17. Mounted photos of: Chapel Royal building interior in 1962, as contrasted with sub-dean James Mansel's improvements of 1972.
18. Chapel Royal building interior after restoration in March 1972.
19. Altar dressings for major feast-tides and special days as used in 1974: Septuagesima & Advent/Lent/Palm Sunday/Easter/Whitsunday/Trinity Sunday.
20. Altar dressings as used in 1974 at Epiphany/Sundays after Epiphany & after Trinity/Conversion of St Paul.
21. Fines for officials who failed to attend or be punctual at the Chapel Royal in 1878.

22. Regulations re boys of the Chapel Royal in 1845.
23. Regulations respecting the children of the Chapel Royal made by the dean, 2 May 1804, mounted on wooden board.

Envelope 4
1. Coronation 1902, a group of king's chaplains.
2. *Vanity Fair* picture of sub-dean Edgar Sheppard in robes.
3. Coronation 1911, a group of king's chaplains.
4. Coronation 1937, a group of king's chaplains.
5. Coronation 1953, a group of queen's chaplains.

Loose photographs
1. Photograph of organ from Whitehall Palace chapel, placed at St Nicholas, Stanford-on-Avon in 1649/50 by Sir Thomas Cave who bought it from Magdalen College, Oxford.
2. Photograph of Thomas Elliott organ from the Chapel Royal, St James's Palace, 1819-1837, and placed in Crick, Northants, in 1841.
3. Tudor brickwork in serjeant of the vestry's basement adjoining the Chapel Royal as revealed in 1984.
4. Photograph of dean, sub-dean, Prince Andrew and Sir John Johnston.
5. Group photograph of choir in colour court in 1985.
6. The Queen talking to the sub-dean & inspecting children of the Chapel outside Chapel Royal, St James's Palace.
7. Chapel Royal choir at Buckingham Palace.
8. Photograph of 1934 'Greek' wedding at Westminster Abbey showing children of the Chapel Royal lining the route within the abbey stalls.
9. Dr Edmund Ayrton, master of the children 1780-1805, by John Hoppner (old child of the Chapel Royal)
10. Children of the Chapel Royal at Choir School, Streatham.
11. Funeral of dean Mandell Creighton, 17 June 1901.

Published sources and MSS from the Chapel Royal archive

Calendar of Close Rolls
A *Collection of Anthems As the Same are now perform'd in his Majesty's Chapels Royal*, published by direction of the Reverend the Sub-Dean of his Majesty's said Chapels Royal (1724). Red leather cover embossed with king's monogram and the words 'Chapels Royal St James's' and gold-edged paper, kindly donated to the Chapel Royal by H.J. Watford in 1989.
A *Collection of Anthems used in His Majesty's Chapels Royal And Most Cathedral Churches in England and Ireland,* published under the direction of Thomas Pearce D.D., Sub-Dean of his Majesty's Chapels Royal (London, 1795). Red leather cover with gold embossed king's monogram and the words 'Chapel Royal St James's' and gold-edged paper.
Hillebrand, H., 'The Early History of the Chapel Royal', *Modern Philology*, vol. 17, September 1920, no. 5 (University of Chicago Press, Illinois), includes transcript of Bodleian Register.
Inventories of the Wardrobe, Plate, Chapel Stuff, etc., of Henry Fitzroy, Duke of Richmond, ed. J.G. Nichols, Camden Series 61 (London, 1854).
Liber Rubeus Scacarii, c. 1135, ed. H. Hall, and published as no. 99 in the Rolls Series.

Bibliography

Liber Regie Capelle, ed. Walter Ullman (Henry Bradshaw Society, 1961). 'Translation of Selected Parts of Liber Regie Capelle' by Canon Gordon Dunstan written 'In the Train, London-Zurich-London', June 1971.

Lists of Payments to The King's Musick in the Reign of Charles II 1660-1685, transcribed, edited and published by Andrew Ashbee (Snodland, 1981).

The Old Cheque Book or Book of Remembrance of the Chapel Royal from 1561-1744, ed. E.F. Rimbault (Da Capo Press, New York, 1966).

Records of English Court Music, vols 1 and 2, 1660-1714, calendared and edited by Andrew Ashbee (1986, 1987).

Scull, C.S., *A List of Masters of the Children, Organists and Composers of the English Chapel Royal from 1444 to the present day* (Chapel Royal, London, 1981).

Scull, C.S., *Notes on the Chapels of St. James's Palace* (Chapel Royal, London, May 1983).

Scull, C.S., *The Offering of The Queen's Gifts of The Feast of The Epiphany* (Chapel Royal, London, 1973).

Stokes, E., 'Lists of the King's Musicians from the Audit Office Declared Accounts'.

Tanner, L.E., 'Lord High Almoners and Sub-Almoners 1100-1980', *Journal of the British Archaeological Association* (1957/8).

Select bibliography

Age of Arthur, The, vols 1-3, ed. J. Morris (Phillimore, Chichester, 1976).

Ainsworth, W.H., *St James's or the Court of Queen Anne* (George Routledge, London, n.d.).

Armours of Henry VIII (HMSO, Norwich, 1977).

Ashe, G., *The Discovery of King Arthur* (Debrett, London, 1985).

Bagni, P., *Benedetto Gennari e la Bottega del Guercino* (Nuova Alfa Editoriale, Bologna, 1987).

Barker, F., & Jackson, P., *London: 2000 years of a city and its people* (Macmillan, London, 1974).

Bede, the Ven., *A History of the English Church and People*, ed. E. Radice (Penguin Books, Harmondsworth, 1984).

Blackmore, H.L., *The Armouries of the Tower of London*, 1 Ordnance (HMSO, Norwich, 1976).

Burrows, D., *Handel and the English Chapel Royal* (CMS, 1984).

Carisbrooke Castle (HMSO, Norwich, 1972).

Charlton, J., *The Banqueting House Whitehall* (HMSO, Norwich, 1964).

Cooke, A.S., *Off the Beaten Track* (Combridge, Hove, 1911).

Cunningham, P., *Extracts from the Accounts of the Revels at Court, in the reigns of Queen Elizabeth and King James I, from the original office books of the Masters and Yeomen* (Shakespeare Society, London, 1842).

Dearnley, C., *English Church Music 1650-1750* (Barrie & Jenkins, London, 1970).

De Lafontaine, H.C., *The King's Musick* (Novello, London, 1909).

Denny, B., *King's Bishop* (Alderman Press, London, 1985).

Denton, J.H. *English Royal Free Chapels 1100-1300* (Manchester University Press, 1970).

Dixon, P., *Excavations at Greenwich Palace 1970-1971* (Greenwich and Lewisham Antiquarian Society, 1972).

Douglas-Smith, A.E., *City of London School* (Blackwell, Oxford, 1937).

Bibliography

Edinburgh Castle (HMSO, Norwich, 1953).

Elliott, W.H., *Undiscovered Ends* (Peter Davies, London, 1951).

English Literature and History, Auction Programme for Thursday 10 July 1986 and Friday 11 July 1986 (Sotheby's, London, 1986).

English Literature: 1575 to the present, Catalogue no. 994 (Henry Sotheran Ltd., London, 1988).

Erickson, C., *Anne Boleyn* (Macmillan, London, 1984).

Erickson, C., *Bloody Mary* (Dent, London, 1978).

Erickson, C., *The First Elizabeth* (Macmillan, London, 1983).

Eusebius, *History of the Church* (Penguin, Harmondsworth, 1988).

Ezard, J. 'Maundy Title Goes North', *Guardian*, 2 April 1985.

Forrest, D., *St James's Square* (Quiller Press, London, 1986).

Fraser, A., *King Charles II* (Weidenfeld & Nicolson, London, 1979).

Fredden, R. & Jockes, R., *The National Trust Guide* (Cape, London, 1973).

Fuller, J.O., *Sir Francis Bacon* (East-West Publications, London and The Hague, 1981).

Garrett, R., *Royal Travel* (Blandford Press, Poole, 1986).

Geoffrey of Monmouth, *The History of the Kings of England*, ed. E. Radice (Penguin, Harmondsworth, 1966).

Giles, P., *The Counter Tenor* (Frederick Muller Ltd., London, 1982).

Glasheen, J., *Round About St. James's: the story of a palace and its neighbourhood* (British Tourist Authority, London, 1980).

Glasheen, J., *St James's London* (Phillimore, Chichester, 1987).

Graeme, B., *The Story of St James's Palace* (Hutchinson, London, 1929).

Gransden, A., *Historical Writing in England, c. 550 to c. 1307* (Routledge & Kegan Paul, London, 1974).

Graves, C., *Palace Extraordinary* (Cassell, London, 1963).

Grimwade, A., 'The Altar Plate of the Chapel Royal', *Connoisseur* (June 1977).

Hammond, P., *Royal Fortress* (HMSO, Norwich, 1978).

Hammond, P., *Sir Walter Raleigh* (Pitkin, Andover, 1984).

Handel and the Chapel Royal, Programme notes for octocentenary celebrations at St. Edmund of Abyngdon, 23 November 1975.

Harrison, F., *Music in Medieval Britain* (Routledge & Kegan Paul, London, 1958).

Heath, G.D., *The Chaepl Royal at Hampton Court* (Twickenham Local History Society, 1979).

Hennell, A., *The History of the King's Body Guard of the Yeomen of the Guard* (Archibald Constable, Westminster, 1904).

'Henry VIII – Charles II', *The Musical Antiquary* (January 1913).

Hepper, F.N., *Bible Plants at Kew* (HMSO, Norwich, 1981).

Hibbert, C., *The Court at Windsor* (Penguin, Harmondsworth, 1982).

History of the King's Works, gen. ed. H.M. Colvin: vols 1 & 2, *The Middle Ages;* vol. 3, *1485-1660 (Part 1)*; vol. 4, *1485-1660 (Part 2)* (HMSO, London, 1963, 1975, 1982).

Holmes M., *The Crown Jewels* (HMSO, London, 1983).

Imperial Calendar (HMSO, London), numerous annual issues.

Jones, J., *King Charles at Carisbrooke Castle* (Carisbrooke Castle Museum, 1985).

Jones, J., *The Royal Prisoner* (Lutterworth Press, Guildford & London, 1965).

Josephus, *Against Apion*, trans H. St. J. Thackeray (Harvard University Press, 1926).

Josephus, *Antiquities*, vols 1-20 (Harvard University Press, 1934-65).

Josephus, *The Jewish War* (Penguin, Harmondsworth, 1959).

Bibliography

King Henry VI (King Henry VI Society, 1973).

Lancing College Magazine (December 1986).

Le Hurray, P., *Music and the Reformation in England 1549-1660* (CUP, Cambridge, 1978).

Letters of the Younger Pliny, ed. E. Radice (Penguin, Harmondsworth, 1963).

Linklater, E., *Ben Jonson and King James* (Cape, London, 1931).

Long, K.L., *The Music of the English Church* (Hodder & Stoughton, London, 1972).

Manly, J.M., 'The Children of the Chapel Royal and their Masters', unpublished thesis deposited at the Chapel Royal.

Mears, K., *The Crown Jewels* (DoE, London, 1986).

Members of the Royal Society of Musicians 1738-1984 (RSCM, London, 1985).

Milner, W.M.H., *The Royal House of Britain: an enduring dynasty* (Covenant, London, 1940).

Mitchell, D., *Pirates* (Thames & Hudson, London, 1976).

Montague-Smith, P. & Montgomery-Massingberd, H., *Royal Palaces, Castles and Homes* (Country Life Books, 1981).

Musica Britannica: a national collection of music XVIII – music at the court of Henry VIII, transcribed and ed. J. Stevens RMA (Stainer & Bell, London, 1973).

Museum of Smuggling History (Botanic Garden, Ventnor, Isle of Wight, 1973).

Musical Times, numerous issues.

Nicholson, S., *The Children of the Chapel Royal: an opera written for the choristers of the College of St Nicholas, Chislehurst, on SS Oronsay and Niagara* (RSCM, 1934).

Ontario: a bicentennial tribute (Key Porter Books, Ontario, 1983).

Paget, J., *The Yeomen of the Guard: five hundred years of service 1485-1985* (Blandford Press, London, 1984).

Perkins, J., *The Crowning of the Sovereign* (Methuen, London, 1953).

Petrie, C., *King Charles, Prince Rupert and the Civil War* (Routledge & Kegan Paul, London, 1974).

Phillips, C.H., *The Singing Church* (Faber & Faber, London, 1945).

Phillips, P.A.S., 'John Cooqus, Silversmith', *Antiquaries Journal* 14 (1934).

Pine, E., *The Westminster Abbey Singers* (Dobson, London, 1953).

Printed Books, Manuscripts and Music, Sotheby's auction programme for Tuesday 27 May and Tuesday 10 June 1986.

Rigold, S.E., *Yarmouth Castle* (English Heritage, 1978).

Robbins-Landon, H.C., *Handel and His World* (Weidenfeld & Nicolson, London, 1984).

Rowse, A.L., *Shakespeare the Man* (Macmillan, London, 1973).

Royal Kalendar (Suttaby & Co., London), numerous annual issues.

Royal Musical Association Research Chronicle no. 2 (RMA, 1962).

Royal Musical Association Research Chronicle no. 5, ed. N. Fortune (RMA, 1965).

St James's or the Court of Queen Anne (William H. Ainsworth, London, n.d.).

St John's Gate Picture Book (Order of Saint John of Jerusalem, 1947).

Salmon, Col. W.A., *Churches and Royal Patronage* (D. Brown and Sons Ltd., Cowbridge, Glamorgan, 1983).

Sheppard, E., *Memorials of St. James's Palace*, vols 1 and 2 (Longmans, London, 1894).

Shire, H.M., *Song, Dance and Poetry of the Court of Scotland* (CUP, Cambridge 1969).

Sibley, P., *Three Famous Men of Brighstone* (Isle of Wight County Council, 1985).

Bibliography

Sinclair, A., *Sir Walter Raleigh and the Age of Discovery* (Penguin, Harmondsworth, 1984).

Sinclair, W., *The Chapels Royal* (Eveleigh Nash, London, 1912).

Sitwell, H.D.W., *The Crown Jewels and other Regalia in the Tower of London* (Dropmore, London, 1953).

Smith, V.T.C., *Defending London's River: the story of the Thames ports 1540-1945* (North Kent Books, 1985).

Stanford-London, H., *Royal Beasts* (Heraldry Society, East Knoyle, 1956).

Steel, T., *Scotland's Story: a new perspective* (Collins, London, 1984).

Stephens, A.J., *The Book of Common Prayer with Notes*, vol. 2 (EHS, 1850).

Stevens, J., *Music and Poetry in the Early Tudor Court* (CUP, Cambridge, 1979).

Stoker, R.B., *The Legacy of Arthur's Chester* (Covenant, London, 1965).

Stopes, C.C., 'Mary's Chapel Royal and her coronation play', *The Athenaeum* 4063 (9 September 1905).

Stopes, C.C., 'William Hunnis and the revels of the Chapel Royal', *Materialen zur kunde des alteren Englischen dramas*, ed. W. Bang, vol. 29 (Louvain, 1910).

Stopes, C.C., 'William Hunnis the dramatist', *The Athenaeum* 3779 (31 March 1900).

Storry, J.G., *Church Heraldry* (Netherbed Press, Oxford, 1983).

Tacitus, *Annals of Imperial Rome* (Penguin, Harmondsworth, 1987).

Tanner, L. *The History of the Coronation* (Pitkin, Andover, 1953).

Taylor, G., *London's Navy* (Quiller Press, London, 1983).

Taylor, G., *The Sea Chaplains* (Oxford Illustrated Press, 1978).

Taylor, J.J. & Drew-Smythe, D., *The Ballad of Salomon Pavey: an Elizabethan ballad opera based on the children of the Chapel Royal* (OUP, Oxford, 1979).

Tower of London: its buildings and institutions, ed. J. Charlton (HMSO, Norwich, 1978).

Tull, G.F., *Henry of Windsor: the scholarly king* (Henry VI Society, 1966).

Wagner, A., *Heralds of England* (HMSO, London, 1967).

Webb, M.J. *The History of the Chapel Royal Brighton 1793-1943* (1977).

Wilson, I., *Undiscovered* (Michael O'Mara Books Ltd., London, 1987).

Woodfill, W.L. *Musicians in English Society from Elizabeth to Charles I* (Da Capo Press, New York, 1969).

Wright, P.A., *Royal Maundy*, 1966, 1971, 1973, 1981 editions (Pitkin, Andover).

Wright, P.A. & Ratcliffe, E.E., *The Royal Maundy*, 7th ed. (The Royal Almonry, Buckingham Palace, 1960).

Wulstan, D., *Tudor Music* (Dent, London, 1985).

Index

The index includes references to all people, places and subjects discussed in the text, but the major sources *Liber Regie Capelle* and *Liber Niger Domus Regis* have not been indexed. References to notes have the letter n following the page number, and references to illustration captions are followed by the letter c. Illustration references are printed in *italic*. Appendix II, Chapel Royal Personnel, has not been indexed.

* Compiled by Elizabeth Wiggans

456

Index

Index

469